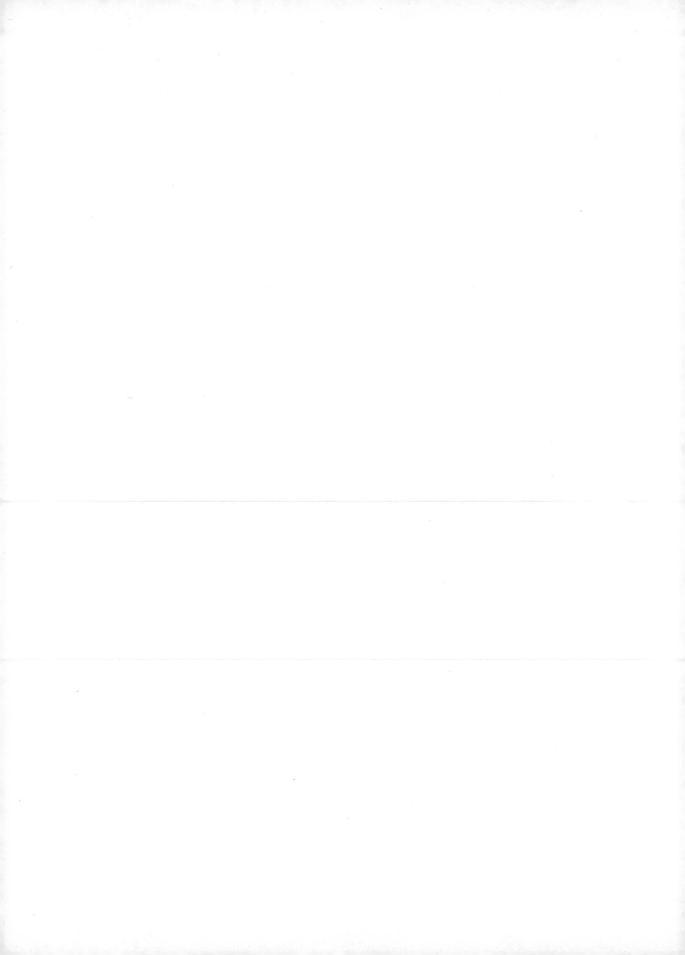

THE
NEW BOOK
OF
KNOWLEDGE

THE
NEW BOOK
OF
KNOWLEDGE

Scholastic Library Publishing, Inc.
Danbury, Connecticut

VOLUME 4

D

D, the fourth letter in the English alphabet, was also the fourth letter in the ancient Phoenician, Hebrew, and Greek alphabets. The Phoenicians and Hebrews called it *daleth*. The Greeks called it *delta*. Many language scholars say that the triangle-shaped *daleth* probably represented a door or archway.

The Greeks built their alphabet on that of the Phoenicians. To the Greeks the letters were just names for sounds. In adapting the alphabet to their own language, they kept the D sound and the triangular shape of the *daleth* but changed its name to *delta*. The *delta* had three sides of equal length: ⊿

The Romans rounded the right part of the triangle and called it *de*, pronounced "day." It is the Roman D that we use today.

Unlike many other letters, the consonant D stands for just one sound—the sound in the words *donkey*, *red*, and *candy*. Some past-tense verbs that end in *-ed*, such as *jumped* and *looked*, are exceptions. In these words the D is pronounced liked a T.

In a series D stands for the fourth member. In music D stands for the second note in the scale of C major.

D is found in many abbreviations. When D is written *'d*, it makes a contraction, or shortening, of a phrase. *He'd* stands for *he had* or *he would*. In Roman numerals it represents 500. D.C. means District of Columbia, and D.A. stands for district attorney. Small d before a date—as in "Jane Austen, d. 1817"—means "died."

The letter D is also connected with a famous event of World War II. On June 6, 1944, the Allied forces invaded Normandy, France. The invasion was an important step toward Allied victory. Since "D day" designates a day set to launch a military operation, the day of the Normandy invasion became known as D day.

Reviewed by Mario Pei
Author, *The Story of Language*

See also Alphabet.

DADDY LONGLEGS. See Arachnids.
DAEDALUS. See Greek Mythology (Profiles).
DA GAMA, VASCO. See Gama, Vasco Da.

SOME WAYS TO REPRESENT D:

The **manuscript** or printed forms of the letter (left) are highly readable. The **cursive** letters (right) are formed from slanted flowing strokes joining one letter to the next.

The **Manual Alphabet** (left) enables a deaf person to communicate by forming letters with the fingers of one hand. **Braille** (right) is a system by which a blind person can use fingertips to "read" raised dots that stand for letters.

The **International Code of Signals** is a special group of flags used to send and receive messages at sea. Each letter is represented by a different flag.

International Morse Code is used to send messages by radio signals. Each letter is expressed as a combination of dots (•) and dashes (––).

This photograph was taken by Louis Daguerre, who helped develop modern photography when he perfected his daguerreotype, the first permanent photographic image.

DAGUERRE, LOUIS (1787–1851)

Louis Jacques Mandé Daguerre was the world's first successful photographer. He was born in 1787 in Cormeilles-en-Parisis, France, a small town near Paris. In 1790, Daguerre's family moved to Orléans. Since the family was not very wealthy, Louis did not have the advantage of a fine education. His father, however, saw that Louis could draw and paint very well and had him study with an architect.

When he was 16 years old, Louis Daguerre decided that he wanted to paint and went to Paris to study. There he studied stage design and worked for Pierre Prévost, a painter of panoramas. Panoramas are huge, curved pictures painted so carefully that anyone looking at them would almost think they were real.

Daguerre became famous as a painter of stage scenery, but his experience with panoramas led him to invent a popular new form of entertainment. In 1822 he and another painter, Charles Bouton, opened the Diorama. The Diorama was similar to a panorama, but it appeared to move by the use of different lighting effects.

Daguerre began to look for other ways to paint realistic images. Scientists had already proved that certain chemicals turned dark when exposed to light. Like others at that time, Daguerre felt that this principle could be used to copy scenes from nature. The camera had already been invented, but there was no way to preserve the images it produced. A French inventor, Joseph Nicéphore Niepce, had found a way to capture images temporarily; in 1829, Daguerre and Niepce formed a partnership and worked to improve this process. After Niepce died in 1833, Daguerre continued the experiments alone.

On January 7, 1839, Daguerre announced the first permanent photographs. These pictures, "fixed" on a tiny, silver-coated copper plate, became known as **daguerreotypes**.

In 1840, Daguerre retired to the town of Bry-sur-Marne. He died there in 1851.

Reviewed by ROBERT A. SOBIESZEK
International Museum of Photography
at George Eastman House

DAHL, ROALD. See CHILDREN'S LITERATURE (Profiles).

DAHOMEY. See BENIN.

DAIRYING AND DAIRY PRODUCTS

Dairying is the branch of farming involved in the production of milk and milk products such as cream, butter, cheese, yogurt, sour cream, and ice cream. Dairy farming is practiced in many countries, with about 600 million tons of milk produced each year. The United States is the world's largest producer, followed by Russia, India, France, Germany, Ukraine, the United Kingdom, and Poland.

Most dairy farms in the United States and Canada are owned and operated by families. These family farms are increasingly becoming large businesses and often have over 1,000 cows. Smaller farms may have 30 to 50 milking cows. Milk is the major source of income for most commercial dairy farmers; some also raise animals to sell to other farmers.

In Canada, the principal dairying regions are in British Columbia and the Atlantic Provinces. In the United States, the greatest concentrations of dairy farms are in the Northeast, the Great Lakes states, and the West Coast—near the markets of large cities. These areas have traditionally had more dairy farms because dairy cattle are more comfortable in cool climates, and the food they eat grows better there.

However, all parts of North America now have dairy farms because farmers today are better able to control the cow's environment. This is due in part to new technologies and farming methods such as improved ventilation and air-cooling equipment and the use of barns that allow the cattle to remain inside at all times.

At the same time, the number of dairy farms in North America has decreased. And between 1970 and 2002, the number of dairy cows dropped from 12 million to about 9 million. This is partly because advances in dairy farming have made it possible for cows to produce more milk. Between 1955 and 1980, for instance, the average cow's milk production doubled. Today, the average cow in the United States produces about 6.2 gallons per day.

▶ **DAIRY FARMERS**

Few other jobs require the broad knowledge needed by modern dairy farmers. They must understand animal nutrition, reproduction, genetics, disease, and management. Since most dairy farms also grow crops, farmers must be familiar with soil chemistry, planting, the use of fertilizers, and insect and pest control. Like anyone who runs a large business, dairy farmers must know about accounting and business management, marketing, and insurance. Computer skills are important as well, since computers are often used to formulate animals' diets and to keep financial records. Most dairy farmers must be good at labor management and maintaining and repairing machinery. Because of this, more and more dairy farmers have bachelor of science degrees and, occasionally, more advanced degrees.

The life of a dairy farmer is very demanding. Cows must be milked and other chores done seven days a week throughout the year. Family members, including children, usually provide much of the labor, especially on average-sized farms. On large dairy farms, there is usually one full-time worker for each 100 cows.

▶ DAIRY COWS

The most common dairy breed in the United States is the Holstein-Friesian. Other major breeds are Jersey, Guernsey, Brown Swiss, Ayrshire, and Milking Shorthorn. Each breed has its own association, which keeps records of the pedigrees (ancestry) of the animals registered with it. Registered animals are often called **purebreds**. Dairy animals that are not registered with breed associations are called **grades**.

Newborn cattle are called calves; female calves are called **heifers** and male calves **bulls**. Most bull calves are sold for meat. A few of the outstanding bull calves are raised to mate with the females. Heifer calves are generally raised to serve as replacements for the cows in the herd.

A dairy cow does not begin producing milk until she has given birth to her first calf, at about 2 years old. She then gives milk for about ten months, at which time she is allowed a "dry" period of six to eight weeks. The rest period allows the mammary (milk-producing) glands to prepare for the next milk-production period. When the cow is about 3 years old, she has her second calf and goes through the milking cycle again. If all goes well, she continues this process of having a calf each year and milking for about ten months thereafter.

Every year the dairy farmer culls (removes) about one-third of the milk cows from the herd. These cows may be low pro-

JERSEY

HOLSTEIN-FRIESIAN

MILKING SHORTHORN

ducers of milk or unable to reproduce. The farmer replaces these cows with young cows.

Feeding and Managing the Herd. One of the most important jobs on a dairy farm, and one of its largest expenses, is feeding the cows the right kind and amount of food. Cows will produce more milk when their feed contains everything they need. A dairy cow eats a combination of pasture, hay, silage, and a concentrate mixture. Pasture is the green grass and other plants an animal may graze on in the fields. Hay is dried grass and other crops such as alfalfa and clover. Silage is a product made from grasses, legumes, and other crops (such as corn) that are placed in a storage bin and allowed to ferment. Pasture, hay, and silage are known as **forages** or **roughages**. Concentrates are high-energy feeds such as grains (for example, corn, oats, and barley) and by-products (for example, wheat bran, soybean meal, and by-products from ethanol plants). Forages are usually less expensive than concentrates, so the diet of the cow is planned to make the most use of forages. However, high-producing cows are fed large quantities of concentrates as well, especially during peak milk production periods. Usually, forages and some of the grain that cows eat are grown on the farm. However, some farms purchase all the cows' food.

On many large dairy farms today, silages and concentrates are blended together with added minerals to provide complete diets. The cow is allowed to eat all it wishes of this mixed feed. Most diets are now planned by computer, which makes the process of blending feedstuffs simpler and less expensive. Complete blended feeds may be fed to cows through automated feeding systems. Blended feeds provide the cow with a completely balanced diet, which help it stay healthy.

In recent years, however, some cows received feed believed to be contaminated with bovine spongiform encephalopathy (BSE), or "mad cow" disease. This disease, which destroys brain tissue and can be transmitted to humans, was first noted in Great Britain in the 1980's. Scientists have since developed tests to identify animals that are infected with BSE.

A dairy calf is usually not allowed to nurse from its mother. It is fed its mother's first milk as soon after birth as possible. Then for

GUERNSEY

BROWN SWISS

AYRSHIRE

A dairy farmer uses a laptop computer and two-way radio. Today's farmers increasingly rely on such devices to keep records and manage their herds.

the first few weeks either milk or a milk substitute is fed, along with grain. Once the calf is eating enough grain, it is weaned away from milk and fed a hay and grain diet.

Today's dairy farm requires a good record-keeping system. Information must be kept on each cow, including records of milk production, feeding, breeding, calving, and health. Many farmers belong to co-operative organizations called dairy herd improvement associations. These organizations help farmers by recording information on the cows and by providing management records that are needed to run and evaluate the business.

Housing. Housing needs for dairy cattle vary according to climate. In many areas of California, for example, the major need may be a roof to provide shade. In Minnesota, New York, or New Brunswick, on the other hand, substantial protection from cold is needed in the winter.

Calves are normally placed in individual calf pens for the first few weeks of life. They are kept under very sanitary conditions to keep them from getting sick. Calf pens are carefully cleaned and disinfected before new calves are brought in. Older calves are usually moved from their individual pens and housed with other calves of approximately the same age and size.

Barn housing is of two general types. In one, the animals are in individual **tie-stalls**, or **stanchions**. Except when released for exercise or milking, they are not free to move from their stalls. Feed is brought several times daily to mangers or feed boxes in front of them. The other general type of barn is a **free-stall**, or **loose-housing**, system. In this system cows can move about freely. Certain areas are for feeding and others for resting, and cows can move from one to the other at any time they wish. Free-stall barns are more efficient than tie-stall barns for mechanized feeding and cleaning. For this reason many newer barns tend to be the free-stall type.

The design of the proper shelter for dairy cows can be complex. Temperature, temperature changes, humidity, air movement, and other factors are important concerns. Dairy cows are most productive when they are kept in neither extremely cold nor extremely hot environments. Hot weather tends to be worse for cows. This is one of the challenges faced by dairy farmers and dairy scientists in tropical and subtropical areas.

Milking. Milking was formerly done by hand. This was difficult and sometimes unsanitary. Today, sanitary modern milking machines remove milk from the cow's udders by a suction process. Most cows are milked twice daily, but more and more dairy farmers are finding it profitable to milk three times daily.

Cows housed in tie-stalls are sometimes milked while in their stalls. The milk may be delivered directly from the milking machine to an around-the-barn pipeline that takes it to a large refrigerated tank in the milkhouse.

Did you know that...

the first cow arrived in America in Jamestown, Virginia, in 1611? By the 1800's, nearly every family in the United States had its own cows. Cows provided the family with an abundant supply of milk, cream, butter, cheese, and other fresh dairy products. They also provided the family with calves, which could be sold or raised for beef.

Above: Dairy calves are usually housed in separate, sanitary pens until they are several weeks old to keep them from getting sick.
Right: A farmer operates a milking machine in a milking parlor.

▶ MILK PROCESSING AND PACKAGING

Milk goes through many processes before it is sold to the consumer. Health laws in most European countries, Canada, and the United States require that it be **pasteurized** if it is to be used without other special treatment.

Cows are sometimes released from their stalls and moved to a **milking parlor** where the milking is done. Milking parlors are always used in free-stall barns.

Milking parlors are partially automated. They are designed in many different ways. One popular type is called a **herringbone parlor** because of the pattern in which the cows are arranged—the cows stand on either side of a pit in stalls arranged like the teeth of a saw. Herringbone parlors can milk from 6 to 20 or more cows at a time. In most parlors the cows stand at a level above the milking operator, so that he or she can easily clean the cows' udders, attach and remove the milking machines, and dip the udders in a disinfectant solution. These solutions help control **mastitis**, an infection of the mammary gland. In milking parlors the milk is transported by pipeline directly from the cow to the storage tank. Another milking parlor is called a **rotary parlor**. Cows enter on a moving circular platform, then back off when milking has been completed. This type of parlor can accommodate up to 60 cows at once.

Health department officials may inspect dairy barns and milking facilities and equipment, which must conform to regulations designed to assure a safe and sanitary product. Milk does not come into contact with air until the consumer opens the container.

Pasteurization is a heating process that kills bacteria in milk. It is named after the French chemist Louis Pasteur, who discovered in the mid-1800's how to make milk safer to drink. Pasteur originally developed this process to keep wine from turning sour. Soon he realized that pasteurization would also kill the disease-producing bacteria in milk. Bacteria that may be present in unpasteurized milk can cause tuberculosis and other serious diseases.

Milk can be pasteurized in three ways. In one method, it is heated to 145°F (63°C) and held at that temperature for 30 minutes. This is the batch, or hold, process. Another method is the high-temperature–short-time process, in which the milk is heated to 161°F (72°C) and held there for 15 seconds. The newest method is the ultra-high-temperature process, in which the milk is heated to 280°F (138°C) and held there for 2 seconds. The first two methods do not change the milk's

frigeration for three months. Milk that has been sterilized in cans, such as evaporated milk, will keep for as long as one year. Milk that does not require refrigeration is easier and less expensive to store and transport.

Milk may also be homogenized and fortified. It is **homogenized** by being heated and forced through tiny openings under high pressure. This breaks the fat into small globules so that it will not separate and rise to the surface. The even distribution of fat makes the milk taste richer. Milk is **fortified** by adding vitamins, minerals, and other nutrients such as extra milk protein. Since milk naturally has only a small amount of vitamin D, this vitamin is commonly added to milk. Vitamin A is sometimes added as well.

Milk may also be modified by adding various flavorings. Milk flavored with cocoa—

Milk must be processed and packaged according to federal health standards before it can be sold. *Above:* Raw milk is pasteurized (heated) to kill harmful bacteria. *Right:* A worker in a milk bottling plant prepares sterile containers for filling.

flavor or food value. The ultra-high-temperature process gives a slight heated flavor to the milk, but it does not change the food value.

Pasteurized milk will keep at the proper temperature for about two weeks. But milk is a good food for bacteria, and the few remaining bacteria will multiply rapidly and cause the milk to sour if it is not kept cold.

In some countries milk is not pasteurized, but people often boil it before use to protect themselves from disease. Boiling changes milk's flavor. Some people choose to drink unpasteurized, or "raw," milk because they believe pasteurization removes nutrients.

In many countries, milk is often sterilized (treated by the ultra-high-temperature process under conditions free from living organisms). It is then packaged in foil-lined cartons. This milk may be stored without re-

chocolate milk—is the most popular variation, especially in the United States.

▶ MILK AND MILK PRODUCTS

Milk is the most widely consumed dairy product. It is usually sold by fat content. That is, it can be whole, skim, or low fat. **Whole milk** is milk that contains all of its natural fat. **Skim milk** is the milk that is left after the cream has been removed. **Low-fat** milk has a fat content of 0.5 to 2.0 percent—less than whole milk but more than skim milk.

Other important dairy products include butter, ice cream, concentrated milk products, and cultured milk products, including cheese.

Butter. Most butter today is made in mechanical churns. The cream is shaken back and forth until the fat collects and separates from the rest of the cream. The part left after butter has been made is called buttermilk.

Buttermilk is used chiefly in making other food products. The buttermilk sold for home use is cultured buttermilk, produced by the action of special bacteria.

The butter is washed with water and then kneaded until it becomes smooth. Salt is often added. Sometimes air is whipped into butter to make the lighter whipped butter. Butter is called the "golden gift" because of its color and because it comes from cream, the richest part of milk.

In India a product known as ghee is eaten. Ghee is made by cooking butter until the curd particles turn brown. The non-fat parts are thrown away, and the fat, or ghee, is used for food.

Ice Cream. Ice cream is one of the best-known and most popular of all milk products. This favorite food is the subject of a separate article in Volume I.

Concentrated Milk Products. Evaporated milk, condensed milk, and dehydrated (dry) milk are concentrated milk products. They have had some of the water removed by

Milk is the most widely consumed dairy product. Other popular dairy products include ice cream, cottage cheese, yogurt, butter, and cheese.

heating the milk in a partial vacuum. The vacuum process permits the milk to boil at a lower-than-normal temperature. These concentrated products are easily prepared for use by adding water.

Evaporated milk is made from pasteurized fresh milk. About half the water content is removed from the milk. Then it is homogenized. Vitamin D is usually added, and the milk is sealed in cans and sterilized.

Sweetened condensed milk has sugar added to it before the milk is put through the vacuum process. The sugar prevents the milk from being spoiled by the action of bacteria.

Dried milk has less than 5 percent moisture. After the milk has been concentrated by the vacuum process, it is sprayed into a large chamber full of rapidly moving hot air. The tiny milk droplets are dried as they fall through the hot air. This drying process is used for whole milk, skim milk, and buttermilk. Dried milk may be stored for long periods. And because of the light weight, it is easily and economically shipped to distant countries.

Cultured Milk Products. Some milk products are made from specially soured milk or cream. Special strains of bacteria are added to the milk to ferment the lactose (milk sugar) and produce the sour flavor. The bacteria do their work under carefully controlled conditions of temperature and cleanliness. Sour cream, yogurt, and cultured buttermilk are well-known cultured milk products. Cheese is also a cultured milk product.

WONDER QUESTION

What is "Grade A" milk?

In the United States, the label "Grade A" on milk means that it meets certain health standards. It must be pasteurized before packaging, for example, and cooled and stored at specific temperatures. Farms that produce Grade A milk must be regularly monitored by government inspectors to make sure that all equipment is properly cleaned and sanitized. Inspectors also test the milk and the cows to make sure they are free of disease.

Milk can also be rated "Grade B." This is referred to as manufacturing grade and is used in products such as cheese and yogurt.

▶ HISTORY OF DAIRYING

People most likely began using milk from animals at about the same time they began domesticating (taming) them. Many historians believe this occurred about 8,000 to 10,000 years ago, probably in Libya. At first, domesticated cows produced only enough milk to feed their own calves. As agriculture developed, however, farmers improved the milk-producing ability of cows through careful breeding and good management and feeding. Milk and other dairy products became an important part of people's diets, and many families kept a few goats, cows, or sheep to provide these products.

With the coming of the industrial age, more people began working in factories and the number of family farms declined. The production of milk and milk products slowly

Dairy products have long been an important part of the human diet. Before the industrial age, many families kept cows, goats, and sheep to provide milk.

HOW CHEESE IS MADE

Little Miss Muffet eating her curds and whey was actually eating the two basic parts of cheese. Curds are the lumpy parts of curdled milk. Whey is the pale, watery liquid that separates from the curds.

Producing curds and whey, or curdling milk, is the first step in the cheese-making process. For hundreds of years milk was curdled by adding **rennet**, an enzyme found in the stomachs of some plant-eating mammals. Today special cultures of beneficial, harmless bacteria may also be added. Sometimes milk is curdled by acids.

In the second step of cheese making, most of the whey is removed from the curdled milk. The curds are then cut into smaller pieces and pressed into molds or hoops to form a larger piece of curd. Swiss is typically shaped into thick wheels and cheddar into rectangular blocks. To make provolone and mozzarella cheese, the curd is placed in hot water to soften it. Then it is stretched and kneaded like dough and molded into pear- or ball-shaped forms.

The flavor of most cheese develops while it is curing (also called aging or ripening). Cheese is held in storage for a specific period of time at a certain temperature and moisture level. Harmless bacteria, yeasts,

and molds are allowed to grow in or on the cheese to develop its flavor, odor, and appearance. Certain cheeses have only one or two of these micro-organisms, while others have all three.

Swiss cheese gets its flavor and appearance from bacteria called *propionibacteria*. While the cheese is curing, the bacteria give off gas. The gas bubbles form the round holes in the cheese.

The blue veins in Roquefort and blue cheeses come from the mold *Penicillium roquefortii*, which produces the flavor and smooth body. A grayish-white mold, *Penicillium camemberti*, grows on the surface of Camembert, which gives it a creamy texture and characteristic flavor.

Some cheeses are not cured. Cottage cheese, for example, is made early in the cheese-making process, from the fresh curds. Cream cheese is made from cream or a mixture of cream and milk. It is ready to eat as soon as it is firm.

While ripening processes go on inside the cheese, wrappings are put over many cheeses to keep them clean and nutritious. Cheddar and Swiss cheese are covered with wax or a thin sheet of plastic. The rind on Camembert and other soft cheeses protects them from harmful bacteria in the air. Colorful red wax seals Edam and Gouda.

became a large scientifically based, highly mechanized industry.

The growth of this industry was closely linked with the development of better crops and animals and with a host of technological changes, such as advances in milk processing and improved transportation and refrigeration. In earlier times, for example, one of the biggest problems was keeping milk fresh so that it would not spoil. People used to keep it cool by putting a container in the shade or in cold spring water near the farm or home. Today milk is automatically cooled as soon as it is removed from the cow; it is carried long distances in large refrigerated tanks and then processed and packaged for placement in refrigerated cases in grocery stores.

▶ FUTURE TRENDS

Since the world's population is rapidly increasing, milk and milk products will be more in demand. But dairy scientists have learned how to greatly increase the productivity of cows, so dairy farmers should be in an excellent position to meet the challenges of the future. And advances in milk processing and the development of new products will make it easier to store, transport, and distribute dairy products to people around the world.

At the same time, there will be more consolidation of the dairy industry as less competitive farmers are forced to give up dairying. This will result in fewer but larger dairy farms, as well as fewer but larger processing plants. Many of these operations may move to states that have a large ethanol industry since the by-products produced by this industry are a good source of inexpensive cattle feed.

Other trends are the result of advances in biotechnology. In addition to artificial insemination, the breeding method called embryo transfer has become more common. Prize cows are given hormones to make them produce many eggs at once. These are fertilized through artificial insemination. The embryos are then transferred to surrogate mother-cows, who give birth nine months later.

The cloning of embryos may become common as well. This would allow the best animals to be precisely duplicated by producing multiple identical calves from a single embryo. Right now animal cloning is in the experimental stages.

Another biotechnical breakthrough, the use of the hormone BST (Bovine Somatroptin), has caused controversy. Introduced in the late 1980's, BST is now given to about 30 percent of all U.S. dairy cows to increase milk production. However, concerns have arisen over its long-term health effects on humans, and some consumer groups are demanding more extensive research.

For many dairy farmers, the use of increasingly sophisticated technology—such as ultra-

Dairy scientists work with bovine cellular material. Advances in biotechnology are helping dairy farmers breed healthier cows and improve milk production.

sound to monitor cows' pregnancies—is likely to become standard practice. Many farmers may also begin using robotic milking machines. These require no labor, since the cow walks to the machine when she feels the urge to be milked. The machine automatically attaches to the udder and the cow is milked.

JEFFREY F. KEOWN
Department of Animal Sciences
University of Nebraska, Lincoln

See also BUTTER; CHEESE; MILK.

DALAI LAMA

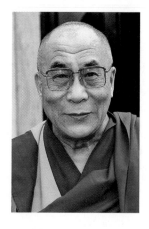

"Dalai Lama" is the title of the spiritual and social leader of Tibetan Buddhists. Each Dalai Lama is believed to be the reincarnation of the previous Dalai Lama, as well as a physical form of Avalokitesvara, the Buddhist deity of compassion.

The current Dalai Lama (the 14th), Tenzin Gyatso, was born Lhamo Dhondrub on July 6, 1935, in Taktser, Tibet. The son of peasant farmers, he was identified as the Dalai Lama when he was 2, after passing a test that required him to recognize the possessions of the former Dalai Lama. When he was 3, he was brought to live at a monastery. Two years later, in 1940, he was installed as the new Dalai Lama.

In 1950, Chinese forces invaded Tibet and the Dalai Lama was made head of the government at age 15. The next year Tibet was incorporated as a self-governing region within China. In 1959, after China violently crushed a Tibetan uprising, the Dalai Lama fled to Dharmsala, India. He established a Tibetan government-in-exile there and continued to serve as the Tibetans' spiritual and social leader.

The Dalai Lama worked to help the thousands of Tibetans who had followed him to India and to preserve Tibetan culture. The Indian government gave the Tibetans land to farm and other means of economic support. Schools and cultural centers were built for the refugees, as well as Tibetan Buddhist monasteries and nunneries.

The Dalai Lama has also worked for Tibetan autonomy. He has traveled extensively, meeting with political and religious leaders, and is a best-selling author in many countries. In addition, he has been an advocate for human rights, the environment, and the resolution of international conflicts. In recognition of his nonviolent approach to conflict, he received the 1989 Nobel Peace Prize.

ROBERT A. F. THURMAN
Jey Tsong Khapa Professor of Buddhist Studies
Columbia University

DALEY FAMILY

Former Chicago mayor Richard J. Daley was one of the country's most powerful Democrats. His sons, Richard M. and William, also became prominent public figures. Over the past several decades, they have become one of America's best-known political families.

Richard J. Daley (1902–76) was born in Chicago, Illinois. He served six terms as mayor of Chicago, from 1955 until his death in 1976. Daley received undergraduate and law degrees from DePaul University in Chicago. He was admitted to the bar in 1933 and served in the state legislature from 1936 to 1946. As mayor, Daley was considered the last of the old-time big-city political bosses. He virtually ruled Democratic politics in Illinois for more than twenty years and acted as an adviser to presidents John F. Kennedy and Lyndon Johnson.

Richard M. Daley (1942–) also received undergraduate and law degrees from DePaul and was admitted to the Illinois bar in 1969. A former state senator and county prosecutor, he has been mayor of Chicago since 1989. He made civic improvement a priority, emphasizing education reform, public safety, and beautification projects.

William M. Daley (1948–) earned an undergraduate degree from Loyola University and a law degree from John Marshall Law School, both in Chicago. Admitted to the Illinois bar in 1975, William became a prominent attorney who practiced in Chicago and Washington, D.C. Between 1977 and 1980 he served under President James Carter on the Advisory Council on Economic Opportunity. In 1993 he served as special counsel to President Bill Clinton on the North American Free Trade Agreement (NAFTA). In 1997, during the second Clinton administration, he became secretary of commerce. He resigned from that post in 2000 to become campaign chairman for Democratic presidential candidate Al Gore.

Reviewed by SARAH MARCUS
Chicago Historical Society

DALI, SALVADOR (1904–1989)

Salvador Dali, the Spanish surrealist painter, used a highly realistic technique to create what he called "hand-painted dream photographs." His painting *The Persistence of Memory* (1931) is among the best known of all surrealist works.

Salvador Felipe Jacinto Dali was born in Figueres, Spain, on May 11, 1904. He studied at the San Fernando Academy of Fine Arts in Madrid from 1921 to 1926. During this period, Dali painted landscapes and still lifes as he experimented with impressionism, cubism, and realism.

On a visit to Paris in 1928, Dali met the artists and writers of the surrealist group. He moved to Paris in 1929 and soon became an important member of this movement. The surrealists were influenced by the theories of Austrian psychoanalyst Sigmund Freud. They believed that people's true thoughts were hidden in their unconscious minds and in their dreams. Surrealist artists tried to show this world of the unconscious by painting images from their imagination.

Dali's surrealist paintings were filled with haunting, bizarre, and even grotesque images. He often depicted familiar objects in an altered or distorted state, such as the melting watches in his famous *Persistence of Memory*. Other paintings feature repeating images or objects that can be perceived as two different things at the same time, as in *Swans Reflecting Elephants* (1937). Dali also used symbols and visual metaphors in such paintings as *The Burning Giraffe* (1937) and *Sleep* (1937).

Dali extended the influence of surrealism beyond painting. He collaborated with the Spanish director Luis Buñuel on the surrealist films *An Andalusian Dog* (1929) and *The Golden Age* (1930) and designed a famous dream sequence for Alfred Hitchcock's film *Spellbound* (1945). He also designed jewelry, furniture, advertisements, and theatrical sets and costumes.

In Dali's later paintings, he turned away from surrealism and began depicting more religious subjects, often using his wife, Gala, as a model. Paintings of this period include *Christ of St. John of the Cross* (1951) and *The Last Supper* (1955).

Dali was also a gifted writer. His literary works include a surrealistic novel, *Hidden Faces* (1944), and autobiographical works, such as *Diary of a Genius* (1965). Museums dedicated to his art are in Figueres and in St. Petersburg, Florida.

After the death of his wife in 1982, Dali spent much of his time in seclusion. He died in Figueres on January 23, 1989.

MARILYN SCHAEFER
New York City Technical College

See also MODERN ART; SURREALISM.

The surrealist artist Salvador Dali tried to show the world of the unconscious in his works. His dreamlike images, such as the limp, hanging watches in *The Persistence of Memory* (1931), are painted in a very realistic style.

DALLAS

Located on the prairies of northeastern Texas, Dallas is the eighth most populous city in the United States. With more than 1.1 million residents, it is the second most populous city in Texas, after Houston.

Dallas was first settled in 1841, when John Neely Bryan set up a trading post there on the upper Trinity River. Within five years, a village had been established. It was named after George Mifflin Dallas, who was then vice president of the United States.

Nicknamed the Big D, Dallas today is a thriving center of finance, trade, distribution, and manufacturing. Retail merchants from all over the Southwest regularly come to the Dallas Market Center, one of the world's largest wholesale trade complexes, to select merchandise for their stores. Among the products made in Dallas are electronics equipment, aircraft parts, processed foods, machinery, and clothing.

The city's major educational institutions include Southern Methodist University, the Dallas County Community College District, Dallas Baptist University, the University of Texas Southwestern Medical Center at Dallas, Dallas Theological Seminary, Baylor College of Dentistry, Baylor University School of Nursing, and the Art Institute of Dallas. The University of North Texas, Texas Woman's

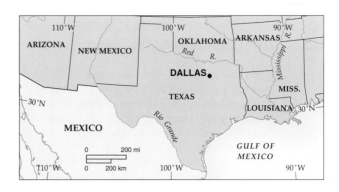

University, the University of Texas at Dallas, and the University of Dallas are also located in the metropolitan area.

Dallas has many cultural institutions. The Dallas Arts District, the nation's largest urban arts district, contains the Dallas Museum of Art and the Morton H. Meyerson Symphony Center, home to the Dallas Symphony Orchestra. Other cultural institutions include the Dallas Opera, the Dallas Theater Center, Dallas Black Dance Theatre, Ballet Dallas, Shakespeare Festival of Dallas, and the Dallas Summer Musicals.

The Dallas Zoo, Old City Park, and the Dallas Arboretum and Botanical Garden are popular attractions. The area around Dealey Plaza, the site of the 1963 assassination of President John F. Kennedy, contains a museum and a memorial dedicated to the slain president. One of Dallas' most familiar landmarks is Fair Park, home to the State Fair of Texas, the largest annual exposition in the United States. On site are the Science Place, Dallas Aquarium, the Museum of Natural History, the Museum of African-American Life and Culture, Starplex Amphitheatre, and the Cotton Bowl football stadium. The Mavericks of the National Basketball Association and the Stars of the National Hockey League play at AmericanAirlines Center. The Dallas Cowboys of the National Football League play at Texas Stadium in Irving, located within the metropolitan area.

Reviewed by CHARLOTTE FOWLER
Greater Dallas Chamber

DALLAS, GEORGE M. See VICE PRESIDENCY OF THE UNITED STATES.

Dallas, the second largest city in Texas, is a major financial, cultural, and educational center in the southwestern United States.

DALTON, JOHN (1766–1844)

In the early 1800's, a little-known English scientist named John Dalton worked out a theory that became the cornerstone of modern science. Dalton's theory explained how different kinds of atoms make up all types of matter.

John Dalton was born on September 6, 1766, in Eaglesfield, a small village in northwestern England. John was raised as a Quaker, keeping the modest ways of the Quakers all his life. He went to a small Quaker school and also took evening lessons in mathematics. By the age of 12, he had started teaching. In 1781 he joined his older brother as a teacher in nearby Kendal. Within a few years the brothers were running the school.

During his twelve years in Kendal, Dalton became friends with John Gough, a blind philosopher. With Gough's help, Dalton studied mathematics and began to keep a diary in which he recorded weather conditions. He continued the diary all his life, making more than 200,000 observations.

Through Gough's influence, Dalton was appointed professor of mathematics and natural philosophy at New College, Manchester, where he went to live in 1793. When the college moved to York, in 1799, Dalton remained in Manchester, supporting himself by tutoring in mathematics and chemistry.

Dalton was also interested in other branches of science. He began to work in botany. When he found that he could not distinguish flower colors, he realized that he was color blind. He studied color blindness and gave such a detailed report of it that this defect came to be known as Daltonism.

After 1801, Dalton's studies of weather led him deeper into the study of chemistry. He found that air was a mixture of gases. Like others before him, he believed that these gases were composed of tiny particles.

Dalton's experiments showed him that all matter—not just gas—is composed of atoms. When the same kind of atoms combine, they form an element. When different kinds of atoms combine, they form a compound.

By 1810, Dalton had written a book called *A New System of Chemical Philosophy*, in which he set forth his atomic theory. He stated that the atoms of each element differ by weight from the atoms of every other element. He expressed this idea with relative weights: that is, he gave an oxygen atom a weight seven times that of a hydrogen atom; an iron atom weighed 50 times as much as a hydrogen atom; and a gold atom weighed 190 times as much as a hydrogen atom.

Dalton worked out a whole table of relative weights. Though most of his calculations were wrong, his theory of atomic weights was correct. The use of atomic weights made chemistry a more exact science.

Dalton also devised a system of chemical notation. In this system, atoms were represented by circular symbols. (For example, hydrogen was represented by a circle with a dot in the middle.) The system proved awkward, however, and never became popular. Instead, the system of letter symbols proposed by Jöns Jacob Berzelius gained acceptance. (See CHEMISTRY, HISTORY OF in Volume C.)

Dalton's work required many hours in the laboratory. He never married and made few trips to London, though in 1804 and 1809 he lectured at the Royal Institution there.

Many honors came to Dalton for his scientific achievements, but he still enjoyed tutoring children. A visiting French scientist was amazed once to find the great Dalton teaching arithmetic to a child on his lap.

After a few years of illness, Dalton died in Manchester on July 27, 1844. He was given a public funeral, and some 40,000 people came to honor the founder of the atomic theory.

Reviewed by LOUIS VACZEK
Author, *Enjoyment of Chemistry*

DALY, MARCUS. See MONTANA (Famous People).

DAMIEN DE VEUSTER, JOSEPH. See HAWAII (Famous People).

DAMON AND PYTHIAS. See GREEK MYTHOLOGY (Profiles).

DAMS

A dam is a barrier placed across a river or waterway that changes the way that water flows. Some small dams simply turn a flow of water from one course to another. Water that is diverted (turned aside) is usually sent through a canal or pipeline to a facility that needs a reliable water supply. Such a facility might be a mill, a power plant, or a water treatment plant. Dams that divert water are called **diversion** dams. Larger dams often hold back or store floodwater and create large reservoirs. These large structures are called **storage** dams.

▶ PURPOSES OF DAMS

Humans have used dams for thousands of years. One of the oldest uses of dams is to divert water from rivers in dry regions so that crops can be grown on arid desert land. The artificial watering of land for agriculture is known as **irrigation**. It is important because it allows food to be produced on land that does not receive enough rainfall to grow crops. Irrigation is often said to "make the desert bloom."

Dams can also be used to produce power by capturing the potential energy of water in a flowing river. Anyone who has ever picked up a bucket of water knows how much energy is needed to lift even a small amount of water just a few feet. Imagine carrying a bucket of water to the top of a ladder and then dropping it. When it hits the ground below, the bucket of water will release a lot more energy than an empty bucket dropped from the same height.

Water flows downward, releasing energy along the way. This energy, harnessed by dams, turns water wheels or turbines, generating mechanical or electric power.

Early gristmills used water wheels to grind grain. Later, water-powered mills were used for textile manufacture, woodworking, stamping (breaking) rock for mining operations, and many other purposes. Beginning in the late 1800's, waterpower was used to rotate electric power generators and produce **hydroelectricity**. Production of hydroelectricity is the main use of waterpower today.

Another important use of dams is to store water for use in cities and suburbs. Many cities depend on dams to store water in reservoirs that are usually located in rural areas many miles away from the cities themselves. Dams that support **municipal water supply** usually capture water from snowmelt and spring floods. This water may be delivered to people later in the year when normal river flow is usually much lower. The water storage provided by large dams can help support urban populations through droughts, when rainfall is scarce and river levels fall.

Irrigation, hydroelectricity, and municipal water supply are the most important uses of dams, but there are other ways that dams serve human society. **Navigation** dams are used to increase the depth of water in rivers so that barges and ships can travel more easily. **Flood-control** dams are intended to prevent flooding of communities in low-lying

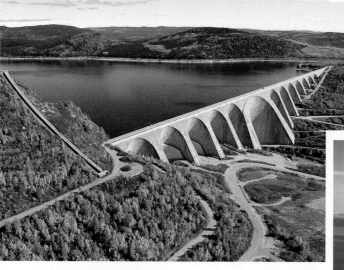

Far left: Hoover Dam, on the Colorado River, is a concrete arch dam. Left: Daniel-Johnson Dam, in northern Quebec, Canada, is a multiple-arch dam. Below left: Grand Dixence Dam, in Switzerland, is a concrete gravity dam. Below: Ataturk Dam, in Turkey, is an embankment dam.

areas. Although water builds up behind these dams after heavy rains, these dams are not meant to store water for long. In fact, their reservoir areas are dry most of the year. Many dams provide opportunities for **recreation**, that is, swimming and boating. Recreational use is often secondary to irrigation or power production. Still, it can promote tourism and thus help the economy of a region.

In the 1900's, engineers and water resource planners began to promote and build large **multiple-purpose** dams. People who wanted to build multiple-purpose dams argued that they would be even more useful than single-purpose dams. For example, Hoover Dam, a large structure across the Colorado River near Las Vegas, Nevada, was promoted as a way to 1) provide flood control, 2) supply water for southern California, 3) produce power for consumers throughout the American Southwest, and 4) offer recreational opportunities.

However, it can be hard to operate a dam meant to serve multiple purposes. The purposes often compete with each other. For example, irrigation competes with power generation. Irrigation is important to farmers, who may feel that dams should release water only when crops need to be nourished (water demand peaks during the summer but falls during the winter). Power generation is important to electricity users, who say dams should release water throughout the year (people use electricity year-round). But water that is released during the winter to generate power will not be available the following summer for irrigation. And during times of drought, boaters will want water to be kept in a reservoir instead of being released for either irrigation or power generation.

▶ TYPES OF DAMS

The simplest dams use a large amount of material to block a waterway. The material in the dam is so heavy (or massive) that the water pressure pushing up against the structure cannot topple the dam or move it downstream. The strength of such dams depends on the force of gravity, which acts on the material in the structure and holds it in place. In fact, massive dams built using concrete or masonry are often called **gravity** dams.

Massive dams can also be built using large quantities of earth fill (soil) or loose rock. Such structures are known as **embankment** dams. They are very good at holding back large bodies of water. However, they can fall apart if water is allowed to flow over them. Flowing water would erode the loose material in the embankment, and the structure would wash away downstream.

Gravity dams of concrete or masonry stand up to flowing water much better than embankment dams, and they often serve as **overflow** dams. These dams allow excess water in a reservoir to safely flow over the top of the structure. To control the flow of water over the structure, dams are often built with **spillways**. A spillway is a channel that guides water over the downstream side of the structure. Water enters the spillway through a notch built into the top edge of the dam. If the spillway is large enough, excess water will keep flowing through the notch into the spill-

way instead of brimming over the top of the dam.

Rather than simply relying on the weight (or mass) of a dam to provide stability, engineers also design dams that resist water pressure because of their structural shape. For example, dams may be built with a curved shape that extends upstream into the reservoir. Known as **arch** dams, these concrete and masonry structures resist water pressure not just by relying on gravity, but also by transferring water pressure from side to side. The best site for an arch dam is inside a narrow canyon that has hard, solid walls. The curved structure of the arch dam can then be used to direct water pressure to these walls. When canyon walls are used to help hold back a reservoir, the dam itself does not have to be built to withstand all the pressure. It can be much thinner than a comparable gravity dam. Because much less material is needed, arch dams are less costly to build.

Another type of structural dam, called a **buttress dam**, relies on a series of thick vertical supports called buttresses rather than on a single solid mass of material. The buttresses rise out of the foundation and support a solid, waterproof wall that faces upstream and holds back the reservoir. The buttresses are usually spaced about 20 to 40 feet (6 to 12 meters) apart. Because of this spacing, buttress dams are sometimes called hollow dams. Designs that use a flat slab of rein-

Electricity is produced at dams by harnessing the power of falling water to turn machines called turbines. The rotating turbines spin the generators, which produce electricity.

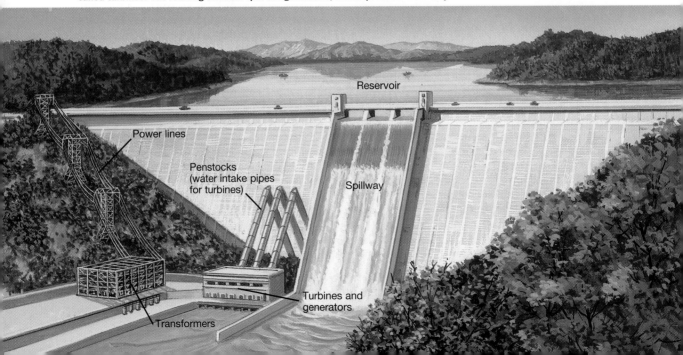

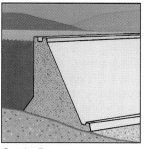

Gravity Dam

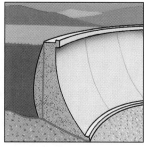

Concrete Arch Dam

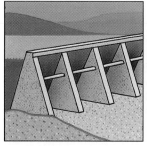

Buttress Dam

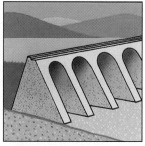

Multiple-Arch Dam
(Massive-Head Type)

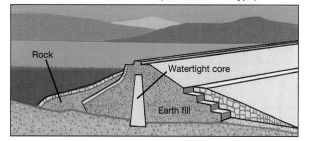

Rock

Watertight core

Earth fill

Embankment Dam

forced concrete to extend across the up-stream side of the buttresses are known as **flat slab** dams. Designs that feature a series of arches to extend across the upstream side are called **multiple-arch** dams.

In a multiple-arch dam, each arch spans the distance between two buttresses. Each arch spreads water pressure to these but-tresses the way a single-arch dam spreads water pressure to canyon walls. Pressure transferred to the buttresses does not have to be handled by the arches themselves, so a se-ries of arches can be lighter than a continu-ous flat slab. Some multiple-arch dams need just 25 percent of the material needed to build a concrete gravity dam.

Some dams combine features of different dam types. For example, the **massive-head** buttress dam combines a flat slab and multi-ple arches.

▶ DAM CONSTRUCTION AND SAFETY

The decision to build a dam requires careful thought. Engineers and water re-source planners must consider many fac-tors, including location and design. For example, they need to measure river flow to be sure there will be enough water to fill the reservoir if a dam is built. They must analyze the geology of the region to be sure the foundations for a possible dam will be strong enough not only to support the dam itself but also to hold back the water that builds up behind the dam. Also, they need to map the topog-raphy (the shapes of the landforms) that will be covered by the reservoir. Without a map, they will not know exactly how much water a dam will store.

Before engineers choose a design for a dam, they must consider the shape of the dam site. (Is it in a narrow canyon, or does it stretch across a wide valley?) They must also consider the availability of building materials. (Is there a nearby supply of earth fill, or is crushed rock readily available for use in making concrete?)

A dam may pose environmental and political risks. Decisions about a dam's location, design, and construction can spark conflict because these decisions often hurt some people and benefit oth-ers. For example, if a dam threatens to create a reservoir that will flood towns or wilderness areas, people may organize to stop the dam's construction or change the dam's location.

Once a proposed dam has been approved, engineers must plan a way to bring equip-ment and materials to the dam site. If a dam is to be built in a remote place, engineers must also build housing and dining facilities for the workers who will be brought to the site. This is important because large dams can take several years to build.

When work on a dam begins, engineers must be sure the structure will rise from a strong foundation. Dirt and loose rock must be excavated (removed). Hard bedrock must be uncovered. But before excavation can even begin, engineers must find ways to con-trol the river flow and "de-water" the site. Sometimes it is possible to drill through canyon walls, creating tunnels that divert water around the dam site. (This method was used to protect workers during the construction of Hoover Dam.) If engineers decide against diversion tunnels, they may build temporary **cofferdams** around parts of the riverbed. Behind a cofferdam, water can be pumped out, opening that part of the site to excavation.

Motorized equipment and large trucks are often used to transport the earth and rock fill for embankment dams. Trucks are sometimes used to transport concrete for gravity and arch dams, but concrete can also be poured from cablecars. These are containers that ride cables strung over the construction site. A cablecar system makes it easy to deliver concrete to any part of the dam.

Safe dams depend on safe designs. To create safe designs, engineers use mathematical tools and computer models. They also invite independent experts to review their work. These experts are often organized into groups called consulting boards. In many states and countries, government agencies may approve or reject dam designs. Reviews by government authorities promote safety, but they also tend to discourage new ideas, especially if the authorities are unfamiliar with new methods.

Once designs are approved, engineers must ensure that their careful plans are actually followed. Dams built over the past several decades have been quite safe. Dam failures have been rare.

▶ **PROBLEMS WITH DAMS**

At first glance, a dam may seem to offer nothing but benefits—municipal water supply, hydroelectricity, flood control, and recreation. But a closer look may reveal large costs. When assessing a dam, it is necessary to weigh the benefits against the costs.

When a dam blocks a river, it changes the environment, including plant and animal habitats. A dam can prevent migratory fish (such as salmon in the Pacific Northwest) from reaching their spawning grounds. Fish ladders and other lift technologies have been developed to help migratory fish get past large dams. However, dams still reduce fish populations along many waterways.

Dams can also affect fish in downstream areas. Dams can change the temperature of water flowing in the stream, and they can block sediment (soil and sand suspended in the river water). Sediment is important because it builds up in sandbars and creates places where fish can lay their eggs.

Large dams can create huge reservoirs that cover hundreds of square miles of land. These reservoirs may cover wilderness areas, destroying habitats for plants and animals. Reservoirs can also cover towns, cities, and farms. When a dam floods a remote desert canyon, the damage caused by a reservoir may seem small. But when a dam floods areas where thousands of people live and where human cultures have thrived for centuries, the costs may seem too high. In fact, large dams in densely populated areas of China and India have sparked protests.

Another problem is the release of carbon dioxide, a greenhouse gas that contributes to global warming. (To read more about greenhouse gases, see the article GLOBAL WARMING in Volume G.) In tropical regions, carbon dioxide may rise from newly filled reservoirs that contain rotting plants and trees. Large stagnant reservoirs in tropical and semitropical areas can provide breeding areas for disease-carrying organisms. And the water stored in large reservoirs can also press down on the ground below, adding to the stresses along any nearby faultlines. Greater stress along a faultline may increase the risk of earthquakes.

Sometimes people decide a dam has outlived its usefulness. If people object to an existing dam, they may argue that it should be **breached** (removed). Conservationists have argued that breaching dams helps restore rivers by bringing back native fish populations. But simply breaching a dam may not restore a river. If a dam has stood for many years, large amounts of sediment may have built up behind it. Removing this sediment without harming the downstream environment can be difficult and expensive.

▶ **HISTORY AND FUTURE OF DAMS**

The oldest known dam is a small earthen structure on the edge of the Black Desert in present-day Jordan. It was built more than 5,000 years ago. Ancient civilizations in Mesopotamia (present-day Iraq) and China used diversion dams to support large-scale irrigation systems. The modern era of dam building is usually considered to have begun in the

NOTABLE DAMS

Name and Location	Type	Height		Length	
		Feet	Meters	Feet	Meters
Aswan High Dam (Egypt)	Embankment	364	111	12,565	3,830
Ataturk (Turkey)	Embankment	554	169	5,459	1,664
Chicoasén (Mexico)	Embankment	869	265	920	280
Fort Peck (Montana, U.S.A.)	Embankment	250	76	21,026	6,409
Grand Coulee (Washington, U.S.A.)	Concrete gravity	550	168	4,173	1,272
Grand Dixence (Switzerland)	Concrete gravity	932	284	2,296	700
Guavio (Colombia)	Embankment	820	250	1,280	390
Guri (Venezuela)	Concrete gravity, embankment	532	162	30,853	9,404
Hirakud (India)	Concrete, masonry, embankment	200	61	15,748	4,800
Hoover (Arizona-Nevada, U.S.A.)	Concrete arch	726	221	1,244	379
Hungry Horse (Montana, U.S.A.)	Concrete arch	564	172	2,115	645
Ilha Solteira (Brazil)	Embankment, concrete gravity	262	80	20,293	6,185
Inguri (Georgia)	Concrete arch	892	272	2,198	670
Itaipu (Brazil-Paraguay)	Hollow concrete gravity, embankment	591	180	25,918	7,900
Kiev (Ukraine)	Embankment	62	19	177,502	54,103
Kishaw (India)	Embankment	830	253	1,181	360
Kurobe No. 4 (Japan)	Concrete arch	610	186	1,603	489
Mangla (Pakistan)	Embankment	380	116	11,000	3,353
Manicouagan No. 5 (Quebec, Canada)	Multiple arch	703	214	4,284	1,306
Mica (British Columbia, Canada)	Embankment	800	244	2,600	792
Nurek (Tajikistan)	Embankment	1,017	310	2,390	728
Oahe (South Dakota, U.S.A.)	Embankment	245	75	9,300	2,835
Oroville (California, U.S.A.)	Embankment	770	235	9,300	2,835
Rogun (Tajikistan)	Embankment	1,066	325	2,506	764
Tarbela (Pakistan)	Embankment	485	148	9,000	2,743
Three Gorges (China)	Concrete gravity (under construction)	607	185	7,648	2,331
Vaiont (Italy)	Concrete arch	858	262	624	190

1600's in Spain, where large masonry storage dams were built for irrigation. By the 1800's, milldams appeared throughout Europe and the United States.

In the late 1800's and early 1900's, rapidly growing cities created demand for large-scale water storage. To satisfy this demand, regional authorities built large gravity dams, many of them rising over 200 feet (61 meters) high. The U.S. Reclamation Service (later renamed the Bureau of Reclamation) sponsored irrigation projects that relied on huge structures. Private electric power companies financed hydroelectric projects.

During the 1920's, planning began for what became the Hoover Dam (also known as Boulder Dam from 1933 through 1947). This dam, which was built on the Colorado river at the Arizona-Nevada border, rose 726 feet (221 meters) high. It was one of the first major multiple-purpose dams in the United States. It was a model for other government-financed multiple-purpose dams during the Great Depression. These included the Grand Coulee Dam, sited on the Columbia River in central Washington, and the Fort Peck Dam, sited on the Missouri River in eastern Montana. In the southeastern United States, the Tennessee Valley Authority was established in 1933 to develop dams throughout a river basin covering parts of six states.

After World War II (1939–45), the large dams that had been built in America served as models. They not only inspired further work in the United States, they also guided development all over the world. At first, the growth in dam construction drew little opposition. However, by the 1970's, many people started to see dams as threats to the environment. People began resisting new dams. By the 1990's, environmental concerns were even greater. People argued that many dams were harming fish populations and that these dams needed to be breached.

Today dams continue to play a vital role in the modern global economy. They also draw opposition from people who believe that many dams bring costs that outweigh their benefits.

DONALD C. JACKSON
Department of History, Lafayette College

See also FLOODS; IRRIGATION; WATER; WATERPOWER.

DANCE

Dance is rhythmic movement of the body, usually performed to music. One of the oldest art forms, dance exists around the world in practically every culture. Like music, dance is a performance art. It may serve a purpose, or it may be performed simply for entertainment or enjoyment. In many cultures, dance is a key element in religious rituals and in marking important events—birth, "coming of age" ceremonies for boys and girls, marriage, and even death. Dancing has prepared people for war, expressed joy in times of peace, and provided entertainment for every level of society, from peasant folk to royalty.

Originally, the word "dance" was derived from the Sanskrit word *tanha*, which means "desire for life." The first "textbook" on dance was the *Natya Shastra*, written in India almost two thousand years ago. Classical Indian dancing still follows the rules that were laid down in this text. Although other ancient cultures did not have written manuscripts as specific as those of India, the dancing figures found on Greek urns and Chinese pottery and in early Egyptian paintings give us clues that dance existed in other cultures long ago.

The purposes of a dance can tell us a great deal about the culture it represents. Over the years, dance has developed along two main lines. There are dances in which everyone can take part, referred to as **communal dancing**. And there are dances performed by highly trained dancers for the entertainment of an audience. This is known as **theatrical dancing**.

▶ ELEMENTS OF DANCE

No matter what its origins or purpose, every form of dance involves one or more of the following main elements.

Steps

A dancer's feet and body move rhythmically in a pattern that relates to the rhythm of musical accompaniment. The motion and patterns made by the feet are called steps.

Steps vary greatly, depending on the purpose of the dance and traditional beliefs. In some cultures, such as those of native peoples of Africa and Hawaii, the spirits worshiped by the people were believed to live underground. Therefore, dancers step heavily, making lots of noise in order to communicate with the gods below.

In ancient India, the dancers wore ankle bells that resounded as their feet forcefully slapped the floor. The steps reflected the complex rhythms of the accompanying music and singing. When migrating gypsies from India settled in Spain, this same rhythmic stamping was blended into flamenco dancing.

oped the ability to rise up on the balls of their feet. Grace and politeness were reflected in court dance through elegant geometrical patterns, stately steps, and controlled turns and balances. During the Romantic era in the 1800's, the use of pointe shoes allowed the female dancer to rise up and balance on the tips of her toes, which made her steps seem to defy gravity.

Gestures

Hand and arm motions that accompany the steps are called gestures. These can be simply ornamental, or they may communicate a message or even tell a story. The most complex use of hand gestures is found in Kathakali, the classical Hindu dancing of India, which has 500 hand positions. These gestures, called mudras, are a form of precise hand language the dancer uses to silently express the words of the accompanying singer, whose song tells a story. In hula, an ancient form of Hawaiian dance, hand gestures also accompany the dancer's steps. The gestures reflect the meaning of the words of ancient chants that tell stories of Hawaiian mythology.

The harvest dances of many African tribes use gestures that imitate working in the fields,

In Native American, Aboriginal Australian, and African tribes, where hunting has traditionally been a necessary activity, dance steps often imitate the movements of birds or the walks of the animals the hunters want to pursue. Through the dance, the tribe asks the gods for luck in a successful hunt and honors the spirit of the animal before the kill.

In western Europe during the Renaissance (1300–1600), dances were often circular, with low gliding steps or with small jumps that allowed the dancers to become airborne. As ballet developed in the courts of France—especially in that of Louis XIV—dancers devel-

cutting down crops, or digging in the soil. Classical ballet uses special gestures that are recognized and understood by the audience to mean, for example, "I pledge my love to you" or "He must leave." In modern dance, dancers find new ways to express joy, sadness, or other emotions through original and powerful movements of the arms and hands.

Technique

Technique is the element of training the dancer must practice in order to master the art of dance. Degrees of training vary widely among cultures, as does the age of the performer. For instance, in classical ballet and classical Spanish bolero, dancers endure rigorous classes at dance academies for at least two hours daily and warm up thoroughly before performing. In general, these dancers are under 30 years old.

In Hawaiian hula, groups of dancers study together in special schools. Their training goes beyond maintaining their dance technique—it is a lifestyle they follow. All students must follow a strict set of rules. If these are broken, the whole group is penalized. Students learn ancient chants and how to weave special plants into their costuming to honor certain gods. They also follow special diets to cleanse their spirit before any performance. Upon graduation, these dancers become respected members of the community.

In dances of Bali, Africa, and Native American tribes, dancers do not warm up through exercising, but prepare for the dance by making offerings to their gods and dressing in elaborate costuming and masks. No special school for training is necessary. In these cultures, people dance well into old age.

The rhythmic stamping and graceful arm movements of Spanish flamenco reflect influences from India and the Middle East.

Music

Musical accompaniment for dance can range from simple percussion instruments made from materials found in nature to more elaborate instruments made of metal and brass. Costumes may also contribute to the percussion that goes along with the dance. In the Middle East, a belly dancer wears many strands of coins, beads, and bells that shake when she moves. Dancers in India and Hawaii also have bells and rattles that sound as they dance.

In Hawaii, percussion music for dances comes from drums made from dried gourds, lava rocks, or bamboo sticks. In Africa, "talking" drums are often made from sacred trees. An elder person in the tribe plays these drums, which imitate the tones of the human voice. When hearing certain rhythms that sound like words, the dancer knows what move he or she should make.

In Bali and Java, every village has its own gamelan, a large orchestra of percussion instruments such as gongs, bells, and metal drums. Most people in Bali grow up learning how to dance at an early age and to play in the gamelan as well.

Stringed instruments are very popular in many forms of dance. The balalaika is important in the folk dancing of eastern Europe. In Japan, the shamisen often accompanies dance. Spanish flamenco dancing is famously paired with the guitar. Early forms of ballet danced in royal courts had elaborate stringed musical accompaniment. Classical ballet today still is typically danced to the music of a large orchestra.

In the early 1900's, modern dance in Germany and the United States explored simple percussion, such as a single drum. Later, many choreographers experimented with using no music at all, or just dancing to the words of a story.

Costuming

Costuming can be one of the most exciting elements of dance. Sometimes costume is intended to have a magical effect in rituals. In the Egungun dance of the Yoruba tribe in Africa, for example, the dancers wear tall masks and headpieces to enable the spirits of their ancestors to return to Earth. When the dancer puts on this headpiece, it is believed that the spirit of a deceased loved one descends into the dancer, who then receives the power to perform antics that remind the community of the person.

The Bambara people of Mali, in West Africa, wear elaborately carved wooden antelope headdresses in agricultural ceremonies. The Bird Dance of the Plains Indians of North America features costumes and headpieces made from large feathers that make the dancers look like eagles.

In Bali, masks are an important part of dance. Many villages in Bali present a dance-play that serves as a cleansing ritual for the community. In this story of a fight between good and evil, Ranga, the witch, wears a terrifying mask. It is believed that once the dancer playing her puts on the mask, spectators can fall into a trance from its power. Representing the fight for goodness is the Calonarong, or dragon, who wears a giant mask. Both these masks are considered sacred and are kept in the temple.

In other forms of dance, costuming is meant to beautify the performer. In bharata natyam, a form of South Indian classical dance for women that was originally danced in Hindu temples, the women dress as brides, indicating their "marriage" to god. Classical ballets such as *The Sleeping Beauty* feature beautiful costumes of jeweled tutus for magical fairies, the princess, and her court.

Face and body paint can also be an important part of costuming. In Japanese Grand Kabuki theater, as well as Kathakali theater of India, the painted faces accentuate the character. The audience can tell whether or not a character is good or evil by the colors he wears. In the dances of the Aboriginal tribes of Australia, the dancers' bodies are painted with elaborate patterns and animal designs that indicate where they are from and what they are dancing about.

▶ COMMUNAL DANCE

Communal dance includes the ritual dances of traditional communities, as well as folk dance and social dance.

Rituals

Rituals are actions or patterns of behavior that are repeated in order to establish a desired effect and to affirm certain values or traditions of the society. In general, communities or tribes that participate in rituals regard the group as more important than the personal feelings or desires of one individual. Since prehistoric times, tribal cultures have used ritual dance to communicate with the

Ritual dance plays an important role in tribal cultures, such as those of Native Americans *(below left)* and Australian Aborigines *(below right)*. Costume, body paint, and movement all have special meaning.

gods, to help with the hunt, to bring rain to crops, or bring healing to their village.

One example of a ritual dance is the Kachina ceremony of the Hopi Indians, who live in the southwestern United States. The Kachinas are considered good spirits who bring rain and healthy crops to the tribe and protect the community from evil. To honor the Kachinas, the dancers wear masks that impersonate the spirits and dance with sacred rattles.

Dance is often an important part of healing rituals, also called exorcisms. The main purpose of such rituals is to free an ailing human body from sickness; some believe illness can come from a spirit possessing the person's soul. In these dances, participants often fall into a state of trance. Some rituals, such as the Navajo Night Chant and the Sanghyang Dedari of Bali, combine dance with chanting, smoking or eating medicinal plants and herbs, and ritual fasting to help heal someone.

Ritual is often part of a culture's religious traditions. In India, dancers called devadasi devoted their lives to the service of their gods. They danced in the temple to stories of Hindu mythology and tended the altar. Some cultures also honored the spirits with seasonal ritual dances. In ancient Greece, the god Dionysus and the coming of spring were celebrated with great dancing and revelry. In autumn, dance ceremonies such as the Yam Festival in Africa and the Green Corn Dance of Native American tribes give thanks for the harvest.

Some Christian religious rituals also involve dance. In Europe during the Middle Ages (500–1500), the Catholic Church sponsored mystery, miracle, and morality plays. These productions, based on stories from the Bible, were presented in church courtyards and town squares. In Spain, a dance for ten young boys called *Los Seises* is performed during the Holy Week in the great cathedral of Seville. The boys sing, dance, and play castanets (wooden clappers).

Rituals with religious roots can become secular, or nonreligious, over time. For example, the pavane, a stately court dance from the Renaissance era, had its origins in the slow, solemn walking used in religious pageants.

Folk Dance

Folk dancing often evolves from rituals or pagan customs. These traditional dances of a community tend to be performed outside and involve no formal training—the steps and melodies are usually simple, though there are exceptions. Some examples include the farmers' dance of the Netherlands and Morris dancing in England. The polka originated as a folk dance in Eastern Europe, but when a Czech dancing master introduced it to Parisian society, it became the rage of ball-

Welsh folk dancers form a circle. Folk dances are often performed outdoors by dancers in traditional costume.

rooms in Europe. In America, square dancing continues to be a form of folk dance enjoyed by many. For more information, see the article FOLK DANCE in Volume F.

Sometimes folk dance illustrates the troubles of the people. In Spain in the 1500's, the gypsies, who originally came from India, were considered lower-class people. Flamenco, the dance form they originated, can be either fiery and fast or slow and mournful. It reflects not only the rhythmic traditions of classical Indian dance and the serpentine arm movements of the Middle East, but the sorrows of the people who originated it.

Tap is a dance form that originated in America during the 1800's. In New York City, Irish immigrants and freed black slaves lived in poor neighborhoods; dancing was an important pastime in both cultures. Tap evolved when African rhythms were combined with traditional Irish step dancing. Although it began as a folk dance, due to its popularity tap has become a theatrical form of dance used in Hollywood films and Broadway musicals.

Social Dance

Between the folk dancing of the common people and the aristocratic dancing found in royal courts is social dance. During the 1700's, people who were not of noble birth began to become wealthy through commerce. The Industrial Revolution also contributed to the development of this rising middle class. Social dancing at balls became an important symbol of good breeding in the upper classes in Europe and the United States in the 1800's and 1900's. Knowing how to dance properly, converse, and use good manners in society was an important part of ballroom etiquette. Social dancing was a way for men and women to meet each other. Dancing together in couples, the man led the woman through a series of dance steps they both had learned.

The waltz was one of the first popular social dances for couples. The close embrace required to dance it was considered scandalous at first.

One of the most famous and earliest examples of social dance is the waltz, which had its origins in folk dance. This "turning" dance for couples became popular in Vienna ballrooms beginning in 1780. It was first thought to be scandalous because of the close way the couples held each other, but it soon became accepted and was wildly popular.

In the 1920's in Europe, the United States, and Argentina, people began to dance in nightclubs, which had a freer atmosphere than the ballroom. Jazz music and African rhythms began to influence dances such as the Charleston and the Lindy Hop. Dances with Latin and African rhythms, such as the rumba and the mambo, became popular in nightclubs in the 1940's.

Partner dancing fell out of fashion when the twist became the rage in the 1960's. Instead of holding hands and dancing steps that matched those of your partner, dancers moved individually, improvising on their own while twisting. The arrival of disco dancing in the 1970's brought partner dancing back.

▶ THEATRICAL DANCE

Theatrical dances are performed for an audience by highly trained, often professional dancers. Although theatrical dances can sometimes be performed just for the sake of dancing, they often tell a story to an audience, with characters portrayed by the dancers. Three great traditions of theatrical dance are Asian and, in the West, ballet and modern dance.

Minuet

DANCE FADS

Dance crazes are not just a phenomenon of modern times. People have taken part in them ever since the rise of social dancing in the 1700's. Following are notable examples from different time periods.

Minuet

The minuet was a stately and elegant court dance that originated in France in the 1700's. Usually a dance for two, the couple made an S or a Z figure while dancing different variations of the minuet step. It stopped being performed after the French Revolution in 1789 because it was associated with the aristocracy, but a simpler form remained very popular in England.

Waltz

Originating from an Austrian folk dance called the *Ländler*, this turning ballroom dance for couples became popular in Europe at the end of the 1700's, replacing the minuet in popularity. It was at first considered scandalous because of the face-to-face position of the couple and the close hold the man kept on the woman's waist. The dance is in 3/4 time.

Tango

Originally a dance for poor immigrants that began in the slums of Buenos Aires, Argentina, the tango is a blend of Spanish dance steps combined with North African rhythms. Like flamenco, the lyrics of tango music often speak of the frustrations of the people. When the dance was exhibited in Paris in the early 1920's, it became enormously popular in the ballrooms of Europe and among the high society of Buenos Aires.

Tango

Lindy Hop

Lindy Hop

The Lindy Hop began in Harlem at the famous Savoy Ballroom in 1926. Dancing to the

Asian Theatrical Dance

India and other parts of Asia have a long tradition of theatrical dance. Asian theatrical dance forms require long periods of training and use elaborate costuming. Kathakali Dance Theater of India, Beijing Opera of China, and Grand Kabuki of Japan are three forms of theatrical entertainment that tell

In Japanese Kabuki and other forms of Asian theatrical dance, all roles are performed by men. Technique is passed down from father to son.

big bands playing the jazz music of the Swing Era, young couples would exhibit their ability to spin, reeling in and unwinding each other at a fast tempo. The Lindy Hop became notorious for its exciting and extremely athletic airborne lifts and daring partnering. Throwing his partner in the air, the man would catch her at breakneck speed and continue dancing. Also known as the jitterbug, this dance continued to be popular with teenagers through the 1930's and 1940's.

Twist

Rumba, Mambo, Cha-Cha

These three dances, originating in Cuba, became tremendously popular in ballrooms during the 1940's and 1950's. The rumba has its roots in the dances of the slaves brought to Cuba from Africa in the 1500's. The exaggerated and fast-paced swaying movements of the hips reflect Spanish and African rhythms. The mambo, a slower variation of the rumba, first became popular in Havana in the 1940's. It led to the development of the cha-cha, which has a triple beat.

Twist

This popular dance originated in teenage culture during the 1960's and was popularized by performers such as Chubby Checker and Elvis Presley. When doing the twist, the feet stay planted on the floor. The knees and the pelvis twist one way, while the upper body twists the other way.

Disco

Disco dancing became the rage in the 1970's. There are many varieties of disco dances, but generally the woman spins constantly while her partner, holding her hand, sends her away and then pulls her back in. The hustle was a line dance that was extremely popular. Examples of disco dancing can be seen in the film *Saturday Night Fever* (1977).

Break Dancing

Break dancing originated in the Bronx in the 1970's. It was performed in the streets to rap music as a form of competition between teams, which usually consisted of young men. Wearing loose-fitting clothing and sneakers, dancers use mock-fighting moves of kung fu or other martial arts. Break dancing is characterized by spinning on the knees, hands, elbows, and head. It has become a part of hip-hop culture.

Break Dancing

stories through dance. All roles, including those of women, are danced by men and boys. Those who are trained to play female characters will do so for their entire careers. In each of these theatrical forms, the boys begin training at about age 7.

Students of Kathakali live in a special academy. The dance training, similar to martial arts, makes the boys very flexible. In addition to mastering the 500 mudras, or hand gestures, they also exercise their facial and eye muscles in order to express emotions—joy, anger, sadness, or bravery—that the audience will recognize in the storytelling.

The Beijing Opera performers are famous for their energetic dances. Battle scenes are full of acrobatic flips and gymnastic tricks. The dancers, who also live at special schools, are trained to be very flexible and to move very quickly.

In Japanese Grand Kabuki, the training is taught to young boys by their fathers or uncles. Kabuki dance training is highly athletic, but the boys must also master the art of

Dancers who perform in China's Beijing Opera *(above left)* are famous for their acrobatic flips. India's Kathakali dancers *(above right)* must master the use of facial expression.

walking, which tells the audience a great deal about the nature of a character. The use of the eyes and facial expressions is also extremely important.

In all three of these theatrical dance forms, the costuming and elaborately painted faces are crucial in transforming the dancer into a character who is part of the story.

Ballet

The theatrical dancing of western Europe had its beginnings in royal courts. When Catherine de Médicis became queen of France, she presented ballets by dancing masters she had brought from Italy. These were so elaborate they bankrupted the court. This rich display of entertainment announced France's cultural superiority to the rest of Europe. Until the French Revolution in 1789, the French royalty continued to send this message to the world by encouraging the best in music and dance.

After the Revolution, many French and Italian dancers, choreographers, and teachers went to work in Russia. During this time, classical ballets such as *The Sleeping Beauty* (1890) and *Swan Lake* (1895) reflected the order of the aristocratic court—the ballerina and her male partner, with the corps de ballet behind them, loosely represented the princess, prince, and their court. See the article BALLET in Volume B.

In Spain during the 1700's, a uniquely Spanish form of classical dancing developed, called bolero. This form of dance closely resembles ballet in that it uses the same five positions of the feet. But many stylized folk steps (called character steps) are also used, and the dancers play castanets.

In the United States, entertainment in the early 1800's involved ballet, but the dancers were imported from Europe. In New York City, a long-running spectacle, *The Black Crook* (1866), influenced the development of

Swan Lake, with its romantic pas de deux (dance for two people), marks a high point of classical ballet, one of the great traditions of theatrical dance in the West.

musical theater in America. Vaudeville, another form of popular entertainment, often featured ballet and ethnic folk dancing such as clogging or skirt dancing. Vaudeville shows toured the United States in the early 1900's and remained popular until the rise of radio and television.

Bolero is a uniquely Spanish form of classical dance. It resembles ballet but also uses elements from folk dance.

Modern Dance

At the very beginning of the 1900's, three American dancers found their fame in Europe: Loie Fuller, Isadora Duncan, and Ruth St. Denis. Each created an innovative way of dancing that contributed to the development of modern dance.

Loie Fuller transformed the skirt dancing of vaudeville with her use of electric lighting, invented only some 20 years earlier. In her Fire Dance, for example, she amazed audiences as blazing orange and red lights projected on her billowing silk costume, giving her the appearance of a flame.

Inspired by the classic beauty of ancient Greece, Isadora Duncan danced as herself, not as a fanciful creature or a fairy tale character. She rejected the technique of ballet in favor of moving her body and arms in a freer way that allowed her to express her emotions. She also shocked many by dancing barefoot, dressed in a loose tunic. See the biography of Isadora Duncan in Volume D.

Ruth St. Denis' career as a solo performer involved transforming herself into a woman from another culture. Through her dress, makeup, and movements, St. Denis became an Indian temple dancer, a Japanese geisha, or a Spanish flamenco dancer.

Rudolf von Laban and his pupil Mary Wigman were dancer-choreographers working in Germany in the 1920's and 1930's. They made important contributions to modern dance. Laban founded several schools and established a system of recording dances called Labanotation. After establishing her solo career, Wigman made dark and serious dances that reflected the somber mood of the time in Germany. Suppressed by Hitler's Nazi regime, modern dance never achieved its potential in Germany. But it flourished in the United States.

The rapid development of American modern dance was due mainly to Denishawn, the first modern dance academy in the United States. Founded in 1916 in Los Angeles by Ruth St. Denis with her husband and partner, Ted Shawn, this important school fostered the careers of three students who later made significant contributions to the development of modern dance: Martha Graham, Doris Humphrey, and Charles Weidman. After touring with the Denishawn dancers, they established their own careers and founded companies; Graham had her own, while Humphrey and Weidman founded a company together. All three of these dancers and choreographers abandoned Denishawn's fascination with portraying dancers from other cultures. Instead, they made works expressing their personal concerns and contemporary issues of the day, and they developed their own dance techniques.

African American choreographers such as Lester Horton, Katherine Dunham, Pearl Primus, and Alvin Ailey made dances that were influenced by other cultures. Horton's

Isadora Duncan

Loie Fuller

Loie Fuller (1862–1928), born in Fullersburg, Illinois, established her career in Europe. Fuller was famous for using electric lighting—still a relatively new technology—in her performances. Her silk costume featured a huge skirt and long sleeves, which she lifted and lowered with long wands hidden within. Ever-changing colored lights projected on her billowing costume allowed audiences to imagine her to be a butterfly, a lily, or a flame.

Isadora Duncan (1877–1927), born in San Francisco, California, created a dance style that laid the foundations for what became modern dance. A biography of Duncan appears in Volume D.

Ruth St. Denis (1878–1968) and **Ted Shawn** (1891–1972), considered pioneers of modern dance, founded Denishawn, the first modern dance academy in the United States. Ruth St. Denis was born in Somerville, New Jersey. She began her solo career by creating dances in which she personified exotic women from other cultures. In 1914, Ted Shawn, born in Kansas City, Missouri, became her dance partner and later her husband. After much touring across America, they founded Denishawn in Los Angeles, California, in 1916. After St. Denis and Shawn ended their partnership, he established the first all-male modern dance company in the United States as well as the Jacob's Pillow Dance Festival in Massachusetts.

Bill "Bojangles" Robinson (1878–1949), one of the legends of tap, was born in Richmond, Virginia, and started his career as a "hoofer" at age 6. He performed in vaudeville, in nightclubs in Harlem, and in musical comedy, beginning with the Broadway production *Blackbirds of 1928*, an all-black revue. Robinson was famous for a routine in which he tapped up and down a flight of stairs. He starred in several Hollywood movies, including *Stormy Weather* (1943), his last.

Martha Graham (1894–1991), born in Allegheny, Pennsylvania, started her dance training at Denishawn at age 22. Her father was an analyst (an early version of a psychotherapist) who taught her that "movement never lies." Graham took this to heart and strove to find her own truthful way of moving. She started a company in 1928, which is still in existence today. Her modern dance technique is still practiced all over the world. Her many dances ranged from American themes, such as *Primitive Mysteries* (1931) and *Frontier* (1935), to Greek myth, such as *Clytemnestra* (1958).

Doris Humphrey (1895–1958) and **Charles Weidman** (1901–75) were pupils at Denishawn and members of its touring company. Humphrey, born in Oak Park, Illinois, was a favorite of Ruth St. Denis,

Martha Graham

interracial company featured theatrical dances inspired by American Indian themes. Both Dunham and Primus were anthropologists whose studies in the Caribbean and Africa served as subject matter for their dances. Ailey used black traditions from the American South as a theme in his works.

Some choreographers who explored modern dance in an experimental way were considered revolutionary. Although modern dance was always innovative, these choreographers went further, rejecting the idea that dance should tell a story or express emotion. Merce Cunningham, originally a dancer with Martha Graham, made abstract dances—with no narrative, or story—that were highly experimental. Another American choreographer, Alwin Nikolais, created dances that were multimedia events: They combined lights, electronic music, and props that transformed the dancers' bodies into odd shapes.

In the 1960's, a new group of choreographers emerged, forming a group called the Judson Dance Theater. The dances of these

Katherine Dunham

Twyla Tharp Dance Company

Twyla Tharp (1941–), born in Portland, Indiana, developed a unique style of movement based on ballet, jazz, and other dance forms. She studied dance in New York City with Martha Graham, Merce Cunningham, and others and danced with the Paul Taylor Dance Company before forming her own troupe in 1965. Her works include *Deuce Coupe* (1973), *Push Comes to Shove* (1976), *The Catherine Wheel* (1981), and the Broadway musical *Movin' Out* (2002).

Mark Morris (1956–), born in Seattle, Washington, studied Balkan folk dancing and Spanish flamenco as a teenager. In 1980, he started the Mark Morris Dance Group in New York City. Morris' modern dances are highly rhythmic and musical and show his wit and humor. Morris borrows widely from the music and dance techniques of other cultures. His own version of the classical ballet *The Nutcracker* is called *The Hard Nut* (1991). The Mark Morris Dance Center, a base for his company and a dance school, is located in Brooklyn, New York.

who gave her the opportunity to develop her choreographic skills by making dances for the Denishawn company. Weidman was born in Lincoln, Nebraska. The two left Denishawn in 1928 to start their own modern dance company. They choreographed dances from an American viewpoint, offering their visions of an equal and democratic society.

Katherine Dunham (1910–), a choreographer, dancer, teacher, and anthropologist, was born in Joliet, Illinois. As a student working on her doctorate in anthropology, she traveled to the Caribbean, where she researched the dances of Haiti and Martinique. She founded the Katherine Dunham Dance Company, the first African American troupe. Dunham was also a social activist who fought for civil rights. In addition to a career in films and theater, Dunham founded schools in New York City and East St. Louis.

Merce Cunningham (1919–), born in Centralia, Washington, started his

career in the dance company of Martha Graham. His solo career began in 1944 when he presented a dance concert with the avant-garde music of American composer John Cage. Cunningham's work continues to be experimental: Choreographic decisions are based on a coin toss, and dances are choreographed on a computer. His company is based in New York City.

Alvin Ailey (1931–89), dancer, choreographer, and founder of his own company, began his career as a dancer for Lester Horton. Ailey's dances often contained autobiographical references to his upbringing in rural Rogers, Texas. Themes of the American South are the subject of his most famous dance, *Revelations* (1960), which is a theatrical stylization of a baptism and the joyous celebrations surrounding it. The Alvin Ailey Dance Company continues to perform and tour; the Alvin Ailey Dance Center in New York City offers classes and scholarships.

Savion Glover (1973–), an actor, tap dancer, and innovative choreographer, was born in Newark, New Jersey. A former student of legendary tapper and actor Gregory Hines, Glover dances to many forms of music as well as jazz, the music traditionally used for tap. He has danced to the baroque music of Vivaldi as well as to hip-hop and funk. Glover is said to be a master at improvisation. He has starred in *The Tap Dance Kid* (1984), *Jelly's Last Jam* (1992), and *Bring In 'da Noise, Bring In 'da Funk* (1996), for which he won a Tony Award.

"postmodern" choreographers often left audiences puzzled. They featured ordinary movements such as walking—or no movement at all. Dancers' actions had nothing to do with the music that played, and they wore everyday clothes instead of costumes. Although considered radical, postmodernism allowed choreographers to experiment with new ways of making dances.

Today it is common for choreographers to borrow freely from other dance forms. Ballet technique can be seen in the work of modern choreographers such as Twyla Tharp or Merce Cunningham. George Balanchine's love of jazz and Broadway musicals is evident in some of his ballets. Mark Morris uses music from around the world and borrows movements from dances of other cultures. This freedom to blend dance styles and music is resulting in dances that are multicultural in feeling. And it is allowing dance to move in new and unexpected directions.

PATRICIA BEAMAN
Tisch School of the Arts, New York University

This painting shows Dante holding his masterpiece, *The Divine Comedy*. Surrounding him are scenes from the epic poem.

DANTE ALIGHIERI (1265–1321)

Dante Alighieri is considered Italy's greatest poet. His epic poem *La divina commedia*, or *The Divine Comedy* (1308–21), is a masterpiece of world literature.

Dante was born in Florence in late May or early June, 1265. His family belonged to the Guelph party, which ruled the city at that time. Dante had a good education and may have finished his studies at the University of Bologna. He married Gemma Donati about 1285.

In Dante's youth his energies were devoted to writing lyric poetry. He also fought in the Battle of Campaldino (1289) against the rival Ghibelline party and began to play an important role in Florentine politics.

Most of Dante's early verse was inspired by his idealistic love of Beatrice Portinari, a Florentine woman he had met when both were children, and who died in 1290. His *La vita nuova* (*The New Life*), composed about 1293 in verse and prose, tells the story of this relationship. *Il convivio* (*The Banquet*, 1303–07) was a work of philosophy in the form of three odes and commentaries on them. In Latin he wrote a study of the Italian language, *De vulgari eloquentia* (*On Eloquence in the Vernacular*, 1303 or 1304) and an argument for world rule by a monarch, *De monarchia* (*On Monarchy*, about 1313).

Because of his opposition to the politics of the so-called Black faction of the Guelphs, Dante was forced to leave Florence in 1302. His first refuge was the court of the Imperial Vicar of Italy, in Verona. Later he wandered from court to court in northern Italy.

The last 13 years of Dante's life were dedicated mainly to the writing of *The Divine Comedy*, a long narrative poem that combines autobiography, commentary on the society and politics of the Middle Ages, and an eloquent lesson in Christian faith. The poem was written in a triple-rhyme scheme (the first and third lines of each stanza rhyme with the second line of the previous stanza) invented by Dante. It is divided into three sections: *Inferno* (Hell), *Purgatorio* (Purgatory), and *Paradiso* (Paradise). Each of these sections represents a different part of the world of the dead, through which Dante travels in the poem. Along his journey, he encounters many notable people from his time.

The poem begins with Dante meeting the Roman poet Vergil in a dark forest. From there, Vergil guides Dante through the circles of Hell, where they find the souls of the damned. The two then scale the Mountain of Purgatory, along whose terraces the remorseful dead are purged, or cleaned, of their sins. At the summit of Purgatory is the earthly paradise, where Dante is reunited with Beatrice. From there, he is led by Beatrice through the various spheres of heaven until they reach God. For richness of subject matter and beauty of language, *The Divine Comedy* has few rivals.

Dante spent his last years in Ravenna, where he served as an ambassador for the prince Guido da Polenta. There Dante died on September 14, 1321.

THOMAS G. BERGIN
Author, *Dante*

DANTON, GEORGES-JACQUES. See FRENCH REVOLUTION (Profiles).

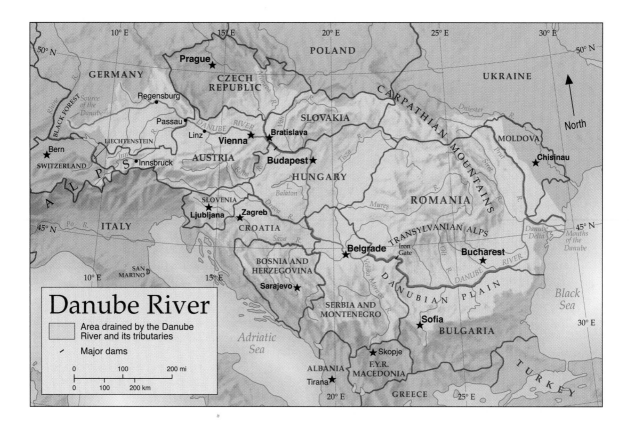

Danube River

Area drained by the Danube River and its tributaries

Major dams

0 100 200 mi
0 100 200 km

DANUBE RIVER

The Danube is the second longest river in Europe, after the Volga. From its headwaters in the Black Forest of Germany, it flows eastward for 1,771 miles (2,851 kilometers), touching on nine different countries—Germany, Austria, Slovakia, Hungary, Croatia, Serbia and Montenegro, Bulgaria, Romania, and Ukraine. The Danube has approximately 300 tributaries, and its drainage basin covers an area of more than 315,000 square miles (815,850 square kilometers). Near the end of its course, the river wends through the Danube Delta, the world's largest reed swamp, then empties into several mouths on the Black Sea.

The Danube has long been an avenue of trade between central and eastern Europe. In ancient times, it formed part of the boundary of the Roman Empire. It later served as the natural boundary between the Austro-Hungarian Empire and the Ottoman Empire.

The Danube is divided into three distinct sections. The upper Danube flows from its source through the German cities of Regensburg and Passau and the Austrian cities of Linz and Vienna (the capital). The only major tributary of the upper Danube is the Inn River, which joins the Danube at Passau, the first navigable port on the river.

The middle and largest of the three sections flows between Vienna and the Iron Gate, a gorge where the Danube crosses the Carpathian Mountains at the border of Serbia and Romania. Major cities along this portion include Bratislava, Budapest, and Belgrade, the respective capitals of Slovakia, Hungary, and Serbia and Montenegro. The landscape, which is generally flat and fertile, is one of Europe's most important agricultural regions. Vast amounts of grain, fruits, and vegetables are grown there. Important tributaries in this region include the Morava, Váh, Tisza, Rába, Drava, Sava, and the Velika Morava.

The lower Danube forms most of the border between Romania and Bulgaria. It has no major tributaries other than the Prut, which forms the Romania-Moldova border.

RONALD WIXMAN
University of Oregon

DANZIGER, PAULA. See CHILDREN'S LITERATURE (Profiles).

DAOISM. See RELIGIONS OF THE WORLD (Taoism).

DAPHNE. See GREEK MYTHOLOGY (Profiles).

DARIUS

Darius (pronounced duh-RY-us) is a Persian name that means "king." Three kings of the ancient Persian Achaemenid dynasty reigned (r.) under this name. The two most notable are discussed below.

Darius I (the Great) (550–486 B.C.) (r. 522–486 B.C.) was the most impressive of the three kings of the Achaemenid dynasty to rule the once vast Persian Empire. The son of Hystaspes and a member of a younger branch of the dynasty, Darius gained the throne in 522 on the death of Cambyses, who had conquered Egypt.

To suppress internal opposition, Darius reorganized the empire under twenty satraps (provincial governors) and promoted major reforms. He standardized weights and measures, introduced coinage, built a widespread system of roads, and established a postal system.

In his efforts to expand his territory, Darius succeeded in conquering Thrace. In 492 B.C., he invaded Greece for the first time. He invaded a second time in 490 B.C. but was badly defeated at the Battle of Marathon, near Athens.

Darius the Great died in 486 B.C. while planning a third invasion of Greece. He was succeeded by his son Xerxes I.

Darius III (380?–330 B.C.) (r. 336?–330 B.C.), the last king of the Achaemenid dynasty, had the misfortune to face invasion by Alexander the Great of Macedonia. Darius was first defeated by Alexander at Issus (333 B.C.) near İskenderun in present-day Turkey. They met again in 331 B.C. at Gaugamela, near Nineveh in present-day Iraq. Though vastly outnumbered, Alexander's forces decisively defeated the Persian army. Darius fled the battlefield. While preparing further resistance, Darius was murdered by Bessus, the satrap of Bactria. Darius was succeeded by Alexander.

JEREMY BLACK
University of Exeter

See also PERSIA, ANCIENT.

DARK AGES. See MIDDLE AGES.

DARROW, CLARENCE SEWARD (1857–1938)

Clarence Seward Darrow was the most famous defense lawyer of the early 1900's. He was known as the attorney for the damned because he often defended people who were political or social outcasts.

Darrow was born in Kinsman, Ohio, on April 18, 1857. He attended law school at the University of Michigan, but poverty forced him to leave without graduating. He worked as a law clerk in Youngstown, Ohio, and was admitted to the bar in 1878.

In 1887, Darrow moved to Chicago, Illinois. He became a junior law partner of John Peter Altgeld, who later became governor of the state. In the early 1890's, Darrow was counsel for the city of Chicago.

Darrow was sympathetic to organized labor. He represented the United Mine Workers during the 1902 anthracite coal strike. He defended labor leaders William D. ("Big Bill") Haywood, who was tried for murder (1907), and the brothers John J. and James B. McNamara, tried for blowing up the Los Angeles Times building (1911). He saved them all from the death penalty.

In 1924, Darrow represented Nathan Leopold and Richard Loeb, two wealthy young Chicagoans who had murdered 14-year-old Bobby Franks, just to see if they could commit the "perfect crime." Darrow also saved them from the death penalty.

Darrow's most famous case came in 1925, when he defended John T. Scopes, a schoolteacher who was tried for teaching the theory of evolution in violation of Tennessee state law. Darrow lost this case but is remembered for his brilliant cross-examination of the prosecutor, William Jennings Bryan.

Darrow was married twice, and he had one son. His numerous books include *The Story of My Life* (1932). He died in Chicago on March 13, 1938.

GERALD KURLAND
Author, *Clarence Darrow:
Attorney for the Damned*

See also SCOPES TRIAL.

DARTS

Darts is a game in which two or more players take turns throwing pointed darts at a numbered board. For many years the game was most popular in England, where it is still played, but today people all over the world enjoy playing darts.

The most familiar and popular kind of darts is the English version, which uses a round dartboard. American darts, popular in some parts of the United States, uses a different kind of dart and a slightly reconfigured dartboard. This article discusses only English darts.

Equipment. Darts are made of wood, plastic, or metal and are feathered like arrows. They cannot measure more than 12 inches (30 centimeters) long or weigh more than 1¾ ounces (50 grams).

The dartboard measures 18 inches (45 centimeters) in diameter and is usually made of pressed fiber (called bristle). It is marked off into 20 equal triangles. The triangles are numbered from 1 to 20 around the outer edge of the board, but they are not numbered in order. A dart scores the value of the triangle in which it lands. At the center of the board is the **inner bull**, or bull's-eye. Surrounding the inner bull is a small circle called the **outer bull**. A dart that lands in the inner bull counts 50 points, and one landing in the outer bull counts 25 points. Near the outer edge of the board is the **double ring**, a narrow circle marked off by two wires. If a dart lands in this section, the score is double the value of that triangle. Halfway between the outer bull and the double ring is another circular band called the **triple ring**. If a dart is thrown there, the score is triple the value. A dart that does not stay on the board or that lands in the area between the double ring and the outer edge of the board does not score any points.

The board is set up with the bull's-eye 5 feet 8 inches (1.7 meters) above the floor. The players stand behind a line at least 7 feet 9¼ inches (2.4 meters) from the board.

Play. There are many different kinds of dart games. One of the most popular, and easiest for beginners to learn, is called 301. It can be played by two people or by teams. Scoring is done by subtraction—each player starts with a score of 301, from which the score for each throw is subtracted. To start

Dartboards are divided into triangles numbered 1 to 20. A dart scores the value of the area in which it lands. The inner bull counts 50 points; the outer bull, 25.

scoring, a player must throw a dart into the double ring. Each player throws three darts per turn. Players must end the game with a double and with exactly the number of points needed to reach zero. The first player to reach zero is the winner. Variations of this game, with the same basic rules, include 501, 601, 701, and 1001.

History. The history of darts is not well documented. It originated in England, perhaps as early as the 1400's, and may have developed from archery. The game soon became highly popular in pubs and taverns. Records show that in 1620 the Pilgrims who were sailing to the New World played darts on the *Mayflower*. Darts became popular in the United States when servicemen learned the game from the English during World War II (1939–45). Today darts can be played on electronic dartboards, which use special soft-tip darts, and even on the Internet.

Reviewed by EDMUND CARL HADY
Executive Secretary, American Dart Association

DARWIN, CHARLES ROBERT (1809–1882)

In the year 1859 a book was published that forever changed people's understanding of themselves in relation to all other living things. The book was *On the Origin of Species*, and its author was Charles Darwin, a quiet English scientist who claimed that all living plants and animals had developed, or evolved, from earlier forms of life.

Before Darwin, most people believed that each of the more than a million species of plants and animals had been created separately and had remained unchanged since the Earth's beginning. They believed that humans were not related to any other species of animal but had been specifically created to rule over all other living things. Darwin's research led him to discover very different ideas, however.

Charles Darwin was born on February 12, 1809, in Shrewsbury, England, into a wealthy and well-known family. His grandfather, Erasmus, was a famous scientist and poet. Charles attended an excellent school, but his record was far from brilliant. He did, however, show a strong interest in nature.

At 16, Charles was sent to Edinburgh University to study medicine. But watching surgery made him so ill that in 1828 he transferred to Cambridge University, where he studied for the clergy. His interest in plants and animals remained very strong.

Darwin graduated in 1831. Through his friendship with John Henslow, his botany professor, Darwin was appointed geologist on the naval vessel H.M.S. *Beagle*. He became the ship's naturalist. The *Beagle* set sail in 1831 on a five-year voyage around the world.

During the voyage of the *Beagle*, expeditions were made into South America, the Galápagos Islands, and other islands of the Pacific. Wherever he went Darwin studied the geology. He searched for fossils. He observed plant and animal life. And he thought about relationships between living creatures and fossil animals. He kept a journal that was to become the basis for his theory of evolution.

On his voyage Darwin read Charles Lyell's book *The Principles of Geology*, which began to have a great influence on his thinking. Unlike most geologists before him, who believed that the face of the Earth was the result of a few great and violent geological changes, Lyell saw that the Earth was continually and slowly shaped by ordinary events. Simple processes, like waves and wind and rain, could act over vast periods of time to gradually alter the Earth's features. These ideas were extremely important to the theory of evolution that Darwin was soon to develop.

In 1836, his earlier plans for the clergy forgotten, Darwin returned to London, where he wrote his account of the voyage. By now he was convinced that all forms of life had evolved from earlier forms. The question was, how did such evolution occur?

Domestic plants and animals, he noted, were bred for certain desirable features. English racehorses were an example of this. Starting long ago with ordinary horses, people carefully selected the strongest and swiftest animals to be bred together. After continuing this practice for many generations, breeders had created a new type of horse—the sleek English racehorse.

Selection by people was the key to breeding in domestic animals. Darwin was convinced that selection also took place in nature, but he wondered how.

Darwin realized that in all species of plants and animals there is a natural range of variation, with no two individuals exactly alike. Those individuals who are more likely to survive and produce offspring are those whose variations better suit them to their environment. Darwin called this sorting out of naturally favored variations **natural selection**. He realized that the result of natural selection over many generations would be a gradual change in the species.

Darwin did not publish his ideas on evolution immediately. In 1839 he married his cousin, Emma Wedgwood, and a few years later they moved to Down, Kent, in southern England. He was in poor health and settled down to a quiet life in the countryside.

Then in 1858, Darwin was sent an essay by Alfred Russel Wallace, an English naturalist. Darwin was stunned to find a theory of natural selection in this manuscript. Wallace's paper was ready for publication; Darwin's huge book—the result of years of work—was not.

Darwin quickly put together a research report that was presented with Wallace's paper at the Linnaean Society meeting in London in 1858. The following year Darwin published his great work, *On the Origin of Species by Means of Natural Selection*. This book contained both the theory of evolution and the evidence for it.

All 1,250 copies of the first edition were sold in a single day. Many people found Darwin's theory of evolution too unsettling and attacked it, and a great controversy followed. The book upset many established scientific ideas and also contradicted firmly held religious beliefs. But Darwin's ideas were supported by many respected scientists, and after a few years Darwin's theory was accepted by much of the scientific community. In 1863, Darwin was awarded the Copley Medal of the Royal Society, Britain's highest scientific honor. During the following years he developed his ideas on evolution further in a number of books. In *The Descent of Man, and Selection in Relation to Sex* (1871), he discussed the evolution of humans, arguing that we along with the apes evolved from a common ancestral species.

Darwin died in Kent on April 19, 1882. He was honored for his achievements by being buried in England's Westminster Abbey, and to this day scientists continue the work he began.

Reviewed by KENNETH A. KOREY
Editor, *The Essential Darwin*

See also EVOLUTION.

DATABASES

Databases are organized collections of data—information such as names, numbers, sounds, and pictures. Today, most databases are computerized. Computers enable quick access to individual pieces of data, even if they are stored in databases that are large and complex.

Computers help many kinds of users store, organize, and retrieve their data. With databases, governments can maintain tax records, doctors can confirm health insurance coverage, and businesses can update inventory and customer information. Individuals can use simple databases to track household expenses or organize personal files. Individuals can also open accounts with banks that have sophisticated databases that process electronic (non-cash) transactions.

People use databases by inputting information in a form that can be understood by a computer. To enter or request data, a user can type on a computer keyboard, press buttons on a telephone keypad, slide a credit card through a credit card reader, or scan an object's bar code. Some systems even respond to spoken commands. Once the user's request has been expressed in the appropriate form, the computer can search through its electronic files, adding, changing, or retrieving information. Finally, the computer can deliver a report in a form that is understandable to the user.

A typical report, such as an account summary, can be printed out or displayed on a computer monitor. In many cases, an actual report is unnecessary. For example, a database-equipped telephone answering system can respond to a caller's telephone keypad input by simply transferring the call to a particular extension.

How did we get along before computers? In the distant past, information was handed down by word of mouth. With the rise of commercial activity and the need for record keeping, people developed handwritten records and accounting methods. Companies developed large product catalogues and detailed customer records. However, the number of transactions was limited by the ability of people to record them by hand.

Most databases are computerized, enabling storage and retrieval of vast amounts of data, which can be displayed on computer monitors.

With the arrival of computerized databases, the number of transactions that could be processed was greatly increased. But for data processing to be truly efficient, databases had to organize data efficiently.

Database Organization. There are many different ways to organize data. The best way to organize data depends on the answers to two basic questions: (1) What questions will we need to ask of our data, and how often will we need to ask each of these questions? (2) What kinds of changes will we need to make in our data, and how often will each of these kinds of changes need to be made?

Here is a simple example: the organization of a database of names, telephone numbers, and addresses. If the purpose of the database is to generate printed telephone directories, and if updated directories will be prepared just once each year, a very simple database structure will work well enough. However, if the purpose of the database is to enable emergency personnel to respond to 911 calls, the database will have to be organized to enable efficient searching. In a typical search, a phone number would be used to look up an address. (Imagine how long it would take to use a phone number to look up an address in a printed telephone book!)

Database Management. Because so many people rely on databases, the management of databases is very complex—especially when many people try to access the same databases at the same time. **Database management systems** ensure that one user's database interactions do not interfere with another's. Some of these systems process database interactions that are enabled by communications lines and wireless technology.

Future Challenges. Rapid progress in communications, finance, medicine, and many other fields has created a need to store more and more data. Of course, in many cases, information stored in a database is linked to the person who provided it. This raises serious questions about the security of private information.

As private information gathers in commercial and government databases, it becomes much easier to use computers to search these databases. All that is needed is a common piece of identifying data, such as a social security number. With this number, it is possible to bring together many pieces of private information about a person.

If database information is not protected, sensitive information can be misused. A serious misuse is **identity theft**—when someone's personal information is taken without permission and then used to commit a crime such as removing funds from a victim's bank account. Laws to prevent identity theft have been proposed. Some would limit the buying and selling of private information. Others would require that security lapses be announced to the public. Technological solutions include fingerprint matching. Some stores are testing systems that can match a fingerprint scan against a digital version of a fingerprint stored in a database.

Another challenge is the design of electronic voting systems. These systems should be easy to use. However, they must also be protected against fraud. In other words, the database for an electronic voting system must be secure even though the data itself must be freely accessed, updated, and processed.

All these challenges show that database designers have a lot of work to do. They must build systems that promote ease of use, protect privacy, and enhance security—all at the same time.

BERNARD A. GALLER
University of Michigan

DATE

Dates are the fruit of the date palm, a tree that has grown in the warmer parts of Southwest Asia and North Africa since prehistoric days. The date palm has a straight, unbranched trunk crowned with feathery leaves up to 20 feet (6 meters) long. The tree may reach a height of 60 to 80 feet (18 to 24 meters). The fruit comes out in large clusters on stalks between the leaves. A cluster may contain more than 1,000 dates and weigh 22 pounds (10 kilograms).

The date is a berry with a single hard seed. Most dates are oblong in shape and are usually more than 1 inch (2.5 centimeters) long. Some varieties of dates turn golden to reddish brown when they become ripe. A few kinds of dates are nearly black. Many dates are picked as soon as they are ripe and spread on mats to dry. The dried fruit contains some moisture, but more than half the date is sugar.

Date palms grow in a warm climate and are usually found near streams or springs. A palm tree growing in the desert has always been a sign to the thirsty traveler that water is not far away. Cultivated date palms are often planted in desert land and then carefully irrigated. The palm will not produce much fruit without plenty of water, but to ripen properly the fruit needs a long hot growing season without rain or humidity.

Date palm trees may be grown either from seeds or from offshoots (known as suckers) that grow out from the trunk when the palm is young. The trees begin to bear fruit in four to eight years. They reach full production in twelve to fifteen years and may bear fruit for 100 years or longer.

Egypt, Iran, and Saudi Arabia are the leading date-exporting countries. Southeastern Spain is the only area in Europe that produces dates. A few date palms are grown in Italy as ornaments and to supply palm leaves for religious festivals. The dates grown commercially in southern California and Arizona come from imported offshoots of Old World varieties.

Throughout the Middle East the date palm's trunk is used for building material and the whole leaves for thatch. The midribs of the leaves go into crates and furniture. Baskets are made out of the leaflets. Leaf bases

From top: The date palm is grown primarily for its fruit, an important food in the Middle East. Dates grow in large clusters. When dried they are chewy and sweet.

make good fuel, and the bud is eaten as a vegetable or salad. Syrup, fermented liquor, vinegar, and alcohol are made from the fruit. The seeds are ground and fed to livestock. The date itself is an important food in desert lands and a delicacy in other regions.

ROY W. NIXON
United States Department of Agriculture

DAUMIER, HONORÉ (1808–1879)

Honoré Daumier, the great French cartoonist of the 1800's, was also a fine painter and sculptor. But the world remembers him best for his many pictures that made fun of French life and politics.

Born in Marseille on February 26, 1808, Daumier moved to Paris with his family in 1816. Because the family was poor, Daumier had no formal education. He worked first as an errand boy in a law court, then as a bookseller. He always loved to draw.

After becoming a lithographer, Daumier began to draw caricatures—drawings that exaggerate and make people look ridiculous—for the newspapers and magazines of Paris. His drawings made fun of the political figures of France and called attention to the weaknesses and dishonesty of government officials. One of Daumier's caricatures was so insulting to King Louis Philippe that Daumier was sentenced to six months in prison.

In 1835 the French government forbade the publication of political cartoons. Daumier then began to make drawings that satirized the social customs of his day. He ridiculed

French artist Honoré Daumier was famous for drawings that ridiculed the life and politics of his day. Here, he presents an unflattering picture of a lawyer in court.

lawyers, middle-class society, and people in the theater. His work was popular, but he was paid little. He did about 4,000 lithographs.

During the 1840's, Daumier turned to painting and sculpture, but even today he is best known for his caricatures. His eyesight failing, he lived his last years in extreme poverty in a cottage outside Paris. He died on February 11, 1879.

Reviewed by EDWARD J. SULLIVAN
New York University

DAVID

David was king of Judah and Israel. His story is told in the Bible, in the books of Samuel and Kings. Son of a landowner, Jesse, of the tribe of Judah, David was the youngest of eight brothers. He tended his father's sheep.

David lived about 1000 B.C., when the Philistines pressed in on the newly established kingdom of Israel. Its first king, Saul, had to fight continually against them. It is said that in one of these battles, David, with a single shot of his sling, killed Goliath, champion of the Philistines. On hearing this, King Saul appointed David his armor bearer.

The king's daughter, Michal, fell in love with David, and they were married. David soon became a popular hero. The Judeans elected him king of the tribe of Judah. After King Saul and his son, Jonathan, died in battle against the Philistines, David became king of all Israel. As king, David's main goal was to weld Israel's twelve tribes into a united kingdom. He waged many wars against the

surrounding nations, proving to be a resourceful general. To bind the tribes more firmly together, David captured Jerusalem and made it his capital. In Jerusalem he housed the ark of the law, a chest containing the two stone tablets on which the Ten Commandments were written.

King David wrote a number of religious poems, called psalms, that are used to this day in churches and synagogues throughout the world. He also helped arrange the religious services later used in the temple built by his son Solomon.

The real greatness of King David lay in his devotion to God. David suffered many disappointments. Being human, he had weaknesses that brought him sorrow. But through it all he remained a faithful leader of his people. He was so loved and admired that in later times people believed the Messiah would come from his family.

MORTIMER J. COHEN
Author, *Pathways Through the Bible*

DA VINCI, LEONARDO. See LEONARDO DA VINCI.

DAVIS, BENJAMIN O., JR. See WASHINGTON, D.C. (Famous People).

DAVIS, BETTE. See MOTION PICTURES (Profiles: Movie Stars).

DAVIS, JEFFERSON
(1808–1889)

Jefferson Davis was president of the Confederate States of America during the U.S. Civil War (1861–65). He was born on June 3, 1808, in Fairview, Kentucky, the youngest of ten children. His family moved to Mississippi when he was only a few years old. There he grew up, a delicate and imaginative child.

At the age of 16, Davis entered the United States Military Academy at West Point. He graduated in 1828 as a second lieutenant in the army and served on the western frontier. In 1835 he resigned from the army to marry Sarah Knox Taylor, daughter of the future U.S. president Zachary Taylor. She died of malarial fever three months after their wedding. Grief stricken, Davis devoted himself to his cotton plantation in Mississippi.

For ten years he led the life of a Southern planter. In 1845, shortly after marrying Varina Howell, he was elected to the U.S. House of Representatives. But the following year he left to fight in the Mexican War as commander of the Mississippi Rifles. Davis returned home a war hero for his bravery at the battles of Monterrey and Buena Vista.

In 1847, the governor of Mississippi appointed Jefferson to fill a vacancy in the U.S. Senate. He was elected to a full term in 1850. An opponent of the Compromise of 1850, Davis resigned in 1851 to run for governor of Mississippi as the candidate for the States' Rights Democrats, but he lost the election.

In 1853, President Franklin Pierce appointed Davis secretary of war. He served until 1857, when he again became a U.S. senator from Mississippi. In the growing quarrel between North and South, Davis argued strongly for states' rights and for slavery.

President of the Confederacy. When Abraham Lincoln was elected president of the United States in 1860, South Carolina seceded from the Union. In 1861, Mississippi followed. Other Southern states seceded, and the Confederate States of America was formed. Some Southerners thought separation without war was possible, but Davis saw war coming. A soldier at heart, he hoped to become general of the Southern armies. To his disappointment, the Confederacy asked him to be its president. In spite of ill health, Davis accepted the task of leading the South. He was formally inaugurated as president on February 22, 1862.

In the U.S. Congress, Davis had been a strong supporter of states' rights. Now he believed that a united South was more important than the rights of each individual state. He fought with his legislature and with his own cabinet. This was partly because Davis and the others had hot tempers. But it was also because Southerners distrusted the strong central leadership that Davis felt was necessary for a nation at war. Davis was dedicated to the Southern cause. But he believed that he was always right and hated to compromise.

In April 1865, General Robert E. Lee, commander of the Southern armies, wired Davis that he could no longer hold Richmond, Virginia, the Confederate capital. Davis fled southward. The war was lost, but he would not believe it. He still thought the South could rally.

In May 1865, Union soldiers captured Davis and put him in jail. The North said he was a traitor. Some accused him of involvement in the assassination of President Lincoln, though he had nothing to do with it. After two years in prison, Davis was released without trial. He could have been returned to the Senate, but Davis would have had to ask a federal pardon. Proud as ever, he refused.

Until his death, Davis defended the cause of the South. But he admitted that the past was dead and urged Southerners to look to the future. He died in New Orleans, Louisiana, on December 6, 1889.

Reviewed by RICHARD B. MORRIS
Columbia University

See also CIVIL WAR, UNITED STATES; COMPROMISE OF 1850; CONFEDERATE STATES OF AMERICA.

DAVIS, MILES. See ILLINOIS (Famous People).

DAVY, SIR HUMPHRY (1778–1829)

Sir Humphry Davy is best known for his invention of the miners' safety lamp. The lamp itself is no longer important, but what it tells us about Davy is important. He was a man who put science to work for people.

Davy was born on December 17, 1778, at Penzance, Cornwall, England. At the age of 16, he went to work for a doctor. At 20, he took charge of a laboratory in Bristol.

While at Bristol, Davy carried out experiments with heat, light, and gas. There he made his first important discovery—that a gas called nitrous oxide (laughing gas) could be used as a painkiller. In 1801, Davy was invited to become a lecturer at the Royal Institution in London.

By 1812, Davy's work was known throughout Europe, and he was knighted. He resigned from the Royal Institution and carried on his research independently.

In 1815, Davy began a scientific attack on a serious problem: gas explosions in coal mines that took many lives each year. The gas occurred naturally in the mines. The fire that sparked the explosion came from the open flame in miners' lamps. To solve the problem, Davy devised a safety lamp with a wire screen. The screen kept the heat of the flame away from the gas in the mine.

In his later years, Davy investigated problems in many fields of science. He studied the relationship between magnetism and electricity. He went to Italy to help unroll papyruses found in ancient ruins. He studied the geology of his native Cornwall.

By 1826, Davy was seriously ill, but even illness could not dull his interest in the world about him. In 1827 he published a book on fishing. He died on May 29, 1829, in Geneva, Switzerland.

Reviewed by LOUIS VACZEK
Author, *Enjoyment of Chemistry*

DAWES, CHARLES G. (1865–1951)

Charles Gates Dawes was an American lawyer, banker, author, and government official. He served one term as vice president of the United States (1925–29) under Calvin Coolidge.

Dawes was born in Marietta, Ohio, on August 27, 1865. He began his career as a lawyer in Nebraska and later became a bank director. In 1895 he moved to Chicago, Illinois, and made a fortune in gas and electric power. He published an influential book defending the gold standard (which determines the value of money based on how much gold is in circulation). As a result, he was chosen finance chairman for the Republican presidential campaign in 1896. After winning the election, President William McKinley appointed Dawes comptroller of the currency (1897–1902) to help supervise the nation's banks. In 1902, Dawes founded the Central Trust Company of Chicago, which billed itself as a "big bank for small people."

After the United States entered World War I in 1917, Dawes purchased food, horses, and other supplies for the American Expeditionary Force (AEF). He achieved the rank of brigadier general. In 1921, President Warren G. Harding appointed him director of the Bureau of the Budget. Within a year, Dawes had cut government spending by one-third.

His money management skills made Dawes a natural choice to lead the Inter-Allied Reparations Committee (1923–24) to review Germany's debt to the Allies for damages caused during the war. The resulting **Dawes Plan** reduced the payment schedule and made it easier for Germany to acquire loans. That achievement led to his election as vice president in 1924 and won him a Nobel Peace Prize in 1925.

When Herbert Hoover became president in 1929, he appointed Dawes ambassador (1929–32) to Great Britain. Later, during the Great Depression, Dawes became head of the Reconstruction Finance Corporation (1932). In 1933, Franklin D. Roosevelt was elected president. Dawes opposed Roosevelt's New Deal programs, so he retired from public life. He remained chairman of the City National Bank & Trust Company of Chicago until he died in Evanston, Illinois, on April 23, 1951.

STEPHEN A. SCHUKER
Corcoran Professor of History
University of Virginia

DAY AND NIGHT. See EARTH.

DAY CARE

Day care is the care of children by paid adults during a part of the day when their parents are away from home. Day care is provided mainly for infants and preschoolers but also for elementary school children before and after school and during school vacations.

▶ REASONS FOR DAY CARE

Day care for children is necessary for several reasons. In many families both parents or the single parent works outside the home. In the past, other relatives often lived with or near the family and could provide some child care. Today fewer grandparents or other family members are able to care for children whose parents work. Therefore working parents must depend more than ever before on the availability of day care.

▶ TYPES OF DAY CARE

Day care can be provided in two main ways. **Day care centers** typically care for large groups of children in settings resembling nursery schools. They may be run by commercial chains or by nonprofit organizations such as churches or civic groups. Some employers provide day care centers for children of employees.

Day care homes provide care for smaller numbers of children in family settings. This type of care, also called **family day care,** is preferred for very young children, who need a great deal of individual attention. Children over three may benefit more from the group activities in day care centers.

▶ ACTIVITIES

High quality day care centers and homes offer a variety of activities for children. During the day children play indoors and outdoors with toys and other play materials. They meet in groups led by the care givers for storytelling, puppet shows, and music. Children receive individual help with a wide variety of projects, such as cooking, science experiments, woodworking, and artwork.

Play materials in centers and homes should encourage both independent play and social play. They should include books, puzzles, blocks, costumes, household objects, dolls, stuffed animals, puppets, clay, paints, crayons, and musical instruments.

A day care center is a place where children are cared for while their parents work outside the home. Supervised by adults, children play together and learn new skills.

▶ CHOOSING DAY CARE

The best way to choose good day care is to interview the care giver and observe the children in the day care setting.

Five important questions should be asked when observing the day care facility. First, are children separated into small groups according to their ages and learning abilities? Second, are there enough adults to supervise the groups and give children individual attention? As a rule of thumb, look for at least one adult for every five preschoolers and at least one adult for every three infants. Third, do the care givers know enough about child development to provide appropriate care? Fourth, is the day care setting safe, attractive, comfortable, and clean? Fifth, do the children in the day care setting appear to be happy and engaged in activities?

Accreditation standards for day care programs in the United States are provided by the Academy of Early Childhood programs of the National Association for the Education of Young Children. For more information, write to NAEYC, 1834 Connecticut Avenue, N.W., Washington, D.C. 20009.

ELIZABETH J. HRNCIR
University of Virginia

DAYS OF THE WEEK

The seven-day week and the names of the days are so old that tracing their history is difficult. It is like trying to follow footprints down a sandy trail that ends in solid rock. We know that the English names for the days came from the Germanic languages. The Germanic names were translations and adaptations from Latin, the language of the Romans.

The ancient Romans worshiped many gods and goddesses. Each day of the week was named for a particular god or goddess, who was worshiped on that day. The Romans adopted this custom from earlier peoples who lived near the Tigris and Euphrates rivers, in the Middle East. And they passed it on to the Germanic-speaking peoples they conquered.

Our name for the first day of the week, Sunday, is from the Germanic *Sunnandag*. This was a translation of the Latin *dies solis*, "day of the sun." The Romans worshiped the sun god on that day.

Monday comes from the Germanic *Monandag*, a translation of the Roman *dies lunae*, "day of the moon." Before the Romans arrived in northern Europe, the tribes there based their calendar on the moon, which they called "teller of time."

The names of the next four days of the week are adaptations of the Roman names to Germanic culture and beliefs. The Germanic peo-

DAYS OF THE WEEK IN MANY LANGUAGES				
ENGLISH	**FRENCH**	**ITALIAN**	**SPANISH**	**GERMAN**
Sunday	dimanche	domenica	domingo	Sonntag
Monday	lundi	lunedì	lunes	Montag
Tuesday	mardi	martedì	martes	Dienstag
Wednesday	mercredi	mercoledì	miércoles	Mittwoch
Thursday	jeudi	giovedì	jueves	Donnerstag
Friday	vendredi	venerdì	viernes	Freitag
Saturday	samedi	sabato	sábado	Samstag

ples knew nothing about the gods for whom the Romans had named those days. They substituted their own gods—gods that we know today from Norse mythology.

The third day of the week was the Latin *dies Martis*, "day of Mars." It honored the Roman god of war. The Germanic peoples had their own war god, Tiu. His name, substituted for Mars, made the day *Tiesdag*, our Tuesday.

The Romans called the next day *dies Mercurii*, in honor of Mercury, messenger of the gods and guardian of spiritual life. The Germanic tribes had no messenger of the gods. But their Woden (or Odin), ruler of the gods, was also the god of spiritual life. They changed *dies Mercurii* to *Wodnesdag*, our Wednesday.

The fifth day, our Thursday, the Romans called *dies Jovis*, "day of Jove" (or Jupiter). This was *Thorsdag* to the Germanic peoples. Both Thor and Jove controlled the thunderbolt and had great physical strength.

The following day was known to the Romans as *dies Veneris*, "day of Venus." Venus was the goddess of love and beauty. The Germanic substitution was Frigga (or Frigg), beloved wife of Woden. Her day was known as *Frigadag* (Frigga's day), our Friday.

Saturn, god of agriculture, was honored by the Romans on the last day of the week, which they called *dies Saturni*. There was no similar Germanic god. Some of the tribes kept the Latin name, calling the day *Saeternesdag*. This became our Saturday. Other tribes ignored Saturn and called the day "bath day." In most of the Scandinavian countries, Saturday is still known as "bath day."

The Romans and the Germanic peoples had stories about these deities. You can read about them in the articles GREEK MYTHOLOGY and NORSE MYTHOLOGY in this encyclopedia.

WILLIAM R. KEYSER
Author, *Days of the Week*

Supreme goddess Frigga (or Frigg) was the inspiration for the naming of Friday. The wife of Woden (or Odin), Frigga was considered the protector of marriage and the home.

Most of the Dead Sea Scrolls were discovered in fragments and had to be pieced together. This one was found in good condition because it had been wrapped and stored in a jar.

DEAD SEA SCROLLS

The Dead Sea Scrolls are one of the most important archaeological finds of the 20th century. In 1947 an Arab shepherd boy, looking for a stray goat, made an amazing discovery. In a cave near the Dead Sea (about 13 miles, or 21 kilometers, from Jerusalem), he found some ancient-looking pots. These pots contained religious writings inscribed on long scrolls that had been hidden almost 2,000 years earlier. Over the next several years many more scrolls were found in nearby caves. Some were nearly complete; others were tiny fragments. In all, over 30,000 pieces of scrolls, making up about 900 different texts, were discovered.

The scrolls were apparently hidden in the caves about A.D. 67, when the Jewish nation revolted against its Roman rulers. Some were written in Hebrew, the ancestral language of the Jews. Others were in Aramaic, a language spoken in Judea in Jesus' time. A few were in Greek and other languages. Most of the scrolls were written on goatskin or sheepskin; a few were on papyrus.

When scholars studied them, they discovered the scrolls contained important information about the history of the Bible and the Jewish religion. Scholars are unsure who hid the scrolls. But most believe they were the work of a Jewish sect called the Essenes, a strict religious group from around the time of Jesus. Many scholars believe a community of Essenes lived at Qumran, an ancient settlement near the place the scrolls were found, and that the scrolls were written there. However, some scholars argue that many of the texts were written elsewhere and brought to the caves for safekeeping during the revolt.

About one-fourth of the texts are copies of books of the Jewish Bible (known to Christians as the Old Testament). These copies are 1,000 years older than any copies of the Jewish Bible known to exist when the scrolls were discovered. They are important because they show that, for the most part, the Bible was accurately copied through the centuries. The texts also caused scholars to debate how much the first-century Jews agreed about which books really belonged in the Bible.

Other scrolls are selections from popular Jewish religious books like Tobit, Sirach, Enoch, and Jubilees. These texts were widely read in the time of Jesus, and their ideas sometimes appear in the New Testament and later Jewish writings. The texts had previously been known only from translations, some made as late as the Middle Ages. The Dead Sea Scroll versions, in the original Hebrew and Aramaic, provided scholars with a more accurate reading of the texts and gave them a better idea of when they were written. They also gave scholars a better basis for thinking about how the texts may have influenced early Christianity and other religious movements.

The scrolls of the religious writings of the Dead Sea Scroll community itself provide some clues about the origins of different Jewish sects, perhaps including Christianity. These texts describe the community's strict lifestyle and how it separated from other Jews in the belief that most of them had misunderstood the laws of Moses and were not keeping them correctly. The community's members believed that God would send leaders who would teach them the truth and lead them in triumph over their enemies.

The Dead Sea Scrolls are housed in the Shrine of the Book in Jerusalem. After many years of study, the last of them was published in 2001.

ANTHONY J. TOMASINO
Bethel College

DEAFNESS

The term "deafness" refers to the inability to understand conversational speech through hearing alone, without visual cues. A person who is hard of hearing has a lesser degree of hearing loss, one in which understanding is difficult but not impossible.

Of the 18 million Americans who have some degree of hearing loss, most are able to benefit from hearing aids. Some 4 million are hard of hearing. Fewer, a quarter to a half million, are deaf. For the deaf, hearing aids do not restore functional hearing.

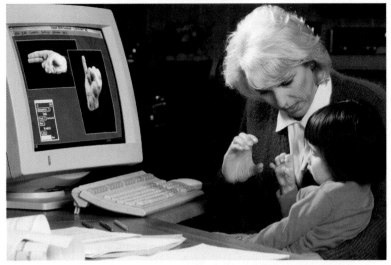

With the aid of a computer program, a woman helps a child learn the manual alphabet. The deaf and hard of hearing use this alphabet along with sign language, a system of special hand shapes and gestures, to communicate.

The degree of hearing loss may be equated with the loudness of sound (measured in decibels) needed for a person to hear. The faintest whisper that most people can hear is 0 decibels. An ordinary conversation between people several feet apart is about 65 decibels. A person is considered deaf if he or she cannot hear sounds below 90 decibels.

▶ **WHAT CAUSES DEAFNESS?**

Hearing loss usually occurs late in life, as a result of long-term exposure to background noise or simply because of normal aging. There are, however, specific causes of hearing loss; several are noted in this section.

Birth Defects. An infant's hearing can be damaged even before birth. For example, if a woman contracts rubella (German measles) during pregnancy, her baby may be born deaf. Abuse of certain drugs by a pregnant woman could also damage or destroy her baby's hearing.

Noise or Injury. Excessive noise (including loud music) can damage hearing structures.

Noise-induced hearing loss is usually gradual and painless, but it is often permanent. Music may be too loud if you have to raise your voice; if you cannot hear someone less than 2 feet (0.6 meter) away; if speech sounds muffled or dull after the music ends; or if you have pain or ringing in your ears afterward. A severe blow to the head also may cause hearing loss.

Disease. Childhood diseases such as measles, mumps, and chicken pox can cause hearing loss. Infection, accompanied by high fever, can damage the hearing at any age.

Heredity. Several patterns of inheritance may lead to deafness. In the most common pattern, **autosomal recessive inheritance**, a child acquires two recessive genes for deafness, one from each parent. Usually neither parent is deaf. Instead, each is a carrier.

Less common is the pattern of **autosomal dominant inheritance**. In this pattern, a child acquires a dominant gene, and it may come from just one parent. That parent's family usually has a history of deafness, with half or

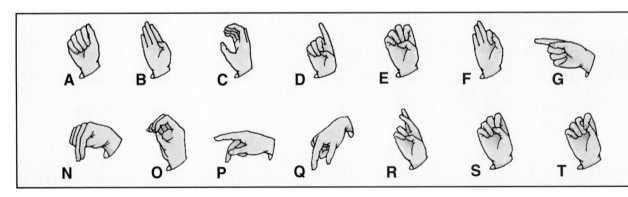

more of the members of the family showing some degree of hearing loss.

Because the recessive pattern is by far the most common cause of inherited deafness, most deaf children (90 percent) are born to hearing parents. Also, most deaf adults (also about 90 percent) have hearing children.

Aging. The progressive deterioration of hearing in older people is called **presbycusis**. It is a natural part of aging. Just as some people get gray hair more slowly than others, some individuals may feel the effect of presbycusis later than others.

▶ **TREATMENT**

Methods to restore hearing vary depending on the cause and severity of hearing loss. **Conductive hearing loss**, which involves the small bones of the middle ear, is often treatable with surgery. But surgery is of no help with **sensorineural hearing loss**, which involves the inner ear or the nerves between the ear and the brain. (To view the internal structures of the ear, see BODY, HUMAN (The Sense Organs) in Volume B.)

Both types of hearing loss may be treated with hearing aids, which amplify sound. However, with sensorineural hearing loss, it is more likely that a sophisticated hearing aid will be needed. A simple hearing aid makes everything louder. A sophisticated hearing aid may boost particular sounds depending on whether they are high or low in pitch. However, even advanced hearing aids may not help those with certain sensorineural losses.

People who have severe or profound sensorineural hearing loss in both ears may be candidates for cochlear implants, devices that may partially restore hearing. The devices consist of several components, some of which are implanted in the skull, and some of which are worn externally, like a hearing aid. However, the device is not a hearing aid. It does not amplify sound. It converts sound into electrical signals, which run to one or more electrodes connected to the cochlea, a winding, cone-shaped organ within the inner ear. These signals stimulate the nerve of hearing, causing it to send electrical impulses from the cochlea to the brain, which interprets the impulses as sound.

Cochlear implants often lead to dramatic improvements in the ability to hear sound. However, their ability to aid speech comprehension varies depending on the individual. Often, people with implants continue to rely on speech reading and sign language.

▶ **DETECTING HEARING LOSS**

Audiologists use machines to detect and measure hearing loss. These machines assess the loudness required for the individual to hear and measure it in decibels. The machines also measure the pitch ranges in which people hear well, less well, or not at all. Pitch, high or low, is measured in Hertz. Testing that assesses pitch response is called pure-tone audiometry. Testing usually includes speech audiometry, which assesses the ability of a person to understand speech.

Today, 90 percent of newborns have hearing tests before they leave the hospital. These tests are important because young children usually acquire language by hearing many thousands of conversations and by listening to television and radio programs. When hearing loss is not discovered until after a child begins formal schooling, the child's development may lag seriously, especially in the areas of speech and language.

▶ **SIGN LANGUAGE**

American Sign Language (ASL) is the fourth most commonly used language in the United States. It consists of hand shapes and movements that stand for concepts. (For example, the sign for "milk" mimics the ges-

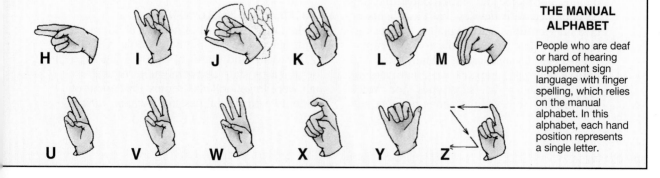

THE MANUAL ALPHABET

People who are deaf or hard of hearing supplement sign language with finger spelling, which relies on the manual alphabet. In this alphabet, each hand position represents a single letter.

tures of cow milking.) To supplement the signs, people use finger spelling. For each letter, and each number, the hand forms a particular shape. (For example, the letter *S* is represented by a closed fist.)

The sign languages of other countries, such as England, France, and Japan, are very different. Japanese sign language displays hand versions of written Japanese. British finger spelling, unlike American finger spelling, uses both hands. Deaf people around the world can learn to understand each other, but it takes a few weeks to adjust.

People who regard ASL as their native language, and who identify with the American deaf community, often observe what is called Deaf culture. Members of this culture identify themselves by their use of ASL and call themselves Deaf with a capital *D*.

▶ **SPEECH AND SPEECH READING**

Many deaf people learn to read lips, or speech read. They memorize lip movements and tongue positions. Because only about 40 percent of speech sounds can be distinguished on the lips, speech readers also rely on facial expressions and gestures. Even expert speech readers often welcome signing and finger spelling. Comprehension is best when all visual cues are available.

Because deaf people cannot hear their own voices, their speech may sound unusual. But how clearly a person speaks has nothing to do with intelligence. Rather, it is a matter of motor memory: People without hearing loss learn how to pronounce words, and how to use intonation to express emotions, by listening to other people and adjusting their own speech accordingly.

▶ **SPECIAL ELECTRONIC DEVICES**

Hearing aids are not the only devices that can help people who have hearing problems. The deaf and hard of hearing may also use special alarms and communication services.

Signaling Devices. Alarm clocks, telephones, doorbells, and smoke detectors may be equipped with devices that flash lights or give off vibrations. Such signaling devices can also alert a deaf person to the cry of a baby.

Electronic Communication. Many deaf and hard of hearing Americans use e-mail and instant messaging as substitutes for voice phone calls. However, the phone network still offers technologies that help the deaf and hard of hearing communicate.

For example, there is a device called the TTY, or teletypewriter. It is also called a TDD, or telecommunication device for the deaf. A TTY user may contact another TTY user or access a relay service. This service features an operator, called a communication assistant, who speaks what the deaf person types (so a person with no hearing loss can listen to it) and types what the speaking person says (so the deaf person can read it).

A TTY has a keyboard similar to a computer keyboard. However, TTY's are much slower than computers. Consequently, more and more users prefer computers to access relay services and contact others who are deaf or hard of hearing.

Additional options are possible with high-speed or broadband communications technologies that support video. With video, deaf people and communication assistants may sign to each other. Also, people with hearing loss may sign to each other.

Captioning. Broadcast television networks deliver programs that may include captions— on-screen text that conveys dialogue, narration, or even nonverbal sounds. The captions may be seen on most television sets. Captions may be "closed" (not visible unless activated) or "open" (always visible).

▶ **CURRENT RESEARCH**

New cochlear implants are better able to provide unique stimulation to specific parts of the cochlea. Because different parts of the cochlea are, in a sense, tuned to certain frequencies, the new implants may better represent how a sound conveys information over a range of frequencies. They may even render human speech with greater accuracy.

Broadband already allows face-to-face visual communication at a distance, but users typically need a desktop computer. In the next big step, such connections will be made with handheld mobile devices.

▶ **EDUCATION AND EMPLOYMENT**

Most deaf and hard of hearing children attend neighborhood public schools. Of the 72,000 deaf and hard of hearing children identified by state departments of education, half were in general classrooms. Placement of students with disabilities into regular classes is known as inclusion. Three out of every ten deaf or hard of hearing children are educated in separate classrooms that are located in neighborhood school buildings. Fewer are still taught in separate schools for the deaf.

Legislation requires that deaf and hard of hearing children be helped by sign-language interpreters, speech and language pathologists, and other professionals. Interpreters translate lessons into ASL. Speech and language pathologists help these children improve their spoken and written English.

Legislation encourages colleges and universities to offer interpreter services to students who are deaf. Gallaudet University in Washington, D.C., is the world's only accredited liberal arts college for the deaf. The National Technical Institute for the Deaf, in Rochester, New York, is the world's largest technical college for deaf students.

Deaf adults can perform any kind of job except those few jobs that are primarily dependent on hearing sounds. They work in many fields, including business, medicine, law, and government. The federal government is the largest single employer of deaf persons.

GARY W. OLSEN
Former Executive Director
National Association of the Deaf

Reviewed by FRANK BOWE
Hofstra University
Author, *Making Inclusion Work*

DEAN, DIZZY. See ARKANSAS (Famous People).
DEAN, JAMES. See INDIANA (Famous People).
DEAN, JOHN W., III. See WATERGATE (Profiles).

DEATH

All people die. To be alive means someday life will end. Most people wonder or worry about this because no one really knows what death is like. What we know for certain is that death is not like sleep. When we sleep, our bodies continue to function. We still breathe; our hearts still beat. When we die, the body's organs and systems stop.

People are living longer than in the past as a result of improvements in medicine, health care, and other factors. For example, the average life span in the United States is 77 years. This compares favorably with life expectancy in the mid-1800's, which averaged 40 years.

Years ago, most people died at home, cared for by family members. As medical science advanced, hospital care for the dying became more common than home care. In the 1970's, a movement called hospice arose. It focuses on providing physical and emotional support for dying people in the home or in homelike settings. At the same time, death and dying became a topic of study and began to be more openly discussed. Today people experiencing the death of a loved one, as well as dying people themselves, are encouraged to express feelings of grief and loss. This may help them move through the grief process.

As children grow, their perceptions of death change. Young children may believe that death is temporary. They may think that something they said or thought may have caused a person's death. By age 9, they realize that neither of these ideas is true. Older children may worry about what would happen to them if one or both of their parents died. They should be reassured that, although such fears are natural, there would always be someone to care for them.

Most people—adults as well as children—wonder about life after death. All the world's great religions offer explanations, and people often base their beliefs on the teachings of their faith. Many believe each person has a soul that lives on in heaven. Others, especially followers of Eastern faiths, believe that people are reincarnated.

Whatever their religious beliefs, there are some things on which everyone can agree: People live on through their children, through the good things they did when they were alive, and through others' memories of them. After a grandmother dies, for example, her grandchildren still bake her special cookies and repeat her familiar stories.

As we think about death, it is important to remember that life is precious. When we are busy living, we do not have time to worry too much about dying.

Reviewed by MARIA TROZZI
Director, Good Grief Program
Boston Medical Center

See also GRIEF.

DEBAKEY, MICHAEL E. See TEXAS (Famous People).

DEBATES AND DISCUSSIONS

Debates and discussions are very important in open societies, where people have the right to express and defend their ideas. In public elections, for example, opposing candidates try to win voters by displaying their qualifications through discussions and face-to-face debates. In schools and colleges, students use the same formats to learn about important issues and gain experience in public speaking.

Differences between Debates and Discussions. A debate is a type of contest in which two sides present arguments in favor of or against an issue. The topic of a debate is one to which you can say, "I agree" or "I disagree." For example: "Resolved, that homework should be abolished." In a debate, the side that agrees with the proposition is called the affirmative side. The side that disagrees is called the negative side.

The speakers on a discussion panel also present opposing viewpoints. But the panel's topic is usually stated as a question to which the speakers provide a variety of answers. An example of a discussion topic would be "Is it a good idea to abolish homework?"

Thus a debate is a contest between two sides, while a discussion is more like an intelligent conversation. In a debate, each side may have one person or a team of two or three people. A discussion is held by a panel of as few as four or as many as eight speakers. In a debate, each team upholds its side of the argument throughout. In a discussion, panelists may change their minds. As with all contests, debates can be won or lost. Discussions do not have judges or result in win-lose decisions.

Preparing for a Debate or Discussion. Participants prepare for debates and discussion panels by studying the history and current background of their topics. They then choose the points they will present and the arguments that support them. They must gather facts and figures to back their arguments, including quotes from authorities who have taken the same position. They must also identify the arguments their opponents are likely to use and decide how to respond to them. Whether taking part in a debate or a discussion, participants must know their topics well and be able to speak and argue clearly.

Conducting a Debate. School debating clubs may use one or more of their own formats, but when they compete with other schools, they must follow the format set by the sponsoring organization. The format covers all the important elements of the debate, including the number of speakers, the order in which they will speak, what materials they can use, and how the event will be judged.

One popular form of debating is policy debate. In the United States, policy debate involves one affirmative and one negative team debating a national topic for an entire school year and thus deeply researching that topic. The topic is always a question about what the government's policy on an issue should be. Usually, each team has two members and each member gives one constructive and one rebuttal speech. The **constructive speeches** come first and are used to construct, or build, the speakers' arguments. The **rebuttal speeches** that follow dispute the other team's points and summarize the case for winning.

Another form popular in schools is parliamentary debate. In this form, students debate in teams. They receive their topic 15 or 30 minutes before the debate, and they use that time to develop their arguments based on what they already know.

In all debates, the side that proves its case wins. A panel of judges may decide who wins when a school debating club holds a debate for other students to watch. Or, the audience may vote on the winner. In tournaments, where many schools compete, there may be one judge for the preliminary round and three judges for the later rounds.

Conducting a Discussion. For a panel discussion, four to eight speakers sit at a table facing the audience. The discussion leader, or moderator, presents the question to be discussed and introduces the panel. It is the moderator's duty to see that every panelist gets an opportunity to talk and that no one speaker takes too much time. In one type of discussion panel, the speakers do all the talking while the audience listens. Another format allows one hour for panel discussion, then the audience is invited to ask questions.

Reviewed by ALFRED CHARLES SNIDER
Lawrence Professor of Forensics
University of Vermont

See also PARLIAMENTARY PROCEDURE; PUBLIC SPEAKING.

DEBS, EUGENE V. (1855–1926)

American activist and politician Eugene V. Debs was a pioneer labor organizer, human rights advocate, Socialist Party leader, and five-time candidate for president of the United States. He was among the first American politicians to promote such basic human rights as restrictions on child labor and voting rights for women. He also promoted workers' rights to form unions and bargain for better pay, working conditions, and job security. Debs once said, "I am for socialism because I am for humanity."

Eugene Victor Debs was born on November 5, 1855, in Terre Haute, Indiana. At the age of 14, he went to work as a fireman on the railroad, where he gained firsthand experience of the hard life of a railroad worker. Debs quit railroad work in 1874 but the following year became an officer of the Brotherhood of Locomotive Firemen, one of the most effective American unions of the late 1800's. Debs edited the *Locomotive Fireman's Magazine* and served as the brotherhood's grand secretary (1878–93).

In 1893, Debs founded the American Railway Union (ARU) to organize all railroad employees by industry rather than by individual craft or skill. It became the nation's largest union. In 1894, to protest pay cuts by the Pullman Company, Debs led the Pullman Strike in Chicago, Illinois. The strike was broken up by federal troops, and Debs was sent to prison for six months.

Debs recognized that labor unions would have to gain political influence to succeed, so thereafter he directed his efforts to politics. He ran five times (unsuccessfully) for president as the Socialist Party candidate (in 1900, 1904, 1908, 1912, and 1920). When he ran in 1920, he was serving a ten-year term in prison for having publicly denounced U.S. involvement (1917–18) in World War I. (His sentence was lifted in 1921 by President Warren G. Harding.)

Debs died in Elmhurst, Illinois, on October 20, 1926. He is honored in the U. S. Department of Labor's Hall of Fame. His home in Terre Haute is preserved as a museum.

CHARLES KING
Secretary, The Eugene V. Debs Foundation

DEBUSSY, CLAUDE (1862–1918)

Claude Debussy, a great French composer, was born in Saint-Germain-en-Laye on August 22, 1862. He began his study of music under a piano teacher who had once been a pupil of Frédéric Chopin. Debussy showed such musical talent that he was admitted to the Paris Conservatory at the age of 11. He began composing music as a teenager and eventually won awards and recognition at the conservatory. Some of Debussy's instructors, though, were annoyed with his innovative harmony and unusual chord progressions.

After further study in Rome and Paris, Debussy began composing the works that made him famous. He admired the work of impressionist painters and symbolist poets and playwrights. His music, like their paintings and poetry, sets a mood and stirs the listener's imagination by suggesting beautiful sights or sounds in nature. Debussy achieved this by developing a new and original kind of harmony. Though dissonant, or clashing, by standards of the 1800's, the harmony sounds dreamlike and strange rather than harsh and unpleasant.

Debussy's first important work in this new style was the *Prelude to the Afternoon of a Faun*, which was inspired by a symbolist poem by Stéphane Mallarmé. Other typical and familiar works of Debussy's are *Claire de Lune (Moonlight)*, for piano, and *Nuages (Clouds)* and *La Mer (The Sea)*, for large orchestra. He also composed an opera, *Pelléas et Mélisande*.

In his last years, Debussy traveled widely, conducting his compositions. He died in Paris on March 25, 1918.

Reviewed by RONALD L. BYRNSIDE
Author, *Music: Sound and Sense*

December

December takes its name from *decem,* the Latin word for "ten," because it was once the tenth month in the ancient Roman calendar. A month of snow and ice in the Northern Hemisphere, December has the shortest day and the longest night of the year at the winter solstice.

Place in year: 12th month.
Number of days: 31.
Flowers: Holly and narcissus.
Birthstone: Turquoise.
Zodiac signs: Sagittarius, the Archer (November 22–December 21), and Capricorn, the Goat (December 22–January 19).

1
- Antarctic Treaty signed in Washington, D.C., assuring peaceful use of the continent by all nations, 1959
- Anniversary of the Proclamation of the Republic in Central African Republic

2
- Monroe Doctrine presented to Congress by President James Monroe, 1823
- National Day in Laos; United Arab Emirates

3
- **Joseph Conrad** born 1857
- Illinois became the 21st state, 1818
- Dr. Christiaan Barnard performed first successful human heart transplant, Capetown, South Africa, 1967

4
- **Wassily Kandinsky** born 1866
- **Francisco Franco** born 1892

5
- **Martin Van Buren** born 1782
- **Christina Rossetti** born 1830
- **Walt Disney** born 1901
- Twenty-first Amendment to U.S. Constitution repealed prohibition, 1933
- National Day in Thailand

6
- Columbus discovered Hispaniola, 1492
- Independence Day in Finland

7
- **Giovanni Lorenzo Bernini** born 1598
- Delaware ratified the Constitution, 1787
- Japanese forces attacked Pearl Harbor, 1941

8
- **Eli Whitney** born 1765
- **Jean Sibelius** born 1865
- American Federation of Labor (AFL) organized, 1886
- Chinese Nationalists left the Chinese mainland to establish their capital in Formosa (Taiwan), 1949

9
- **John Milton** born 1608

10
- **César Franck** born 1822
- **Emily Dickinson** born 1830
- Mississippi became the 20th state, 1817
- Wyoming Territory allowed women to vote and hold office, 1869
- Spain ceded the Philippines to the U.S., 1898
- Human Rights Day celebrated by United Nations member nations

11
- **Louis-Hector Berlioz** born 1803
- **Fiorello La Guardia** born 1882
- Indiana became the 19th state, 1816
- Edward VIII of Great Britain abdicated, 1936
- UNICEF Anniversary Day celebrated by United Nations member nations

12
- **John Jay** born 1745
- Pennsylvania ratified the Constitution, 1787
- Marconi received the first radio signal across the Atlantic Ocean from England to Newfoundland, 1901
- Independence Day in Kenya

13
- **Heinrich Heine** born 1797
- Council of Trent opened, 1545
- Sir Francis Drake began voyage around the world, 1577
- St. Lucia Day in Sweden

14
- **Tycho Brahe** born 1546
- Alabama became the 22nd state, 1819
- Roald Amundsen reached the South Pole, 1911

15
- Bill of Rights, the first ten amendments to U.S. Constitution, ratified, 1791
- *Bill of Rights Day*

16
- **Jane Austen** born 1775
- **Margaret Mead** born 1901
- Boston Tea Party, 1773
- Battle of the Bulge started by Germans, 1944
- National Day in Bahrain

17
- **Sir Humphry Davy** born 1778

18
- **Edward MacDowell** born 1861
- **Paul Klee** born 1879
- New Jersey ratified the Constitution, 1787
- Thirteenth Amendment to U.S. Constitution, ending slavery, proclaimed, 1865
- National Day in Niger

19
- **Leonid Ilyich Brezhnev** born 1906
- Continental Army camped at Valley Forge, Pennsylvania, for the winter, 1777

20
- U.S. Government lifted its ban on cultural exchanges with the U.S.S.R., 1968

21
- **Benjamin Disraeli** born 1804
- **Joseph Stalin** born 1879
- Pilgrims landed at Plymouth, Massachusetts, 1620

22
- **James Oglethorpe** born 1696
- **Giacomo Puccini** born 1858

23
- U. S. Federal Reserve system established, 1913

24
- **Kit Carson** born 1809
- Treaty of Ghent, ending War of 1812, signed by U.S. and Great Britain, 1814
- First radio program broadcast at Brant Rock, Massachusetts, 1906

25
- **Isaac Newton** born 1642
- **Clara Barton** born 1821
- **Maurice Utrillo** born 1883
- **Anwar el-Sadat** born 1918
- Washington and troops crossed Delaware River to Trenton, New Jersey, 1776
- *Christmas Day* celebrated in all Christian countries

26
- **Mao Zedong** born 1893
- Battle of Trenton, 1776
- Boxing Day in the United Kingdom

27
- **Johannes Kepler** born 1571
- **Louis Pasteur** born 1822
- U.S.S.R. invaded Afghanistan, 1979

28
- **Woodrow Wilson** born 1856
- Iowa became the 29th state, 1846
- National Day in Nepal

29
- **Charles Goodyear** born 1800
- **Andrew Johnson** born 1808
- **William Ewart Gladstone** born 1809
- Texas became the 28th state, 1845
- First YMCA in U.S. opened in Boston, Massachusetts, 1851

30
- **Rudyard Kipling** born 1865
- U.S.S.R. established, 1922

31
- **Henri Matisse** born 1869
- **George C. Marshall** born 1880
- *New Year's Eve*

Holiday that may begin in November or December: *Hanukkah* (lasts for eight days).

The calendar listing identifies people who were born on the indicated day in boldface type, **like this.** You will find a biography of each of these birthday people in *The New Book of Knowledge.* In addition to citing some historical events and historical firsts, the calendar also lists the holidays and some of the festivals celebrated in the United States. These holidays are printed in italic type, *like this.* See the article HOLIDAYS for more information.

Many holidays and festivals of nations around the world are included in the calendar as well. When the term "national holiday" is used, it means that the nation celebrates an important patriotic event on that day—in most cases the winning of independence. Consult *The New Book of Knowledge* article on the individual nation for further information on its national holiday.

DECIMAL SYSTEM

Thousands of years ago, people who used their ten fingers for counting developed a number system that used ten as its base. This type of system is called a **decimal system**. The word "decimal" comes from a Latin word meaning "tens" or "tenths."

Although people in ancient civilizations used written numerals, it was not until about A.D. 600 that the symbols, or digits, 1, 2, 3, 4, 5, 6, 7, 8, and 9 were developed by the Hindus in India. They then invented the symbol 0 for zero. About 200 years later, Arab mathematicians adopted the Hindu numerals and introduced them to the Western world. Today the Hindu-Arabic numerals and the decimal system are used throughout the world.

Place Value. The decimal system that we use is a **place-value system**, or **positional system**. In a place-value system, the value of each digit in a numeral depends on its position or place in the numeral. In the decimal system, the value of each digit in a numeral is multiplied by ten as you move from right to left. As Figure 1 shows, the far-right place is the ones, or units, place. The next place to the left is the tens place, and the next is the hundreds place.

Figure 1.

Can you tell the value of each digit in the numeral 236? The 6 stands for 6 x 1 or 6 ones or simply 6, the 3 stands for 3 x 10 or 3 tens or 30, and the 2 stands for 2 x 100 or 2 hundreds or 200. The total value of the number is determined by adding 200 + 30 + 6 to get two hundred thirty-six. What value does the digit 6 have if we change 236 to 623? The 6 now stands for 6 x 100 or 6 hundreds or 600.

Although zero is a number, the symbol for zero, 0, also serves as a placeholder when there is an empty place, or missing value, in a number. For example, in the numeral 202, the 0 tells us that there are no tens.

One of the benefits of the decimal place-value system is that it allows us to write very large numbers easily. In Figure 2, the place-value chart has been extended to show places through the millions. The numeral is read nine million, two hundred ninety-five thousand, two hundred ninety-seven. Large num-

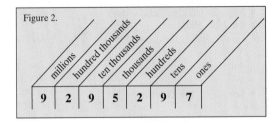

Figure 2.

bers are usually written with the digits in groups of three, separated by commas, as in 9,295,297. The grouping begins at the right. Sometimes the digits are in groups of three without using commas, as in 9 295 297.

Decimals Smaller Than 1. Values for fractions, or parts, of whole numbers can also be written in the decimal system. The position of each digit in the fractional part of a numeral represents decreasing powers of ten, and the value of each position is $\frac{1}{10}$ the value of the position to its left. Look at Figure 3. Notice that in the numeral 63.546, a decimal point

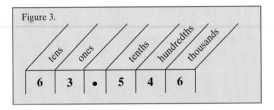

Figure 3.

is written to the right of the ones place. The place to the right of the decimal point is the tenths place. The next place to the right is the hundredths place, and the next is the thousandths place. The numeral 63.546 is read sixty-three and five hundred forty-six thousandths. The decimal system makes it possible to write very small numbers—numbers in the millionths or even smaller.

The decimal system is popular throughout the world because it is easy to use, enables us to write numbers of any size, and provides an efficient way of doing arithmetic calculations.

Reviewed by BRYAN BUNCH
Instructor,
Pace University

See also ARITHMETIC; FRACTIONS AND DECIMALS; NUMERALS AND NUMERATION SYSTEMS.

A copy of the Declaration of Independence, one of the most important documents in American history, is prominently displayed at the National Archives in Washington, D.C.

DECLARATION OF INDEPENDENCE

Every July 4, Americans celebrate the birthday of the United States. On that day in 1776, the members of the Second Continental Congress, meeting in Philadelphia, signed a Declaration of Independence cutting the last link between the 13 original colonies and the government of Great Britain. Only their president, John Hancock, signed the Declaration that day, in large and graceful handwriting. Fifty-five other delegates added their signatures one month later.

Soon Americans were reading the Declaration in their newspapers. George Washington, the commander of the American army, had it read aloud to his soldiers. He hoped it would inspire them to fight the British army that was trying to keep the colonies within the British Empire.

In 1783, after seven more years of fighting, Americans finally won their independence.

Later, July 4 became a national holiday. At large public meetings, Americans listened carefully as every word of the Declaration was again read aloud. They liked one sentence in particular, the one that said "all men are created equal."

Those words were put in the Declaration by its author, Thomas Jefferson, a Virginia lawyer and planter who owned many slaves. When Jefferson wrote about equality in the Declaration, he meant that the American people had the same rights to liberty and self-government as the British people across the Atlantic Ocean. He was not using the Declaration to tell Americans that they should all be equal to each other. But Jefferson's choice of words has led many Americans to think in just those terms ever since.

▶ WHY IT WAS ADOPTED

When the Continental Congress approved the Declaration in 1776, it ended a debate that had begun over a decade earlier. With its

The committee that drafted the Declaration of Independence included (from left to right) Thomas Jefferson, Roger Sherman, Benjamin Franklin, Robert R. Livingston (cousin of signer Philip Livingston), and John Adams.

goods, hoping that British merchants would ask Parliament to repeal the law. Most important, Americans argued that they did not have to obey this law because they sent no representatives to Parliament.

In the spring of 1766, Parliament did repeal the Stamp Act. But it passed another law, called the Declaratory Act, which said that Parliament could still make laws for the Americans "in all cases whatsoever." The next year it adopted a new tax, the Townshend duties, forcing colonists to pay duties (taxes) on various goods imported into America. Once again the colonists protested. They argued that they should not have to obey laws passed by a parliament in which they were not represented. In 1770, Parliament repealed all the duties except for the one on tea.

Three years later, Parliament passed the Tea Act, which was designed to help the East India Company sell its excess tea in America. To help the company even more, Parliament could have removed the duty on tea. But King George III and his chief minister of government, Lord North, insisted on keeping the duty. Removing it would suggest that the Americans had been right to argue that Parliament had no power to govern them.

In November 1773, ships carrying East India Company tea began arriving in American ports. The colonists again organized protests. In nearly every case, they forced the ships and their cargo to return to England. In

victory in the Seven Years' War (1756–63), Great Britain was the most powerful European empire in North America. In Canada, France had surrendered its colony of Quebec. France and Spain recognized the British claims to most of the land east of the Mississippi River.

The war had been very expensive, and to win it, Britain had taxed its citizens heavily. Victory would not be cheap either. Now Britain had an even larger empire to run. British troops would have to remain on the frontier, for example, to keep peace between the Indians who lived on these lands and the colonists who hoped to settle them. The British government thought the Americans should pay their fair share of these costs. After all, Britain had fought the war to protect its colonists against the French to the north.

In 1765, the British Parliament adopted the Stamp Act as one way to make the Americans help pay the costs of maintaining the British Empire. The act placed a tax on various paper products and legal documents. The colonists fought back. They forced the men appointed to distribute the stamps to resign their offices. They also stopped buying British

Jefferson composed the Declaration of Independence on this writing box, which he designed himself. A man of many talents, he was chosen to draft the Declaration because of his skill as a writer.

TWO KINDS OF EQUALITY

The equality that the Declaration of Independence defended belonged to the American people as a whole. As British colonists, they insisted that they should enjoy the same rights as the countrymen their ancestors had left behind when they sailed to the New World. Just as the British people elected representatives to frame the laws that would govern them, Americans had an equal right to be governed by laws that their own representatives had adopted. When a government acted like a tyrant, denying a people their just rights, the same people had a basic right to replace that government with a new one.

Jefferson and the other members of Congress did believe that all *free persons* should be equal before the law. In matters of religion, for example, everyone had the same right to believe what he or she wished, according to their personal sense of conscience. But they also accepted a great deal of inequality that later Americans would find troubling. Men without property could not vote; neither could women or children. The Declaration of Independence was not concerned with these kinds of inequality.

Some Americans had no rights at all. These were the hundreds of thousands of slaves who worked the plantations of the southern states. By 1776, a majority of these slaves were American-born, but many thousands had been captured in Africa before being shipped to the New World and sold. The equality that the Declaration of Independence proclaimed did not apply to slaves, either as individual men and women, or as a distinct people.

Yet as years passed, many Americans began to read the Declaration of Independence as proof that all men should be able to live equally in freedom. Some of the first Americans to read the Declaration this way were the African Americans who gained their freedom from slavery during or after the Revolution. In the 1800's, the other parts of the Declaration seemed less important than its opening statement of "self-evident truths" about equality and "inalienable rights" that no one should ever be forced to surrender. Americans no longer needed to be reminded of all the bad deeds George III had done. They knew that the United States enjoyed "the separate and equal station" among the nations of the world that the Declaration had announced it was about to assume. But the question of why slavery still existed in a nation founded on the idea that "all men are created equal" had yet to be solved. The part of the Declaration that mattered most now became the first two paragraphs—and so we still read it today.

Boston, however, Governor Thomas Hutchinson refused to allow the tea ships to depart, and the colonists refused to allow the tea to be unloaded. On the night of December 16, a party dressed like Mohawk Indians boarded the three ships and threw 342 chests of tea into Boston harbor.

The king, Lord North, and Parliament were all outraged by this event. They agreed that the town of Boston and the colony of Massachusetts had to be punished. This punishment came in the form of the four Coercive Acts that Parliament passed in 1774. The first, the Boston Port Act, was enough to spark a great crisis throughout the colonies. It closed the entire port of Boston until the colonists agreed to repay the East India Company for the destroyed tea.

In September 1774, representatives from twelve of the 13 colonies (excluding Georgia) assembled in Philadelphia for the First Continental Congress. They agreed that the only laws of Parliament the colonies had to obey were those regulating the overall trade of the empire. Congress also agreed that because the king had given the charters of government to the original colonies, he was the only authoritative link between the colonies and the empire. Congress wanted George III to agree that the legislatures of his American colonies were equal in authority to the Parliament of Great Britain. The colonies, in other words, were "independent" of Parliament but "dependent" on the king.

There was one critical problem with this idea. George III rejected it. In his view, Par-

In this 1786 painting by John Trumbull, the members of the drafting committee present the proposed Declaration of Independence to the Continental Congress.

liament was the supreme legislature for his entire empire, and the Americans had to obey it, whether or not they ever sent representatives there. The king also believed that the colonists had to be taught the costs of defying the British government. When war broke out between royal troops and the Massachusetts militia in April 1775, the king strongly favored sending more soldiers to America. In August 1775, the king even told Parliament that he believed the Americans already wanted independence.

Most Americans still disagreed. But once it became clear that the king favored using his army against them, Americans believed they were free to declare their complete independence of all British authority, the king as well as Parliament. The only question was when to do so. By the spring of 1776, many Americans agreed that the time for a declaration of independence was near. If the British continued to make war against them, the Americans would need to get aid from other nations (especially France) to fight them. But the French government would not risk war if it thought Britain and its colonies might still settle their dispute.

By early June 1776 the Continental Congress was ready to take the final steps toward independence. It appointed three committees. One would propose articles of union for the 13 colonies. A second would prepare a plan for making treaties with foreign allies. The third would write a declaration of independence. This third committee had five members. The best known were Benjamin Franklin of Pennsylvania and John Adams of Massachusetts, who had been the leading supporter of independence in Congress. The others were Roger Sherman of Connecticut, Robert Livingston of New York, and Thomas Jefferson of Virginia. The other members of the committee knew Jefferson was an outstanding writer, and they asked him to draft the declaration. The committee read his work before it was presented to Congress.

▶ WHAT THE DECLARATION SAYS

The Declaration is divided into three parts of unequal length. An introduction of two paragraphs states the general ideals of government that justify the colonists' decision to become an independent nation. The second and longest section charges King George III with many violations of American rights. The final three paragraphs explain that the colonists have tried to solve their dispute with Britain peacefully. But because Britain has ignored all their efforts, the united colonies can now ask other nations to recognize that Americans have the same rights of self-government as any other people. Each of these points added an important element to the case for independence.

The most famous lines appear in the opening sentences. Jefferson stated three propositions in rapid order, saying "We hold these truths to be self-evident." First, "all men are created equal." Second, they possess "certain

inalienable rights"—rights they can never surrender—to "life, liberty, and the pursuit of happiness." Third, governments are formed for the purpose of securing these rights. Therefore, any time a government acts without the consent of the governed (as Parliament had tried to do by passing laws affecting the American colonists), the people have a right to disobey that government and establish a new one.

But it was not Parliament that the Declaration then went on to blame for the current crisis, but the king. The Declaration listed 27 specific charges against "the present king of Great Britain" and the kings who had ruled before him. George III was accused of trying to establish "an absolute tyranny" over the colonies. Some of the charges cited problems that had bothered Americans long before

1765, such as the fact that the British monarch had often vetoed laws that the colonists had adopted for their own benefit. Other charges were much more recent. The charges that mattered most were that the king had approved laws punishing the colonists for trying to protect their just rights, and then made war against them. A king who acted this way could no longer expect Americans to give him their allegiance. Because the king was the one link to the empire that Americans had said they would accept, rejecting his rule meant rejecting all political ties to Britain.

These charges were more than an attack on George III, however. They were also an attack on the idea that a people like the Americans should be ruled by kings at all. Americans deserved a different kind of government. It would rely only on the consent of the people, not the wishes and orders of a distant king.

Jefferson included one other charge in the draft of the Declaration that Congress was unwilling to approve. This was to blame the British monarchy for its role in promoting the slave trade between Africa and America. Jefferson may have wanted to use this charge to awaken his fellow citizens to the evils of slavery. But he himself was a slaveowner, as were other members of Congress. Delegates from the southern states knew that their fellow citizens still believed that slavery was both legal and necessary. To blame the king for their own actions seemed improper, even embarrassing.

The third part of the Declaration explained what Congress was now going to do. Before, Americans had tried to resolve their differences with Britain peacefully. They had sent petitions to Britain and tried to explain to the British government and people why they should be allowed to enjoy the rights they claimed. All those efforts had failed, and war had begun. Therefore, the Declaration concluded, "these united colonies are, and of right ought to be, free and independent states." As such, they were equal in authority with all the other nations of the world.

JACK N. RAKOVE
Original Meanings: Politics and Ideas in the Making of the Constitution

See also FOUNDERS OF THE UNITED STATES; INDEPENDENCE DAY; INDEPENDENCE HALL; JEFFERSON, THOMAS; REVOLUTIONARY WAR.

TEXT OF THE DECLARATION OF INDEPENDENCE

IN CONGRESS, JULY 4, 1776
THE UNANIMOUS DECLARATION OF THE THIRTEEN UNITED STATES OF AMERICA

When in the Course of human events, it becomes necessary for one people to dissolve the political bands which have connected them with another, and to assume among the powers of the earth, the separate and equal station to which the Laws of Nature and of Nature's God entitle them, a decent respect to the opinions of mankind requires that they should declare the causes which impel them to the separation.—We hold these truths to be self-evident, that all men are created equal, that they are endowed by their Creator with certain unalienable Rights, that among these are Life, Liberty and the pursuit of Happiness.—That to secure these rights, Governments are instituted among Men, deriving their just powers from the consent of the governed,—That whenever any Form of Government becomes destructive of these ends, it is the Right of the People to alter or to abolish it, and to institute new Government, laying its foundation on such principles and organizing its powers in such form, as to them shall seem most likely to effect their Safety and Happiness. Prudence, indeed, will dictate that Governments long established should not be changed for light and transient causes; and accordingly all experience hath shewn, that mankind are more disposed to suffer, while evils are sufferable, than to right themselves by abolishing the forms to which they are accustomed. But when a long train of abuses and usurpations, pursuing invariably the same Object evinces a design to reduce them under absolute Despotism, it is their right, it is their duty, to throw off such Government, and to provide new Guards for their future security.—Such has been the patient sufferance of these Colonies; and such is now the necessity which constrains them to alter their former Systems of Government. The history of the present King of Great Britain is a history of repeated injuries and usurpations, all having in direct object the establishment of an absolute Tyranny over these States. To prove this, let Facts be submitted to a candid world.—He has refused his Assent to Laws, the most wholesome and necessary for the public good.—He has forbidden his Governors to pass Laws of immediate and pressing importance, unless suspended in their operation till his Assent should be obtained; and when so suspended, he has utterly neglected

IN CONGRESS, July 4, 1776.

The unanimous Declaration of the thirteen united States of America,

When in the Course of human events, it becomes necessary for one people to dissolve the political bands which have connected them with another, and to assume among the powers of the earth, the separate and equal station to which the Laws of Nature and of Nature's God entitle them, a decent respect to the opinions of mankind requires that they should declare the causes which impel them to the separation. ———— We hold these truths to be self-evident, that all men are created equal, that they are endowed by their Creator with certain unalienable Rights, that among these are Life, Liberty and the pursuit of Happiness. ———— That to secure these rights, Governments are instituted among Men, deriving their just powers from the consent of the governed, ———— That whenever any Form of Government becomes destructive of these ends, it is the Right of the People to alter or to abolish it, and to institute new Government, laying its foundation on such principles and organizing its powers in such form, as to them shall seem most likely to effect their Safety and Happiness. Prudence, indeed, will dictate that Governments long established should not be changed for light and transient causes; and accordingly all experience hath shewn, that mankind are more disposed to suffer, while evils are sufferable, than to right themselves by abolishing the forms to which they are accustomed. But when a long train of abuses and usurpations, pursuing invariably the same Object evinces a design to reduce them under absolute Despotism, it is their right, it is their duty, to throw off such Government, and to provide new Guards for their future security. ———— Such has been the patient sufferance of these Colonies; and such is now the necessity which constrains them to alter their former Systems of Government. The history of the present King of Great Britain is a history of repeated injuries and usurpations, all having in direct object the establishment of an absolute Tyranny over these States. To prove this, let Facts be submitted to a candid world. ———————

We, therefore, the Representatives of the united States of America, in General Congress, Assembled, appealing to the Supreme Judge of the world for the rectitude of our intentions, do, in the Name, and by Authority of the good People of these Colonies, solemnly publish and declare, That these United Colonies are, and of Right ought to be Free and Independent States; that they are Absolved from all Allegiance to the British Crown, and that all political connection between them and the State of Great Britain, is and ought to be totally dissolved; and that as Free and Independent States, they have full Power to levy War, conclude Peace, contract Alliances, establish Commerce, and to do all other Acts and Things which Independent States may of right do. ———— And for the support of this Declaration, with a firm reliance on the protection of divine Providence, we mutually pledge to each other our Lives, our Fortunes and our sacred Honor.

to attend to them.—He has refused to pass other Laws for the accommodation of large districts of people, unless these people would relinquish the right of Representation in the Legislature, a right inestimable to them and formidable to tyrants only.—He has called together legislative bodies at places unusual, uncomfortable, and distant from the depository of their public Records, for the sole purpose of fatiguing them into compliance with his measures.—He has dissolved Representative Houses repeatedly, for opposing with manly firmness his invasions on the rights of the people.—He has refused for a long time, after such dissolutions, to cause others to be elected; whereby the Legislative powers, incapable of Annihilation, have returned to the People at large for their exercise; the State remaining in the mean time exposed to all the dangers of invasion from without, and convulsions within.—He has endeavoured to prevent the population of these States; for that purpose obstructing the Laws for Naturalization of Foreigners; refusing to pass others to encourage their migrations hither, and raising the conditions of new Appropriations of Lands.—He has obstructed the Administration of Justice, by refusing his Assent to Laws for establishing Judiciary powers.—He has made Judges dependent on his Will alone, for the tenure of their offices, and the amount and payment of their salaries.—He has erected a multitude of New Offices, and sent hither swarms of Officers to harass our people, and eat out their substance.—He has kept among us, in times of peace, Standing Armies without the Consent of our legislatures.—He has affected to render the Military independent of and superior to the Civil power.—He has combined with others to subject us to a jurisdiction foreign to our constitution, and unacknowledged by our laws; giving his Assent to their Acts of pretended Legislation:—For quartering large bodies of armed troops among us:—For protecting them, by a mock Trial, from punishment for any Murders which they should commit on the Inhabitants of these States:—For cutting off our Trade with all parts of the world:—For imposing Taxes on us without our Consent:—For depriving us in many cases, of the benefits of Trial by Jury:—For transporting us beyond Seas to be tried for pretended offences:—For abolishing the free System of English Laws in a neighboring Province, establishing therein an Arbitrary government, and enlarging its Boundaries so as to render it at once an example and fit instrument for introducing the same absolute rule into these Colonies:—For taking away our Charters, abolishing our most valuable Laws, and altering fundamentally the Forms of our Governments:—For suspending our own Legislatures and declaring themselves invested with power to legislate for us in all cases whatsoever.—He has abdicated Government here, by declaring us out of his Protection and waging War against us.—He has plundered our seas, ravaged our Coasts, burnt our towns, and destroyed the lives of our people.—He is at this time transporting large Armies of foreign Mercenaries to compleat the works of death, desolation and tyranny, already begun with circumstances of Cruelty & perfidy scarcely paralleled in the most barbarous ages, and totally unworthy the Head of a civilized nation.—He has constrained our fellow Citizens taken Captive on the high Seas to bear Arms against their Country, to become the executioners of their friends and Brethren, or to fall themselves by their Hands.—He has excited domestic insurrections amongst us, and has endeavoured to bring on the inhabitants of our frontiers, the merciless Indian Savages, whose known rule of warfare, is an undistinguished destruction of all ages, sexes and conditions. In every stage of these Oppressions We have Petitioned for Redress in the most humble terms: Our repeated Petitions have been answered only by repeated injury. A Prince, whose character is thus marked by every act which may define a Tyrant, is unfit to be the ruler of a free people. Nor have We been wanting in attentions to our British brethren. We have warned them from time to time of attempts by their legislature to extend an unwarrantable jurisdiction over us. We have reminded them of the circumstances of our emigration and settlement here. We have appealed to their native justice and magnanimity, and we have conjured them by the ties of our common kindred to disavow these usurpations, which, would inevitably interrupt our connections and correspondence. They too have been deaf to the voice of justice and of consanguinity. We must, therefore, acquiesce in the necessity, which denounces our Separation, and hold them, as we hold the rest of mankind, Enemies in War, in Peace Friends.—

We, THEREFORE, the Representatives of the United States of America, in General Congress, Assembled, appealing to the Supreme Judge of the world for the rectitude of our intentions, do, in the Name, and by Authority of the good People of these Colonies, solemnly publish and declare, That these United Colonies are, and of Right ought to be FREE AND INDEPENDENT STATES; that they are Absolved from all Allegiance to the British Crown, and that all political connection between them and the State of Great Britain, is and ought to be totally dissolved; and that as Free and Independent States, they have full Power to levy War, conclude Peace, contract Alliances, establish Commerce, and to do all other Acts and Things which Independent States may of right do.—And for the support of this Declaration, with a firm reliance on the protection of divine Providence, we mutually pledge to each other our Lives, our Fortunes, and our sacred Honor.

Roger Sherman of Connecticut

George Read of Delaware

Button Gwinnett of Georgia

Connecticut

Samuel Huntington (1731–96), born in Windham, Conn., was a self-taught lawyer who was admitted to the Bar of Connecticut at age 23. He was a delegate to the Continental Congress (1776–84) and was serving as its president (1779–81, 1783) at the time the Articles of Confederation were negotiated. Huntington later served as lieutenant governor and chief judge of the Superior Court of Connecticut (1784–86) and as governor of Connecticut (1786–96).

Roger Sherman. See CONNECTICUT (Famous People) in Volume C.

William Williams (1731–1811), born in Lebanon, Conn., fought at Lake George during the French and Indian War (1754–63). He later established himself as a merchant. During the Revolutionary War, Williams personally helped gather supplies for the Continental Army and served as a delegate to the Continental Congress (1776–78, 1783, 1784). For more than 50 years he held a variety of public offices in Connecticut, including town clerk of Lebanon, state legislator, and county court judge.

Oliver Wolcott (1726–97), born in Windsor, Conn., was the 14th and youngest child of Connecticut colonial governor Roger Wolcott. He served in a volunteer militia against the French in North America before graduating from Yale in 1747. About 1751 he became sheriff of Litchfield County. He was a delegate to the Continental Congress (1775–78, 1780–84) and commander of the Connecticut militia. He later served as lieutenant governor (1787–96) and governor (1796–97) of Connecticut.

Delaware

George Read (1733–98), born in Cecil County, Md., was a lawyer and delegate to the Continental Congress (1774–77).

During the war he served as acting governor of Delaware (1777–79) and later became a judge (1782–86). As a delegate to the Constitutional Convention (1787), Read upheld the rights of smaller states. And because Read led the fight to get the Constitution approved, Delaware became the first state to ratify the document. Read went on to serve as a U.S. senator (1789–93) and chief justice of Delaware (1793–98).

Caesar Rodney. See DELAWARE (Famous People) in Volume D.

Thomas McKean (1734–1817), born in New London, Pa., was a major political figure in both Delaware and Pennsylvania. A lawyer, he served as a member (1762–79) and as speaker (1772–73, 1777) of the Delaware Assembly. He served as a delegate to the Stamp Act Congress (1765), delegate to the Continental Congress (1774–76, 1778–83), president of the Continental Congress (1781), president of Delaware (1776), chief justice of Pennsylvania (1777–99), and governor of Pennsylvania (1799–1808).

Georgia

Button Gwinnett (1735?–77), born in Gloucester, England, was a merchant who immigrated to America in the 1760's. He later bought land in Georgia, established himself as a planter, and became involved in politics. He was a delegate to the Continental Congress (1776, 1777) and president of Georgia (1777). He died of wounds he received in a duel.

Lyman Hall (1724–90), born in Wallingford, Conn., gave up the ministry to become a

physician. In the 1750's, he moved to Georgia, cofounded the town of Sunbury, and became a planter. He was a delegate to the Continental Congress (1775–78, 1780) and served as governor of Georgia (1783).

George Walton (1741–1804), born near Farmville, Va., was a prominent lawyer, who moved to Georgia in 1769. He fought in the Georgia militia during the war and was captured and held prisoner (1778–79). A delegate to the Continental Congress (1776–81), he also served the state of Georgia as governor (1779–80, 1789–90), chief justice (1783–89), superior court justice (1790–92, 1793–95, 1799–1804), and U.S. senator (1795–96).

Maryland

Charles Carroll of Carrollton. See MARYLAND (Famous People) in Volume M.

Samuel Chase (1741–1811), born in Somerset County, Md., was a lawyer and judge. A delegate to the Continental Congress (1774–78, 1784, 1785), he opposed the signing of the U.S. Constitution. He later served as chief justice (1791–96) of the General Court of Maryland and was appointed an associate justice of the Supreme Court in 1796. Charged with partisan conduct by Thomas Jefferson's supporters, Chase was the only Supreme Court justice ever impeached (1804) by the House of Representatives. Acquitted by the Senate, he remained on the court until his death.

Charles Carroll of Carrollton, Maryland

William Paca (1740–99), born near Abingdon, Md., was a prominent lawyer and judge. He was first elected to the Maryland state legislature in 1771 and was later appointed a delegate to the Continental Congress (1774–79). He served as chief judge of the Maryland general court (1778), chief judge of the court of appeals (1780–82), and three terms as governor (1782–85) of Maryland. He ended his career as U.S. district judge for the state of Maryland (1789–99).

Signers of the Declaration of Independence

Thomas Stone (1743–87), born in Charles County, Md., was a lawyer, a delegate to the Continental Congress (1775–76, 1777–78, 1783–84), and a member of the Maryland state senate (1777–80, 1781–87). Haberdeventure, the home Stone built for his family in Port Tobacco, Md., is preserved as a National Historic Site.

Massachusetts

John Adams. See ADAMS, JOHN in Volume A.

Samuel Adams. See ADAMS, SAMUEL in Volume A.

Elbridge Gerry. See VICE PRESIDENCY OF THE UNITED STATES (Profiles) in Volume UV.

John Hancock. See HANCOCK, JOHN in Volume H.

Robert Treat Paine (1731–1814), born in Boston, Mass., was a lawyer who prosecuted the British soldiers responsible for the Boston Massacre. He was a member of the Massachusetts state legislature (1773–75, 1777) and a delegate to the Continental Congress (1774–76). He later served as the first attorney general (1777–90) of Massachusetts and as a state supreme court judge (1790–1804). In 1780, he cofounded the American Academy of Arts and Sciences.

New Hampshire

Josiah Bartlett. See NEW HAMPSHIRE (Famous People) in Volume N.

Matthew Thornton (1714?–1803), born in Ireland, was just a boy when his parents immigrated to the American colonies. Thornton practiced medicine (1740–79) in Londonderry, N.H. and became involved in local politics. He served as president of the New Hampshire legislature (1775–76). A delegate to the Continental Congress (1776), he later served as a state supreme court judge (1778–82) and state senator (1784–86).

John Hancock of Massachusetts

John Witherspoon of New Jersey

William Whipple (1730–85), born in Kittery, Me., was a sailor and merchant before serving as a delegate to the Continental Congress (1776–79). During the war, he commanded militia groups at Saratoga (1777) and Rhode Island (1778). He later served as an associate justice (1782–85) of the New Hampshire superior court.

New Jersey

Abraham Clark (1726–94), born in Elizabethtown, N.J., was a farmer, surveyor, and self-taught lawyer, known for helping poor farmers in land disputes. He was known as "Congress Abraham" for his various congressional offices. He was a delegate to the Continental Congress (1776–78, 1779–83, 1787–89) and a member of the New Jersey state legislature (1776, 1783–85) and the U.S. House of Representatives (1791–94).

John Hart (1711?–79), born in Stonington, Conn., was a longtime member of the New Jersey provincial assembly (1761–71) and state legislature (1775–76). He was a delegate to the Continental Congress (1776) and was the oldest member of the group to sign the Declaration of Independence. He later served as chairman of the New Jersey Council of Safety (1777–78).

Francis Hopkinson (1737–91), born in Philadelphia, Pa., was a lawyer and member of the New Jersey

Josiah Bartlett of New Hampshire

delegation to the Continental Congress (1776). He later served as a U.S. District judge for eastern Pennsylvania (1789–91). Hopkinson also wrote political satires and in 1777 helped design the American flag.

Richard Stockton (1730–81), born in Princeton, N.J., was a prominent lawyer who served New Jersey as a member of the executive council (1768–76), associate supreme court justice (1774–76), and delegate to the Continental Congress (1776). In late 1776, while supporting the war effort, he was captured by the British. His harsh imprisonment contributed to his early death.

John Witherspoon (1723–94), born near Edinburgh, Scotland, was a Presbyterian minister who immigrated to America in 1768 to serve as president of the College of New Jersey (now Princeton University), a job he held until his death. He was a delegate to the Continental Congress (1776–79, 1780–81, and 1782) and the only clergyman to sign the Declaration. He later played a major role in organizing the Presbyterian Church in the United States and establishing Princeton as one of the nation's leading universities.

New York

William Floyd (1734–1821), born in Brookhaven, N.Y., was a prominent civic leader on Long Island and a general in the local militia. He was a delegate to the Continental Congress (1774–77, 1778–83) and later served as a member of the U.S. House of Representatives (1789–91) and the New York state senate (1808).

Francis Lewis (1713–1803), born in Llandaff, Wales, was a merchant who immigrated to America in 1738 to set up businesses in New York and Philadelphia.

Philip Livingston of New York

Joseph Hewes of North Carolina

John Morton (1724?–77), born in Ridley, Pa., was a longtime member of Pennsylvania's provincial assembly (1756–75). He attended the Stamp Act Congress (1765) and was later named a delegate to the Continental Congress (1774–77). He held various civil offices in Pennsylvania, including justice of the peace, high sheriff, and associate judge of the supreme court.

George Ross (1730–79), born in New Castle, Del., established a law practice in Lancaster, Pa. He was a member of Pennsylvania's provincial assembly (1768–76), a delegate to the Continental Congress (1774, 1776–77), and vice president of the Pennsylvania Constitutional Convention (1776). He also served as a colonel in the Continental Army during the war.

Benjamin Rush (1745–1813), born in Byberry, Pa., was a physician and a professor of chemistry and medicine at the College of Philadelphia (1769–91). He was named a delegate to the Continental Congress (1776–77) and served as a surgeon-general in the Continental Army. In 1786 he opened the first free clinic in the United States. He later served as treasurer of the U.S. Mint (1797–1813) and as a professor of medical theory and clinical practice at the University of Pennsylvania (1791–1813).

James Smith (1719?–1806), born in Ireland, was a boy when he immigrated to the American colonies, where he became

In 1756, while serving as a British aide to General Mercer, he was captured by the French at Fort Oswego and taken to France as a prisoner. On his return to America, he devoted himself to the patriots' movement. A delegate to the Continental Congress (1774–79), he lost all his property on Long Island during the Revolutionary War. His son Morgan (1754–1844) later served as governor of New York (1804–07).

Philip Livingston. See LIVINGSTON FAMILY in Volume L.

Lewis Morris (1726–98) was born in Morrisania, in what is now New York City. While a delegate to the Continental Congress (1775–77), Morris also served as a brigadier-general in the New York militia. In 1777, his half-brother, Gouverneur, took his seat in Congress. (See the biography of Gouverneur Morris in Volume M.) Lewis Morris also served as a judge and as a member of the state legislature (1777–90).

North Carolina

Joseph Hewes (1730–79), born near Kingston, N.J., established a successful shipping business in Wilmington, N.C. He was later elected to North Carolina's provincial assembly (1766–75). A delegate to the Continental Congress (1775–79), he served as its secretary of naval affairs until his death at age 49.

William Hooper (1742–90), born in Boston, Mass., was a lawyer who settled in Wilmington, N.C. He served as a member of the provincial assembly (1773–76, 1777–78) and as a delegate to the Continental Congress (1774–77). In 1786, he became a federal judge.

John Penn (1741?–88), born near Port Royal, Va., practiced law in Virginia before moving to North Carolina in 1774, where he became a member of the provincial congress. He was named a delegate to the Continental Congress (1775–77, 1779–80), serving in the latter term on the Board of War.

Pennsylvania

George Clymer (1739–1813), born in Philadelphia, Pa., was a successful merchant when he became a delegate to the Continental Congress (1776–78, 1780–83). As a member of the Constitutional Convention (1787), he signed the U.S. Constitution and served in the first U.S. Congress (1789–91). He was later named president of both the Philadelphia Bank and the Philadelphia Academy of Fine Arts.

Benjamin Franklin. See FRANKLIN, BENJAMIN in Volume F.

Robert Morris (1734–1806), born in Liverpool, England, immigrated to the American colonies in 1747 and became a successful merchant in Philadelphia. When the Stamp Act hurt his business, he joined the patriots' protests against the British. A delegate to the Continental Congress (1775–78), he personally helped finance the Revolutionary War. From 1781 to 1784, he served as superintendent of finance, founding the national Bank of North America in 1782. He later served as a delegate to the Constitutional Convention (1787) and as a U.S. senator (1789–95) from Pennsylvania.

Robert Morris of Pennsylvania

Edward Rutledge of South Carolina   Richard Henry Lee of Virginia

a lawyer and surveyor. In 1774, as a provincial assemblyman, Smith encouraged a boycott of British goods and organized a volunteer militia in York, Pa. He was named a delegate to the Continental Congress (1776–78) and helped draft the Pennsylvania state constitution. In 1782 he became brigadier general of the Pennsylvania militia.

George Taylor (1716–81), born in Ireland, was about 20 when he immigrated to America. He became an iron manufacturer, operating a furnace in Bucks County, Pa. He served in the provincial assembly (1764–69), on the Committee of Correspondence (1774–76), and as a delegate to the Continental Congress (1776–77).

James Wilson (1742–98), born in Carskerdy, Scotland, immigrated in 1765 to America, where he became a lawyer and politician. A delegate to the Continental Congress (1774, 1775–77, 1782, 1783, 1785–87) and the Constitutional Convention (1787), he was largely responsible for writing the Pennsylvania state constitution of 1790. He later served as an associate justice on the U.S. Supreme Court (1789–98).

Rhode Island

William Ellery (1727– 1820), born in Newport, R.I., was a merchant and lawyer. An early abolitionist, he served as a delegate to the Continental Congress (1776–81, 1783–85), chief justice of the Rhode Island superior court (1785), commissioner of the Continental Loan Office (1786–90), and customs collector (1790–1820) at Newport.

Stephen Hopkins (1707– 85), born in Providence, R.I., was a lawyer and educator. He served several terms as colonial governor of Rhode Island (1755, 1756, 1758–61, 1763–64, 1767). An early and outspoken advocate for colonial union and independence,

Stephen Hopkins of
Rhode Island

he was a delegate to the Albany Convention (1754) and the Continental Congress (1774–78).

South Carolina

Thomas Heyward, Jr. (1746–1809), born in St. Luke's Parish, S.C., was a lawyer and delegate to the Continental Congress (1776–78). During the Revolutionary War, he was captured by the British while commanding a South Carolina militia force. He later served as a judge (1783–98).

Thomas Lynch, Jr. (1749–79), born near Georgetown, S.C., was a lawyer. During the Revolutionary War he served as captain of a South Carolina regiment and as a delegate to the Continental Congress (1776). After sailing for the West Indies, he was never heard from again. It is presumed he was lost at sea.

Arthur Middleton (1742–87), born near Charleston, S.C., served in the colonial legislature and provincial assembly of South Carolina (1765–76), where he helped write the state constitution. He then became a delegate to the Continental Congress (1776–77, 1781). In 1780, during the war, Middleton was captured by the British near Charleston and held for one year.

Edward Rutledge. See SOUTH CAROLINA (Famous People) in Volume S.

Virginia

Carter Braxton (1736–97), born in Newington, Va., was a son of a wealthy plantation owner. He served many years in the Virginia House of Burgesses (1761–71, 1775–76). In 1776, he replaced the late Peyton Randolph as a delegate to the Continental Congress (1776). He later served in the Virginia House of Delegates (1776–83, 1785–86, 1790–94).

Benjamin Harrison (1726? –91), born in Charles City County, Va., was a longtime member of the Virginia House of Burgesses (1749–75). He served as a delegate to the Continental Congress (1774–78) and as governor of Virginia (1782–84). His son, William Henry Harrison, was elected U.S. president in 1840. Benjamin's great-grandson, also named Benjamin, was elected president in 1888.

Thomas Jefferson. See JEFFERSON, THOMAS in Volume JK.

Francis Lightfoot Lee. See LEE FAMILY in Volume L.

Richard Henry Lee. See LEE FAMILY in Volume L.

Thomas Nelson, Jr. (1738–89), born in Yorktown, Va., was a planter. He served in the Virginia House of Burgesses (1774) and in 1775 founded the Virginia Militia, serving as its first commander. He was a delegate to the Continental Congress (1775–77, 1779) and later served as governor of Virginia (1781).

George Wythe (1726–1806), born in Elizabeth City County, Va., began practicing law in 1746 and became one of Thomas Jefferson's teachers. He was a member (1754–55, 1758–68) and clerk (1769–75) of the Virginia House of Burgesses and a delegate to the Continental Congress (1775–77) and the Constitutional Convention (1787). He also served as a judge (1788–1801) and taught law at the College of William and Mary (1779–89).

For more information on the signers, see the article CONTINENTAL CONGRESS in Volume C.

Young American Medals for Bravery (*left*) and Service (*right*) are awarded to deserving young people under age 19 by the United States Department of Justice.

DECORATIONS AND MEDALS

Medals and decorations are given to members of the armed services for bravery, outstanding service, being wounded, and taking part in a war or a campaign. Medals can be awarded to civilians for service, bravery, or saving lives. Medals are also awarded for sports achievements, as in the gold, silver, and bronze medals of the Olympic Games.

In ancient Greece and Rome the decoration for merit, military or otherwise, was a laurel wreath. It was placed on the victor's head like a crown. Roman coins bore the head of the emperor crowned by a wreath. On later coins, the wreath was placed around the edge of the coin, as can still be seen on the back of some U.S. pennies.

During the Crusades, medals were used to identify the Knights Templar, the Knights of Saint John of Jerusalem, and others. For centuries most medals were given to nobles or officers for military deeds. England's Queen Elizabeth I ordered medals for Sir Francis Drake and the other captains who defeated the Spanish Armada in 1588. Medals were rarely given to common soldiers.

▶ U.S. DECORATIONS AND MEDALS

Decorations are usually awarded for individual meritorious achievement or bravery, many times for a single accomplishment. For example, the Navy Cross is a decoration given by the U.S. Navy to an individual for exceptional heroism in action. Other examples of decorations are the Distinguished Service Cross (Army), and the Silver Star. Some awards are called medals even though they are, in fact, decorations—for example, the Air Medal, the Navy/Marine Corps Medal, and the Medal of Honor. The Medal of Honor is the highest award for valor in action against an enemy force bestowed upon an individual serving in the U.S. armed services.

Medals usually fall into the areas of individual service or participation in a military operation or series of operations. For example, in 2003, U.S. president George W. Bush issued an executive order establishing the Global War on Terrorism Expeditionary Medal and the Global War on Terrorism Service Medal for those who served in military operations to combat terrorism on or after September 11, 2001. Other examples are the World War I Victory Medal, the National Defense Medal, and the Armed Forces Reserve Medal.

The first badge for meritorious service or bravery for the common soldier was the **Badge of Military Merit**, established by George Washington in 1782 during the American Revolution (1775–83). It was a heart-shaped patch of purple cloth trimmed with lace. Although called a badge, it can be considered America's first decoration. The badge allowed its wearer to pass guards and sentinels without challenge and to have his name and regiment inscribed in a Book of Merit. The badge specifically honored the lower ranks, where decorations were unknown in European armies. Only three Badges of Military Merit were awarded during the Revolution. The award was revived in 1932 as the **Purple Heart**. In design, it appears as a purple enameled heart within a gold border showing a relief profile of George Washington in Continental uniform.

After the Revolution, the U.S. Congress awarded some special medals. One went to Washington for driving the British out of Boston.

After the Badge of Military Merit fell into disuse, there were few military awards for individual valor until the Civil War (1861–1865). This was in part because Americans tended to associate awards with the European system of knights, nobles, and kings.

The Medal of Honor. In 1861, President Abraham Lincoln approved a decoration for enlisted Navy men who distinguished themselves by their gallantry in action during the Civil War. Later he approved a similar one for the Army. This was the Medal of Honor, often mistakenly called the Congressional

DECORATIONS AND MEDALS OF THE UNITED STATES

Medal of Honor (Army)

Distinguished Service Cross

Navy Cross

Air Force Cross

Distinguished Flying Cross

Silver Star

Civilian Distinguished Service Medal

Bronze Star

Purple Heart

European-African-Middle Eastern Campaign Medal (World War II)

Presidential Unit Citation (Army)

Legion of Merit (Chief Commander)

Presidential Unit Citation (Navy)

Victory Medal (World War I)

NASA Distinguished Service Medal

National Security Medal (CIA)

NASA Pins

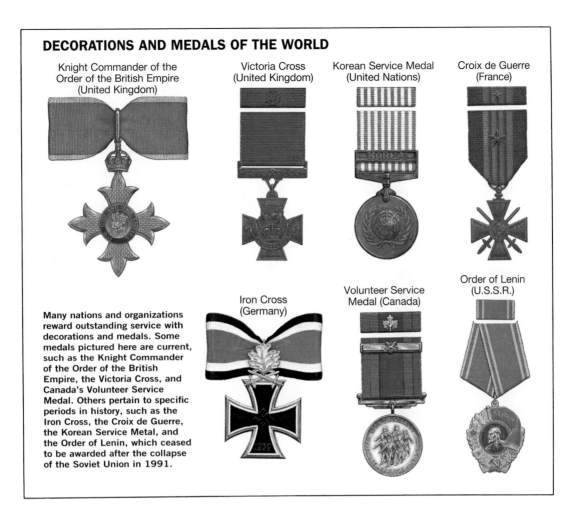

DECORATIONS AND MEDALS OF THE WORLD

Knight Commander of the
Order of the British Empire
(United Kingdom)

Victoria Cross
(United Kingdom)

Korean Service Medal
(United Nations)

Croix de Guerre
(France)

Iron Cross
(Germany)

Volunteer Service
Medal (Canada)

Order of Lenin
(U.S.S.R.)

Many nations and organizations reward outstanding service with decorations and medals. Some medals pictured here are current, such as the Knight Commander of the Order of the British Empire, the Victoria Cross, and Canada's Volunteer Service Medal. Others pertain to specific periods in history, such as the Iron Cross, the Croix de Guerre, the Korean Service Metal, and the Order of Lenin, which ceased to be awarded after the collapse of the Soviet Union in 1991.

Medal of Honor. Later, Congress voted to award the Medal of Honor to both officers and enlisted men and made it a permanent decoration.

At first, because there were no lesser medals, the Medal of Honor was given out freely. On one occasion, for example, President Lincoln promised one to every man in a regiment who would re-enlist. After the Civil War, Congress reviewed the awards and canceled 911 of the 2,438 medals that had been given out. Later, a committee of generals and admirals established stricter rules governing who would be eligible for the Medal of Honor. It was to be given only to those who performed "a deed of personal bravery or self sacrifice above and beyond the call of duty while a member of the armed forces in actual combat with an enemy of the nation."

The U.S. president, in the name of Congress, has awarded some 3,400 Medals of Honor to the nation's bravest soldiers, sailors, airmen, marines, and members of the coast guard. By a special act of Congress it was awarded to one civilian, Charles A. Lindbergh, for his nonstop transatlantic plane flight in 1927. The Medals of Honor for the Army, Navy, and Air Force are of different designs.

Civilian Awards. The highest honor that can be conferred on civilians in peacetime by the president is the Presidential Medal of Freedom. It is presented to Americans who have made exceptional contributions to the national interest, public service, or culture. The Distinguished Service Medal of the National Aeronautics and Space Administration is presented to astronauts who have made spaceflights. The Young American Medals for Service or Bravery are given to Americans under age 19 for courage or public service.

FRANK R. DONOVAN
Author, *The Story of the Medal of Honor*

Reviewed by DEAN S. VEREMAKIS,
CAPT, USNR (RET); MED, MA
President, Orders and Medals Society of America

Objects that are both beautiful and useful have been produced by nearly every culture over time. *Clockwise from above:* An ancient Roman bronze lamp; a wooden headrest from Africa; an Indian rug from the 1600's; a black-figure vase from ancient Greece; a Persian dagger from the 1800's; a modern teapot; an art nouveau vase; a jade ring made in China.

DECORATIVE ARTS

The term "decorative arts" refers to a kind of art that is useful as well as beautiful. Furniture, glassware, ceramics, woodwork, metalwork, and textiles are among the most important decorative arts.

The term "decorative arts" was developed in the 1800's by English and American art historians to distinguish pottery, weaving, woodworking, and similar arts from what they considered the "fine arts," such as painting, sculpture, and architecture. The historians explained that decorative arts had a clear purpose, while fine arts were simply admired for their beauty. This distinction has often led to the fine arts being more valued, or respected, than other types of art. Outside of Europe and the United States, however, most cultures have made no distinction between fine arts and decorative arts; all kinds of art are equally appreciated.

▶ EARLY DECORATIVE ARTS

The oldest surviving pieces of decorative art, made out of wood and bone, date from the Stone Age. They were created for personal adornment, weapons, or tools, and they were typically decorated with animal and human figures.

About 6000 B.C., people in the Middle Eastern region called Mesopotamia changed from a nomadic (wandering) society to a farming society. They began to make tools, textiles, and pottery decorated with scenes of everyday life or with abstract patterns.

Artists soon learned how to hammer copper, gold, and silver into different shapes to make jewelry, goblets, and weapons. The people who lived around the Mediterranean Sea made gold objects decorated with the forms of

The simple clay pots of Mesopotamia were decorated with abstract patterns.

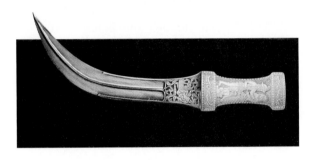

in everyday activities. Because many Egyptian gods were represented as real or imaginary animals, Egyptian decoration is full of snakes, lions, cats, eagles, and sphinxes.

Early Egyptian craftsmen used stone for vessels and many other objects. Some stone vessels had two handles and straps so that they could be hung on the wall. Of the many different kinds of stone used, the blue lapis lazuli was the most prized.

The Egyptians were also skilled at working metal, which they used to make vessels, statues, and jewelry and to decorate furniture. Gold was easily shaped and decorated with raised designs, called **reliefs**, or designs formed by hammering wire of different metals into the surface. Metal was

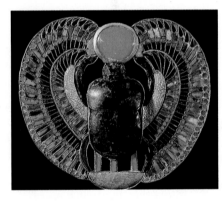

The ancient Egyptians combined gold and other metals with colored stones such as lapis lazuli to create stunning pieces of jewelry.

animals, humans, and plants. Artists in northern Europe used geometric shapes, such as circles, squares, spirals, crosses, and triangles.

As more cultures arose around the world, each developed its own style of decorative art. But neighboring cultures also learned about each other's artistic styles through trade and warfare, so some similarities in style can be found in various regions around the world.

▶ ANCIENT EGYPT

Most of what is known of ancient Egyptian decorative arts comes from tombs. It was usual to provide the person who died with everything he or she might need in the afterlife, including furniture to sit or sleep on, weapons to hunt with, jewelry to wear, and games to play. Tomb walls were often decorated with paintings of the deceased engaged

This article provides a general overview of decorative arts through history and throughout the world. More information on specific kinds of decorative art can be found in the articles ENAMELING, FURNITURE, GLASS, ILLUMINATED MANUSCRIPTS, JEWELRY, MOSAIC, POTTERY, STAINED-GLASS WINDOWS, and TAPESTRY.

often combined with stone to make jewelry in the shape of animals. Ivory was also carved and often used with ebony (a hard, black wood). Simple designs of lotus and papyrus plants were used on furniture, tools, and tableware. These plant forms were often combined with human or animal heads. Sometimes the bodies of people had the heads of sacred animals.

▶ SUB-SAHARAN AFRICA

As in Egypt, the oldest objects from sub-Saharan (south of the Sahara desert) Africa have been found in graves. Tools, weapons, and ornaments were often made from bones and shells. Large sculptures of gods and rulers were carved from rock. Wood was used

African cultures south of the Sahara Desert created ritual masks from metals such as bronze and iron.

for furniture, including special royal stools with seats supported by carved heads. Tools, amulets, bells, and ritual masks were made from bronze and iron. Elephant tusks were carved with battle scenes or bands of braided patterns. Members of the upper class also wore ivory masks carved like human faces. Textiles were woven from raffia, cotton, and imported silk and were decorated with brightly colored geometric and abstract patterns. Basket-weaving, which included mats and wall coverings, was the most widely practiced of all the crafts.

▶ CHINA AND JAPAN

The decorative arts of China and Japan were flowing and graceful because they were closely tied to **calligraphy** (the art of beautiful writing). Materials such as jade, porcelain, silk, and lacquer, which were unknown in Europe for centuries, were commonly used. Painted decorations focused on nature, with flowers, birds, and mountainous landscapes.

Chinese craftsmen were famous for their mastery of any material they used, such as bronze, jade, ceramics, and silk. Chinese decoration featured several successive styles, including animal forms, plant shapes, and depictions of people. Symbols such as the dragon and phoenix appeared in Chinese art about 2000 B.C.

The earliest and finest bronzes ever made date from the Shang (1523–1000's B.C.) and Zhou (1000's–221 B.C.) dy-

Japanese artisans used lacquer (a hard, shiny coating) to decorate many objects, such as this screen.

nasties. (A dynasty is a period of time when one family rules.) Vessels for cooking, serving liquids, and holding food each had unique shapes and were decorated with carvings of dragons, snakes, locusts, birds, and imaginary beings. These vessels were cast by a technique called lost wax casting. The original model was made of wax, or clay covered with wax. Then the artist would cover the model with a thick layer of plaster or clay, with several holes in it. The model in its shell was then heated. The wax melted and flowed out through the holes. Next, melted bronze was poured into the shell through the same holes, replacing the wax. When the bronze cooled and hardened, the shell was broken away, and a candlestick, doorknob, or plate had been created.

The Chinese made bells and other musical instruments out of the colorful gemstone jade, which makes a unique sound when struck. Artists of the Shang and Zhou dynasties skillfully carved jade rings, disks, axes, and knives and then polished them to a shine. But the high point of Chinese jade-carving was during the Han dynasty (202 B.C.–A.D. 220), when artists carved miniature figurines, ornaments for sashes, and little jade trees with many graceful curves. During the Ming dynasty (1368–1644), jade was so richly carved it resembled lace.

The Chinese developed a new kind of pottery called porcelain. When porcelain is fired (baked in a kiln), it hardens into a fine, almost transparent, white material. The most famous porcelain was decorated with blue-and-white glazes, as well as with "secret" carved designs that were not visible unless the piece was viewed directly in strong light. Over the centuries the Chinese developed exquisite new shapes in porcelain and painted them with floral designs.

The use of silk, obtained from the cocoon of the silkworm, was a carefully guarded secret among Chinese artisans for many years. This fine material was woven into clothing and tapestries.

Japanese decorative arts were strongly influenced by Chinese art, but the Japanese eventually developed their own unique designs. Japanese ornament is based on a feeling for the harmony of nature and for human beings, carefully placed in compositions. The result is a style that has strongly influenced European art.

The Japanese believed that an object is truly beautiful only when it serves a purpose. They therefore decorated all kinds of objects used in their everyday lives. Artisans created beautiful lacquer (shiny-coated) objects, some featuring imaginary landscapes filled with people and dainty buildings, which were varnished with different colors.

Like the Chinese, the Japanese were highly skilled in ceramics. The development of the tea ceremony encouraged a love of simplicity and ritual, and teacups and pots were made with simple shapes and glazes. Artists introduced colorful designs to porcelain, and even ornamented porcelain with gold and silver. Small decorative figures were cast in bronze.

Woodblock printing in Japan was adopted from China in the 700's. This technique was used mostly to reproduce inexpensive religious works. It reached its highest development in the 1700's, when the skills of the designer, woodcutting specialist, and painter combined to create full-color illustrations.

The Chinese were famous for porcelain, such as this incense burner, decorated with blue-and-white glazes.

▶ INDIA

Indian art first arose around places of worship, and it continues to be influenced by some of the country's major religions, such as Hinduism, Buddhism, and Islam. Symbolic geometric designs decorated some of the earliest shrines and temples. Later, huge stone pillars were heavily decorated with reliefs and three-dimensional carvings of human or animal forms. Baskets, beautifully worked brass bowls, and brightly colored textiles were also created. Jars were carved from wood and decorated with natural scenes, and wood printing blocks were used to decorate vibrantly colored fabrics.

▶ PRE-COLUMBIAN DECORATIVE ARTS

Pre-Columbian art is the art created by native civilizations in Latin America before the arrival of Columbus and other Europeans beginning in the late 1400's. The Aztecs, Maya, and other civilizations developed arts to serve important religious or political functions. Many decorations show planets, stars, and the sun, which was the symbol of the ruler or emperor. Most Maya temples were crowded with ornaments and relief carvings of figures in ceremonial dress. Gold was worked into jewelry and ritual objects. Fine designs of gold or silver wire were also applied to gold or silver surfaces, a technique called **filigree**. Textiles and architecture were often decorated with geometric forms and mythological creatures. Paintings on walls and pottery provide an accurate picture of daily life, and large sculptures were carved of gods, chieftains, and priests.

The Maya, Aztecs, and other pre-Columbian cultures decorated pendants and other objects with astronomical images.

GREECE AND ROME

The decorative arts of ancient Greece and Rome were very similar. The Romans, who conquered Greece in 148 B.C., chose to model much of their society after Greece and adopted many styles of Greek art. Unlike the highly stylized arts of Asia and Africa, Greek and Roman art was more realistic and closer to nature.

The ancient Romans often covered their floors with mosaics, pictures formed by arranging small colored stones or pieces of enameled glass.

Among the earliest examples of Greek decorative art are paintings on vases. In one technique, called **black-figure painting**, the subjects were painted on the vase with liquid clay that turned black after firing in a kiln. In another technique, **red-figure painting**, the backgrounds were painted black and the figures were formed by the areas of red clay left unpainted. These paintings were typically scenes of everyday life or of characters from Greek mythology.

Gold jewelry decorated with filigree was very popular in the Greek and Roman worlds. Vessels were made of iron about the year 600 B.C., but bronze was the favorite material of Greek artisans. Out of bronze they fashioned statues and many useful objects for everyday use, such as weapons, vessels, and medals.

The columns of Greek temples supported decorative panels of relief sculptures, which featured animal or plant-like forms as well as scenes from mythology and battles. Other common types of sculpted ornament included **bucrania** (an ox skull surrounded by ribbons) and acanthus leaves.

Although no Greek paintings beside those on vases have survived to modern times, many Roman frescoes (paintings made on wet plaster) have been found decorating walls in the cities of Pompeii and Herculaneum. Because Pompeii and Herculaneum were buried by a volcanic eruption in A.D. 79, houses, furniture, and many examples of decoration were preserved. These included gold bracelets and necklaces, vessels cut out of semi-precious stones, and glassware of many different colors. Rich textiles once hung on walls. The Romans also covered their floors with **mosaics**, pictures formed by arranging small stones or pieces of enameled glass in cement.

BYZANTINE EMPIRE

When the Roman Empire split into two sections in A.D. 395, the eastern half was centered on the city of Byzantium (Constantinople) and became the Byzantine Empire. Byzantine art combined many features from the Western and Eastern worlds. The forms were based on shapes found in nature, but Byzantine artists tried to make them into pleasing patterns and designs by flattening them and varying their sizes.

Byzantine monks were masters of enamel work, in which powdered glass is melted to form a hard, shiny surface. A design was made with thin ribbons of gold attached to a gold plate. Each separate area in the design was filled with enamel, and then the piece was baked in a kiln until the enamel and metal joined together. The gold base gleaming through the enamel gave the object a distinctive glow.

Churches were decorated with gold mosaics. Fine gold jewelry with gemstones was also made for wealthy rulers. Brightly colored combs, fans, religious tablets, and book covers were crafted from ivory.

MIDDLE AGES

During Europe's Middle Ages (500–1500), most art was made for rulers or the church and featured bright colors, rich decorations, and stylized forms. Sculptures, paintings, stained-glass windows, and gold reliquaries (containers holding the remains of a Christian saint or martyr) filled major cathedrals. Colorful tapestries, jewelry, clothes, and armor were made for powerful lords and their families.

Monasteries produced a large amount of decorative art. The covers of Bibles and other religious books were decorated with gold, silver, ivory, enamel, and delicately painted leather. The monks painted the pages with brilliantly colored illustrations, some showing scenes of the seasons.

German iron and bronze workers were known for their candlesticks and church doors. Gates and screens for cathedrals were beautifully made, and fancy metal hinges held together the wooden slats of great doors.

Stained-glass windows were a distinct feature of the Gothic style of architecture, which developed during the 1100's. The decorative quality of these windows was enhanced by ornate stone supports that divided each window into separate panes. The patterns formed by these supports, called **tracery**, consisted of arcs and circles combined with shapes from nature. Large windows illustrated stories from the Bible.

The Gothic period also brought a greater use of armor decoration. Designs were engraved or etched into the metal. Sometimes the engraved lines were filled with hard black or silver paste to create a bolder pattern.

Fewer religious articles were made toward the end of the Middle Ages. Rich merchants wanted objects for their homes. Vases, handwoven rugs and clothing, and the corners of tables were decorated with the same imaginary animals that appeared on the lord's shields or flags.

▶ RENAISSANCE

The Renaissance ("rebirth"), which began in Italy in the 1400's, was an age of rediscovery. European artists tried to find new ways to express themselves and turned to the arts and ideas of classical Greece and Rome. They studied Greek and Roman ruins, trying to imitate not only the forms but also the materials. The shapes of animals, plants, and people were also studied in an effort to create

The decorative quality of Gothic stained-glass windows was often enhanced with tracery, ornate stone supports dividing the window into separate panes.

more natural forms in painted and carved decoration. Churches were no longer built with pointed arches, and their roofs were now supported by columns topped with capitals.

New types of furnishings were developed to satisfy a growing demand for rugs, ceramics, tapestries, glassware, and paintings. One method of decorating wooden furniture was **intarsia**. Small pieces of wood of different colors were set into the surface to form special patterns or scenic designs such as landscapes. Another method was to create geometric designs by setting little pieces of ivory and bone into the wood. Low wooden chests were decorated with thin fabric, on which a design was built up with a plaster-like paste called gesso. Final details were carved into the gesso, and the piece was gilded (covered with thin gold leaf).

The Italians invented a kind of ceramic decoration

Italian ceramics known as majolica were decorated with brilliantly colored scenes from religion, history, or mythology.

called **majolica**. Majolica pottery was decorated with brilliantly colored scenes from Greek mythology, the Bible, or Italian history. Large majolica plates and vessels were not meant to be used but only displayed and admired.

Gold was engraved or decorated with enamel, and craftsmen rediscovered how to cast gold and bronze with the lost wax method. They also developed new ways of making glassware in all sorts of shapes and colors.

BAROQUE AND ROCOCO

"Baroque" is the name given to European art of the 1600's and early 1700's that was characterized by ornate designs and curved shapes that gave the impression of motion. Baroque decoration was heavy and dramatic.

Large pieces of furniture such as cabinets and desks were common during this period. The popular form of decoration was **marquetry**, in which veneers (thin layers) of ivory, bone, mother-of-pearl, brass, bronze, tortoiseshell, and different kinds of wood were set onto the wooden panels of furniture to create decorative designs.

The rococo style developed in the early 1700's. Rococo also featured curved shapes to evoke movement, but it had a lighter and more delicate appearance than baroque. Decoration was now swirling and moving, with

A gilded bronze clock in the rococo style has an ornate and flowing design.

clouds, garlands, or draperies. Depictions of rocks, shells, scrolls, flowers, fruits, and leaves were used on nearly all the decorative art of the day, as well as on architecture and in painting. Rooms became oval or round, and furniture was curved and swayed. Everything had light gold borders, and angels and cherubs played in smoke and clouds.

During this period, European artists also studied the designs found on Chinese and other Asian silks, furniture, and porcelain. The forms that developed, called **chinoiserie**, were not copied directly from the Chinese but were combined with European forms. They copied the lacquer style and the light, airy paintings of the Japanese as well. And the secrets of silk and porcelain were finally discovered.

THE INDUSTRIAL AGE

The Industrial Revolution, which began in the mid-1700's, was a time of great technological growth throughout Europe and the United States. By the mid-1900's, many objects that were once made by hand were now mass-produced by machines and sold to millions of people. At first manufacturers of decorative objects tried to copy the appearance of handmade art, but the results were not always very pleasing. However, artisans who made handcrafted objects found it difficult to compete with the speed and low cost of mass production. Mass-produced goods—even though they lacked the quality of earlier decorative art—came to dominate the markets.

Some architects and designers rebelled against these developments. The most prominent was William Morris of England, who with his followers founded the **arts and crafts movement** to revive craftsmanship and good design. Although many people did not agree with the arts and crafts movement, Morris' ideas slowly began to affect decorative art. Other artists agreed that machine-made products were ugly, but they did not think that art should return to the past. These artists were part of the **art nouveau** ("new

Baroque furniture was often decorated with marquetry, designs formed by placing veneers of ivory, bone, brass, and various kinds of wood onto a wooden surface.

art") movement, which featured a style of flowing, curved lines and flat color patterns. It affected all the arts, from posters to architecture.

Another movement, **art deco**, also arose about this time. Art deco designers wanted to join art and industry, and they chose materials and forms that could be easily mass produced. Glass, plastic, and chrome were often used, and the designs had a sleek, streamlined look. The style was used for clothing, jewelry, and furniture as well as for household objects such as clocks and teapots.

With the development of the artistic movement called **modernism** in the early 1900's, many architects and designers argued that the form or shape of an object should be dictated by its function, or what it is supposed to do, and that all kinds of ornament should be avoided. Architects such as Le Corbusier and Walter Gropius believed that the most pleasing object is one that works the best; a teapot is useless if its design makes the tea drip when it is poured. Ornament was extra, and therefore unnecessary. Students at the Bauhaus, a German design school founded by Gropius, dedicated themselves to the development of objects that were practical as well as beautiful.

Modernism also encouraged a new exploration of materials for their own decorative ef-

Left: A Tiffany "dragonfly" lamp in the art nouveau style. *Above:* An art deco radio made of plastic has a sleek, streamlined appearance.

fects. Plastic was molded into useful and pleasing shapes for wastepaper baskets, wall surfaces, and even kitchenware. Steel frames, synthetic textiles, and flexible materials were used to create new kinds of furniture that were both comfortable and light.

▶ **DECORATIVE ARTS AS DESIGN**

The term "decorative arts" is rarely used today. Instead, decorative objects are now referred to as "design," because most of them are planned and drawn by designers and then made by machines. The label "design" applies not only to traditional decorative objects such as jewelry and ceramics, but also to coffee makers, computers, and even buildings. In the United States, architects such as Michael Graves have designed furniture and appliances that are mass-produced and sold in department stores. In the 1960's, Swedish designers developed a line of inexpensive but well-designed wood furniture that could be sold in kits and assembled by the consumer.

Today there is perhaps a greater appreciation for handicraft than ever before. African masks, jewelry, and textiles are part of tribal art collections in museums, and contemporary Asian ceramics are highly prized. Whether mass-produced or handmade, everyday objects are appreciated if they have beautiful form, material, or detailing.

RICHARD W. IRELAND
Maryland Institute College of Art
Revised by ISABELLE FRANK
Editor, *The Theory of Decorative Art*

DEEP-SEA DIVING. See OCEANOGRAPHY; SKIN DIVING; UNDERWATER EXPLORATION.

Molded plywood and leather furniture by designer Charles Eames is typical of the modernist style of the 1900's.

DEER

The deer, a hoofed mammal, is among the most graceful of animals. Deer are distinguished by their antlers, which are grown by the males of nearly all species and by female caribou. About 40 species of deer belong to the Cervidae family, from the familiar Bambi (white-tailed deer) to elk, reindeer, and moose.

Fossils indicate that deer lived in Asia at least 30 million years ago, and 25 million years ago in North America. Deer are currently found throughout the Northern Hemisphere and have been introduced in New Zealand and elsewhere. They have adapted to virtually every land habitat, from dry deserts to woodlands, prairies, marshes, and Arctic regions. Some even live in densely populated suburban areas.

▶ SPECIES OF DEER

One of the traits that can vary considerably among deer species is size. In every species, however, the female (a doe or cow) is always smaller than the male (a buck or bull). **Moose** are the largest members of the deer family, standing more than 7 feet (2 meters) tall at the shoulder and weighing up to 1,800 pounds (800 kilograms). They have broad, flattened antlers that can weigh more than 75 pounds (34 kilograms), with projecting tines, or points. Moose are found in Alaska and other northern states and Canada.

The smallest deer is the **Chilean pudu**. This animal, one of ten deer species that are native to South America, measures only about 10 to 16 inches (25 to 40 centimeters)

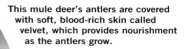

This mule deer's antlers are covered with soft, blood-rich skin called velvet, which provides nourishment as the antlers grow.

high and weighs approximately 13 to 30 pounds (6 to 14 kilograms).

In North America, the most common species is the **white-tailed deer**. It is found from Canada to South America and weighs up to 300 pounds (135 kilograms). The endangered Florida Key deer, a small subspecies of white-tailed deer, weighs only 45 to 75 pounds (20 to 34 kilograms).

The **mule deer**, a close relative of the white-tailed deer, is found west of the Mississippi River. Mule deer have larger ears than white-tailed deer and black-tipped tails. **Elk**, also called **wapiti**, are found in Canada and the western United States. Male elk weigh more than 880 pounds (400 kilograms).

Caribou live in Alaska and Canada. Both male and female caribou have antlers, but the female's antlers are much smaller than the male's. Some herds of barren ground caribou remain on the Arctic tundra year-round, while others migrate south each winter to northern forests. Woodland caribou live in the northern forest all year.

There are many other deer species as well. **Musk deer**, **water deer**, and **muntjacs** are

Moose are the largest members of the deer family. They can stand more than 7 feet (2 meters) tall and weigh nearly a ton.

small, primitive deer native to Asia. The musk deer weighs 15 to 37 pounds (7 to 17 kilograms), and the water deer weighs 24 to 31 pounds (11 to 14 kilograms). Muntjacs, also called barking deer, are slightly larger at 30 to 60 pounds (14 to 27 kilograms). Male

The Chilean pudu, which is native to South America, is only 10 to 16 inches (25 to 40 centimeters) tall and is the smallest of all deer.

musk deer fight with their tusks rather than with antlers. Some scientists place musk deer in a separate family.

Fallow deer, found throughout Europe, have broad, flattened antlers like moose. The **reindeer** of northern Europe and Asia are the same species as the caribou of North America, while the **red deer** in Europe are the same species as North American elk.

▶ CHARACTERISTICS OF DEER

Deer are the only animals with antlers, which, among males, are used in contests to gain the right to mate with females. Made of bone, antlers are shed after each mating season and regrown several months later. Growing antlers are covered with soft, blood-rich skin called velvet, which provides them with nourishment. Later the velvet dries up and the antlers become dead tissue with no nerves or blood flow.

Deer have long, slender legs, each with two toes tipped by strong, curved hooves. These hooves are actually modified fingernails. Although deer usually walk slowly, they will run

short distances if suddenly alarmed, at speeds of more than 40 miles (64 kilometers) per hour.

Like cattle, deer are **ruminants**, or cud chewers, and have four-chambered stomachs. This means they do not fully chew their food before it is swallowed into the first chamber, where fiber-digesting bacteria carry out the first stage of digestion. Later, the partially chewed food, or cud, is brought back up into the mouth and chewed again. When the food particles are small enough, they are swallowed again and passed to the other chambers of the stomach, where chemical digestion occurs.

Food preferences depend upon the deer species. Smaller deer prefer high-quality food. Larger deer tend to eat lower-quality food, but more of it. Foods include grass, forbs (herbs), twigs, lichens, acorns, and fruits. Deer also eat farm and garden crops.

▶ DEER AND THEIR YOUNG

Deer in northern latitudes breed in the fall, when days get shorter and nights get longer. Deer that have been brought into the Southern Hemisphere breed six months later than the same species of deer in the Northern

Young deer, called fawns or calves, may be hidden by their mothers after birth and usually stay with them until they are 4 months old.

Hemisphere. White-tailed deer breed in October and November in northern latitudes, January and February in Mexico, and any month of the year in South America.

Female deer usually give birth for the first time when they are 2 years old. Males are physically capable of breeding at 18 months but generally do not breed until they are 3 to 4 years old, or even older in species that form large breeding groups.

Young deer, called fawns or calves, are born 160 to 270 days after the parents have

White-tailed deer, the most common species in North America, are found even in heavily populated areas and can cause problems for homeowners.

mated. This period tends to be longer for larger deer. One exception is the roe deer. It breeds in the summer, but the embryo does not begin growing until late fall. Deer usually have one or two fawns, but some species may have three or four.

Females that are about to give birth move away from other deer. In some species the mother hides the young and only visits it occasionally during the day to nurse it. However, the calves of other species, such as caribou and reindeer, can follow their mothers shortly after birth.

Young deer nurse for four months or longer, then separate from the mother. Al-

though young females often establish territories nearby, young males tend to spread to other areas. In species that migrate, migration paths can be passed from generation to generation among related females.

▶ PREDATORS OF DEER

Deer predators include large carnivores (meat eaters) such as coyotes, wolves, bears, mountain lions, and wolverines. Predators usually attack the old and sick deer, as well as young fawns and calves. Although deer and their predators have survived this way for thousands of years, this natural balance is altered today because humans have greatly reduced both prey and predator populations. Musk deer, barasingha, brow-antlered deer, and even subspecies of the white-tailed deer (the Key deer) are now considered endangered or threatened.

Yet some species have survived and even thrived, despite human interference. In fact, there may be as many white-tailed deer now as there have ever been. In certain areas, increased numbers of deer have led to problems such as crop destruction and deer–motor vehicle accidents. However, millions of people continue to hunt white-tailed deer in the United States. These human hunters have replaced predators as a means of keeping the population in check.

Other deer species have recovered with the help of humans. Pere David's deer, which was native to China, died out there in 1922. Luckily, several of these deer had been brought to Europe in the 1800's. In the 1950's, Pere David's deer from England were sent back to China to re-establish a population there.

RONALD A. MOEN
Research Associate
University of Minnesota, Duluth

See also ELK AND MOOSE; REINDEER AND CARIBOU.

DEFENSE, UNITED STATES DEPARTMENT OF

The Department of Defense (DOD) is the federal agency responsible for maintaining the national security of the United States. Its purpose is to coordinate America's military armed forces in times of war and to plan for the nation's defense in times of peace.

The Department of Defense is one of the 15 executive departments of the United States government. It is commonly referred to as the Pentagon. The Pentagon is actually a massive five-sided, five-story building that serves as the department's headquarters. The Pentagon is recognized around the world as a symbol of U.S. power and influence.

Organization

Several divisions make up the Department of Defense. They include the Office of the Secretary; the Department of the Army; the Department of the Navy; the Department of the Air Force; the Joint Chiefs of Staff; the Unified and Specified Commands; and the Defense Agencies.

The Office of the Secretary. The department is headed by a secretary of defense, who is a civilian (a nonmilitary person). The secretary is appointed by the president with the Senate's approval and is a member of the president's cabinet, the National Security Council, and the North Atlantic Council. The secretary's many responsibilities include making defense policy; advising the president on all matters concerning defense and national security; and managing a budget of roughly $300 billion, which is second only to that of the Department of Health and Human Services. Every year the secretary must report to Congress to define the department's priorities and explain how its resources are being used.

The secretary of defense is assisted by a deputy secretary; an undersecretary for acquisition; an undersecretary for policy; a general counsel; an inspector general; and eleven assistant secretaries, who handle a wide range of responsibilities. These include budgets and finances, international security and policy; health, legislative, and public affairs; and reserves, logistics, and personnel.

The Three Branches of the Military. The three service branches of the military are the Army, the Navy, and the Air Force. These branches organize, train, equip, and maintain the nation's armed forces. Each branch has a department within the Department of Defense that is headed by a civilian secretary, who reports to the secretary of defense. In addition, each branch has a noncivilian chief military adviser. They are the chief of staff of the Army, the chief of staff of the Air Force, the chief of naval operations, and the commandant of the Marine Corps (which is part of the Navy). These chiefs report to a chairman and vice chairman, who rank above all other officers in the United States Armed Forces. All together, these military advisers are known as the **Joint Chiefs of Staff**.

The chairman of the Joint Chiefs of Staff serves as the principal military adviser to the secretary of defense, the president, and the National Security Council and directs the operations of the unified and specified commands. **Unified commands** are forces made up of two or more service branches working together. They are the Central, European, Joint Forces, Northern, Pacific, Southern, Special Operations, Strategic, and Transportation commands. **Specified commands** are represented by only one service branch, such as Strategic Air Command and Forces Command.

The Defense Agencies. In addition to the secretary's office and military departments, 16

Secretaries of Defense		
Name	**Took Office**	**Under President**
James V. Forrestal	1947	Truman
Louis A. Johnson	1949	Truman
*George C. Marshall	1950	Truman
Robert A. Lovett	1951	Truman
Charles E. Wilson	1953	Eisenhower
Neil H. McElroy	1957	Eisenhower
Thomas S. Gates, Jr.	1959	Eisenhower
Robert S. McNamara	1961	Kennedy, L. B. Johnson
Clark M. Clifford	1968	L. B. Johnson
Melvin R. Laird	1969	Nixon
Elliot L. Richardson	1973	Nixon
James R. Schlesinger	1973	Nixon, Ford
Donald H. Rumsfeld	1975	Ford
Harold Brown	1977	Carter
Caspar W. Weinberger	1981	Reagan
Frank C. Carlucci	1987	Reagan
*Richard B. Cheney	1989	G. Bush
Les Aspin	1993	Clinton
William J. Perry	1994	Clinton
William S. Cohen	1997	Clinton
Donald Rumsfeld	2001	G. W. Bush

*Subject of a separate article or profile. Consult the Index.

agencies are administered by the DOD. They are Advanced Research Projects, Missile Defense, Commissary, Contract Audit, Contract Management, Finance and Accounting, Imagery and Mapping, Information Systems, Intelligence, Legal Services, Logistics, National Security, Security, Security Cooperation, Pentagon Force Protection, and Threat Reduction.

History

The Department of Defense was established by the National Security Act of 1947 following World War II. This act combined the Department of War and the Department of the Navy (both of which had existed since 1789) into a single department. For its first two years, the department was called the National Military Establishment.

The Pentagon, one of the world's largest office buildings, was built in 1943 in Arlington, Virginia, near Washington, D.C. The building covers 34 acres (14 hectares) and has approximately 3.7 million square feet (333,000 square meters) of usable floor space.

On September 11, 2001, 189 Pentagon workers and air passengers were killed when terrorists crashed a hijacked airplane into the southwestern side of the building. The attack—coupled with the almost simultaneous destruction of the twin towers of New York City's World Trade Center—was the worst terrorist assault in American history.

BETH HEINSOHN
ANDREW COHEN
Coauthors, *The Department of Defense*

DEFOE, DANIEL (1660?–1731)

Daniel Defoe, famed as the author of *Robinson Crusoe,* was born in London, probably in 1660. Little is known of his early life. His family were "dissenters"—people who did not support the established Church of England. At 14, Daniel was sent to a school run by dissenters. He studied to be a minister, but in 1685 he decided to go into business.

Throughout his life, Defoe was active as both a businessman and a journalist. He not only wrote about business, but he was himself an investor, wholesaler, and manufacturer. He had his own periodical called *The Review* from 1704 to 1713, and he wrote many books and articles on political and social issues.

Defoe took an active part in many of the major political events of his time. These events often were related to religious struggles. In 1685 he joined in an unsuccessful revolt against the Catholic king of England, James II. In 1688 he supported the Protestant William of Orange, who became king after James II was deposed.

In 1702, Defoe wrote a satiric pamphlet called *The Shortest Way with Dissenters,* in which he pretended to be a prejudiced member of the Church of England who wished to destroy all dissenters. This pamphlet was Defoe's way of mocking the extreme supporters of the Church of England. He was punished publicly for the satire by having to stand in the pillory (a wooden device locked around the head and hands). But even after this, Defoe continued to write about politics.

The works of fiction for which Daniel Defoe is remembered today were not written until late in his life. *The Life and Strange Surprising Adventures of Robinson Crusoe* was published in 1719. It tells of a young man who travels to distant lands and finally returns home a wealthy man. The major part of the book is an account of Crusoe's shipwreck on a deserted island. Through this story, Defoe raises questions about a human being's ability to survive apart from society.

Another of Defoe's best-known works, *Moll Flanders,* appeared in 1722. This is the story of a poor girl, born in prison, who eventually becomes a rich landowner in Virginia.

One of Defoe's most remarkable books is *A Journal of the Plague Year* (1722). From writings about the terrible London plague of 1665, Defoe put together what seems to be a vivid eyewitness account. For such achievements, Defoe is now ranked as one of the first great realistic novelists. He died in London on April 26, 1731.

EVERETT ZIMMERMAN
Author, *Defoe and the Novel*
An excerpt from *Robinson Crusoe* follows.

▶ROBINSON CRUSOE

Robinson Crusoe has spent many years learning to survive on the remote island where he has been shipwrecked. One day he is astonished to discover the footprint of another human being in the sand. But it is not until much later, when a group of cannibals come to the island for their feasts, that he finds a companion. In the following episode, Crusoe rescues one of their prisoners, whom he later names Friday, after his day of rescue.

It came now very warmly upon my thoughts, and indeed irresistibly, that now was my time to get me a servant, and perhaps a companion or assistant, and that I was called plainly by Providence to save this poor creature's life. I immediately ran down the ladders with all possible expedition, fetched my two guns, for they were both but at the foot of the ladders, as I observed above, and getting up again, with the same haste, to the top of the hill, I crossed toward the sea, and having a very short cut, and all down hill, clapped myself in the way between the pursuers and the pursued, hallooing aloud to him that fled, who, looking back, was at first perhaps as much frightened at me as at them; and I beckoned with my hand to him to come back; and, in the meantime, I slowly advanced towards the two that followed; then rushing at once upon the foremost, I knocked him down with the stock of my piece. I was loth to fire, because I would not have the rest hear; though, at that distance, it would not have been easily heard, and being out of sight of the smoke too, they would not have easily known what to make of it. Having knocked this fellow down, the other who pursued with him stopped, as if he had been frightened, and I advanced apace towards him; but as I came nearer, I perceived presently he had a bow and arrow, and was fitting it to shoot at me; so I was then necessitated to shoot at him first, which I did, and killed him at the first shot.

The poor savage who fled, but had stopped, though he saw both his enemies fallen and killed, as he thought, yet was so frightened with the fire and noise of my piece, that he stood stock-still, and neither came forward nor went backward, though he seemed rather inclined to fly still, than to come on.

I hallooed again to him, and made signs to come forward, which he easily understood, and came a little way, then stopped again, and then a little farther, and stopped again; and I could then perceive that he stood trembling, as if he had been taken prisoner, and had just been to be killed, as his two enemies were. I beckoned him

Robinson Crusoe finds a single mysterious footprint in the sand of his desert island: "I stood like one thunder-struck, or as if I had seen an apparition."

again to come to me, and gave him all the signs of encouragement that I could think of; and he came nearer and nearer, kneeling down every ten or twelve steps, in token of acknowledgment for my saving his life. I smiled at him, and looked pleasantly, and beckoned to him to come still nearer. At length he came close to me, and then he kneeled down again, kissed the ground, and laid his head upon the ground, and taking me by the foot, set my foot upon his head. This, it seems, was in token of swearing to be my slave for ever. I took him up, and made much of him, and encouraged him all I could. But there was more work to do yet, for I perceived the savage whom I knocked down was not killed, but stunned with the blow, and began to come to himself; so I pointed to him, and showing him the savage, that he was not dead, upon this he spoke some words to me; and though I could not understand them, yet I thought they were pleasant to hear; for they were the first sound of a man's voice that I had heard, my own excepted, for above twenty-five years.

Degas loved the ballet. It was the theme of many of his paintings, such as *Dance Class* (1874). Louvre, Paris.

DEGAS, EDGAR (1834–1917)

The French painter Edgar Degas was born on July 19, 1834, in Paris. His father was a wealthy banker who was raised in Italy. His mother, descended from French nobility, was born in New Orleans. Degas grew up in elegant Paris society. He spent many hours in museums, theaters, and concert halls. After studying painting briefly in Paris, Degas went to Italy to learn directly from the works of the old masters. While there, he painted masterful portraits of his Italian relatives. He returned to Paris in 1859.

In 1865, Degas met a group of young artists later known as the impressionists. He helped organize their exhibits, and from 1874 to 1886, he was a leading exhibitor. At the Paris cafés where the impressionists met, he was known for his aloof manner and biting wit.

Degas took his subjects from everyday life, choosing poses that showed the human body in action—women ironing, ballet dancers practicing or rubbing their tired ankles, women bathing or combing their hair. In these pictures he seemed to catch a passing moment. Whether he worked in oil paints, charcoal, or pastels, Degas was always a master of line.

The last years of Degas' life were bitter and lonely. He lived alone and saw few people. For a long time, Degas had suffered from failing eyesight, and work became more and more difficult. He turned to sculpture because he could shape it without seeing it. He did many statues of horses and dancers in motion. Finally he was unable to work at all. He died on September 27, 1917, at the age of 83.

Reviewed by FRANK GETLEIN
Author, *The French Impressionists*

DE GAULLE, CHARLES (1890–1970)

The French general and political leader Charles de Gaulle was born in Lille, France, on November 22, 1890. As a boy, he read about the heroes of bygone days and the lives of the Catholic saints and martyrs, as well as the history of France. The serious-minded boy became a patriotic and religious man.

De Gaulle entered the military academy of Saint-Cyr and graduated as a second lieutenant in 1912. He fought in the infantry during World War I and was captured by the Germans. After the war, de Gaulle served at various army posts and taught military history at Saint-Cyr. In 1921 he married Yvonne Vendroux. The couple had three children.

In books and articles, written mainly in the 1930's, de Gaulle set forth his ideas on the role of a leader. He felt that a leader should stand apart from and above other people. He stated that the army of the future would have to rely on armored equipment and air power.

World War II proved de Gaulle's military theories right. In 1940, German mechanized forces swept over France. De Gaulle was promoted to brigadier general and appointed undersecretary of war. In spite of his pleas, France signed an armistice with Germany in June, 1940, and de Gaulle left for London. There he broadcast a call to all French people to keep fighting. Thus began the Free French Movement. It gained in power and influence, and in June, 1944, de Gaulle became head of the provisional government of France. He served until October, 1945, when he was elected president-premier by a constitutional convention. In January, 1946, he abruptly resigned because of a conflict over a new constitution. De Gaulle felt that the new constitution must create a powerful president. From 1947 to 1953 he led a movement for amending the constitution. When this failed, he left public life.

De Gaulle was again made premier in June, 1958, when France faced civil war over Algeria. A new constitution for the Fifth Republic, which provided for a strong president, was adopted by popular vote. De Gaulle was elected president and took office in January, 1959. He was elected to a second term in 1965. As president, de Gaulle undertook to restore France to its former position of world greatness. A high point in his presidency came in 1962 when France recognized Algeria's independence. De Gaulle also signed a treaty with West Germany, recognized Communist China, encouraged France to develop nuclear power, and fought Britain's entry into the European Economic Community (Common Market). In 1966 he withdrew all French forces from the North Atlantic Treaty Organization.

De Gaulle retired in 1969 after his proposals for changes in the French constitution were rejected. He died on November 9, 1970, at his home in Colombey-les-Deux-Églises.

JEAN T. JOUGHIN
American University (Washington, D.C.)

DELACROIX, EUGÈNE (1798–1863)

Eugène Delacroix was a leader of romantic painting in the 1800's. Throughout his life he painted the way he wanted to paint and paved the way for other artists to try new styles. He also became famous for his writings, especially his *Journal.*

Delacroix was born near Paris on April 26, 1798. As a boy he attended drawing classes and showed talent in writing and music. When he was orphaned at 16, Delacroix had to select a career. He chose art.

Unlike most other painters of his time, Delacroix used rich, bright colors to illustrate tragic scenes, and his drawing was not exact and detailed. Critics attacked his work. They said that his colors were too splashy and that his drawing was not realistic enough. Few people bought his pictures, but Delacroix would not change his manner of painting.

Delacroix went to Morocco in 1832. There he filled his sketchbooks with drawings of the North African desert, Arabs in flowing robes, lions, and horses. He used these drawings for some of his greatest paintings.

Upon his return to Paris, Delacroix became a celebrity. People liked to hear about his adventures in North Africa. But few could appreciate his paintings until other artists began to paint in his romantic style. Gradually Delacroix's work gained admirers, and Delacroix became one of the most popular painters in France. He died in Paris on August 13, 1863.

The journal that Delacroix began to keep when he was 24 is valued as a work of literature as well as a record of Delacroix's life and his thoughts on art. His other writings include articles and several volumes of letters.

Reviewed by EDWARD J. SULLIVAN
New York University

DELANY, MARTIN ROBINSON. See CIVIL WAR, UNITED STATES (Profiles: Union).

Delacroix's forceful style can be seen in this detail from *Horses Coming out of the Sea* (1860). Phillips Collection, Washington, D.C.

DELAWARE

State flag

Delaware gets its name from the river and bay that separate it from New Jersey. The river and bay, in turn, were named by an English ship captain, Samuel Argall, who was employed by the Virginia Colony. In 1610, during a storm, Argall took refuge in a bay that was unnamed on his navigational map. He named the bay for the governor of the Virginia Colony, Lord de la Warr, and later the river was given the same name.

Over the years the state has had many nicknames, but the most important is First State. Delaware earned this nickname because it was the first state to ratify the United States Constitution (December 7, 1787).

Delaware, one of the original 13 states, lies along the Atlantic seaboard, bordered by New Jersey, Pennsylvania, and Maryland. It is the second smallest state after Rhode Island, extending only 96 miles (154 kilometers) from north to south and 39 miles (63 kilometers) from east to west at its widest point.

Situated midway between New York City and Washington, D.C., Delaware has always been a crossroads between the North and the South. During the Civil War (1861–65), Delaware was considered a border state—it stayed within the Union but allowed slavery until the 13th Amendment to the Constitution abolished the practice in 1865.

A mixture of agriculture and industry has made Delaware a prosperous state. Its northernmost county, New Castle, has always ranked first in population, ethnic diversity, and industrial and commercial development. It is the site of Delaware's largest city, Wilmington, and the state's largest employer, the DuPont Company, a major manufacturer of chemical products. Delaware's other two counties, Kent and Sussex, have traditionally had fewer people and more farms. Kent County, in central Delaware, contains the state capital, Dover, and a major U.S. Air Force base. Sussex County leads the nation in production of broilers (young chickens), and it has popular beaches on the Atlantic coast. Rehoboth Beach calls itself the Nation's Summer Capital because it draws many visitors from Washington, D.C. Besides long stretches of public beaches, Delaware has many protected wetlands and wildlife refuges.

Above: Pleasure boats dock at Lewes, the site of Delaware's oldest settlement. *Opposite page, clockwise from left:* Elegant gardens grace Nemours, a mansion near Wilmington that is open to the public. Dairy cattle graze near Centerville. Rehoboth Beach is a popular resort on the Atlantic Ocean.

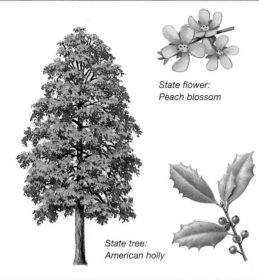

State flower:
Peach blossom

State tree:
American holly

FACTS AND FIGURES

Location: Northeastern United States; bordered on the north by Pennsylvania, on the east by New Jersey, and on the south and west by Maryland.

Area: 2,396 sq mi (6,206 km²); rank, 49th.

Population: 783,600 (2000 census); rank, 45th.

Elevation: *Highest*—442 ft (135 m), in Newcastle County; *lowest*—sea level.

Capital: Dover.

Statehood: December 7, 1787; 1st state.

State Motto: *Liberty and independence.*

State Song: "Our Delaware."

Nickname: First State.

Abbreviations: DE; Del.

State bird:
Blue hen chicken

Workers stack hay on an Amish farm in Kent County. Level farmland is found throughout central and southern Delaware.

▶ LAND

Delaware covers about one-third of the Delmarva Peninsula, which lies between Delaware Bay and the Atlantic Ocean on the east and Chesapeake Bay on the west. The name Delmarva was made by putting together parts of the names of Delaware, Maryland, and Virginia. Each of these states occupies a part of the peninsula.

Land Regions

Most of Delaware—95 percent of it—lies in the Atlantic Coastal Plain. The rest is in the Piedmont, or foothills of the Appalachian Mountains.

The Coastal Plain is nearly flat. It rises from sea level to about 70 feet (20 meters) near the midpoint of the southern border. Then the plain slopes gently toward Maryland's Eastern Shore. Much of the eastern side of

Delaware descends into broad tidal marshes, especially along Delaware Bay.

The Piedmont Plateau covers the northern tip of New Castle County. This is the hilly part of Delaware. At a few points it rises more than 400 feet (120 meters) above sea level.

Rivers, Lakes, and Coastal Waters

Delaware's eastern boundary is formed by water—the Atlantic Ocean, Delaware Bay, and the Delaware River. The United States Supreme Court has ruled that the Delaware River belongs to Delaware, all the way over to the low-water mark on the New Jersey side of the river.

Two-thirds of Delaware's land drains into the Delaware River and the ocean. The rest drains into Chesapeake Bay. Streams, usually called creeks, are small but numerous. In northern Delaware the principal ones are the Brandywine and the Christina. In the south they are the Murderkill, Mispillion, and Broadkill.

In eastern Sussex County there are two small bodies of salt water, Rehoboth Bay and Indian River Bay. They are separated from the ocean by a long strip of coastal beach. Little Assawoman Bay lies west of Fenwick Island in the southeastern corner of the state. In western Sussex County the principal stream is the deep, tidal Nanticoke River, which flows into Chesapeake Bay.

Delaware has only one small natural lake, at Rehoboth Beach. But there are many good-sized millponds, which were created in early days by building dams in streams.

The quiet waters of Brandywine Creek flow south from Pennsylvania into Delaware. The Brandywine is the chief tributary of the Christina. The two rivers join east of Wilmington, then flow into the broad Delaware River.

Huge flocks of snow geese and other wild birds gather at Bombay Hook National Wildlife Refuge, near Smyrna, and at other protected sites on Delaware Bay.

Climate

Delaware experiences all four seasons. Summers are hot, and days of extreme heat are common, especially inland. Winters are relatively mild because Delaware is sheltered by mountains in Pennsylvania. Average temperatures range from 35°F (2°C) in winter to 76°F (24°C) in summer, but on many days temperatures are well below or above those marks. Delaware's location on the Atlantic Ocean makes it humid throughout the year. Snowfall is normally greatest in February. Northern Delaware receives an average of 18 inches (46 centimeters) of snow a year; southern Delaware, about a third less. Rainfall is evenly distributed over the state. In all, the state averages about 46 inches (1,170 millimeters) of precipitation a year. Periods of drought are frequent in summer, and many large farms have irrigation systems to guard against crop losses.

Plant and Animal Life

About one-third of the land in Delaware is forested. Common hardwoods include oak, beech, hickory, and sweet gum trees. The woods of Sussex County contain mostly softwoods, particularly loblolly pine. Swamp magnolia and holly trees are also common.

Delaware has a wide variety of wildflowers, including more than 100 rare plants. The *Wolffrella floridiana*, the smallest known flowering plant, can be found in Dragon Marsh, near Delaware City on the Delaware River—one of only two known locations for the plant.

Wildlife is abundant in the Delaware Valley. Deer, squirrels, cottontail rabbits, skunks, raccoons, and opossums are common. Muskrats live in the marshes. Several kinds of snakes are found in Delaware. Only one of these, the copperhead, is poisonous. There are several kinds of turtles. One is the highly valued diamondback terrapin. It is native to the tidal marshes. Another is the snapping turtle.

Many kinds of birds live in Delaware. The great blue heron and the green heron can be seen along the shores, as can smaller fish-eating birds and gulls. In late autumn and early winter, huge flocks of red-winged

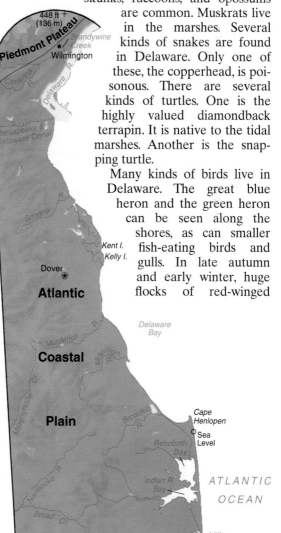

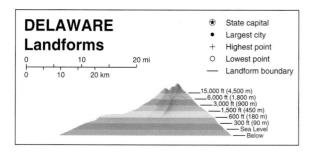

DELAWARE Landforms

| 0 | 10 | 20 mi |
| 0 | 10 | 20 km |

* State capital
• Largest city
+ Highest point
○ Lowest point
— Landform boundary

15,000 ft (4,500 m)
6,000 ft (1,800 m)
3,000 ft (900 m)
1,500 ft (450 m)
600 ft (180 m)
300 ft (90 m)
Sea Level
Below

blackbirds, cowbirds, grackles, and starlings can be seen heading for their nightly roosts in river marshes. These birds spend the day feeding in fields and pastures. Canada geese, snow geese, and wild ducks come in great numbers in the fall to spend the winter at Bombay Hook National Wildlife Refuge on Delaware Bay, near Smyrna, and at the Prime Hook National Wildlife Refuge in Sussex County.

Delaware has a rich variety of fish and shellfish. Carp, trout, bass, white perch, and eels can be found in the ponds and streams in the state. Clams, crabs, oysters, sea trout, and striped bass inhabit the coastal waters.

Natural Resources

Delaware is poor in mineral resources but it has fertile soils. In the north the soil is rich in clay and stony loam, which is good for agriculture. The rest of the state has silt loam and sandy loam soils, which become still more sandy in the southern part of the state. The light soils of downstate Delaware are highly productive when properly drained and fertilized.

▶ PEOPLE

Delaware's population has grown slowly for much of the state's history. In the 1900's, it enjoyed two growth spurts, one from 1920 to 1960 and another in the 1990's. Today three-fourths of Delaware's people live in urban areas—cities, suburbs, and towns. Two-thirds live in the northern part of the state, in New Castle County.

Delaware's people are ethnically and culturally diverse, and have been almost from the beginning. The first Europeans to arrive found the region sparsely inhabited by Native Americans, chiefly of the Lenape (also called Lenni-Lenape or Delaware) and Nanticoke tribes. Under the pressure of European settlement, the Native Americans moved west and north. By 1750 only a small number remained in Delaware.

Ocean beaches attract summer vacationers from many neighboring states. At Rehoboth Beach, visitors can stroll on the boardwalk and sample saltwater taffy. Children especially enjoy playing in the sand.

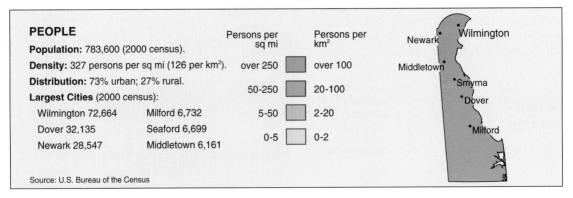

PEOPLE

Population: 783,600 (2000 census).

Density: 327 persons per sq mi (126 per km²).

Distribution: 73% urban; 27% rural.

Largest Cities (2000 census):

Wilmington 72,664	Milford 6,732
Dover 32,135	Seaford 6,699
Newark 28,547	Middletown 6,161

Persons per sq mi	Persons per km²
over 250	over 100
50-250	20-100
5-50	2-20
0-5	0-2

Source: U.S. Bureau of the Census

Newark • Wilmington
Middletown
• Smyrna
• Dover
• Milford

Today two small groups of mixed ancestry, one at Cheswold and the other on the shores of the Indian River, trace their descent to the state's early Native Americans.

Delaware's earliest European settlers—Swedes, Finns, and Dutch—arrived in the 1630's, but their numbers were small. After Delaware became an English colony in 1664, more English settlers came. During the 1800's, English and Irish immigrants were joined by Germans, Poles, Italians, and other European nationalities.

Olde Dover Days, an annual festival in the state capital, celebrates Dover's colonial heritage.

Today Delaware's largest immigrant groups are from Asian and Spanish-speaking countries. Many immigrants have been attracted to the northern part of the state, where economic development has provided the most job opportunities.

African Americans have been in Delaware about as long as people of European ancestry. Less than a year after the first Swedish settlers arrived, a black man was brought from the West Indies. He was probably the only one in the Swedish colony, but many African slaves were brought in under Dutch and English rule. In the 1900's, especially during World War II, many African Americans moved to Delaware to take advantage of job opportunities. In 2000, African Americans accounted for about 20 percent of the state's population.

Education

In the 1700's, before public schools were founded, people in Delaware sent their children to private schools if they could afford to do so. In 1748 the Quakers of Wilmington started a free school for children who could not pay. This school, the Friends School, is still in existence as a private school. Delaware's public school system dates from 1829, but until the 1920's many rural areas had only one-room schools, open just a few months a year.

Delaware's educational system improved after new laws required children to attend school and provided for public funding of education. In 1978, the courts ordered the busing of children into and out of Wilmington in an attempt to achieve better racial balance between city and suburban schools. Court supervision of schools in New Castle County ended in 1997, but the mandate for racial balance remains in place. Today, statewide, nearly 100,000 students are enrolled in public elementary and high schools.

Delaware's oldest and largest institution of higher learning is the University of Delaware in Newark. It traces its beginning to the New London Academy, founded in 1743, and received a state charter in 1833. It is especially noted for its chemical engineering programs. Other public institutions of higher education are Delaware State University, in Dover, and Delaware Technical and Community College,

Green lawns, shade trees, and red brick buildings grace the campus of the University of Delaware in Newark.

PRODUCTS AND INDUSTRIES

Manufacturing: Chemicals and allied products, processed foods, rubber and plastic products, products of printing and publishing, fabricated metal products, nonelectrical machinery.

Agriculture: Broilers, soybeans, corn, milk, hogs, eggs, mushrooms.

Minerals: Sand and gravel, clays.

Services: Wholesale and retail trade; finance, insurance, and real estate; business, social, and personal services; transportation, communication, and utilities; government.

*Gross state product is the total value of goods and services produced in a year.

Percentage of Gross State Product* by Industry

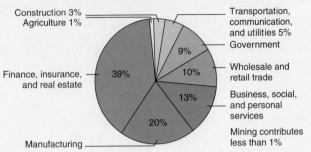

Construction 3%
Agriculture 1%
Transportation, communication, and utilities 5%
Government — 9%
Wholesale and retail trade — 10%
Business, social, and personal services — 13%
Finance, insurance, and real estate — 39%
Manufacturing — 20%
Mining contributes less than 1%

Source: U.S. Bureau of Economic Analysis

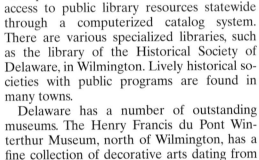

Above: The Hagley Museum and Library, near Wilmington, preserves several mill buildings from the 1800's. Exhibits explain the history of Delaware's early industries. *Right:* The Delaware Agricultural Museum, in Dover, provides a history of farm life from colonial to recent times. Farm equipment on exhibit includes an airplane used for crop dusting.

with campuses in all three counties. There are three private colleges: Wesley College in Dover, Wilmington College in New Castle, and Goldey Beacom College in Wilmington.

Libraries, Museums, and the Arts

The largest library in Delaware is at the University of Delaware in Newark. The Wilmington Institute Free Library in Wilmington is the largest public library. Many towns also have public libraries, and Delawareans have access to public library resources statewide through a computerized catalog system. There are various specialized libraries, such as the library of the Historical Society of Delaware, in Wilmington. Lively historical societies with public programs are found in many towns.

Delaware has a number of outstanding museums. The Henry Francis du Pont Winterthur Museum, north of Wilmington, has a fine collection of decorative arts dating from 1640 to 1860, displayed in galleries and period rooms. The Hagley Museum and Library, on Brandywine Creek near Wilmington, is on the site of the original DuPont powder mills. Exhibits tell the story of early industries in the area. The Delaware Art Museum in Wilmington specializes in the works of local artists, such as the famous Delaware illustrator Howard Pyle. It also has a notable collection of Pre-Raphaelite paintings and literature. Other museums devoted to history, natural history, agriculture, and art are located throughout the state.

Performing arts are represented by the Delaware Symphony, Opera Delaware, the Russian Ballet Theater of Delaware, and the Delaware Theatre Company. Most performances take place at the Grand Opera House in Wilmington, which serves as the state's center for performing arts.

Delaware's people work in many fields—manufacturing, research and development, banking, tourism, agriculture, and the service professions. Delaware has often been called the nation's chemical capital because it is home to the international headquarters of the DuPont Company.

Delaware has also been called the nation's corporate capital. The state's lenient corporate tax laws have made it attractive for major business firms and banks to incorporate there. The state is thus their legal "home," even though their offices and factories may be located elsewhere.

Services

Most Delawareans work in service industries. Financial services are a growing sector. In the 1980's, the state legislature passed new laws favorable to banks and other financial institutions. Since then the number of banks, especially banks providing credit-card services, has increased. Health care, tourism, and wholesale and retail trade are among the other service industries that employ many workers. The state's many corporations also employ an unusually high number of corporate lawyers.

Manufacturing

Delaware's early factories were mills that harnessed waterpower to make flour, lumber, textiles, and gunpowder. Today manufacturing accounts for about one-third of the total value of goods and services produced in the state. Chemicals are the most important products, and Delaware is an important center for research and development in the fields of chemicals, pharmaceuticals, and biotechnology. Synthetic fibers, paints, plastics, and many other products based on chemicals are manufactured in the state.

Other Delaware industries produce paper and rubber products and a variety of other goods. The factories with the most employees are two automobile assembly plants, both in New Castle County. Food processing is also important to the state.

Agriculture

Delaware was once a farming state. But since World War II (1939–45) the number of farms and acres of land devoted to farming have declined. In 1950, there were 8,300 farms, covering about 70 percent of the state's total area. In 1997 there were just 2,400 farms, and less than half the state's land was devoted to agriculture.

Broilers (young chickens) are by far the most important agricultural product. Delaware produces about 1.5 billion pounds (6.8 billion kilograms) of broilers a year. Large plants in Sussex County process the chickens for sale in national and international markets.

Delaware's farms also produce fruits, vegetables, and dairy products for regional and national markets. Soybeans and corn, both used as chicken feed, are the chief grains.

Mining and Construction

As Delaware has grown, construction companies large and small have helped build housing developments, malls, research and industrial centers, office towers, schools, govern-

A container cargo ship is unloaded at Wilmington, which has port facilities equipped to handle large oceangoing vessels.

ment buildings, and ocean resorts. Today about 5 percent of Delaware's workers are in construction, although the number varies with economic conditions.

Sand and gravel are mined in Delaware and are used primarily in the construction industry. However, mining is not an important part of the state's economy today.

Places of Interest

Winterthur Museum and Gardens, near Wilmington

Zwaanendael Museum, in Lewes

Fort Christina Park, near Wilmington

Killens Pond State Park

Bombay Hook National Wildlife Refuge, near Smyrna, is a haven for migrating birds. Each spring and fall, bird-watchers come to observe the flocks of ducks, geese, and other birds that pause to rest here.

Dickinson Mansion, near Dover, attracts many visitors. It was the family home of John Dickinson, Revolutionary War leader and writer.

Fenwick Island, on the Atlantic coast at the Maryland border, has a historic lighthouse built in 1857. Much of the island remains wild and untouched.

Fort Christina Park, near Wilmington, preserves the history of the early Swedish settlers. It includes Kalmar Nyckel Museum and Shipyard, with a replica of the ship that brought the first Swedish settlers to Delaware. Old Swedes Church, founded in 1698, is nearby.

The Green, in Dover, is a public square surrounded by historic buildings. Among them is the Old State House, seat of the legislature from colonial to modern times. The Green was laid out in 1717 by an order of William Penn's dating from 1683.

Hagley Museum and Eleutherian Mills are near Wilmington, on Brandywine Creek, where E.I. du Pont founded his powder mill in 1802. Several old buildings have been restored. Visitors can see how the early mills operated and how mill workers lived.

Henry Francis du Pont Winterthur Museum and Gardens, near Wilmington, is a showplace for decorative arts from the 1600's to 1840. Some 80,000 paintings, textiles, ceramics, pieces of historic furniture, and the like are displayed in room settings. A tram carries visitors through the formal gardens.

Nemours, a Du Pont family estate near Wilmington, includes a replica of a French château and extensive gardens that are open to the public.

Zwaanendael Museum, in Lewes, is a replica of a historic Dutch building. It commemorates the Dutch settlement of 1631 and houses exhibits on colonial and Native American life.

State Areas. Nearly 100,000 acres (40,000 hectares) of land are protected in Delaware, including two national wildlife areas. Delaware's many state parks and forests include Delaware Seashore State Park, with 7 miles (11 kilometers) of beaches on Rehoboth Bay, and Fort Delaware State Park, a preserved fort dating from the Civil War. For information on state areas, contact the Delaware Tourism Office, 99 Kings Highway, P.O. Box 1401, Dover, Delaware 19903.

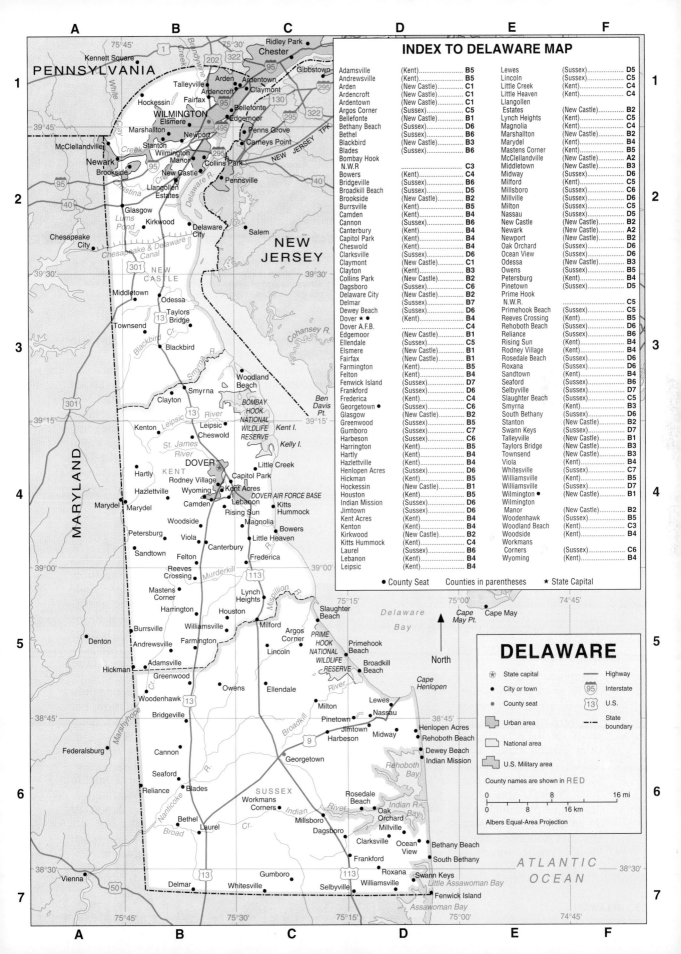

INDEX TO DELAWARE MAP

Adamsville (Kent)................. B5
Andrewsville (Kent)................. B5
Arden (New Castle)............. C1
Ardencroft (New Castle)............. C1
Ardentown (New Castle)............. C1
Argos Corner (Sussex)............. C5
Bellefonte (New Castle)............. B1
Bethany Beach (Sussex)............. D6
Bethel (Sussex)............. B6
Blackbird (New Castle)............. B3
Blades (Sussex)............. B6
Bombay Hook N.W.R. C3
Bowers (Kent)............. C4
Bridgeville (Sussex)............. B6
Broadkill Beach (Sussex)............. D5
Brookside (New Castle)............. B2
Burrsville (Kent)............. B5
Camden (Kent)............. B4
Cannon (Sussex)............. B6
Canterbury (Kent)............. B4
Capitol Park (Kent)............. B4
Cheswold (Kent)............. B4
Clarksville (Sussex)............. D6
Claymont (New Castle)............. C1
Clayton (Kent)............. B3
Collins Park (New Castle)............. B2
Dagsboro (Sussex)............. C6
Delaware City (New Castle)............. B2
Delmar (Sussex)............. B7
Dewey Beach (Sussex)............. D6
Dover ★ ● (Kent)............. B4
Dover A.F.B. C4
Edgemoor (New Castle)............. B1
Ellendale (Sussex)............. C5
Elsmere (New Castle)............. B1
Fairfax (New Castle)............. B1
Farmington (Kent)............. B5
Felton (Kent)............. B4
Fenwick Island (Sussex)............. D7
Frankford (Sussex)............. D6
Frederica (Kent)............. C4
Georgetown ● (Sussex)............. C6
Glasgow (New Castle)............. B2
Greenwood (Sussex)............. B5
Gumboro (Sussex)............. C7
Harbeson (Sussex)............. C6
Harrington (Kent)............. B5
Hartly (Kent)............. B4
Hazlettville (Kent)............. B4
Henlopen Acres (Sussex)............. D6
Hickman (Kent)............. B5
Hockessin (New Castle)............. B1
Houston (Kent)............. B5
Indian Mission (Sussex)............. D6
Jimtown (Sussex)............. D6
Kent Acres (Kent)............. B4
Kenton (Kent)............. B4
Kirkwood (New Castle)............. B2
Kitts Hummock (Kent)............. C4
Laurel (Sussex)............. B6
Lebanon (Kent)............. B4
Leipsic (Kent)............. B4

Lewes (Sussex)............. D5
Lincoln (Sussex)............. C5
Little Creek (Kent)............. C4
Little Heaven (Kent)............. C4
Llangollen Estates (New Castle)............. B2
Lynch Heights (Kent)............. C5
Magnolia (Kent)............. C4
Marshallton (New Castle)............. B2
Marydel (Kent)............. B4
Mastens Corner (Kent)............. B5
McClellandville (New Castle)............. A2
Middletown (New Castle)............. B3
Midway (Sussex)............. D6
Milford (Kent)............. C5
Millsboro (Sussex)............. C6
Millville (Sussex)............. D6
Milton (Sussex)............. C5
Nassau (Sussex)............. D5
New Castle (New Castle)............. B2
Newark (New Castle)............. A2
Newport (New Castle)............. B2
Oak Orchard (Sussex)............. D6
Ocean View (Sussex)............. D6
Odessa (New Castle)............. B3
Owens (Sussex)............. B5
Petersburg (Kent)............. B4
Pinetown (Sussex)............. D5
Prime Hook N.W.R. C5
Primehook Beach (Sussex)............. C5
Reeves Crossing (Kent)............. B5
Rehoboth Beach (Sussex)............. D6
Reliance (Sussex)............. B6
Rising Sun (Kent)............. B4
Rodney Village (Kent)............. B4
Rosedale Beach (Sussex)............. D6
Roxana (Sussex)............. D6
Sandtown (Kent)............. B4
Seaford (Sussex)............. B6
Selbyville (Sussex)............. D7
Slaughter Beach (Sussex)............. C5
Smyrna (Kent)............. B3
South Bethany (Sussex)............. D6
Stanton (New Castle)............. B2
Swann Keys (Sussex)............. D7
Talleyville (New Castle)............. B1
Taylors Bridge (New Castle)............. B3
Townsend (New Castle)............. B3
Viola (Kent)............. B4
Whitesville (Sussex)............. C7
Williamsville (Kent)............. D7
Williamsville (Sussex)............. D7
Wilmington ● (New Castle)............. B1
Wilmington Manor (New Castle)............. B2
Woodenhawk (Sussex)............. B5
Woodland Beach (Kent)............. C3
Woodside (Kent)............. B4
Workmans Corners (Sussex)............. C6
Wyoming (Kent)............. B4

● County Seat   Counties in parentheses   ★ State Capital

DELAWARE

★ State capital
● City or town
● County seat
Urban area
National area
U.S. Military area

County names are shown in RED

Highway
95 Interstate
13 U.S.
State boundary

0 — 8 — 16 mi
0 — 8 — 16 km
Albers Equal-Area Projection

Transportation

Delaware has less than 50 miles (80 kilometers) of interstate highway, the least of any state. Interstate 95 crosses the northern part of the state, linking it to New Jersey, Pennsylvania, and Maryland. The Delaware Memorial Bridge, built in 1951, crosses the Delaware River south of Wilmington to connect with the New Jersey Turnpike.

Delaware's main commercial airport is Greater Wilmington Airport, just south of the city. Dover Air Force Base, near Dover, is a major military cargo and transport center. Amtrak passenger trains link Wilmington to Philadelphia, Pennsylvania, and Baltimore, Maryland. Freight travels a

Restored homes and brick sidewalks line the streets of the historic district in New Castle. Before independence, New Castle was the capital of the Delaware colony.

similar route, and there is a north-south freight line as well.

Water transportation has always been important in Delaware. Freight still travels on the Delaware River, and the Wilmington Marine Terminal at Wilmington provides modern port facilities for large oceangoing vessels. The Chesapeake and Delaware Canal extends across the northern part of the Delmarva Peninsula. It connects the upper Chesapeake Bay with the lower Delaware River.

Communication

Delaware has two daily newspapers. *The News-Journal*, published in Wilmington, has the largest circulation. The *Delaware State News*, in Dover, is the second daily. Most towns and suburban regions have weekly papers. There are radio stations throughout the state. Wilmington has one public television station, but Delaware has no commercial stations.

▶ CITIES

The one large city in Delaware is Wilmington. It has a population of about 73,000. But its metropolitan area, which includes counties in New

Jersey and Maryland, contains more than 500,000 people.

Dover, the capital, is near the geographical center of the state. It has been the seat of the state's government since 1777 and is also the seat of Kent County. Dover has long been a market and shipping center for the surrounding countryside. It has a variety of local industries. The U.S. Air Force Base near Dover is one of the largest military air cargo terminals in the world, employing thousands of people. Wesley College and Delaware State College are located in Dover.

Wilmington is a seaport on the lower Delaware River. Although it was the site of the original Swedish settlement in 1638, the town did not really

begin to grow until the flour-milling industry was established there a century later. In the charter granted by King George II in 1739, it was named for George Spencer-Compton, Earl of Wilmington.

Wilmington is the industrial, commercial, and financial center of Delaware. It is known especially as the headquarters of the DuPont Company and other companies that make products from chemicals. Since 1981, it has become the home of many banks that provide credit-card services nationwide.

New Castle, on the Delaware River, was first settled by the Dutch in 1651. Under Dutch, Swedish, and English rule it was the capital of the Delaware colony. During the days of sailing vessels, New Castle was a port of call for ships heading for Philadelphia. Later, the New Castle and Frenchtown (Maryland) Railroad was an overland link between the Delaware River and the Chesa-

Delaware's legislature, the General Assembly, meets in the stately brick Legislative Hall, in Dover. Other government buildings are located nearby.

GOVERNMENT

State Government
Governor: 4-year term
State senators: 21; 4-year terms
State representatives: 41;
  2-year terms
Number of counties: 3

Federal Government
U.S. senators: 2
U.S. representatives: 1
Number of electoral votes: 3

For the name of the current governor, see STATE GOVERNMENTS in Volume S. For the names of current U.S. senators and representatives, see UNITED STATES, CONGRESS OF THE in Volume U-V.

peake Bay. New Castle's Old Court House (1732) and its many old brick houses and churches, clustered around the shady Green, make it a pleasant place to visit.

▶ **GOVERNMENT**

The present state constitution was adopted in 1897. It is Delaware's fourth constitution. The state's chief executive is the governor, who is elected for a 4-year term. For a long time the governor's office was a rather weak

Famous People

Joseph Robinette Biden, Jr. (1942–), born in Scranton, Pennsylvania, has served as a U.S. senator from Delaware since 1973. He is the ranking Democratic member of the Senate Judiciary Committee. He was also a candidate for president in 1988.

Emily Perkins Bissell (1861–1948), born in Wilmington, led a fight against tuberculosis by introducing the sale of Christmas seals in the United States in 1907. She served as president of the Delaware Anti-Tuberculosis Society from 1908 until her death.

Annie Jump Cannon (1863–1941), born in Dover, was a leading astronomer. At Harvard Observatory, where she worked for most of her career, she discovered so many stars she was called "the census-taker of the sky."

Wallace Hume Carothers (1896–1937), born in Burlington, Iowa, was a chemist with the DuPont Company in Wilmington. In 1935 he developed nylon, the world's first successful synthetic fiber.

John Dickinson (1732–1808), born in Talbot County, Maryland, was called the Penman of the Revolution because he wrote many articles in support of independence. Dickinson represented Pennsylvania, and later Delaware, in the Second Continental Congress. He was a delegate from Delaware to the Constitutional Convention of 1787.

Éleuthère I. du Pont (1771–1834) was the founder of what is today the vast DuPont Company. He was born in Paris, France, and studied under Lavoisier, the famous French chemist. He came to America in 1799 and in 1802 established a powder mill on a farm near Wilmington.

Caesar Rodney

Pierre S. du Pont (1870–1954), a great-grandson of E. I. du Pont, was born in Wilmington. An industrialist and a public benefactor, he headed the DuPont Company in its greatest period of expansion, during and after World War II. He devoted much time and money to improving public education in Delaware.

Oliver Evans (1755–1819), born near Newport, Delaware, has been called America's first engineer. He was a pioneer in the designing and building of high-pressure steam engines. He worked with his brothers, who were flour millers in Wilmington. His inventions there mechanized the milling of flour.

---

one in Delaware. Only in 1897 did the governor get the power to veto laws. In 1970, the chief executive's powers were greatly strengthened when many different state agencies were brought directly under the governor's control.

The state legislature is called the General Assembly. It consists of a senate and a house of representatives.

The state's highest court is the supreme court. Its three justices are appointed by the governor, with the senate's approval, for 12-year terms. An unusual feature of Delaware's judiciary is the Court of Chancery, which decides many corporate legal disputes. The respect that this court has earned is partly responsible for Delaware's position as the legal home of thousands of corporations.

▶ **HISTORY**

The first European settlement in what is now Delaware was made by the Dutch on the present site of Lewes in 1631. That settlement was destroyed by Native Americans, and the project was abandoned. Meanwhile, a Swedish company, backed by Dutch and Swedish investors, was formed to establish a colony overseas. This company founded the colony of New Sweden at the mouth of the Christina River in March 1638.

The colony grew slowly, and in 1655 it was conquered by a Dutch expedition from New Amsterdam (present-day New York). The Swedish governor and other officials returned to Sweden, but the settlers remained on their farms under Dutch rule.

Delaware Becomes an English Colony

In 1664, during a war between Holland and England, the Dutch settlements on the Hudson and Delaware rivers came under the rule of James, Duke of York, the brother of King Charles II of England. In 1682 the duke gave the Delaware settlement to William Penn. Penn, a Quaker, had already received Pennsylvania as a grant from King Charles II. From then until the Revolutionary War, Penn and his descendants held the title to all the land in Delaware and Pennsylvania.

Delaware was governed by courts in each of three counties—New Castle, St. Jones (later renamed Kent), and Deale (later Sussex). William Penn assured the people that under his rule they would be governed by laws of their own making. Beginning in 1682, a legislative assembly met each year. It was

Pierre S. du Pont

Howard Pyle

Howard Pyle (1853–1911), born in Wilmington, became famous as an artist, author, and teacher. He is remembered best for his illustrations in a long series of children's books. The first one, *The Merry Adventures of Robin Hood*, appeared in 1883.

Jay Saunders Redding (1906–), born in Wilmington, gained renown as a scholar and author in the field of African American history. Among his best-known works are *The Lonesome Road: The Story of the Negro in America* (1958) and *They Came in Chains* (1973).

Caesar Rodney (1728–84), born near Dover, was a member of the Continental Congress. He was home on business when the vote for independence came up in July 1776, and Delaware's two other delegates were split on the question. Rodney rode all night, through a thunderstorm, to reach Philadelphia in time to break the tie and cast Delaware's vote for independence. Rodney served as commander of Delaware's militia during the Revolutionary War and also as governor (1778–81).

composed of an equal number of members from each of the counties of Delaware and Pennsylvania. But the people of Delaware and Pennsylvania could not agree on policies, and in 1704 Penn reluctantly permitted their legislators to meet separately. He and his descendants continued to appoint one governor for Pennsylvania and the region they called "the three lower counties on the Delaware."

The Revolutionary War and Statehood

The only Revolutionary battle fought on Delaware soil was won by the British. It took place at Coochs Bridge near Newark on September 3, 1777, during the British march from Chesapeake Bay to Philadelphia. A few days later the British defeated Washington's army at the Battle of Brandywine, in Pennsylvania, and took control of Wilmington. At this time, Delawareans moved their capital from nearby New Castle to Dover.

During the Constitutional Convention of 1787, Delaware's representatives argued that small states should have the same voice in government as large states. Pleased with the compromise that gave every state two senators, regardless of its population, Delaware was the first state to ratify the Constitution. The date of ratifica-

Swedish colonists arrived at the mouth of the Christina River in March 1638. They founded New Sweden, Delaware's first permanent European settlement.

tion—December 7, 1787—is celebrated each year as Delaware Day.

Statehood to the Civil War

After the war, Delaware's industries prospered and its population grew, especially in New Castle County around Wilmington. The Chesapeake and Delaware Canal, which opened in 1829, shortened the water route linking Baltimore, Wilmington, and Philadelphia. Steamboats replaced sailing vessels on the Delaware River, and railroads were built.

In 1802 Éleuthère I. du Pont, a French immigrant, established a black powder (gunpowder) factory on Brandywine Creek, north of Wilmington. His company, later run by his descendants, became the nation's largest manufacturer of explosives. Other industries that sprang up around Wilmington included carriage making, leather tanning, shipbuilding, and railroad-car manufacturing. Job opportunities in these industries attracted immigrants, especially from Ireland, England, and Germany. Agriculture prospered, too. By the mid-1800's, commercial peach orchards had been developed to such an extent that Delaware was widely known as the Peach State.

The Civil War and After

Slavery existed in Delaware from early times. By 1860 more than 90 percent of the African Americans in Delaware were free, but Delawareans were deeply divided on the issue of abolition—whether slavery should be abolished. Wilmington's free blacks and Quakers strongly favored abolition. In southern Delaware, however, some farmers still relied on slave labor, and they resisted efforts to end it.

At the beginning of the Civil War, in 1861, the General Assembly of Delaware expressed its complete disapproval of secession. Delaware remained in the Union. But in 1862 it refused to accept a plan devised by President Abraham Lincoln under which the government would buy slaves from their owners and free them. Lincoln gave up on this plan for "compensated emancipation" after it failed in Delaware.

Delaware supplied many soldiers to the Union armies. But there was also much sympathy for the South, and many young men from Delaware joined the Confederate forces. Slavery did not end in Delaware until it was banned under the 13th Amendment to the Constitution, in 1865.

After the war, little Delaware remained divided between the populous, urban upstate region and the rural downstate region. The Chesapeake and Delaware Canal has long been recognized as the dividing line between those regions. Toward the end of the 1800's, Italian, Russian, and Polish immigrants added to the diversity of the Wilmington area. Southern Delawareans remained largely descendants of the earlier English and African American population.

The 1900's

As a major supplier of explosives to the United States and its allies in World War I (1914–18) and World War II (1939–45), the DuPont Company expanded dramatically. On the basis of its wartime profits and research, the company branched out into other chemical-based products, including paints and synthetic fibers, such as nylon and rayon. As the headquarters for DuPont and other chemical companies, Wilmington became an important business and research center.

Southern Delaware's agriculture changed dramatically in the 1920's, after a highway was built to link the region to northern cities. In 1923 Cecily Steele, a farm wife from Ocean View, Delaware, began shipping young chickens to urban markets by truck. Her success led other farmers to concentrate on raising broilers, and within twenty years the commercial broiler business had more than doubled the total cash farm income of the state.

Today the ocean resorts along Delaware's Atlantic coast—especially at Rehoboth Beach, Dewey Beach, Bethany Beach, and Fenwick Island—have brought a new vitality to southern Delaware. The Coastal Zone Act, passed in 1971, protects the fragile ecosystem of the state's river, bay, and ocean shores. Statewide, the people of Delaware are working to create new jobs, improve schools, and protect the natural environment. Their efforts will be important as Delaware continues to grow.

H. CLAY REED
Formerly, University of Delaware
Reviewed by BARBARA BENSON
Historical Society of Delaware

DELHI

The vast and historic city of Delhi is located in northwestern India on the western bank of the Yamuna River. Through the centuries there have been at least seven different cities where modern Delhi now stands. The earliest one dates from the 1100's.

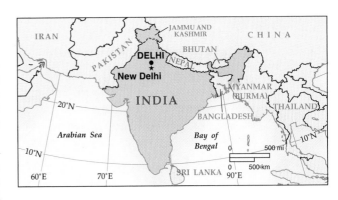

Modern Delhi is made up of two cities— Old Delhi and New Delhi. New Delhi is the capital of India. With a population of more than 7 million people, Delhi is India's third largest city after Calcutta (Kolkata) and Bombay (Mumbai). It is part of the National Capital Territory of Delhi, which has a population of 9 million and encompasses most of greater Delhi and a large number of surrounding villages.

Old Delhi. Amid the narrow twisting streets, crowded bazaars, and sprawling slums of Old Delhi are constant reminders of bygone ages. The Red Fort, built by the Mogul emperor Shah Jahan in the 1600's, still dominates the skyline of the old city. Within its red sandstone walls are marble palaces, gardens, and the shimmering Moti Masjid (Pearl Mosque). Nearby is the Jama Masjid, one of the world's largest mosques (Muslim houses of worship).

Its brilliant domes and slender minarets (towers) reach high into the sky.

The Mogul emperors and other former rulers built many tombs that are still admired for their beauty and design. Among the most famous are the tombs of the Lodi Gardens, the tombs of Jamali and Sultan Ghari, and the tomb of the emperor Humayun, which was erected after his death in 1556.

Chandni Chowk (meaning "Street of Silver") is the main street of Old Delhi and one of the oldest streets in all of India. It was named for the silversmiths who worked and sold their wares there centuries ago. Today it is one of Delhi's busiest places, crowded with

Old Delhi's tomb of the Muslim emperor Humayun (1508–56) is one of the finest surviving monuments of Mogul art and architecture.

avenue lined with government buildings, links a triumphal arch known as India Gate to the splendid Rashtrapati Bhavan, or Presidential Palace. Not far from the Rashtrapati Bhavan is Parliament House, where India's federal legislature meets. Parliament Street is flanked by tall modern office buildings, including the Reserve Bank of India and Broadcasting House. The road leads to Connaught Place, the city's main shopping center, which is laid out in a circle with a park at its center. New Delhi also has many elegant homes and gardens.

Above: Chandni Chowk ("Street of Silver") is Old Delhi's main commercial street.
Right: The boulevard known as the Raj Path (or King's Way) leads to the India Gate triumphal arch, New Delhi's most famous landmark.

traffic, people, and shops of all kinds. Consumer goods, textiles, handicrafts, and publishing are Old Delhi's leading industries.

Between Old Delhi and New Delhi is a shrine called the Raj Ghat. On January 31, 1948, the great Indian leader Mahatma Gandhi was cremated on this spot. A simple memorial, set in a peaceful park, marks the last resting place of the man who has been called the father of the Indian nation. A similar memorial was built in honor of Jawaharlal Nehru, the first prime minister of India, who was cremated there in 1964. Nehru's daughter, Prime Minister Indira Gandhi, who was assassinated in 1984, was also cremated nearby.

New Delhi. New Delhi, located to the south of Old Delhi, is a planned city, built specifically to serve as a capital. Most of New Delhi's attractive red stone buildings are devoted to government and other public service activities.

New Delhi's broad streets radiate from the city's center like spokes of a giant wheel. The Raj Path (or King's Way), a broad tree-lined

History. Some scholars believe that Delhi dates back to a time before recorded history. There is a legend of a city, known as Indraprastha, that stood on the site some 3,000 years ago. This legend is told in the *Mahabharata*, the epic story of old India. Most historians, however, date the founding of Delhi to the 1100's.

The city's importance grew in 1638, when the emperor Shah Jahan made it the capital of the Mogul Empire, which then ruled much of India. In 1739 the city was attacked and partly destroyed by the Persian conqueror Nadir Shah.

In 1803, Delhi came under the control of the British, and in 1912 it replaced Calcutta as the capital of India. In 1931, the construction of New Delhi was completed and was made the capital of British India. When India gained its independence in 1947, New Delhi became the capital of the new nation.

In 1992, the Union Territory of Delhi became the National Capital Territory of Delhi. Now self-governing, the territory is generally classed as a state, although it does not have the formal status of statehood.

Reviewed by BALKRISHNA G. GOKHALE
Author, *The Making of the Indian Nation*

DEMETER. See GREEK MYTHOLOGY (Profiles).

DE MILLE, CECIL B. See MOTION PICTURES (Profiles: Directors).

DEMING, W. EDWARDS. See WYOMING (Famous People).

DEMOCRACY

The word "democracy" comes from the Greek word *demokratia*. This is a combination of *demos*, the Greek word for "people," and *kratos*, meaning "rule."

Athens was the most famous Greek democracy. In the 400's B.C., Athens had an assembly that all citizens could attend. A council of 500 citizens elected each year did most of the important government work.

Although this sounds very democratic, more than half the people of Athens, including women and slaves, were excluded from taking any part in the government because they were not considered citizens.

Democracy in the United States

The Revolutionary War, as well as almost every other political revolution in history, took place because the people wished to rule themselves. The founders of the United States favored a republic—a government of elected representatives who would answer to the people. But by "people" they meant men of wealth, or property, and social position. Ideas that were accepted in the late 1700's and early 1800's sound undemocratic today. People are no longer denied the vote because they are poor or because they do not own property. Nobody would even suggest this in a modern democracy.

The United States form of government has changed in many ways since its infancy. The benefits of democracy have spread gradually to more people than ever before.

Meaning of Democracy

Democracy is government by the many instead of by the few. It is based on the belief that all should have the same basic rights and freedoms and that people should be free to govern themselves.

In a **direct democracy**, the people decide questions by voting. However, direct democracy is practical only in small communities. Most democratic nations are **representative democracies**. In representative democracies, the people elect public officials, who act according to the people's wishes.

Californians gather to express their views on gun control. First Amendment Freedoms, which include freedom of speech, are among the most cherished rights of United States citizens.

Democracy is a philosophy of government, not a form of government. The United States is a democracy with a republican form of government. A republic has an elected head of state, a president. England is also a democracy, but it is a monarchy as well. It has a king or queen—a hereditary ruler, or head of state. In both countries the representatives of the people are chosen in free elections.

Privileges of Democracy

The rights and responsibilities that make up a democratic system are not unlimited, of course. Some restrictions are necessary. There are limits of fair play, of common sense, of safety. While people in a democracy are free, they may not injure the health or the good name of others.

Recognizing these necessary limits, let us examine the substance of democracy.

First of all, there is **freedom of speech and the press**. This means that all citizens have the right to speak their minds without fear of punishment. A person who cannot speak freely cannot think freely.

The term "freedom of speech" includes freedom of expression in forms of communication such as television, radio, and films. It extends to the arts—theater, dance, music, literature, painting.

The right of free speech, press, and thought includes the right to publish and read newspapers, magazines, and books. It includes the right to disagree, to take a different view from the popular, accepted one. In a democracy a citizen may express an opinion even though it is contrary to the opinion of others.

Freedom of Assembly. Citizens in a democracy may join in a meeting or convention to support their government or to criticize it, to debate foreign policy, to start a new political party, or to reshape an old one. They may discuss controversial issues that are important to them. They may argue, pass resolutions, or send petitions to the mayor, the governor, or even to the president.

Popular Sovereignty. This is the heart of democracy. It means that the people are supreme —not a king, not a leader, not a clique of despots, but the people. Popular sovereignty gives to the voters the right to keep their officials in office or to vote them out. Balloting is free, and it is secret. The privacy of every voter is assured.

In some Swiss cantons, the people still practice a form of direct democracy. The entire adult population meets to vote on important issues and to make laws.

Officials in a democracy are responsible to the people. When the officials' terms are over, they must go before the people for re-election. They have no hereditary rights in their jobs. They may not hold office by force or fraud.

Political Freedom. Citizens in a democracy may belong to the party of their choice. This may be a major party—Democratic or Republican in the United States—or a minor party. The minor parties may propose ideas that are unpopular or even freakish. But citizens are free to vote for them just the same. Often a major party supports an idea that was first suggested years earlier by a minor party.

Civil Rights. These include the right to vote, to hold office, to have a fair trial, to enjoy the privileges of full citizenship.

Religious Freedom. The Constitution of the United States prohibits government support to any religion or interference with anybody's religious beliefs. People may not be barred from holding office because of their religion or lack of religion. Some democracies—England, for example—support a state church. But religious freedom is guaranteed to all.

Freedom of Movement. All citizens in the United States may choose the city or state where they want to live. They are free to move about the country if they wish. They need neither permission nor passport.

Economic Opportunity. In a democracy, people may go into business for themselves. If they prosper, they enjoy the rewards that go with success. If they fail, they may try again or change their work. The decisions, the risks, and the rewards are their own.

Workers may join unions. They may strike without losing their rights as citizens.

In a democracy, people may seek work in any profession, craft, or industry, without regard for race, creed, or sex. People may work in private industry or become civil servants. The choice of occupation is theirs—based on their own abilities.

Education. A democracy provides equal educational opportunities for all of its citizens, without regard for race, creed, color, or social position.

DAVID E. WEINGAST
Assistant Superintendent, Newark Public Schools

DEMOCRATIC PARTY. See POLITICAL PARTIES.

DENG XIAOPING (1904–1997)

Deng Xiaoping was for many years China's most powerful political figure and the architect of its practical approach to economic reform. He belonged to the first generation of Communist revolutionary leaders, who first came to power in China in 1949.

Deng was born on August 24, 1904, in Sichuan province. He grew up in a well-to-do family and received a traditional Chinese education until 1920, when he went to France. There he joined the Communist Party. He studied briefly in the Soviet Union, before returning to China in 1927.

Deng distinguished himself in politics, party work, and military affairs. He served as a political officer in the Chinese Communist forces that fought both the ruling Nationalist government and invading Japanese armies. In 1945 he became a member of the Central Committee of the Communist Party.

After the victory of the Communists over the Nationalists in 1949, Deng held various important posts. He was, among other things, minister of finance, vice premier, a member of the Politburo (the highest decision-making body), and general secretary, or head, of the party. He resigned from his last post, chairman of the Military Affairs Council, in 1989.

During his long career, Deng weathered the most violent political storms. On several occasions he was stripped of power and subjected to the harshest criticism, but each time he managed to bounce back. As paramount leader, he brought about drastic changes in China, particularly in the area of economics.

Deng Xiaoping, China's elderly paramount leader, came to power in the late 1970's. He was praised for his economic policies, which opened China to the outside world, increased industrialization, and helped raise the Chinese people's standard of living. But he also was condemned for his brutal crackdown on the 1989 student pro-democracy movement in Tiananmen Square.

He opened up China to the outside world, released the productive energy of Chinese farmers, hastened the pace of industrialization, and raised the people's standard of living.

These accomplishments earned Deng respect and even affection. However, the brutal crackdown on student pro-democracy demonstrators in Tiananmen Square in Beijing, the capital, in 1989 hurt his image abroad. After his death on February 19, 1997, China's future path was unclear.

C. T. HU
Coauthor, *China: Its People, Its Society,
Its Culture*

See also CHINA (History: The People's Republic).

DE NIRO, ROBERT. See MOTION PICTURES (Profiles: Movie Stars).

DENMARK

Denmark proper (not counting its vast overseas island region of Greenland) is the smallest in area of the Scandinavian nations. Its population, however, is greater than that of Norway and more than half that of Sweden, two Scandinavian countries many times larger than Denmark. The people of Denmark are called Danes.

Located in northern Europe, Denmark is made up of the Jutland peninsula, which is part of the European mainland, and about 480 islands, most of them small and uninhabited. Denmark's largest island is Zealand (Sjælland). It is the site of Copenhagen, Denmark's capital and one of the two largest cities in Scandinavia. For more general information on the Scandinavian

Right: A young Dane enjoys an ice cream treat. *Below:* Colorful houses line a boat-filled canal in Copenhagen's Nyhavn (New Harbor).

countries, see the article SCANDINAVIA in Volume S.

▶ **PEOPLE**

Language. Danish is the official language of Denmark. It is related to Faroese, Icelandic, Norwegian, and Swedish, which all trace their origins to Old Norse, a Germanic language. The Danish alphabet has the same letters as the English alphabet, plus the three additional letters æ, å, and ø.

Religion. All religions may be practiced freely. About 95 percent of the Danes are Lutheran. Muslims make up the largest minority, with about 2 percent.

Education and Libraries. Almost all education in Denmark is free. Most Danish children attend preschool and at the age of 7 start their nine-year compulsory education. Then they may either complete a tenth year before moving

into the three-year upper secondary school system, *gymnasia*, or test directly into it. Students who attend *gymnasia* are usually preparing for admission to one of the country's universities. Business and technical tracks are also options.

The Danes value education highly. In 1844 they established their first Folk High School. Today there are about 100 such schools, where teenagers, adults, and retirees can add to their knowledge and skills.

The government supports a national system of libraries. The country's most important library, the Royal Library, is located in Copenhagen.

Home Life. Danes are proud of their homes, and much of their social interaction takes place there. Cut flowers and candles are used to offset the often-dreary climate. Houseplants grow on nearly every windowsill. Home furnishings often include pieces that represent the leading role Danes have played in modern design.

Sports and Recreation. In recent decades, Denmark has seen growing participation in organized sports. Soccer is by far the most popular; the country has had professional soccer teams since 1977. Danes have also been successful in international and Olympic competition, especially sailing.

Many Danes vacation in southern Europe or elsewhere abroad during the winter. As the weather grows warmer, Denmark's long beaches attract many people. Near the cities, summer garden colonies come to life as thousands of families move to little cottages on tiny plots of land.

Food and Drink. Probably the best-known Danish specialty is *smørrebrød*, an open-faced sandwich spread with butter and topped with cheese, fish, smoked meat, or another Danish delicacy. Other favorites include roast pork stuffed with prunes and apples, and *frikadeller*, or meat patties. Cheese and fruit often accompany desserts. Danish beer is famous worldwide.

▶ **LAND**

Denmark's terrain was formed over a period of many thousands of years by the actions of glaciers—enormous, slow-moving sheets of ice. Pushing down from the north, the glaciers carved out the surface features of present-day Denmark. After climate changes

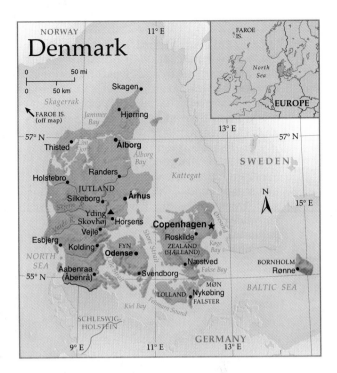

some 20,000 years ago caused the glaciers to retreat northward, they formed the bodies of water that surround the island of Denmark. The glaciers also deposited a mix of soils, which gave Denmark the most fertile land in Scandinavia.

FACTS and figures

KINGDOM OF DENMARK (Kongeriget Danmark) is the official name of the country.

LOCATION: Northern Europe.

AREA: 16,368 sq mi (42,393 km²), not counting the Faroe Islands and Greenland. Faroe Islands: 540 sq mi (1,399 km²). Greenland: 840,000 sq mi (2,175,600 km²).

POPULATION: 5,400,000 (estimate, Denmark proper).

CAPITAL AND LARGEST CITY: Copenhagen.

MAJOR LANGUAGE: Danish (official).

MAJOR RELIGIOUS GROUP: Evangelical Lutheran.

GOVERNMENT: Constitutional monarchy. **Head of state**—monarch (queen). **Head of government**—prime minister. **Legislature**—Folketing.

CHIEF PRODUCTS: Agricultural—grain, potatoes, sugar beets, pork and beef, dairy products, fish. **Manufactured**—processed foods and beverages, machinery and instruments, textiles, chemicals, electronics, wood products, ships, windmills. **Mineral**—limestone, kaolin, lignite (brown coal).

MONETARY UNIT: Krone (1 krone = 100 øre).

Land Regions. Denmark generally has a low, rolling landscape, with occasional small hills and many lakes and rivers. The average elevation is less than 100 feet (30 meters) above sea level. The highest point in Denmark, Yding Skovhøj, is 567 feet (173 meters) and is located in east central Jutland.

The Jutland peninsula makes up about two-thirds of the country's total land area. Western Jutland consists largely of a sandy heath and is one of the few regions with poor soil. Denmark's only land boundary, with Germany, crosses the southern part of the peninsula. About 100 of the Danish islands are inhabited. Aside from Zealand, the im-

Approximately 60 percent of Denmark's land is farmable. Windmills—used to generate electricity—are a common sight on the low, rolling landscape.

portant islands include Fyn, Falster, Lolland, and Møn. Bornholm, southeast of Sweden, has a land formation unlike the rest of Denmark. Its northern coast has jagged cliffs of granite, the only hard stone in Denmark.

Overseas Regions. The Danish kingdom includes two semi-independent territories located far from the heart of the country: the Faroe Islands and Greenland. The Faroes, consisting of 18 rocky islands and three islets, are located in the North Sea about halfway between Norway and Iceland. The islands were settled in the 800's by Scandinavians who established an economy based on sheep and wool. The name "Faroes" means "sheep

islands." Sheep raising ranks second in importance to fishing, the mainstay of the islands' economy. The Faroes have been self-governing since 1948 but are not fully independent. The islands are represented by two delegates in the Danish parliament, the Folketing. The people speak their own language (Faroese) and have their own flag.

Greenland, off the northeast coast of Canada, is the largest island in the world. Except for narrow coastal strips, Greenland is covered by an ice shield. Most Greenlanders are of Inuit descent; the rest are of Northern European ancestry. Greenland has had home rule since 1979 and is represented in the Danish parliament by two delegates. The official languages are Danish and East Inuit, and the island has its own flag. A separate article on Greenland appears in Volume G.

Climate. Although Denmark lies as far north as the panhandle of Alaska, it has a temperate climate. Moist air blows in over the country from the North Sea. This makes winters mild and keeps summers cool. The coldest month is usually February, when the temperature averages 32°F (0°C). The warmest month is July, when the temperature averages 65°F (18°C). Annual precipitation, mostly rain, is about 25 inches (635 millimeters).

Natural Resources. Denmark's soil is its most important natural resource, and about 60 percent of the land is farmable. Approximately 10 percent of the land is forested and supplies wood for building materials. Sand and gravel deposits are used to make cement. Bornholm has granite and kaolin, a clay used in making porcelain. There are deposits of limestone and lignite, a low-grade brown coal. Deposits of oil and natural gas exist, but not enough to meet the country's energy needs. Denmark has almost no waterpower for generating electricity. About 10 percent of its electricity is generated by wind.

▶ **ECONOMY**

Denmark is a prosperous country and has one of the world's highest standards of living.

Left: Workers empty fishing nets at one of the country's many ports. Denmark's location on the North Sea makes fishing one of the nation's most important industries.

Below: Spanning the Øresund (the Sound), the Øresund Bridge links Copenhagen, Denmark, with Malmö, Sweden. The bridge is part of a vast transportation network that runs from Scandinavia to Italy.

Agriculture was long the most important part of Denmark's economy, but in the 1900's it was supplemented by growth in manufacturing and trade. Since World War II (1939–45), the fastest-growing sectors have been in services such as transportation, tourism, and health care.

Manufacturing. Industrial goods are vital to Denmark's economy and make up the most important exports. At the same time, Danish industry depends heavily on imported raw materials. Leading manufactures include marine engines, windmills, and industrial measurement tools. Danish modern furniture is known worldwide, as are the country's fine silver, dinnerware, and porcelain figurines.

Agriculture. Only about 4 percent of the Danish workforce is engaged in agriculture, but the land is cultivated intensively. Marshy regions have been drained and areas of poor soil fertilized, so that about 65 percent of the land is now devoted to agriculture. Many Danish farmers specialize in raising livestock. Meat and dairy products are among Denmark's most important exports, along with fish. Main cash crops include grain, potatoes, and sugar beets.

Since the late 1800's, the country's farmers have been well organized. It was then that they built a modern system of production based on cooperatives, in which farmers pool their money to buy modern machinery, fertilizer, and animal feed. The farmers also control processing and then share in the profits.

Transportation. Denmark has a well-developed transportation system. However, an efficient system was long needed to link the country's many islands. Accessibility improved greatly in 1998, when the Great Belt Bridge (*Storebæltbroen*) opened, connecting the islands of Fyn and Zealand. The connection—actually a complex of two bridges and a tunnel—serves car, truck, and rail traffic. Also key was the opening of the Øresund Bridge in July 2000, connecting Denmark and Sweden and completing a ground-based travel network that runs from far northern Scandinavia to southern Italy.

Denmark's main international airport is Kastrup, near Copenhagen. Additional airports are located in the country's major cities.

MAJOR CITIES

Copenhagen is not only the capital and by far the largest city of Denmark but also its busiest port and chief industrial center. About one-fourth of the Danes live in Copenhagen and its suburbs. The population of the Copenhagen area is about 1.8 million; the city's population is nearly 500,000. Founded in 1167 as a fortified fishing harbor, Copenhagen soon became an important seaport and trade center. It became the capital in the 1400's after the Danish monarchs established their residence there. A separate article on Copenhagen appears in Volume C.

Århus is the chief port on the Jutland peninsula and the country's second largest city. Its population is approximately 214,000; Greater Århus, which includes the city and its suburbs, has a population of about 250,000. The city is home to Århus University, several important museums, and an annual festival dedicated to the performing arts.

CULTURAL HERITAGE

Denmark has a rich cultural heritage. In literature, one of the best-known Danish literary figures is Hans Christian Andersen, whose fairy tales, written in the 1800's, made him one of the most widely read authors in the world. (See the article on Andersen in Volume A.) The philosophical works of Søren Kierkegaard, who lived in the 1800's, have influenced philosophers of the present day. One of the most widely read Danish authors of the 1900's, Isak Dinesen (who wrote under the pen name Karen Blixen), is best known for her *Seven Gothic Tales* and *Out of Africa*. (For more information on Danish literature, see the article SCANDINAVIAN LITERATURE in Volume S.)

Denmark's most influential composer was Carl Nielsen. Spanning the late 1800's and early 1900's, Nielsen's symphonies and other musical works contained elements of both romanticism and modernism.

Famous Danish scientists include Tycho Brahe, an astronomer of the 1500's, and Niels Bohr, who made important discoveries in the first half of the 1900's in nuclear physics. Other Danes who have contributed to human knowledge are Saxo Grammaticus, considered one of the great historians of the Middle Ages; and navigator Vitus Bering, who led Alaskan explorations in the 1700's.

GOVERNMENT

Denmark is a constitutional monarchy, and the government is based on the constitution of 1953. The monarch is the head of state and holds executive power, including the right to approve all legislation and to act independently in a national emergency. The monarch governs with a council made up of about 18 ministers and headed by a prime minister. The government is appointed by the monarch but determined by the outcome of the national elections. Legislative power lies with the unicameral (one-house) 179-seat parliament, or Folketing, for which elections are held at least every four years. The judicial branch has three levels: local courts, two regional appeals courts, and a supreme court. Judges for all courts are appointed by the monarch, who acts on recommendations from the Justice Department. Judges serve for life but can be removed for cause.

HISTORY

Early History. Denmark's history begins some 10,000 to 15,000 years ago, as the last glaciers began to melt. As the ice disappeared, the sea level rose and a variety of animals appeared, including reindeer and wild boars. Fish and wild fowl abounded in the marshy coastal areas. Nomadic hunters and fishers followed. Gradually they learned how to tend livestock and grow crops.

About the A.D. 700's, the Danes began to sail far from their home waters on expeditions of trade, plunder, and settlement. These voyages took them throughout the Baltic and to western Europe and the British Isles. During the late 700's, the contacts became more frequent and more aggressive. By the mid-800's much of eastern England was under control of the Danes. The Danish and other Scandinavian sea rovers were collectively known as Vikings or Northmen. A separate article on the Vikings appears in Volume UV.

The Growth of Denmark. The first Christian king of Denmark, Harald Bluetooth, united the country during the 900's. King Canute ruled over Denmark, England, and Norway until his death in 1035.

Egeskov Castle, on the island of Fyn, is the best-preserved moat castle in Europe. The castle is one of many located in the countryside surrounding the city of Odense.

Denmark became an important power during the Middle Ages. One of the greatest Danish monarchs of the period was Queen Margrethe I, who in 1397 united Denmark, Norway, and Sweden in what is called the Kalmar Union. Sweden left the union in 1523, but Norway was tied to Denmark until 1814.

Decline of Danish Power. During the 1500's, Denmark was the leading power in the Baltic, but its position faded with the rise of Sweden as a European power in the 1600's and the growing strength of Russia in the 1700's. Still, the country was able to build an overseas empire that included colonies in Africa, India, and the Caribbean. Denmark lost Norway to Sweden in 1814 as a result of the Napoleonic Wars but kept the former Norwegian possessions of Greenland, the Faroes, and Iceland. (Iceland gained complete independence in 1944.)

In 1864, Denmark lost the Schleswig-Holstein, an area bordering the southern part of Jutland, in a war with Prussia, Austria, and their German allies. Shortly after World War I (1914–18), the people of North Schleswig voted to return to Denmark; the rest of the territory remains part of Germany.

Modern Times. Denmark was neutral in World War I, but during World War II it was occupied by Germany from 1940 until 1945. Denmark joined the United Nations in 1945 and became a member of the North Atlantic Treaty Organization (NATO) in 1949. The decades following World War II were prosperous; a key to this prosperity was economic cooperation. Denmark joined the European Community (EC) in 1973.

Danish voters rejected the Maastricht Treaty on European Union (EU) in 1992 but approved it in a second referendum in 1993. However, in 2000 they decided not to adopt the euro, the common currency of the EU.

Denmark Today. In recent years, Denmark's governments have been coalitions of different parties that have steered a steady course in political and economic affairs. The country's social advances in such areas as education, health services, and care for the young, the old, the disabled, and the unemployed have made it an outstanding example of the modern social-welfare state, in which the government takes responsibility for the well-being of all its citizens.

Elections in 2001 brought a shift to the right in politics, as a Liberal-Conservative coalition, led by Prime Minister Anders Fogh Rasmussen, ousted the Social Democratic Party. Rasmussen and his party were returned to power in 2005.

VINCENT MALMSTRÖM
Dartmouth College

Reviewed by BYRON J. NORDSTROM
History and Scandinavian Studies
Gustavus Adolphus College

DENSITY. See FLOATING AND BUOYANCY.

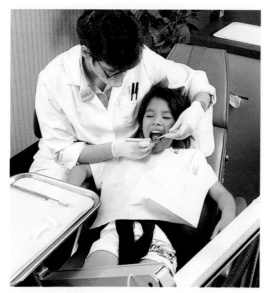

Regular visits to the dentist are important. During each checkup, a dentist helps keep your teeth healthy through careful examination and treatment.

DENTISTRY

In the old days, if you had had a toothache, your mother would have used a folk remedy, such as putting a clove in your mouth, to help ease your pain. If the pain had continued, she would have taken you to the village blacksmith, the barber, or if you were lucky, to the physician.

There were no dentists in those days to repair a tooth and try to save it. The blacksmith or the barber would have taken a good, strong pair of pliers and given a mighty pull. The trouble with that kind of mouth care was that most people had few, if any, teeth left by the time they were middle-aged!

Today dentistry is an important part of modern health care. Dentists are the professionals whose primary job is to take care of the teeth and mouth. They are educated in the field of health care that involves the teeth, gums, cheeks, lips, tongue, and palate (roof of the mouth), as well as the occlusion, or "bite."

▶ A VISIT TO THE DENTIST

Regular visits to the dentist are an important part of good health care. A typical visit, which lasts about 30 minutes, might happen like this:

After checking in and waiting your turn to see the dentist, you will be called in by an assistant who helps you get comfortable in the dental chair. This chair moves and turns to suit your size and also to help the dentist get a good view inside your mouth. The dental hygienist will probably see you after this. He or she looks over your teeth and may check for decayed areas by probing your teeth with a pointed, but not sharp, instrument.

A teeth cleaning is next. This involves flossing between the teeth to remove food particles, scraping off tough tartar, and then using a cleaning substance on the tooth surfaces. This substance is something like gritty toothpaste. It is put into a tiny rubber cup that spins to polish your teeth clean.

Sometimes the cleaning is followed by dental X rays of the teeth and jaws. Dental X-ray examinations are made with a large machine that takes X-ray pictures, or radiographs, of your teeth and jaws. The procedure is completely painless, and the amount of radiation used is very small. X rays are an important tool. They help the dentist recognize and diagnose abnormalities of the teeth that are hidden from view, such as areas around the roots of teeth, or abnormalities of the jawbone. Dental radiographs of the crowns of the teeth only are called bitewing radiographs. They are done periodically to help the dentist diagnose cavities, particularly those that may be hidden between the teeth.

After looking at the X rays, the dentist carefully checks your teeth and gums for any sign of disease or injury. (If you are seeing the dentist for a dental emergency, such as a toothache or a lost or broken tooth, the dentist will focus on treating the injury and will try to repair the damage.)

A more routine visit involves a thorough check for cavities. Dentists treat cavities, which are parts of teeth that have been damaged by dental caries (decay), by removing all of the diseased tissue. It is replaced with a special type of filling material that may be a metal alloy, a type of cement, or a polymer (plastic). The dentist will carefully work the filling material into the tooth. Sometimes a tooth is completely covered with a crown. The crown is made of either metal or plastic and is used when damage to the teeth is extensive.

Although the dentist's primary interest is in the structures of the mouth, dentists are also concerned about the total health of the patient. Disease and abnormalities of the teeth and jaws can lead to a decline in general health and overall well-being. The reverse is also possible: disease and abnormalities elsewhere in the body may first show up in changes in the tissues of the mouth. The dentist is alert to such changes that would suggest a health disorder.

▶ IMPROVEMENTS IN DENTAL CARE

Research in dentistry has resulted in significant improvements in dental health and dental treatment. Dental caries have been greatly reduced in recent years largely due to the fluoridation of many public water supplies and to fluoride treatments provided by dentists in areas where water is not fluoridated.

The dental instrument used to remove diseased parts of teeth, commonly called the dental drill, has improved dramatically since the 1940's. At that time the drill rotated at a very slow 2,000 to 4,000 revolutions per minute (rpm). Today this instrument spins at 300,000 to 500,000 revolutions per minute. It is an air-driven tool that cuts away diseased tooth parts almost painlessly.

In addition, teeth that are seriously diseased can often be restored to full function using special surgical techniques. In the past a diseased tooth meant a lost tooth, but today this is not true. If properly cared for, your teeth can last throughout your lifetime.

▶ DENTAL SPECIALTIES

Most dentists are general practitioners—they can provide most of the treatments needed by their patients. However, there are a number of dentists who specialize in specific areas of treatment. For example, a dentist may specialize in the surgery required to remove severely diseased teeth or in the techniques required to treat the interior of the tooth. Specialists in dentistry complete additional educational programs to gain the necessary skills for treating more complicated problems.

There are eight specialty groups recognized by the dental profession in the United States today. **Oral and maxillofacial surgeons** are specialists for surgical procedures of the mouth and jaws. **Orthodontists** are specialists for correcting irregularities of the teeth and bite (malocclusions). **Pedodontists** (pediatric dentists) are specialists for treating children. **Periodontists** treat the tissues around the teeth, called the periodontium, or gums. Dentists who specialize in replacing missing teeth are **prosthodontists,** and dentists who specialize in treating the dental pulp—the nerve and nerve chamber—are **endodontists. Oral pathologists** are specialists in the diagnosis and identification of disease in the oral tissues. **Public health dentists** are specialists in preventing and controlling dental disease on a community basis.

On a limited basis, general dentistry includes all these phases of dental care. Most dental problems can be solved by the general practitioner, so referrals to specialists are usually limited to complicated and unusual cases. Only 14 percent of the dentists in the United States are specialists.

▶ DENTISTRY AS A CAREER

A career in dentistry is a very rewarding one. Dentists must be knowledgeable in the biological sciences as well as skilled in the procedures needed to treat dental problems.

To become a dentist, a person must complete at least seven years of education after high school. Three to four years of science courses in college are usually required to qualify for admission to a dental school. Dental schools then provide four years of intensive dental study. Upon graduation, a new dentist often completes a one-year dental residency program before entering into dental practice. Like physicians, dentists must also pass a test and receive a license from the state in which they intend to work.

In addition to opening an office for private practice, a dentist may choose to become a dental researcher. He or she may hope to discover new information about the causes and methods of treatment of dental diseases.

There are careers for dentists in the Armed Forces as well as in Veterans Administration hospitals. Until recently, people in hospitals, nursing homes, and other institutions had little dental care. Now dentists have portable equipment so that they can go to the patient if the patient cannot visit them.

Women are becoming a growing part of the dental profession. In some countries, such as Norway and Russia, there are many women dentists. But until 1970 in the United States, female enrollment in dental schools was less than 1 percent. From 1970 on, however, first-year enrollment of women in dental schools has increased significantly, rising to 35 percent by the early 1990's.

Other Dental Careers

In addition to the dentist, other health professionals provide dental care. The dental hygienist cleans teeth, removes dental plaque and calculus (tartar) from teeth, and provides instruction on brushing and flossing.

The dental laboratory technician is a skilled person who makes artificial dentures, dental bridges, and other dental devices. The technician is employed by commercial dental laboratories and by some dentists. They are prohibited by law from working directly on patients.

The dental assistant performs a wide variety of duties in the dentist's office. He or she helps the patient get ready for an examination, hands instruments to the dentist, and performs clerical duties.

All of these jobs require special skills, education, and training. Each plays an important part in providing good care to dental patients.

▶ DENTISTRY IN THE UNITED STATES

Dentistry as an independent profession in the United States began in the 1800's. The first dental school in the United States, the Baltimore College of Dental Surgery, opened in 1840. The first publication devoted to dentistry, the *American Journal of Dental Science,* began in 1839, and the first dental society in America, the American Society of Dental Surgeons, was organized in 1841.

With these developments, the dental profession became identified with a formal course of education, a professional society, and a body of literature devoted to dentistry. Since then, the dental profession has grown to occupy a unique place in health care. Without regular attention to the teeth and their supporting tissues, health care would be incomplete.

GORDON H. ROVELSTAD
Executive Director, American College of Dentists
See also FLUORIDATION; ORTHODONTICS; TEETH.

DENVER

Denver, the capital of Colorado, is the largest city and center for trade and industry in the entire Rocky Mountain region. The elevation at Denver's state capitol building is 1 mile (1.6 kilometers) above sea level. This extraordinarily high altitude has given Denver the nickname the Mile High City. Denver has also been called the Western Capital of the United States. Other than Washington, D.C., it has the largest number of federal agencies, including a branch of the United States Mint.

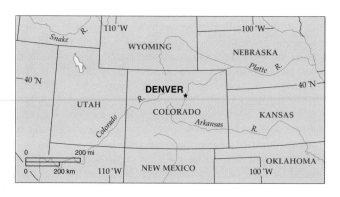

Located on the South Platte River, where the mountains meet the Great Plains, Denver is the gateway to the mountains and all the recreational opportunities they offer. Dry, sunny weather and an abundance of winter snow make the area popular for outdoor sports and recreation all through the year. Much of the city's economy is based on tourism, as well as the aerospace, oil, computer, and cable television industries. Other important industries include brewing, food processing, health care, and printing and publishing services. The city also serves as the financial, manufacturing, and supply center

for the region's mining, cattle ranching, and farming businesses.

Denver is home to about 555,000 people. About 2.6 million people live in the greater metropolitan area, which includes five of the largest cities in the state—Aurora, Lakewood, Arvada, Boulder, and Westminster. The population of Denver is about 12 percent African American, 3.4 percent Asian American, and about 2 percent Native American. About 32 percent claims some Hispanic heritage. Besides fast-growing suburbs, Denver has well-preserved historic neighborhoods such as Capitol Hill, Country Club, Auraria, Highlands, and Lower Downtown.

Several colleges and universities are located in Denver. The University of Denver,

Amid modern downtown skyscrapers, the gold-domed state capitol shines as a reminder that Denver got its start as a gold-rush town.

founded in 1864, is the city's oldest institution of higher education. The Denver branch of the University of Colorado shares a campus with Metropolitan State College of Denver and the Community College of Denver. Regis University, a Jesuit college, is also located in the city.

Denver has facilities for a number of professional sports teams. New Mile High Stadium houses the National Football League's Denver Broncos. Coors Field, opened in 1995, is home to the Colorado Rockies baseball club of the National League. The Pepsi Center is home to the Denver Nuggets of the National Basketball Association and the Colorado Avalanche of the National Hockey League.

▶ PLACES OF INTEREST

In the late 1800's, many grand buildings were constructed with the fortunes made from gold and silver. Among the most notable are the Brown Palace Hotel, the Molly Brown House Museum, and the Byers-Evans House Museum. The state capitol building shares Civic Center Park with the Colorado History Museum, the Denver Public Library, and the Denver Art Museum. The Denver Museum of Natural History and the Denver Zoo are located in City Park. Denver Botanic Gardens, in Cheesman Park, features a variety of tropical plants.

The Denver Center for the Performing Arts houses the Colorado Symphony Orchestra, Colorado Ballet, Opera Colorado, and four theaters. Elitch Gardens, the city's largest and oldest amusement park, has been relocated in central Denver on the bank of the South Platte River.

Residents also enjoy a large Denver Park system, as well as the Denver Mountain Parks, which include a buffalo herd visible from Highway I-70 at Genesee Park. Winter Park is a large family ski area, while Red Rocks Park has a stunning outdoor amphitheater made of natural sandstone slabs.

▶ HISTORY

Denver was founded on November 22, 1858, after prospectors discovered gold in the South Platte River near its junction with Cherry Creek. The Colorado gold rush lured some 100,000 fortune seekers, and Denver boomed as it became the main supply town for the miners.

The settlement was named for James Denver, governor of the Kansas Territory, which included much of Colorado before the Colorado Territory was created in 1861. In 1867, Denver became the territorial capital. After statehood was achieved in 1876, Denver became Colorado's state capital.

Denver's initial prosperity depended on silver as well as gold. During the 1870's, the opening of the silver mines in Leadville, Aspen, and other mountain sites made many of Denver's citizens rich. By 1890 more than 100,000 people lived in Denver.

Denver's many railroads made it the transportation hub of the Rockies. The 1927 opening of the Moffat Tunnel provided a reliable winter route under the high mountains west of Denver. This 6.2-mile (10-kilometer) tunnel put Denver on a direct transcontinental railroad route. Today the 54-square-mile (140-square-kilometer) Denver International Airport, like the city's early railroads, makes Denver the hub for the Rockies and the High Plains.

THOMAS J. NOEL
Coauthor, *Denver: Mining Camp to Metropolis*

DE PAOLA, TOMIE. See CHILDREN'S LITERATURE (Profiles).

DEPARTMENT STORES

A department store offers for sale, under one roof, almost anything you might want to buy. Each type of merchandise—men's, women's, and children's clothing; home furnishings; and more—is grouped together and sold in a separate department.

Some department stores offer a more complete selection than others. Some even sell food, plants, pets, bicycles, appliances, auto accessories, and paints and hardware. Department stores employ buyers, who travel throughout the world to find the best values at the best prices. Buyers generally purchase goods for their own particular departments, such as children's wear, housewares, cosmetics, women's sportswear, or furniture.

Department stores need many customers to do enough business to make a profit. Therefore they are usually found in cities and suburban areas with large populations. City department stores are often situated in the business district, close to public transportation such as subways and buses. In the suburbs, a department store is often the "anchor" store in a shopping center or mall.

Like most large businesses, department stores are organized into several divisions. The selection and purchase of goods are the function of the merchandising division. Other divisions include financial, credit management, human resources, marketing and sales promotion, and information systems.

Competition is keen, so a department store must always try to attract customers in order to sell more merchandise if it wants to succeed. Through advertising, stores can announce events taking place in the store, what is new, or upcoming sales. Stores advertise in their cities' local newspapers, in local and national magazines, and on radio and television.

Another way to draw customers is by means of attractive window displays. Large downtown department stores often spend vast amounts of money trying to have the best window displays in their community. Appealing interior displays are important, too.

Special events and promotions, such as fashion shows and makeup demonstrations, also attract people and draw them from one department to another. Thanksgiving Day parades, concerts, and charitable balls sponsored by department stores help to bring

Macy's is among the best-known department stores in the United States. Events such as its spectacular Thanksgiving Day parade help attract shoppers.

people in and to establish the good will that is all-important to the life of the business.

Many department stores offer charge accounts and accept bank credit cards. This allows customers to buy merchandise on credit and pay for it when they get a bill.

One of the first true department stores was Bon Marché, which opened in Paris, France, about 1870. Among the earliest U.S. department stores were Marshall Field, founded in Chicago, Illinois, in 1865, and Filene's, founded in Boston, Massachusetts, in 1881. In the 1920's, J.C. Penney began the first department store chain, with branches in many locations. The years after World War II (1939–45) saw the movement of large department stores from cities to the growing suburbs. Today many national department stores sell goods through catalogs and Internet sites.

BEN LICHTENSTEIN
Saks Fifth Avenue
Reviewed by TOMI BLOCK
National Retail Merchants Association

DEPRESSION, GREAT

The Great Depression was the worst worldwide economic crisis of the modern industrial era. It began in late 1929 and lasted until after the outbreak of World War II in 1939. From 1929 to 1933, industrial production in the United States fell by nearly 50 percent, and unemployment rose from about 4 percent to at least 25 percent. Stock prices fell to about 20 percent of their 1929 worth, and well over 30 percent of the nation's banks failed, wiping out the life savings of depositors.

Previous economic collapses had usually been called "panics." Therefore, when U.S. president Herbert Hoover at first referred to this new economic crisis as a "depression," he was trying to avoid the frightening implications associated with the word "panic." "Depression" implied that the economy had merely taken a brief downturn—a small dip—and was not in the same category as the panics that had hit the economy repeatedly in the 1800's. But the depression of the 1930's turned out to be much worse than the previous panics. The term "Great Depression" later distinguished this particular period of economic collapse from less severe episodes, both before and since.

Causes of the Great Depression. Although the great stock market crash in October 1929 is often identified as the major cause of the Great Depression, it is more accurate to see the sudden drop in stock prices as a reflection of the underlying problems that already existed in the economy. These were the real causes of the Great Depression.

The decade preceding the Great Depression, often called the Roaring Twenties, was for many people a time of unprecedented prosperity. But beneath the carefree surface of the 1920's, serious economic problems were brewing throughout the world. Some of the problems resulted from the high costs of World War I (1914–18). Several European nations owed large debts to the United States, which contributed to a weak international banking structure. Germany, which lost the war, was particularly burdened. The peace treaty that ended the war required the Germans to make massive reparation payments to pay for the destruction the war had caused in other countries.

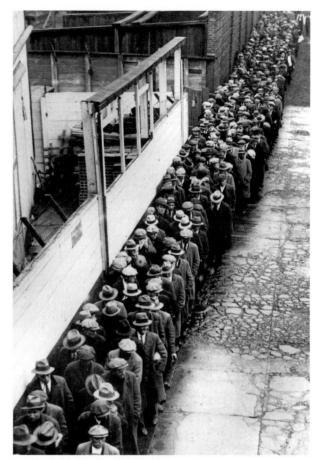

In the winter of 1932–33, when the Great Depression was at its worst, long lines of jobless and homeless men waited for free meals in New York and many other cities.

The global economy, however, was also weakened by the same mass-production industries that had generated the prosperity of the 1920's. More than ever before, the mass production of goods—such as automobiles, radios, and household appliances—placed a higher standard of living within reach of many more people, both in the United States and in other industrial countries. But mass production requires mass consumption to keep the economy in balance. In other words, people have to buy all the products that come off assembly lines. In the 1920's, most of the profits from mass-produced goods went to the factory owners and investors, not to the average worker. Most working people did not make enough money to buy all the goods that were being produced. To solve this problem, consumers were encouraged to purchase expensive goods on credit, which allowed them to pay for them over an extended period of time. Thus, many people went into debt, owing money for goods they really could not afford to own.

By 1929, so many consumers had gone into debt that they could no longer buy much of the new merchandise, even on credit. As manufacturers saw unsold goods piling up in their warehouses, they reduced their levels of production and laid workers off. This further reduced demand (because unemployed people could buy nothing beyond the basic necessities) and set in motion a downward spiral in which even fewer goods were sold and even more workers lost their jobs.

Effects of the Great Depression. Although the Great Depression was caused mainly by economic imbalances in the most advanced industrial nations, it also ravaged the world's developing nations and remaining colonies. Their economies depended on selling raw materials to the industrialized nations, who no longer wanted them.

Migrant Mother, a famous photograph by Dorothea Lange, captured the desperation of many Depression-era families.

By early 1933, when the Great Depression hit its lowest point, at least one-quarter of all American workers—more than 15 million people—were unemployed. Even those who managed to keep their jobs were often required to work only part-time and at greatly reduced wages. At the time, the United States had no federal system of unemployment insurance or welfare, and large numbers of Americans were reduced to waiting in breadlines for food handouts. During this decade traditional American optimism was severely shaken. The hardships suffered by so many people made them extremely cautious in their spending and saving habits, even after prosperity returned.

In the United States the Great Depression produced other enduring changes. It discredited the pro-business Republican Party, which had dominated politics in the 1920's. In the 1932 presidential election American voters elected a Democrat, Franklin D. Roosevelt, by a large margin. His response to the crisis was to create dozens of new programs, collectively known as the New Deal.

The New Deal. The Great Depression created public support for a greatly expanded role for the federal government in regulating the economy and providing social programs that gave citizens some protections, such as old age pensions and unemployment insurance through the Social Security Act. Although the Roosevelt administration's measures in response to the Great Depression did not bring the economic crisis to an end until military spending for World War II stimulated the economy, the New Deal was so popular that it brought together a political coalition that kept the Democrats in power until the 1950's.

Global Impact. The Great Depression threw the future of both the capitalist economic system and the democratic political system into question around the world. The collapse of the U.S. economy seemed to prove that an unregulated free market system did not work. Similarly, many people questioned whether a democratic government was sufficiently equipped to handle the crisis. Communists and fascists began gaining support, claiming their economic systems were better suited to maintaining a functioning economy and providing for people's basic needs.

In Japan, the economic turmoil caused by the economic downturn strengthened the arguments of militarists who believed they needed to expand into China and other parts of Asia to create new markets for their products. This way of thinking placed Japan on the road to war. At the same time, economic desperation in Germany opened the way for Adolf Hitler to seize power. By promising to restore Germany to prosperity and international power, Hitler and his Nazi followers took their country down the path of totalitarianism that resulted in World War II and the Holocaust.

ROBERT S. MCELVAINE
Author, *The Great Depression*

See also NEW DEAL; ROOSEVELT, FRANKLIN DELANO (His Presidency).

When major industries are affected by recessions or depressions, entire towns can fall into an economic slump. Empty storefronts are sure indicators of a depressed area.

DEPRESSIONS AND RECESSIONS

Economic news often dominates newspaper headlines and radio and television newscasts. This news is almost always about things going up and down. Perhaps some things are going up—prices, interest rates, or unemployment. Other things may be going down—profits, the stock market, or the gross national product. A **depression** can be described as a time when all of these things are moving in the wrong direction. A **recession** is similar, but conditions are not as severe, and a recession does not last as long as a depression.

You might think of an economy as somewhat like a growing child. A child has periods of rapid growth, and so does an economy. These are periods of prosperity. Unemployment falls as new jobs are created. Business profits and wages rise, causing incomes to rise. But sometimes a child may have periods of very slow growth or what seems to be no growth. An economy has similar times, and they are called recessions. Unemployment rises when there are more workers available than jobs. Incomes fall slightly because profits and wages decline. For a child, periods of slow growth are usually followed by noticeable growth. It is normally the same for an economy. But there the similarity ends. It is possible that the growth process of an economy can be reversed. In other words, an economy can shrink. Then the economy moves from a recession to a depression. During a depression, unemployment is very high, incomes fall dramatically, and many businesses fail.

▶ WHY DEPRESSIONS AND RECESSIONS OCCUR

Experts who study depressions and recessions closely do not understand all the reasons why they occur. They used to be explained in terms of a yo-yo. Good times were followed by bad times in a regular pattern. Like a yo-yo, the economy was always going up and down. But the worldwide Great Depression of the 1930's did not fit this theory. The pattern since World War II (1939–45), with no depression and infrequent recessions, does not fit either.

Each recession is a little different from all others. But there are some factors common to all.

Unemployment Rises. During a recession, very few new jobs are created, and many jobs are eliminated. Workers find it very difficult to find jobs, and the number of unemployed workers rises.

Income Does Not Grow. Governments keep track of the total value of goods and services produced in the country during a certain period. This figure is called the gross national product, or GNP. During a recession, the GNP falls, or at least it does not rise. In the United States a recession is officially defined as any period of nine months or longer during which the GNP does not rise.

Business Profits Fall. Recessions do not affect each industry equally. But in every recession, some business profits fall and some small firms fail.

Stock Prices Fall. Ownership of stock gives an individual the right to share in a firm's profit. Because business profits fall during times of recession, the price of stocks usually also falls.

Inflation Rates Fall. During a recession, people buy fewer products than they do when their incomes are rising. For this reason, there is less pressure for the prices of products to rise. The result is that the rate of inflation falls. This does not mean that prices will fall. They simply will not rise as fast.

The fact that recessions usually slow down the rate of inflation means that they are not all bad. In fact, governments at times appear to try to start very short recessions to try to slow down the rate of inflation. But recessions are not always successful at doing this. A recession occurred in many countries in 1974–75, after the Organization of Petroleum Exporting Countries (OPEC) increased oil prices sharply. This was a recession in which inflation rates rose dramatically in many parts of the world.

▶ **DEPRESSIONS IN MODERN TIMES**

Modern economic conditions started to cause depressions in the early 1800's, when much of the Western world became industrialized. Before then, events such as war and disease were the chief causes. For 100 years before World War II (1939–45), most countries in the world had gone through a series of depressions. The last of these started in the United States in the late 1920's and spread quickly to the rest of the world. This particular one was so severe that it is called the Great Depression. Fear of the return of such a depression has been an important influence on economic policy.

There is some disagreement about all the factors that caused the Great Depression. But many experts believe that the government contributed to it. At first the government raised interest rates and some tax rates.

These actions are the opposite of those generally recommended by economists today.

The government eventually started to try to increase the demand for products. President Franklin D. Roosevelt's New Deal policies slowly helped the economy recover. The Federal Deposit Insurance Corporation (FDIC) was created to insure bank deposits. The Securities and Exchange Commission (SEC) was created to regulate activities on the stock market. The Social Security Administration (SSA) was established to provide incomes for retired workers. Agencies such as these, together with increased knowledge of how to react to recessions, should help governments avoid further depressions. For more information, see the article DEPRESSION, GREAT preceding this article.

▶ **DEALING WITH DEPRESSIONS AND RECESSIONS**

Modern economic theory focuses on the ability of the government to avoid conditions that cause depressions and recessions. This theory is based on the idea that a depression or recession begins when people buy fewer products in one part of the economy. If this is not stopped, firms lose business and need fewer workers. This slowdown in business activity then spreads to the rest of the economy. Modern theory also suggests that the government of a country can stop this process by lowering taxes or interest rates and by encouraging people and firms to increase spending. The government can also increase its purchases to help stop the slowdown in spending.

The theory that government should play an important role in stopping depressions and recessions has been adopted by most industrialized countries. The United States made this idea part of the Employment Act of 1946. So far these policies have been partly successful. There has not been a major depression in an industrialized country since World War II. But recessions still occur. In the early 1980's and 1990's, for example, many countries around the world suffered severe recessions. In the early 2000's, the United States experienced a more moderate downturn in the economy.

ROBERT B. ARCHIBALD
College of William and Mary

See also INFLATION AND DEFLATION; UNEMPLOYMENT AND UNEMPLOYMENT INSURANCE.

DERMATOLOGY

Dermatology is the study of the skin. Dermatologists are medical doctors who treat skin diseases. Some of these diseases occur only on the skin, but some reflect systemic conditions, which affect the whole body. Many dermatologic conditions are caused by chemicals, metals, medications, and other substances that contact the skin. Some conditions occur rapidly (poison ivy), and others take years to develop (skin cancer after sun exposure).

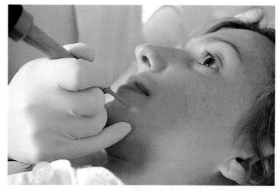

A dermatologist uses a hand-held laser to focus light and heat on a small area of the skin. The laser burns away warts and moles but leaves surrounding skin unharmed.

▶ DERMATOLOGIC CONDITIONS

A selection of common dermatologic conditions is described in this article.

Acne is a common skin condition that begins in the teenage years. It may be caused by a surge of hormones. These hormones stimulate and enlarge the glands that produce sebum (skin oil). Bacteria on the skin attack sebum and dead cells, resulting in redness and swelling. Washes, creams, antibiotics, and medications that contain vitamin A are useful. Acne does not result from a lack of cleanliness. (Too much scrubbing may make acne worse.) No foods cause or worsen acne.

Dermatitis (eczema) is an inflammatory skin condition. The main symptom is intense itchiness. Scratching causes—and worsens—rashes. Atopic dermatitis often occurs with allergies. It may run in families that include members affected by asthma or hay fever. However, the exact cause is unknown. Atopic dermatitis usually begins in infancy. It makes the skin more sensitive to water and soap, which tend to dry the skin. Moisturizers and prescribed creams or pills may bring relief. Most cases resolve on their own by puberty. However, no cure is available.

Contact dermatitis may result if some substance or activity irritates the skin, damaging it faster than it can repair itself. Contact dermatitis may also result if the body damages itself. This can happen through contact with an allergen (substance that causes an allergic reaction). A well-known allergen is poison ivy. Actually, the allergic trigger is an oil inside the plant. Avoid touching the plant or anything that has contacted it. Do not inhale the smoke of burning plants. If you are exposed to poison ivy, wash with soap and water right away. Creams or pills may decrease the allergic reaction and stop the itch. Consult a doctor before taking over-the-counter products or prescription drugs.

Impetigo is a bacterial infection common in children. It causes blisters that ooze fluid and develop a honey-colored crust. They usually appear on the face and hands. Impetigo may itch, and scratching may spread it. Objects that touch infected skin may pass the disease to others. Impetigo is treated with antibiotics.

Moles occur when melanocytes, cells that make pigment, multiply beyond what is normal. Moles are usually harmless, but a few may lead to a cancer called malignant melanoma. (Melanocytes in normal skin may lead to this cancer, too.) A mole should be checked if it is large, if it has an irregular border or a variety of colors, or if it develops symptoms such as itching, pain, or bleeding.

Psoriasis is a lifelong disorder in which areas of the skin are red, swollen, and covered with a silvery white scale. Psoriasis may affect the nails, and it may cause joint pain. To treat psoriasis, drugs are used that slow skin cell production and reduce inflammation. Light therapy, moisturizers, and scale-removing agents are also important

Ringworm has nothing to do with worms. It is an infection caused by tinea fungi that leads to itching and red, scaly rings. Ringworm of the body, which affects the legs, trunk, and face, is caused by tinea corporis. Ringworm of the scalp, which may lead to hair loss, is caused by tinea capitis. Ringworm that affects the foot (athlete's foot) is caused by tinea pedis. Medicated creams and pills kill the fungi.

Skin cancer is the most common cancer in humans. There are three major types of skin cancer: basal cell carcinoma (BCC), squamous cell carcinoma (SCC), and malignant melanoma. Malignant melanoma needs to be treated aggressively. If it is found early, surgical removal may be the only treatment needed. If the cancer has already spread, treatment may include additional tissue removal, chemotherapy, and radiotherapy.

Most skin cancers are BCC's or SCC's. They can be prevented by reducing sun exposure and wearing hats and sunscreen. They may be treated with drugs and surgery.

Warts are caused by a virus. It usually enters the skin after direct contact with an infected person. The common wart typically develops on the hand. Common warts are gray to flesh-colored, raised from the skin surface, and covered with rough projections. Many treatments try to irritate the wart and prompt an immune reaction. Warts can be covered with liquids or pads that contain a weak acid. Other treatments include freezing sprays and laser surgery.

▶ **FUTURE OF DERMATOLOGY**

Scientists improve dermatology by studying skin conditions and how they occur. One approach is to study the relationship between skin conditions and immunology, the body's response to a disease. Research on immunology may help identify disease pathways that can be targeted by new medications.

New treatments include laser surgery and light therapy. These treatments are being used to help patients with dermatological conditions such as psoriasis, acne, and scars.

Cosmetic dermatology, which is aimed at enhancing a patient's appearance, includes chemical peels and botox injections. Telemedicine uses cameras and computers to link patients and doctors in different locations. This technology is helpful for patients who live far from dermatologists.

BRIAN BERMAN, M.D., PH.D.
DEBORAH ZELL, M.D.
SARI FIEN, M.D.
Skin Research Group, University of Miami

DESCARTES, RENÉ (1596–1650)

René Descartes, French philosopher and mathematician, tried to understand how we come to know what is real. His statement, "I think; therefore I am," reflects his idea that the individual mind is the starting point of all knowledge.

Descartes was born on March 31, 1596, at La Haye, France. His mother died of tuberculosis shortly afterward, and his father, fearful of losing René too, kept careful watch over his son's delicate health. René was a thoughtful child who asked many questions. His father called him "my little philosopher."

When René was 8, he was sent to a Jesuit school at La Flèche. Because of his delicate health, he was allowed to stay in bed in the morning, meditating and reading the classics. It was a habit he followed all his life.

From 1612 to 1616, Descartes studied law at the University of Poitiers. Then he went to Paris and joined a group of young men devoted to gambling. Descartes won easily by working out his chances mathematically. But he soon tired of this life, and he spent the next two years in mathematical investigation. Seeking activity once again, he became a sol-

dier. In his leisure time he developed a method of reasoning that resulted in the philosophy called Cartesianism, after his name. And he developed analytic geometry, the basis of modern mathematics.

After two years as a soldier, Descartes traveled and lived in Paris, developing his theories, before moving to the Netherlands. He lived a secluded life, but he carried on a wide correspondence with the leading intellects of Europe. He did not publish his first book, *Le Monde* ("The World"), for fear its revolutionary theories would cause the Catholic Church to persecute him as it had Galileo. But friends persuaded him in 1637 to publish his *Discourse on the Method of rightly conducting the Reason and seeking Truth in the Sciences*. This book gave the world analytic geometry and established Descartes's reputation.

In 1649, Descartes moved to Sweden, where the queen invited him to teach philosophy. But he soon caught pneumonia, and he died on February 11, 1650.

Reviewed by HOWARD OZMON
Author, *Twelve Great Philosophers*

Desert landscapes are varied. *Top:* Some are sandy, such as the Sahara, in northern Africa. *Left:* Some are cold, such as the Dry Valleys, in Antarctica. *Above:* Some support diverse plant life, such as the Sonoran, in the United States and Mexico.

DESERTS

Deserts are dry places. They receive little rain and hold on to little or no liquid water. In warm deserts, water quickly evaporates. In cold deserts, water is locked in ice and snow.

Although all deserts are dry, their landscapes are varied. Some deserts are covered by towering sand dunes. Some are covered with gravel plains and flat (or almost flat) sheets of sand. And some are covered by thick layers of ice that were deposited long ago. In polar areas (the Arctic and Antarctica), surprisingly little snow falls. However, it stays so cold that the snow is able to build up year after year.

Desert landscapes are beautiful, with many different colors and diverse plants, animals, and people. Many deserts contain valuable mineral and ore deposits. And many deserts attract settlers, including farmers who depend on irrigation to water their crops.

Desert ecosystems are sensitive to human activities. If we damage these ecosystems, they may never recover, and we may lose our chance to learn how valuable they truly are.

▶ DEFINING DESERTS

Deserts are often classified by how arid they are, that is, by how little rainfall they receive. In extremely arid deserts, rain may not fall for more than a year at a time. In arid deserts, yearly rainfall is less than 10 inches (25 centimeters). In semiarid deserts, yearly rainfall is between 10 and 20 inches (25 and 50 centimeters).

It is possible, however, for a place to be arid without being a desert. An arid place is considered a desert only if it quickly loses the water it receives. In most arid deserts, water is lost because sunshine is abundant, winds are strong, and temperatures are high. In fact, many deserts can lose more water to evaporation than they ever receive from rainfall.

Some arid lands do not lose enough moisture to qualify as deserts. For example, in Alaska, the North Slope of the Brooks Range receives very little rain, but has many lakes and rivers. The cool temperatures help limit evaporation, and drainage is poor. Also, some semiarid lands do not qualify as deserts. These places are called steppes, which are treeless plains covered with short grasses.

▶ WHERE ARE THE DESERTS?

Deserts occur on every continent and wherever there are arid lands. Arid or semiarid lands cover about 41 percent of the Earth's surface. About 33 percent of the Earth's surface is desert.

Arid conditions and deserts result from a combination of complex factors, including the general circulation of the atmosphere, the location of large landmasses, and local geography. In some deserts, certain factors count more than others. This explains why deserts occur at different latitudes, longitudes, and elevations. But most deserts are found in certain latitudes, reflecting the influence of Earth's prevailing wind systems.

Trade Wind Deserts

The trade winds are strong, steady winds that blow over the tropics and subtropics toward the equator. When they blow over large land areas, the trade winds are quite dry. They are sometimes called desert makers. (For more information, read the article TRADE WINDS in Volume T.)

Trade winds are just part of the general circulation of the atmosphere. This circulation is driven by the unequal heating of the Earth's surface by the sun. Warm air from the equator flows toward the poles, and cool air from the poles flows toward the equator. However, this circulation is far from simple.

When the Earth spins on its axis, it helps create a complex pattern of air circulation with great belts of winds circling the globe. (For more information about these winds, read the article WEATHER in Volume WXYZ.) Between these belts, winds are relatively light, and air tends to rise or fall. Between the belts dominated by the trade winds and the belts dominated by the westerlies, air tends to flow downward. When this air descends, it becomes warmer and picks up moisture, drying the land below. Also, when this dry air flows towards the equator, it **dissipates** (thins out) the cloud cover, which means more sunlight reaches the surface, heating the land.

Most of the world's large deserts are found in the trade wind latitudes. In fact, nearly 6 million square miles (15.5 million square kilometers) in this zone are occupied by deserts, of which the Sahara is the largest. Other notable trade wind deserts are found in Australia. Here, the Simpson, the Great Sandy, and other deserts cover about a third of the continent.

Midlatitude Deserts

Some deserts lie farther from the equator, between latitudes 30° and 50° N and between latitudes 30° and 50° S. (To read more about latitudes, read the article LATITUDE AND LONGITUDE in Volume L.) These deserts typically receive a little more rainfall than the trade wind deserts. They tend to have a wide range of temperatures and to be rocky and stony, without the large sand sheets and areas of dunes that characterize the trade wind deserts.

Rain Shadow Deserts

High mountain ranges, at any latitude, force rain-bearing winds to compress, condensing the moisture in clouds, causing precipitation to fall on the windward side of the ranges. The air that crosses the mountains and reaches the leeward side is dry. The result is a "rain shadow" desert. Examples of rain shadow deserts include the Tian Shan Desert in China and Death Valley in California.

Coastal Deserts

Two coastal deserts, the Namib in Africa and the Atacama in South America, receive more moisture from fog than rain. Air heated during the day by the land surface flows over cold ocean currents and condenses as fog, which blows onshore overnight. Fog can drift inland some 30 miles (50 kilometers) in the Namib, resulting in up to 5 inches (13 centimeters) of precipitation a year.

Polar Deserts

The Arctic and Antarctica are desert regions where the annual precipitation is less than 10 inches (25 centimeters) and the average temperature in summer is less than 50°F (10°C). These are not sandy deserts. Instead, there are gravel plains and rocky mountains. Where snow falls, there may be wind-sculpted snow dunes.

▶ DESERT ENVIRONMENTS

Lack of precipitation is the main factor that helps create a desert environment. But other factors also help define deserts, including water erosion, temperature, and wind. Desert plants and animals have developed special adaptations that enable them to survive in such environments.

Precipitation

Not only is rainfall low in deserts, it is extremely unreliable and unevenly distributed. Some deserts receive all their precipitation as snow in winter. Others receive heavy rain for a short period, often during summer thunderstorms. A few may receive a little rain in either summer or winter.

Drought (an extensive period of below-average rainfall) is a normal and recurring event in desert ecosystems. Drought limits the productivity of both animals and plants and causes hardship and insecurity for desert peoples. (For more information, read the article DROUGHT in Volume D.)

Although the Atacama Desert, along the coast of Chile and Peru, receives fog moisture, it is believed to be the driest place on Earth. Measurable rainfall (more than 0.04 inch, or 1 millimeter) may not occur for many years. The inland Sahara averages less than 1 inch (2.5 centimeters) of rain a year, but the Chihuahuan, Sonoran, Great Basin, and Mojave deserts of the southwestern United States and Mexico can average as much as 12 inches (30 centimeters) a year.

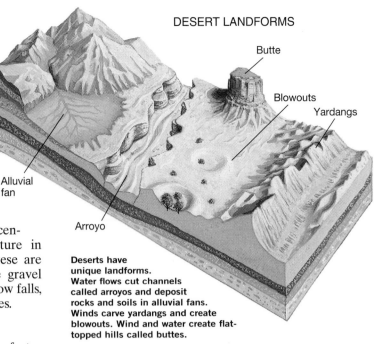

DESERT LANDFORMS

Butte

Blowouts

Yardangs

Alluvial fan

Arroyo

Deserts have unique landforms. Water flows cut channels called arroyos and deposit rocks and soils in alluvial fans. Winds carve yardangs and create blowouts. Wind and water create flat-topped hills called buttes.

Water Erosion

Brief and intense rainfall is characteristic of desert storms. It often saturates the ground and then becomes runoff, which quickly fills small surface channels and short-lived desert drainage channels (called **arroyos** or **wadis**).

Over many centuries, such storms and runoff create steep-sided canyons like the Grand Canyon in Arizona. They can also wash rocks and soils down mountain slopes. At the bottom, the rocks and soils form spreading piles called alluvial fans. These deposits can sometimes be dated, providing records of the how the climate and landforms have changed over thousands of years. Water erosion, along with wind erosion, may also create isolated flat-topped hills called **mesas** or **buttes**. (For more information, read the article EROSION in Volume E.)

Temperature

The deserts in subtropical and some mid-latitude areas experience daily extremes in temperature because the air is so dry that it does not block the sun's heat during the day or slow heat loss at night. The Sahara and the Mojave are the hottest deserts, with average monthly temperatures above 86°F (30°C) during the summer. Extreme highs exceed 122°F (50°C). The daily range is typically 60 to 70°F (15 to 25°C), and winter nights are often below freezing.

Semiarid deserts, farther from the equator, are cooler, with summer averages from 70 to 80°F (21 to 27°C) and nights about 50°F (10°C). Coastal deserts are even cooler. However, they are still dry, with mean summer temperatures in the 55 to 75°F (13 to 24°C) range. Annual highs are about 95°F (35°C), and annual lows are about 40°F (5°C).

The polar deserts are much colder and have long, dark winters. These factors pose serious challenges for plant, animal, and human inhabitants.

Wind

In the desert, wind processes are important because the surface is covered by loose clay, silt, and sand. These materials are easily carried by the wind. Dust storms are part of desert life. These storms are so large they can even be seen from space.

China is working to reduce the effects of dust storms, planting shelter belts of trees to

During China's dust-storm season, winds pick up dust from the Mongolian desert, carry it hundreds of miles, and drop it in Beijing and other cities.

slow the wind and cause it to "drop" its load of dust. Desert dust is sometimes carried long distances. For example, storms in the Sahara occasionally deposit fine layers of yellowish dust as far away as southern England and the northern areas of continental Europe.

Winds form sand dunes of various shapes and sizes. They also create **yardangs** (streamlined sculptures) from rock outcrops. **Deflation** (removal of ground surface sediments by the wind) frequently exposes plant roots and

creates **blowouts** (hollows), which may be more than a half mile across.

Soil

Desert soils have low amounts of organic matter (decomposing plant and animal remains) in their top layers, which means that they are sometimes not very fertile. Lower soil layers are often cemented by salts and clays, creating a barrier to plant roots.

Sand dunes cover about 20 percent of desert land surfaces. Other areas are covered by sheets of sand and gravel. There are also areas covered by stones, which may be closely packed together, forming "desert pavement." Crusts, formed by rainfall, soil gases, and micro-organisms, can form a layer over $1/10$ inch (3 millimeters) thick in some places. Although these crusts slow erosion, they also restrict plant growth.

Plants

Plant life largely depends on the amount of rain and when it falls. In the desert, scarce rain usually results in sparse vegetation. The plants that are able to grow often show special adaptations. Some desert plants have seeds that can remain dormant for several years, waiting for enough rain at the right time. When conditions are right, the seeds germinate, and the desert appears lush and green—but for just a few weeks.

Trees are rare in deserts and usually occur only along dry river channels or in depressions where groundwater is close to the surface. Many plants tolerate high salt content in soils and can store water in their leaves, roots, and stems. By opening their **stomata** (tiny openings in the leaves) at night rather than during the day, plants are able to take in carbon dioxide for photosynthesis while limiting water loss by evaporation.

Some desert plants are spiny or hairy. These adaptations help shade parts of the plant. Some plants have very shiny leaves, which help reflect sunlight. Another adaptation is slow growth. An unusually long lived plant is the *Welwitschia mirabilis*, which grows in the deserts of Namibia. It lives up to 2,000 years. It grows about 3 feet (1 meter) in height and has only two leaves. They become split and ragged because the wind thrashes them against the ground. Deep taproots serve more to anchor the plant against the wind than to obtain water, for the welwitschia absorbs most of its moisture—in the form of precipitation from fog—through the stomata on its leaves.

Another long-lived desert plant is the Saguaro cactus, which grows in the Sonoran Desert. It may live more than 200 years. The Saguaro and other types of cactus have special adaptations that help them survive in the desert. (For more information, read the article CACTUS in Volume C.)

Animals

Many animals have both bodies and behaviors adapted to life in the desert. For example, the gemsbok (a type of large antelope) has complex nasal passages and blood vessels that help cool its blood. It also stands on top of dunes to reach cooling winds. Sidewinder rattlesnakes and adders twist their bodies as they move so that only two or three spots on their undersides touch the ground at any moment. Tenebrionid beetles climb to Namibian dune crests in the early morning and angle their bodies into the wind so that the moisture in the fog condenses on them.

Many desert animals are nocturnal (active at night), spending the day either underground or in the shade. Most desert animals rarely drink. They get most of the moisture they need from their food.

Large mammals are relatively rare in the desert. With the exception of camels, they cannot store enough water in their bodies to survive. Camels can drink a very large amount of water and absorb it slowly from their stomach and intestines. A camel's kidneys concentrate urine to reduce water loss. It can become thick, syrupy, and twice as salty as seawater.

DESERT PEOPLES AND CULTURES

Many of the 1 billion people who live in the world's arid and semiarid lands have skin that contains abundant melanin, a brownish pigment that absorbs and scatters ultraviolet radiation from sun-

Some plants adapt to the desert by growing and maturing very slowly. An extreme example is the welwitschia, which can live up to 2,000 years.

light. Melanin-rich skin resists sunburn. There is no other adaptation of the human body that enhances survival in harsh desert environments. People survive in the desert because they are able to adapt their behaviors and their cultures.

Desert peoples living traditional lifestyles include farmers, especially in green, fertile areas called **oases**. Traditional peoples also include nomads, who move when seasons change or when new supplies of water or other natural resources are needed. Although many people in the desert now live in towns and cities, traditional lifestyles still exist. To stay on the land, some people are trying new ways to earn livelihoods.

Some people in the desert use farming methods that protect soil and limit environmental harm. One such technique is agroforestry, in which trees and bushes are grown along with crops and livestock on the same land. Agroforestry helps maintain watersheds, restore soil fertility, and check erosion.

Other activities that can help people stay on the land include photo and hunting safaris, crafts production, and the gathering and marketing of organic wild plants. Some people practice ecotourism, running campgrounds and lodges. Conservation areas are becoming more common in deserts.

Animals such as the gemsbok can survive in the desert because they have adaptations that help them withstand the hot and dry conditions.

In China and India, some desert communities help fight **desertification** (the spread of deserts). They work to stabilize sand dunes and limit the effect of dust storms.

▶ DEVELOPMENT IN THE DESERTS

Many people live in towns and cities in the semiarid areas on the edges of truly arid deserts. In the western United States, urban areas may double by 2050. Much of the growth will take place in arid and semiarid areas.

People are attracted to deserts because they are often rich in resources. For example, there are oil deposits below the Middle Eastern deserts and in some other semiarid and Arctic areas. Desert areas are also rich in precious metals and minerals, some of which have been concentrated by evaporation of shallow lakes in arid regions or by leaching and redeposition.

The Atacama Desert contains abundant sodium nitrate, which is mined for fertilizer and explosives. Chile and Peru are also rich in copper, as is Iran and the southwestern United States. Australia has the world's largest known economic resources of bauxite,

A green, fertile area in the desert is called an oasis. Some oases support farming, such as the Djanet oasis in Algeria.

iron ore, lead, zinc, silver, uranium, industrial diamonds, and mineral sands; 15 percent of the country's income results from mining.

Mining in desert areas often causes environmental damage and pollution. However, since the 1950's, many countries have taken steps to restore damaged areas and to limit the harm caused by mines.

Because they are dominated by grassland, arid and semiarid regions have often been used for raising livestock. Traditionally, the animals were tended by nomadic or semi-nomadic people. These shepherds would leave little or no lasting changes on the landscape. However, since the late 1800's and early 1900's, permanent ranches have been established, and fences have been raised to protect domestic animals such as sheep, goats, and cattle. Wild animals are kept out.

Semiarid areas, with abundant sunshine and a long growing season, attract farmers who see the potential for growing two crops a year—provided there is sufficient water. However, any farming in the desert that depends on rainfall is very risky. In arid and semiarid areas, abandoned fields are common, with ruins of villages showing that people tried to farm but failed.

Large-scale agriculture, which depends on irrigation, may appear to be more successful. However, if the soil is repeatedly soaked with water, salt deposits can build up in the soil. If fertilizers are used, chemicals can build up in the soil.

▶ FUTURE OF THE DESERTS

Development in dry regions has shown that desert and near-desert environments are not only harsh,

In some deserts, people rely on ecotourism for their livelihoods. Organizing camel rides is one example.

The world's largest oil deposits are underneath the deserts of the Middle East. Most are found in Saudi Arabia, which maintains a complex network of wells, pipelines, and refineries. This refinery at Ras Tanura is also a marine terminal where oil tankers are filled.

they are also fragile. Development can cause desert conditions to arise in near-desert drylands. It can also disrupt a desert ecosystem (a term for the interactions between the living organisms of a certain environment and their nonliving surroundings). To continue reaping the benefits of desert development, it may be necessary to better manage deserts and drylands.

Water Extraction

Desert ecosystems often suffer when water is pumped out of the ground and taken from the region by canal or pipeline. Water extraction can lower groundwater tables, causing the desert to become a source of dust. In fact, this has happened in Owens Valley, in the southwestern United States. Dust from the valley is transported by wind several hundred miles, causing air pollution and respiratory problems. The ecosystem of the valley itself has also suffered. In China, the World Heritage Site of Crescent Lake in the Gobi Desert is threatened because dams on major rivers have lowered the water table. The lake level has dropped 23 feet (7 meters).

Desertification

Arid and semiarid lands are sensitive to natural climate changes and are sometimes prone to desertification. In fact, dry places everywhere are at risk whether or not they border actual deserts. Desertification affects 250 million people, and it may soon affect 1 billion more. Desertification not only affects people and their livelihoods, it also disrupts large-scale environmental processes (interac-

tions between a landscape's soil, water, and vegetation) and reduces biodiversity (the variety of plant and animal species).

When scientists try to assess desertification, they measure changes in the numbers and types of plants, groundwater depth, crop yields, and animal populations. To help limit desertification, scientists study new ways to manage desert resources. Scientists also participate in the United Nations Convention to Combat Desertification.

New Research Techniques

Scientists are trying to gain a broader understanding of deserts. They are learning more about the climate patterns that create deserts and the development practices that may worsen desertification. Increasingly, scientists are relying on tools such as remote sensing, the use of satellite images to gather information about deserts.

Remote sensing can be combined with global climate modeling, a tool that relies on powerful computers to predict future weather conditions, such as rainfall amounts. Together, remote sensing and climate modeling can help scientists warn people of the potential for drought.

Scientists share their knowledge to help people wisely manage desert resources. By protecting desert resources, it may be possible to limit desertification and ensure the continued health of desert ecosystems.

DAVID MOUAT
Desert Research Institute

See also BIOMES.

DESERT STORM. See PERSIAN GULF WAR.

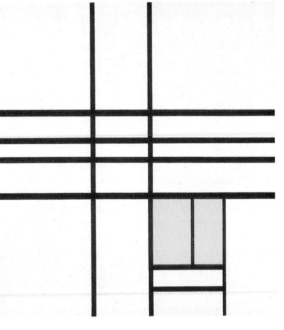

Whether found in nature or made by people, a good design must have balance, rhythm, and proportion. These three principles contribute to the unity of the design. *Left:* The leaves, arranged in groups of three and evenly sectioned by veins, are a good example of a well-balanced design. *Top left and right:* The circular shape of the spider web and the spiral design of the shell create pleasing rhythms. *Above:* In *Composition* (1936) by Piet Mondrian, lines divide the canvas into shapes of different but proportioned sizes.

DESIGN

"Design" refers to the way in which the parts that make up an object are put together. Whether it is found in nature or made by people, every object has its own arrangement of parts—its own design. If an object that a person creates is designed well, every individual part of it contributes to the whole thing—just as each branch, root, and leaf contributes to the structure of a tree. Only when every part helps the whole object is a design unified, and unity is probably the most important characteristic of a successful design.

When a person designs an object, the material used must be suited to the object's purpose. Material is as important to unity as are the three design principles: balance, proportion, and rhythm.

▶BASIC DESIGN PRINCIPLES

In order to be unified, a design must be well balanced. Each part must be in proportion to every other part, and the design should seem to have movement, or rhythm. These characteristics are the principles, or basic issues, of design.

Balance can be bisymmetrical or asymmetrical. In bisymmetrical balance both halves of an object or surface are equal. Your body is bisymmetrical. If you drew a line down the middle of your body, each half would be equal to the other. If you drew an imaginary line down the center of a design with asymmetrical balance, the parts on either side would be unequal. But each half is given equal importance or weight in the design. To be unified, a design must be balanced in a way that does not call attention to an unimportant part but at-

Left: The lively rhythm of *Number 3* (1949) by Jackson Pollock leads the viewer's eye rapidly across the canvas. *Below:* The still, motionless quality of the ancient Egyptian statue forces the eye to look slowly.

tracts attention to the whole. Balance is often achieved in the designs of such things as tapestries, wallpapers, and floor coverings by use of repetition, in which one or more shapes are repeated throughout, forming a pattern.

Proportion refers to the relationship of the size of each part of a design to the other parts. The designer tries to make the size of one shape in his design complement the size of the other shapes. There is no rule for judging proportions. Sometimes one large shape among many tiny ones may appear clumsy and out of proportion; but at other times this same kind of relationship may be very effective.

Rhythm is usually thought of as a musical term, but it is very important in design. It is the force that leads our eye from one part of the design to another and draws our attention to the most important parts. The rhythm of some Egyptian statues makes us look slowly, and we seem to feel the stillness of an ancient Egyptian religious rite. In contrast, a modern action painting can make us feel as excited as when we listen to the lively rhythm of jazz.

Above: This 1958 woodcut by Antonio Frasconi has asymmetrical balance: the two halves of the picture are unequal. *Below:* The design on this Pennsylvania Dutch chest is balanced bisymmetrically. The two sides almost mirror each other.

Left: Line, an important design element, can be expressed in three dimensions as well as on flat surfaces. The lines in *Encounter* (1975), by Richard Lippold, are made of metal rods. *Above:* The way that colors interact when used together is another key design consideration. In *Blue and Green Music* (1919), Georgia O'-Keeffe uses a combination of cool colors.

▶THE ELEMENTS OF DESIGN

The tools that a designer works with include more than drawing materials and technical instruments. A designer's most important tools are the design elements—line, color, value, texture, planes, and solids and space.

Line. The very first marks in the history of art were probably lines drawn by a caveman in the ground or on the walls of his cave. As children, the first images we create are usually scribbles made with lines. To make expressive lines has always been a goal of artists.

Very exact lines may be made with instruments. Architecture, furniture design, and industrial design call for great accuracy, and exact lines must be used. For other purposes lines can be free, sketchy, and flowing. Most of the time we think of lines on flat surfaces, such as in drawings. But line is an important element in three-dimensional design (sculpture, architecture, and useful objects) as well.

Color. Through their choice of color, artists can indicate feelings or create a mood. For example, vibrant, warm colors such as red and orange often are used to depict strong emotions or action. And a cool color such as blue can convey a calm, peaceful feeling. Identical designs can look very different when made in different colors. The way colors interact when used together is another key design consideration. You can read more about the properties of color in the article COLOR in Volume C.

Value. In art, selecting the value—the lightness or darkness—of a color is as important as selecting the color itself. For example, blue and green used together can look calm if both colors are soft and close in value. But blue and green together can also look very bright if the blue is rich and dark and the green is yellowish and light. The unity of a design is affected by the relative lightness and darkness of its parts.

Texture is the quality of an object that we learn about through our sense of touch. After we become familiar with a texture, we no longer have to touch an object to know what it feels like. We do not have to touch a brick wall to know how it feels; our eyes tell us of its roughness.

Texture is extremely important in design. The appearance of a building can be completely changed if marble walls are substituted for wooden ones. Artists have actually glued sandpaper, newspaper, and fabric onto their canvases to emphasize textures. In paintings, forms painted with thin, glossy paint give an entirely different effect than the same shapes painted thickly and with a dull finish. Many designs are enriched by use of contrasting textures—rough with smooth, soft with hard, shiny with dull.

Planes are flat surfaces. Some artists today create pictures by using only such plane figures as squares, circles, triangles, and rectangles. These paintings do not have realistic subject matter. Early in the 20th century other artists, known as cubists, took their subjects from nature. But the cubists tried to show the many planes of a three-dimensional object at once on a two-dimensional surface, the canvas.

In three-dimensional design, lines and planes are sometimes used together. In the kind of sculpture called mobiles, wires represent lines, and flat, cutout shapes represent plane figures. The shapes, suspended from the lines, move and capture light from time to time. Mobiles are interesting not only for their sculptural qualities but for the ever-changing shadows they cast on walls.

Left: Mobiles, such as *Red Petals* (1942) by Alexander Calder, combine three-dimensional lines and planes to create sculpture that moves. *Below:* Cubist paintings show the many planes of a three-dimensional object on a flat surface, the canvas. In Pablo Picasso's *Girl with a Mandolin* (1910) the girl, her instrument, and the background are painted as combinations of planes.

Left: The space shapes created by Henry Moore's sculpture *Rocking Chair II* (1950)— between the mother and child and between the chair legs, for example—are as important to the design as the solid forms. *Above: Grandmother* (1925), a collage by Arthur Dove, combines the contrasting textures of fabric, paper, and wood.

Solids and Space. Solids have height, width, and thickness and are the basis of three-dimensional design. Sculpture, pottery, decorative objects, tools, furniture, and buildings are all solids, and the materials used to create them are extremely important. The designer must learn every characteristic of the material in order to create the best and strongest solid forms.

When making a statue, a sculptor is filling space. Beginning in the 20th century, sculptors began to pay special attention to space as an element of design in their work. The space shapes created by the sculpture can be as important as the solid shapes that surround and define them.

A building encloses space. When we talk about the shape of a room, we are in fact talking about the shape of the unit of space enclosed by walls, ceiling, and floor. The very nature of the architect's job is to enclose, divide, and rearrange space.

▶ **THE CHANGING STANDARDS OF GOOD DESIGN**

What is liked and disliked in art and design constantly changes. Furniture made in colonial America is different from the furniture of England in the Victorian Age, and Victorian design is quite unlike modern Danish and Italian furniture. The blankets made by 16th-century South American Indians have little in common with the tapestries made by the Flemish at about the same time. Different things inspire artists and designers in different cultures. But the basic characteristics of design tend to remain the same. These characteristics are not laws that bind artists; they are guides that help to free them.

RUTH P. TAYLOR
Pratt Institute

See also FURNITURE; INDUSTRIAL DESIGN; INTERIOR DESIGN.

DE SMET, PIERRE JEAN. See MONTANA (Famous People).
DES MOINES. See IOWA (Cities).

DE SOTO, HERNANDO (1500?–1542)

The Spanish conquistador (conqueror) Hernando De Soto is usually given credit for being the first European to discover the Mississippi River. Leading a ragged Spanish army, De Soto first saw the great river near the site of the present city of Memphis, Tennessee, on May 21, 1541.

De Soto was born about 1500 in Extremadura, then a poor region of Spain. As a boy he met Pedro Arias de Ávila—called Pedrarias—who was governor of the Darién colony (now in Panama). Pedrarias took a liking to the young De Soto and became his patron—a kind of guardian and benefactor. Pedrarias paid De Soto's way to the University of Salamanca. When the boy was 19, he brought him to Darién.

For the next several years, De Soto took part in exploring and treasure-hunting expeditions in Central America. He achieved a reputation for recklessness and bravery. In 1532 he joined the conquistador Francisco Pizarro on an expedition to conquer Peru. After months of hard fighting, De Soto withdrew, taking with him a large bounty of gold.

With his fortune, De Soto returned to Spain and married Isabel, Pedrarias' daughter. But he soon grew restless. The Holy Roman emperor Charles V (who was also King Charles I of Spain) then appointed De Soto governor of Cuba and gave him the right to conquer Florida.

With more than 600 soldiers, De Soto sailed from Spain in 1538. After stopping in Cuba, they crossed to Florida, landing south of Tampa Bay on May 30, 1539. His army marched northward, and soon they made a lucky find. While fighting some Native Americans they discovered that one was actually a Spaniard, Juan Órtiz, who had been captured twelve years before. Órtiz then served with De Soto as a guide and interpreter.

De Soto's men marched in a wide path through what is now Georgia, part of North and South Carolina, Mississippi, and Tennessee. Along the way, they plundered the villages of the Native Americans, seeking gold and jewels. While looting the settlement of Cofachiqui, in present-day South Carolina, they found large quantities of freshwater pearls. But food had become scarce, and their clothes were now in tatters. Their weapons and armor were rusted and battered. And all around them were hostile natives.

The Native Americans who could be persuaded to talk always said that great treasure lay ahead—perhaps a day's march beyond. Each time De Soto and his men were seized with new eagerness. But each time they were disappointed. At last they reached the broad Mississippi River. De Soto's men built barges and they crossed to the Arkansas side. They continued west to the Neosho River in Oklahoma, then turned back east. On May 21, 1542, De Soto fell ill and died of fever. He was buried in the Mississippi River.

Only one-third of De Soto's men remained alive. But they continued the expedition, and it is believed they explored as far as the Brazos River in Texas. After many hardships they finally made their way to a Spanish settlement in Mexico.

Reviewed by FAYE GIBBONS
Author, *Hernando De Soto: A Search for Gold and Glory*

DETECTIVES. See POLICE.

DETECTIVE STORIES. See MYSTERY AND DETECTIVE STORIES.

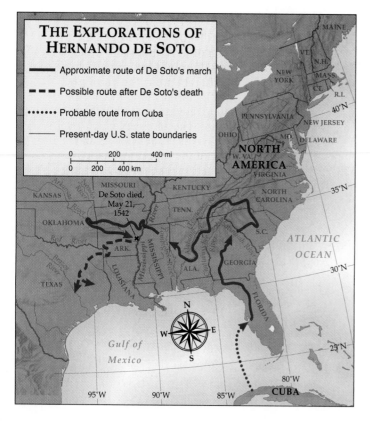

THE EXPLORATIONS OF HERNANDO DE SOTO

—— Approximate route of De Soto's march

- - - Possible route after De Soto's death

•••••• Probable route from Cuba

—— Present-day U.S. state boundaries

0   200   400 mi
0   200   400 km

Since colonial times, soap has been made by combining the same basic ingredients—fats and an alkali. The colonial housewife made lye (an alkali) from water and wood ashes in a process called leaching. This was one of several tedious steps needed to obtain a single barrel of soap. Modern machinery has automated the entire process. The large metal vat (*right*) can handle several hundred thousand pounds of material at one time.

DETERGENTS AND SOAP

Detergents and soap are substances that make things clean. Soap is actually a kind of detergent. But in ordinary use, **soap** means a cleaner made with naturally occurring materials. **Detergent** refers to a variety of synthetic cleaners that are manufactured in chemical plants.

Soap and detergents work by the same action to clean soiled materials. The ingredients in the detergents or soap that do the actual cleaning are called **surface-active agents,** or **surfactants** for short. A surfactant is a type of molecule that will attach itself to and surround a dirt particle.

Surfactants are long and narrow. One end of the molecule is attracted to water. For this reason scientists call this end the **hydrophilic,** or water-loving, end of the molecule. The other end of the molecule is repelled by water, but it is attracted to oily dirt and grease. Scientists call this the **hydrophobic,** or water-hating, end of the molecule.

In a washing machine full of dirty clothes, for example, the water-hating ends of the soap molecules are attracted to the oily dirt in the soiled fabric. They dig into and soften the grease, fat, or oil that holds the dirt. Then they split up the grease and dirt into tiny particles. The swishing motion of the washing machine helps this process.

As the water-hating ends of surfactants embed themselves in a particle of greasy dirt, the water-loving ends form a shell around the outside of the particle. This pulls the dirt away from the clothes and toward the wash water. The shell around each tiny particle of dirt prevents it from returning to the cleaned fabrics. The surfactant-surrounded dirt particles remain suspended in the wash water until they are rinsed away.

▶USES FOR DETERGENTS AND SOAP

In addition to being used in the washing machine, bathtub, and kitchen sink in our homes, soap and detergents are used in a wide variety of industries.

Soap is used as a lubricant in making tiny wires for electrical appliances such as television sets and telephones. Soap is also used as a lubricant in making aluminum and tinfoil.

Soap is used to wash away polish in making jewelry. It holds rust preventers in suspension in antifreeze solutions for automobile engines. Soap softens leather before it is made into shoes and handbags. Soap helps to make the glossy, slick paper used for the pages of many magazines and books.

Detergents are used in some cosmetics. Chemical sprays for agriculture can contain detergents. The petroleum industry uses detergents to increase crude oil production, and chemical manufacturers use detergents when making synthetic rubber. Cotton, silk, and wool fabrics are washed in detergents to make them clean and soft before they are made into dresses, suits, and other articles of clothing.

▶PIONEER SOAPMAKING IN AMERICA

The natural materials required to make soaps are fats and chemicals called alkalis. Early settlers in North America made their own soap at home. They used fat drippings that they saved in large kettles and alkali made from wood ashes. This soap, which was harsh and smelly and had a tendency to irritate the skin, did only a passable job of cleaning.

After a while a few people got the idea of making soap in large quantities and selling it to busy pioneer housewives. These people collected waste fats from villagers and made soap outdoors in great iron kettles. They stirred the big batch of boiling soap with wooden paddles and poured it into wooden frames for hardening. Then they cut the soap into bars and peddled it from door to door. This was the beginning of the American soap industry.

▶SOAPMAKING TODAY

There have been many changes in soapmaking since colonial days. Better ways of making soap have been developed. Soaps now come in many shapes, colors, and sizes. Even the smell has been improved.

The kettle-boiling method of making soap is still used by a few soapmakers. But the "kettle" is actually a steel tank standing three stories high. The kettle has steam coils in the bottom for heating and is large enough to handle several hundred thousand pounds of material at one time.

The basic ingredients for soapmaking are the same as in the past—fats and an alkali. The fats are usually tallow (animal fats) and coconut oil. (Olive oil is used for castile soap.) The alkali is caustic soda (sodium hydroxide).

Most soapmakers now use a process in which soap is made continuously, rather than one batch at a time. The fats are broken down chemically, which eliminates some of the steps in the kettle-boiling method.

Soap can be made this way in about six hours from start to finish. (The kettle method requires about a week to make the same amount of soap.) This method also has the advantage of producing soap that is more uniform in quality.

▶HOW DETERGENTS ARE MADE

The first step in manufacturing a detergent is making the surfactant. Surfactants can be made from a wide variety of raw materials, including petroleum, animal fats, and vegetable oils. Different kinds of surfactants are used for different jobs. Some varieties go into cold water detergents. Other surfactants work well in hard water. Still others are chosen because they do not foam.

The chemical processes that are involved are quite complicated. For example, animal fat may be treated with a series of different chemicals—an alcohol, hydrogen gas, sulfuric acid, and an alkali—to make just one kind of surfactant used in modern household detergents. The surfactant must be mixed with

Surfactants are the substances in both detergents and soap that do the actual cleaning. One end of each surfactant molecule is attracted to oily dirt. The other end is attracted to water and thus suspends the dirt particles so that they can be rinsed away easily.

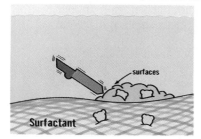

other chemicals that help it remove dirt more thoroughly and keep the dirt from settling back on the cleaned material. Enzymes are sometimes added to split the greasy dirt into small pieces. Special bleaches, coloring, fabric softeners, and suds stabilizers also may be added. These complicated reactions and the special equipment they call for make the manufacture of detergents a far more complex process than that of soap.

▶ ENVIRONMENTAL CONCERNS

Although soap is a good cleaning agent, it tends to leave deposits—such as a ring in the bathtub—when used in water with a lot of mineral salts. Therefore, after World War II many people began to use detergents instead of soap. Unfortunately, the increased use of large quantities of detergents created several environmental problems that neither the manufacturers nor the public had expected.

One problem involved the surfactants. Certain bacteria feed on the natural waste materials in sewage and break them down into harmless substances. Soap molecules are rapidly broken down by these bacteria. (For this reason soap is said to be **biodegradable.**) But the bacteria could not break down the molecules of the surfactants that were first used in detergents. Keeping all their original foaming ability, surfactants caused billowing masses of foam in sewage plants and in rivers and lakes. Foam was even found in some drinking water.

To help solve the foaming problem, detergent manufacturers developed new types of surfactants whose molecules would break down quickly after use. By 1965 the changeover to the new surfactants was complete.

Another problem involved detergent builders—the chemicals used in detergents to keep the dirt from settling back on the cleaned material. Phosphates (chemical compounds containing phosphorus and oxygen) are widely used in detergents because they are the most effective, inexpensive builders. Phosphates are not removed by bacteria and are not changed in the treatment of sewage.

When phosphate-rich sewage reaches lakes and rivers, it acts like a huge dose of fertilizer. Algae—tiny plantlike organisms—multiply at a fantastic rate, in time choking out other water life. When the huge masses of algae die and decay, they use up the oxygen in the water, so that fish cannot survive. Eventually,

The use of biodegradable surfactants and a reduction in the amount of phosphates used in detergents represent progress in solving detergent-related pollution problems.

the lake is filled with rotting vegetation. This process is called **eutrophication.** Synthetic phosphates pouring into lakes speed up the pace of eutrophication many times.

The eutrophication problem cannot be blamed on detergents alone. A great deal of phosphate from farm fertilizers gets into lakes and streams. Natural wastes in sewage also contain phosphates.

Eutrophication has been slowed down by reducing the amount of phosphates in detergents. However, no new builder has been discovered that can take the place of the phosphates and is environmentally safe. Today's detergents often contain a mixture of different builders in order to decrease phosphate levels. The U.S. Environmental Protection Agency is studying phosphate substitutes to determine which ones can be used without harm to people or to the environment.

Reviewed by SCOTT E. PATTISON
California State Polytechnic University
Author, *Fatty Acids and Their Industrial Applications*

DETROIT

Detroit, located in southeastern Michigan, is the largest and most populous city in the state. A sprawling industrial center covering some 140 square miles (363 square kilometers), Detroit is home to about 900,000 people. Its greater metropolitan area, with approximately 5.5 million residents, contains more than half of Michigan's total population. The city has long been associated with automobile manufacturing, earning it the nickname Motor City.

In 1701 the French official Sieur Antoine de la Mothe Cadillac founded a small fur-trading post, Fort Pontchartrain du Détroit, at the site of the present-day city; the French word *détroit* means "strait" and refers to the short Detroit River that links Lake St. Clair with Lake Erie. During the French and Indian War (1754–63), British forces took control of the Detroit region away from the French and held the area as late as 1796, even though it had been officially ceded to the United States in 1794. The British held Detroit again, briefly, during the War of 1812.

Detroit served as the capital (1805–37) of the Michigan Territory and then as the first state capital (1837–47). The city's location and access to the Great Lakes made it an important port and commercial center.

In 1903, Henry Ford organized the Ford Motor Company in Detroit. Soon afterward, Walter Chrysler and Ransom Olds also set up automobile plants in the area. The automobile industry provided jobs to thousands of European immigrants and African American migrants from the South. In the 1950's, however, many people started moving out of Detroit and into the suburbs. This migration out of the city accelerated in 1967, following a series of race riots, and Detroit fell into decline.

Detroit, nevertheless, remains an important center for manufacturing, health care, education, and shipping. A 1,500-acre (600-hectare) working salt mine lies beneath the city. The downtown area has been experiencing a cultural revival, and new residential housing and commercial buildings are being developed. The Civic Center stretches along the riverfront and includes the Cobo Conference/Exhibition Center, Cobo Arena, and the Joe Louis Arena. Nearby is the ultramodern Renaissance Center. Detroit's many schools include Wayne State University and the University of Detroit Mercy.

The city is home to several professional sports teams, including the Detroit Tigers of baseball's American League, the Detroit Red Wings of the National Hockey League, the Detroit Lions of the National Football League, the Detroit Pistons of the National Basketball Association, and the Detroit Shock of the Women's National Basketball Association.

Interesting places to visit include the Detroit Zoo, the Motown Historical Museum, the Detroit Institute of Arts, the Detroit Historical Museum, and the Charles H. Wright Museum of African American History. Belle Isle Park, located in the Detroit River, includes a public beach and the Dossin Great Lakes Museum. The Henry Ford Museum and Greenfield Village, located in nearby Dearborn, are also major attractions.

Reviewed by FRANCIS X. BLOUIN
The University of Michigan, Ann Arbor

Detroit's Renaissance Center includes a circular tower and high-rise office buildings. The focus of the city's downtown revival, it has become a riverfront landmark.

DEVELOPING COUNTRIES

A country's level of development reflects how much income it produces and how well its people live relative to other countries. Countries with high incomes and high standards of living are considered developed. Countries with lower incomes and standards of living are classified as developing. Of the 6.3 billion people alive today, 1 billion live in developed countries and 5.3 billion live in developing ones, mostly in Africa, Asia, Latin America, and the former Soviet republics.

Measuring Development. A basic measure of development is how much income a country produces per person each year. This shows the amount of goods and services each person in a country would be able to buy in a year if income were divided equally. An average high-income, or developed, country produces seven times more income per person each year than a developing one.

About 20 percent of the world's countries are in the developed category, including Japan and the Republic of Korea in Asia; Canada and the United States in North America; Australia in Oceania; and France, Germany, and the United Kingdom in Europe.

The remaining 80 percent of the world's countries are in the developing country category, but not all of them are at the same level. For example, middle-income developing countries produce three times more income per person each year than low-income developing ones. Examples of middle-income developing countries include Argentina, Brazil, and Mexico in Latin America; China and Malaysia in Asia; and South Africa. Low-income countries include most sub-Saharan African countries, Bangladesh in Asia, and the former Soviet republic of Uzbekistan.

Measures such as yearly income per person are good for distinguishing groups of countries, but they do not indicate the range of income within a country. For example, the average yearly income per person in a high-income country may be $30,000, but not every person in that country earns that much money. Some people earn more and some less. Some people are rich, some middle class, and others poor. Compared to the developed countries, however, many people in the developing countries are poor. Over 1 billion of them are extremely poor and live on about $1 day; 2.8 billion live on $2 a day or less.

Other important measures focus on the quality of people's lives, including **life expectancy**, or how long people can expect to live; the **literacy rate**, or how many can read and write; and **school enrollment**. People in a developed country tend to live longer, healthier lives; have a higher literacy rate; and acquire more knowledge through education than people living in a developing country. People in a developed country can expect to live 78 years compared with 65 years in a developing country. In sub-Saharan Africa, where some of the poorest people in the world live, life expectancy is 46 years.

Poverty in the developing world is especially difficult for children. According to the United Nations Children's Fund (UNICEF), half the children in developing countries are severely deprived of at least one of the essential goods and services they need to survive, grow, and develop. Some 640 million do not have adequate shelter; 400 million lack safe water; 270 million lack access to health care services; and 140 million, the majority of them girls, have never been to school.

Millennium Development Goals. Most developing countries use strategies designed to raise their income and the quality of life of their people. Development is also a cooperative effort. In 2000, 189 countries agreed to the UN Millennium Declaration, which sets goals for creating a better world. Many nations have adopted them as their own.

The first Millennium Development Goal (MDG) is to wipe out extreme poverty and hunger in the world. The remaining are to promote gender equality; improve health for mothers; achieve universal primary education; combat HIV/AIDS, malaria, and other diseases; help children survive; protect the environment for future use, which is known as **sustainable development**; and create a global partnership for development.

Many international organizations, such as the UN, work to help both the developed and developing countries meet the MDG's. In the UN, over 130 developing countries, known as the G-77, support the MDG's.

Reviewed by LAURA RANDALL
Professor Emerita, Hunter College, CUNY

See also FOREIGN AID; GLOBALIZATION; INDUSTRY.

DEW. See FOG AND SMOG.

DEWEY, GEORGE
(1837–1917)

Spanish-American War hero Commodore George Dewey commanded the U.S. squadron that defeated the Spanish in 1898 at the Battle of Manila Bay in the Philippines.

Born in Montpelier, Vermont, on December 26, 1837, Dewey graduated from the U.S. Naval Academy in 1858. In 1861, he became a lieutenant. During the Civil War (1861–65), Dewey served as executive officer of six ships and saw action at New Orleans, Port Hudson, Charleston, and Fort Fisher.

After the war, Dewey taught at the U.S. Naval Academy, commanded ships in the Pacific and waters around Europe, and held other positions before taking command of the Asiatic Fleet in Nagasaki, Japan, in 1898.

On the eve of the Spanish-American War (1898), when the USS *Maine* sank in the harbor of Havana, Cuba, Dewey was en route to Hong Kong in his flagship, the USS *Olympia*. Shortly after arriving, he received a telegram from Assistant Secretary of the Navy Theodore Roosevelt. Roosevelt wrote that if war should break out between the United States and Spain, Dewey was to make sure that the Spanish squadron did not leave the Philippine Islands, then a colony of Spain. Next, he was to attack the Spanish forces in those islands.

The United States declared war on Spain on April 25, 1898. Dewey sailed for Manila three days later and early on May 1, 1898, led his squadron into Manila Bay. Engaging the Spanish, Dewey told his flag captain, "You may fire when ready, Gridley," and in six hours the entire Spanish squadron was destroyed.

Dewey sailed home from Manila to a hero's welcome. For the next 16 years Dewey, now Admiral of the Navy, a rank Congress created for him, headed the Navy's General Board. It helped the U.S. Navy become one of the most powerful in the world. He died on January 16, 1917, and was buried in Arlington National Cemetery.

JAMES C. BRADFORD
Texas A&M University

DEWEY, JOHN (1859–1952)

John Dewey was an American philosopher, educator, and psychologist, whose theories had a great influence on U.S. education.

Dewey was born on October 20, 1859, in Burlington, Vermont. He graduated from the University of Vermont and earned his doctor of philosophy degree from Johns Hopkins University in Baltimore. From 1884 to 1894 he taught philosophy at the University of Michigan and the University of Minnesota.

From 1894 to 1904, Dewey was professor of philosophy, psychology, and education at the University of Chicago. He then taught philosophy at Columbia University until his retirement in 1930.

Dewey's main theory of education is often summed up as "learning by doing." He sought to replace the traditional teaching method of having students learn through memorization. He said that "education is a process of living" and that students must learn to adapt to a changing world. He believed that education should prepare children to take part in a democratic society, not teach them subjects they probably would never use.

Dewey believed that the value of an idea lay in the practical purposes to which it could be put. This philosophical theory is known as pragmatism. He stressed the importance of experience in learning and sought to combine his ideas of education and philosophy. In response to attacks on his ideas, Dewey said, "It is less important that we all believe alike than that we all alike inquire freely and put at the disposal of one another such glimpses as we may attain of the truth …."

Dewey spent many years lecturing and participating in public affairs. He died in New York City on June 1, 1952. His books include *The School and Society* (1899), *How We Think* (1910), and *Democracy and Education* (1916).

Reviewed by WILLIAM W. BRICKMAN
University of Pennsylvania

DIABETES

Diabetes mellitus, commonly known as diabetes, is a disease that disrupts the body's ability to use glucose, a sugar that is the body's main fuel. After we eat, glucose from digested food enters the bloodstream. Cells in the pancreas, an organ behind the stomach, sense the glucose and release the right amount of insulin, a hormone that moves glucose from blood into cells.

In diabetes, the pancreas does not make enough insulin, or the body's cells do not respond properly to the insulin that is produced. Blood glucose rises, and may cause extreme thirst, fatigue, frequent urination, weight loss, and blurred vision. In time, diabetes damages tissues and organs. The damage can be severe, leading to blindness, heart disease, and kidney failure. However, such damage may be avoided if diabetes is properly managed.

Several kinds of blood tests are used to diagnose diabetes. Some require people to fast or consume a premeasured glucose drink before blood is drawn. If the proper test shows a high glucose level, a second test on another day confirms the diagnosis.

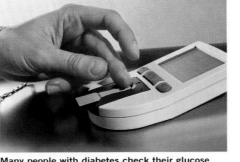

Many people with diabetes check their glucose levels using a small device called a glucometer. It runs a test with just one drop of blood.

Types of Diabetes. In the United States, about 18.2 million people have some form of diabetes. **Type 1 diabetes** may appear at any age but most often arises in children and young adults. In type 1 diabetes, the body's immune system mistakenly destroys the insulin-making cells of the pancreas. People with type 1 diabetes must have several insulin injections daily or an insulin pump to live. If not treated quickly, a person can fall into a coma, a state known as diabetic ketoacidosis.

Type 2 diabetes affects 17 million people in the United States, and it is by far the most common form of diabetes. It usually occurs in adults who are overweight and inactive and who have diabetes in their family. Some ethnic groups—African Americans, Hispanic Americans, and American Indians—are more likely to develop it. Older people are at highest risk, but doctors are now seeing type 2 diabetes in children who are overweight and have type 2 diabetes in their family.

When type 2 diabetes starts, the body cannot use insulin effectively, a condition called insulin resistance. In time, insulin production falls and glucose levels rise. Type 2 diabetes is treated with diet and exercise, oral medicines, and sometimes insulin.

Gestational diabetes develops during pregnancy. It occurs more often in minority groups and in women with a family history of diabetes. Women who have had gestational diabetes have a greater chance of developing type 2 diabetes later in life.

Managing Diabetes. Although there is no cure for diabetes, people with diabetes are living longer, healthier lives than they did 20 years ago. Timely action is important. For example, before developing type 2 diabetes, people often have **pre-diabetes**. In pre-diabetes, glucose is higher than normal but not as high as in diabetes. The condition, which affects about 41 million Americans, has no symptoms. However, if it is detected, a person with pre-diabetes may prevent or delay type 2 diabetes by losing weight and increasing physical activity.

If people do develop diabetes, they can often avoid its complications by following a healthy diet, exercising, checking their glucose levels, and taking medicines to control glucose, cholesterol, and blood pressure.

Hope for a Cure. Although the causes of diabetes are not fully understood, some genes make a person more likely to develop it. Scientists have not yet learned how to prevent type 1 diabetes, but they are studying how immune cells attack insulin-making cells. They hope to find ways to stop the attack and protect the cells.

JUDITH FRADKIN, M.D.
JOAN CHAMBERLAIN
National Institute of Diabetes and Digestive and
Kidney Diseases, National Institutes of Health

DIAGNOSTIC IMAGING. See IMAGING, DIAGNOSTIC.

DIAMONDS

Diamonds, the hardest of all substances, are also among the most valuable. Some are used for jewelry, especially engagement rings, but most are used in industry.

▶ PROPERTIES

Diamonds are minerals that consist largely of crystallized carbon. They can be natural or synthetic. Their hardness enables them to scratch every other mineral and to resist being scratched. Diamonds can take a steady, hard pressure without cracking or being worn down, but they can be easily shattered by a sharp blow.

Diamonds are also good conductors of heat. The heat does not melt them or distort their shape. Because diamonds do not react with other substances at ordinary temperatures, they do not corrode or tarnish. But in the absence of oxygen, temperatures over 1830°F (1000°C) will turn diamonds into graphite, a soft black form of carbon. If dia-monds are heated in the open air, they will vaporize at 1652°F (900°C).

Diamonds come in many different sizes and shapes. The weight of a diamond is expressed in carats. One carat equals about $\frac{1}{142}$ ounce (200 milligrams).

Rough natural diamonds look like glassy pebbles. Some have light, clear colors and contain almost no impurities. These can be made into gems. Other diamonds contain many impurities and are brown, yellow, or gray. These stones have many industrial uses.

Gem diamonds are cut and polished to reveal their brilliance. The gem's shape depends on the shape of the original crystal. In a properly cut diamond, light that enters is reflected back through the top. This light is often colored because diamonds break up white light into the colors of the spectrum.

The quality and price of gem diamonds depend on four factors—clarity, color, cutting, and size. The best diamonds contain the fewest flaws, such as cracks and dark areas. With the exception of some rare colors, the most valuable stones are transparent and colorless. The more brilliant the cut, the greater the value. Finally, the heavier the stone, the greater its value.

▶ FORMATION AND OCCURRENCE

Natural diamonds, formed below the Earth's crust by tremendous heat and pressure, are brought to the Earth's surface via magma (molten rock) during volcanic eruptions. They are mined by digging out the soil that forms after the magma has hardened and broken down—usually in the necks of extinct volcanoes. Diamonds are also found in deposits of volcanic soil in streambeds. Most diamond mines close down after the soft layer at the top of the volcanoes has been removed. Because of the expense, only areas that are very rich in diamonds are mined more deeply.

▶ WHERE DIAMONDS ARE FOUND

Historians believe that the earliest diamonds came from the Hyderabad region of central India. In the 1720's, diamond deposits were found in Brazil by miners looking for gold in the Jequitinhonha River. More than a century later, in 1867, children playing along the banks of the Orange River at Hopetown found the first South African diamond. The stone weighed about 22 carats. In 1869 a stone almost four times larger was uncovered in a stream east of Hopetown. This led to a diamond rush in South Africa and the discovery of the famous Kimberley fields.

Today most of the world's natural diamonds come from South Africa and nearby Botswana. Many other countries also contain deposits and there are huge diamond fields in Russia, Australia, and Canada. There are even diamonds in the sea. Dredges that work like vacuum sweepers suck the diamond-bearing gravel from the ocean floor off the southwest coast of Africa.

▶ DIAMOND MINING AND PRODUCTION

During the mining process, the material removed from the mine includes dirt, rock, and

A gem diamond must be cut and polished to reveal its brilliance. It is shaped according to the shape of the original crystal.

gravel. This is crushed and mixed with water, then rocked back and forth on a sloping steel table that is thickly covered with grease. As the table rocks, the gravel slides off and the diamonds stick to the grease. Skilled sorters can then pick out the diamonds.

The sorters put the leftover gravel through many tests to make sure that even very small diamonds are recovered. The diamonds are then cleaned before being sent to diamond centers. At the diamond centers, they are graded as either gem or industrial diamonds.

Synthetic diamonds are manufactured in a laboratory. These are created by duplicating the pressure and temperature below the Earth's crust where diamonds were originally formed. The process also involves adding a catalyst to carbon to force a chemical reaction and placing the mixture in a pressure cell. Industrial diamonds were first manufactured by companies in Sweden and the United States in the mid-1950's. The first synthetic gem diamonds were made in 1970.

Diamonds are often mined from soil deposits in the necks of extinct volcanoes. Those with light, clear colors and no impurities (*below right*) can be made into gems. The rest, which are usually more opaque and brown, yellow, or gray (*right*), are used in industry.

USES OF INDUSTRIAL DIAMONDS

Approximately 80 percent of mined diamonds are used in industry. These are ideal for mechanical parts that must resist wear and undergo sudden temperature changes and that must not change size, create friction, or rust or tarnish.

Diamond bearings are used in instruments for laboratories. They are so hard and smooth that rubbing them together or against another material creates almost no friction. Some machines turn at 90,000 revolutions a minute. Even at this high speed, no lubrication is needed to keep the bearings from wearing away.

Diamond cutting tools cut much faster and more accurately than other tools. A diamond blade used in laboratories can slice metal (except steel) thinner than a human hair. Some saws have diamond-studded edges that can cut hard materials like rocks, concrete, and some metals. The diamonds act as saw teeth.

Diamonds are also used to help manufacture fine wire, such as the wire that is used in electric toasters. The wire is pulled through holes in a special tool called a die. Many small diamonds, called diamond dust, are used to polish the holes so that the wire can slide through easily.

Diamonds so small that they can be seen only with a magnifying glass are used to polish hard metal. Thousands of these diamonds are used together to wear down uneven parts of the surface. To the human eye the metal will look so brilliant that a reflection can be seen. Often these small diamonds are mixed with a paste. The paste keeps the diamonds separated. It also keeps the diamonds wet and makes them easier to use. The glass in telescopes is shaped with diamond dust.

Reviewed by JOHN KOIVULA
Gemological Institute of America

See also GEMS; GRINDING AND POLISHING; JEWELRY; MINERALS; ORES; ROCKS.

DIANA, PRINCESS OF WALES (1961–1997)

A dazzling appearance and sparkling personality made Diana, Princess of Wales, an international celebrity. Married to the heir to the British throne, she became a humanitarian and defender of oppressed people.

Diana Spencer was born in Sandringham, England, on July 1, 1961, into the nobility. Her father became Earl Spencer in 1975. After attending boarding schools in England and Switzerland, Diana worked briefly as a kindergarten teacher. Then came her storybook courtship with Charles, Prince of Wales, and their marriage in 1981. Millions worldwide viewed the televised wedding ceremony.

Diana, Princess of Wales, shown here with victims of land mines, promoted many humanitarian causes.

Diana gave birth to Prince William (1982) and Prince Henry (Harry) (1984). But the marriage was not a happy one. After years of conflict, Charles and Diana were separated in 1992 and divorced in 1996. The royal couple's stormy breakup embarrassed the British royal family. It resulted in enormous publicity, during which Diana received much more sympathy than Charles.

Followed by the media, Diana traveled widely to promote many humane causes. Her popularity ensured that huge sums of money were raised for her charities, which included the plight of homeless people, sick children, and AIDS victims, and the movement to outlaw land mines.

"Princess Di," as everyone called her, died in a car accident in Paris on August 31, 1997. Diana's funeral produced a remarkable outpouring of grief—over the death of a woman born to privilege but possessing a unique human touch.

DON M. CREGIER
University of Prince Edward Island

DIARIES AND JOURNALS

The words "diary" and "journal" refer to the same thing: a written record of a person's experiences and observations as they occur in his or her life. People keep diaries and journals to remember things they did, people they knew, and places they visited; to learn about themselves or explore personal problems; or just to express themselves in an enjoyable and creative way.

Most diaries are of interest only to their owners, who consider them very personal and so keep them private. But throughout history, some diaries have been of such great general interest that they are published for all to read. They may contain valuable historical details, reveal the innermost thoughts of a famous person, or record great achievements.

▶ HISTORY OF DIARIES AND JOURNALS

The earliest existing diaries were written in Japan during the 900's by ladies of the royal court, who wrote poetic accounts of their lives. Among the early colonists of North America, the Puritans kept diaries to develop self-discipline and record their history, while the Quakers used their diaries for spiritual guidance. These early journals have important historical value because they tell us what daily life was like in earlier times.

The diary most famous for its historical descriptions is one that was never meant to be read by others. The British naval administrator Samuel Pepys lived in London during the 1600's, and he was interested in everything about the city—its politics, music, theater, gossip, parties, and pubs. In his diary (which he wrote in a special code), he described in vivid details what he saw,

Samuel Pepys

heard, smelled, tasted, and touched. His diaries provide first-hand accounts of what it was like to witness the great plague of 1665–66 and the fire that nearly destroyed the city in 1666.

The French author Aurore Dupin, better known by her pen name George Sand, used her diary to help her deal with the frustration of trying to be a novelist at a time—the 1800's—when that career was not thought proper for women. She was the first diarist to write imaginary dialogues, a technique used by many diarists today. In her journal she wrote conversations between the part of her that had to act like a male writer to the outside world and the part of her that was private and feminine. She found that writing in a diary helped her mature and come to terms with her situation.

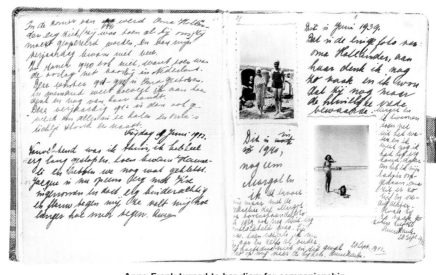

Anne Frank turned to her diary for companionship, recording her thoughts and feelings as she and her family hid from the Nazis during World War II.

One of the most famous diaries was written by the young Jewish girl Anne Frank while she and her family hid from the Nazis during World War II (1939–45). Unable to go to school or see her friends, the young girl turned to her diary for companionship. In her first entry she wrote "I hope I shall be able to confide in you completely, as I have never been able to do in anyone before, and I hope that you will be a great support and comfort to me." Her diary is remarkable not only for

How to Start Your Own Journal

After you have read some published journals, you may want to start one of your own. School-supply stores, bookshops, and stationers sell blank journals in many sizes and prices. Ask for a lined one. You can also write your journal on a computer using a word-processing program.

Although you do not have to write in your journal every day, doing so is a good way to get into the writing habit. Start small. Record your daily activities or describe your class at school or a sporting event. If you go on a trip, write down where you went and what you saw. Draw pictures of your friends. Write about some of the things that worry you, and about things that make you happy. You can do all this in just a few paragraphs in each entry.

Later, you can begin to write at greater length about important experiences and your reactions to them. For example, you might try to describe how you felt when a family pet died. You might take a closer look at your family and how it has changed over a period of time. Or you might describe your feelings about moving to a new neighborhood.

The best audience to write to in your diary is yourself, perhaps to your older self who will one day read the diary. The privacy of a diary will help you develop a natural writing style. Honesty in your observations and your writing is key.

---

its historic account of the Nazis' persecution of the Jews but also for the clarity and warmth with which she expressed her thoughts and feelings. For more information, see the article on Anne Frank in Volume F.

Diary writing in the later 1900's was influenced by the realization that keeping a journal can help people heal and guide themselves. The Swiss psychologist Carl Jung recorded his dreams in a journal that he used to help him develop his theories about the unconscious mind. The American author Anaïs Nin began to write a diary at the age of 11 to help her through a difficult childhood. She used a free and expressive style when writing in her diary, an activity she said was "a process of nature, not of the ideal. The diary is a place where you don't have to worry about being perfect." But she later edited her diaries for publication.

Today diarists have found a new outlet in the form of Web logs, or blogs, on the Internet. Unlike other kinds of diaries, blogs are interactive. They offer readers the opportunity to make comments or ask questions. They can also include photographs, videos, and sound. Blogs can serve as a way for people with very different backgrounds and living in different parts of the world to learn about each other.

Today newspapers, radio, television, and the Internet provide highly accurate records of historical events. But people will continue to turn to their diaries to confide their deepest thoughts, dreams, and wishes.

TRISTINE RAINER
Author, *The New Diary*

DIATOMS. See PLANKTON.

I'm a recent graduate of... well, a university in Dallas that likes horses and the colors red and blue... with a degree in political science. I presently work for the Dallas County Democratic Party, but *nothing* I say here (or anywhere else, for that matter) should ever be taken as the official opinion of the party office. I'm also the Vice President of Communications for the Dallas County Young Democrats.

While I'll try not to get too underfoot around here, I will be posting from time to time about things going on in the Dallas area. We've got some great Democratic candidates coming together for the 2006 election cycle. Next year is going to be an exciting time to be a progressive in North Texas!

I'd like to thank Karl-Thomas, Byron and the others here at BOR for giving me the opportunity to post here.

Posted at 06:04 AM to About Burnt Orange | Permalink

| Comments (5) | TrackBack (0)

TEXAS   MEDIA

abilene
abilene reporter news

alpine
alpine avalanche

amarillo
amarillo globe news

austin
austin american statesman
austin chronicle
daily texan online
keye news (cbs)
kut (npr)
kvue news (abc)
kxan news (nbc)
news 8 austin

beaumont
beaumont enterprise

brownsville
brownsville herald

Web logs, or blogs, are interactive diaries. Readers can post, or submit, comments or questions as they communicate with people from all over the world.

DICKENS, CHARLES
(1812–1870)

Charles Dickens is regarded as one of the greatest English writers of all time. His novels, which often combined autobiography with social commentary, exposed the harsh realities suffered by the poor and underprivileged of his day.

Dickens was born on February 7, 1812, in a modest little house on the outskirts of Portsmouth, a town on the south coast of England. His father was an underpaid civilian clerk to the navy, and the family was always poor. Charles was taken out of school when he was 11, since there was no money to pay the fees. In 1824, his father went to prison for debt; about the same time, the 12-year-old boy was sent to work in a factory that made blacking for boots. Working long, hard days, he earned only enough for his food and lodging. The hardships of his childhood are described in his novel *David Copperfield* (1849–50), whose early chapters are largely Dickens' own story.

At 13, Dickens went for two years to the school of the cruel Mr. Jones, known as the Slasher because he gave the boys more beatings than lessons. After more schooling and a job as a clerk, Dickens worked as a newspaper reporter and discovered that he was born to write.

His first novel, *The Pickwick Papers* (1836–37), told of the hilarious adventures of a group of comic would-be sportsmen. Like most of his novels, it was first published in monthly installments. It was a huge and immediate success, and readers waited eagerly for each new installment. Each of his following books was also popular, and Queen Victoria herself called him to her palace to tell him how much she loved his stories.

In 1836, Dickens married Catherine Hogarth, and they had ten children. Although Dickens was always busy, working for hours every day on novels, short stories, and magazine articles, he was a wonderful father when the children were small. Birthdays were grand celebrations, and Christmas in the Dickens house in London was a riot of feasting and laughter and comic plays that he wrote for the children and their friends to perform.

Despite the successes and comfortable home life of his adulthood, Dickens never forgot the hardships he experienced as a child; he remained keenly aware of the misery, sickness, and neglect of the poor. He sought to right such wrongs not only by sponsoring charitable organizations but also through his novels, many of which satirized the selfishness, greed, and materialism of Victorian society.

In *Oliver Twist* (1837–39), he wrote of the wretched inmates of the poorhouse. The "ragged schools" in the north of England, where unwanted boys were beaten into idiocy or starved to death, were exposed in his book *Nicholas Nickleby* (1838–39) and abolished as a result. He wrote of working conditions that were more like slavery, conditions like those endured by Tiny Tim's father, Bob Cratchit, in *A Christmas Carol* (1843). *Bleak House* (1852–53), considered the first detective novel in the English language and perhaps Dickens' greatest work, satirized the injustices and delays of British legal procedure. And in *Little Dorrit* (1855–57), he exposed the corruption and inefficiency of government bureaucracy.

Dickens' books were also very popular in the United States. In 1842 he visited Boston and New York and got a great reception. He was the friend and guest of the authors Henry Wadsworth Longfellow, Washington Irving, and Edgar Allan Poe. The great orator Daniel Webster declared that Dickens had done more to improve the life of the English poor than all the statesmen who had ever been in the British government.

However, Dickens' popularity with Americans dimmed when he began to lash out at the things that roused him: slavery, which still flourished in the South; the pirating of his books by publishers who paid him no money (the laws of copyright came later, largely due to Dickens' efforts); and the appallingly crude manners and primitive conditions he found in the still-young American West.

What he loved about the best of America—and what he despised about the worst of it—he put into a travel book called *American Notes* (1842). It unleashed a storm of protest, and so at first did his next novel, *Martin Chuzzlewit* (1843–44), part of which was set in what were then the foul, disease-ridden swamps of frontier America.

Dickens' marriage, always stormy, ended in 1858 after 22 years. In the period that followed, he wrote four more novels. They included *A Tale of Two Cities* (1859), a historical novel of the French Revolution, and *Great Expectations* (1860–61), about the life and experiences of a young orphan named Pip. Dickens also edited and contributed to newspapers and magazines and traveled widely.

In 1867, though tired and already ill with a heart condition, he was persuaded to revisit America and make a tour, giving public readings from his works. The tour was a huge success, and people traveled long distances to see and hear him. Among those who attended a reading in New York was Samuel Clemens (Mark Twain).

Dickens returned to England in 1868 and continued to write and give public readings. However, he was still in poor health and he told his friends that he was "nearly used up." He grew weaker and weaker until, on June 9, 1870, he died of a stroke at his home at Gad's Hill, in Kent. His 15th novel, *The Mystery of Edwin Drood*, was left unfinished.

MONICA DICKENS
Reviewed by JOHN O. JORDAN
Editor, *The Cambridge Companion to Charles Dickens*

Excerpts from two of Charles Dickens' best-known novels, *David Copperfield* and *Oliver Twist*, follow.

DAVID COPPERFIELD

David Copperfield's stepfather was a cruel and stingy man. One day, David bit him on the hand. In punishment his stepfather sent him away to Salem House, a school near London run by a brutal headmaster named Creakle, "a stout man with a bull-neck, a wooden leg, over-hanging temples, and his hair cut close all round his head."

I gazed upon the schoolroom into which he took me, as the most forlorn and desolate place I had ever seen. I see it now. A long room, with three rows of desks, and six of forms, and bristling all round with pegs for hats and slates. Scraps of old copy-books and exercises litter the dirty floor. Some silkworms' houses, made of the same materials, are scattered over the desks. Two miserable little white mice, left behind by their owner, are running up and down in a fusty castle made of pasteboard and wire, looking in all the corners with their red eyes for anything to eat. A bird, in a cage very little bigger than himself, makes a mournful rattle now and then in hopping on his perch, two inches high, or dropping from it; but neither sings nor chirps. There is a strange unwholesome smell upon the room, like mildewed corduroys, sweet apples wanting air, and rotten books. There could not well be more ink splashed about it, if it had been roofless from its first construction, and the skies had rained, snowed, hailed, and blown ink through the varying seasons of the year.

Mr. Mell having left me while he took his irreparable boots upstairs, I went softly to the upper end of the room, observing all this as I crept along. Suddenly I came upon a pasteboard placard, beautifully written, which was lying on the desk, and bore these words. "*Take care of him. He bites.*"

I got upon the desk immediately, apprehensive of at least a great dog underneath. But, though I looked all round with anxious eyes, I could see nothing of him. I was still engaged in peering about, when Mr. Mell came back, and asked me what I did up there?

"I beg your pardon, sir," says I, "if you please, I'm looking for the dog."

"Dog?" says he. "What dog?"

"Isn't it a dog, sir?"

"Isn't what a dog?"

"That's to be taken care of, sir; that bites?"

"No, Copperfield," says he, gravely, "that's not a dog. That's a boy. My instructions are, Copperfield, to put this placard on your back. I am sorry to make such a beginning with you, but I must do it."

With that he took me down, and tied the placard, which was neatly constructed for the purpose, on my shoulders like a knapsack; and wherever I went, afterwards, I had the consolation of carrying it.

What I suffered from that placard nobody can imagine. Whether it was possible for people to see me or not, I always fancied that somebody was reading it. It was no relief to turn round and find nobody; for wherever my back was, there I imagined somebody always to be. That cruel man with the wooden leg aggravated my sufferings. He was in authority, and if he ever saw me leaning against a tree, or a wall, or the house, he roared out from his lodge-door in a stupendous voice, "Hallo, you sir! You Copperfield! Show that badge conspicuous, or I'll report you!" The playground was a bare gravelled yard, open to all the back of the house and the offices; and I knew that the servants read it, and the butcher read it, and the baker read it; that everybody, in a word, who came backwards and forwards to the house, of a morning when I was ordered to walk there, read that I was to be taken care of, for I bit. I recollect that I positively began to have a dread of myself, as a kind of wild boy who did bite.

OLIVER TWIST

Oliver Twist, born in a poorhouse, was apprenticed to a casket maker. He was so unhappy that he ran away to London and fell in with a gang of young thieves led by the evil Fagin, who taught the reluctant Oliver the art of picking pockets. One day Oliver and two of Fagin's gang, the Artful Dodger and Charley Bates, robbed an old gentleman.

George Cruikshank's illustration from *Oliver Twist* shows Oliver watching in alarm as the Artful Dodger and Charlie Bates pick Mr. Brownlow's pocket.

But the old gentleman was not the only person who raised the hue-and-cry. The Dodger and Master Bates, unwilling to attract public attention by running down the open street, had merely retired into the very first doorway round the corner. They no sooner heard the cry, and saw Oliver running, than, guessing exactly how the matter stood, they issued forth with great promptitude; and, shouting "Stop thief!" too, joined in the pursuit like good citizens.

Although Oliver had been brought up by philosophers, he was not theoretically acquainted with the beautiful axiom that self-preservation is the first law of nature. If he had been, perhaps he would have been prepared for this. Not being prepared, however, it alarmed him the more; so away he went like the wind, with the old gentleman and the two boys roaring and shouting behind him.

"Stop thief! Stop thief!" There is a magic in the sound. The tradesman leaves his counter, and the car-man his waggon; the butcher throws down his tray; the baker his basket; the milkman his pail; the errand-boy his parcels; the school-boy his marbles; the paviour his pickaxe; the child his battledore. Away they run, pell-mell, helter-skelter, slap-dash: tearing, yelling, screaming, knocking down the passengers as they turn the corners, rousing up the dogs, and astonishing the fowls: and streets, squares, and courts, re-echo with the sound.

"Stop thief! Stop thief!" The cry is taken up by a hundred voices, and the crowd accumulate at every turning. Away they fly, splashing through the mud, and rattling along the pavements: up go the windows, out run the people, onward bear the mob, a whole audience desert Punch in the very thickest of the plot, and, joining the rushing throng, swell the shout, and lend fresh vigour to the cry, "Stop thief!" There is a passion for hunting something deeply implanted in the human breast. One wretched breathless child, panting with exhaustion; terror in his looks; agony in his eyes; large drops of perspiration streaming down his face; strains every nerve to make head upon his pursuers; and as they follow on his track, and gain upon him every instant, they hail his decreasing strength with still louder shout, and whoop and scream with joy. "Stop thief!" Ay, stop him for God's sake, were it only in mercy!

Stopped at last! A clever blow. He is down upon the pavement; and the crowd eagerly gather round him; each new comer, jostling and struggling with the others to catch a glimpse. "Stand aside!" "Give him a little air!" "Nonsense! he don't deserve it." "Where's the gentleman?" "Here he is, coming down the street." "Make room there for the gentleman!" "Is this the boy, sir!" "Yes."

Oliver lay, covered with mud and dust, and bleeding from the mouth, looking wildly round upon the heap of faces that surrounded him, when the old gentleman was officiously dragged and pushed into the circle by the foremost of the pursuers.

"Yes," said the gentleman, "I am afraid it is the boy."

"Afraid!" murmured the crowd. "That's a good'un!"

"Poor fellow!" said the gentleman, "he has hurt himself."

"I did that, sir," said a great lubberly fellow, stepping forward; "and preciously I cut my knuckle agin' his mouth. I stopped him, sir."

The fellow touched his hat with a grin, expecting something for his pains; but, the old gentleman, eyeing him with an expression of dislike, looked anxiously round, as if he contemplated running away himself: which it is very possible he might have attempted to do, and thus have afforded another chase, had not a police officer (who is generally the last person to arrive in such cases) at that moment made his way through the crowd, and seized Oliver by the collar.

"Come, get up," said the man, roughly.

"It wasn't me indeed, sir. Indeed, indeed, it was two other boys," said Oliver, clasping his hands passionately, and looking round. "They are here somewhere."

"Oh no, they ain't," said the officer. He meant this to be ironical, but it was true besides; for the Dodger and Charley Bates had filed off down the first convenient court they came to. "Come, get up!"

"Don't hurt him," said the old gentleman, compassionately.

"Oh no, I won't hurt him," replied the officer, tearing his jacket half off his back, in proof thereof. "Come, I know you; it won't do. Will you stand upon your legs, you young devil?"

Oliver, who could hardly stand, made a shift to raise himself on his feet, and was at once lugged along the streets by the jacket-collar, at a rapid pace. The gentleman walked on with them by the officer's side; and as many of the crowd as could achieve the feat, got a little ahead, and stared back at Oliver from time to time. The boys shouted in triumph; and on they went.

DICKINSON, EMILY (1830–1886)

Emily Dickinson's poetry was virtually unknown during her lifetime. It was not until after her death that the unique style and heartfelt words of her verse were revealed, placing her alongside Walt Whitman as one of America's greatest poets.

Emily Elizabeth Dickinson was born in Amherst, Massachusetts, on December 10, 1830. Her father, Edward, was a lawyer, a church leader, and one of the wealthiest men in the village. Her mother, also named Emily, was timid and often ill. There were two other children in the Dickinson family besides Emily—Austin, 18 months older than Emily, and Lavinia, 2 years younger.

The Dickinson children attended an academy in Amherst, where Emily discovered the modern authors of her time, such as Henry Wadsworth Longfellow and Sir Walter Scott. After reading Scott's *Kenilworth*, she said, "This then is a book! And there are more of them!" English was her best subject in school, and her friends admired her humorous contributions to the school paper. One of her teachers even told her that perhaps someday she would become a poet.

When she was almost 17, Dickinson went to Mount Holyoke Female Seminary, the future Mount Holyoke College. However, she found that she could not fully embrace the religious instruction offered there and she re-

turned home after a year. She would later explore her faith in her poems.

Dickinson's earliest existing poem was written in 1852. Her most productive period of writing occurred between 1858 and 1862, when she wrote more than 300 poems. The reason for her great output during those years, for the abrupt decrease in her writing afterward, and for her subsequent decision to isolate herself from almost everybody has been the subject of much speculation. One theory was that she and a friend of her brother's fell in love, but her father forbade their marriage because the boy was poor. Whatever the reason, a profound change came over Dickinson in the latter part of her life. She avoided social gatherings, including church, and began wearing white clothes all the time. Despite her solitude, she continued to write poetry in relative secrecy, and she remained devoted to her family and a group of friends with whom she frequently exchanged letters.

One of the few people who knew of her poetry was abolitionist and author Thomas Wentworth Higginson, whose work she had read and admired. In 1862, Dickinson sent him four of her poems and asked him if her verse was "alive" and "breathed." Higginson found her poems to be new and original, different from anything he had ever read. He did not like them, but he offered her advice. Despite his advice, Dickinson continued to write in her own special style while working hard at her craft. She studied words, with her dictionary as her "only companion." Everything around her—the wooded hills, her flower garden, a train coming down the track, even a little snake—became a part of her poetry.

Instead of copying old forms, Dickinson discovered new ways of writing poetry. She ignored literary conventions (such as sentence structure, grammar, punctuation, and poetic form) and used a minimum of words to best capture her feelings or reveal the truth of the experience she was describing. Her poems, which varied from joyful to somber, are clever and passionate explorations of the self, faith, death, and the fleeting joys of life.

Dickinson died in Amherst on May 15, 1886. Soon after, her sister discovered more than 1,000 poems Dickinson had written and hidden in a bureau in her room. The first volume of her poetry was published in 1890, although much of her unconventional style was edited to appeal to the readers of the time. It was not until 1955, when her poems were finally published in the same form she had written them, that the world was introduced to the full talent of Emily Dickinson.

LOUISE HALL THARP
Author, *Tory Hole*;
The Peabody Sisters of Salem

These two poems by Emily Dickinson demonstrate the unconventional grammar and spare use of words that are typical of her work.

A Bird Came Down the Walk

A bird came down the walk:
He did not know I saw;
He bit an angle-worm in halves
And ate the fellow, raw.

And then he drank a dew
From a convenient grass,
And then hopped sidewise to the wall
To let a beetle pass.

He glanced with rapid eyes
That hurried all abroad,—
They looked like frightened beads,
  I thought
He stirred his velvet head

Like one in danger; cautious,
I offered him a crumb,
And he unrolled his feathers
And rowed him softer home

Than oars divide the ocean,
Too silver for a seam,
Or butterflies, off banks of noon,
Leap, plashless, as they swim.

I'll Tell You How the Sun Rose

I'll tell you how the sun rose,—
A ribbon at a time.
The steeples swam in amethyst,
The news like squirrels ran.

The hills untied their bonnets,
The bobolinks begun.
Then I said softly to myself,
"That must have been the sun!"

But how he set, I know not.
There seemed a purple stile
Which little yellow boys and girls
Were climbing all the while

Till when they reached the other side,
A dominie in gray
Put gently up the evening bars,
And led the flock away.

DICTIONARIES

A dictionary is a book in which the words of a language are arranged in alphabetical order. Dictionaries give many different kinds of information in many different ways.

People use a general-purpose dictionary mainly to find out how a word is spelled or what it means. But a dictionary also shows you how to divide a word into syllables and how to pronounce it. It provides histories of words; lists all of their different senses, or meanings; and indicates whether there is more than one way to spell them. A dictionary will also tell you whether the word can be used as more than one part of speech. For example, the word "walk" can be used as a verb or a noun. Some dictionaries give examples of the correct use of a word in sentences. A dictionary will also tell you the spelling of different forms of words, such as plural forms.

Some dictionaries give information about famous people and places. They may also include other proper nouns, abbreviations, illustrations, maps, diagrams, and special charts and tables.

Many people talk about "the dictionary" as if there were only one. There are in fact many different dictionaries of the English language—from small pocket dictionaries to very large ones that try to record the entire language. Some dictionaries deal only with specific subjects, such as law, music, geography, or science. There are bilingual, or two-language, dictionaries, such as Spanish-English and French-English dictionaries. These dictionaries often have two parts. Each part translates the words of one language into the other language.

▶ **HISTORY OF ENGLISH DICTIONARIES**

Dictionaries of the English language began to appear during the 1600's. The first great English dictionary was written by the English author Samuel Johnson and was published in 1755. It contained more than 40,000 words. Modern dictionaries contain more words, partly because there are more words in the language now. Many of the new words evolved from new technologies. Indeed, it has been estimated that 25 to 30 percent of the entries in current college-level dictionaries are scientific or technical. The basic organization of dictionaries, however, has remained the same.

The American Noah Webster believed that the new United States needed its own schoolbooks and dictionaries that were different from their British counterparts. In 1828, he published *An American Dictionary of the English Language*. It defined about 70,000 words. Joseph Worcester, another American **lexicographer** (dictionary author or editor), published rival dictionaries during the 1800's, but Webster's dictionaries remained the more popular.

A children's dictionary may provide colorful illustrations along with other information about words.

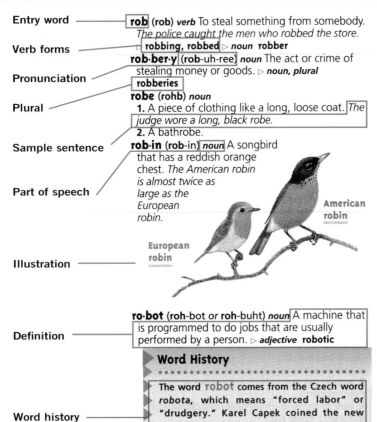

Entry word	**rob** (rob) *verb* To steal something from somebody. *The police caught the men who robbed the store.*
Verb forms	▷ **robbing, robbed** ▷ *noun* **robber**
	rob·ber·y (rob-uh-ree) *noun* The act or crime of stealing money or goods. ▷ *noun, plural*
Pronunciation	**robberies**
	robe (rohb) *noun*
Plural	**1.** A piece of clothing like a long, loose coat. *The judge wore a long, black robe.*
	2. A bathrobe.
Sample sentence	**rob·in** (rob-in) *noun* A songbird that has a reddish orange chest. *The American robin is almost twice as large as the European robin.*
Part of speech	
Illustration	European robin / American robin
Definition	**ro·bot** (roh-bot *or* roh-buht) *noun* A machine that is programmed to do jobs that are usually performed by a person. ▷ *adjective* **robotic**

Word History

The word robot comes from the Czech word *robota*, which means "forced labor" or "drudgery." Karel Capek coined the new meaning in his 1921 play called *R.U.R.* or *Rossum's Universal Robots.*

Word history

Beginning in 1857, a group of scholars in England began to put together the most thorough dictionary of the English language. Later named the *Oxford English Dictionary*, its first volume was published in 1884. By 1928, the dictionary consisted of twelve thick volumes. The *O.E.D.*, as it is called, provides the **etymology** (history and origin) of words, including numerous examples of their use in writing, and contains some 500,000 entries. Several supplements to this famous dictionary have since appeared.

Many American dictionaries have been produced since the time of Webster and Worcester. *The Century Dictionary and Cyclopedia*, which was published in 1889–1899, remained a landmark in the United States among dictionaries that give the etymology of words.

Although Noah Webster died in 1843, his name lives on in the titles of many other dictionaries published in the United States. In 1909 the first of the international dictionaries of English, containing words used in all the English-speaking countries, was published by the firm now known as Merriam-Webster, Inc. In 1961 the same company issued *Webster's Third New International Dictionary*, which contains more than 450,000 words.

Most adults use a "college" dictionary, such as *The American Heritage College Dictionary*, *Random House Webster's College Dictionary*, *Webster's New World College Dictionary*, and *Merriam-Webster's Collegiate Dictionary*. The spelling and division of words used in *The New Book of Knowledge* are based on *Merriam-Webster's Collegiate Dictionary*.

▶ **TECHNOLOGY AND THE DICTIONARY**

Computers have revolutionized the way dictionaries are compiled and used. Lexicog-

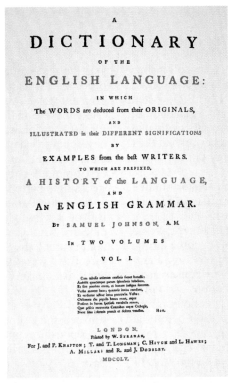

A
DICTIONARY
OF THE
ENGLISH LANGUAGE:
IN WHICH
The WORDS are deduced from their ORIGINALS,
AND
ILLUSTRATED in their DIFFERENT SIGNIFICATIONS
BY
EXAMPLES from the beſt WRITERS.
TO WHICH ARE PREFIXED,
A HISTORY of the LANGUAGE,
AND
AN ENGLISH GRAMMAR.
By SAMUEL JOHNSON, A.M.
IN TWO VOLUMES
VOL. I.

LONDON.
Printed by W. STRAHAN,
For J. and P. KNAPTON; T. and T. LONGMAN; C. HITCH and L. HAWES;
A. MILLAR; and R. and J. DODSLEY.
MDCCLV.

The first major English dictionary was Samuel Johnson's *A Dictionary of the English Language*, published in 1755.

raphers use computer programs to ensure that all words included in definitions are also defined in the dictionary. They also use computer programs to count the number of times words appear in various publications, which helps them decide what words to include in dictionaries. Lexicographers have traditionally used examples from these sources to show the meanings of words, whether they are new to the language or already known. Computers have made it easier to use dictionaries as well. Many dictionaries are available online and on CD-ROM. Those that come with word-processing programs can automatically correct spelling, suggest synonyms, and even spot grammatical errors. Some Web sites also let users look up words in many different online dictionaries at once.

▶ **CHILDREN'S DICTIONARIES**

Until the 1930's, any adult dictionary edited to contain fewer words was thought suitable for children. About that time, Dr. Edward L. Thorndike, a psychologist, began scientifically studying the words children used most often and the words children would need to know to do their schoolwork. His studies were the basis of the *Thorndike-Century Junior Dictionary*, published in 1935. Soon other dictionaries for young people began to appear. Word lists were based on careful studies of schoolbooks and other school materials. Among the notable children's dictionaries available today are *The American Heritage Children's Dictionary*, the *Macmillan Dictionary for Children*, and the *Scholastic Children's Dictionary*. These include many colorful illustrations.

HOWARD R. WEBBER
Houghton Mifflin Company

See also REFERENCE BOOKS.

DIEFENBAKER, JOHN GEORGE (1895–1979)

John George Diefenbaker, Canada's prime minister from 1957 to 1963, was born on an Ontario farm on September 18, 1895. When he was 8, his family moved to Saskatchewan and later settled in Saskatoon. He graduated from the University of Saskatchewan and then served with the Canadian Army during World War I.

After returning home Diefenbaker studied law. In 1919 he opened a law office in Wakaw and later in Prince Albert, Saskatchewan.

Diefenbaker's early political career gave no sign that he would someday become prime minister. Twice he was a Conservative Party (later renamed the Progressive Conservative Party) candidate in federal elections and twice in Saskatchewan provincial elections. Each time he was defeated. It was 1940 before he won a seat in the Canadian Parliament.

The turning point in Diefenbaker's career came in 1953. In that year he won the seat for Prince Albert, Saskatchewan. In 1956 he won the Progressive Conservative Party leadership, and in 1957 he became prime minister. He was the first member of that party to hold the office in 22 years. But the Diefenbaker government was a minority government. In 1958, Diefenbaker called another election. His forceful appearance and his "New Vision" for developing Canada won him many votes. His party gained 208 of the 265 seats in the House of Commons—the largest number ever won by a single party in the history of Canada.

In 1960, Parliament passed the Canadian Bill of Rights to guarantee the liberties of all citizens. But Canada was troubled by economic problems. So many Progressive Conservatives were defeated in the 1962 election that Diefenbaker again led a minority government. In 1963 his government fell, and the Liberal Party came to power. Lester B. Pearson became prime minister. Diefenbaker led the Opposition until 1967. He was serving his 13th term in Parliament when he died on August 16, 1979.

JOHN S. MOIR
University of Toronto

See also PEARSON, LESTER.

DIES AND MOLDS

Many of the things we see and use every day are made with dies or molds.

Dies are special tools that shape and cut metal and plastic by pressure. If you have ever watched cookies being punched out of a sheet of dough by a cookie cutter, you have seen a simple type of die in action.

Molds are also special tools, used to shape materials in a liquid form. Metal or plastic is poured or forced into the cavity of the mold and is allowed to solidify. If you have ever watched a mold of gelatin being made, you have seen a simple type of mold in action.

Dies are used in industry to make parts like the hoods and fenders of automobiles. Molds are used to make parts like refrigerator door handles, radio casings, and many automobile parts, including transmission parts, engine parts, and grilles.

Dies and molds are especially useful for rapidly producing large numbers of identical parts. Another advantage of dies and molds is that the parts they turn out usually have a good surface finish, with no blemishes or marks. Sometimes, however, difficult parts may require a little grinding or polishing to remove rough edges.

Molds and dies in general are made in two halves. When brought together they will make the shape of the part.

Molds and dies are made by skilled artisans called journeymen. These skilled workers serve a four- or five-year apprenticeship learning the trade. They learn to operate a wide variety of machine tools, such as grinders, drills, planers, and lathes. Journeymen work with extremely precise measurements—some as precise as one ten-thousandth of an inch (.00025 centimeter). Many of the machine tools that are used to make dies and molds are computer-controlled.

There is a variety of dies and molds. A die that pierces, cuts, or forms material in thin sheets is called a **stamping die.** Stamping dies can form curved surfaces without wrinkling or cracking the metal. Typewriter parts, gears of

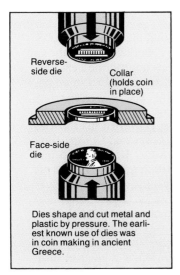

Reverse-
side die

Collar
(holds coin
in place)

Face-side
die

Dies shape and cut metal and plastic by pressure. The earliest known use of dies was in coin making in ancient Greece.

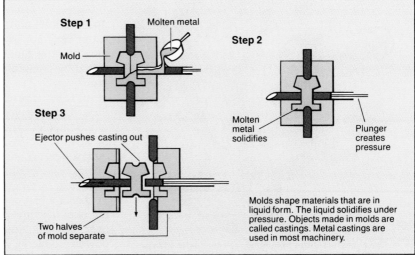

Step 1

Molten metal

Mold

Step 2

Molten metal solidifies

Plunger creates pressure

Step 3

Ejector pushes casting out

Two halves of mold separate

Molds shape materials that are in liquid form. The liquid solidifies under pressure. Objects made in molds are called castings. Metal castings are used in most machinery.

clocks, radio and television chassis, and knives, forks, and spoons are some of the many things that are made with stamping dies. Automobile body parts and metal furniture are also made with stamping dies.

A **coining die** is a special type of stamping die. Coining dies are used when an impression, or design, must be made on the face or back of a piece. An important use of a coining die is in making coins. Coining dies are also used for making small objects like metal cuff links, tie clasps, and costume jewelry.

A **draw die** is a special type of stamping die that forms deep objects like coffeepots and cooking pots. Draw dies are so named because they draw the metal out to form the object.

A **forging die** is one that forms the piece by striking the object. Sometimes one blow is enough. In other cases the die strikes the object many times, like a blacksmith forming a horseshoe. Forging dies are used to make heavy, solid metal parts such as engine crankshafts, locomotive axles, heads of axes, hammers, and wrenches.

In **die casting,** molten metal is forced into a mold under pressure. When the material has solidified, the two halves of the mold are separated, and the part pops out. Die castings vary greatly in size. Scale model airplanes, cars, and trains are examples of die-cast parts.

Plastic molding is similar to die casting except that molten plastic instead of metal is forced into the mold under pressure. Components of model kits are frequently made of molded plastic, as are telephones and sections of automobile bodies.

▶**DIES FOR WIREDRAWING**

Metal rods and wires (which are really nothing but very thin rods) are made by pulling a bar of metal through a series of round dies. Each die in the series has a hole a little bit smaller than the one before it. In this way the rod or wire is gradually made thinner. This type of die may be made of very hard metal, carbide, or diamond.

▶**HISTORY**

The earliest known use of dies was in 650 B.C. Greek metalworkers used them to produce silver coins. The coins were made by pounding metal into a pattern cut into a harder metal block. A hammer and a hand-held punch were used for this.

These hand-held dies often slipped, ruining the work. About A.D. 1500, artisans working for Pope Julius II developed a better method. They mounted the dies on a screw press, a device that kept the dies in place and provided more even pressure.

Die forming was limited to soft metals—such as copper, gold, silver, and lead—until the Industrial Revolution. The reason was that dies must be harder and tougher than the material they are used on. Otherwise, instead of forcing the other metal into shape, the dies themselves would be squashed out of shape. Steels that were hard and tough enough to be used for shaping ordinary steel and iron were not developed until that time.

Reviewed by BRUCE BRAKER
Tooling and Manufacturing Association
See also IRON AND STEEL; WIRE.

Diesel engines differ from other internal-combustion engines in that diesels use the heat of highly compressed air, rather than a spark, to ignite the fuel.

DIESEL ENGINES

A young German engineering student was listening to a lecture on engines by one of his professors. The time was the 1870's. The young student was Rudolf Diesel. The professor spoke of the steam engine and its wastefulness. The best-designed steam engines at that time used only about one tenth of the potential energy in their fuel. The rest went up the smokestack. It should be possible, the professor said, to build an engine that could use nearly all the energy in its fuel.

Young Diesel never forgot his professor's ideas. Years later he was able to carry them out in the engine he invented. Although Diesel's engine never did reach perfect efficiency, it is still more efficient than any other type of engine. Today diesel engines (named after their inventor) are supplying power for trucks, tractors, power shovels, railroad locomotives, and ships all around the world.

▶ THE INVENTOR OF THE DIESEL ENGINE

Diesel studied engineering at the Munich Polytechnic Institute. One of his professors was the famous scientist Carl von Linde. It was Linde who sparked Diesel's interest in engines.

After graduating, Diesel went to work for Professor Linde's refrigerating-machine company. One day he was watching the compressors at an ice factory. (In those days there were no kitchen refrigerators. Ice was made in large central plants and peddled from door to

door.) Diesel noticed that the compressors became very hot as they worked. Suddenly an idea came to him. Why not use the heat produced by compression to ignite fuel in an engine?

In 1892, Diesel took out a patent on his idea. The next year he published his theories in a pamphlet called *Theory and Construction of a Rational Heat Motor*. He designed and built a one-cylinder working model to test his theory. The fuel for this first diesel engine was coal dust.

Diesel's first engine blew up with a deafening roar. The inventor was nearly killed. However, he had proved that he could set off a power-producing explosion without an electric spark or a flame.

With financial help from the wealthy industrialist Friedrich A. Krupp, a steel and cannon maker, Diesel set to work to redesign his engine. He switched from coal dust to oil as the fuel and strengthened weak parts. By 1898, Diesel was able to exhibit his improved engine. It quickly became a success.

Engineers in many countries developed better materials and more efficient designs for the diesel engine. By the end of the 1920's, diesel engines had become light enough to use in trucks and buses. Since then they steadily have become more and more important in transportation.

▶ HOW THE DIESEL ENGINE WORKS

The diesel engine is a type of internal-combustion engine. An internal-combustion engine burns its fuel right inside the chamber where it does its work. The gasoline engine is an internal-combustion engine. Gas turbines and jet engines are also internal-combustion engines. (The article INTERNAL-COMBUSTION ENGINES may be found in Volume I.) Engines that burn their fuel outside of the chamber are called external-combustion engines. The steam engine, which burns fuel under a separate boiler, is an external-combustion engine.

Most internal-combustion engines are of the reciprocating type. They burn fuel internally in a combustion chamber consisting of a capped cylinder and piston. As the fuel is burned, violently expanding gases press against the pistons and drive them down into the cylinders. The up-and-down, or reciprocating, motion of the pistons is converted by the connecting rods and crankshaft into rotary

Four-Stroke Cycle in a Diesel Engine

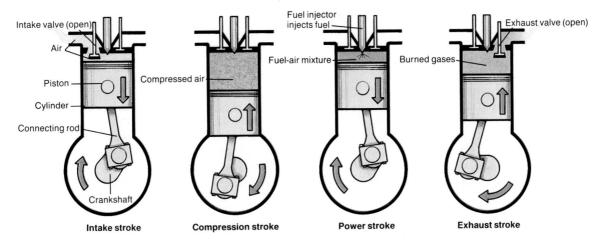

Intake stroke   **Compression stroke**   **Power stroke**   **Exhaust stroke**

motion. This rotary motion can be harnessed to turn wheels and propellers. There are also valves or ports to control intake and exhaust gases. All of these components are located in the engine block.

The chief difference between gasoline and diesel engines is in the way the fuel is ignited (set on fire). In gasoline engines the fuel is ignited by an electric spark. Diesel engines do away with the spark plugs, distributors, and generators needed to produce the electric spark. The heat of the highly compressed air trapped in the cylinders is enough to ignite the fuel.

Many diesel engines use what is called a four-stroke cycle of operation. That is, only one of every four movements of the piston produces power. The other three movements, or strokes, are needed to get the engine ready for the next power stroke. The cycle goes through the following steps.

At the beginning of the **intake stroke,** the piston is at the top of the cylinder. As the piston moves down, it sucks in air through a valve in the top of the cylinder. When the piston reaches the bottom of its stroke, the air intake valve closes, so that no air can escape.

The piston now starts to move upward. This upward stroke is called the **compression stroke.** As the piston moves up, it compresses the air in the cylinder to about 500 pounds per square inch (35 kilograms per square centimeter). Compressing the air so tightly raises its temperature to about 1000°F (538°C), more than hot enough to ignite the fuel.

At the top of the compression stroke, a powerful pump called a fuel injector sprays fuel into the cylinder through a tiny opening. When the fuel hits the hot air, it burns immediately. The burning of the fuel creates gases that expand with tremendous force in the enclosed cylinder, forcing the piston down in the **power stroke.**

When the piston reaches the bottom of the power stroke, an exhaust valve in the top of the cylinder opens. As the piston moves up in the **exhaust stroke,** it forces the burned gases out of the cylinder through the open valve. At the top of the exhaust stroke, the exhaust valve closes, and the whole cycle begins over again.

Two-Stroke Cycle in a Diesel Engine

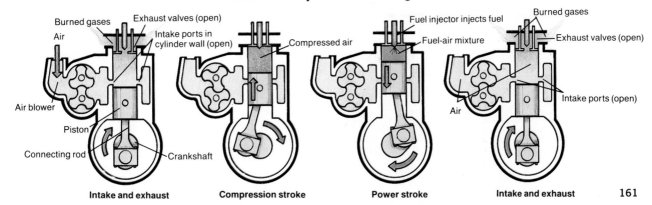

Intake and exhaust   **Compression stroke**   **Power stroke**   **Intake and exhaust**

161

This cycle is repeated several hundred times each minute.

Some diesel engines have a two-stroke cycle. As the piston travels downward near the end of the power stroke, it uncovers openings, or ports, in the cylinder. An air blower forces fresh air into the cylinder, at the same time driving out the exhaust gases through the exhaust valve in the top of the cylinder. As the piston rises in the compression stroke, it covers the ports, so that no more air enters the cylinder. The piston continues to rise, compressing the air trapped in the cylinder. At the top of the compression stroke, the fuel is injected into the cylinder, and the power stroke follows. Thus the two-stroke engine produces power on every second stroke instead of every fourth stroke.

Diesel engines can run on a wide variety of fuels, from kerosene to fuel oil. These fuels are cheaper than the highly refined fuels today's gasoline engines need.

The high compression ratio of the diesel engine enables it to make use of as much as 40 percent of the energy in its fuel. The best gasoline engine can use only about 30 percent.

The compression ratio is a figure that tells how tightly the air in the cylinder is squeezed during the compression stroke. For example, if the air takes up the whole cylinder at the beginning of the compression stroke and only $\frac{1}{16}$ of the space in the cylinder at the end of the stroke, the compression ratio is 16 to 1. Twelve to 1 is the lowest compression ratio at which a diesel engine will work. Below that, the air does not get hot enough to make the fuel burn. The highest compression ratio that is practical is 20 to 1. The average is 16 to 1.

▶ USES

Diesel engines can deliver large amounts of power over long periods of time. They are cheaper to run than gasoline engines. They are also heavier and larger. For these reasons diesel engines generally are used for heavy-duty work.

Diesel engines are now the main source of power for ships and locomotives. Usually the diesel engine does not drive the ship or locomotive directly. Instead it turns an electric generator. This generator supplies power for electric motors that turn the propeller of the ship or the wheels of the locomotive. This is called a diesel-electric system.

Before nuclear power was invented, all submarines used diesel engines for cruising on the surface of the water. The invention of the snorkel, a long air tube that reached up to the surface, has made it possible for submarines to use their diesel engines even when they are submerged.

Most long-distance trucks and buses are diesel-powered. So are heavy earth-moving machines. Farm tractors also are big users of diesel power. Diesel engines are being used in increasing numbers in automobiles.

Diesel engines run electric power plants and air compressors, pump water and other fluids, and turn the mighty, rock-piercing bits of oil-well drills. The list of uses keeps growing.

Because there are so many diesel engines, diesel exhaust contributes greatly to air pollution. To help limit air pollution, the Environmental Protection Agency has set emission standards for non-road diesel engines, diesel engines that power highway trucks and buses, and diesel fuels.

Reviewed by JOSEPH W. DUFFY
Central Connecticut State University

DIET. See HEALTH; NUTRITION.

DIETRICH, MARLENE. See MOTION PICTURES (Profiles: Movie Stars).

Diesels cost less to run than comparable gasoline engines, but they weigh more. Diesel power is preferred for heavy work where engine weight is not a problem.

DIGESTIVE SYSTEM

Biting into an apple, sniffing the aroma of a cake baking, or even thinking about your favorite food is enough to start your mouth watering. That is the first step in a process called digestion, by which the foods you eat are changed into forms that the body can use for energy and building materials.

During digestion, food passes through the body along a sort of assembly line, which is equipped with work stations where foods are chopped up, churned around, and soaked in chemical baths. These treatments gradually reduce the solid lumps of food to a soupy semi-liquid and finally to individual chemicals small enough to pass into the bloodstream and be carried as nourishment to the body's cells.

▶ORGANS OF THE DIGESTIVE SYSTEM

The digestive tract is one long, continuous tube running from the mouth down through the neck and into the trunk of the body, finally ending at the opening called the anus. Along the way, the tube curves and loops repeatedly. In an adult, about 30 feet (9 meters) of digestive tract are packed into the area of the body between the mouth and the anus.

The mouth is the receiving chamber for food. It is equipped with a set of 32 teeth, which are specialized for cutting, tearing, and grinding all kinds of foods. The **esophagus,** a muscular tube, acts like a conveyor belt for chewed food. It carries food from the mouth down to the **stomach** for further processing.

In the stomach, food is churned around and mixed with digestive chemicals to help break it into smaller particles that the body can use.

The stomach leads into the **small intestine,** which is a tube about 20 feet (6 meters) long that is looped and coiled to take up most of the space inside the abdomen. The inner wall of the intestine is covered with microscopic fingerlike projections, called **villi.** There are hundreds of villi in 1 square inch (6 square centimeters) of intestinal wall. They provide a great amount of surface area for nutrients to be absorbed into the body. The three main parts of the small intestine are the **duodenum,** the C-shaped first part, the **jejunum,** the coiling middle section, and the **ileum,** the final section that empties into the **large intestine.**

The last organ of the digestive tract is the large intestine. It is made up of two parts: the **colon,** which passes up, across, and down the abdomen, and the **rectum,** which leads out of the body through the anus.

In addition to the organs of the digestive tract itself, the pancreas and liver are also part of the digestive process. They produce chemicals that aid digestion in the small intestine. Bile, a product of the liver used in digestion, is stored temporarily in the gall bladder.

▶A TRIP THROUGH THE DIGESTIVE SYSTEM

It is lunchtime, and you are sitting down to a tempting meal: a hamburger on a bun, a glass of milk, and a juicy apple for dessert. What happens when you eat this food? How does your body get the nutrients it needs?

This sample lunch provides plenty of all the main kinds of food substances. There are proteins in the hamburger, bun, and milk; carbohydrates in the bun, milk, and apple; and fats in the hamburger and milk. These foods also contain water, vitamins, and minerals. (But they will not need to be digested—the body can absorb them just as they are.)

Your mouth is starting to water as you bite into the hamburger. Your teeth grind the bread and meat as they are mixed with a watery fluid, **saliva,** produced by salivary glands in the mouth. An enzyme (a substance that speeds up a chemical reaction) in the saliva begins the digestive process already. It starts to break down the carbohydrates from the bun into sugars. (If you chewed long enough, the bread would start to taste sweet.)

After chewing and a big swallow, the food slips down your throat. Passing through the **pharynx,** a shared passageway for food and air, it travels down into the esophagus. There waves of muscle contraction, known as **peristalsis,** carry it to the stomach. Gravity helps move the food, but it is not essential. Astronauts in space can eat normally even when they are in weightless environments.

In the Stomach. Some substances are absorbed directly through the stomach wall. These are generally small molecules, such as water, salt, simple sugars, and alcohol. Some of the sugar from your apple will pass into the bloodstream directly from the stomach.

If the human digestive tract were stretched out in a long line, it would be 30 feet long—more than five times taller than an average adult.

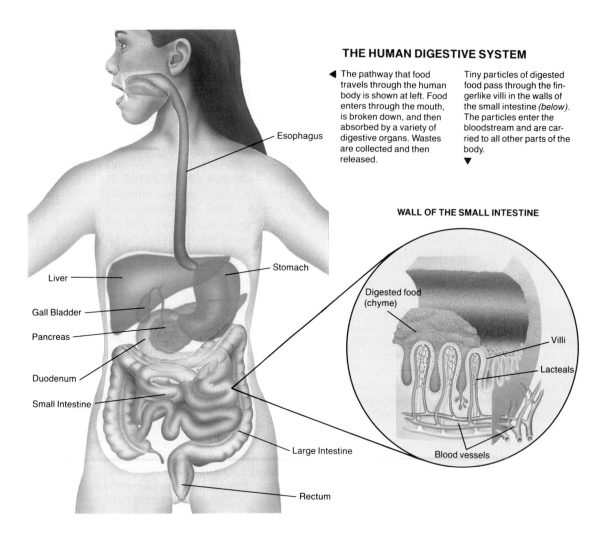

THE HUMAN DIGESTIVE SYSTEM

◄ The pathway that food travels through the human body is shown at left. Food enters through the mouth, is broken down, and then absorbed by a variety of digestive organs. Wastes are collected and then released.

Tiny particles of digested food pass through the fingerlike villi in the walls of the small intestine (below). The particles enter the bloodstream and are carried to all other parts of the body.

▼

Esophagus

Liver

Gall Bladder

Pancreas

Duodenum

Small Intestine

Stomach

Large Intestine

Rectum

WALL OF THE SMALL INTESTINE

Digested food (chyme)

Villi

Lacteals

Blood vessels

Most other food must undergo further digestion, however. Contractions of the muscular stomach wall produce a churning motion that mixes the food with strong chemicals produced in special glands in the stomach lining. One of these chemicals, hydrochloric acid, is strong enough to curdle milk, changing it into soft lumps. An enzyme called pepsin helps to digest the proteins from the hamburger bun and meat by breaking them down into chemically simpler substances. (The proteins are not completely broken down here. They must travel to the small intestine for further digestion.)

Through the Small Intestine. By the time the food is ready to leave the stomach, it has turned into a soupy semi-liquid called **chyme.** This is squirted down into the duodenum part of the small intestine. Here muscular contrac-

tions move the chyme along as a number of digestive chemicals work on it.

The pancreas contributes a salt, sodium bicarbonate, that neutralizes the acid from the stomach. This creates the alkaline conditions that are best for the work of the digestive enzymes in the intestines. Some of these enzymes also come from the pancreas. They are amylase, which breaks down carbohydrates into sugars; lipase, which breaks down fats into fatty acids and glycerol; and trypsin, which breaks down proteins into their building blocks—the amino acids.

Glands in the walls of the intestines also produce digestive enzymes. Some of these are sucrase and lactase, which change complex sugar molecules into simple sugars; and aminopeptidase, which breaks down partially digested proteins into amino acids. Bile, made by the liver, breaks down large fat globules (droplets) into tiny ones so lipases from the intestines can digest them more readily.

The products of digestion are absorbed through the villi in the lining of the small intestine. These villi contain tiny blood vessels that carry most of the nutrients into the bloodstream. The sugars from digested carbohydrates and the amino acids from digested proteins pass into these tiny blood vessels. Minerals, such as iron from the hamburger meat and calcium from the milk, also pass into these blood vessels. Vitamins are also absorbed into the bloodstream. The blood vessels from the villi lead to the liver, where some of the food materials are stored for later use.

Something different happens to the products of fat digestion. They are absorbed into **lacteals,** which are structures in the villi that are connected to the lymphatic system. This system eventually empties into the bloodstream.

Through the Large Intestine. By the time the remains of the meal reach the large intestine, the work of the digestion is basically complete. The main job of the large intestine is to remove water from the undigested food matter and form this matter into solid masses, called **feces,** which are eliminated from the body. Bacteria live in the large intestines and feed on the undigested matter, helping to break it down further. Much of the bulk of the feces is actually formed by huge numbers of bacteria, and the gases sometimes produced here are the result of their action.

▶ **DISORDERS OF THE DIGESTIVE SYSTEM**

Nearly everyone suffers now and then from a digestive system problem. Some disorders are due to poor eating habits, but others can be serious and must be treated by a doctor.

Stomachache is a rather vague term that most people use for discomfort in the abdomen, where the intestines are, rather than in the stomach. Eating spoiled food or drinking water contaminated by bacteria can cause painful muscle cramps in the intestines; an emotional upset also can have this effect.

Heartburn is a painful burning sensation in the middle of the chest that actually does not involve the heart. It occurs when acidic digestive fluids in the stomach squirt up into the esophagus and cause irritation.

The stomach lining is normally protected from these acids by a coating of gooey mucus. But sometimes the acid gets through this coating, producing a painful sore called an **ulcer.**

In diarrhea, muscle contractions move the contents of the intestines along too quickly. There is not enough time for water to be absorbed, and the feces are soft and even liquid instead of solid. Infection in the digestive tract is a common cause of diarrhea. If diarrhea continues, the body may lose too much water and become dangerously dehydrated.

In constipation, the contents of the intestines do not move along fast enough. Waste materials stay in the large intestine so long that too much water is removed and the feces become hard. Elimination may then be painful, which adds to the problem.

▶ **DIGESTION IN THE LIVING WORLD**

All animals, from single-celled creatures such as the amoeba to human beings with trillions of body cells, must digest the foods they take in. Even plants have to digest some of the stored food materials that they have manufactured themselves during photosynthesis.

Digestion in a single-celled amoeba is a simple matter. A bit of food is enclosed in a bubble called a **vacuole,** and digestive enzymes flow in. As the food is broken down into usable chemicals, they pass through the membrane that surrounds the vacuole and are absorbed by the cell. When only waste products remain, the vacuole moves to the surface of the cell, opens up, and releases its contents.

All complex organisms, beginning with the earthworm, have a tube-type digestive system in which food moves through a long tube in the body, starting with the mouth and ending at the anus. Such a system permits an efficient assembly-line arrangement where specialized work stations along the digestive tract handle various kinds of food materials. Each animal's digestive system is carefully matched to the kinds of foods the animal eats. Some systems are highly specialized. You can find out about the specialized digestive systems of such animals as birds, ruminants (cows, for example), and even termites by consulting the Index.

ALVIN SILVERSTEIN
VIRGINIA SILVERSTEIN
Coauthors, *The Digestive System*

See also BODY, HUMAN; STOMACH.

DILLON, DIANE AND LEO. See CHILDREN'S LITERATURE (Profiles).

DIMAGGIO, JOE. See BASEBALL (Great Players).

DINOSAURS

Dinosaurs were real animals that once lived on the earth, but they died out about 65 million years ago. Since the very first kind of human did not appear on the earth until about 3.5 million years ago, it is clear that no one has ever seen a living dinosaur. Yet, almost everyone has some knowledge about dinosaurs and can picture what at least one or two kinds of these prehistoric creatures looked like. This information about animals that lived so long ago comes from scientists who have pieced together the dinosaur's ancient world from fossil remains.

Fossil remains can be in the form of bones, found either in skeletons or separately; footprints in rock; impressions of skin, also in rock; and eggs. Most of the dinosaur specimens that have been collected are in museums. But at Dinosaur National Monument, near Vernal, Utah, a museum has been built around rocks holding dinosaur bones.

▶ WHAT WERE DINOSAURS?

Dinosaurs were reptiles that lived in what is known as the Age of Reptiles. This age began in the geological period called the Triassic period, which began about 230 million years ago. Dinosaurs are last found in the rocks of the late Cretaceous period. This period ended about 65 million years ago. The dinosaur age thus lasted for some 165 million years.

General Characteristics

Dinosaurs were primarily land-living reptiles. Although some of them went into water, these waters were mainly on the land—in rivers, lakes, or swamps. Dinosaurs included flesh eaters and plant eaters, bipedal forms (those that walked on their two hind legs), and quadrupeds (those that walked on all fours).

Like modern reptiles, most dinosaurs had scaly skins. Some also had large plates of bone covering their skin, and this sometimes included a very heavily armored head. Based on actual finds of fossil dinosaur eggs and

Triassic Period

Jurassic Period

Plateosaurus

Diplodocus

Allosaurus

Herrerasaurus

Procompsognathus

Archaeopteryx

hatchlings, we know that at least some dinosaurs were egg layers.

But in many ways dinosaurs were unlike modern reptiles (which are not dinosaur descendants). Many dinosaurs walked and ran on their hind legs only. Some looked like long-tailed birds without wings and others more like kangaroos. Some may have even climbed trees. And of course, many dinosaurs were enormously large.

The name "Dinosauria" was given in 1841 to the earliest known forms of these animals by Richard Owen, an English anatomist. Owen said that he made the name up from the Greek words meaning "fearfully great lizards." We now know that not all dinosaurs were fearfully large. In fact, some dinosaurs were quite small. More recent scientific discoveries have shown that the classification made by Owen is out of date. The word "Dinosauria" is no longer used by scientists, but it continues to be used in the common form "dinosaur."

Paleontologists (scientists who study fossils, the evidence of ancient life-forms) are not certain whether dinosaurs were cold-blooded as other reptiles of today are, or warm-blooded. A warm-blooded animal regulates its body temperature by internal processes, while a cold-blooded animal depends on external sources of heat, such as the sun and shade, to regulate its body temperature.

The question of whether dinosaurs were cold- or warm-blooded is important. The answer would help scientists understand more about how dinosaurs lived. Could dinosaurs move quickly at all times? Or were they slow, as many reptiles are when they are very cold? How much food did dinosaurs need? (Cold-blooded animals do not need as much food as warm-blooded ones.) Perhaps more fossil evidence will help answer these questions.

Millions of years ago, there lived some extraordinary reptiles called dinosaurs. They ruled the land for nearly 150 million years — from the Triassic period through the Cretaceous period — before disappearing from the earth. Shown below are just a few of these remarkable creatures within the period they lived.

Cretaceous Period

Iguanodon

Tyrannosaurus rex

Utahraptor

Brachiosaurus

Iguanodon

Fossil Finds

There is some doubt as to when the first recognizable dinosaur bones were discovered. Footprints have been known for many years. A dinosaur skeleton may have been uncovered in Haddonfield, New Jersey, toward the end of the 1700's. The first bones that are still available for examination and identification are some discovered in England. One set was found in 1822 by Mary Ann Woodhouse and is now in the British Museum of Natural History in London, England; the bones were from the dinosaur called *Iguanodon*. Another set was carefully studied and became the basis for the first scientific description of a dinosaur. These bones were named *Megalo-*

Unearthing fossils long buried in rock is a painstaking task. A skeleton of *Tyrannosaurus rex* (*above*) slowly emerges from a Montana excavation site. A paleontologist (*left*) carefully uses hammer and chisel to search through rock.

saurus ("large lizard") in 1824 by Professor William Buckland of Oxford University.

Since then many dinosaur remains have been discovered. Large deposits in the United States can be found at Dinosaur National Monument in Utah; at Ghost Ranch in New Mexico; near Cleveland, Utah; and in Como Bluff, Wyoming. Bones have been found at Dinosaur Provincial Park in Alberta, Canada; in the Gobi Desert of Mongolia; in the coal mines at Bernissart, Belgium; and near Trossingen, Germany. Significant remains have also been found in Argentina, Brazil, India, China, France, Portugal, South Africa, Tanzania, and the former Soviet Union.

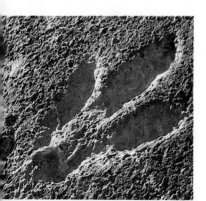

Fossilized footprints supply clues to how dinosaurs lived. "Dinosaur freeways," paths made up of large numbers of footprints, suggest that some dinosaurs were very mobile creatures and may have migrated in herds over long distances.

Each year, new kinds of dinosaurs are being found and they are being found in new places. From the dinosaur bones and other fossil remains that are found, paleontologists are able to piece together evidence that tells what kind of dinosaurs there were and how they lived. Since the discovery and identification of the first dinosaur bone in 1822, scientists have found fossils from many kinds, or species, of dinosaurs—of varying shapes and sizes. With this information, they are able to estimate that at least 300 different kinds of dinosaurs have existed throughout history.

When dinosaur bones were first discovered, it was hard for people to believe that such creatures had really lived on earth. Dinosaurs were not only mysterious but they were also terrifying because of their size. Today, every fossil is another important clue to the mystery of what the dinosaur's anatomy, behavior, and life-style were like. Sometimes only fragments of fossils are found and

A steady hand and a patient temperament are needed when it comes to cleaning a skeleton. First, the protective jacket of plaster or polyurethane foam that is used to transport the skeleton is removed. Then a museum worker begins the long task of removing the rock and earth that cling to the fossil. Chisels, drills, and sometimes chemicals are used to clean away the excess rock.

the skeleton cannot be accurately reconstructed. Other times, the fossils that are found are not assembled correctly and one skeleton reconstruction will actually be made up of bones from more than one kind of dinosaur.

One such incident occurred when an almost complete fossil skeleton of the dinosaur called *Apatosaurus*, which used to be known as *Brontosaurus*, was dug up. The skeleton was almost complete when it was found, except for the head. When the dinosaur was reconstructed, the head from another kind of dinosaur that was found nearby was incorrectly paired with the body skeleton. It was not until the late 1970's that the mistake was corrected.

Because fleshy tissues are not usually preserved as fossils, scientists must guess at what some dinosaur features were like. For years dinosaur artists placed the nostrils high up on the snout, toward the brain. But evidence reported in 2001 suggests that dinosaur nostrils were much closer to the tip of the snout.

Using information gained through studying fossils, scientists have been able to create life-size models that show how different events in a dinosaur's life may have occurred. This baby dinosaur emerging from its egg (*above*) is one example.

Museum workers put the final touches on a reconstruction of an *Allosaurus* skeleton (*right*).

ORIGINS OF DINOSAURS

The dinosaurs probably had their origins in a small reptile that has been found in the Triassic rocks of South Africa, the United States, and Scotland. These little reptiles are known as Pseudosuchia, or "false crocodiles." Many had small front limbs and were able to run upright on their hind legs, using their long tails for balance.

Animals other than dinosaurs evolved from similar small reptiles. These include two groups that, like the dinosaurs, became extinct: the soaring pterosaurs, or "flying lizards," and the sea-dwelling ichthyosaurs, or "fish lizards." Two other dinosaur-related groups exist today—the true crocodiles and the birds. Fossils of reptilelike prehistoric birds, such as *Archaeopteryx*, and of small feathered dinosaurs suggest that birds arose directly from dinosaurs.

While dinosaurs ruled the land, this pterosaur, *Pterodactylus*, flew over the seas and came to rest on land at nesting time.

The great number of dinosaur bones discovered in recent years and still other evidence tell us that the various dinosaurs are not all closely related to one another. They must have evolved along at least two distinct lines. The differences are seen in the arrangement of the teeth in the jaws and in the arrangement of the hipbones. These differences are quite constant in the two main kinds of dinosaurs, and they form the basis for classifying these animals into two distinct groups.

THE SAURISCHIA

The first main group is called the Saurischia, which means "lizardlike hip." The hipbones of these animals were similar to those of modern crocodiles. This group is divided into two subgroups: the Theropoda, which were meat-eating dinosaurs that walked upright on their hind legs, and the Sauropoda—plant-eating dinosaurs that walked on all fours.

A lizardlike hip structure distinguishes the dinosaurs belonging to the group called Saurischia from all other dinosaurs.

The Theropoda, or "Beast Feet." This group of dinosaurs was carnivorous, or meat eating. They had strong jaws and large teeth with sharp edges. Unlike most animals they could not stand or run on all four legs. Their front limbs were very small and were designed for grasping and tearing their prey. They walked or ran with their bodies leaning forward and their tails outstretched for balance. Their huge feet usually had three or more toes.

The Triassic Period. The Theropoda in the Triassic period (when dinosaurs first appeared) were relatively small, though they soon increased in size and became more ferocious in appearance. *Coelophysis*, for example, was about 9 feet (2.7 meters) long when fully grown. But it was light and agile and could run across the dry plains in search of food or to escape from its enemies. In what is now

The strong hind limbs of the *Allosaurus* ended in birdlike feet with curved claws. The meat-eating *Allosaurus* used its clawed hands and feet to tear its prey to shreds.

Europe there were already heavier, slower relatives of *Coelophysis*. From these larger dinosaurs there came even larger and more remarkable dinosaurs. Heavier, slower dinosaurs evolved in North America as well.

The Jurassic Period. In North America during the Jurassic, the next geological period, lived *Allosaurus* (also called *Antrodemus*). It had a proportionately larger skull, more solid bones, and an overall length of 30 feet (9 meters). The knifelike teeth and the curving claws on hands and feet already marked this as a creature that tore its prey to shreds. *Ceratosaurus* was a similar kind of dinosaur. It bore a bony horn on its snout—a most unusual feature in these flesh-tearing creatures.

The Cretaceous Period. From the next geological period, the Cretaceous, the rocks of Canada and the United States have produced the remains of the biggest carnivorous dinosaurs of all times. *Gorgosaurus*, 40 feet (12 meters) long with a jaw 4 feet (1.2 meters) long, was a huge and impressive creature. Yet as time passed, a new giant meat-eating dinosaur began to walk the land. This was *Tyrannosaurus*, 50 feet (15 meters) long, whose name comes from words meaning "tyrant lizard." Its head was almost 6 feet (2 meters) long.

These fearsome creatures had large heads, very short necks, and massive bodies, tails, and hind legs. Yet the forelegs were very feeble and the hand was reduced to two fingers. However, each finger had a sharp, curved claw. Obviously such animals could not crash their way with speed through the swampy grasslands, and they were unable to stalk their prey efficiently. Whatever they did was done by sheer bulk and the strength of their heavy jaws, which were equipped with long teeth. Both *Gorgosaurus* and *Tyrannosaurus* must have weighed about 7 tons—much more than the largest African elephant of today.

Not all of the carnivorous dinosaurs were large, however. In western North America and in Asia, small meat-eating predators like *Deinonychus*, *Dromaeosaurus*, and *Velociraptor* have been found. Smaller than ostriches, these animals had sharp claws on their feet for killing and slicing up prey. *Deinonychus* may even have hunted in packs like wild dogs do today.

The huge head of *Tyrannosaurus rex* (*below*) shows the long, powerful jaws equipped with dozens of sharp, flesh-tearing teeth that it and its relatives, such as *Tarbosaurus* (*left*), used to devour prey.

The Sauropoda, or "Lizard Feet"

A second group of dinosaurs in the Saurischia family is the Sauropoda. The early relatives of the Sauropoda, a group called Prosauropoda, were relatively small—about the size of a rhinoceros. However, the Sauropoda, or "lizard feet" as this group is known, included some of the largest animals that have ever existed. The feet were massive and five-toed, only the inner three toes having claws, as a rule. The characteristic footprints (often capable today of holding many quarts of water) are found in several parts of the United States, but especially in Texas. The feet, large as they were, certainly were not out of proportion to the rest of the giant body.

The Triassic Period. The Sauropoda ancestors originated in the Triassic period—in a lumbering Prosauropoda dinosaur called *Plateosaurus*. Unlike the Theropoda, this creature had forelegs almost the same length as the hind legs. It probably lived near lakes or rivers, but scientists are not sure whether it ate meat or only plants. The descendants of *Plateosaurus* rapidly spread throughout the world and attained enormous size.

The Jurassic Period. Common during the late Jurassic was the best-known member of the Sauropoda, the *Apatosaurus*, which for many years was identified by the name *Brontosaurus*, meaning "thunder lizard."

The *Plateosaurus*, which flourished about 200 million years ago, was the ancestor of such giants as *Apatosaurus* and *Diplodocus*. The *Plateosaurus* measured about 16½ feet (5 meters) high when standing erect and weighed about 2,200 pounds (998 kilograms). Although it was small compared to its gigantic relatives, *Plateosaurus* was the largest reptile of the Triassic period. It was essentially a plant eater that moved on all four legs to feed at ground level and reared up on its hind legs when it wanted to reach the tasty leaves of the upper branches.

Apatosaurus was an enormous animal and is typical of the group Sauropoda. Such animals had a long slender head like that of some lizards, at the end of a very long neck. The body was elephantine, and the tail was very long, ending in a thin whiplike section. The legs were massive. Their gigantic skeletons when clothed in flesh and muscle—with heart and other organs and with blood flowing through arteries and veins—resulted in animals that must have weighed 30 or 40 tons.

The massive skeletons are wonders of natural engineering. Although we may have difficulty in picturing the living animals now, they must have been able to move, find plants to eat, and survive many changes over the years.

How could such animals move? At one time it was thought that *Apatosaurus* lived in the water. Scientists believed that the buoyancy,

The land-dwelling *Apatosaurus* was so huge that scientists originally thought it must have lived in water to support its enormous weight.

or uplift, of the water took a great deal of the burden off the dinosaur's feet. But studies have shown that the leg bones of *Apatosaurus* could support and move the huge animal. Scientists now think that this dinosaur lived on land and swung its long neck from side to side, browsing for ferns and shrubs.

Even though it could walk, *Apatosaurus* surely must have been a slow-moving animal. As such, it was easy prey for carnivorous dinosaurs. *Apatosaurus* skeletons have been found with tooth marks from flesh eaters like *Allosaurus*.

Diplodocus and *Brachiosaurus* were also Sauropoda of the Jurassic period. *Diplodocus,* a close relative of *Apatosaurus,* was an extremely long animal 90 feet (27 meters) in length. Others, like the shorter *Brachiosaurus,* held their very long necks high off the ground. Standing about 60 feet (18 meters) tall, *Brachiosaurus* was three times taller than the tallest giraffe of today. And it may have weighed more than 70 tons.

The Cretaceous Period. Although the giant plant-eating Sauropoda dominated the Jurassic period, they were of minor importance in the Cretaceous period. As time passed, many varieties of the once-thriving giants died out; the forms that lingered on were found mainly in the Southern Hemisphere. South America, India, and Australia had interesting giants of this kind. Smaller relatives, such as *Euthelopus,* were also found in the early Cretaceous.

The *Diplodocus* used thin, pencil-shaped front teeth like a rake to gather in its plant-food diet.

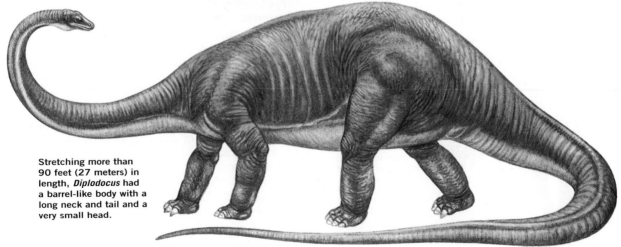

Stretching more than 90 feet (27 meters) in length, *Diplodocus* had a barrel-like body with a long neck and tail and a very small head.

▶THE ORNITHISCHIA

The second main group of dinosaurs is called the Ornithischia, which means "bird-like hip." The hipbones of these animals resemble the hipbone arrangement of modern birds. Members of this group include the Ornithopoda, which were plant-eating dinosaurs that could walk on two legs, and all the armored and horned dinosaurs—also plant eaters.

The Ornithopoda, or "Bird Feet"

Some of these dinosaurs had so many bird-like characteristics that for a long time scientists thought that they were closely related to or were the ancestors of the birds. The feet bear noticeable similarities to those of some birds and have given this subgroup its name, Ornithopoda, or "bird feet." As we have seen, however, the dinosaurs and the birds may have shared a common ancestor long before this group evolved.

The Triassic Period. The earliest Ornithopoda were found in the middle and late Triassic period. In South America, *Pisanosaurus* was found; in Africa, *Heterodontosaurus*. Because these early forms are represented only by scraps of bone, there is little information

The different groups of ornithischian dinosaurs vary greatly in outward appearance; however, all have a birdlike hip structure.

The *Anatosaurus* was one of the most common crestless hadrosaurs. Like other hadrosaurs, it was a large plant-eating dinosaur, used to walking on its strong hind legs. The feet of these (and other) hadrosaurs had three toes. In its mouth were hundreds of teeth growing together in a dense mass. It used its large array of teeth and its powerful jaws to grind and shred tough, fibrous plants. As teeth were worn down and shed, they were replaced from the growing mass of teeth.

about their structure. However, *Heterodontosaurus* was known to be a tiny, fast-moving dinosaur. It was only about 3 feet (1 meter) long. Like other Ornithopoda, it was a plant eater, even though it had three different types of teeth.

The Jurassic Period. The *Camptosaurus* was a thick-bodied dinosaur of the late Jurassic period. Some species reached lengths of more than 23 feet (7 meters) and weighed up to 845 pounds (383 kilograms). They were slow-moving plant eaters with toothless beaks.

Also appearing in the late Jurassic was the *Iguanodon*. This was a large animal, measuring about 30 feet (9 meters) along the backbone and tail. It walked on muscular hind legs with three-toed feet. *Iguanodon* carried its head more than 14 feet (4 meters) from the ground. It weighed more than 4 tons.

Iguanodon had a single row of teeth in each jaw. Its leaf-shaped teeth and their arrangement show that it was a vegetarian. It roamed the countryside of the late Jurassic and the early Cretaceous, feeding on the pine, palm, or cycad trees that were then among the most common land plants.

The Cretaceous Period. The *Iguanodon* and its close relative, called a hadrosaur, thrived

The tail of the *Stegosaurus* ended in sharp spikes that could inflict a deadly wound when the tail was swung against the soft underbelly of an enemy.

during the Cretaceous period. Similar to the *Iguanodon*, the hadrosaur was a large dinosaur, used to walking on its strong hind legs. However, the foot of the hadrosaur had three toes, ending in hooves like those of a horse. With hooves such as these, the dinosaur could run on soft, as well as hard, ground.

Its head ended in a bill like a duck's and it is often called the duck-billed dinosaur. Many of the hadrosaurs had odd-shaped heads with bumps or crests of bone on them. Depending on how they were formed, the crests may have been used to smell or to produce sound. Based on their heads, the duckbills are divided into two subgroups: the crested hadrosaurs and the flat-headed (crestless) hadrosaurs.

The tail was flattened from side to side, and this suggests that it could have been used in water like an oar. We can picture this dinosaur

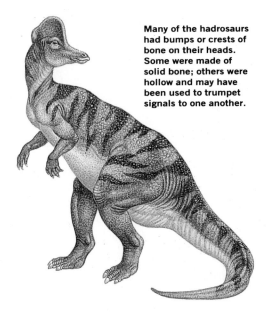

Many of the hadrosaurs had bumps or crests of bone on their heads. Some were made of solid bone; others were hollow and may have been used to trumpet signals to one another.

taking to water to escape from the large flesh-eating dinosaurs already described. In the water it could swim by moving the tail from side to side. The animal may have fed on plants growing in the water, but fossil plant remains found in the stomach section of one duck-billed dinosaur indicate that these dinosaurs also fed on land plants such as pine trees.

By the end of the Cretaceous period, the Ornithopoda (which were the most successful of the Ornithischia) were the most plentiful of the plant-eating dinosaurs.

The Plated, Armored, and Horned

The plated, armored, and horned dinosaurs represent the other main group of the Ornithischia family. Fossil evidence shows that this group of dinosaurs first emerged in the Jurassic period. These animals walked on all four legs and were covered with bony outgrowths of some kind. The great weight they carried around must have made them very slow movers. Scientists are quite sure that these animals could not catch prey and have concluded that they were plant eaters.

The Jurassic Period. One of the oldest and most familiar members of the plated Ornithischia family is the *Stegosaurus*, which means "plated lizard." This plant-eating dinosaur, which originated in the Jurassic period, had a small head with a walnut-sized brain. It had very short front legs and large hind legs that seem to have pushed the heavy body along.

Stegosaurus reached sizes of 30 feet (9 meters) in length and several tons in weight. The distinctive feature of *Stegosaurus* was its two rows (or possibly a single row) of bony plates set in the skin just above the backbone. Scientists think that these plates were a kind of body-cooling system for *Stegosaurus*. Blood flowing through the plates was cooled by breezes blowing across the plates. If this was so, it means that *Stegosaurus* may have been partly warm-blooded, at least after strenuous activity. (Muscular exercise generates heat that somehow must be lost.)

The Cretaceous Period. The greatest variety of plated, armored, and horned dinosaurs existed in the Cretaceous period. *Scolosaurus* had a heavily armored skull and a bony knob at the end of its tail. Its body was covered by plates of bone separated by strips of softer skin

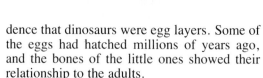

For *Protoceratops* (*right*), early child rearing included a communal egg nest. Some watched the eggs while others searched for food. For its descendant *Triceratops* (*below*), which traveled in packs, it included forming defensive circles around the young when there was danger.

that contained small pieces of bone. As a result, the armor was somewhat flexible. The weight of such an armored animal 18 feet (5.5 meters) long must have been great.

Scolosaurus was broad and low, and it was probably quite safe even from *Gorgosaurus* and *Tyrannosaurus*, the great flesh eaters of its time. But if it slipped and fell on its back, it was at the mercy of any animal that came upon it. It had no protective covering for its underbelly. If it slipped in water, it would immediately drown.

Scolosaurus was only one of a group of somewhat similarly armored creatures that all lived at about the same time in North America and Asia. *Nodosaurus* and *Edmontonia* were similar reptile "tanks." Another was called *Dyoplosaurus*, and it had a great bony knob on its tail, which must have been very threatening as a weapon.

The most successful of this group of dinosaurs were the horned dinosaurs, or Ceratopsia, which means "horned faces." Fossil remains of one of the earliest horned dinosaurs were first uncovered in Asia. This dinosaur was named *Protoceratops*, which means "primitive horned face." *Protoceratops* was small—about 6 feet (2 meters) long. The head had little horns or what appeared to be the beginnings of horn development.

The remains of *Protoceratops* were found near nests of eggs—the first conclusive evidence that dinosaurs were egg layers. Some of the eggs had hatched millions of years ago, and the bones of the little ones showed their relationship to the adults.

Little is known of what happened in later times to *Protoceratops*. But the fossil record shows that millions of years later, similar horned dinosaurs lived in North America. These animals were huge. They had skulls 7 feet (more than 2 meters) long, with large horns on the face and a great frill of bone extending over the neck. They probably looked like giant rhinoceroses. The body was unarmored, but the sharp horns on the head kept off most of their enemies. One of the best known of these animals was *Triceratops*, which had a large horn on the nose and a long horn over each eye.

These dinosaurs lived in the last days of the Cretaceous. When the Cretaceous ended about 65 million years ago, the days of the dinosaurs were over.

▶THE END OF THE DINOSAURS

The disappearance of the dinosaurs is in some ways a great mystery. During the time the dinosaurs lived, many new kinds developed and other older kinds died out. Not all kinds died out at once, but by the end of the Cretaceous period, the last of the dinosaurs had disappeared. Scientists have proposed several theories to explain the disappearance of the dinosaurs.

One theory suggests that dinosaurs were unable to keep up with the many changes that were occurring on the earth toward the end of the Cretaceous period. During the dinosaur age, the earth was very different from the earth today. The climate was generally warmer than it is in the same part of the world today. Large masses of land were covered with inland seas bordered by swamps. And it was in the waters of the seas and on the banks and swamps beside them that the vast number of dinosaurs lived.

Then very slowly, the geography of the earth changed. As the land changed, the habitats that the dinosaurs were used to disappeared, leaving many dinosaurs homeless. Changes in the land brought changes in the vegetation, and the plant-eating dinosaurs were affected. As the plant eaters began to die out, the flesh eaters began to be short of meat. All these changes in geography, plant life, and climate became too much for animals used to other conditions.

The Asteroid Theory

Some scientists believe that the end of the dinosaur may have been caused by an object or event in the earth's solar system or beyond. (This is based on the observation that great extinctions seem to have occurred at intervals of about 26 million years.) As a result, astronomers and astrophysicists—as well as geologists and paleontologists—have begun to study the puzzle of dinosaur extinction.

In 1980 the asteroid theory was proposed by Luis and Walter Alvarez. This theory is based on the discovery of unusually high concentrations of the rare metal iridium at rock levels close to the level of the last dinosaur remains. Iridium is more common in meteorites than in rocks found in the earth's crust.

The impact of an extraterrestrial object, such as a giant asteroid, smashing into the earth could have led to the dinosaurs' final extinction.

According to this theory, a large asteroid crashed into the earth about the time the dinosaurs disappeared. The force of the collision caused a huge cloud of dust to circle the earth. The dust blocked the sun's light for as long as five years. This killed many plants, and without food, the dinosaurs died too.

Other Theories

In addition to the asteroid theory, there is the theory of the exploding star, or supernova. This theory suggests that a supernova showered the earth with deadly radiation that killed off the dinosaurs.

Another theory suggests the existence of an unseen companion star to our sun. It has been called the death star, or Nemesis. Its theoretical orbit would bring it close to the sun about every 26 million years. When it comes close to the sun, it disturbs the gravitational balance of the solar system causing showers of comets to crash into the earth. This could cause catastrophes including the extinction of the dinosaurs. Other theories include the Planet X hypothesis. This suggests the presence of an unseen tenth planet in our solar system. Its orbit could also cause comet showers on earth. The result, again, would be periodic extinctions.

Still another theory is that the dinosaurs died from disease. As land bridges formed between masses of land that were once far apart, it became possible for dinosaurs to migrate. Epidemics could have spread during these migrations.

None of these theories has yet been documented. However, we do know that the conditions that supported dinosaur life changed irreversibly. The huge reptiles that walked the earth for more than 165 million years were not, in the end, able to survive the changes.

W. E. Swinton
Massey College, University of Toronto

Reviewed by John H. Ostrom
Peabody Museum of Natural History
Yale University

See also Birds (The First Birds); Earth, History of (Mesozoic Time); Fossils.

DIONYSUS. See Greek Mythology (Profiles).

DIPHTHERIA. See Diseases (Descriptions of Some Diseases).

DIPLOMACY. See International Relations.

DIRECT MAIL. See Mail Order.

DISABILITIES, PEOPLE WITH

A disability is a permanent condition that significantly limits the kind or amount of activity a person can perform. The most common are physical disabilities, which can restrict mobility, use of the hands, and even speaking. Other disabilities, such as deafness and blindness, affect the senses. Still others are mental, emotional, or behavioral.

The United Nations estimates that there are some 600 million people with disabilities in the world today. In the United States, some 36 million people, roughly one out of every eight, have disabilities. When lesser impairments are added, the total rises to 56 million people. All people with disabilities also have abilities, which they use to study, work, support their families, and contribute to their communities.

▶ TYPES OF DISABILITIES

In many countries, wars and violent conflicts are a major cause of physical disabilities in children and adults. Such disabilities can also be caused by accidents or by diseases such as cerebral palsy, which typically occurs at birth. Physical disabilities are most common among senior citizens and among teens who are injured playing sports or while driving. Most people with physical disabilities require help to move around.

Physical disabilities related to the senses include problems hearing or seeing. The term "deafness" is used when a person's hearing loss is severe or profound. Blindness is defined as 20/200 vision. That is, a blind person can see a letter or a chart at 20 feet (6 meters) that a typically sighted person can see at 200 feet (60 meters), or ten times 20 feet.

Blindness and deafness occur most often in people in their 60's or older, but younger people may become so through accidents or illnesses. Some children are born blind or deaf (seldom both). Many people who are not blind or deaf may still have problems seeing or hearing well. They often benefit from hearing aids and eyeglasses.

Learning disabilities can hamper a person's ability to speak or write, solve mathematical problems, pay attention, or even understand when other people speak. Such disabilities are life-long conditions, but most people learn ways to cope with them. One of the most common types of learning disabilities is a reading disorder sometimes called dyslexia.

ADHD, a behavioral disorder, is also very common. In one type of ADHD, people find it hard to pay attention or concentrate; they are easily distracted. In the other type, they find it hard to sit still, stop talking, or wait their turn.

Mental retardation limits the amount people can learn and how fast they can learn. Emotional disabilities include mild disturbances and more serious mental illnesses, such as psychosis, in which a person may lose the ability to deal with reality.

Other diseases are becoming more common as more people live longer, including Alzheimer's, a disease of the brain. There are also a growing

Above: A woman on the U.S. team skis to a gold medal victory at the 2002 Paralympic Games, an event held for athletes with disabilities. *Right:* A young Iraqi boy injured during a bomb attack learns to use an artificial leg that will improve his mobility.

number of children and young people with autism, a severe brain disorder that limits attention, communication, and other interaction with people. To date there are no cures for either of these diseases.

▶ PREVENTION AND TREATMENT

Some disabilities can be prevented by early detection, diagnosis, and treatment of the diseases that lead to them. An example is glaucoma, a disease of the optic nerve of the eye. It can cause blindness if not treated. Other disabilities can be prevented by reducing violence and by cutting back accidents on the road, in the workplace, and at home.

Proper diagnosis and treatment are critical in aiding people with disabilities. Almost anyone with disabilities can benefit from **rehabilitation**, which is the process of helping people with disabilities make the most of their abilities.

Rehabilitation includes medical care and treatment; counseling; physical therapy; speech and hearing therapy; self-care and job training; and devices that help people with disabilities live independently.

For people with physical disabilities, the first step is often medical and surgical treatment. For example, doctors prescribe digital hearing aids to some patients with hearing problems so that they may hear better. Many thousands of Americans who are deaf receive cochlear implants, which are surgical devices that can restore some hearing. Doctors may perform surgery to help restore sight to some of those who are blind. They may also use a technique called microsurgery to replace severed limbs. Or they may implant special aids such as artificial joints, including hips and knees, to help people walk again.

Even when abilities cannot be restored surgically, much can be done to help people with disabilities lead better lives. For example, an occupational therapist can teach someone who has difficulty walking to use a motorized or manual wheelchair, crutches, or a walker. With these aids, people with physical disabilities find it easier to go to school or work or to engage in community activities.

Many products are available that assist people in dressing, eating, communicating, and other everyday activities. There are more than 100,000 such devices.

Most people with mental retardation can learn to become less dependent on others. Through one-on-one instruction, and much practice, people with mild or moderate mental retardation can often master daily living skills. People with emotional disorders can be helped with special forms of therapy as well

A therapist helps a boy with cerebral palsy improve his coordination. Almost anyone with disabilities can be helped through rehabilitation.

as medications, which, if taken as directed, alleviate symptoms in many cases.

The most common treatment for people with disabilities is special education, which uses specially designed teaching materials and methods. For example, deaf students are taught to read lips and use sign language. Children with writing disorders may be taught to do their assignments on a computer keyboard or take oral rather than written tests. Most people with ADHD learn to cope with their limitations through special education, along with supportive treatments.

Increasingly, students with disabilities are benefiting from technologies adapted for them. For example, children with reading disorders or vision problems can view words printed in big letters on a computer screen or have text read aloud by the computer. For the blind there are Braille keyboards. Those who have difficulty moving their hands can use a special mouse that does not require a precise movement to click on an item on the computer screen.

▶ EMPLOYMENT

Some 13 million, or about one-third, of the 36 million American adults with disabilities have jobs. With education, job training, and modern technology, people with disabilities can do almost any job their abilities and interests lead them to try. There are newspaper and magazine writers and editors who are blind, school and college teachers who are deaf, business executives who have physical limitations, and counselors and social workers with learning disabilities.

Advances in technology are helping people with disabilities to work. For example, people who are blind use e-mail and word-processing programs that respond to verbal commands. Those who are deaf make and receive phone calls via high-speed telecommunications connections known as broadband. With broadband, people may sign to each other over phone lines. Those same broadband connections allow people with severe health or mobility problems to telecommute—that is, to work from their homes.

▶ ROLE OF GOVERNMENT

The United States has a number of laws and programs that demonstrate the role governments can play in helping people with disabilities. The Rehabilitation Act of 1973 helps many adults with disabilities get job training. The Individuals with Disabilities Education Act of 1975 provides special education through high school for all students with disabilities. The 1990 Americans with Disabilities Act (ADA) prohibits discrimination against people with disabilities in employment, transportation, public accommodation, communications, and government activities.

Largely because of ADA, in most cities and towns in America, people using wheelchairs or other mobility devices can access

A musician uses an artificial hand to play the keyboard. Advances in technology offer new ways for people with disabilities to make the most of their abilities.

public buildings, stores, recreational facilities, airports, bus terminals, train stations, and other transit facilities. There is not as much suitable access to private homes and apartments.

The two-thirds of people with disabilities who do not have jobs depend on government Medicare and Medicaid programs to help pay their medical bills. In addition, Social Security Disability Insurance and Supplemental Security Income provide them with some money. Since people with disabilities cannot use such programs unless they have little or no job income, many are discouraged from working.

In addition to the federal regulations cited above, rehabilitation services are offered in all 50 states through state vocational rehabilitation agencies. Important support is also provided by private organizations, including Easter Seals, United Cerebral Palsy, the American Foundation for the Blind, and the Arc.

▶ THE WAY AHEAD

Too often, people without disabilities see those who have them only in terms of their limitations, not in terms of their abilities. Just as medicine helps people with disabilities live longer and better lives, society needs to help them be full participants in their communities. This means hiring more people with disabilities and providing them with more accessible housing.

Governments can contribute by supporting medical research that will help today's people with disabilities live better lives and that will prevent or lessen disabilities in the future. They can also support prevention, including safety regulations and the early detection, diagnosis, and treatment of diseases that lead to disabilities.

FRANK BOWE
Hofstra University
Author, *Making Inclusion Work*

See also ADHD; ALZHEIMER'S DISEASE; BLINDNESS; DEAFNESS; LEARNING DISORDERS; MENTAL ILLNESS; OCCUPATIONAL THERAPY; RETARDATION, MENTAL.

DISARMAMENT

Disarmament means controlling, limiting, or reducing armed forces and weapons. By disarming, governments hope to prevent wars. The efforts to disarm have been many; the successes have been few.

Some historians have estimated that since 3600 B.C. the world has had only about 300 years of peace. During this time there probably have been over 14,000 wars, large and small, in which more than 1 billion people have been killed.

Disarmament is known to have taken place as long ago as the 500's B.C. A league of Chinese Yellow River states defeated a warlike Yangtze state, brought it into the league, and made a treaty of disarmament. But most disarmament efforts have been made in the past several hundred years, when weapons have become more powerful than ever.

The efforts toward disarmament grew in the 1900's. After World War I (1914–18), there was a burst of hope for worldwide disarmament. In 1919 the Treaty of Versailles was signed, ending the war. The treaty required Germany to disarm so that the other nations of the world could disarm, too. But Germany rearmed when Adolf Hitler came to power in the 1930's. Twenty years after the Treaty of Versailles was signed, the world was at war again.

After the end of World War II in 1945, disarmament became more important than ever before. This was due to the fact that the United States and the Soviet Union, as well as some other nations, built up enormous stores of nuclear weapons. In the event of a new war, these weapons of mass destruction were capable of wiping out civilization.

▶ NUCLEAR DISARMAMENT

The first plan to control nuclear weapons was proposed in 1946 by the United States at the United Nations. The plan was called the Baruch Plan in honor of Bernard Baruch, the United States representative to the United Nations Atomic Energy Commission. At the time, only the United States had atomic weapons. The Baruch Plan called for these weapons to be destroyed. American atomic secrets would be turned over to an international atomic control agency. The agency would then be in charge of all activities—peacetime

as well as wartime—involving atomic energy. Unfortunately, the Baruch Plan was turned down by the Soviet Union. The Soviets wanted veto power in the atomic control agency. They wanted the power to vote down any decision on their own. The United States, which did not want any nation to have the veto, would not accept this proposal by the Soviet Union.

The United States made a number of other proposals for disarmament during the following years. Among these were plans to reduce the size of armed forces and reduce the number of weapons, both nuclear and non-nuclear; to ban nuclear testing; to stop production of nuclear materials; and to use nuclear materials for peace.

The Soviet Union also put forward its own disarmament plans. These generally dealt with matters similar to those contained in the United States plans. But, among other things, the two sides could not agree on one basic question: how each nation could make sure the other kept its end of the agreement. The United States insisted that inspectors be allowed on Russian and American soil to see that there was no cheating. The Soviet Union argued that inspection and control would merely be cover-ups for American spying.

Although no disarmament came out of these long years of discussion, the United States did have some success with the Atoms for Peace Plan presented in 1953. Four years later this led to the establishment of an International Atomic Energy Agency.

▶ TWO APPROACHES TO DISARMAMENT

In the years since the Baruch Plan was proposed, the disarmament question has been discussed at more than 100 international conferences. Generally two approaches have been taken to the problem. One approach is to try to work out a total disarmament program. The other approach is to attempt to agree on any single measure or group of measures that would add to world peace and security.

Total Disarmament

The first approach—toward general and complete disarmament—gives little promise of quick success. Total disarmament means reducing armed forces and weapons step by step until there are none (or almost none) left. The differences between Americans and

Soviets on getting total disarmament centered on three main issues. These issues were balance, inspection (monitoring), and methods of keeping the peace during disarmament and afterward.

Balance means disarming in such a way that neither side ever gains a military advantage. The United States and the Soviet Union agreed that there ought to be balance. But in the past, each believed that the proposals made by the other side would give that side an advantage.

The United States also said that inspection was needed so that each side could be sure the other was disarming. But the Soviets long claimed that inspection was necessary only after nations had completely disarmed.

Finally, there was the disagreement about keeping the peace during and after disarmament. The United States wanted a permanent organization to make sure that world peace and security would be protected as armed forces were reduced. The Soviet Union agreed with the idea of some international control of disarmament but disliked the idea of forming a permanent organization.

Limited Disarmament

Agreement among the world's nations on total disarmament will be difficult to accomplish. However, in recent years there has been considerable progress in agreements to greatly limit armaments of various kinds.

In 1968, after years of negotiations, the Nuclear Nonproliferation Treaty was signed. ("Nonproliferation" means controlling the spread of something.) More than 120 countries have ratified this treaty, which seeks to prohibit the spread of nuclear weapons to countries that do not have them. The treaty also requires countries that already have nuclear weapons to try to reduce the numbers they have.

Beginning in 1969, the Soviet Union and the United States held Strategic Arms Limitation Talks (SALT). These talks were aimed at limiting and eventually reducing the numbers of their strategic nuclear arms. ("Strategic" arms are weapons capable of reaching targets in an enemy's homeland.) A strategic arms limitation treaty was finally agreed upon. It was signed in 1972. The pact limited the numbers of certain weapons each nation could maintain. In 1979 the two nations agreed upon a second SALT pact, imposing further limitations.

In 1987 improved relations between the United States and the Soviet Union led to the signing of the INF treaty, which banned all intermediate-range nuclear forces. For the first time, both sides agreed to permit inspections of military facilities to verify that the terms of the treaty were being carried out.

In 1990 the United States and the Soviet Union reached an agreement in principle on a new arms pact that would greatly reduce conventional weapons. The Strategic Arms Reduction Treaty (START), cutting long-range nuclear missiles, was signed by the United States and the Soviet Union in 1991. A second START treaty was signed between the Russian Federation and the United States in 1993. In 2002, the United States and Russia signed the Treaty of Moscow, pledging to eliminate two-thirds of their long-range nuclear warheads by 2012.

In 1996 the United Nations General Assembly approved the Comprehensive Test Ban Treaty, banning all nuclear testing, but it was rejected by the U.S. Senate in 1999.

Biological and Chemical Warfare. Infecting the enemy with diseases is called biological warfare. A 1975 treaty prohibiting the production of biological weapons has been ratified by over 100 nations.

Chemical warfare is the military use of chemicals that kill people or destroy food supplies. In 1997, 165 nations signed the Chemical Weapon Convention Treaty, prohibiting the use or sale of poison gas weapons.

▶ THE FUTURE

When the Cold War ended with the collapse of the Soviet Union in 1991, there was great hope that weapons of mass destruction might be eliminated and funds diverted to peaceful causes. But in 2003, the nuclear menace was renewed when North Korea threatened to step up its weapons program. That same year, the United States cited the threat of secret nuclear weapons development as the main reason for invading Iraq.

WILLIAM C. FOSTER
Former Director, United States Arms Control and
Disarmament Agency

DISCOVERY AND EXPLORATION. See EXPLORATION AND DISCOVERY.

DISASTERS

Disasters are unforeseen and often sudden events that cause great destruction and human suffering. They are often caused by nature but can also be caused by people. Disasters, including earthquakes, droughts, and wars, cause damage wherever they occur. However, they tend to cause greater loss of property than life in the developed, or richer countries, and greater loss of life than property in the developing, or poorer, ones.

The U.S. state of Kansas, for example, suffers from a drought nearly every ten years. The corn fails to grow, and farmers earn very little money from their crops. But the farmers do not starve. They are insured, and they receive government payments that help them carry on until the next harvest.

In contrast, when the same drought hits farmers growing the same crops in a developing country such as Sudan or Niger in Africa, the results are devastating. The farmers have no insurance, and their government is too poor to assist them. The drought destroys their crops, taking away their food. There is famine, which means that many people have too little to eat and are liable to die.

Disasters cause great destruction, leaving people homeless, as seen here in Indonesia, where a tsunami demolished the town of Banda Aceh in 2004.

▶ WHAT TRIGGERS DISASTERS?

Disasters can be triggered by a natural event, such as a hurricane, or by human-made events such as wars or technological accidents, which include chemical spills. They can happen rapidly or build slowly.

Sometimes disasters are caused by a combination of events. Global warming is the rise in the average temperature of the Earth's surface caused largely by the burning of coal, gasoline, and other fossil fuels. This warming is causing the climate in parts of Africa to become dryer. The result is crop failures in those areas, which means the people living there can neither grow food to eat nor earn money from crop sales to buy food.

Over time, as a result of the combination of global warning and crop failures, famine sets in and people die from diseases that hunger makes them too weak to resist.

▶ DISASTER TRENDS

Between 1900 and 2004, the number of people reported killed by disasters tended to fall, while the number affected by disasters rose steeply. On the positive side, this shows that most countries have gotten better at responding to disasters and providing medical care to disaster victims. On the negative side, there are growing numbers of survivors who require immediate disaster relief, including water and sanitation, food, medical help, shelter, and protection. Many may also have lost their homes and their ability to earn a living.

Disasters can be a major cause of poverty, particularly in developing countries such as China or Vietnam, where floods or droughts hit villages year after year, preventing people from rebuilding and improving their lives.

Around the world each year, disasters kill an average of 67,000 people, but they injure and destroy the homes, schools, jobs, and livelihoods of an average of 260 million people. In December 2004, a massive earthquake in the Indian Ocean caused deadly tsunamis (series of huge waves) that badly damaged India, Indonesia, Maldives, Sri Lanka, and Thailand. In this one disaster, some 300,000 people in a total of twelve countries were killed or remain missing. Millions lost their homes and their ability to earn a living.

Most natural disasters happen in Asia, including earthquakes, hurricanes, floods, and droughts. On average, 90 percent of people affected by disasters live in Asia, and 71 per-

NOTABLE DISASTERS

Drought—Ethiopia: 2002 to 2004. 13.2 million people affected.* Brazil: 1998. 10 million people affected.

Earthquake—Pakistan: October 8, 2005. Over 86,000 people killed; over 100,000 injured; more than 3 million lost their homes.

Epidemic—Bangladesh: April 1991. Diarrhea. 1,000 killed; 1.5 million affected.

Flood—Bangladesh: April 30,1991. 138,866 people killed; 138,849 injured; 300,000 lost their homes; 15 million people affected. $1.8 billion in damage.

Hurricane—United States: August 2005 (Hurricane Katrina). Over 1,000 people killed; 500,000 affected. $25 billion in damage.

Landslides and mudslides—Kyrgyzstan: April 14, 1994. 111 people killed; 13,500 lost their homes; 45,000 affected. $36 million in damage.

Technological accident—Bhopal, India: December 3, 1984. 2,500 people killed; 100,000 injured. 200,000 affected.

Tsunami—Aceh province, Indonesia: December 26, 2004. 65,708 people killed; 532,898 lost their homes. $452 million in damage.

War—Democratic Republic of the Congo: 1998 to 2002. At least 2.5 million people killed.

*Affected people require immediate disaster relief, including food, water, shelter, sanitation, and medical help.

cent of all deaths related to disasters happen in Asia.

Drought leading to famine, which is the biggest killer by far, takes the lives of nearly three times as many people as earthquakes each year. Water-related disasters, such as floods and hurricanes, cause the most damage.

▶ WHO HELPS IN DISASTERS?

Most help for the victims of disasters comes from their families and local communities. Relatives living abroad often send home money to help. Local government agencies also provide assistance, and many countries have a national disaster response agency.

International help comes from other governments, either directly or working together through the United Nations. It may also be provided by the National Red Cross and Red Crescent Societies, which assist some 233 million people each year. There is a Red Cross or Red Crescent organization in nearly every country in the world.

Disaster relief also comes from private organizations formed by people who want to help. These are called nongovernmental organizations (NGO's) and include Oxfam, CARE, and Save the Children Fund. These groups raise money from private citizens in order to provide relief around the world.

▶ DISASTER RELIEF

Disaster relief always aims to accomplish two things: to save lives and to do so regardless of who is suffering. It does not matter to a disaster relief agency whether the victims are on one side of a war or another, if they are Christian or Muslim, black or white. All that matters is that people are suffering and need assistance.

Each disaster is unique, but response efforts tend to occur in the following phases: search and rescue, immediate relief, reconstruction of homes and other buildings, and long-term development, including programs to reduce poverty. Fast search and rescue is vital after a disaster such as an earthquake, in which many buildings and other structures may be destroyed. People trapped in collapsed buildings can die very quickly from their injuries. About 90 percent of all the people who are pulled out of the rubble alive

In New Orleans, Louisiana, the U.S. Coast Guard rescues a survivor of Hurricane Katrina (2005). Search and rescue is usually the first response to a natural disaster.

a. A tsunami crashes over an island where no people live.

b. A tsunami smashes into a seaside resort where the people have been warned the wave is coming and have moved to the safety of higher ground.

c. A tsunami arrives at a quiet little fishing port where no one was expecting it. As it crashes in, hundreds of people are killed.

The correct answer is c. Disasters tend to be unforeseen and cause human suffering and loss of property, particularly when people are unprepared for them.

after an earthquake are rescued in the first day; after that, far fewer people survive. This means that search-and-rescue teams need to be local or on standby and ready to work at a moment's notice.

Immediate relief consists of providing:

Water and Sanitation. Water must be provided quickly to disaster victims—without it, people can die within days. Good sanitation and toilets are also needed, because disease spreads fast in the aftermath of a disaster.

Food. In many disasters, people need food urgently. In developing countries, food may be available, but the disaster victims are often too poor to buy it. Disaster relief agencies may supply food, or they may help people earn money so that they can buy food.

Medical Care. After a disaster, many people are weak from hunger and thirst and so can die more easily from malaria, measles, or even diarrhea. International aid agencies, such as the group Doctors without Borders, often provide emergency health care.

Shelter. After earthquakes, hurricanes, floods, and even drought, people often find that their houses have been destroyed. In famines people leave their villages in search of food. Relief agencies provide such people with emergency shelter to protect them from the weather, including rain or the hot sun. Often the shelters are made from tree branches around which blue plastic sheeting is thrown, forming a simple enclosure. But these basic shelters provide disaster victims with somewhere to call home.

Protection. Soldiers and other groups often attack people caught in and around wars as the victims flee for their lives. Women and young men are those most often attacked. Aid agencies try to protect disaster victims by coming between them and their attackers and by making the attacks public to discourage further violence.

As people recover from disaster they often form local organizations to help them plan

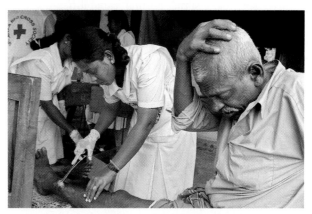

A Red Cross nurse provides medical care to a man injured in a natural disaster in Sri Lanka. More people survive disasters today than a century ago.

for the future. International aid agencies work with these local groups to better prepare people for future disasters and to make future disasters less likely, including, for example, by adopting early warning systems.

▶ THE FUTURE

Most disasters should not happen. Hurricanes hitting Bangladesh used to claim the lives of tens of thousands of people every year. That does not happen today, because the government has learned how to prepare for disasters and to protect its people, so that fewer of them are affected or die. It is impossible to stop earthquakes, droughts, and other destructive natural events, but with enough effort it may be possible to prevent them from turning into disasters.

PETER WALKER
Director, Feinstein International Famine Center
Friedman School of Nutrition Science and Policy,
Tufts University

DISCOVERY AND EXPLORATION. See EXPLORATION AND DISCOVERY.

DISEASES

A disease is a disturbance of a body structure or function. It may make a person physically or mentally ill, limit his or her activities, or even lead to death. Sometimes disease brings obvious changes in body structures, such as swelling of the jaw in mumps or the open sores in certain types of cancer. Sometimes no changes in body structures can be found, even under a microscope, but the person loses some normal capabilities—cannot see clearly, for example, or is unable to become pregnant.

Subjective changes—things that the sick person feels, such as pain or weakness—are called **symptoms** of disease. Objective changes, which other people can observe, are referred to as **signs** of disease. Unusual redness or a spotty rash on the skin, a higher than normal body temperature, an increase in the number of white blood cells, and various other changes that can be seen or discovered through tests can all be signs of disease.

▶ KINDS OF DISEASES

An illness that comes on suddenly, such as an attack of vomiting after eating spoiled food, is referred to as **acute**. In a **chronic** condition, on the other hand, symptoms either continue or return from time to time for a period of months or years. Some diseases can be chronic but then become acute. For exam-

This article describes the many kinds of diseases, the diagnosis and treatment of disease, and the prevention of disease. It includes a feature that contains descriptions of selected diseases, in alphabetical order.

Cardiovascular diseases are covered in HEART and CIRCULATORY SYSTEM; dermatological diseases in DERMATOLOGY; gastrointestinal disorders in DIGESTIVE SYSTEM; liver disorders in LIVER; mental and emotional disorders in MENTAL ILLNESS; musculoskeletal disorders in MUSCULAR SYSTEM; renal and urologic disorders in KIDNEYS; and respiratory disorders in LUNGS.

The article MEDICINE provides a general overview of medical practice and research and the history of medicine. Specific methods used to diagnose illnesses are described in IMAGING, DIAGNOSTIC and X-RAYS. Nontraditional healing practices are discussed in ALTERNATIVE MEDICINE and HOLISTIC MEDICINE. Other articles on treatment and prevention include ANTIBIOTICS, DRUGS, HEALTH, and PUBLIC HEALTH. Immunity, or how the body resists disease, is covered in ANTIBODIES AND ANTIGENS, IMMUNE SYSTEM, and VACCINATION AND IMMUNIZATION.

ple, diabetes is a chronic disease in which the body does not use and store sugars properly. By exercising, eating a special diet, and taking certain drugs or injections of the hormone insulin, diabetics (people who have diabetes) can usually keep their symptoms under control and lead a relatively normal life. But a diabetic who takes in too much sugar or injects too much insulin may have a sudden acute attack that can result in unconsciousness.

Diseases can have many causes. **Infectious** diseases are the result of invasions of tiny microbes such as bacteria and viruses, which get into the body and multiply to huge numbers. Some of the symptoms of microbe-caused diseases are actually the effects of **toxins**, poisons produced by the germs. Some signs, such as fever and swelling, are actually a part of the body's defenses against infection.

Not all diseases are the result of infection. **Noninfectious** diseases are usually the result of something going wrong with organs or functions of the body. In **immunological** diseases, for example, the body's immune de-

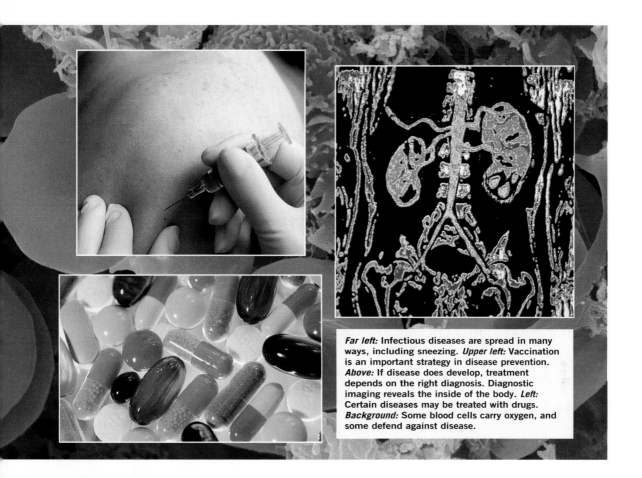

Far left: Infectious diseases are spread in many ways, including sneezing. *Upper left:* Vaccination is an important strategy in disease prevention. *Above:* If disease does develop, treatment depends on the right diagnosis. Diagnostic imaging reveals the inside of the body. *Left:* Certain diseases may be treated with drugs. *Background:* Some blood cells carry oxygen, and some defend against disease.

fenses do not work properly. They may turn against the body's own cells, damaging them instead of protecting them. Some noninfectious diseases are **congenital**, meaning they are present at birth. Others are **hereditary**, passed on from parents to children. In **hormonal** diseases, the body's chemistry can be disrupted by endocrine system disorders. In **degenerative** diseases, various parts of the body break down and lose their ability to work normally. In **neoplastic** diseases, including the many forms of cancer, the processes of cell growth and reproduction run wild and form tumors.

Failure to eat a balanced diet or conditions in which the body is unable to use certain foods properly may result in **nutritional** diseases. Chemicals in the air, water, and food as well as radiation, noise, and other influences that can affect people at home or at work may have damaging effects on the body. They can produce various **occupational** and **environmental** diseases. **Mental** and **emotional** diseases, such as depression, may be the re-sult of disorders in the body or influences in the environment. The mind can also have positive and negative effects on the health of the body. You can read more about mental and emotional diseases in the article MENTAL ILLNESS in Volume M.

Infectious Diseases

Until the 1940's, infectious diseases were the major cause of death in many parts of the world. **Bacteria** and **viruses** are the main groups of microbes that can cause infectious diseases. Bacteria damage the body by producing poisons called toxins, and viruses may kill the cells they infect. Various **parasites** (tiny creatures that live off a host's body), including plantlike fungi, microscopic animal-like protozoa, and a number of worms, can also be **pathogenic** (disease-causing) for humans. Abnormally shaped proteins called **prions** can cause a rare, fatal brain disease.

Disease-Causing Bacteria. Bacteria are single-celled organisms too small to be seen without a high-powered microscope. There are three main kinds: **coccus**, shaped like tiny, round balls; rod-shaped **bacillus**, which may be covered with hairlike projections; and corkscrew-shaped **spirillum**. Pictures and further information on each kind appear in the article BACTERIA in Volume B.

Not all bacteria are pathogenic. Harmless bacteria swarm on the skin and in the mouth and digestive tract. Some of them even make vitamins the body can use. But when pathogenic forms enter the body, they can lead to illness. Many bacterial infections affect a particular part of the body. However, untreated bacterial infections can spread to the bloodstream. Common disease-causing bacteria include the bacilli responsible for tuberculosis, typhoid fever, and botulism (a deadly type of food poisoning); the cocci that cause strep throat and rheumatic fever, "staph" infections, and some forms of pneumonia; and the spirillum responsible for the sexually transmitted disease syphilis.

Disease-Causing Viruses. Viruses are much smaller than bacteria—so small they cannot be seen with an ordinary light microscope. Only electron microscopes provide enough magnification to show viruses. A virus is the simplest form of life, consisting of a core of nucleic acid, containing the instructions for making new viruses, and an outer coat of protein. Viruses cannot live on their own. They invade cells and turn them into tiny virus factories, making them manufacture new virus particles that can go out and infect new cells. You can read more about them in the article VIRUSES in Volume UV.

Diseases caused by viruses include the common cold and influenza, chicken pox, measles, mumps, and AIDS. Viruses are linked to some cancers, such as certain cervical and liver cancers.

Parasites and Other Microbes. In addition to bacteria and viruses, other types of microbes can also cause infectious diseases. They include

DESCRIPTIONS OF SOME DISEASES

Acne
See DERMATOLOGY in Volume D.

AIDS
See AIDS in Volume A.

Allergies
See ALLERGIES in Volume A.

Alzheimer's Disease
See ALZHEIMER'S DISEASE in Volume A.

Anemia
Anemia occurs when there is a shortage of red blood cells or a shortage of iron-containing hemoglobin, the molecule that carries oxygen and gives red blood cells their color. There are many different causes of anemia. The most common cause in children is a diet low in certain nutrients needed to make hemoglobin, especially iron, folic acid, or vitamin B12. Temporary anemia may occur after loss of blood from an injury. Sickle-cell anemia (described later in this feature) is an inherited disease that causes the premature destruction of red blood cells.

To determine what kind of anemia is involved, a doctor performs a blood test. Then the doctor may prescribe an appropriate medicine or suggest a change in diet.

Anorexia Nervosa
See MENTAL ILLNESS (Eating Disorders) in Volume M.

Anthrax
Anthrax is caused by a type of bacteria called *Bacillus anthracis*. The disease usually occurs in animals such as cattle and sheep, but in rare cases it can affect humans. Human infections occur when a person comes in contact with anthrax bacteria spores, usually through contact with an infected animal or infected animal products.

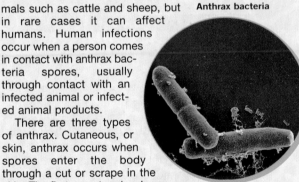

Anthrax bacteria

There are three types of anthrax. Cutaneous, or skin, anthrax occurs when spores enter the body through a cut or scrape in the skin. The first symptom is a bump or pimple on the skin, which grows into a sore with a dark center. If left untreated, blood poisoning can result. Inhalation of anthrax spores causes an infection of the lungs. The infected person may experience severe difficulty breathing as toxins (poisons) produced by bacteria cause swelling and bleeding in the lungs. Inhalation anthrax is often fatal. The third type of anthrax is gastrointestinal anthrax. This form of the disease is very rare in the United States.

Anthrax is diagnosed using a test to look for anthrax bacteria in the blood. Doctors prescribe antibiotics, including ciprofloxacin and doxycycline, to treat anthrax. Anthrax is not spread from person to person. Bioterrorists infected 22 people in the United States in 2001 by mailing spores.

Appendicitis
At one spot along the large intestine, there is a little tube that branches off. It is about 4 inches (10

various kinds of **fungi**, such as the ringworm pathogen, and microscopic, animal-like **protozoa**, such as the ones that cause malaria (the most widespread disease in the world), amebic dysentery, and African sleeping sickness. Flatworms (such as tapeworms) and roundworms (pinworms and trichina worms, for example) produce various **parasitic diseases**.

Transmission of Infectious Diseases. Bacteria, viruses, and other disease-causing microbes can be transmitted, or passed, from one person to another in various ways. A sneeze can carry the microscopic particles through the air on droplets of moisture, which another person may breathe in. Sharing food or a drinking glass can spread germs. The hands, constantly touching things, can pick up microbes and then carry them to the mouth or eyes.

In areas where sanitation is poor, microbes from the feces and urine of sick people may pass into the food or drinking water. Any time the skin is broken, microbes can swarm into the wound, producing infection.

Flies walking on filth and then landing on food can spread germs. Some biting insects such as mosquitoes and fleas may carry microbes in their bodies and inject them into people they bite. Ticks may carry *Rickettsia* bacteria. The *R. rickettsii* species causes Rocky Mountain spotted fever. How some microbes are carried by other animals and cause disease in humans is described in the article VECTORS OF DISEASE in Volume UV.

Insect repellent sprays help prevent bites from disease-carrying pests such as mosquitoes and ticks.

People may acquire infections in hospitals and clinics. People may spread infections

---

centimeters) long and is closed at the end. It is called the appendix. As far as scientists can tell, the appendix serves no purpose in human beings. The dead-end tube makes a good place for bacteria to collect and grow. When they do, the appendix becomes sore and painful.

An infection in the appendix is called appendicitis. The chief symptom of appendicitis is pain, usually in the lower right side of the abdomen. The person may also feel like vomiting and may have a slight fever. At this point, an operation is usually done, and the appendix is removed. If an operation is not done and the infection keeps building up, the appendix may burst, letting bacteria spread to other organs in the abdomen. Once the infection has spread, the person is in serious danger and requires extensive care.

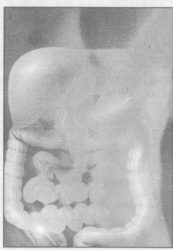

Appendicitis (lower left, in yellow)

Arteriosclerosis

See CIRCULATORY SYSTEM in Volume C and HEART in Volume H.

Arthritis

Arthritis means sore, inflamed, or stiffened joints. There are two chief kinds of arthritis: osteoarthritis, which is the most common kind, and rheumatoid arthritis.

In **osteoarthritis** the springy tissue, called cartilage, at the ends of the bones is worn away. The ends of the bones, rubbing together without their natural cushion, get rough and sore. Most people over 65 years of age are affected by some osteoarthritis.

Rheumatoid arthritis can occur at any age, often in persons as young as 30 or even younger. In rheumatoid arthritis a tough layer of inflammatory tissue grows around the joints and cripples them. Fluid may develop in the joints. The joints become enlarged, painful, and stiff. The cause of this disease is not fully understood. Treatments with anti-inflammatory substances, such as aspirin, are used to reduce the pain and swelling.

Bronchitis

Bronchitis is a disorder of the passageways, called the bronchi, that carry air to the lungs. The bronchi become inflamed, and mucus and pus form in them. The main symptom of bronchitis is frequent noisy coughing. The coughing helps clear the bronchi of mucus and other secretions. To help loosen the mucus, doctors may prescribe medications or the breathing of moist air from a vaporizer.

Bronchitis may be caused by viruses and bacteria that live in the nose and throat. Chemicals that irritate the bronchi—especially chemicals in smog

wherever they travel, and food exports may spread infections wherever they are distributed. These means of transmission grow more important as global travel and trade become more common.

After pathogenic microbes enter the body, there is a period of time, called the incubation period, when nothing seems to be happening. The person seems healthy. But the microbes are multiplying. If the body's defenses cannot cope with them, eventually they produce symptoms of disease. The length of the incubation period varies from one disease to another. It can last just a few hours in certain types of food poisoning or up to decades for some kinds of "slow viruses." During this period, when there are no signs of illness, a person may unsuspectingly transmit the bacterium or virus to others.

Exposure to an infectious disease does not necessarily mean a person will catch that disease. The body's immune system, including the microbe-eating white blood cells and antibodies (chemical defenses that attack particular kinds of germs), helps protect the body from infection. Viruses also trigger another kind of defense: Infected cells produce a substance called interferon, which protects other cells from infection. (You can find more information about the body's immune response in the article IMMUNE SYSTEM in Volume I.) Sometimes, however, the disease organisms overwhelm the body's defense against disease, and the person becomes ill.

Treating Infectious Diseases. Bacterial diseases are treated with **antibiotic** drugs such as penicillin and streptomycin. These drugs are not effective against viruses, but recently some **antiviral** drugs have been developed. However, viral diseases are still controlled mainly by preventing them with **vaccines**. A harmless form of the virus is injected into the body and stimulates the production of antibodies that work against the pathogen. The

Bronchial tubes: normal (*top*) and inflamed (*bottom*)

or tobacco smoke—may also be a cause of bronchitis.

Some people suffer from bronchitis for years and never fully recover. Such people are said to have **chronic bronchitis**. Cigarette smoking is the most significant cause of chronic bronchitis.

Bulimia
See MENTAL ILLNESS (Eating Disorders) in Volume M.

Cancer
See CANCER in Volume C.

Cataracts
See EYE in Volume E.

Cerebral Palsy
Cerebral palsy is one of the most common diseases that cause handicaps in children. It begins when lack of oxygen or an injury causes brain damage in a newborn baby. The damage affects the child's ability to use and control muscles. The area of the brain that is damaged determines the handicaps of the child with cerebral palsy. The typical victim of cerebral palsy may have trouble walking, speaking, and using the hands. A child with cerebral palsy can have normal intelligence.

The damage to the brain cannot be repaired, but doctors can relieve some of the physical problems of the cerebral-palsied child.

Chicken Pox
Chicken pox is a common virus disease of children. The virus is in the nose and throat and is probably spread through the air from person to person.

It takes two to three weeks for chicken pox to develop after exposure. It begins with a mild headache and fever. In a day or so, a red rash appears and then progresses to bumps called pox. A chicken pox bump looks like a drop of water on a red base. The bumps appear mostly on the upper part of the body, but they can occur anywhere, including inside the mouth. As they dry up, they form scabs, which later drop off. When all the bumps are dried and have scabs, the disease is no longer contagious. A chicken pox vaccine is available and recommended in the United States for children over 1 year old.

Common Cold
The cold is a common disease that is caused by a virus, usually the rhinovirus. Most people have two or three colds a year. Having a cold does not protect against future colds because so many different viruses can be the cause. Cold viruses are transferred from one person to another. Hands provide the most frequent route for transmission of a cold virus. People pick up the virus from contami-

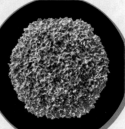

Common cold virus

person thus becomes **immune** to the disease. Young children receive vaccines to protect them against various bacterial diseases (diphtheria, whooping cough, and tetanus; also tuberculosis in some countries) and viral diseases (measles, rubella, mumps, and polio). Vaccination against smallpox has not been routine since 1977, when the last naturally occurring case in the world was recorded. Smallpox vaccine has been stockpiled, however, in case the smallpox virus ever becomes an agent of bioterrorism.

Immunological Diseases

Normally the immune system works to protect the body and keep it healthy. White blood cells not only detect and destroy invading microbes, but they also constantly inspect the body's own cells for changes that might be harmful. This **immune surveillance** is the main defense against cancer. White blood cells are continually spotting and destroying body cells that have gained the ability to grow uncontrollably and form tumors. When the immune system itself goes wrong, serious illness can result.

Some immunological diseases are **immune deficiencies**: Key parts of the immune system are missing or do not work properly. Depending on which part is lacking, the person will be defenseless against certain kinds of infections or may develop cancerous tumors. Immune deficiencies may be hereditary, or they may be acquired later in life, usually as a result of a virus infection or the action of a drug. Depending on the type of deficiency, it may be treated with bone marrow transplants or extracts of hormones from the thymus gland. (Important types of white blood cells develop in the bone marrow and thymus.)

Some types of immunological diseases develop when the immune system is too active and damages the body. In **autoimmune diseases**, the white blood cells turn against the

nated surfaces; they then carry the virus on their hands to the eyes, nose, or mouth, where it can easily enter the body. Careful hand washing is one of the best methods for preventing the spread of colds.

There is no cure for colds. Nose drops and cold pills may give some relief from the watery eyes, runny nose, and dry throat that go with a cold. But the cold pills that contain antihistamines make some people sleepy and dizzy. Antibiotics such as penicillin are not useful against cold viruses.

Croup and Laryngitis

The **larynx** is a boxlike organ at the entrance of the windpipe. It contains the vocal cords that produce the sounds of speech. When the larynx becomes inflamed during a respiratory illness, a person may be unable to speak above a whisper for several days. This condition is called laryngitis.

In a baby or young child, laryngitis is more serious than it is in an adult. A child's air passageways are much smaller than an adult's. When the tissues lining the passageways become inflamed and swollen, the space through which air may pass is made smaller. It becomes hard for the child to breathe. Taking a breath makes the child cough. The cough sounds like the bark of a seal. This condition is known as croup.

The best immediate treatment for croup is breathing in moist air. The hot water in the bathroom shower may be turned on to make a large amount of steam quickly, and the child can be taken into the bathroom to breathe in this steam. All cases of croup should be reported to the doctor immediately. Hospital care is often needed.

Cystic Fibrosis

Cystic fibrosis is a hereditary disease that affects mucus-secreting glands, such as those that line the airways of the respiratory system and the ducts of the pancreas. Because of this hereditary defect, the mucus that these glands secrete becomes thick and hard, plugging the airways and ducts. The disease also affects the sweat glands, causing the production of "salty" sweat. Babies with cystic fibrosis often taste salty when they are kissed.

When the pancreatic ducts are plugged, the flow of enzymes necessary for the digestion and absorption of food is blocked. Drugs that replace the pancreatic enzymes are available. However, the most serious problem for the person with cystic fibrosis is the accumulation of mucus in the air passages of the lungs. The thick mucus blocks the normal flow of air in and out of the lungs and leads to infection and destruction of lung tissue. At present, many persons with the disorder die at an early age because of lung disease. Scientists have identified the cystic fibrosis gene and are working on ways to correct the disorder.

People with cystic fibrosis may benefit from chest physical therapy, which includes clapping the back and chest, turning, deep breathing exercises, and coughing. This therapy is usually combined with treatments designed to remove secretions.

Diabetes

See DIABETES in Volume D.

Diphtheria

Diphtheria is a highly contagious disease. The bacteria that cause this disease most commonly

body's own cells or substances and begin to produce antibodies against them. That is the way a strep throat infection can develop into rheumatic fever: Antibodies against the *Streptococcus* bacterium may also attack cells in the joints and in the heart, producing pain and damage. Rheumatoid arthritis and systemic lupus erythematosus are two of the most common autoimmune diseases. These diseases are treated with drugs that reduce inflammation, such as aspirin and cortisone.

Allergies are another type of immunological disease. Cells that normally produce antibodies against worms and other parasites become sensitized to harmless things in the

Allergies are abnormal responses by the immune system to substances such as grass or pollen.

environment, such as dust, pollen, or foods. These cells produce inflammation, which can result in a runny nose and sneezing, difficulty in breathing, a rash on the skin, or various other annoying, painful, or even dangerous symptoms, depending on what part of the body has become sensitized.

Congenital and Hereditary Diseases

Both congenital and hereditary diseases are present at birth, but their causes are very different. **Congenital conditions** arise during the period of development before birth or during the birth process, whereas **hereditary diseases** are those that were determined at the moment of

---

infect the tonsils and other tissues in the throat, producing a toxin (poison) that circulates in the bloodstream. Symptoms include a fever, sore throat, and swollen glands. A thick, white membrane forms on the tonsils and may make breathing and swallowing difficult. The heart and nerves may also be affected, causing heart failure, paralysis, and sometimes death. The disease can be treated with a drug that neutralizes the toxin.

Diphtheria was once a widespread childhood disease that caused many deaths. Today routine vaccination of infants has nearly eliminated the disease in the United States.

Emphysema

Emphysema is a disorder that affects the tiny air sacs within the lungs. These air sacs become stretched and flabby like balloons that have been blown up many times. Eventually, the weakened

Air sacs in lungs damaged by emphysema

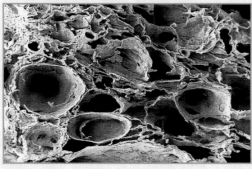

walls of the air sacs may be destroyed. Emphysema develops most often in people who have had chronic bronchitis for a long time. (Bronchitis is described earlier in this feature.) Cigarette smoking is the most significant cause of emphysema. Air pollution tends to make it worse.

People who have emphysema always feel short of breath and tire easily. This is because they cannot breathe in enough oxygen or breathe out enough carbon dioxide to keep the body cells in good working order. People can live with this disease for many years. Breathing exercises and medication can bring them some relief. Oxygen from a tank may be delivered to the nose via plastic tubes.

Epilepsy (Seizure Disorders)

Seizures, sometimes called convulsions, result when there are disturbances in the electrical activity of the brain. They are much like an electrical storm in the brain.

Seizures are not a disease, but rather a symptom of brain dysfunction. They may occur during almost any serious illness or injury affecting the brain, including infections, tumors, drug abuse, and high fevers in small children. When seizures occur on a repeated basis, the condition is sometimes called epilepsy or a seizure disorder.

There are many types of epilepsy or seizure disorders. Two common types involve **grand mal** seizures and **petit mal** seizures. Grand mal seizures cause a sudden loss of consciousness and wild jerking of the arms, legs, and other parts of the body. People with petit mal seizures experience short staring spells. There are drugs that help control seizures.

conception, programmed into the genes inherited from the parents.

Infection of a pregnant woman with the rubella (German measles) virus and certain other microbes can interfere with her child's development and result in congenital birth defects. Smoking, drinking alcoholic beverages, and taking certain drugs can also have harmful effects on a baby's development before birth.

Hereditary diseases may be dominant or recessive. A dominant condition appears in the parent and is passed on to the children. Recessive conditions must be inherited from both parents, who may have no signs or symptoms but carry the genes for the disease. (You can read more about how this works in the article GENETICS in Volume G.) Some hereditary diseases are sex-linked, affecting mainly members of one sex. Hemophilia, the "bleeders' disease," occurs mostly in males but can be carried by females.

Hereditary diseases may affect many systems of the body; Down syndrome, for example, produces characteristic changes in the face and body, mental retardation, and usually a shortened lifetime. Many hereditary diseases are **metabolic diseases**, resulting from a change in some important chemical reaction in the body. Children born with phenylketonuria (PKU), for instance, cannot use one of the amino acids that are normal building blocks of proteins. If the condition is not treated, the child becomes mentally retarded. Fortunately, phenylketonuria can be detected by a simple test of a baby's urine, and its harmful effects can be prevented with a special diet.

People who know or suspect that a hereditary disease runs in their family can undergo **genetic counseling** to determine their chances of having a child with the disease. When a woman is pregnant, tests such as amniocentesis or chorionic villi sampling can be used to

In brain X-rays of a person with a seizure disorder, abnormalities are seldom found. But an electroencephalograph—a machine for measuring brain waves—may reveal trouble. Most often the trouble is in only the part of the brain that controls the muscles, not the part that reasons and thinks.

Food Poisoning

See FOOD PRESERVATION in Volume F.

German Measles

German measles—sometimes called **rubella**, or three-day measles—is a virus disease that causes a rash of pinkish bumps. It is not related to regular measles, which is called **rubeola**, or ten-day measles. (See the entry Measles in this feature.) Roseola is a different disease, one that affects young children.

If a mother gets German measles from six to nine months before her baby is born, the baby may have a damaged heart, brain, eyes, or ears. Otherwise, it is a mild disease, causing little fever, if any. The rash begins on the face and spreads over the body. It is usually gone in three days. A vaccine that protects against rubella is now available.

Glaucoma

See EYE in Volume E.

Rash caused by German measles

Gonorrhea

Gonorrhea is a bacterial disease. It begins as an infection of the sexual organs and is spread by sexual contact. If it is not treated, gonorrhea can make a person sterile—that is, unable to have children. It can also spread to other internal organs and to the joints.

Antibiotics will usually cure gonorrhea. The early symptoms are a discharge from the sexual organs and slight pain with the passing of urine. Females with gonorrhea may have no early symptoms at all. Only a physician is qualified to diagnose and treat gonorrhea.

Heart Disease

See CIRCULATORY SYSTEM in Volume C and HEART in Volume H.

Hemophilia

Hemophilia is the name for two inherited diseases in which the blood does not clot normally. Several different proteins must be present for blood to clot properly. If one of the proteins is missing, or present at low levels, blood clots very slowly. People with hemophilia A have low levels of one kind of blood clotting protein, and people with hemophilia B have low levels of another kind. In a person with hemophilia, bleeding from a small cut can last for hours, and even a minor bump can cause a large bruise. Drug therapy and blood transfusions are used to replace the missing clotting pro-

check for various hereditary diseases. Women in their late thirties or forties, who have a higher than average chance of giving birth to a child with Down syndrome, may also choose to have such a test. (See the article DOWN SYNDROME in Volume D.)

Hormonal Diseases

Hormones are chemical messengers produced in structures called **endocrine glands**. Hormones help control growth, reproduction, and many other body functions. Endocrine disorders resulting in the production of too much or too little of a hormone can cause serious diseases. Disorders of the pituitary gland, for instance, can result in dwarfism

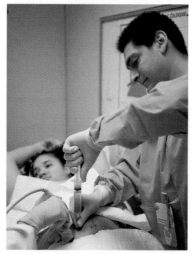

A doctor performs amniocentesis on a pregnant woman. Testing amniotic fluid can reveal genetic defects in the fetus.

(too little growth hormone) or gigantism (too much). Thyroid hormones help determine how fast the body's chemical reactions take place. Too little of these hormones makes a person sluggish and fat; too much makes a person "hyper," causing nervousness, weight loss, and sleeplessness.

The various endocrine hormones act on each other in many complicated ways. Normal sexual development, for example, is influenced not only by the sex hormones that are produced in the reproductive organs (ovaries in females and testes in males) but also by hormones that are released from the pituitary and adrenal glands.

teins. Treatments that incorporate gene therapy are also being researched.

Hemophilia A and hemophilia B are caused by recessive genes carried on the X chromosome. Females can carry the genes for these diseases, but usually only males will be born with hemophilia.

Hepatitis

See HEPATITIS in Volume H.

Herpes Simplex I and II

Herpes simplex I is a viral infection that causes blisters to form on the lips and inside the mouth. These blisters, also called cold sores, can develop into painful ulcers. Some people also have swollen gums and fever. The infection is usually mild in children and more severe in adults. Even after the infection is gone, the virus can remain. Another infection, such as a cold, or exposure to sun and wind often triggers another attack.

Herpes simplex virus

Mild cases require little treatment. This common infection usually presents no health risk. The major problem is transmission of the virus to the eye by touching it after contact with the cold sore. This can cause an ulcer to form on the eye.

Herpes simplex II is another infection caused by a herpes virus. People with this condition develop groups of blisters in the genital area. These blisters rupture and become small ulcers. Herpes simplex II is transmitted through sexual contact. About a week after contact with an infected person, pain, tenderness, and itching develop on the sexual organs. Blisters and sores soon appear and last from one to three weeks. Because the virus can remain in the body after the attack subsides, many people with herpes simplex II have repeated outbreaks of symptoms. Doctors may prescribe antiviral drugs to reduce the severity of symptoms and the frequency of outbreaks.

The risk of transmission of herpes simplex II is reduced, but not eliminated, if sexual contact is avoided until the blisters and sores clear up. Using condoms during sexual activity will also reduce the risk of transmitting the herpes infection.

Hypertension

Blood is pushed through the blood vessels by the pumping of the heart. It has to be pushed up from the heart to the brain, and it has to get back to the heart from the feet. The strength of this push is called the pressure of the blood.

Blood pressure changes with many other body changes. If the heartbeat is weak, the blood pressure may fall. If the blood vessels become narrow, the blood pressure may rise. It rises with hard exercise, fear, or excitement. It may fall with rest or sleep. The chemicals in the blood and the nerve impulses to the blood vessels control these changes.

Two numbers are used to describe a person's blood pressure. One number represents the pressure that develops as the heart contracts, or beats, pumping the blood into the blood vessels. This is called the **systolic pressure**. The other number rep-

Hormonal disorders may be treated by giving replacements of the lacking hormones. If a gland is producing too much of a hormone, the condition may be treated with surgery or radiation.

Degenerative Diseases

Body cells are constantly being destroyed and replaced. But as a person grows older, the systems that repair damage to body structures become less effective. Some kinds of cells (brain cells, for example) are not replaced; once they are lost, they are gone forever. Thus, the constant wear and tear of daily living gradually makes various body organs less able to do their jobs. Degenerative diseases are the result of a general breakdown of body structures. Some of the diseases may be a part of the natural aging process. Certain types of arthritis and cardiovascular diseases (diseases of the heart and blood vessels) are common degenerative diseases. Other examples are cirrhosis of the liver, osteoporosis of the bones, and emphysema of the lungs.

The development of effective drugs and vaccines to control infectious diseases has helped people live longer, but the result of longer life spans is that larger numbers of people now develop degenerative diseases. These diseases have become the greatest causes of disablement and death in the developed countries of the world.

Neoplastic Diseases

Neoplastic diseases are the result of changes in the body's own cells. The cells begin to divide uncontrollably, and they lose their normal **contact inhibition**—the cell's ability to recognize when it is in contact with other cells. When this inhibition is lost, cells continue to multiply, piling up and spreading out into surrounding tissues. Neoplastic cells also tend to lose their **differentiation**, or the

resents the pressure that occurs when the heart relaxes between heartbeats. It is called the **diastolic pressure**. In grown-ups and teenagers, the normal systolic pressure ranges from 100 to 140. The normal diastolic pressure is about 65 to 90. Low blood pressure usually causes no trouble. But high blood pressure, called hypertension, may cause serious health problems.

Moving the blood at a higher pressure is a strain on the heart. If the heart cannot supply enough blood to the important organs of the body, then these organs will not work properly. And if the walls of a blood vessel break under pressure—like a hose that springs a leak—the part of the body served by that blood vessel will be injured.

When blood pressure gets too high, attempts to lower it may include reducing salt intake and losing weight. If these methods fail, drugs may be used. Drugs do not cure high blood pressure, but they can lower it and keep it under control.

There is no cure for hypertension, but scientists are looking for ways to prevent it. They believe that the conditions leading to the most common kind of hypertension may begin to develop during childhood or even infancy. They believe that many cases may be prevented if the growing child gets enough exercise, avoids salt in the diet, and maintains a normal weight. This is especially important if hypertension tends to run in the family. (For more information, read the articles CIRCULATORY SYSTEM in Volume C and HEART in Volume H.)

High blood pressure can also be a symptom of certain kidney diseases, damaged heart valves, or an imbalance of body hormones. In these cases the doctor has to treat the condition that causes the high blood pressure.

Impetigo

See DERMATOLOGY in Volume D.

Infectious Mononucleosis

Infectious mononucleosis is more likely to affect children and young people than older people. It rarely causes any lasting damage, but individuals need weeks and sometimes months to get over it. Direct contact between people can spread the disease.

Infectious mononucleosis is a virus infection of the lymphatic system. (The lymphatic system is a network of vessels that carry fluid, called lymph, from the spaces between body cells and empty it into the bloodstream.) All along the lymph channels are little nodes, or glands. The lymph nodes make a kind of white blood cell called a **lymphocyte**. The blood of a person who has mononucleosis has far more lymphocytes than normal. Many of them are not properly formed.

The early symptoms of infectious mononucleosis are similar to influenza, usually a sore throat and headache. Then the lymph nodes begin to swell. Sometimes the liver, spleen, and tonsils are also enlarged. The person often feels weak and has a fever. Rest, a great deal of liquids, and nourishing food are needed. Gradually, the body's own defenses will get rid of the infection. Sometimes infectious mononucleosis becomes chronic, or long lasting. Such cases seem to be caused by the presence of the **Epstein-Barr virus** in the body.

specific characteristics of the tissue in which the cells developed.

The result of unregulated cell division is a **neoplasm** (meaning "new growth"), also called a **tumor**. When a tumor is **cancerous**, cells from it may break away and travel through the body by way of the blood or lymph circulation. They may settle in other places and form new tumors. This process of migration is called **metastasis**. When this happens, the cancer is said to have metastasized. Cancer is the leading cause of death in some age groups.

Recent research suggests that cancer may be caused by **oncogenes**, which are special cancer-causing genes that act by controlling cell multiplication. Normally the oncogenes are in a harmless, "turned-off" form. But exposures to radiation, cancer-causing chemicals (**carcinogens**), or virus infections may turn on the oncogenes in a cell, causing it to become neoplastic. Tobacco contains many carcinogens and is the leading cause of lung cancer and emphysema.

The body's immune defenses normally guard against cancer. White blood cells recognize new neoplastic cells by their chemical changes and destroy them before they can spread. If these immune defenses are weakened, cancer can develop. (You can read more about this in the article CANCER in Volume C and the article IMMUNE SYSTEM in Volume I.)

Nutritional Diseases

In many parts of the world, malnutrition is one of the most serious health problems. When children do not get enough to eat, they cannot grow and develop properly. Adults suffer from starvation, too. They lose weight and have little energy for doing things, and they have poor defenses against infectious diseases. Worldwide, over 800 million people are undernourished.

Influenza

See INFLUENZA in Volume I.

Leukemia

In leukemia, which is sometimes called cancer of the blood, the bone marrow and lymph glands produce millions of abnormal, useless white blood cells and not enough normal red or white blood cells. The disease is serious because we rely on certain kinds of white blood cells to fight infection. People with leukemia are anemic and have low resistance to infection. They bruise and bleed easily.

Leukemia cell

Chronic leukemia develops slowly, and a person may have it for a long time without any symptoms. In acute leukemia, symptoms appear suddenly.

Once all leukemias were considered incurable. But research has led to more successful treatments. Radiation and chemotherapy are used to destroy the cancer cells. Bone-marrow transplants are used to produce new, healthy blood cells.

See also CANCER in Volume C.

Mad Cow Disease

See the entry Variant Creutzfeldt-Jakob Disease in this feature.

Malaria

See MALARIA in Volume M.

Measles

At one time measles, also called rubeola, was one of the most common childhood diseases. In the 1960's a vaccine was developed to prevent the disease. Most children get a measles shot when they are about 15 months old.

Rash caused by measles

Measles starts with high fever, a cough, and a runny nose. Then tiny white spots appear inside the mouth, and a rash appears all over the body. The fever goes down and the rash fades in several days. In rare cases, measles can cause inflammation of the brain and death.

Measles is caused by a virus. (The virus is different from the one that causes German measles—see the entry German Measles in this feature.) The virus passes from one person to another through the air. A person who has the disease can spread it to others for a few days before and a few days after the rash appears. It takes from 7 to 14 days for measles to develop once a person has been exposed to it. Measles is a disease that people have only once.

Mononucleosis

See the entry Infectious Mononucleosis in this feature.

In the United States and other industrial countries, though, eating too much is more of a problem. Overeating leads to obesity (excessive fatness) and contributes to cardiovascular disease, diabetes, and other harmful conditions. Obesity rates have increased over the last several decades. In 2000, nearly one in three American adults was obese.

Good nutrition means more than just eating the right amount of food. People also need to eat the right kinds of food. Proteins, carbohydrates, and fats are needed as building and energy materials for growth, repair, and other body functions. Water is vital, too. Vitamins and minerals are important in the body's chemical reactions. A failure to eat enough of a particular vitamin or mineral can result in a **deficiency disease**. A lack of calcium or a lack of vitamin D, for example, can result in bone diseases such as rickets and osteoporosis. Vitamin deficiencies can result in such diseases as scurvy, beriberi, and pellagra.

Doctors prescribe vitamin or mineral supplements for deficiency diseases. Some people take vitamin pills on their own. But many medical experts say that eating a balanced diet is the best way to avoid nutritional diseases. (For more nutritional information, refer to the article VITAMINS AND MINERALS in Volume UV.)

Occupational and Environmental Diseases

Certain jobs, such as fire fighting and construction work on tall buildings, are well known for being dangerous. Mine workers may develop a disabling lung disease called silicosis from breathing in rock dust. Workers in asbestos-manufacturing plants suffer from a lung disease called asbestosis and may develop an unusual type of lung cancer. Pesticides used to protect food crops from insects may be poisonous to manufacturing and agricultural workers and to the public if proper safety measures are not taken.

Multiple Sclerosis

Multiple sclerosis (MS) is a disorder of the nervous system that often affects young adults. The symptoms of multiple sclerosis are vision problems, poor control of muscles, and trouble in speaking distinctly. These problems are caused by the destruction of the outer covering of certain nerves. The covering insulates the nerves and keeps the messages traveling efficiently along the nerve pathways. Without the covering, many messages go astray.

Most scientists believe MS occurs when immune system cells mistakenly attack and destroy other body cells. In this type of disease, called an autoimmune disease, the immune system turns on, but fails to turn off. A virus or some other factor may be responsible for turning the immune system on.

People with MS are encouraged to eat well and to live a healthy lifestyle. Other treatments, which include drugs, depend on the symptoms that appear.

Nerve damage caused by multiple sclerosis

Mumps

Mumps is a viral disease that causes swelling of the salivary glands. These are the glands that make saliva, the moisture in the mouth. The glands are found under the tongue and jawbone and in front of the ear. Those found in front of the ear, the parotid glands, are the glands that swell most often in mumps. When they become swollen, it hurts to chew and swallow. Headaches are another symptom of mumps.

Mumps may cause the swelling of other glands, such as the pancreas and testes, especially when adults get the disease.

But mumps is mainly a disease of children between 5 and 15 years of age. The virus is spread from one person to another through the air or through contaminated objects. It takes from 14 to 21 days for mumps to develop after a person has been exposed to the virus. Usually people have mumps only once. Most children are immunized against mumps when they are 15 months old.

Muscular Dystrophy

Muscular dystrophy is the name of a group of genetic diseases that involve the wasting away of the muscle fibers. In most cases the disease begins early in childhood, with the person growing weaker and weaker as the muscles become more affected. Exercise and braces make it easier to move around and keep a good posture. There is no cure for muscular dystrophy, and death usually results when the heart or breathing muscles fail.

Nephritis

Acute nephritis is a disease in which parts of the kidney become inflamed. It usually affects children

More ordinary jobs and even daily living have their own, less obvious dangers. Repetitive motions, such as those needed to operate power tools or type at a keyboard, may cause carpal tunnel syndrome. Tendons become irritated and thickened, pressuring nerves and causing pain in the hand and wrist.

Automobiles, factories, and home furnaces all burn fuels and send soot particles and various gases such as carbon monoxide, hydrocarbons, and oxides of sulfur and nitrogen into the air. This air pollution can contribute to emphysema, allergies, and lung cancer. Factories may also produce solid or liquid toxic wastes, which are sometimes discharged into rivers and oceans or buried underground. Heavy metals such as mercury, lead, and cadmium are dangerous pollutants that can damage the muscles and nerves if they are breathed in or get into the food we eat. These pollutants may exist in very, very tiny amounts in the soil or in water, but they can

Carpal tunnel syndrome is an occupational disease that can result from repetitious tasks such as keyboarding. A brace can prevent further injury.

be concentrated many times by food chains. That is, the pollutants are first taken in by plants or micro-organisms, which are then eaten by animals, which in turn may be eaten by other animals or humans. Each creature in the chain keeps more of the pollutant in its body tissues.

Noise is a type of pollution that can contribute to disease. People subjected to high

and young people. Sometimes the word "glomerulonephritis" is used to identify the disease.

A **glomerulus** (plural: glomeruli) is a clump of tiny blood vessels, or capillaries. It is enclosed in a little cup from which a **tubule**, or little tube, leads into the central area of the kidney. Together, the glomerulus and the cup with the tubule form the working units of the kidney, called **nephrons**. There are about a million nephrons in each kidney. They cleanse the blood and regulate the fluid in the body.

The blood carries dissolved wastes—materials the body does not need. The wastes are filtered out of the blood through the walls of the glomeruli into the tubules. There the waste materials and some of the liquids are made into urine. The urine passes through the urinary tract and out of the body.

In acute glomerulonephritis, the glomeruli do not filter the blood properly, and the amount of fluid entering the tubules is poorly regulated. Fluid collects in the tissues. The body becomes swollen and puffy. Vital blood cells and proteins may pass through the defective walls of the glomeruli, and they may be lost in the urine.

The person with acute nephritis often has headaches and feels weak. There is blood in the urine, and the blood pressure may rise.

Acute nephritis occurs most often following a certain kind of streptococcal infection. But it may also occur following infections by other organisms, including staphylococci. Symptoms appear about three weeks after infection. Most people with acute nephritis recover completely without any permanent kidney damage. (See also Streptococcal Sore Throat in this feature.)

Peptic Ulcer

A peptic ulcer is an open sore that occurs in the inner lining of the esophagus, stomach, or duodenum. The duodenum is the upper part of the small intestine that connects with the stomach.

Cells in the walls of the stomach make hydrochloric acid, pepsin, and other strong digestive juices. These juices begin the digestion of protein in the food a person eats. The cells of the digestive tract also contain protein, but they are coated with a protective lining of mucus. Physicians once thought that peptic ulcers were caused by acid in stomach juices eating away at the protective lining. More recently, scientists have found that most peptic ulcers are caused by a bacterium called *Helicobacter pylori*. Overuse of certain pain medications, such as aspirin and ibuprofen, can also cause ulcers.

People with ulcers may feel pain or burning in the upper abdomen early in the morning or when they have not eaten for a while. Medications to reduce the amount of acid the stomach pro-

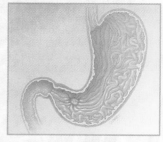

Stomach wall damaged by peptic ulcer

duces help relieve pain while the ulcer heals. Today most ulcers are treated with antibiotics to kill the *Helicobacter pylori*. If the ulcer is caused by overuse of pain medications, they should no longer be taken. Ulcers that are left untreated can become

noise levels, such as those listening to loud music, working in factories, or living near a busy airport, may not only suffer hearing losses but also develop hypertension (high blood pressure) and may suffer from heart disease. The constant stress from the noise may also lower their resistance to infectious diseases and cancer.

After the 1986 nuclear reactor accident at Chernobyl in the former U.S.S.R., many people became worried about **radiation sickness**. Nuclear reactors and nuclear weapon explosions are not the only sources of radiation. In some areas radon given off by rocks in the ground accumulates inside buildings and can be a serious health hazard. Even X-rays can be dangerous, contributing to the risk of cancer and other diseases. (Modern medical X-ray tests use very small amounts of radiation, below the danger level.)

Many people do not realize that too much exposure to sunlight can be very dangerous.

Ultraviolet radiation can not only burn the skin and make it dry and leathery but also lead to skin cancer. People who lie in the sun or under ultraviolet lamps to get a suntan are taking a serious risk.

▶ **DIAGNOSIS AND TREATMENT OF DISEASE**

In the past, lack of medical knowledge about disease often meant that a person's chances of recovering from an illness were small. When a person became ill, doctors were frequently unable to identify the illness accurately or to determine its cause. Treatment often consisted mainly of sympathy, rest, and simple home remedies. As a result, the expected human life span was quite short.

This situation, which existed throughout most of human history, changed dramatically in the 20th century. An explosion of medical knowledge has enabled doctors to diagnose and treat many illnesses with great accuracy and success. Improvements in diagnosis and

bleeding ulcers. An ulcer that bleeds slowly over a long period of time can result in anemia and other complications that may require surgery.

Periodontal Disease

This disease, also called periodontitis or pyorrhea, causes inflammation of the gums and deterioration of the bone that surrounds and supports the teeth. It is the main cause of bad breath in adults and is responsible for most of the teeth lost as people age.

Sometimes a person has such minor symptoms that he or she may not realize that periodontal disease is present. As the disease progresses, symptoms include pain, bleeding and swollen gums, and a foul taste in the mouth.

The primary cause of periodontal disease is the buildup of dental plaque around the gum line of the teeth. Plaque is a thin film of bacteria that sticks to the teeth and gums. If not removed, plaque can cause the tissues and bone to break down, leading to tooth loss.

Periodontal disease can usually be prevented with regular brushing, flossing, and dental checkups. If not too far advanced, the disease can be treated by specialized plaque removal techniques and by surgery on the gums and bones in the mouth.

Phenylketonuria (PKU)

Phenylketonuria (PKU) is a rare inherited disease that causes brain damage in infants and young children. To function properly, the body needs protein, which is made up of chemicals called amino acids. Excess amounts of amino acids are broken down and excreted (eliminated) from the body. People with PKU are unable to break down one amino acid called phenylalanine.

Because mental retardation can occur quickly if PKU is not treated, newborn infants are now tested for PKU. If this testing reveals PKU, the newborn is given a special diet low in phenylalanine. A primarily vegetarian diet eliminates many of the effects of PKU. When the nervous system develops fully, usually after age 10, the child can often change to a regular diet.

Pinworms

Many worm infections that people get are common in warm climates, usually where there are outdoor toilets. Pinworm infection is different. Anyone in any climate can get pinworms. Pinworm eggs have been found on toilet seats and on desks and floors in clean and modern schools.

Pinworm eggs can pass from the hands into the food and then be swallowed. By the time the female worm works her way down through the intestines, she is ready to lay her eggs. As she leaves the intestines, the small white worm lays as many as 11,000 eggs, some just inside and some just outside the person's body. These eggs, which are too small to see without a microscope, may get on the clothing and hands. Thus the eggs may be spread almost anywhere among children and adults. Pinworm infection may go unnoticed until itching near the anus occurs or the white, hairlike worms are found on the clothing. Anal itching is always worse at night.

Taking a single dose of a special medicine can cure pinworms. Usually everyone in the family must take the medicine to get rid of this problem. This is because pinworms are passed back and forth from person to person.

treatment have helped people today live healthier and longer lives.

Methods of Diagnosis

To diagnose disease, doctors must think like detectives. They question the patient, examine his or her body, and gather more information about the problem with specialized tests. Once the diagnosis is made, the doctor can accurately determine an appropriate treatment.

Medical History. Like any good detective, a doctor who examines you first wants to know the background of the case. He or she will ask you for your medical history.

The medical history begins with the story of your sickness. Because many different illnesses produce similar symptoms, the doctor may want to know when you first became ill, what you were doing at the time, and whether you have been exposed to any contagious diseases. For example, if you walked in the woods, you may have brushed against poison oak or poison ivy plants, which later gave you an itchy rash. If you drank creek water while in the woods, it may have contained bacteria that infected your stomach and intestines, causing cramps or diarrhea.

The next part of the medical history determines how your body feels with this particular sickness. The doctor needs to know your symptoms. These may be ailments such as headaches, sore throat, chest pain, stomach cramps, burning on urination, fever or chills, arm or leg aches, or skin problems. If you have received an injury, the doctor needs to know how it happened and exactly where and how severe the pain is.

Your past medical history may also be important. For instance, a urinary infection often recurs, but measles rarely appears again. Anyone who has had chicken pox is at risk for shingles, an outbreak of blisters on the skin caused by the same virus as chicken

Pneumonia

Most cases of pneumonia, a disease of the lungs, are caused by bacteria, usually **pneumococcus** bacteria. Pneumonia may also be caused by viruses, by fungi, or by breathing chemicals that irritate the lungs.

When harmful organisms are breathed in, they enter the alveoli (tiny air sacs in the lungs). The alveoli become irritated and filled with fluid. Large numbers of white cells from the blood then enter the alveoli. These cells fight and destroy disease organisms. The white cells form a solid mass in the tiny air sacs, halting the exchange of oxygen and carbon dioxide. If a great many alveoli are blocked off, the lungs cannot supply the body with sufficient oxygen. Gradually, the white cells may destroy the organisms, and the alveoli are able to function again.

The organisms that can cause pneumonia are all around us. But when we are healthy, our bodies are able to resist their effects.

People with AIDS or certain other diseases have severely weakened body defenses. They are prone to develop a rare fungal pneumonia called *Pneumocystic carinii* pneumonia.

In the 1970's a severe form of pneumonia, called **Legionnaires' disease**, was discovered. This disease is caused by bacteria that live in water, especially warm standing water. It is thought that the

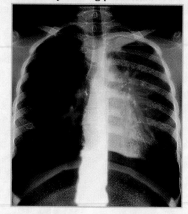
Chest X-ray showing pneumonia

disease can be spread through some air-conditioning systems.

Pneumonia was greatly feared before antibiotics were found to be effective against bacterial forms of the disease. Now, some bacteria have developed a resistance to certain antibiotics, prompting the development of new antibiotics. A vaccine that protects against pneumococcal pneumonia can also be used.

As yet, there is no cure for viral pneumonia. Most people who have it get well by themselves. The patient must have bed rest, liquids, and nourishment. Medicines to ease the cough and lower the fever may be needed.

Polio

Poliomyelitis is the medical name for polio, also known as infantile paralysis. Usually this disease is caused by a virus that is swallowed. Infected individuals pass the polio virus in their feces, which, in turn, may get on their hands and be spread to other people.

In one form of polio, the virus invades the brain and spinal cord and destroys certain nerve cells. As a result, some muscles lose their nerve supply and become paralyzed.

Polio is mainly a disease of children. Because polio can leave muscles paralyzed for life or even cause death, it was once one of the most feared of diseases.

pox. A recurring cough, headache, or fatigue might point to allergies.

Your medical history also includes your family's history of illnesses. You may have inherited a tendency to have certain diseases. For example, if your blood relatives have had diabetes, asthma, or allergies, your chances of having these particular diseases are greater than those of a person with no family history of these illnesses.

A patient may discuss his or her medical history with a genetic counselor. The genetic counselor uses the information to determine if the patient, or the patient's offspring, risks inheriting a genetic disorder.

Genetic counseling may include genetic testing, which is able to scrutinize a patient's genes in great detail, down to the level of the chemical sequences that make up the genes. The medical importance of this kind of genetic information is discussed in the article GENETICS in Volume G.

Medical records contain a patient's complete medical history. They are kept on file for future reference.

In the 1950's a vaccine against polio became available. This was the vaccine developed by Dr. Jonas E. Salk. Several years later a second vaccine, developed by Dr. Albert B. Sabin, became available. The Sabin vaccine gives strong protection against the disease and is the most commonly used form of the oral polio vaccine. However, many babies now receive a strengthened version of the Salk vaccine, which is given as an injection.

Polio virus

The number of cases of polio in the United States has dropped steadily since the discovery of the first vaccine. But the disease has not been wiped out. There are still some outbreaks of polio in other countries, but increased use of vaccinations may bring the end of polio in a few years.

Psoriasis

See DERMATOLOGY in Volume D.

Rabies

One of the most dangerous diseases humans can catch from animals is rabies. Most animals that have rabies are wild, such as skunks, foxes, raccoons, and bats. Wild animals may infect people directly or by infecting domestic animals, such as cats and dogs, which then pass the disease to people. In the United States, success in controlling canine rabies has made human rabies very rare. Worldwide, canine rabies is still widespread and a major source of human rabies.

The disease is caused by a tiny virus in the saliva of an infected, or rabid, animal. When the animal bites a person, rabies is passed on through a break in the skin. But even the lick of an infected animal is dangerous if there is already a cut on the skin through which the virus can enter the body.

Rabies attacks the nervous system. Without treatment, a person bitten by a rabid animal will develop symptoms that include fever, headache, and muscle pain followed by seizures, muscle spasms, and death. Treatment for a person bitten by a rabid animal includes immediate cleaning of the bite and a series of injections with anti-rabies vaccine.

Reye's Syndrome

Reye's syndrome affects the brain and some abdominal organs such as the liver. It usually occurs in children under age 18. Although the exact cause is unknown, it often follows a viral infection such as flu. Many experts think that aspirin used during the viral illness may cause Reye's syndrome.

The symptoms in Reye's syndrome are similar to those of encephalitis, a condition in which brain cells are inflamed. Most cases are mild, with fever, headache, and loss of appetite. More severe inflammation results in irritability, drowsiness, or even coma. In the most serious cases, the person may have double vision, loss of muscle function, and difficulty hearing or speaking.

Rheumatic Fever

The symptoms of rheumatic fever are pains in the arms, legs, and joints. The joints may be red and

Illness can also be caused by the stress of being upset, anxious, or afraid, so doctors need to know about your life and feelings. Are you happy or unhappy with school or work, with family or friends? Confide in your doctors freely when they ask you personal questions. They can help you. If they do not ask you personal questions about something that bothers you, volunteer the story. Doctors respect your confidence and do not tell other people about your problems. Sometimes just talking with a physician whom you respect and like can help you find some of the answers to your problems. Or the doctor may be able to suggest someone else to talk with who would meet your particular needs.

As you give your medical history and answer questions, the doctor usually begins your physical examination.

The Physical Examination. Your physical examination actually begins when the doctor or nurse observes the way you walk into the office. They note the way you look and act, whether or not you limp, if you seem to be in pain, have a rash or a lump, or if you appear sick or feverish. Your temperature, pulse, and blood pressure may be taken.

For some illnesses, the doctor may go over you from head to toe. For other illnesses, like sore throats with headaches, the doctor may only examine your eyes, ears, nose, throat, neck, and chest. Looking through an **otoscope** allows the doctor to see your eardrums and to look for mucus or infection in your middle ear. Checking behind the mucus membranes of your eyelids may reveal signs of an infection or allergy. An examination of the inside of your eyes with an **ophthalmoscope** shows the eye's lining, or retina. Examination of the retina may reveal damage caused by high blood pressure or diabetes. By tapping your cheeks and forehead, tender infected sinuses may be detected. If your breath smells foul, you may have a bacterial

---

swollen, but they are not seriously damaged by the disease. The disease also affects the heart and can seriously harm that organ.

Rheumatic fever usually comes on shortly after an infection caused by one of the streptococcal bacteria. (Information about infections of this kind is included under the heading Streptococcal Sore Throat in this feature.) The bacteria are never found in the sore joints or in the hearts of people who have rheumatic fever. Doctors think that some people are sensitive to certain toxins made by the organism. The swollen joints and the scarring of the heart are probably caused by the toxin. Large doses of penicillin will get rid of the streptococci. Persons who have had rheumatic fever once are often given regular doses of penicillin to keep them from getting another "strep" infection.

Ringworm
See Dermatology in Volume D.

Rocky Mountain Spotted Fever
Rocky Mountain spotted fever is a painful and dangerous disease. It is carried by a tick, a small, insectlike animal that lives in woods and underbrush.

Tick that carries Rocky Mountain spotted fever

Within four to eight days after being bitten by an infected tick, the person develops fever, headache, muscle aches, and nausea. A rash that starts on the wrist or ankle follows. The symptoms can become severe, and the person who is bitten needs to be hospitalized. Antibiotics are used to treat the disease.

A vaccine preventing Rocky Mountain spotted fever is suggested for those who are frequently exposed to ticks. For others occasionally involved in activities in the woods, protective clothing, insect repellents, and careful removal of ticks can prevent the disease. Ticks should be removed with tweezers to avoid crushing them.

SARS
Severe acute respiratory syndrome (SARS) first appeared in China in November 2002 and was recognized as a global threat in March 2003. Before the 2003 outbreak was contained, it had spread to

Children wearing masks to avoid catching SARS

infection like strep throat. Holding your tongue down with a tongue depressor allows a look at your tonsils and the back of your throat. Swollen lymph glands in the neck usually indicate a throat infection.

The doctor also watches the way you breathe, listens to the lungs and heart with a **stethoscope**, and taps your chest to see if the lungs sound normal. Pressing down on areas of the abdomen checks for liver, spleen, stomach, and bowel problems. The doctor checks bones and joints and the back for an abnormal curve called scoliosis.

Checking your body in these and other ways helps the doctor collect the information he or she needs to help you. In doing so, the doctor may even detect hidden problems that may contribute to your current illness or to future difficulties.

Laboratory Studies and Specialized Tests. Because of the many different signs and symptoms of diseases, a medical history and

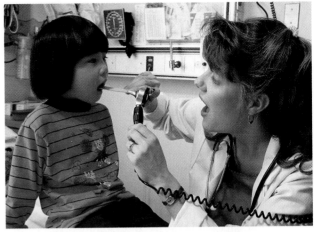

During a physical examination, a doctor inspects the patient for any signs of disease. Special instruments are often used to better observe the eyes, ears, and throat.

physical examination do not always allow an accurate diagnosis. Even a sore, red throat with swollen glands may be caused by one of hundreds of different viruses, one of many

more than two dozen countries in North America, South America, Europe, and Asia. Over 8,000 people became sick, and nearly 800 died. SARS is a dramatic example of how quickly a contagious disease can spread in a world in which global travel is common.

SARS is caused by a coronavirus. Although coronaviruses usually cause mild illness, the SARS virus somehow evolved into a potentially deadly form.

SARS usually begins with a high fever, and most patients develop pneumonia. The disease spreads by close person-to-person contact, such as when an infected person coughs or sneezes. Also, a person may become infected from touching a surface contaminated with infectious droplets and then touching his or her mouth, nose, or eyes. Once infected, a person usually becomes sick in two to seven days. Patients are most contagious during the second week of illness.

There is no effective treatment to counter the SARS virus. Patients with SARS receive the same treatment that would be used for a patient with serious pneumonia. Research into new treatments includes work on antiviral drugs. To deal with SARS, public health officials emphasize the rapid recognition of new outbreaks, which will trigger responses such as travel advisories and the isolation of sick travelers.

Scarlet Fever

Scarlet fever is one of several diseases caused by hemolytic streptococci. (Information about these bacteria is included under the heading Streptococcal Sore Throat in this feature.) Children between 2 and

8 years of age are most likely to develop scarlet fever, but it is not a common or serious disease in the United States today.

Scarlet fever, which is passed from person to person, develops three to five days after exposure to the bacteria. The disease usually begins with a sore throat, fever, headache, and vomiting. In a day or two a rash appears on the body. The rash begins to fade after about a week. Penicillin is given in most cases to kill the streptococci.

Sickle-Cell Anemia

Sickle-cell anemia is an inherited disease caused by a flaw in the structure of the hemoglobin molecule (a complex chemical in the red blood cell). Under certain conditions of stress, such as infection or lack of oxygen, the abnormal hemoglobin changes the round red blood cell to a sickle shape. These sickle-shaped red blood cells clog the blood vessels, producing great pain and causing tissue damage.

Blood cells affected by sickle-cell anemia

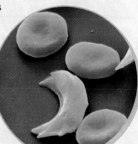

Sickle-cell anemia is a condition that affects mostly people of African descent. However, some individuals of Mediterranean, Middle Eastern, and East Indian descent can also be affected. A less serious form of the condition, called sickle-cell trait, may not trouble the person at all. But if two people with sickle-cell trait marry, their children may inherit the more severe disease,

different bacteria, or even an allergy. So doctors order laboratory tests.

To take a throat culture, for example, mucus is taken from a sore throat with a cotton swab. The mucus is put on a culture plate (a special dish used to cultivate bacteria) to see if streptococcus or other bacteria will grow. By growing and identifying the bacteria, the doctor can determine which antibiotic will best kill the germ.

Blood tests must be done to diagnose some illnesses. A high number of white blood cells usually signifies a bacterial infection requiring an antibiotic. A low number of white blood cells can mean a viral infection. Urine can be examined under the microscope, cultured, or checked for chemicals that appear during illness. Sometimes a bowel movement, or stool specimen, has to be examined in the laboratory to reveal an intestinal problem. Skin tests may be performed to diagnose bacterial and fungal infections, to determine the causes of allergies, and to distinguish between cancerous and non-cancerous growths.

X-rays, which go through skin and muscle to make pictures of bones and organs, are used to look for injuries such as broken bones or illnesses such as diseased lungs. The electroencephalograph (EEG) is a machine that measures brain waves. It is used when a doctor suspects a problem involving a patient's brain. The electrocardiograph machine (ECG) examines the electric currents produced by a beating heart. From it the doctor can tell if the heart is working normally.

For especially complex problems, the doctor may order very specialized tests. Computed tomography (CT) scans are X-rays of many different layers of the body. When put together by a computer, they can show your internal organs and bones in three dimensions. Magnetic resonance imaging (MRI) uses radio waves and magnets to create pictures of the molecules and chemicals in body

sickle-cell anemia. A blood test can detect both sickle-cell anemia and sickle-cell trait.

Spinal Curvature

Normally the spine, or backbone, arches gently down along the middle of the back. But sometimes, in the rapidly growing body of a child, the spine may begin to grow into a curve shaped like the letter C or S. There can be many causes for the condition.

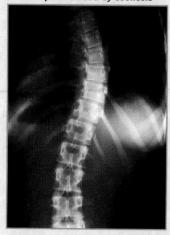

Curved spine caused by scoliosis

Three important causes of spinal curvature are poorly formed spinal bones (vertebrae), bad posture, or weak back muscles. Spinal curvature can cause pain, fatigue, and sometimes serious problems in the lungs and heart.

Scoliosis is one of the most common back problems for teenagers, especially teenage girls. In scoliosis, the spine begins to grow in a side-to-side curve, which often causes few problems for the person at first. Undetected, the curve can become severe. Then a close look will reveal that one hip, shoulder, or shoulder blade is higher than the other. Fortunately, most schools have screening programs that allow early detection. Treatments for scoliosis include exercises to strengthen the muscles that support the spine, a brace to halt the curving of the spine, and surgery.

Kyphosis is a spinal condition in which the spine begins to curve back to front, producing a rounded hump in the upper back. Treatment for kyphosis is similar to that for scoliosis.

Streptococcal Sore Throat

Various kinds of viruses and bacteria can cause sore throats. One group of bacteria, the **hemolytic streptococci**, causes a sore throat that can be more serious than most. Strep throats, as they are called, are most common in children 5 to 15 years of age.

Different kinds of hemolytic streptococci can infect other parts of the body. These infections can be very dangerous because the bacteria can produce different kinds of toxins that injure the body. The red rash of scarlet fever is caused by one of these toxins. Other streptococcal toxins can harm the heart and the kidneys. Scientists believe it is possible to develop an immunity to some of these toxins.

A doctor can often recognize a streptococcal sore throat by the way it looks. The tonsils are red, swollen, and coated with a whitish substance. To be certain of the diagnosis, the doctor may take a specimen, or sample, of the moisture from the throat and have it tested. This is called a **throat culture**. If the throat culture reveals that the organism causing the sore throat is streptococcus, then the doctor will prescribe penicillin or some other antibiotic. The medicine usually helps the patient feel better within four days; still, the patient must take all the medicine, which usually lasts ten days.

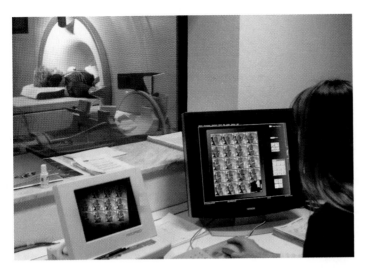

Magnetic resonance imaging (MRI) is an important diagnostic tool. The images produced are displayed on a computer monitor.

organs. (You can read more about specialized tests in the article IMAGING, DIAGNOSTIC in Volume I.)

These and many other techniques help the physician diagnose an illness or injury. After a diagnosis is made, treatment follows.

Treating a Disease

More often than not, your body will heal itself. Many of the signs and symptoms of disease actually give evidence of how your body fights a particular disease. Fever, even though it makes you uncomfortable, helps suppress or kill the germs that make you sick. The pus in an infected wound comes from your white blood cells, which ingest (take in) and kill the bacteria causing the sore. Your lymph glands enlarge while they manufacture antibodies, which fight infections. If you accidentally swallow a poisonous

Stroke

Stroke is a condition involving damage to the brain caused by an interruption of the blood supply. The brain must have oxygen. If the brain is left without oxygen for even a few minutes, many brain cells will die. Oxygen is brought to the brain by the blood carried in four main arteries. Each of the main arteries has many branches. Sometimes one of these branches can be blocked by a blood clot. Sometimes one of the branch arteries breaks. When either of these things happens, we say that the person has had a stroke. This means that some of the brain cells have been destroyed by lack of oxygen.

The aftereffects of a stroke depend on what part of the brain was damaged. Certain parts of the brain control certain parts of the body and certain actions. For instance, there is one area in the brain that controls speech. If anything seriously injures that area in the brain, the person can make sounds but cannot form the sounds into words. Many people who have strokes are paralyzed—that is, they cannot move certain muscles. Others have trouble remembering things.

Some people may have frequent little strokes, or attacks, which do not cause much damage. After the small attacks, they may just be forgetful or unsteady on their feet for about a day. But in many cases, these small attacks are followed by a full stroke that does a lot of damage. Doctors at major hospitals can sometimes prevent stroke damage if a patient reaches the emergency room within three hours. Emergency care is important.

Many of the handicaps caused by strokes can be overcome. The cells of the brain, unlike most other cells in the body, can actually learn to do new jobs. The person who has had a stroke can often force the good cells in the brain to take over the jobs of the cells that were destroyed. Often the patient can learn to walk or talk all over again.

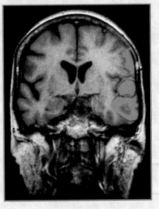

MRI of skull showing bleeding that led to a stroke

Syphilis

Syphilis is a disease that is usually spread by sexual contact. The syphilis organism, *Treponema pallidum*, is a spirochete, or spiral-shaped, bacterium. The syphilis spirochete cannot live on any surface that is dry. It can live only in warmth and moisture. Thus it is almost impossible to get syphilis from objects that a person with the disease has touched. The most common way of catching syphilis is by coming in contact with an open syphilitic sore on the sex organ of an infected person.

For the first couple of years, syphilis can cause a variety of symptoms that come and go. There can be sores and rashes on the skin, fever, sore throat, nausea, and inflamed eyes. After that, the symptoms go away. This does not mean the disease is gone. It has gone into a latent, or inactive, stage. Sometimes it remains in the inactive stage for the rest of a person's life. But often the disease comes back and does more damage.

substance, you may react by vomiting and expelling the substance from your stomach. Or the substance may be expelled from the body by diarrhea.

One of the first rules in the treatment of disease should be to help the body's own defenses. For example, if you have a sore throat, you may be able to wash some of the infection away by gargling with a weak, hot salt water solution (one half level teaspoon of salt to eight ounces of water). When you suffer from diarrhea or vomiting, your body loses a large amount of water and salts, which need to be replaced by drinking liquids. And do not forget rest as a treatment. It helps your body use all its energy to fight the illness.

Drugs. Drugs are an important part of treating many diseases. They can be used to relieve pain and other disease symptoms or to cure the disease itself. For example, throat lozenges containing benzocaine numb the pain that accompanies strep throat, while penicillin fights the germs that cause the illness. Drug research is a vast and changing area, where old drugs are being improved and new drugs are tested. Tailoring drugs to individuals on the basis of their genes is a kind of research still in its infancy.

Drugs work in a variety of ways. Antibiotics kill molds and bacteria and are used to treat illnesses, such as bacterial meningitis, pneumonia, and strep throat, and localized infections, such as boils. However, if antibiotics are overused, bacteria may become resistant. Chemical fungicides kill fungi, such as those causing ringworm and athlete's foot. Only a few antiviral drugs have been developed, including some for herpes, AIDS, and influenza. However, many serious viral infections can be prevented with vaccinations, which stimulate the body to develop its own disease defenses. (You can read more about this in the article VACCINATION AND IMMUNIZATION in Volume UV.)

When syphilis attacks the heart, it can destroy some of the heart tissue. The main artery wall may be weakened. Eventually such a weak place may break, and the person dies.

Many different symptoms can result when syphilis attacks the brain or the spinal cord. When the nerve from the eye to the brain is damaged, the person gradually becomes blind. Other nerves can be damaged and people will have trouble walking. Sometimes their arms and legs become numb. The person may also have trouble remembering and thinking.

Syphilis can be stopped in its early stages by antibiotics. But the damage already done to the body cannot be repaired.

Tapeworms

There are many kinds of flatworms, called tapeworms, that can live in the human intestines. All tapeworms consist of a head, which fastens itself to the intestinal wall, followed by a chain of segments, or parts. Each segment is a kind of separate unit, able to make tapeworm eggs. New segments grow from the head, and older segments drop off from the opposite end, breaking up and releasing the eggs.

Four kinds of tapeworms are found in the United States.

Magnified image of a tapeworm

One is the pork tapeworm. (It is not the worm that causes trichinosis, which has a separate entry in this feature.) The beef tapeworm is somewhat longer, and it infects more people. The fish tapeworm is usually found in fish from the Great Lakes region. The dwarf tapeworm is passed between people and is the most common source of infection. The best way to prevent infection with tapeworms is to properly dispose of human feces. The next best strategy is to thoroughly cook or freeze all meat and fish before it is eaten. Proper food handling will kill any live tapeworm larvae.

Tapeworms usually do not make people very sick. Sometimes people who have tapeworms feel only a hungry, gnawing discomfort. It is possible to have a tapeworm infection for a long time and not know it. It may be discovered only when some segments of the worm pass from the body. Several medicines are given to kill tapeworms.

Tay-Sachs Disease

Tay-Sachs is an inherited disease caused by abnormally high storage of fatty substances in the brain of a young child. Tay-Sachs victims, who are mostly of Eastern European Jewish ancestry, usually do not survive beyond the third year. Normal, healthy people can carry one gene for Tay-Sachs disease. They are called carriers. If two carriers marry, their children may inherit both Tay-Sachs genes, causing the disease. Carriers can be identified by a blood test.

Tetanus

This disease, also known as lockjaw, makes all the muscles stiff, usually beginning with the jaw

A pharmacist fills a prescription. Drugs, both prescription and over-the-counter, have a major role in the treatment, management, and prevention of disease.

Drugs called anti-inflammatories help reduce inflammation and swelling caused by diseases such as arthritis or from injuries such as sprained ankles. Aspirin is the oldest drug of this type.

The endocrine glands in the body produce another type of drug—chemical messengers called hormones. Too much or too little hormone production can cause disease. For example, when the thyroid gland does not produce enough thyroid hormone, a person feels sluggish and cold, becomes constipated, and may have swelling of the face and feet. For this problem, doctors order thyroid pills to make up for the body's inability to produce the hormone.

Surgery. Some diseases cannot be cured by the body's own defenses or by drug therapy alone. These illnesses may require surgery. Surgery is performed for several reasons. It may be performed to remove all or part of a diseased or infected organ. For example, ton-

muscles. It is caused by the tetanus bacteria, which live in the soil. When tetanus bacteria find their way into a warm, moist place where there is no air, such as a deep cut or wound, they begin to make a poison, or toxin. As the amount of tetanus toxin increases in the body, the muscles cramp and twitch. Sometimes they may tighten so hard that the person's bones are broken by the force. Many people have died of lockjaw.

For this reason, it is recommended that everyone have a tetanus toxoid shot. Most children have three tetanus toxoid shots when they are babies. The tetanus toxoid shots cause the body to start making antibodies against the toxin. Usually people need booster shots every ten years so that their bodies will keep making antibodies. A booster shot is also given promptly after a deep or dirty cut.

Persons who already have a tetanus infection need immediate help in counteracting the toxin made by the bacteria. Doctors give antitoxin to such persons. This antitoxin contains antibodies against the toxin.

Tonsillitis

The tonsils are two small clumps of lymph tissue on each side of the back of the throat. The tonsils are full of small white blood cells called lymphocytes. The lymphocytes trap and kill the bacteria that get into the throat through the nose or the mouth.

Sometimes the tonsils have so many bacteria to fight that they begin to lose the battle. The wrinkles and grooves in their surface are filled with bacteria, and the tonsils become swollen and sore. Then the person is said to have tonsillitis.

If a person has many attacks of tonsillitis, the doctor may remove the tonsils. Once the person is put to sleep with an anesthetic, the doctor cuts out the tonsils, often removing the **adenoids** at the same time. They are tissue like the tonsils and are usually enlarged and infected if the tonsils are. Swollen adenoids can make breathing difficult. They can also cause ear infections and deafness.

At one time doctors thought that all enlarged tonsils were diseased and often chose to remove them. Now doctors often advise leaving them alone because as children grow older, their tonsils and adenoids shrink. But it is still thought better to have them out if a child has many sore throats, earaches, and much trouble breathing.

Trichinosis

Trichinae are tiny worms that live in the muscles of meat-eating animals, including humans. People get these worms from eating meat, usually pork, that contains trichinae larvae, or newly hatched worms.

In the human intestine, the larvae become adult worms and begin hatching more larvae, which travel in the bloodstream all through the body. They settle in the muscles where they may live ten years or more.

Trichinosis, or infection with trichinae, causes an upset stomach and high fever at first. As the larvae invade the muscles, the muscles become swollen and painful. Eating food heavily infected with trichinae can kill a person. Cooking pork and wild game until it is no longer pink will kill the trichinae.

Tuberculosis

See TUBERCULOSIS in Volume T.

sils may be removed if they are repeatedly infected and cause related health problems. A cancerous organ or tumor may be removed in an effort to prevent cancer from spreading throughout the body.

Doctors also perform surgery to repair or replace a damaged organ. A heart that does not work properly can often be repaired by surgery. When a heart is hopelessly damaged, a heart transplant (replacing the heart with a healthy one) may save the person's life. Many other body parts—including skin, kidneys, bone, and even the cornea of the eye—can be replaced in surgery.

Laparoscopy is a procedure in which a viewing tube is inserted through a small incision. The procedure enables doctors to diagnose some diseases, and it may be used in combination with special surgical instruments

Typhoid Fever

Typhoid fever is an infection of the stomach and intestines. It is caused by a bacterium called *Salmonella typhosa*. The patient gets a fever that rises

Typhoid bacteria

higher and higher for about three weeks. During the time the fever is on the rise, the typhoid victim may suffer nosebleeds, a cough, constipation or diarrhea, and a rash of rosy spots over the abdomen. In severe cases, the infection may eat into the walls of the intestines, causing sharp pain, serious bleeding, and sometimes death.

The feces of the typhoid patient are a dangerous source of infection to others. Where people get their drinking water from shallow wells, rivers, or streams, there is danger that typhoid bacteria may get into the water supply from outdoor toilets or septic tanks. Eating shellfish that lived in water contaminated with feces can give a person the disease. Flies can carry the bacteria. Typhoid bacteria can also live in food, such as milk.

Occasionally the typhoid bacteria will remain in the body of the typhoid victim after recovery from the disease. The organisms pass out of the person's body in the feces and can contaminate water and food, giving others the disease. Such people who carry the typhoid bacteria in their bodies—but do not have the disease—are called **typhoid carriers**.

An antibiotic called chloramphenicol is used to treat typhoid. It has prevented many typhoid deaths. There is also a vaccination against typhoid.

Typhus

Typhus is an infectious disease caused by bacteria. Lice, fleas, mites, or ticks carry the bacteria and transfer it to humans when they bite. Throughout history there have been outbreaks of typhus in times of war and whenever people must live in crowded conditions. Sanitation methods that kill rats and other rodents carrying infected lice and fleas help keep typhus under control.

A person with typhus develops fever, headache, chills, and a rash. Antibiotics are given to treat typhus. There is also a vaccine that can prevent the disease. The vaccine is often given to people who travel in areas with typhus outbreaks.

Variant Creutzfeldt-Jakob Disease

Variant Creutzfeldt-Jakob disease (vCJD) is a disorder of the brain. It is one of a group of diseases, known as spongiform encephalopathies, that occur in humans as well as cattle, sheep, elk, cats, and other animals. In cattle the disease is called bovine spongiform encephalopathy (BSE), or "mad cow" disease. A similar disease in sheep is called scrapie. The classic form of CJD is a rare disorder that occurs primarily in elderly adults around the world. In the mid-1990's, a new, or variant, form was diagnosed in several young people in Britain. It is believed to be caused by exposure to meat contaminated with BSE. The incubation period (the time between exposure to BSE and onset of symptoms) ranges from 10 to 30 years.

Most experts believe that vCJD and BSE are caused by infectious particles called **prions**. Prions are proteins. Unlike viruses and bacteria, which cause many infectious diseases, prions do not

that are also inserted through small incisions. These instruments can reduce the invasiveness of some kinds of surgery, such as removal of the appendix or gall bladder.

Other Therapy. Some diseases may require treatments other than drugs or surgery. For example, cancer that has spread through a vital organ cannot simply be cut out. Instead, doctors may resort to radiotherapy, beaming intense therapeutic X-rays through the organ to kill the cancer cells.

Chemotherapy fights cancer by using medicines that reach the whole body and kill rapidly dividing cells. Gene therapy, in which abnormal or missing genes are replaced, has been tried with very limited success, but it is still being researched.

Special diets are crucial in treating certain diseases. For example, sugars and starches are limited for people with diabetes, calcium-containing foods for some patients with kidney stones, and cholesterol-containing foods for people with arteriosclerosis (hardening of the arteries). For other diseases, some dietary components need to be increased. Potassium-containing foods, such as prunes, raisins, potatoes, and bananas, replace salts lost by diarrhea.

For some injuries and diseases, physical therapy is needed to restore or improve muscle strength and flexibility. It may be used, for example, to help a handicapped child, an injured worker or athlete, or a stroke victim. Treatments may include massage, exercise, whirlpool baths, hot or cold compresses, electrical stimulation, and ultrasound. Rehabilitation therapy includes physical, occupational, aquatic, balance, and other therapies to improve a patient's physical abilities.

Last but not least, the physician heals by reassuring, listening, and helping the patient understand and cope with stress, which can lead to a variety of illnesses, such as backache and indigestion.

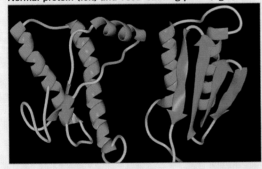

Normal protein (*left*) and vCJD-causing prion (*right*)

contain any genetic material. Scientists do not yet understand how prions cause disease.

Brain tissue is progressively destroyed in vCJD, giving the brain a "spongy" appearance. The brain damage leads to symptoms of depression or anxiety, loss of muscle control, and eventually dementia and death. There is no cure for vCJD.

Cases of vCJD have been reported in Britain and several other European countries, but not in the United States. Scientists believe the risk of human-to-human transmission of vCJD is low. But as a precaution, health authorities in the United States and other countries have placed restrictions on blood donations from people who might have been exposed to BSE.

Vitamin Deficiency
See Vitamins and Minerals in Volume UV.

Warts
See Dermatology in Volume D.

Whooping Cough
Whooping cough is a highly contagious disease. People of any age can catch it, but it is mainly a disease of childhood. Its medical name is pertussis, because it is caused by a bacterium called *Brodetella pertussis*. This bacterium infects the nose, throat, and lungs. The bacteria are coughed into the air by someone who has whooping cough. Then they are breathed in by other people. It takes from 7 to 14 days after this for the disease to develop.

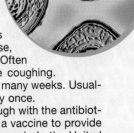

Whooping cough bacterium

Whooping cough begins mildly. In the beginning, it seems like a slight cold with a dry cough. But in a week or so whooping cough patients develop fits of coughing. They may cough ten times in a row, before stopping to breathe. As the person inhales, a sound like a "whoop" is produced. This sound, so typical of the disease, provides its common name. Often vomiting goes along with the coughing. Whooping cough may last for many weeks. Usually people have this illness only once.

Doctors treat whooping cough with the antibiotic erythromycin. There is also a vaccine to provide protection against whooping cough. In the United States, babies receive this vaccine at about 2 months of age. Several booster shots are given within the first year of age as well.

Christine L. Williams, M.D., M.P.H.
American Health Foundation

PREVENTION OF DISEASE

As scientists and doctors have learned more about the human body and the nature of disease, they have become aware of the importance of preventing illnesses as well as treating them. They have learned that the body has many natural defenses against disease. They have also discovered that certain diseases can be prevented when conscious efforts are made to avoid exposure to disease organisms and to strengthen the body's natural defenses. These efforts, when put into practice by individuals, by doctors, by communities, and even by entire nations, play a vital role in helping everyone maintain good health.

The Body's Defenses

The body has many ways of defending against invading microbes. The skin that covers the body acts as a barrier that keeps most germs out. The membranes that line the mouth, nose, and other openings also act as barriers.

The body may protect itself by tolerating certain kinds of bacteria called resident bacteria. These usually harmless organisms live on the skin, in the mouth, and in the intestines. They deter harmful organisms by crowding them out, and the "good" bacteria in the intestines aid digestion. Resident bacteria can be harmful, though, if they enter the bloodstream or go past their usual bounds in some other way.

When microbes do manage to get into the bloodstream or body cells, several kinds of defenses go into operation. Cells damaged by the invading microbes send out chemical messengers. Some of the messengers cause blood vessels to leak, so that fluid accumulates in the tissues and causes swelling. (The redness and swelling are referred to as inflammation.) Other chemical messengers may reach a special control center in the brain and produce a fever—a rise in the body temperature.

White blood cells monitoring the tissues pick up the chemical "Help!" signals and travel to the site of the infection. There they gobble up the microbes, literally eating and digesting them. Other types of white blood cells recognize "foreign" particles such as disease microbes, distinguishing them from the body's own substances. Still other white cells produce antibodies, very specific defenses that attack particular kinds of germs.

These defenses are important in preventing disease, but they are not always effective against every kind of illness. The body may be invaded by microbes that cause new kinds of diseases. A prominent example is the virus that causes AIDS. (See the article AIDS in Volume A.) Other examples include microbes that reach people through microbe-carrying organisms, or vectors. Such microbes cause Lyme disease and West Nile virus. (See the article VECTORS OF DISEASE in Volume UV.) New microbes may be revealed in sudden outbreaks, such as those associated with Legionnaire's disease and SARS (both these diseases are discussed in the feature that accompanies this article). Deadly diseases once thought under control, such as malaria, tuberculosis, and yellow fever, are resurging. Tuberculosis has appeared in a drug-resistant strain.

The Part the Individual Plays

It is important to do all you can to protect your health. A healthy person is much better able to fight off disease germs than a person who is weak and run-down. A person who stays healthy while he or she is young also has a better chance of enjoying continuing good health in later years.

The best ways to protect your health are to have a balanced diet (including fish, meat, milk, green and yellow vegetables, and fruit), to enjoy some form of exercise every day, to sleep eight to ten hours every night, to practice good hygiene, and to go to the doctor regularly.

In order to avoid disease, it is sensible to avoid going near people if you know they have illnesses that can be spread. If you get a cut or scrape, you can avoid diseases such as blood poisoning by cleaning the wound with soap and water and using local antiseptics to prevent infection. Using condoms for sexual activity prevents the spread of AIDS and some other sexually transmitted diseases.

If you do become ill, you can take steps to prevent your illness from becoming worse or being complicated by a more serious disease. The best way to overcome illness (or to avoid becoming even more ill) is to follow your doctor's instructions for getting rest, eating properly, and taking medications.

What the Doctor Can Do

The doctor plays an important part in disease prevention by educating people on how to avoid diseases and by giving them protection against certain illnesses. The doctor does this with an inoculation or vaccination against a particular disease. This means that he or she places in a healthy person's body some of the dead or weakened germs that cause the disease or one very like it. The body then makes substances called antibodies to fight the disease germs. These substances remain in the body and protect the person from the disease. This method of protection is used against one type of meningitis, whooping cough, polio, measles, mumps, rubella (German measles), and hepatitis B. (You can read more about this in the articles ANTIBODIES AND ANTIGENS in Volume A and VACCINATION AND IMMUNIZATION in Volume UV.)

One example of how effective vaccinations are is that they have completely wiped out the disease smallpox. Smallpox used to make millions of people ill and in some epidemics killed 40 percent of those infected with the disease. Polio was nearly wiped out by vaccinations in 2004, but some cases of it have appeared since then in countries where not enough vaccinations were given.

In another disease prevention measure, the doctor may place a preparation called a toxoid in a healthy person's body. This preparation is made from the poisons, or toxins, that are formed when the germs of a particular disease enter a person's body.

When the toxoid is given to a healthy person, it causes the formation of antibodies that overcome or neutralize the toxins. This form of protection is used against diphtheria and tetanus (lockjaw).

In their first year of life, babies receive protection against diphtheria, whooping cough, tetanus, polio, and measles. As children grow older, doctors repeat the protection according to a definite timetable so that there are always enough antibodies present to fight a particular disease.

A vaccination against typhoid fever, yellow fever, cholera, typhus, Rocky Mountain spotted fever, or plague is usually given only when a person knows he or she will be in an area in which the disease is found. However, tetanus immunization typically involves a series of vaccinations. (For details, see Tetanus in the feature accompanying this article.)

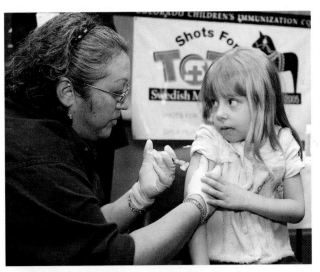

Vaccinations are usually given as injections. They have been especially effective in children, protecting against diseases such as measles, mumps, and rubella.

Another way in which doctors help prevent disease is by giving their patients complete checkups each year. Often an illness is found before it becomes serious or spreads to other people.

How the Community Helps

The community helps prevent disease by seeing that the water supply is kept pure, that human wastes and garbage are disposed of in sanitary ways, and that food supplies are kept clean. These measures are necessary in order to protect the people in the community from such serious diseases as typhoid fever, cholera, and dysentery.

These diseases are all caused by germs and are spread in very much the same way. When the germs of one of these diseases enter a healthy person who then develops the disease, the person passes out some of the germs in body wastes. If the germs reach the person's hands and he or she handles food that others will eat, the germs may be passed on.

In communities with poor sanitation, there may be few indoor toilets. There are usually flies on or near the outdoor toilets. Some of the disease germs in the waste material may be carried by flies to other places in the community. In this way diseases reach the food supplies.

In communities that do not have modern sanitation, human wastes may be drained off into a nearby lake or river. The lake or river may supply the town with water. If disease germs reach the water supply, the entire town may become ill.

Modern communities keep drinking water and the water in swimming pools pure by adding chemicals to it. Chlorine is often used as a water purifier. (In addition to chlorine, some communities add chemicals called fluorides to the water supply. These have been found to lessen tooth decay in children.)

Water treatment plants ensure that the public water supply is kept pure. By using chlorine to kill disease germs, these plants protect the community from serious diseases.

Human wastes are piped to sewage disposal plants, where they are purified by treatment with chemicals or by other means. Once they are purified, the wastes can safely be carried off into a lake or river or spread on the ground.

To discourage the breeding of flies, garbage is collected in closed trucks, and in many cities it is carried to a large garbage disposal plant. There it is dried and burned in large incinerators. Other methods of garbage disposal are also used. These include using garbage to fill in low-lying land, then covering the garbage with dirt.

To make sure that milk and food are kept free of disease germs, health inspectors exam-

ine dairies and farms and check the health of dairy workers. Health officers check the cleanliness of restaurants, food markets, and food-packing plants—and the health of workers in all of these places.

The community also works to control diseases that are spread through insects and animals. Cows with tuberculosis or brucellosis (undulant fever) can pass on either of these diseases to humans through their milk. Today cows are inspected for tuberculosis, and milk is pasteurized to destroy disease germs. (Raw milk may harbor many harmful organisms. Symptoms of illness caused by these organisms include diarrhea, stomach cramps, and fever.) When animals are to be killed and eaten as meat, the meat is examined before it is packed or shipped to markets.

The germs of yellow fever, malaria, and typhus are passed to humans through the bite of an insect. Plague is a disease caused by a bacterium found in rodents, usually rats and ground squirrels, and it may spread to people by rodent or flea bites. To prevent these diseases, programs of rodent and insect control are carried on in many countries. Rats hide in ships and are carried from one country to another. That is why special efforts must be made in seaports to poison rats and to keep them from breeding. Public health workers check fleas from ground squirrels for plague bacteria. To kill insects, the swamps in which they breed are sprayed with chemicals. But care must be taken that the chemicals do not destroy all plant and animal life in an area.

There are other ways, too, in which the community can act to help prevent disease. Health services, including sight and hearing tests for schoolchildren, can be provided. Modern engineering methods can be used to control smoke and harmful fumes that rise from chimneys. Factory workers can be protected from chemicals, fumes, and dust that may cause disease. Authorities can regulate the use of radioactive materials.

Nonprofit organizations provide important disease-prevention services. In the United

States, for example, the American Heart Association helps educate the public on the prevention of heart attacks. The American Lung Association campaigns against cigarette smoking to help reduce lung cancer. The American Red Cross tests for disease in donated blood in order to prevent others from becoming infected. And many groups in countries around the world collect money to use for research to find cures for such diseases as cancer and muscular dystrophy.

What a Nation Does

Many preventive measures take place at the national level. This is especially evident when a new disease, such as AIDS, starts to become a widespread health threat. The increased incidence of the disease is noted by physicians, who report this to their professional organizations and often, in the United States, to the U.S. Department of Health and Human Services. These groups then publish articles in medical journals and speak to physicians at medical meetings about the new disease. A federal agency, the Centers for Disease Control and Prevention, collects statistics and carries out research on the new disease. It also collects and compares research from medical schools, private research groups such as the Rockefeller Institute, and government research agencies such as the National Institutes of Health.

Pharmaceutical companies spend great amounts of money and time in efforts to find and produce effective drugs to treat disease. Research for drugs and treatments is very important in the fight against disease. When new drugs or treatments are developed, they are evaluated by the federal Food and Drug Administration and approved for use if they seem helpful and safe.

The Surgeon General of the United States alerts the public to critical dangers and problems affecting the public health and offers ways to avoid them. The U.S. Congress and sometimes state governments vote to give special funds to speed research on diseases that are a serious threat to public health.

The Department of Homeland Security oversees the development of vaccines, toxins, and other forms of treatment of diseases that may be deliberately spread by terrorists through biological and chemical warfare. The World Health Organization (WHO) has updated its guidelines for public health responses to terrorism.

How Nations Help One Another

To prevent disease on a worldwide scale, nations also must work together. Today the WHO, formed under the United Nations, is the major group through which different countries work together to prevent disease. Their work includes sharing information and passing on warnings whenever there is serious outbreak of disease in any part of the world. Through the Global Outbreak and Response Network, the WHO sends healthcare workers to the site, collects samples for testing, helps in local quarantines, and does everything possible to bring an outbreak under control quickly.

The WHO also helps prevent disease by setting up international quarantine regulations. These are rules concerning the passage of travelers from one country into another. Quarantine laws are intended to prevent the introduction into a country of a contagious, or catching, disease. Any traveler who may have the disease is placed in quarantine (separated from other people). There is an international quarantine on cholera, plague, and yellow fever. Many countries are working together against smoking through the WHO's Framework Convention on Tobacco Control. In addition to its other effects, global warming may favor the spread of diseases into new regions. Such trends may be slowed if the Kyoto Protocol and other efforts to reduce global warming succeed.

There are still areas in which disease prevention is not practiced. Some developing countries lack the medical and health workers, the equipment, and the funds that are necessary for the work of disease prevention. But many organizations are working to change this situation and bring the benefits of disease prevention to all people.

ALVIN SILVERSTEIN
College of Staten Island, CUNY

VIRGINIA SILVERSTEIN
Coauthors, *Allergies;
Cancer; Heart Disease*

GLENN AUSTIN, M.D.
Author, *The Parents' Medical Manual*

Reviewed by MARGARET O. HYDE
Coauthor, *Drugs 101: An Overview for Teens*

See also MEDICINE.

DISINFECTANTS AND ANTISEPTICS

Chemical germicides are substances that kill germs. One type includes the chemicals that are used on nonliving objects, such as floors and washbasins. These are called **disinfectants.** A second type includes those that can be put directly on the skin. They are called **antiseptics.**

There are more good disinfectants than antiseptics. This is because most chemicals that kill germs thoroughly also can damage living human tissue.

Antiseptics are less poisonous than disinfectants. Yet even antiseptics must be used only on the outside of the body. They are too strong to be swallowed or used in injections.

A third group includes chemicals that destroy germs but can be used inside the body. These are the antibiotics. You can read about them in the article ANTIBIOTICS in Volume A.

▶DISINFECTANTS

The use of disinfectants is most important in hospitals and medical offices. Disinfectants usually are wiped or sprayed on large surfaces like floors and tops of tables. Small objects, such as dentists' instruments, may be soaked in disinfectant.

Disinfectants are also used in restaurant kitchens for washing dishes and silverware.

Before any procedure that breaks the skin—such as a shot or surgery—medical personnel scrub their hands as well as the patient's skin with antiseptics.

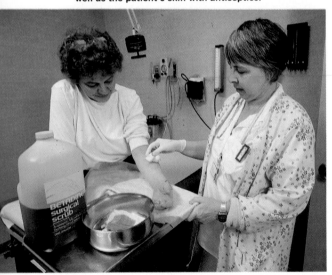

The dishwashers rinse away the chemical so that it does not remain on the utensils.

In the home, bleaches and washing soda are often used as disinfectants, particularly in bathrooms and kitchens.

Some disinfectants are effective even in very weak solutions, provided they are given a long time to work. Calcium hypochlorite is one. Very small amounts of it can be put into water supplies and swimming pools, where it dissolves and releases the chemical chlorine. The solution is too weak to harm people, but over a period of hours the number of germs is reduced.

▶ANTISEPTICS

Antiseptics are put on the skin to reduce the number of germs. Surgeons scrub their hands and arms with a germicidal, or germ-killing, soap before they perform an operation. Antiseptics are put on a patient's skin before an operation.

Many persons use an antiseptic soap for ordinary skin care. Deodorants contain an antiseptic. Most families keep an antiseptic in the home for treating cuts and scratches.

Some of the preparations for home use are bacteriostatic instead of germicidal. That means they stop the bacteria from growing. Their action is not as quick as that of chemicals that kill the germs outright.

But even the true germ-killers cannot completely rid the skin of bacteria. Some will survive in the tiny perspiration channels and in channels through which hairs grow.

▶STERILIZATION

It is almost impossible to kill all forms of germs with either disinfectants or antiseptics. Some germs form spores, small seedlike particles that wait to grow until they have warmth and moisture. Many spores are not affected by chemical germicides. Many viruses also survive germicides.

Making an object completely germfree is called sterilization. To kill all the spores and viruses, the object usually must be exposed to intense heat. Sterilization is done with steam under pressure, with boiling water, or with dry oven heat.

EARLE SPAULDING
Professor of Microbiology
Temple University School of Medicine

See also FIRST AID; BACTERIA.

DISNEY, WALT (1901-1966)

Walt Disney began by making a mouse the world could love—and then went on to create a family entertainment empire.

When people think of animated cartoons, one name immediately comes to mind—Walt Disney. While he did not invent animated cartoons, Disney was responsible for improving their quality and making them into an art form. Out of his work came what is probably the world's best known cartoon character—Mickey Mouse.

Walter Elias Disney was born in Chicago, Illinois, on December 5, 1901, the fourth of five children of Elias and Flora Disney. When he was a baby, the family moved to a farm near Marceline, Missouri. It was here that Walt spent his early years and developed his interest in drawing. In 1910 the family moved again—this time to Kansas City. There Walt delivered newspapers and went to school. When he was 14, he was enrolled in art classes at the Kansas City Art Institute.

The Disney family moved back to Chicago in 1917, and Walt attended one year of high school there before joining a Red Cross unit and spending nine months as an ambulance driver in France at the end of World War I.

When Disney returned from France in 1919, he decided to make art his career. He soon joined the staff of the Kansas City Film Ad Company, which was producing a simple type of animation. He and a colleague, Ubbe Iwerks, learned enough about animation to try doing some of their own. They formed a company called Laugh-O-Gram Films, where they made crude animated cartoons.

In 1923, Disney moved to California, and in partnership with his brother Roy he began Walt Disney Productions. After five years of making silent cartoons, he produced *Steamboat Willie,* the first cartoon to use synchronized sound (sound that matches what is going on in the film). Walt Disney's cartoon creation, Mickey Mouse, appeared in that 1928 cartoon, using Disney's own voice. Disney's success led to the film series *Silly Symphonies,* which was introduced in 1929 and first used color in 1932. Soon full-color Disney cartoons, such as *Three Little Pigs* and *The Tortoise and the Hare,* were winning Academy Awards. The 1930's brought fame to Walt Disney as Mickey Mouse and his pals Donald Duck, Pluto, Minnie Mouse, and Goofy appeared not only in cartoons but on merchandise items licensed by Disney.

Disney's most famous creation, Mickey Mouse, first appeared in *Steamboat Willie* in 1928. Mickey soon became a movie "star" around the world.

Disneyland, in Anaheim, California, was a dream of Walt Disney's for many years. The dream came true in 1955. Millions of people flock to Disneyland and its sister park, Disney World in Orlando, Florida, each year.

Mickey Mouse cartoons featured a supporting cast of such popular characters as Minnie Mouse, Donald Duck, Goofy, and Pluto.

Two of Disney's earliest, and still most popular, feature-length cartoons were *Snow White and the Seven Dwarfs* (*below*), made in 1937, and *Bambi* (*left*), made in 1942. *Fantasia*, in 1940, combined cartoons with classical music.

Disney's *The Mickey Mouse Club*, a weekly television series in the 1950's, featured teenage singers and puppeteers.

EPCOT (for *Experimental Prototype Community of Tomorrow*) opened in Disney World in 1982. The Center features displays of new technology and exhibits from many countries.

In 1937 the Disney studio produced the world's first animated feature film, *Snow White and the Seven Dwarfs*. Then came *Pinocchio* and *Fantasia* in 1940, *Dumbo* in 1941, and *Bambi* in 1942. *Song of the South*, in 1946, used cartoon characters with live actors.

During World War II the Disney organization designed military insignias and made training films for the United States armed forces. After the war Disney continued to make animated films, such as *Alice in Wonderland* (1951), *Peter Pan* (1953), and *The Jungle Book* (1967). He also turned to live-action films such as *Treasure Island* (1950) and *20,000 Leagues Under the Sea* (1954).

Moving into a totally new area, Walt Disney opened Disneyland in Anaheim, California, in 1955. He had wanted to design an amusement park where families could have fun together. Disneyland had exciting rides and attractions but was also spotlessly clean and run by smiling, friendly employees. The park eventually came to be one of the most popular tourist attractions in the United States.

During the next decade, Disney added new attractions to Disneyland while continuing to make films the whole family could enjoy. *Mary Poppins*, in 1964, is considered by many to be the pinnacle of his filmmaking career. Disney won a record 32 Academy Awards for his technical innovations in film.

Walt Disney also pioneered the production of feature films for television. Some of these appeared on his weekly series *The Mickey Mouse Club* (1955–59) and on *Walt Disney's Wonderful World of Color*, which aired, under several titles, for 29 seasons.

Shows prepared for the New York World's Fair in 1964 enabled Disney to show off his Audio-Animatronics figures in such attractions as *It's a Small World* and *Great Moments with Mr. Lincoln*. The lifelike figure of Abraham Lincoln, which recited passages from his speeches, never ceased to amaze fairgoers.

Walt Disney never rested. Even as he died, on December 15, 1966, he was planning for a whole new Walt Disney World vacation kingdom in Florida, and EPCOT, an experimental prototype community of tomorrow. Both came into being after his death, Walt Disney World opening in 1971 and EPCOT Center in 1982.

SHARON DISNEY LUND

See also ANIMATION; MOTION PICTURES.

DISRAELI, BENJAMIN (1804–1881)

Benjamin Disraeli, who was to become prime minister of Great Britain, was born in London on December 21, 1804. He was the second child of Isaac D'Israeli, author of a well-known book, *Curiosities of Literature*.

Isaac D'Israeli was Jewish, but Benjamin was baptized a Christian. After attending school, which he hated, he taught himself Greek and Latin, spent 3 years in a lawyer's office, and helped start an unsuccessful newspaper. At the age of 22 he wrote an anonymous novel, *Vivian Grey,* which was violently attacked when its author's name leaked out. Intensely ambitious, he drew attention to himself by appearing in brightly colored clothes and speaking only when he had something witty to say.

With the money he made on the novel, young Disraeli toured Greece, Turkey, Palestine, and Egypt. Returning home, he continued to write while trying hard to enter politics. He failed several times as a candidate for Parliament, but consoled himself with a love affair that inspired another novel.

Queen Victoria's accession to the throne in 1837 caused a general election, and Disraeli was elected to Parliament for the borough of Maidstone. But his first speech was received with shouts of derision. He made the memorable reply: "I sit down now, but the time will come when you *will* hear me." It came when he attacked Prime Minister Sir Robert Peel's repeal of the Corn Laws, which regulated the price of wheat and other grains. The brilliance of Disraeli's speeches was such that he was recognized as the leader of the Tory "Young Englanders." In 1844 he wrote a novel, *Coningsby,* which projected the ideals of the group. Two more novels, *Sybil* and *Tancred,* established his reputation as an author. He was not a great novelist. But he could depict the political scene with authority, and nearly all his works contain witty comments on life.

In 1839 Disraeli had married a wealthy widow, Mrs. Wyndham Lewis, known to history as Mary Anne. Their affection for each other lasted throughout their lives.

Disraeli's own party, the Tories, distrusted him; his opponents, the Whigs, detested him; and his slow rise to power is perhaps the greatest personal achievement in the history

Benjamin Disraeli, Earl of Beaconsfield.

of politics. When the Tories at last took office, he was appointed chancellor of the exchequer. He enraged the Whigs by producing a reform bill, the first step in his concept of Tory democracy. It was passed in 1867, much to the mortification of his chief opponent, William E. Gladstone.

When out of office, Disraeli continued to write novels. One, *Lothair,* was a huge success in America as well as England. In 1874 a general election gave the Tories a handsome majority, and Disraeli became prime minister for 6 years. His term of office was mainly notable for the creation of Queen Victoria as Empress of India and the purchase of the controlling shares in the Suez Canal, which gave England power over Egypt. But Disraeli's greatest moment came in 1878. Having stopped the war between Russia and Turkey by sending a fleet to the Dardanelles, he attended the Berlin Congress. There he compelled Bismarck, the German chancellor, to back England's policy of keeping Russia out of the Mediterranean Sea.

By now Disraeli's wife had died and his adoring sovereign, Queen Victoria, had created him Earl of Beaconsfield. In 1880, ill with asthma and gout, he asked the Queen to dissolve Parliament and call a new election. The Liberals under Gladstone were returned, and Beaconsfield retired. After writing a final novel, *Endymion,* the most vivid and versatile personality in England's political history died on April 19, 1881.

HESKETH PEARSON
Author, *Dizzy; The Life and Personality
of Benjamin Disraeli*

See also GLADSTONE, WILLIAM EWART.

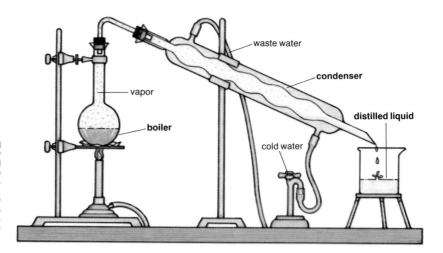

Distillation is being carried out with a simple still. Vapor is rising off the boiling liquid and is moving through the connecting tube to the inner part of the condenser. Here the vapor is cooled by cold water flowing in the condenser's outer chamber. As it cools, the vapor changes back to a liquid.

Labels: vapor, boiler, waste water, condenser, cold water, distilled liquid

DISTILLATION

When a liquid is boiling, it gives off vapor, or gas. When the vapor is trapped and cooled, it turns back into liquid. This process is called distillation.

Distillation has been used for nearly 2,000 years to purify liquids and to extract perfumes and flavorings from plants. Today it is used in refining petroleum, manufacturing alcohol. and purifying some industrial wastes.

▶DISTILLING EQUIPMENT AND HOW IT WORKS

The equipment used for distilling is called a **still.** The simplest kind of still has two parts. One part (the boiler) is a container in which the liquid is heated and vaporized (turned to vapor). The other part is a tube connected to the container, in which the liquid is cooled and condensed (turned back to liquid). The tube is called a **condenser.** The boiler is closed (except where the tube is joined to it) to prevent the vapor from escaping into the air and being lost. As the vapor condenses it forms drops of liquid on the walls of the condenser tube and trickles down, drop by drop, into another container called a receiver.

The condenser is generally cooled by running a stream of cold water over it. This condenses the vapor rapidly so that little escapes and is lost.

The stills that are used today in industry are much more complicated, but they work on the same basic principles.

▶PURIFYING WATER BY DISTILLATION

Very pure water is needed for filling automobile batteries, for preparing intravenous feeding solutions or contact lens cleaning so-lutions, and for carrying out some chemical manufacturing processes. Water from rivers, wells, and reservoirs is not pure enough for these uses because it contains some dissolved mineral salts. Water can be removed from these mineral salts by distillation. The water is boiled off and then turned back into liquid in the condenser. The mineral salts are left behind in the boiler.

Distillation also may be used to obtain fresh water aboard ships and space capsules.

▶SEPARATING MIXTURES OF LIQUIDS

Sometimes one liquid is in fact a mixture of several different liquids. For example, wine is made up of alcohol and water; crude oil is made up of gasoline, kerosene, and different kinds of light and heavy oils. The different liquids can be separated by distillation.

How is it possible to separate one liquid from another simply by boiling them together? The answer is that each liquid boils at a different temperature. By properly controlling the temperature, one liquid can be vaporized while the other remains liquid.

For example, suppose a mixture of methyl alcohol (wood alcohol) and water is to be separated. Methyl alcohol boils at 149°F (65°C). Water boils at 212°F (100°C). If the mixture is heated to just over 150°F (66°C) and is not allowed to become hotter, the alcohol will vaporize. When the vapor is condensed, it will yield nearly pure methyl alcohol. (The distilled liquid will contain a very small amount of water, because the water gives off some vapor as it is heated.)

The process just described is called simple distillation. Simple distillation works well for liquids whose boiling points are far apart, and when only one liquid needs to be separated from a mixture. It does not work as well for separating liquids that boil at nearly the same temperature.

Two or more liquids can be separated from a mixture by the process called fractional distillation. (Fractional distillation gets its name because the liquid mixture that is being distilled is separated into portions called fractions.) As the mixture is heated gradually, each component boils separately when its particular boiling point is reached. The vapor of each is collected and condensed separately.

▶OTHER TYPES OF DISTILLATION

Vacuum Distillation. Some substances cannot be distilled in the ordinary way because they would be destroyed by the heat before they reached their boiling points. Such substances are distilled in a partial vacuum. Decreasing the pressure on a liquid makes it boil at a lower temperature. The liquid is vaporized before it can get hot enough to break down. High-quality lubricating oils are sometimes vacuum-distilled.

Steam Distillation. This is sometimes used for substances that have low boiling points and are easily damaged by heat. Steam is injected into the still under pressure. The heat of the steam vaporizes the substance to be distilled. When the vapor is condensed, the steam collects in the condenser as water. For this reason steam distillation can only be used with substances that do not mix with water, such as perfume and flavoring oils from plants.

Dry Distillation. This is used to distill liquid chemicals from solid materials. For example, creosote, methyl alcohol, and many other useful chemicals may be obtained from wood by dry distillation. The wood is heated in a closed chamber, and the vapor is collected and condensed. Charcoal is all that remains after the vapor is driven off. Coal tar, a source of many important chemicals, is obtained from certain kinds of coal in the same way.

Sublimation. A few solid substances behave in an unusual way when they are heated. Instead of melting into a liquid, they turn directly to vapor. This process is called sublimation. When the vapor condenses, it becomes solid again, usually as a fine powder. Impurities in the substance that has been sublimed remain behind in the heating vessel. The sublimation process can be used to purify solid iodine.

▶HISTORY

When and where distillation was first used is uncertain. It is believed that around A.D. 200, liquids were being distilled by the alchemists of Alexandria, a center of learning in ancient Egypt.

During the Black Death (1348–50) doctors prescribed distilled alcoholic drinks to ward off the terrible plague. The drinks did not prevent the disease, but they became very popular anyway. For several hundred years distilling was used mainly in the production of brandy, gin, whiskey, and other strong alcoholic beverages.

Around the middle of the 19th century a new use was discovered for distillation. This was oil refining. At first oil refining was a crude, slow process. Each fraction—gasoline, kerosene, lubricating oils—had to be distilled off separately, at a different temperature. The invention of fractional distillation greatly simplified the process. Today the oil-refining industry is the largest user of distillation.

Reviewed by JOHN H. STROHL
West Virginia University

DISTRICT OF COLUMBIA. See WASHINGTON, D.C.

Two liquids in a solution can be separated by distillation. Because the liquids boil at different temperatures, one can be vaporized while the other remains a liquid.

DIVING

Diving is a form of acrobatics performed in the air over water. A diver can make many different kinds of movements between the platform or springboard and the water. The water provides a safe place to land after completing the acrobatic movements in the air.

Diving is a demanding sport, requiring a high degree of muscular development and coordination and a good sense of timing. It is essential that no person should attempt to dive unless he or she is a good swimmer.

Platform diving is usually performed from a high, firm platform. In springboard diving a long flexible board that bends easily is used. Springboard diving, which was developed after platform diving, is performed closer to the water than platform diving. It is beautiful to watch and enjoyable to perform.

In a well-executed dive, the body straightens and stretches for the entry into the water, whether it be feet first or head first. The good diver does not strike the water flat with the back or stomach. A good dive looks easy and effortless, but much practice and work are needed to achieve it.

To become a good diver, one must understand the fundamentals of the sport and receive careful instruction from a qualified diving teacher or an experienced diver. Daily practice is also most important for the person who wishes to become an expert.

As do most sports, diving requires strong arms and legs and flexibility. The training program for competitive divers includes weight training for strength, ballet for grace and flexibility, and, of course, diving practice. Dives may be practiced from a diving board, trampoline, or platform. For safety and for better training, all dives should be practiced under the supervision of a diving coach.

If you wish to train to be a diver, you can practice at home by doing push-ups and sit-ups for strength. A very good exercise involves hanging by your arms from a high bar (chinning bar), keeping your legs straight, your feet together, and your toes pointed, and then lifting your legs toward your chest. This exercise is similar to the motion you must perform in certain dives. The exercise also strengthens your abdominal and thigh muscles. Divers also practice handstands—to learn balance and to strengthen the arms, shoulders, and wrists. All head-first entries into the water are done in a handstand position.

In a head-first dive, your legs and feet will be the last part of your body the judges see. So it is helpful to practice—even at home—stretching and pointing your feet and toes. This will help you create a graceful form as your body enters the water.

▶**BEGINNING DIVES**

The feet-first jump is the simplest and easiest dive to learn (Figure 1).

The best method of learning to enter the water head first is to start from a kneeling position (Figure 2).

After you have learned to dive with the one-leg method (Figure 3), you are ready to do a front header, using both feet for a push-off (Figure 4).

Feet-first jump

A: Stand at the edge of the pool, your arms extended in a V position. **B:** Swing your arms downward in a circular motion, bending your knees and body slightly. **C:** Your arms continue forward and upward in the same circular motion as you jump. Keep your chest up, your head and back straight, and your feet and toes pointed. Your hands reach to the sky at the height of your jump. **D:** Bring your arms to your sides as you enter the water. To soften your landing on the bottom of the pool, flatten your feet after they have broken the surface of the water.

Figure 1

Head first, kneeling

A: Kneel on one knee at the edge of the pool. Extend your arms forward. Lock your thumbs together. Your head should be tucked in between your arms. Grip the edge of the pool with the toes of one foot. **B:** Gently roll into the water.

Figure 2

Head first – one leg

A: Stand at the edge of the pool. Extend one leg behind you. Bend forward, your arms over your head as in the kneeling dive. **B:** As you begin to fall toward the water, continue to lift the lower leg, raising it to meet the upper leg. Your legs should be together as they enter the water.

Figure 3

Head first — both legs push off

A: Stand with your toes over the edge of the pool, knees together and straight. Keep your arms over your head. Bend forward, reaching for a spot on the water close to you. **B:** Do not bend your knees as you fall. **C:** Straighten your body as you enter the water. If you wish to do this dive with a spring, kick your heels upward by snapping the ankles and quickly pointing the feet as you fall.

Figure 4

Back jump takeoff (from diving board)

Figure 5

A: Stand with your back facing the water, your arms extended in the V position. The balls of your feet should be on the diving board. **B:** Swing your arms downward in a circular motion, bending your knees and body slightly. **C:** Your arms continue forward and upward in the same circular motion. Your heels will drop as the board bends. **D** and **E:** With a slight backward lean, take off by pushing away with your feet. **F** and **G:** As you enter the water, your feet should be directly beneath your body, and your arms should be at your sides.

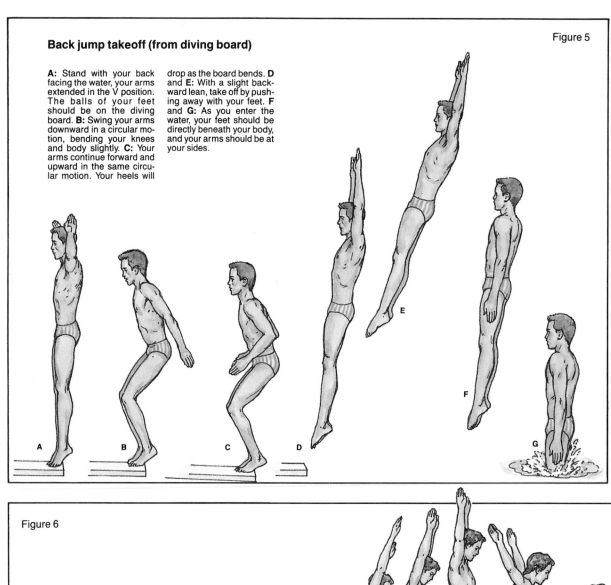

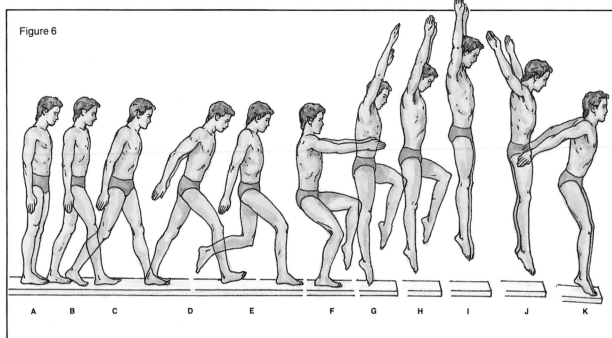

Figure 6

DIVING SAFETY

1. Never dive alone. A lifeguard or other person qualified in water safety should be present.

2. Look before you leap. Make sure that the preceding diver has cleared the diving area and that no swimmer has swum into the diving area. Also look for floating objects, such as a kickboard used in swimming practice.

3. Never dive head first into any body of water unless you know how deep it is. Always jump feet first the first time.

4. Even if the depth of a pool is marked, check the bottom of the pool. Where does the shallow water begin? Where does the incline from deep to shallow begin? How deep is the water directly under and to the sides of the diving board?

5. Be sure that the diving board is not too close to the sides of the pool, for it is possible to hit the pool's wall after an improper takeoff.

6. In head-first dives, always have your hands hit the surface of the water first, and be ready to do an armstand on the bottom of the pool.

7. Never take part in horseplay on or around diving boards or diving areas.

8. Dive only from boards and platforms that have a surface of nonskid material.

9. Do not dive from a springboard if the front end is noticeably higher than the rear end, for uneven pitch may throw you back toward the board.

10. Never dive from the side of a springboard.

11. Only one person at a time should use a diving board.

12. When learning a dive, do not turn your head to the side when you hit the water, as this can cause a broken eardrum. Never dive with a head cold, as this can cause sinus or ear infections. When jumping feet first, exhale through your nose to keep water from rushing up into your nose and sinuses.

After you have practiced diving from the side of the pool, you are ready to try the dives shown in Figures 1 through 4 from the end of a springboard. As a beginner, you should practice these and all other dives only under proper supervision.

Before diving from a board, it is important to test how much the board bends. Some boards have more "spring" than others. The amount of spring depends on the material of which the board is made and on the setting of the fulcrum, a bar under the board that can be adjusted forward or backward. If the fulcrum is set forward (toward the end of the board), the board bends more quickly and stiffly. If the fulcrum is set toward the back, the board is slower and more flexible.

After you have mastered the first four dives off the diving board, the next step is to learn the back jump take-off (Figure 5), in which you stand with your back to the water and enter it from a backward position.

Some dives are begun from a standing position at the end of the board or platform. Other dives are begun with a walk (or run)—called the approach—to the end of the board or platform. Learning the forward approach (Figure 6) is essential if you want to become a good diver.

Three-step approach and hurdle

A: Position yourself on the springboard to give yourself enough room for three steps and a hurdle. (The first two steps of the approach should be about the same length. The third step should be a bit longer. Let your arms move naturally. Your speed should increase as you near the end of the board.) **B:** As you walk you must keep your back straight with a slight forward lean. Keep your head straight, with your eyes on where your last step will be. **C:** One step before the hurdle step, swing your arms forward above the hip line. **D:** As you step into your hurdle step, your arms will fall back behind the hip line. This generates power for the arm swing. **E, F,** and **G:** Swing your arms forward and up over your head. The hurdle is a one-legged jump. The opposite thigh lifts, timed to add more power and height. **H:** Push your body into the air as high as possible. **I:** When you reach the peak of the hurdle, straighten your legs and point your toes. **J, K,** and **L:** As you drop back to the board, you should touch first with the balls of your feet. Forcefully bring your arms down in a circular motion. **M** and **N:** Bend your knees to push up and **O** and **P:** away from the board. Complete your arm circle to get maximum lift off the board.

In the four-step approach, one additional step is taken before the hurdle. The first step and the hurdle are made with the same foot.

Figure 7

Forward dive straight (layout position)

This dive is also known as the swan dive. **A:** Begin by using the three- or four-step approach and hurdle. **B** and **C:** After you have swung your arms up over your head, extend them in a T position. **D:** Keep your body straight and stomach in. Don't arch your back. **E:** As you enter the water, your arms should be close to the sides of your head. Your body should be stretched but not arched out.

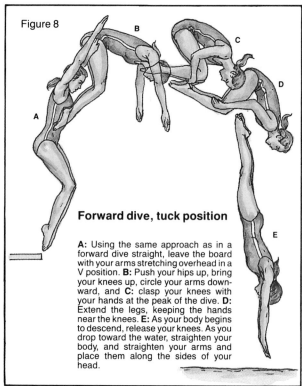

Figure 8

Forward dive, tuck position

A: Using the same approach as in a forward dive straight, leave the board with your arms stretching overhead in a V position. **B:** Push your hips up, bring your knees up, circle your arms downward, and **C:** clasp your knees with your hands at the peak of the dive. **D:** Extend the legs, keeping the hands near the knees. **E:** As your body begins to descend, release your knees. As you drop toward the water, straighten your body, and straighten your arms and place them along the sides of your head.

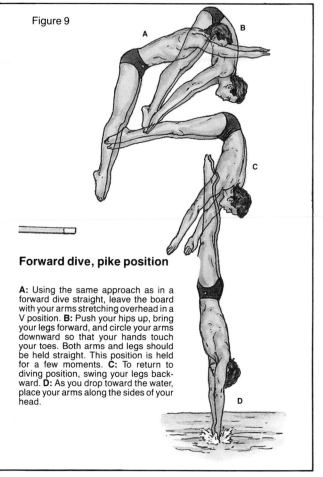

Figure 9

Forward dive, pike position

A: Using the same approach as in a forward dive straight, leave the board with your arms stretching overhead in a V position. **B:** Push your hips up, bring your legs forward, and circle your arms downward so that your hands touch your toes. Both arms and legs should be held straight. This position is held for a few moments. **C:** To return to diving position, swing your legs backward. **D:** As you drop toward the water, place your arms along the sides of your head.

Figure 10

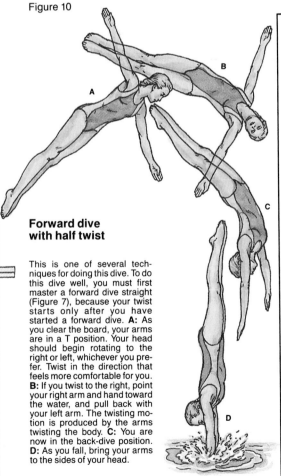

Forward dive with half twist

This is one of several techniques for doing this dive. To do this dive well, you must first master a forward dive straight (Figure 7), because your twist starts only after you have started a forward dive. **A:** As you clear the board, your arms are in a T position. Your head should begin rotating to the right or left, whichever you prefer. Twist in the direction that feels more comfortable for you. **B:** If you twist to the right, point your right arm and hand toward the water, and pull back with your left arm. The twisting motion is produced by the arms twisting the body. **C:** You are now in the back-dive position. **D:** As you fall, bring your arms to the sides of your head.

▶ BASIC DIVING POSITIONS AND DIVES

The three basic diving positions are the layout (Figure 7), the tuck (Figure 8), and the pike (Figure 9). When the body remains straight, with the legs extended, the diver is in the layout position. In the tuck position, the legs are bent up to the diver's chest, and the hands clasp the shins to form the body into a tight "ball." In the pike position, the body is bent forward, and the legs are straight. A fourth diving position, called the free position, applies to dives involving twisting and somersaulting.

The five basic dives are the front dive (Figure 7, Figure 8, and Figure 9); the twist dive (Figure 10); the back dive (Figure 11, Figure 12, and Figure 13); the inward dive, formerly known as the cutaway (Figure 14); and the reverse dive, formerly called the gainer (Figure 15). All the variations and combinations of diving come from these five.

Each of the basic dives heads a group. The front dive is the first in Group I, the **forward** group of dives. In this group, the diver dives away from the board or platform, doing a front somersault, executing a half turn, or advancing to the 1½ somersault. The last dive in this group is the forward 3½ somersault.

In Group II, the **backward** dives, the diver stands at the edge of the board or platform.

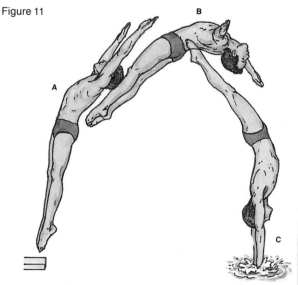

Figure 11

Back dive, straight position

Review the back jump takeoff (Figure 5) before attempting a back dive. **A:** On takeoff, lean slightly backward and extend your arms upward. Push your chest upward, and follow your hands with your eyes. **B:** At the peak of your lift, stretch your arms out to a T position. Tilt your head slowly back to see the water. **C:** Extend your arms over your head as you fall toward the water. Your body will have very little arch as it enters the water.

Rotating backward in the air, the diver may perform a half turn to 2½ somersaults.

Dives in Group III, the **reverse** group, start with a forward takeoff. But instead of continuing forward to the water, the direction is reversed and the dive is performed in the same direction as the back group. In this form of diving, the diver can rotate in reverse from 1½ to 2½ turns. This group requires advanced skill.

Dives in Group IV, the **inward** group, start with the back dive. The diver stands at the outer edge of the board or platform and jumps into the air as for a simple back dive. But the direction of the diver's body then changes, and the dive is completed in the direction of the board or platform.

The basic dive for the Group V, the **twisting** group, is the front dive with a half twist. In this group the diver may combine dives from the first four groups with one or more twists. This is the largest of all groups because a twist may be added to any dive in any direction.

Dives from Groups I through V are done in both springboard and platform diving. A final group, Group VI, the **armstand** group, is done from the platform only. The diver must begin the dive from an armstand position at the end of the platform.

There are more than 60 different dives in Groups I through V that may be taken from the springboard. There are some 50 dives in Groups I through VI that may be taken from the diving platform.

Figure 12

Back dive, pike position

A: Begin as if you were going to do a backward dive, springing up and outward. **B:** Take a pike position, with your hands touching your toes, at the peak of the dive. Your eyes should be looking at your hands. **C:** To get out of the pike position, keep your legs in the same position they were in when your hands touched them. Pull your upper body away from your legs. **D:** Get into a straight position for entry into the water.

Figure 13

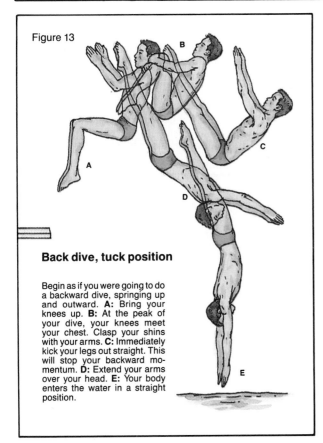

Back dive, tuck position

Begin as if you were going to do a backward dive, springing up and outward. **A:** Bring your knees up. **B:** At the peak of your dive, your knees meet your chest. Clasp your shins with your arms. **C:** Immediately kick your legs out straight. This will stop your backward momentum. **D:** Extend your arms over your head. **E:** Your body enters the water in a straight position.

Figure 14

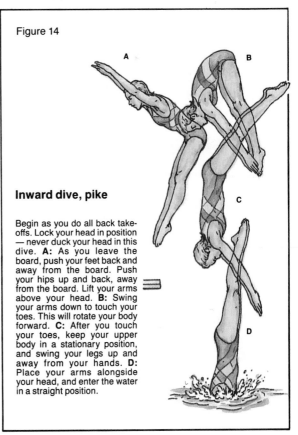

Inward dive, pike

Begin as you do all back take-offs. Lock your head in position — never duck your head in this dive. **A:** As you leave the board, push your feet back and away from the board. Push your hips up and back, away from the board. Lift your arms above your head. **B:** Swing your arms down to touch your toes. This will rotate your body forward. **C:** After you touch your toes, keep your upper body in a stationary position, and swing your legs up and away from your hands. **D:** Place your arms alongside your head, and enter the water in a straight position.

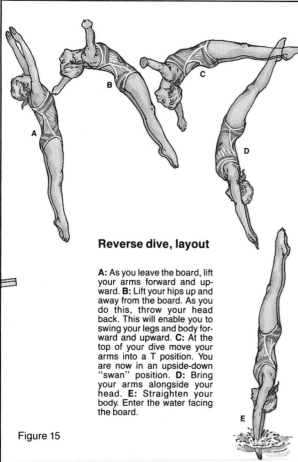

Reverse dive, layout

A: As you leave the board, lift your arms forward and upward. **B:** Lift your hips up and away from the board. As you do this, throw your head back. This will enable you to swing your legs and body forward and upward. **C:** At the top of your dive move your arms into a T position. You are now in an upside-down "swan" position. **D:** Bring your arms alongside your head. **E:** Straighten your body. Enter the water facing the board.

Figure 15

▶ COMPETITIVE DIVING

In addition to Olympic and national championships, diving is part of the competitive swimming programs for interscholastic and intercollegiate swimming meets and championships. United States Diving, in the United States, and the Canadian Amateur Diving Association, in Canada, regulate diving competitions in their respective countries. Both are connected with the International Amateur Swimming Federation, known as FINA, from its name in French.

Dives used in competition are classified as **compulsory** (a dive that the diver is required to do) and **optional** (a dive that the diver chooses, but not a repetition of a required dive). The compulsory dives are the basic dives in Groups I through V—forward, back, reverse, inward, and forward dive with a half twist—performed in layout, pike, or tuck. The number of dives a diver must perform depends on the age group in which the diver is competing. The number of dives increases as the diver competes in the older brackets.

All dives are rated numerically, according to the relative difficulty of the dive. The rating, from 1.2 for the easiest dive to 3.0 for the most difficult dive, is called the **degree of difficulty.** The compulsory dives all have generally low degrees of difficulty. (Tables listing all recognized dives with their difficulty ratings are published each year by the national diving organizations.)

Before a contest each diver lists on a form the names of the dives he or she will do, the diving position in which he or she will perform each dive, and the degree of difficulty for each dive.

Judges evaluate a dive and award points in whole or half numbers ranging from 0 (completely failed) to 10 (perfect). Depending on the importance of the particular competition, three, five, or seven judges may be used. With five or more judges, the high and low scores are canceled; only the middle scores are added. The total score for a particular dive is calculated by multiplying the degree of difficulty of the dive by the total of the awards given by the judges. (With seven judges, this score must then be multiplied by $\frac{3}{5}$, in order to equate the score with a score that would be given by five judges.) At the end of the competition, the diver with the highest total of points is the winner.

It is believed that people learned to dive shortly after they learned to swim. They probably started by jumping into the water and then found that they could enter the water more gracefully by diving head first. But it was not until the late 1800's that acrobatic, or fancy, diving developed. European gymnasts, wishing to improve their acrobatic technique, found that water was softer to land on than the ground or tumbling pads. As a result, the sport of fancy diving, now called competitive diving, developed in Europe.

By 1904 there was great international interest in diving. Enough different types of dives had been developed to hold a diving championship contest during the Olympic Games of that year. This event was listed in the program as high diving.

Since the 1904 Olympics, old dives have been dropped and new ones added. Synchronized diving, in which two divers dive simultaneously and try to match each others' moves exactly, was introduced at the 2000 Games.

A number of great divers have distinguished themselves in Olympic competition. In the Olympic Games of 1924, Albert White of the United States became the first diver to win gold medals in both springboard and platform (high) diving. Others who accomplished this "double" were, among the men, Peter Desjardins of the United States (1928) and Greg Louganis of the United States (1984, 1988); and among the women, Victoria Draves of the United States (1948), Patricia McCormick of the United States (1952, 1956), Ingrid Kramer of Germany (1960), and Fu Mingxia of China (1996).

Dr. Sammy Lee of the United States was the first man to win gold medals in platform diving in successive Olympics (1948, 1952). Robert Webster of the United States was the next to do so (1960, 1964), and Klaus Dibiasi of Italy won three in a row (1968, 1972, 1976). In addition to Greg Louganis, the only other man to win successive gold medals in springboard diving is Xiong Ni of China (1996, 2000).

In addition to Patricia McCormick, the other women who have won successive gold medals are Dorothy Poynton of the United States (1932, 1936) and Fu Mingxia of China (1992, 1996) in platform diving; and Ingrid

Greg Louganis of the United States joined the ranks of the greatest divers in history when he won two gold medals at both the 1984 and 1988 Olympic Games.

Kramer (1960, 1964), Gao Min of China (1988, 1992), and Fu Mingxia (1996, 2000) in springboard diving.

Great advances have been made in diving in recent years. Today divers from all over the world perform much more complicated stunts with ease. They may somersault through the air 4½ times forward or 3½ times backward, or perform combinations of spins and twists as effortlessly as an eagle soars through the sky.

SAMMY LEE, M.D.
Olympic Platform Diving Champion
(1948, 1952)

DIVING, UNDERWATER. See SKIN DIVING; UNDERWATER EXPLORATION.

DIVORCE

Divorce is the legal end of a marriage. When couples marry, they promise to share love, relationships, money, children, and often religion. They also take on certain legal rights and responsibilities. A divorce ends the legal obligations of marriage, but many experts say that spouses who separate must also get "divorced" in other ways. By this they mean that the husband and wife need to separate emotionally, learn to deal with their friends and relatives on their own, and eventually make enough money to support themselves alone. For many people, these changes are harder than the legal divorce.

People most commonly get divorced because they have serious differences they cannot resolve. Divorces also occur because one spouse has a serious problem, such as alcoholism, drug addiction, or mental illness. Or one spouse may have fallen in love with someone else.

While divorce laws differ among countries, most societies permit divorces only when there are serious problems between a husband and wife. Divorce laws differ from state to state in the United States and from province to province in Canada. In the United States, most couples now get a no fault divorce, which means that legally neither husband nor wife is responsible for the divorce.

Obtaining a divorce often requires a husband and wife to hire lawyers to represent them in court. In the United States, an increasingly popular alternative is for couples to hire a mediator. A mediator helps a husband and wife draw up a mutually acceptable agreement on how to divide their marriage property and arrange for the custody of any children they may have. The divorce agreement may then be put into legal terms by a lawyer, or prepared by the couple themselves, for final approval by the court.

The terms of the divorce set out any future financial obligations the partners may have to each other. For example, the court may order one spouse to make payments to support the other. These payments are called maintenance and are based on income and financial need.

About 60 percent of people who get divorced have children. Divorced parents must make legal and practical arrangements for the custody of their children. Some divorced parents agree to share equal custody of their children, but this is not the most common arrangement. In most cases, children live mainly with one parent, usually the mother but sometimes the father. In these cases, children usually see their other parent on weekends or at some other arranged time.

Some children may wish to live most of the time with one or the other parent after a divorce. When parents divorce, the parents and the legal system are supposed to take the child's wishes and needs into account. If the parents disagree, experts say, they should work out their differences without putting the children in the middle.

Historical Background. Before the 1700's, divorce as we know it was rare. During medieval times in Europe, only a church court could grant a divorce. Later the laws governing divorce were transferred from the church to the state. During the 1800's and 1900's, divorce laws were further extended and made more liberal.

Divorce is more common in the world than ever before. The United States has the highest divorce rate in the world, with nearly half of all marriages ending in divorce. Many divorced Americans remarry. In fact, over 40 percent of U.S. marriages involve people who were previously married.

Effects on the Family. Divorce may bring relief from a very unhappy family life, but it can also be very painful. One spouse may not want to get divorced and may feel hurt, angry, and alone. The spouse who wanted the divorce may believe the decision was right but may have feelings of anger and guilt. Divorced parents worry about their children. They may miss their children when the children are with the other parent but feel overwhelmed when caring for them all by themselves. Parents also worry that their children will be harmed by the divorce.

Most children find divorce very painful. Some do not realize their parents are having problems until they learn they are going to separate. Children react to divorce in different ways. Many, especially young ones, may blame themselves, even though divorce is never a child's fault. Some children get angry with one or both parents. Others are too embarrassed to tell their friends. Some really miss a parent or their former family life. Some develop problems: They may behave badly, do poorly in school, or get depressed.

Frequently, children wrongly believe it is their job to keep their parents together or to help them get along better after a divorce. They may try to make one or both parents happy or to be a "parent" to their brothers or sisters. But while children sometimes have to take on more responsibility after a divorce, their real job is to continue being children. That means working hard in school, doing chores at home, having fun with friends, and letting the adults solve the big problems. Whatever the situation, talking can help. Children can talk to a friend, relative, teacher, coach, or religious leader or to a professional such as a psychologist.

Starting a New Life. After a divorce, both parents and children often face new challenges. The children may have to change schools and make new friends. Their parents may start to date other people. One or both of them may remarry. Those events can lead to more changes, including having a stepparent, stepbrothers and stepsisters, or a new baby in the family.

Parents and children can adjust to the changes that occur after a divorce if they are patient, talk about their feelings, and respect and care for each other. After a time, most children and their parents find ways to go on with their lives.

ROBERT E. EMERY
University of Virginia, Charlottesville
Author, *The Truth about Children and Divorce*

See also FAMILY.

DIX, DOROTHEA LYNDE (1802–1887)

American social reformer Dorothea Dix devoted her life to helping the mentally ill by persuading state legislatures to build special hospitals for them.

Dorothea Lynde Dix was born on April 4, 1802, in Hampden, Maine. As a young girl, she went to live with her grandmother in Boston, Massachusetts. When she was 14, Dorothea became a schoolteacher. She opened her own school for young girls in 1821 and later wrote several books for children.

Dorothea Dix began her life's work by accident. In 1841 she agreed to teach a Sunday school class in a Massachusetts jail. She discovered that mentally ill people were kept in a room without heat. She protested to the authorities. Then she spent the next two years investigating the treatment of the mentally ill in jails and poorhouses throughout the state. She was horrified by what she found. Mentally ill people were kept chained and caged. Often they were beaten by their keepers. She appealed to newspapers and public officials for help.

With their assistance, she convinced the Massachusetts legislature to provide money for mental hospitals.

For the next 13 years, Dorothea Dix continued her work. She traveled widely, although she was often in poor health. Because of her efforts, new hospitals were built, or old ones improved, in New England, Pennsylvania, New Jersey, and the southern and western states and in Canada. In 1854 she went to Europe to carry on her work there.

During the Civil War, she served the federal government as superintendent of women nurses. Her ideas and her forceful personality made her somewhat unpopular in this position. After peace came in 1865, she returned to her work for mental hospitals. She continued to travel and work until she was 80, when she retired to Trenton, New Jersey. There she made her home until her death at the age of 85, on July 17, 1887.

Reviewed by ALLEN F. DAVIS
Temple University

DJIBOUTI

Djibouti is a very small nation on the northeastern coast of Africa. Once known as French Somaliland, it won independence from France in 1977. Largely a desert land with few natural resources, Djibouti is a poor country. Its economy is based on services and commerce, reflecting its strategic location on the shipping routes between the Mediterranean Sea and the Indian Ocean.

▶ **PEOPLE**

Djibouti's two main groups are the majority Issas, who are related to the people of nearby Somalia, and the Afars, who are related to a people in neighboring Ethiopia. Nearly all are Muslim. Diverse immigrant groups of more recent origin also live in the city of Djibouti, the country's capital and largest city. French, Somali (spoken by the Issas), Afar, and Arabic are among the languages spoken by Djiboutians.

Over 80 percent of Djiboutians live in urban areas. The rest are mostly nomads, who trade with neighboring countries and raise camels, sheep, and goats.

▶ **LAND**

Djibouti is located just north of the large region known as the Horn of Africa. Most of the country consists of arid plains, but there also are mountains that rise to a height of 5,000 feet (1,500 meters). The land is barren and desolate with sharp cliffs and deep ravines. About 90 percent is desert. Most of the rest is pastureland. In the few areas where reliable water supplies exist, people have planted irrigated orchards, small vegetable gardens, and date palm groves.

Djibouti has a very hot, dry climate. From May to October, temperatures average 92°F (33°C) but can reach 113°F (45°C). It is slightly cooler between November and April.

▶ **ECONOMY**

Most of Djibouti's land cannot be cultivated and there is little industry, except for some food processing and construction. Djibouti exports few locally made goods and imports most of its food.

The bulk of Djibouti's income comes from services and commerce. The country provides port and transport services for the region. It also receives goods shipped from countries outside the region and forwards them to more distant ports. Central to those activities are Djibouti's airport and harbor, and a railroad that links Addis Ababa, the capital of Ethiopia, with the port of Djibouti. Much of landlocked Ethiopia's imports and exports pass through Djibouti by way of the railroad and the port of Djibouti. Other sources of income include French and U.S. military gar-

Below: The city of Djibouti, the country's capital, and a view of its port facilities, through which pass goods from around the world. *Right:* Port workers unload a shipment of wheat.

risons. Djibouti also receives financial aid from France and other countries.

Djibouti's greatest economic challenge is overcoming the poverty of its people. Poverty is serious and widespread and greater in rural areas than in the capital city. Nearly half of Djibouti's people live below the poverty line, which means they cannot afford adequate food, housing, education, and health care. Unemployment is extremely high, over 50 percent officially. Boys outnumber girls in the country's schools, putting women at a disadvantage in finding employment.

▶ **MAJOR CITIES**

Djibouti is a port city, the country's capital and major city, and home to two-thirds of its population.

▶ **HISTORY AND GOVERNMENT**

Because of its nearness to the Asian continent, Djibouti was long an arrival point for people migrating from Asia to Africa. Between the 700's and 900's, Arabs converted the people of the region to Islam. The French became interested in the area in the 1800's and signed treaties with the local chiefs. The French wanted influence in the region to counter that of the British. In 1885, France claimed a protectorate over the area, which became known as French Somaliland.

Djibouti remained a protectorate until 1958, when it became a French overseas territory renamed, in 1967, the French Territory of

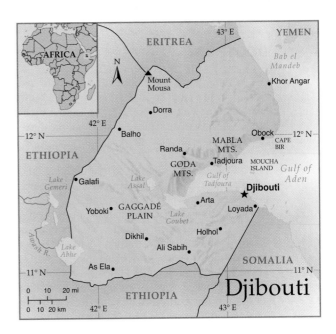

Djibouti

the Afars and the Issas. Ten years later, the people voted for independence, which was declared on June 27, 1977. The new nation was named the Republic of Djibouti.

Hassan Gouled Aptidon became Djibouti's first president and soon installed a one-party state that was dominated by his own Issa community. He served three 6-year terms, during which Afar discontent grew. In 1991 that dissatisfaction led to a civil war between the government and the largely Afar rebel group, the Front for the Restoration of Unity and Democracy (FRUD).

Aptidon sought to weaken the Afar rebels by holding multiparty elections in 1992–93, but these elections brought accusations of fraud by minority parties and were boycotted by about half the eligible voters. FRUD was defeated militarily by the Aptidon regime and a peace accord was signed in 1994. However, ethnic problems continue.

In 1999 another Issa, Ismail Omar Guelleh, succeeded Aptidon as president. On April 8, 2005, Guelleh was re-elected president for a 6-year term in a race in which there were no other candidates. During the race he vowed to reduce poverty and the country's dependence on imported food.

Djibouti is a republic. The president is the chief of state. Members of parliament are elected for 5-year terms.

GAIL M. GERHART
Columbia University

FACTS and figures

REPUBLIC OF DJIBOUTI (République de Jibouti in French; Jumhouriyya Djibouti in Arabic) is the official name of the country.

LOCATION: Northeastern Africa.

AREA: 8,500 sq mi (22,000 km²).

POPULATION: 477,000 (estimate).

CAPITAL AND LARGEST CITY: Djibouti.

MAJOR LANGUAGES: French, Arabic (both official), Somali, Afar.

MAJOR RELIGIOUS GROUP: Muslim.

GOVERNMENT: Republic. **Head of state**—president. **Head of government**—prime minister. **Legislature**—Chamber of Deputies.

CHIEF PRODUCTS: Agricultural—livestock (camels, goats, sheep), fruits, vegetables. **Manufactured**—construction, agricultural processing.

MONETARY UNIT: Djibouti franc (1 franc = 100 centimes).

DOCTORS

Doctors are highly trained professionals, skilled in the science and art of healing, who are concerned about people's health and well-being. For many centuries, sick people have looked to doctors for help and advice. Doctors, in turn, have identified disease and injury, provided helpful treatments, and established preventive measures as they supplied medical care to their patients.

The kind of doctor who cares for a person's health is called a **physician**. A physician is often identified by the initials M.D. after his or her name, such as Robert Kelly, M.D. These initials mean medical doctor, which is a degree granted by a recognized medical school. In the United States, medical schools must be approved by the American Medical Association. In some countries the letters M.O. (medical officer) or M.B. (bachelor of medicine) are used. Other physicians are doctors of osteopathy and have D.O. after their names. These doctors emphasize the importance of body structures, such as muscles and bones, in the cause and treatment of disease.

The word "physician" comes from the Greek word *physis*, which refers to nature. Thus a physician is one who has an understanding of the nature of people and their problems. Greece was also the birthplace of Hippocrates, the physician who is called the "father of medicine." At the time Hippocrates practiced medicine (about 400 B.C.), the people of Greece believed that the gods they worshiped were responsible for causing disease. The physicians of the time used witchcraft and magic to treat disease. Contrary to the general beliefs, Hippocrates started to show that disease occurred through natural causes. He became the first physician known to separate medicine from religion and to treat patients using knowledge gained from scientific writings and experience.

THE FATHER OF MEDICINE

Physicians and scholars wrote of Hippocrates and his methods of practicing medicine. He became associated with all that was considered good in medicine. In his honor, an oath was written that reflected his high ideals.

Since ancient times, the Hippocratic oath has been used as an ethical code for physicians. Many of today's doctors start their careers by taking a modern version of the Hippocratic oath, called the Declaration of Geneva.

Declaration of Geneva

At the time of being admitted a member of the medical profession:
I solemnly pledge myself to consecrate my life to the service of humanity;
I will give my teachers the respect and gratitude which is their due;
I will practice my profession with conscience and dignity;
The health of my patient will be my first consideration;
I will respect the secrets which are confided in me, even after the patient has died;
I will maintain by all the means in my power, the honor and the noble traditions of the medical profession;
My colleagues will be my brothers;
I will not permit considerations of religion, nationality, race, party politics or social standing to intervene between my duty and my patient;
I will maintain the utmost respect for human life from the time of conception; even under threat I will not use my medical knowledge contrary to the laws of humanity.
I make these promises solemnly, freely and upon my honor.

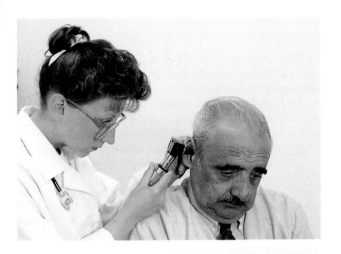

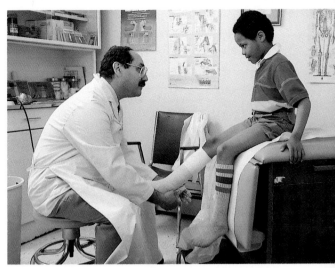

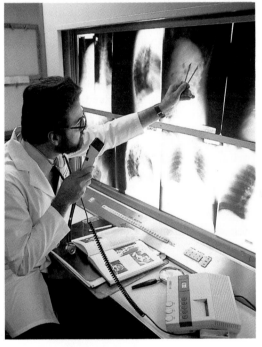

▶THE NEED FOR DOCTORS

People visit a doctor for many reasons. Some go because a fever, sore throat, or stomach ache tells them that they are sick. Others have been injured or have an ache or pain in a certain part of their body. Children may go to the doctor for these reasons, but most often they go for regular or special checkups. Children (like adults) must also keep their immunizations up to date. These are medicines that keep us from contracting certain serious diseases like measles or polio.

Today people also seek help from doctors to achieve wellness. Wellness includes taking an active part in one's own health. With the help of doctors, people are able to take steps to prevent illness and strive for the best possible health and well-being. People turn to doctors to help them lose or gain weight, deal with sorrow or tension, begin a family, or change unhealthy habits such as smoking tobacco or drinking too much alcohol or coffee. Doctors also help people develop healthful habits such as getting more exercise or learning to eat better.

▶KINDS OF DOCTORS

There are many different kinds of doctors. Some doctors limit their patient practice to taking care of certain parts of the body or certain types of problems. Others care only for patients in certain age groups. Each doctor is

Is the Surgeon General really a surgeon?

Although the Surgeon General may be a specialist such as a surgeon, the title refers to the person who is the United States' chief health adviser. The position of surgeon general was established in 1870 to direct the Marine Hospital Service. In fact, the Surgeon General has a rank equal to that of vice admiral in the U.S. Navy. This important government doctor works in Washington, D.C., and observes and protects the health of the people in the United States. As the chief executive of the Public Health Service in the Department of Health and Human Services, the Surgeon General commissions and reviews research concerning health issues and makes statements about major health problems such as smoking and AIDS.

a specialist in his or her medical area of choice. Even the family doctor is a specialist; he or she takes care of the most common health problems and pays attention to each family member over a number of years.

Sometimes medical practices differ not only in the methods used but in the focus of practice. Homeopathy is the treatment of disease by the administration of small doses of drugs that have an effect on a healthy body similar to that of the disease itself. For example, poison ivy causes rashes, so the homeopathic physician treats rashes with poison ivy. Holistic, or wholistic, medicine is a kind of medical practice that attempts to view and treat the whole individual as well as the disorder. Doctors who practice holistic medicine place great emphasis on an individual's nutrition, environment, emotions, and values, as well as on his or her physical symptoms.

Still other doctors choose not to be directly involved in patient care. Today there are many other interesting and exciting choices. Doctors work for private companies or medical groups as medical advisers or administrators. These include companies that make drugs or medical supplies, sell insurance, or run big hospital and clinic groups.

Doctors also work as researchers in medical schools or universities. They may become teachers and train others to work in the medical profession. And some doctors work as medical examiners who determine causes or times of death, especially as they relate to criminal investigations.

The United States government employs doctors who advise public officials or study the cause and spread of disease. In many countries, health care is owned and operated by the government, and all doctors work for the government.

▶ WHAT DOCTORS DO

A doctor's duties can differ greatly from place to place and according to the type of medical practice or health care setting. But no matter where or in what specialty doctors practice, they make all the major decisions regarding patient care. Doctors are the leaders of the health care team that includes physician's assistants, nurses, therapists, pharmacists, and other skilled technicians.

Most doctors are involved in the direct care of patients. Their day usually begins with a trip to the hospital. There the doctor may perform operations, visit patients, or order treatments or tests from the laboratory, X-ray and other imaging departments, pharmacy, or other hospital department.

Some doctors are at the hospital all day to complete these activities but most leave for their offices after the morning visit, which is often called morning rounds. At the office, doctors do many different things. They may set broken bones and put on casts or splints, listen to hearts and lungs, look into ears and eyes, give inoculations (shots), and do a variety of tests.

Sometimes a patient cannot come to the office so the doctor must go to the patient's home. This is called a house call. House calls are usually done when a person has a physical condition that prevents him or her from getting out of bed or leaving home. However, severe problems or medical emergencies are best handled by members of an ambulance team on the way to the hospital emergency room. Here the patient might arrange to meet his or her own doctor or will be cared for by an emergency room doctor, along with other care givers.

A doctor's day often includes non-patient-related activities as well. He or she must keep up to date with medical information. This is called continuing medical education. To do this, the doctor reads medical journals and books, attends meetings, and uses audio and video tapes. Sometimes this involves sharing information with other doctors by giving talks or writing articles.

Many factors affect how doctors practice medicine. The rising costs of health care and new technology mean that doctors, and patients, spend less time in the traditional hospital setting. Instead, patients are being seen and treated in places where they do not have to stay overnight. The creation of specialized health care centers (for such problems as emergencies, minor surgery, or medical tests) and of what are called shopping-center doctor's offices (open 24 hours a day, seven days a week) has resulted in new options for both the patient and the doctor.

▶ISSUES FACING TODAY'S DOCTORS

In some ways a doctor's job never changes. A doctor cares for sick people and helps healthy people stay healthy. But some things, such as medicines, laws relating to doctors, and the availability of modern treatments, do change, and they can sometimes create difficulties that today's doctors must face.

Medical Ethics

Medical ethics are the rules that tell doctors how to behave when caring for patients. For example, doctors must honor patients' privacy. Any information a patient tells the doctor or any diagnostic findings cannot be told to anyone without the patient's permission.

Since modern medical technology may prolong a very sick person's life, doctors today sometimes face serious problems with medical ethics. When a patient permanently loses consciousness, for example, or has no hope of recovery, the doctor and the patient's family must decide when to treat the illness, how long to treat it, and when to stop treatment. These are very difficult decisions to make. Some people believe that stopping treatment is a form of **euthanasia**, or mercy-killing. The ethics of such actions are an issue of intense debate and disagreement. Doctors must weigh these issues and at the same time respect their patients' rights and wishes.

Malpractice

Another real problem facing doctors today is malpractice. This means treatment that was

THE FIRST APPOINTMENT

When the doctor and patient meet, a number of things usually happen. First, the doctor talks with the patient and asks many questions about the patient's problem or concern. These questions include information about the patient's health history (such as broken bones or severe illnesses), family, habits (such as smoking), and daily routines (such as diet and number of hours of sleep). All of this is called the patient's medical history.

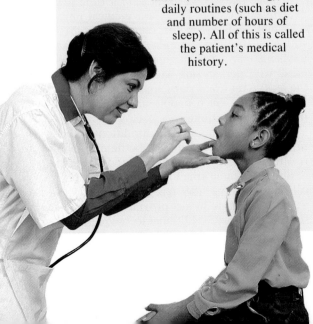

Next the doctor performs a physical exam (*left*). This is a careful examination of the body that gives the doctor additional information about the patient's physical health. Sometimes the doctor uses special lights or instruments for looking at and listening to the workings of the body.

After the medical history and physical exam, the doctor may need even more information. This is obtained from laboratory tests of body fluids (such as blood or urine), X rays, or other special procedures. With all this information, the doctor comes to a conclusion, or **diagnosis**, about the patient. Then the patient receives treatment or recommendations from the doctor. These might include taking medicines, having an operation, or starting a special diet or an exercise program. The doctor's recommendations might also include advice on achieving a health benefit such as stopping smoking, or education such as how to take a temperature.

MEDICAL EDUCATION

Because modern medical care and the issues facing doctors are continually changing, medical schools must adapt their content and style according to the times. In today's schools, students study medical subjects ranging from anatomy, biochemistry, and physiology to pediatrics, surgery, and psychiatry. Their learning takes place in the classroom (*right*) as well as the hospital and clinic. They also discuss problems in medical ethics. Equally important, they learn how to relate to their patients in an understanding and helpful way.

After four years of college and four years of medical school, the student receives a medical degree. He or she then enters a residency training program in a hospital to become a specialist in a chosen area. This is called graduate medical education and can last from two years to more than ten years. It gives the new doctor additional experience in patient care.

During medical school or residency, the student completes a special examination. This exam plus the M.D. or D.O. degree and the residency training allow the doctor to obtain a license to care for patients in his or her state. No doctor in the United States can practice without a license. Look for it on the wall of your doctor's office.

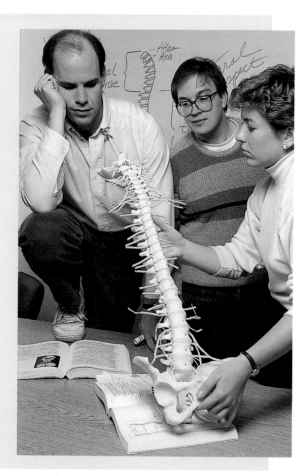

not proper and may have caused injury or harm to the patient. Today more people start lawsuits (a legal action to get paid for damages) against doctors then ever before. Some say there is a crisis.

This problem has caused a strain between many doctors and their patients. To protect themselves, most doctors pay large sums of money to buy malpractice insurance. This insurance is used to pay for damages awarded in a lawsuit, but it has also increased the cost of health care. Certainly mistakes sometimes happen and situations occur where medical treatment was not proper. The patient involved in such situations deserves proper help and support. Doctors, elected officials, and the public are now working together to try to solve this problem.

International Health Care

Most countries of the world have doctors. But some countries have very few doctors, and health care is hard to find. From country to country, there are differences in the education of doctors and in the kind of care they provide. The World Health Organization (WHO), the World Medical Association, and other groups are helping to bring together doctors from around the world and to help them solve common problems in patient care.

In some places people still care for the sick with folk medicine. These are medical practices that are based in part on religion, superstition, or social custom. An American Indian medicine man, or healer, giving the herb foxglove to a person sick with dropsy (fluid in the legs) is an example of someone practicing folk medicine. Such people are described as **traditional practitioners**.

Many treatments used by traditional practitioners have been found to be helpful. This is often because the plants or foods used in treatment contain small amounts of chemical substances (some now recognized as powerful drugs) that do in fact provide relief to the sick person. Some traditional techniques, such

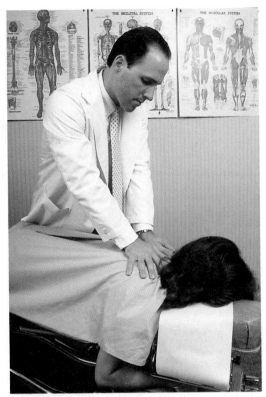

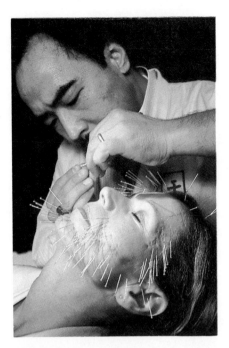

People seek health advice and care from a variety of sources. Some people rely on medical doctors; others search out traditional practitioners or health professionals that use special techniques, such as chiropractic treatments (*above*), acupuncture (*above right*), and biofeedback (*right*).

as acupuncture, have also been found to be helpful and are still used today. The ancient Chinese developed the practice of acupuncture, which uses needles inserted into parts of the body to restore the balance of the body's life forces.

The dances, chants, and other rituals that are often part of folk medicine practices are not widely recognized as valid treatments, though they are still used in some parts of the world. Slowly, more modern health care is being brought to these areas, and university-educated doctors are replacing (or coexisting with) traditional health practitioners.

▶ DOCTORS AND HEALTH CARE

Many exciting changes in health care are affecting doctors. Technical inventions that combine lasers, X rays, and computers are being developed. New drugs and vaccines are being approved for use almost every day.

Computer programs are helping doctors to record and review a patient's health history.

Despite these changes, doctors still treat patients with direct one-to-one contact. There can be no substitute for this type of care.

WILLIAM E. JACOTT, M.D.
Chairman, Council on Medical Education
American Medical Association

See also HOSPITALS; MEDICINE; SURGERY.

DODGE, GRENVILLE MELLEN. See IOWA (Famous People).

DODGE, MARY MAPES. See CHILDREN'S LITERATURE (Profiles).

DODGSON, CHARLES LUTWIDGE. See CARROLL, LEWIS.

DOENITZ, KARL. See WORLD WAR II (Profiles: Axis Powers).

DOGS

Can you imagine a world without dogs? Most people would find that hard to do. Dogs are an important part of so many people's lives. Herding sheep, catching criminals, guiding people who are blind, and providing companionship are just a few of the many things dogs can do. They are a very special kind of animal because they live and work so closely with human beings.

> *Dogs are our link to paradise. They don't know evil or jealousy or discontent. To sit with a dog on a hillside on a glorious afternoon is to be back in Eden, where doing nothing was not boring—it was peace.*
>
> MILAN KUNDERA

Domestic dogs (*Canis familiaris*) are members of the family of mammals called Canidae. There are more than 30 different species, or kinds, of animals in this family. Called canines, they also include wild dogs, wolves, coyotes, jackals, and foxes. Canines are native to most parts of the world, except Antarctica and some ocean islands. They have adapted to habitats ranging from deserts to tundras.

Some of the wild canines are familiar and look a lot like domestic dogs. Others are quite unusual and hardly resemble dogs at all. Whatever their appearance, all canine species existing today share a common ancestor named *Leptocyon*. *Leptocyon* lived in North America between about 7 and 10 million years ago. Domestic dogs evolved from wolves about 50,000 years ago.

Dogs have been by our side since ancient times, when they helped us hunt for food. Today dogs provide companionship at rest and at play; amaze us with their agility; perform valuable police work; and offer us unconditional love.

▶ CHARACTERISTICS OF DOGS

Dogs are warm-blooded carnivores, or meat-eaters. Like other mammals, they have hair covering their bodies, they produce live offspring, and the females produce milk for nourishing the young.

Although dogs may look very different from one another, their differences are really limited to size, shape, and surface characteristics. All breeds of dog share the same body structure, with the same number of bones and muscles.

Body

Dogs typically have muscular, deep-chested bodies with long, slender legs. They have four toes on each foot and a thumblike toe, or **dewclaw**, on each front foot and sometimes on the rear feet as well. Dogs walk on their toes, which are well padded with fat and protected with tough, leathery skin.

Most dogs have 42 teeth, which include four sharp, pointed teeth (called canines) that are adapted for tearing flesh. They also have broad, flat teeth (called premolars and molars) that are adapted for grinding and crushing food.

Some of the familiar parts of a dog's anatomy, such as ears, tail, muzzle (snout), and fur, differ greatly in appearance between breeds. Some ears are erect and pointed, as in the German shepherd dog; others are erect but not pointed, as in the French bulldog and chow chow. Many dogs have hanging ears, such as those found on the golden retriever. Basset hounds and bloodhounds have especially long hanging ears. The whippet and bulldog, among other breeds, have what are described as rose-shaped ears, which are set relatively far back on the dog's head.

Not all dogs have tails. Boxers and Pembroke Welsh corgis have short tails that are usually docked, or cut very short, a few days after birth. Akitas and pugs are examples of breeds with curled tails. Some breeds, such as the Scottish deerhound and the borzoi, have

The ears of dogs vary greatly, from long and floppy (basset hound, *left*) to short and erect (basenji, *below left*).

exceptionally long tails.

The muzzle of most dogs is long and some-what pointed. Several breeds have short, flat-tened muzzles. These dogs sometimes have trouble breathing be-cause of their unusual face shape. You may hear bulldogs, Boston terriers, and pugs pant-ing or snorting, espe-cially when they are excited.

A dog's fur, or coat, is often its most strik-ing feature. The beauti-ful dark red coat of the Irish setter and the curly coat of the poodle make these two breeds widely recognized. Many terriers have a coat of straight, stiff fur, called a wiry coat. Old English sheepdogs have long, woolly coats; Great Danes have short, smooth coats. A working dog called a komondor has very long, wavy fur that twists together like tassels. There are even dogs without coats, such as the Mexican hairless.

Dog coats come in almost every color imaginable. They may be black, white, gray, tan, brown, or yellow. Sometimes unusual names are used to describe the colors of dogs' coats. A reddish-brown coat is called liver, and a light tan is described as fawn. A blue coat is actually steely gray.

The combinations of colors that can be found in dogs' coats also have special names. Brindle coats have black stripes on a lighter base, pied coats are white with patches of an-other color, roan coats have many fleckings of two different colors, and merle coats have fleckings and patches of several colors.

Most dogs, such as the greyhound (*left*), have long and tapered muzzles. But the muzzles of some breeds, such as the French mastiff (*right*), are short and flattened.

Senses

Because dogs evolved from wolves, their senses are specially adapted for finding and catching prey. This is still true, even though modern domestic dogs are usually fed by their human owners.

Hearing. Dogs have excellent hearing. They can hear sounds at a much greater dis-tance than humans can. They also can distin-guish between very similar sounds. More remarkably, dogs are able to hear ultrasonic sounds—those sounds that are too high-pitched for a person to detect at any distance.

Smell. Perhaps the most developed sense a dog has is its sense of smell. They can detect

DOG "TALK"

Did you know that dogs communicate through body language? *Left to right:* A dog signals that it wants to play by crouching down and raising its rear in a "play bow." To show submission, a dog crouches down and folds its ears back. When a dog wants

the faintest scent many days or even weeks after the source of the scent is removed. This is one reason that dogs are used to sniff out illegal drugs, bombs, and missing people. Dogs can smell things that no human—and no machine—could ever detect.

Sight. Although their vision is less developed than their senses of smell and hearing, dogs do have good eyesight. They probably do not see colors well, although this is difficult to determine for sure. The widely spaced position of their eyes—toward the sides of the face—means that dogs can see farther to the sides of their bodies than people can.

One group of dogs, called sighthounds, are able to see better than other kinds of dogs. These dogs are bred to chase game over long distances. They rely on their eyesight to spot prey and their powerful legs to chase and catch the prey. Greyhounds, whippets, and borzois are several examples of sighthounds.

Touch. Dogs are very sensitive to touch. It is one of the most important ways they communicate. How dogs touch others depends on their relationship and the message they want to communicate.

Dogs respond to touch in much the same way as their ancestors, the wolves. Dogs that

Dogs have a wide range of vocalizations, including barks, growls, and whines. Like their wolf relatives, these sled dogs howl to communicate with each other.

live together lick one another, sleep close together, and lean or rub against each other. They shy away from pain and respond with pleasure to gentle stroking. They also snap or bite at certain times, such as when they are angry or threatened.

Taste. Dogs have a well-developed sense of taste. They have obvious likes and dislikes when it comes to what they will eat. Not everything they eat would appear to be good for them. Dogs may eat sticks, small rocks, dirt, grass, and even dung. However, these are likely to be an infrequent addition to a dog's diet.

Communication: Barks, Growls, and Other Sounds

Barking is the most familiar sound a dog makes. It is often used as a warning, such as when there is a knock at the door or when a stranger approaches. Barking can also mean that the dog is aggressive and is looking for a fight. Or barking can be an expression of excitement or joy.

Some barks from the same dog can sound more high-pitched than others. These barks mean that the dog needs help, such as when it is standing at the back door waiting to be let into the house. Other high-pitched barks mean that the dog is trying to avoid a fight and that it does not want to be hurt.

to show complete submission, it rolls over on its back and exposes its belly. A frightened dog tucks its tail between its legs, holds its body low,

and folds its ears back. An aggressive dog has a stiff posture, upright tail and ears, bared teeth, and raised hair on its back and shoulders.

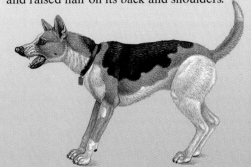

FROM WOLF TO DOG

From a common ancestor, the wolf, domestic dogs have developed into a variety of shapes and sizes. *Clockwise from top:* Sleek and muscular greyhounds are fast runners. The medium-sized collie is an agile herder. The American Staffordshire terrier is a powerful guard dog. The dachshund's short legs and long body allow it to follow small game into tunnels. The Saint Bernard's great size makes it well suited for hard work and harsh weather conditions. The small and almost hairless Chinese crested makes a fine house pet. The thick double coat of the Lhasa apso keeps it warm during cold winters.

Growling is usually used by dogs as a serious warning. It may mean "Stay away" or "I'm going to bite you." Some dogs growl when they play roughly. When a mother dog growls at her pups, she is usually saying "Stop what you are doing immediately!" She does this to teach them that she is in charge—that they cannot bite her or take her food.

Howling is an interesting, sometimes beautiful sound that many dogs are able to make. Not all dogs howl, however. The northern breeds, such as the Siberian husky, Alaskan malamute, and Samoyed, seem to howl frequently. This may be because these breeds are still very much like the wolf, which howls a great deal. Hounds are known for a sound similar to a howl, called baying. Baying sounds like a mixture of a bark and a howl.

Dogs also whimper and whine. These sounds mean that the dog needs something or that it is hurt. Sometimes dogs whimper when their owners return home, especially after a long absence. These sounds mean "Please notice me" or "I missed you!"

▶ DOG BREEDS

Dogs have been bred for thousands of years to help humans do specific tasks. With each task, a new kind of dog was created. A hunter who needed dogs to sniff out game would breed together dogs that had a good sense of smell. A farmer who wanted to keep sheep safe from wolves or coyotes would breed together dogs that were brave and had guarding skills.

After a great many years, this careful breeding for certain traits, called **selective breeding**, produced dogs that were very different from each other. For instance, the hunter's selective breeding helped create beagles, while the farmer's selective breeding produced collies. Although both are still domestic dogs, they have become different breeds. There are more than four hundred different breeds of purebred dogs in the world today. A dog is called a purebred when its father, or **sire**, and mother, or **dam**, belong to the same breed.

There is great variety in the age of the different breeds. Ancient records show that some breeds have existed for more than a thousand years. From engravings and sculptures, we know that the greyhound could be found in ancient Egypt. The Saint Bernard was brought to Europe by the ancient Romans. The breed was then developed by monks living near the Great Saint Bernard Pass in the Swiss Alps. Other breeds are so new that they are still being developed by selective breeding.

Breed Groups

Organizations of dog breeders, called **kennel clubs**, use a registration system to keep

Cerberus

DOGS IN MYTHOLOGY AND FOLKLORE

Animals are common figures in mythology and folklore, and the dog is no exception. In the ancient stories and beliefs of many cultures, the dog is frequently associated with death and the underworld.

Many cultures speak of dogs that guard the boundary between the land of the living and the land of the dead or who accompany travelers on the road to the underworld. In Greek mythology, the three-headed dog Cerberus guarded the entrance into Hades. The English countryside is full of tales about ghostly black dogs that foreshadow someone's death or haunt certain locations. Anubis, the ancient Egyptian god of the dead and embalming, was depicted as a jackal (or a person with a jackal's head).

Dogs may have been linked to death long ago because they were frequently used in hunting and would eat dead animals (carrion). Dogs may even have been allowed to eat the remains of dead people as part of funerary rituals.

THE AMERICAN KENNEL CLUB (AKC) BREED GROUPS

Italian Greyhound

TOY DOGS

Most tiny dogs fall into the American Kennel Club's toy breed category. These breeds have been valued as house pets for hundreds, and in some cases thousands, of years. Toy dogs are small enough to carry around in your arm or cuddle on your lap (they are sometimes referred to as lap dogs), and they are often preferred by people living in small homes or apartments. These breeds are especially popular as show dogs. Dogs in this group include the Chihuahua, the Yorkshire terrier, the Italian greyhound, and the shih tzu.

Affenpinscher

Papillon

Pug

SPORTING DOGS

Clumber Spaniel

The energetic sporting, or gun, dogs are widely used in hunting. In fact, they have been selectively bred to specialize in different kinds of hunting. For example, the German shorthaired pointer, the English setter, and the Brittany are used to find game birds and show the hunter where they are. They do this with a special pose called **pointing**. Dogs such as the English springer spaniel and the cocker spaniel are used to find game birds and chase them into flight (a process called **flushing**) and then retrieve the bird after it has been shot, or downed. The golden retriever, the Labrador retriever, and the Chesapeake Bay retriever are used to retrieve birds from land or water after the birds have been downed. Because these dogs have been bred for outdoor activity, they need a lot of exercise.

English Setter

Weimaraner

NONSPORTING DOGS

Chinese Shar-Pei

The nonsporting breeds are popular house pets and show dogs. They vary widely in appearance, from the short and heavyset bulldog to the tall and lean dalmatian. Some have short hair, such as the Boston terrier and the Chinese shar-pei, while others have long hair, such as the Lhasa apso and the löwchen. Schipperkes make good watchdogs, and the Finnish spitz is sometimes used to hunt small game. Other nonsporting breeds recognized by the American Kennel Club are the bichon frise, the chow chow, the keeshond, the American Eskimo dog, and the Tibetan spaniel.

Boston Terrier

American Eskimo Dog

Dalmatian

WORKING DOGS

The American Kennel Club's working breeds are large and intelligent dogs often used in police, guard, and rescue work. This group includes well-known breeds such as the rottweiler, the Doberman pinscher, the boxer, and the Saint Bernard. The Siberian husky, the Alaskan malamute, and the Samoyed are frequently used to pull sleds. As the name implies, the Portuguese water dog is a skilled swimmer and has been used by fishermen to retrieve nets and even herd fish. The massive and wrinkled Neapolitan mastiff was developed to guard Italian estates. The Great Dane was developed in Germany to hunt boar.

Doberman Pinscher

Neapolitan Mastiff

Rottweiler

Komondor

HOUNDS

The American Kennel Club once grouped the hounds with the sporting dogs because, like sporting dogs, they are used in hunting. They are especially good at finding and tracking game, such as rabbits, raccoons, and foxes. One of the best-known hounds is the beagle, which is an excellent rabbit hunter. The black-and-tan coonhound is commonly used in parts of the United States to track raccoons and chase them up trees. Hunters on horseback often follow a pack of English foxhounds as they trail a fox. The bloodhound is a "human hunter" that is often used by police departments to follow the scent of people who are lost or who are wanted for breaking the law. Other hounds, such as the whippet, Afghan hound, and greyhound, are fast runners with sleek bodies and keen eyesight.

Afghan Hound

English Foxhound

Pharaoh Hound

Saluki

TERRIERS

These energetic, spirited dogs were once widely used to hunt rodents and other small mammals, though they are no longer hunting specialists. Breeds such as the Manchester terrier and the cairn terrier could catch mice and rats and shake them to death. Some terriers are still kept around barns and stables for this purpose. However, in most parts of the world these breeds are now used primarily as pets. Other terrier breeds recognized by the American Kennel Club include the Dandie Dinmont terrier, the American Staffordshire terrier, and the Glen of Imaal terrier.

Airedale Terrier

Dandie Dinmont Terrier

Cairn Terrier

Bull Terrier

HERDING DOGS

These intelligent and easily trained dogs make good pets, though they have been bred to chase and direct farm animals such as sheep, cattle, and poultry. Their job might be to round up strays and drive them back into the flock or to move herds from one area to another. Many herding dogs also have a strong instinct to protect their flocks or herds from dangerous predators, such as wolves and coyotes. Although people tend to think of the German shepherd dog as a police or guard dog (like the dogs in the working group), the American Kennel Club puts them in the herding group. Other breeds in this group include the collie, border collie, and bearded collie; the Shetland sheepdog; the Belgian Tervuren; and the Cardigan and Pembroke Welsh corgis.

Belgian Tervuren

Pembroke Welsh Corgi

Puli

Briard

MISCELLANEOUS CLASS

The miscellaneous class is for relatively new dog breeds that are not yet recognized as official breeds by the AKC but that have developed a widespread following among breeders. Dogs in the miscellaneous class are permitted to compete in official AKC competitions, such as obedience and agility events. They can also compete in breed, or conformation, shows but cannot earn championship points. Breeds become recognized by the AKC when they have demonstrated continued development in the miscellaneous class. They are then admitted into one of the main breed groups. This class has in-cluded breeds such as the plott, an agile and tireless hunting dog; the beauceron, a French herding dog; and the Tibetan mastiff, a large and robust pet and guard dog.

Redbone Coonhound

Tibetan Mastiff

Beauceron

THE IDITAROD

The Iditarod is the world's premier dogsled race. It is run every March between the Alaskan cities of Anchorage and Nome, covering more than 1,000 miles (1,600 kilometers) of rugged terrain.

About 65 teams participate each year. Each team is made up of one sled driver, called the **musher**, and 12 to 16 dogs. The musher guides the dogs with verbal commands. It takes each team from nine to twelve days to complete the race. The first place winner is awarded a cash prize. A Junior Iditarod for youths between the ages

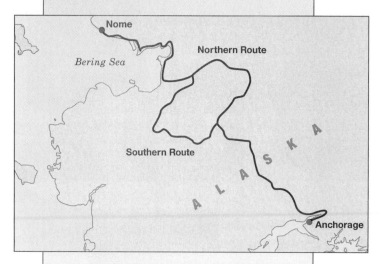

of 14 and 18, first held in 1978, is run on a course about 750 miles (1,207 kilometers) long. The winner is given a trophy and a scholarship.

The health and welfare of the dogs is a primary concern in the race, and any musher who does not provide proper care for his or her dogs is penalized. All dogs are given a thorough physical exam before the race by a veterinarian, and veterinarians are available at checkpoints all along the racing route. The dogs even wear special booties to protect their feet from sharp ice.

The Iditarod follows the trail used by early settlers and miners on their journey inland from the coast. During the harsh winters, the only way to get mail and supplies to the remote settlements and mining towns was by dogsled team, and this led to the establishment of what is today called the Iditarod Trail. The race alternates every other year between a northern route and a southern route.

track of pure-bred dogs. When a dog is registered, it receives papers showing its breeding— much like a birth certificate names the father and mother of a person. The American Kennel Club (AKC) groups pure-bred dogs into eight categories: **working**, **sporting**, **hound**, **terrier**, **herding**, **toy**, **non-sporting**, and **miscellaneous**. The miscellaneous class is for dog breeds that are relatively new. After these breeds have become well established, the AKC may fully recognize them by admitting them into one of the main breed groups. For a discussion of each of these breed groups, see the feature American Kennel Club (AKC) Breed Groups accompanying this article.

> *The dog is a gentleman; I hope to go to his heaven, not man's.*
>
> MARK TWAIN

Rare Breeds

Nearly everyone has seen a beagle, a poodle, and a German shepherd dog, but how many people have encountered a Greater Swiss mountain dog, a Karelian bear dog, or a tosa? These breeds are much better known in their native lands of Switzerland, Finland, and Japan. They are not widely known in North America.

Dogs that are rare, or uncommon, in one part of the world may be quite common in another. Unless a breed is brought outside the region where it was developed, few other people know about it. Thus, where you live helps determine which breeds you consider rare.

There are, however, some dog breeds that are virtually unknown in any part of the world. Because there are so few dogs in these breeds, they can be considered truly rare. One of the rarest of all breeds is the Chinook, a large, sturdy dog bred in the United States to pull sleds. Chinooks are similar in appearance to other sled dogs, such as the Siberian husky and the Alaskan malamute. They have a fluffy coat that ranges from a deep reddish gold to a light tan. According to some estimates, there are only about 500 Chinooks alive in the world today.

Puppies are born in groups called litters. They depend on their mother to feed and care for them until they are about 7 weeks old.

▶ THE LIFE OF A DOG

The many different breeds of dogs go through the same stages as they grow and develop. The amount of time that any one stage takes varies depending on the specific breed. All dogs are born helpless and dependent on their mothers for care and protection. As puppies, dogs go through a period of rapid growth. Just after 6 months, most dogs reach sexual maturity. By 2 years old, they are full-grown adults.

The Puppy

Puppies are born about nine weeks after the male and female have mated. The puppy, which grows within the female dog in a fluid-filled sac, is tiny and wet when it is born. Sometimes it is still covered by the thin membranous sac. The mother dog licks her newborn puppies to remove the sac. Her licking also cleans and dries the puppies.

The group of puppies that are born at one time is called a **litter**. The size of the litter depends on the breed, age, and health of the parent dogs. An average litter is about 4 to 8 puppies. They are born one at a time, and it may require many hours for all the puppies in a large litter to be born. Soon after birth, the puppies will begin to nurse on the mother dog's warm milk.

Newborn puppies spend the first few weeks of life nursing, sleeping, and eliminating waste. They cannot yet see or hear, so the mother dog takes care of all their needs. At about 2 weeks, the puppies' eyes begin to open and their ears begin to function. Their sight and hearing improve each day.

The next phase in the puppies' lives is very significant for their development. From the time they are 3 weeks old until they are about 4 months old, puppies learn how to get along with other dogs. They learn this by interacting with their littermates (brothers and sisters) and with the mother dog. They growl, bark, wrestle, chew, and try to be first to eat or play with a toy. By doing this, the puppies figure out which of them is the toughest, or most **dominant**, and which is the weakest, or most **submissive**.

DOG WELFARE

Some people believe that dogs should not be used for any purpose that does not directly benefit the dog, such as greyhound racing, dog fighting, sled-pulling races, breed showing, and scientific experiments. Although not everyone agrees on what are safe and acceptable uses for dogs, most people agree that dogs should never be used in ways that could cause them pain or injury. That is why dog fighting has been outlawed in all fifty states and in the District of Columbia.

Dogs do a great deal to serve their human owners, but people also do a great deal to help dogs. Organizations such as the American Society for the Prevention of Cruelty to Animals (ASPCA) promote humane treatment of dogs and other animals. Local animal shelters and rescue organizations provide safe refuge for lost or unwanted dogs. Some organizations focus on a single breed, such as those that take in racing greyhounds when the dogs retire or are unable to race anymore. These groups provide health care to the homeless animals, sometimes at great cost, and find them new homes with loving families.

DOG SPORTS AND COMPETITIONS

There are many kinds of sports in which dogs compete to demonstrate various traits or skills. Among the most popular are breed shows, obedience trials, field trials, agility trials, and races.

Breed, or Conformation, Show

Breed Shows

Breed shows are probably the most familiar kind of dog competitions. These are contests where dogs are judged by a set of **standards** that describe the ideal size, shape, color, temperament, and movement for each recognized breed. Because these shows judge how closely dogs conform to the standards, they are also called **conformation** shows. These kinds of shows are held in countries all around the world and are typically sponsored by large clubs or organizations, such as the American Kennel Club and the Canadian Kennel Club.

Dogs of the same breed are judged together first. Judges watch the dogs' movements as they walk around the show ring, and they examine each dog individually, checking the dog's size, its coat, ears, teeth, and other features. The individual who conforms the closest to the standard is awarded first place. With each win, the dog earns a certain number of points. Kennel clubs set the number of points that must be earned for the dog to be awarded the title Champion. Once a dog receives the title, the letters "Ch." are used in front of the dog's name in all official publications.

After a dog becomes a champion, it is eligible to compete against other champions for the title Best of Breed (BOB). Winners in each breed group are then judged against one another at the show. For example, the winning retrievers, pointers, spaniels, and setters all compete for best sporting dog. When the winners of each group have been chosen, the very best dog is selected for the top award: Best in Show (BIS).

Perhaps the most famous dog show is the Westminster Kennel Club Dog Show, held every year in New York City since 1877. The world's largest dog show is Great Britain's Crufts Dog Show, first held in 1891, at which more than 20,000 dogs compete each year.

Obedience Trials

During an obedience trial, the dogs are judged on how well they respond to commands as they perform specific obedience exercises, such as sitting and staying, heeling, and jumping over obstacles. Each exercise is worth a certain number of points. Points are deducted for each mistake. Only the very best dogs and handlers make no mistakes and finish the trial with a perfect score. After earning several obedience titles and winning additional competitions, a dog may accumulate enough points for the very highest award: Obedience Trial Champion (OTCH).

Field Trial

Field Trials

Field trials are designed to demonstrate a dog's tracking and hunting skills in a simulated hunting situation. **Retriever trials** are for breeds that retrieve upland game birds (such as pheasant and quail) and waterfowl. **Pointing trials** are for breeds whose job it is to find and point out upland game birds and then retrieve them when downed. Breeds used in these trials include the pointers and setters. In **dachshund trials**, **beagle trials**, and **basset**

trials (each held separately), the dogs are tested on their ability to find and chase rabbits and respond to the commands of their handlers. **Spaniel trials** test the dog's skills at locating, flushing, and retrieving game birds on land and water. Champions are named for each kind of trial, as well as for each breed that participates in the trials.

Agility Trial

Agility Trials

In agility trials, a handler is given a set amount of time to guide a dog through an obstacle course. This course typically includes tunnels, ramps, jumps, and a see-saw. These trials test the training and handling skills of the handler and the speed and agility of the dogs. Any breed of dog, as well as mixed breeds, may compete in agility trials. The heights of the jumps and the time permitted to run the course are adjusted according to the dog's size.

Races

The major kinds of dog races are greyhound races and sled-dog races. In greyhound races, the dogs chase a mechanical lure around an enclosed oval track. People typically make wagers, or place bets, on which dog they think will be the first to cross the finish line. In recent years, concern has grown outside the industry over the welfare of the dogs used in such races.

In sled-dog races, a team of dogs pulls a sled, ridden and guided by a person called the musher, over snow-covered terrain. The most famous race is the Iditarod, held in Alaska every year since 1967. The race, which follows the trail used by early settlers on their journey inland from the coast, covers more than 1,000 miles (1,600 kilometers) of mountains, forests, and tundra. For more information, see the feature on the Iditarod accompanying this article.

Protection Competition (Schutzhund)

Other Competitions

Other kinds of dog competitions may not be as well known as those just discussed, but they are just as popular with their followers. **Protection** competitions, which include sports such as Schutzhund (German for "protection dog") and French Ring, rate large working dogs in their ability to perform various protection, tracking, obedience, and agility exercises. In **weight-pull** contests, dogs wear special harnesses to pull a loaded sled or cart across a set distance within a set time. The acrobatic leaps and twists of dogs as they catch a tossed Frisbee make **canine disc**, or **disc dog**, competitions especially popular with spectators. There are even **canine freestyle** competitions, which feature choreographed performances by handlers and their dogs set to music.

Sled-Dog Race

However, the mother dog is still in charge. When puppies get too rough while nursing or playing, she may growl. If this does not stop the puppies, the mother dog may snap at them. This teaches the puppies that a growl means to stop what they are doing. The puppies continue learning from the mother dog until they leave the litter to go to new homes.

Puppies that are about 4 weeks old can begin to get some of their nourishment from soft, mushy food. Breeders of domestic dogs may start to give the puppies oatmeal, rice, or wet dog food. Wild canine mothers, such as wolves and coyotes, bring food back up from their stomachs to feed the puppies. This behavior of regurgitating partially digested food helps the young dogs stop nursing and get used to eating solid food.

Puppies are ready to leave their mother at about 6 to 8 weeks. The transition to a new home is smoothest about this time. The puppy is a willing and eager learner. Owners should use this to their advantage and start teaching the puppy important behaviors, such as how to eliminate waste outside.

At 4½ months old, puppies begin to lose their primary teeth. Just as in humans, these primary teeth are pushed out by adult teeth.

> *The great pleasure of a dog is that you may make a fool of yourself with him and not only will he not scold you, but he will make a fool of himself too.*
>
> SAMUEL BUTLER

By 6 months of age, all the adult teeth are in. The puppy is considerably bigger, too. Its days of puppyhood soon will be over.

The Adult Dog

Dogs mature at a much faster rate than people do. Just after 6 months old, most dogs reach sexual maturity. This means that they are able to mate and produce offspring. Male dogs usually start to lift their hind leg when urinating. Their urine is a scent indicator to other dogs. It warns males to stay away and lets females know that a male dog is nearby.

A female dog experiences a reproductive cycle, which is often described as coming into heat, sometime after she reaches 6 months of age. This heat cycle lasts for about three weeks. Most female dogs have two heat cycles a year. Although a male is willing to mate at any time of the year, a female canine is willing to mate only when she is in heat.

Young dogs go through a rapid growth process. By the time they are 8 or 9 months old, most dogs have reached their full height. They usually continue gaining weight for a few months before reaching their adult size. By the time a dog is 18 months to 2 years old, it is a full-grown adult.

The Great Dane (*below*), one of the largest dog breeds, can weigh more than 175 pounds (79 kilograms) at adulthood. Chihuahuas (*right*), the smallest breed, may weigh only about 3 pounds (1.5 kilograms).

The size of the adult dog can vary greatly between breeds. The smallest breed, the Chihuahua, measures only 6 to 8 inches (15 to 20 centimeters) at the withers (top of the shoulders). This tiny dog may weigh only 2 or 3 pounds (about 1 kilogram) when fully grown. One of the largest breeds, the Great Dane, can be more than 34 inches (86 centimeters) at the withers and weigh more than 175 pounds (79 kilograms).

Life Span

Depending on its breed, a healthy dog may live for only seven years or as long as twenty years. Giant breeds, such as the Saint Bernard or Newfoundland, typically have very short life spans. It is not unusual for a Great Dane to die of old age at 7. Indeed, a 10-year-old Great Dane is a very old dog!

One of the longest living dogs is the little black schipperke. It is not rare to meet a 20-year-old schipperke. However, these breeds are examples of dogs with the longest and shortest life spans. The average life span for most breeds of dogs is about fourteen years.

▶ DOGS AND PEOPLE

Dogs were one of the first animals to be domesticated, or tamed and raised by people. This happened more than 50,000 years ago, when human beings lived by hunting and gathering their food. Dogs as we know them today did not exist then. Instead, wolves roamed the countryside, hunting for food just as human beings did.

We will never know for certain how wolves and people first came together. Perhaps early hunters learned that they could find food by following wolves who were hunting. Perhaps some wolves followed human hunters, hoping to take some of their catch. Early humans may have allowed wolves near their camp, glad to have their keen senses and loud bark to warn of dangers. Wolves near the camp may have been given scraps of food and so learned to stay nearby.

Over time, the wolves and humans came to trust one another. Puppies that were born may have been cared for and protected by people. They grew up less wild and aggressive. After many hundreds of years, these friendlier animals were no longer true wolves. They had changed, or evolved, into a new species: the domestic dog.

*Near this spot
Are deposited the remains of one
Who possessed beauty without vanity,
Strength without insolence,
Courage without ferocity,
And all the virtues of man without his
   vices.
This Praise, which would be unmeaning
   flattery
If inscribed over human ashes,
Is but a just tribute to the memory of
Boatswain, a Dog.*

GEORGE GORDON, LORD BYRON;
EPITAPH TO HIS DOG (1808)

Domestic dogs depend on human beings for food, shelter, and safety. Dogs give a great deal in return. Depending on a dog's breed and its individual abilities, it can learn to perform many remarkable tasks that aid people.

Guard Dogs

For thousands of years, domestic dogs have been used mainly to guard and protect the home and the family. As time has passed, the job of the guard dog has expanded to assist industry, the military, and the police.

A guard dog can assist a police officer in catching criminals or can protect the officer from attack. Just one well-trained dog and a single officer can control a large crowd of people. Other guard dogs are trained to guard military bases and patrol borders. Dogs that are often used for guard duties include the Doberman pinscher, the German shepherd dog, and the Rottweiler. (For more information on dogs in the military, see the feature Military Working Dogs in the article UNITED STATES, ARMED FORCES OF THE in Volume UV.)

Herding Dogs

Dogs such as the collie, Shetland sheepdog, and Belgian sheepdog can be a great asset on ranches or farms with sheep, cattle, goats, or poultry. These breeds have herding skills. They round up stray livestock and move them where the rancher directs. Their help in protecting livestock from wild predators saves the farmers and ranchers thousands of dollars every year.

Tracking and Hunting Dogs

Did you know that the bloodhound has been described as a nose with a dog attached to it? This is because bloodhounds

have a remarkable sense of smell. Many other breeds do, too, and their noses have been put to work to sniff out everything from game animals to explosives.

At large international airports, dogs are often used to check for illegal drugs and hidden bombs. Dogs can smell even a tiny amount of a drug packed deep inside a large suitcase.

Another interesting job for a dog's nose is at the scene of a fire. Specially trained dogs can recognize many different kinds of chemicals, some of which are used illegally to start fires (an act called arson). Arson dogs have even been known to catch people who start fires by smelling the fire-starting chemicals on their clothes.

Dogs are frequently used by police to locate missing people or victims of violent crime. Rescue workers also use dogs to find the remains of people buried in rubble after a building has collapsed.

Helper Dogs and Pet Therapy

Dogs of many breeds are trained to assist people in special ways. People who are blind,

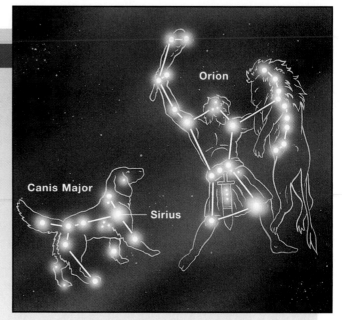

WONDER QUESTION

What are the dog days?

The dog days are the hot, muggy days of summer. They were named for the star Sirius, called the Dog Star because it is the brightest star in the constellation Canis Major (the Big Dog). Centuries ago ancient astronomers noticed that this bright star rose above the horizon just ahead of the sun each morning during the hot summer months from July to September. Minutes later the sun rose and Sirius disappeared into the sun's glare.

The early Romans believed that the combination of the Dog Star and the hot sun so close together caused drought and illness. In order to pacify their gods, the Romans often sacrificed dogs during the midsummer months.

In Greek mythology Sirius was the faithful dog of Orion, a great hunter. Orion was mistakenly and fatally wounded by the goddess

Artemis. To atone for the deed, Artemis placed Orion and his hunting dog among the stars. To this day, Sirius follows just behind Orion in an eternal march across the sky.

Dogs help people in many ways. *Above:* A rescue dog searches for earthquake survivors. *Above right:* A helper dog assists a girl with disabilities. *Right:* A pet therapy dog gets a hug from a nursing home resident.

deaf, or confined to a wheelchair can be helped by these dogs to achieve greater independence in their daily lives. A seeing-eye dog can safely lead a blind person from place to place. A trained hearing-ear dog can signal to a deaf individual when the telephone is ringing or when there is a knock on the door. A dog trained to aid a person who uses a wheelchair can help by picking up dropped objects or turning wall light switches on or off.

Dogs that aid people in these ways are very special. They are permitted by law to go wherever their handlers go, including stores, restaurants, and even hospitals. Among the breeds chosen for this kind of work are the Labrador retriever, the golden retriever, and the German shepherd dog.

If you see a person using a dog for assistance, remember that the dog is working and must use all its senses to help its handler. Do not pet the dog or distract it in any way. You may greet or touch the dog only if invited to do so by the handler.

A dog's companionship is something that many people take for granted. But for those who are in a hospital, a nursing home, or another health-care facility, a visit with a dog can bring many important benefits. This is called **pet therapy** because the dogs can help improve the patients' physical or mental health. Petting and cuddling a dog has been shown to lower blood pressure and pulse rate, which in turn can improve heart function. Patients in an unconscious, or comatose, state have been known to respond to the presence of a dog.

A dog's visit can help people, especially children, be more at ease in the unfamiliar and sometimes frightening setting of a hospital. Petting or brushing a dog can also provide important physical therapy to those with injured arms or hands. Simply being near a dog can help people who are withdrawn or depressed feel some happiness.

Companion Dogs

The most common role dogs serve is as a companion, or pet. But owning a dog is a lot of responsibility, and there are many things you must do to ensure that you and your pet

Left: Choosing a dog is an important decision that is best made by the entire family. *Above:* One of the responsibilities of owning a dog is making sure your pet receives daily exercise.

enjoy a long and happy relationship that benefits both of you.

▶ A DOG IN THE FAMILY

The first step in bringing a dog into your family is choosing the right dog for you. Keep in mind that a dog is a living creature that will become attached to you and your home. With good care, a dog is a friend that will live with you for many years. Take the time to find the right dog for you.

Choosing a Dog

Finding the right dog can sometimes be a difficult process. You might first want to decide whether you want a purebred dog or a mixed breed. There are benefits to either decision. A purebred dog offers predictability. Its size, color, and type of coat match certain breed standards. There is a good chance that its personality will be like other dogs of the same breed.

If you are not particular about personality and appearance traits, there are many beautiful and wonderful mixed-breed dogs to choose from. Animal shelters and dog pounds have all kinds of mixed-breed dogs (and often purebred dogs as well) needing good homes.

You must also decide if you want to raise a puppy or adopt an adult dog. Puppies certainly are appealing, but they require a lot of supervision and training. An adult dog may be easier to bring into a busy household.

Deciding which is the best dog breed for a pet is a very personal matter. A breed (or mix of breeds) that is wonderful for one person might be disastrous for another. When choosing a breed, be sure to consider your physical size, energy level, and lifestyle. For example, a person who cannot spend time exercising a dog should not choose a breed that has been bred to hunt or work for long periods. A toy or nonsporting breed that does not require as much activity might be better.

You can research dog breeds by reading books, visiting dog shows, or talking with breeders. You also can obtain valuable information from veterinarians, professional dog trainers, and the Web sites of kennel clubs around the world.

Care of the Family Dog

There are some basic supplies that you will need right away. When you bring your new dog home, make sure that you have food, a food bowl, and a water bowl ready. A leash and collar with a tag for identification are also important. You may want to purchase a kennel crate or build a safe area to confine your dog for short periods when you cannot be there to supervise. Your new dog, particularly if it is a puppy, should have something to chew on, such as squeaky toys, nylon bones, and rawhide bones. Do not give your dog scrap bones from the kitchen. They are dangerous because they may splinter and injure the dog.

Feeding. Regular feedings are an important part of taking good care of a dog. How much and how often a dog should eat are determined by the dog's age, size, health, and activity level. You can obtain information on a proper diet and feeding schedule for your dog from the dog's breeder or from a veterinarian.

There are a variety of high-quality commercial dog foods on the market. Some are moist products that come in cans; others are dry and may need to have water added.

> *I've seen a look in dogs' eyes, a quickly vanishing look of amazed contempt, and I am convinced that basically dogs think humans are nuts.*
>
> JOHN STEINBECK

These prepared dog foods are intended to provide a dog with a balanced diet. They contain all the necessary nutrients a dog needs.

Shelter. Most pet dogs live in the house with their owners. There are many different kinds of dog beds and indoor kennels that will correspond to your dog's needs. Be sure to choose a bed or basket that is the right size and shape for your dog. If your dog will be spending much time outdoors, you will need to provide a doghouse or kennel. Keeping your dog in a fenced-in area will ensure its safety.

Exercise. It is an important part of a dog's development to exercise and play. Most dogs need to be walked daily for exercise. However, the pet owner must be careful to match the amount of exercise to the age and ability of the dog.

Puppies under 6 months of age have not developed enough physically nor do they have enough energy for long walks. Working

See For Yourself

How to Train Your Dog

Whether your dog is a household pet or a show dog, it is important to teach it some basic obedience commands, such as "sit," "stay," and "come." A dog that can follow these commands is a welcome companion. Obedience behaviors can also help protect a dog from accidents when it is around traffic or other hazards.

A puppy can begin its obedience training when it is about 10 to 12 weeks old. During training, it is important to establish a leadership relationship with your puppy. This does not mean hitting or hurting your dog in any way. Use your voice to correct mistakes. A gruff-sounding "No!" is often very effective. Praise is important, too. When your puppy does what you ask, be sure to say, "Good dog!"

Keep in mind that obedience training is a learning experience for your dog. Always show your dog what you want it to do. For example, gently push down on the dog's hind end as you say the word "sit." Practice this every day. Soon your dog will understand what you want and will respond reliably to your command.

Before you attend an obedience school with your dog, be sure to get references for the school from your veterinarian, groomer, or other professionals. Good obedience instructors can make the job of training your dog a little easier. And a group training class is a fun way for your dog to make new canine friends.

dogs have a lot of energy and need large amounts of exercise, including tasks such as chasing and fetching. Other dogs, such as toy breeds, have limited amounts of energy and are happy with just their daily walks.

Through play, dogs become outgoing pets that are eager and friendly in their interactions with people and other animals. Play not only helps develop a dog's personality, it can also help develop working skills. The puppy

Bringing your dog to the veterinarian for regular checkups will help your pet have a long and healthy life.

that runs after a ball or other toy and returns it to its owner is learning how to retrieve. As they chase and try to catch a moving object, dogs are learning some of the skills used in hunting.

Training. After meals, naps, and play, the puppy must be taken right outside to eliminate. This will teach the puppy that it must eliminate outside.

Puppies also like to chew, especially when they reach about 4 months of age. Close supervision and a safe, puppy-proofed area are absolutely necessary during this period. A constant chewer who destroys household items can quickly take the joy out of dog ownership. As the puppy grows older, you should teach it basic obedience commands, such as to come when called and to sit or lie down when told. Other important behaviors include walking on a leash without pulling, greeting people without jumping on them, and staying in place. A dog who knows these

behaviors is a dog that you—and others—will enjoy being around. You can learn how to train your dog to do all of these things by enrolling in a qualified dog obedience school. For more information, see the feature How to Train Your Dog accompanying this article.

Health Care. A new puppy should be taken for a veterinary exam as soon as possible. Along with checking the dog's health and vaccinating the dog against diseases such as rabies and distemper, the veterinarian can give you advice on proper diet, exercise, and grooming for your dog. A dog should have a routine checkup each year.

When your dog is between the ages of 6 months and 1 year old, your veterinarian may recommend that the dog be spayed (if it is a female) or neutered (if it is a male). These are surgical procedures that prevent dogs from producing offspring.

Spaying involves the removal of the female dog's uterus and ovaries. After being spayed, the female dog no longer comes into heat. She is incapable of producing puppies. Neutering involves the removal of the male dog's testicles. A neutered male dog can no longer produce puppies. Both of these surgeries are part of the daily routine of most veterinary hospitals. Healthy older dogs can also be spayed or neutered.

Responsibility and Companionship

Each person who owns a dog has a responsibility to take care of it: to feed and water the dog every day and to provide it with shelter from bad weather. Taking care of a dog includes spending time with it. By giving back the companionship that a dog so generously gives, you continue the long history of partnership between dogs and humans.

BARBARA McKINNEY
JOHN ROSS
Coauthors, *Dog Talk: Training Your Dog Through a Canine Point of View*

See also ANIMALS; COYOTES; FOXES; MAMMALS; WOLVES.

DOLE, ELIZABETH. See NORTH CAROLINA (Famous People).

DOLE, ROBERT J. (BOB). See KANSAS (Famous People).

DOLE, SANFORD B. See HAWAII (Famous People).

DOLLAR

The dollar is the basic unit of U.S. currency. Several other countries also call their currency the dollar, including Australia, the Bahamas, Canada, Hong Kong, Jamaica, and Singapore. In all these countries, a dollar consists of 100 cents and appears as a coin or bank note. The dollar sign ($) is often used to designate a figure in dollars.

The word "dollar" comes from the German word *thaler* (TAH-ler), which is short for *Joachimsthaler*, a silver coin first struck in 1484. This coin was widely used in Europe. English-speaking people gradually changed the pronunciation to DAH-ler.

British and Spanish coins were the best-known currencies in the American colonies by the time of the American Revolution. The most accepted coin was the Spanish peso, which Americans called a Spanish dollar. The value of a Spanish peso was eight reales (ray-AHL-ays). A merchant making change for an eight-reales coin would cut it into smaller

pieces. This resulted in a fraction, such as one-half (four reales), one-quarter (two reales), or one-eighth (one real, also called one bit). This is the origin of "pieces of eight," a familiar phrase in pirate tales.

The United States began its own coinage system in 1792. Because Americans were used to seeing prices stated in Spanish dollars, the United States selected the dollar as its basic unit. Thomas Jefferson thought that dividing money by eight was impractical. As a result, Congress adopted the decimal system, whereby each dollar is divided into 100 cents (from the Latin *centum*, meaning "100").

▸ **DOLLARS IN CIRCULATION**

The United States Treasury Department is responsible for producing U.S. paper money and coins through two of its bureaus, the U.S. Mint and the Bureau of Engraving and Printing. The U.S. Mint produces the coins. The bills are printed by the Bureau of Engraving and Printing. The bureaus ship the finished bills and coins by truckloads to the U.S. Federal Reserve, which is responsible for putting the currency into circulation.

Since the early 1970's, the Federal Reserve has issued only Federal Reserve Notes. Be-

All Federal Reserve Notes except $1 and $2 bills have been redesigned since 1996. The following bills are pictured: $1 (George Washington), $5 (Abraham Lincoln), $10 (Alexander Hamilton), $20 (Andrew Jackson), $50 (Ulysses S. Grant), and $100 (Benjamin Franklin).

How can you tell if a bill is counterfeit?

The best way to tell if a bill is counterfeit is to compare it with a real bill of the same value.

Serial number — Type of note
Federal Reserve letter and bank number
Federal Reserve seal
Plate position letter
Portrait   Series
Plate number
Treasury seal
Serial number
Color-shifting ink

Real bill:	Counterfeit bill:
1. Small red and blue fibers are in the paper. (These fibers may not be visible if the bill is old or worn.)	1. Small red and blue fibers are missing entirely or are printed on the surface of the paper.
2. The portrait appears lifelike and stands out clearly from the background. Hair lines and lines forming the background should be distinct.	2. The portrait is lifeless and merges into the background. The background is too dark. Hair lines are indistinct.
3. The saw-tooth points around the rim of the Treasury Seal are clear and sharp.	3. The saw-tooth points around the rim of the Treasury Seal may be uneven, broken, or blunt.
4. Serial numbers are evenly spaced and line up perfectly. Ink color should be the same as that of the Treasury Seal.	4. Serial numbers may be unevenly spaced, out of line, or poorly printed. Ink color may be different from that of the Treasury Seal.
5. All ornamental work should be clear and distinct with unbroken lines.	5. Ornamental work may be blurred and broken.
6. The denomination printed on the security strip embedded in the Series 1990 and later $5, $10, $20, $50, and $100 bills matches that of the note. (The strip appears in different places on the different denominations.) Printing on the strip should be visible when viewed from either side of the note. Additionally, the security strips glow different colors when held under ultraviolet light: $5—blue, $10—orange, $20—green, $50—yellow, and $100—red.	6. Security strip may be absent. Printing may be visible from only one side. Under ultraviolet light, the strip may fail to glow or may glow an incorrect color.
7. The watermark on the Series 1999 $5 and $10 notes and the Series 1996 $20, $50, and $100 notes should appear as a shadow-like image. It can be seen from either side when the bill is held up to the light and should resemble the central portrait on the note.	7. A watermark may be pressed into the paper rather than embedded. Resemblance between the watermark and the note's central portrait may be poor. Watermark may be of incorrect portrait.
8. On the front side of $10, $20, $50, and $100 notes, color-shifting ink at lower right changes color. On notes dated Series 1996 through Series 2003, the shift is from green to black. On Series 2004 and newer notes, the color shift is from copper to green.	8. Color-shifting ink may be absent, or may not shift between the proper colors.
9. The Series 2004 $20 note features green, peach, blue, and yellow background colors. The Series 2004 $50 note has blue, red, and yellow background colors.	9. Green, peach, blue, and yellow background colors may be missing from the Series 2004 $20 note. The Series 2004 $50 note may be missing blue, red, and yellow background colors.

The U. S. Secret Service is the part of the U. S. Department of the Treasury that enforces the laws against counterfeiting.

According to the Secret Service, if you receive a counterfeit bill,

1. do not return the bill to the person who gave it to you;

2. contact the police or the nearest office of the Secret Service. Be ready to provide a complete description of the person who gave you the counterfeit bill;

3. write your initials and the date on the bill and give it to the police or Secret Service only.

In 2000 the U.S. Mint released the Golden Dollar (*right*), featuring the image of Sacagawea. In Canada, the dollar coin (*below*), featuring Queen Elizabeth II, has replaced the dollar note.

fore that, from 1929 until the early 1970's, Silver Certificates, Gold Certificates, U. S. Notes, Treasury Notes, and National Bank Notes were used. Currently in use are $1, $2, $5, $10, $20, $50, and $100 notes.

In the past, $500, $1,000, $5,000, and $10,000 notes were also issued. The highest-value note ever issued was worth $100,000. The government created it to help banks transfer large sums of money. It was never circulated in public.

The United States does not recall or lower the value of its outmoded bills. They remain legal tender—that is, they are valid for payment. A genuine $1,000 bill from 1890, for example, is still redeemable at a bank for $1,000. Many outmoded bills, however, are worth more than their face value to collectors.

The Federal Reserve is responsible for shredding and disposing of worn-out bills. Banks replace older notes with new ones as the notes circulate.

▶ COUNTERING COUNTERFEITERS

Between 1996 and 2000, the United States redesigned its $5, $10, $20, $50, and $100 bills. It was the first major change in paper money since 1929. The notes were redesigned mainly to make it harder for them to be counterfeited (illegally copied). The 1996–2000 security changes included intricate engravings, special paper, fluorescent fibers, and strips of film embedded in the paper.

Did you know that...

on average, a $1 bill lasts 22 months before it is too worn to continue circulating? As a result, an almost constant stream of $1 bills is necessary to maintain the supply. More than 4.1 billion $1 bills were produced in the government's fiscal year 2004, part of the nearly $128 billion printed in that period. The $20 note is generally second in terms of number produced, followed by the $5 note. In 2004, $719.9 billion were circulating worldwide.

In 2003, the Federal Reserve began circulating a new $20 note as the first in the Series 2004 currency redesign. The design was the first in modern American history to include colors other than black and green in U.S. bills. The Series 2004 $20 bill features green, peach, blue, and yellow background colors (see Wonder Question).

According to the Bureau of Engraving and Printing, the new $20 bill is safer because it is easier to check and harder for counterfeiters to fake.

The next Series 2004 redesigned bill, a $50 note, appeared in September 2004. The bill has blue, red, and yellow background colors. New $10 and $100 bills will be included in the Series 2004 redesign. All bills in the series will have unique color combinations, making it easier to tell the different quantities apart.

Even with the security changes, the use of electronic scanners and computer imaging to forge U.S. paper money remains a problem. To stay ahead of counterfeiters, the U.S. government plans to redesign its currency about every seven to ten years.

▶ DOLLAR COINS

The United States has issued dollar coins since 1794. The first ones were made of silver. Dollars made of gold were minted from 1849 to 1889. Both the silver and gold dollars depict different views of a female figure of Liberty on the front side of the coin.

In 1971, the United States issued a copper-nickel dollar featuring President Dwight D. Eisenhower. The same design was minted in silver for collectors. Susan B. Anthony was portrayed on a copper-nickel $1 coin minted from 1979 to 1981 and again in 1999. In 2000, the United States introduced a gold-colored $1 coin that depicts Sacagawea, a Native American who guided much of the Lewis and Clark expedition of 1804–06. The coin has copper, zinc, manganese, and nickel layers.

The U.S. Mint produces coins in Philadelphia, Denver, San Francisco, and New York.

DAVID C. KRANZ
Managing Editor, F&W Publications, Inc.
Bank Note Reporter;
Numismatic News; *World Coin News*

In the 1700's, wealthy English aristocrats built dollhouses (then called baby houses) that were miniature copies of their own homes. The Tate Baby House (shown here from the rear) was built about 1760 in the Georgian style of architecture. Today it is part of the Victoria and Albert Museum of Childhood collection in London.

DOLLHOUSES

A dollhouse is a miniature house built to contain dolls and their furniture. Dollhouses are part of a tradition that dates back about 4,000 years to the ancient Egyptians and Chinese. In both cultures, people made miniature versions of their homes and businesses. Miniature figurines, also made throughout the centuries, can add to our understanding of what life was like at different times in history. A 100-year-old dollhouse, for example, can show us not just the type of house that people lived in back then, but what sort of beds they slept in, what manner of stoves kept them warm, and what sort of cooking utensils they used.

Scale. The standard proportion, or scale, used in today's dollhouses is 1:12. This means that every dimension of the miniature item is $\frac{1}{12}$ the size of the real item. This proportion may also be expressed as 1 inch to 1 foot. For example, if a real table is 3 feet high, the miniature table would be 3 inches high. Smaller scales are also used.

History. The first dollhouse on record was ordered in 1558 by Duke Albrecht V of Bavaria, for his daughter. Although it no longer exists, we know it had four floors and included a ballroom, a chapel, and a bathroom. In days when even the nobility washed very little, the presence of a bathroom shows what an elegant household this was.

The oldest dollhouses still in existence were built in Germany and the Netherlands in the 1600's. They were made for adults and were very expensive. Model rooms, containing elaborate knickknacks and toys, were displayed in magnificent art cabinets. In the 1700's, English aristocrats built dollhouses that were small copies of their stately homes. These pieces, then called baby houses, were beautifully produced in miniature, usually by the estate carpenter or a cabinetmaker.

In the 1800's, industrialization allowed dollhouses to be mass-produced, and they became affordable as toys. They often still had elaborate furnishings, such as embroidered rugs and silk curtains. As less expensive materials became available, the popularity of dollhouses spread.

Today, the world of miniatures is divided between toy and collector dollhouses. Some people collect only dollhouses and furnishings of the past. Such collecting can be very costly. Sometimes a young person is fortunate enough to inherit an antique dollhouse. In that case, experts recommend that the house be changed as little as possible.

Famous Dollhouses. Possibly the most famous dollhouse ever built is the Queen's Dolls' House, created for Queen Mary of England in the 1920's. Designed by the noted architect Sir Edwin Lutyens, the house is actually a miniature palace. It stands more than 7 feet (2 meters) tall and has functioning plumbing and electricity. The furnishings include silver thrones, copies of the crown jewels, paintings by famous artists, and miniature books by Rudyard Kipling and Sir Arthur Conan Doyle. The Queen's Dolls' House is one of the most popular attractions at Windsor Castle.

In 1922, before her dollhouse was completed, Queen Mary presided at the opening of the exhibition of another celebrated miniature mansion, in Dublin, Ireland. It was called Titania's Palace, in honor of the Fairy Queen. It took Sir Neville Wilkinson, a celebrated painter of miniatures, 15 years to build. The palace is 10 feet (3 meters) wide and contains approximately 3,000 miniatures. Some of the pieces are original historical miniatures, such as a brass cannon crafted during the 1600's and a pair of gold figurines cast during the 1500's. Some pieces, such as the throne, were handcrafted from rubies, diamonds, and other precious materials. Today Titania's Palace is exhibited at Legoland in Denmark.

Another fairy home was built in America for the former silent movie star Colleen Moore. Created by a Hollywood set designer and more than 700 artisans, it stands 7 feet tall and houses more than 2,000 items, some of them extraordinary. The mirror in the Prince's Bathroom is made of gold, a sapphire, and diamonds. The chandelier in Cinderella's Drawing Room is also gold, hung with diamonds, emeralds, and pearls. Many of the floors in the house are made from materials such as mother-of-pearl, quartz, and jade. Colleen Moore's Fairy Castle, which was completed in the mid-1930's, is now exhibited at the Museum of Science and Industry in Chicago.

Other famous dollhouses include the Stettheimer Dollhouse, built in the 1920's by Carrie Walter Stettheimer, a New York society hostess. In addition to depicting the lifestyle of the upper class during the Roaring 20's, this dollhouse displays original miniatures by several important artists of the day, among them Marcel Duchamp and Gaston Lachaise. The Stettheimer Dollhouse is exhibited at the Museum of the City of New York.

FLORA GILL JACOBS
Author, *A History of Dolls' Houses*

MICHILINDA KINSEY
Coeditor, *Dollhouse Miniatures*

See For Yourself

How to Make Your Own Dollhouse

For your first dollhouse, start with something simple—a plain box or empty drawer, a kit, or a pre-made dollhouse (available at your local craft store). You will also need some basic tools—scissors, tweezers, notepaper, pencil and eraser, sandpaper, glue, ruler, measuring tape, paintbrushes, sewing kit, and a drop cloth.

Begin by planning your dollhouse. What kind of house or room will it be? Will it depict a real time or place, or a fantasy land? Sketch windows, decorations, and furniture. Measure real items and draw them in miniature (using the standard scale, 1 inch equals 1 foot) to see how they will fit within your dollhouse.

Next, look around you. Many household items can be used to decorate and furnish your dollhouse. Here are some examples:

- Use gift wrap or scrapbooking paper for wallpaper. Use ribbon, plain or decorated, as borders.
- Build furniture from small boxes. For example, glue fabric to a rectangular box to form a bed. Glue lace trim around the middle as the bed skirt, then cut rectangles of fabric for the top sheet and bedspread. Cut dry sponges into pillows and glue on pillowcases.
- Use the lid from a tube of lip balm for a planter. Fill it with dry loose tea, and then add a plant made from tiny dried flowers.
- Cut pictures of paintings or photos from catalogs. Using pinking shears, cut frames from cardstock. Paint the frames, and then glue the pictures in the center.
- For glasses and vases, cut lengths of clear plastic drinking straw. Punch circles out of a clear plastic lid, and then glue the straws to the circles.

Dolls can be whatever you wish them to be. They have been a part of the fantasy world of childhood for thousands of years.

DOLLS

Dolls have been loved by children for centuries. No one knows when dolls were first made. But it is known that primitive people used dolls as religious or magical objects before dolls were toys. Today collecting dolls is a hobby that adults and children share.

Dolls thousands of years old have been found in Egyptian tombs. Some were made of baked clay; others were brightly painted wooden dolls, with long hair made of strings of clay beads. In the ancient city of Cyrene, in North Africa, dolls of carved ivory have been found. Early Greek and Roman books mention wax dolls. However, none of these old wax dolls can be seen today. They have all been destroyed or have melted away.

▶DOLLS OF WOOD

Every suitable material you can imagine has gone into doll making. But from earliest times wood has been the favorite material from which to carve or whittle a toy baby or a small figure of a boy, a girl, a man, or a woman.

The first wooden dolls to be made from a pattern so that they all looked alike came from Germany. Records show that a doll maker named Ott worked in Nuremberg as early as 1413. Later the peasants of the Thuringian Forest made wooden dolls in quantity. During the long winter months, the foresters occupied themselves by carving dolls. It was not long before traveling merchants discovered the dolls and began to sell them all over Europe. In time they were also sold in the United States. These dolls became known as peg dolls or Pennywoodens.

Hand-carved wooden dolls still are made in almost every country. Among the most famous wooden dolls made in the United States were the Springfield dolls introduced by Joel Ellis in 1873. They were named after the little town in Vermont where Mr. Ellis started his factory. The heads of these dolls were made of hardwood that was steamed and pressed into shape. The bodies were molded on a lathe, and the arms and legs were joined to them with steel pins. The Springfield dolls set the pattern for other doll makers to follow.

▶WAX DOLLS

Even though the Egyptians, Greeks, and Romans knew how to make wax dolls, the Germans were the first to produce them in quantity, during the 17th century. Somewhat later, wax dolls were produced in England by two Italian families of doll makers, Pierotti and Montanari. Madame Montanari, working in London in the mid-1800's, perfected a way of making wax dolls with rooted hair, instead of attached wigs. Her method was to set the hair into the wax strand by strand with a hot needle. Pierotti also used this method. Modern doll makers use the same method, with composition and plastic materials.

During the 19th century many interesting wax doll heads were produced in England and the United States. Some of the dolls had their hats molded right onto their heads. Other dolls were made with two, three, or four faces. The different faces were made over a pivot hidden by the doll's wig. When the pivot was turned, a new face appeared from under the stationary wig. Each face wore a different expression, so that the doll could look serious or happy or could appear to be crying or to be asleep. Dominico Checkeni of Marion, Connecticut, patented the design for the first of these many-faced dolls in the United States in 1866.

▶ DOLLS OF PAPIER-MÂCHÉ, CHINA, AND BISQUE

Dolls made in the 19th century seem quaint to modern eyes. In those days most of the dolls were made to look like grown-ups rather than children. By the end of the century, the dolls wore dresses with tiny waists, bustles, and short jackets. Doll collectors now call one of the early types the Milliner's Model. The heads of these dolls were made of papier-mâché, a paper pulp mixed with glue and allowed to harden. The Milliner's Model had long, spindly wooden arms and legs, and the body was made of kid or cloth stuffed with sawdust. Sometimes the hairstyle was very elaborate, with puffs at the sides and the back hair gathered into a knot or loops on top of the head. Then, for a final effect, the doll makers might insert combs, flowers, feathers, or other decorations.

The Chinese made ceremonial dolls of papier-mâché long before the use of this material was discovered in Europe or America. In Europe the first papier-mâché doll heads were made about 1810, in Sonneberg, Germany. The earliest papier-mâché doll heads in America were made in Philadelphia by Ludwig Greiner, who came to the United States in 1840. Mr. Greiner learned his trade in Germany. Two early Greiner models were a boy doll with short, curly hair showing brush marks at the temple, and a girl doll with sausage curls. After Ludwig Greiner died in 1874, two of his sons carried on the business until the early 1900's.

Two other very popular 19th-century dolls were the china and the bisque-headed dolls, People not too familiar with these materials sometimes confuse china and bisque. Bisque is unglazed china. Most bisque dolls are flesh-colored. When bisque dolls are left white and polished well, collectors call them Parian. Parian dolls made in Dresden, Germany, between 1850 and 1880 were called Dresden dolls. These dolls had very fancy hair arrangements of flowers, ribbons, and combs, all molded of the same china as the head and shoulders. Beautiful bisque dolls were also made in

The peg wooden doll from Germany (*left*) and the wax doll from England (*center*) both date from about 1850. At right is a German-made papier-mâché Milliner's Model.

"China dolls," popular in the 1800's, were so called because their heads were made of glazed china (*left*). Dresden dolls, made in Germany, had bisque china heads (*right*).

France. The most famous French dolls were made by the Jumeau factory. The Jumeau dolls were very elegant. They were often accompanied by a doll's trunk containing four costumes complete with all accessories and jewelry.

▶DOLLS OF OTHER MATERIALS

For generations farm families all over the world have made dolls of hemp and straw and braided flax. In colonial America children played with dolls made from corn husks. The top strips of green were folded over the ear of corn and tied across to make the doll's head. A tassel of dried brown corn silk peeking out at the top made very fine hair. Once the husks were dry, the eyes, nose, and mouth were painted on.

In many countries cloth dolls were popular. The earliest ones were probably made from a table napkin or a large handkerchief. The cloth was rolled and folded, and knotted to form the head. The features were drawn on the head with a pencil or paint. Later, rag dolls were sewn together and stuffed with cotton, rags, or other soft material. The features were embroidered, and linen threads were used to make the doll's hair.

Stocking dolls have been favorites of many children. They were easily made by filling a stocking with rags or sawdust and sewing on strands of colored wool for the hair. Then a gay face was made by chain stitching a nose and mouth in red thread and sewing on shiny buttons for eyes. Though never things of beauty, these dolls were soft and cuddly and greatly pleased their owners.

Dolls were made of hard rubber long, long ago. One rubber doll was found at the bottom of an ancient well in Yucatan, in southeastern Mexico. Scientists say that this rubber doll is about 1,000 years old.

In the United States and Europe in the late 19th century, some doll heads were made of metal. Much earlier than this, dolls of silver and gold were made for the children of wealthy families. There still exist tiny, fully jointed dolls of gold and white metal that measure no more than $1\frac{1}{8}$ inches (3 centimeters) high.

Frank E. Darrow of Bristol, Connecticut, took out a patent in 1866 to manufacture leather doll heads. But rats found the heads so tasty (they even nibbled away at the power belts that ran the machines) that Darrow had to abandon his factory in 1877. Today fine leather dolls are made in Morocco. A few are made in the southern United States for doll collectors.

▶FASHION DOLLS

In the days before there were any fashion magazines to show pictures of the latest styles

In colonial America children played with dolls made of corn husks (*left*). Russian children enjoy wooden stacking dolls made to fit one inside the other (*right*). Mechanical dolls were particularly popular in 19th-century Germany (*center right*). "Fashion dolls" were once used as models by French clothing designers. The elaborately dressed dolls were sent abroad to potential buyers (*bottom right*).

in women's clothes, clever dress designers in France made "fashion dolls." These dolls were dressed in the newest Paris fashions and sent abroad. This made it possible for distant buyers to order the dresses they wanted. As early as 1391, dolls were sent to the Queen of England to show her what the ladies of the French court were wearing. When fashion magazines were printed, it became unnecessary to send dolls, and the fashion doll soon disappeared.

Today paper dolls are sometimes made with such elaborate wardrobes that they might be called fashion dolls. Some plastic dolls are sold with many different costumes, and these also might be called fashion dolls. But they do not serve the same purpose as the original fashion dolls, which was to let people see the latest in fashion design. Today magazines, newspapers, and television do that.

▶ MECHANICAL DOLLS THAT WALK AND TALK

Since very early times, mechanical dolls have danced, twirled, kicked, bowed, and jumped their way into popularity. In Europe during the 18th and 19th centuries, there were unusual mechanical dolls that nodded and smiled and fanned themselves as gracefully as any lady of the day. Other dolls had built-in mechanisms that squeaked out the words "Pa-pa" or "Ma-ma" as they walked across the floor with outstretched arms.

Three of the most extraordinary mechanical dolls were made about 200 years ago in France. Two of these large dolls are dressed in 18th-century boys' costumes. One could draw and was able to sketch a portrait of Queen Marie Antoinette of France. The other, which was also widely exhibited, was noted for its excellent penmanship. The third doll was a lady 45 inches (115 centimeters) tall. She was seated at a harmonium, a kind of organ, and played a melody especially composed for her. As she played, she seemed to breathe so naturally that a red flower on the bodice of her dress rose and fell. She turned her head from side to side as her hands moved across the keyboard, and each finger touched a note as though the doll were really playing. When the tune ended, she stood up and bowed to the audience, just as a real performer does. The dolls are part of a collection in a museum of Neuchâtel, Switzerland.

Today mechanical dolls are made to dance like a ballerina or talk at the pulling of a string. Some of them can blow out candles. Others blow bubbles or party horns.

▶ PORTRAIT DOLLS OF FAMOUS PEOPLE

Since the Middle Ages, dolls have been made that look like kings and queens and other persons of note. These portrait dolls have been sculptured in wax, wood, papier-mâché, china, and bisque.

Modern dolls are also made to look like famous people. Perhaps the most famous and popular of all was the Shirley Temple doll. Today, celebrities often have dolls made to resemble them. A recent popular subject for dolls has been Diana, Princess of Wales. Children also collect dolls that resemble characters from favorite books, movies, and television series. Space themes like *Star Trek* and *Star Wars* are popular, as are Westerns. Also popular are singing stars and cartoon characters like Superman and Batman.

▶ SPECIALTY DOLLS

One of the most popular dolls in history is the 11½-inch (29 centimeters) teenage fashion doll Barbie, introduced in 1959. Barbie and her friends have huge wardrobes, and the clothing and accessories through the years have reflected current fashion and trends. Other teenage fashion dolls also became popular as a result of the success of Barbie.

Until the early 1900's, most dolls looked like adults rather than children, but today youngsters seem to prefer dolls that resemble themselves. Infant and toddler dolls such as those at left and below are favorites of young children. Older children are fond of dolls fashioned after real or fictional characters. The Shirley Temple doll (*right*) has long been a popular character doll.

In the 1980's the "real-looking" Cabbage Patch Kids dominated the market. In addition to ordinary "children" and babies, there were Cabbage Patch twins and dolls in ethnic costumes from foreign countries.

G.I. Joe was first introduced in 1964 and was an instant success. He was 11½ inches (29 centimeters) tall and had many outfits and accessories. In 1982 he was re-introduced in a 3¾-inch (9.5 centimeters) size. In response to the popularity of the 1985 film character Rambo, a Rambo doll was introduced. These action dolls are particularly popular with boys, who also enjoy transformers (robot-like dolls that can be converted into other objects).

▶ **DOLL COLLECTING**

Because of the popularity of doll collecting as a hobby, there are many doll clubs for serious collectors. The United Federation of Doll Clubs is the largest club of this type, with more than 735 clubs across the United States and abroad. It boasts a membership of nearly 17,000. A national convention is held every August at various cities in the United States. The oldest doll club in the United States is the Doll Collectors of America, Inc., founded in 1935.

Some of the doll clubs publish their own magazines on a regular basis. Doll magazines published by independent publishers are also very popular.

Today's doll collectors also can find many books on dolls, with color illustrations, that deal with every aspect of collecting, dressing, repairing, and making dolls. Photographs of rare dolls have made their identification simpler.

Collectors may attend doll shows all over the world. Sponsored by doll clubs, promoters, or individuals, such shows may feature modern, collectible dolls, as well as antique dolls. A collector may find dolls at general antique shows as well.

There are many doll museums all over the world. Fine doll museums in Europe include Bethnal Green Museum in London, and the Musée Carnavalet in Paris. Excellent doll collections in the United States may be found at the Margaret Woodbury Strong Museum in Rochester, New York; the Wee Lassie Museum in Homestead, Florida; Yesteryears Museum in Sandwich, Massachusetts; and the Museum of the City of New York.

Today's trend toward realism in doll making has led to many new kinds of dolls, among them Hal's Pals (*right*), a collection displaying physical disabilities. The perpetually teenage "Barbie" doll (*center*) is one of the most popular dolls ever made. Characters from the movie *Star Wars* were among the first of many action-doll collections (*bottom*). Action dolls are usually modeled after comic book, television, or movie characters.

Dolls in traditional costumes (*left*), Raggedy Ann dolls (*center*), and kachina dolls (*right*) are among the handcrafted dolls prized by collectors.

▶HANDCRAFTED DOLLS TODAY

Today handcrafted dolls are being made all over the world. In the United States and other countries where most of the dolls are made by machine, people still make beautiful dolls by hand. Probably the most popular ones are the stuffed fabric dolls. Among these are Raggedy Ann and Andy, which have been favorites for decades. Also popular are fabric dolls with faces created by stitches that pull the fabric into position to make the nose, mouth, and other features. Folk dolls, including cornhusk and corncob dolls, are being made in Appalachia and the Ozarks in the United States.

Indians following old tribal ways continue to make dolls. The Hopi Indians of the Southwest are famous for their kachina dolls. The Seminole Indians of Florida still make dolls with fiber from the palmetto and dress them in bright patchwork clothing.

In Europe, dolls are often handmade to show the traditional costumes, which the people now wear only for festivals. In South America, dolls such as the Peruvian ones shown at left above are dressed in modern native costumes made from the same hand-loomed fabrics that the people wear. In the Caribbean islands, dolls are popular tourist souvenirs. Most are female dolls dressed in bright skirts and blouses. They frequently wear turbans and balance baskets on their heads.

In Africa, carvers continue to make interesting dolls from ebony and other woods. In Japan, doll making is a respected art practiced by both women and men. They make beautiful display dolls from kits available from schools of doll making. Also popular in Japan are the wooden dolls called *kokeshi*. They are sold at vacation resorts. In each area the dolls are a little different, and many people have large collections of these dolls. Dolls are even given their own holiday in Japan. On March 3, little girls display special dolls that have been handed down from mother to daughter. The dolls represent the emperor and empress, knights, warriors, and court attendants. After being shown on this occasion, they are put away until the following year.

▶FRIENDSHIP DOLLS

Dolls are also used to promote world friendship. The first exchange of dolls was made in 1927, when the Committee on World Friendship Among Children sent a collection of American dolls to the children of Japan. Japanese children in turn gave American children a gift of 58 beautiful museum dolls.

In the years that followed, many other countries have continued this idea, and dolls all over the world have been sent as ambassadors of peace and friendship from the children of one nation to those of another.

CLARA H. FAWCETT
Author, *A New Guide for Collectors*
Reviewed and updated by ZELDA CUSHNER
Former Editor, *Doll News*

The dolphins' ability to learn and perform an astonishing number of tricks has made them well-known "stars" of marine showplaces as well as motion pictures and television.

DOLPHINS AND PORPOISES

Dolphins and porpoises are members of the most playful and intelligent group of animals living in the sea. They have been known since ancient times for their frolicsome habits around boats and human divers. Their ability to be trained easily and to carry out complex behaviors has made them popular attractions at many ocean aquariums.

Which Name to Use

Dolphins and porpoises are actually small whales that range in length from 4 to 12 feet (1.2 to 3.6 meters), except for the killer whale, which can be up to 30 feet (9 meters) long. The habits and characteristics of most of these creatures are very similar, and people often use the terms dolphin and porpoise interchangeably.

The names of both of these animals have their roots in ancient times. "Dolphin" comes from the Greek *delphis,* a word that probably referred to the shape of the common dolphin's long snout. The word "porpoise" comes from the Latin *porcus piscis,* meaning "fish hog." Fishermen of long ago considered these animals to be fish hogs because they devoured so many fish from their nets.

Scientists today distinguish between dolphins and porpoises based on the shapes of their snouts and teeth. Some group porpoises in a separate family, called the Phocoenidae, because porpoises have a rounded snout rather than the beaklike snout that most dolphins have. In addition, porpoise teeth have a spade-like shape rather than the cone shape of the teeth in most dolphins. Other scientists, however, do not think that porpoises belong in a separate family and group them in the main dolphin family, the Delphinidae.

For the purpose of this article, the word dolphin will be used as the general term to describe all of these small whales. When a particular species is discussed, however, it will be identified more specifically as a dolphin or porpoise.

▶TYPES OF DOLPHINS AND PORPOISES

About 50 species of dolphins and porpoises are known today. Certain members of the major dolphin family have become river or lake dwellers, but most inhabit the oceans of the world. Some live in the deep seas, rarely venturing close to land. Others are found in coastal waters. They may be seen along beaches and in bays and harbors. Of them all, the best known is the bottlenose dolphin.

Best known of all dolphins, the bottlenose is named for its narrow snout, which is lined with small teeth shaped for catching and holding fish.

The Bottlenose Dolphin

The scientific name of the bottlenose is *Tursiops*. Its common name comes from the shape of its snout—something like an old hand-blown bottle. There are several different species in the world, but the best known of all is the bottlenose of the Atlantic Ocean. It is the one that is most often seen in large sea aquariums. Because it lives well in captivity, it has been studied more than any other small whale.

Tursiops is gray on its back and sides, shading to white underneath. It has a dorsal (back) fin shaped something like that of a shark. Its two flippers also somewhat resemble the fins of a shark. But within each flipper is a bone structure very similar to that of a human arm. The skeleton of the flipper even includes five "fingers." The flippers represent the forelimbs of the distant ancestors of dolphins; these were animals that lived on dry land and went about on four legs. No dolphin has a trace of hind legs. But buried in the flesh are two small bones—all that remains of the hipbones.

The powerful tail is thin, as if it had been pressed together from either side. This form permits it to move up and down readily in the water, driving the fins, which are at the end of the tail. These fins are called flukes. They resemble a fish's tail except that they lie flat in a horizontal plane instead of upright, or vertical.

In many ways the bottlenose dolphin is a typical representative of its family. It is about average in size, ranging from 8 to 9 feet (2.4 to 2.7 meters) long when grown. It has 80 to 90 teeth, which is between the two extremes—some species have only 6 to 12 teeth, while others possess 200 or so. The teeth of the bottlenose are often worn flat at the ends. They are not used for chewing, however, but only for catching and holding food. Usually the dolphin's meal—a fish or squid—is swallowed head-first and whole.

Common Dolphins

Common dolphins are found worldwide in warm or tropical seas. They have black or brown backs with light stripes on the sides and are slightly smaller than the bottlenose. Common dolphins are often sighted playing around ships and are also frequently found swimming with schools of tuna.

The Common, or Harbor, Porpoise

The common porpoise, also called the harbor porpoise, is the most abundant small whale in the Atlantic coastal waters of Europe. It is a relatively small animal, growing only about 6 feet (1.8 meters) long. Like all porpoises, it has a blunt snout and spade-shaped teeth. The common porpoise usually travels in small groups and tends to avoid people. It does venture near land, however, and sometimes swims up rivers looking for food.

The Killer Whale

This is the largest member of the Delphinidae family, with males measuring up to 30 feet (9 meters) long and weighing 11,000 pounds (5,000 kilograms). The killer whale earned its name because it preys on seals, sea lions, dolphins, and other whales as well as fish and squid, which are its primary diet. Contrary to legend, the killer whale is not a ferocious killer that attacks humans.

Killer whales are found worldwide. They typically live and hunt in packs of four to 40 animals. Their distinctive black and white coloring, large size, and ability to be trained have made them popular attractions at ocean aquariums.

Most dolphins, such as these playful bottlenose dolphins (*left*), are found in the world's oceans and seas. Others, such as the bouto dolphin (*below left*) that inhabits the Amazon River, are found in fresh water.

River Dolphins

These animals belong to a separate family of primitive, freshwater dolphins, the Platanistidae. There are four species of river dolphins. All have long snouts and feed mostly on fish. Their vision is poor, and the eyes in one species even lack a lens. The animals in this family live in rivers and lakes in Asia and South America.

▶ LIVING IN A MARINE ENVIRONMENT

Little was known about the habits of dolphins before Marineland of Florida was completed in 1938. Here a colony of bottlenose dolphins was established in a huge "oceanarium" tank. The tank had glass portholes in the sides so that everything its inhabitants did could be observed.

Over the years the dolphins have mated, given birth, and raised their young in the oceanarium. Much of what is known about the behavior and way of life of all dolphins has come from the many observations made at Marineland.

Surfacing to Breathe

Unlike fish that can breathe underwater through their gills, dolphins must come to the surface in order to breathe. In the course of living in a marine environment, dolphins have acquired the means to get a breath of air quickly and efficiently while swimming at full speed.

In most animals the nostrils are located at the end of the snout. In dolphins they have moved back to the top of the head, where they form a single opening called the blowhole. This permits the dolphin to take a breath while swimming at full speed. Its horizontal flukes, which move up and down rather than from side to side like a fish's tail, also enable the dolphin to rise quickly for air.

A dolphin surfaces with a rolling motion. It exhales and inhales all in a fraction of a second—then it holds its breath. *Tursiops*, the bottlenose, normally surfaces and "blows" two or three times a minute. But it can hold its breath much longer—probably from five to ten minutes.

Distinguishing characteristics of the dolphin family include the rounded snout of the common porpoise (*above*) and the large size of the pilot whale (*below left*) and the killer whale (*below*).

A baby dolphin is born tailfirst into a watery world (*top*). The mother will help her infant to the surface for its first breath of air. Then for several weeks the young dolphin will swim close to its mother's side.

Giving Birth

A female dolphin carries her calf (as baby dolphins are called) for twelve months. The calf is usually born tailfirst into its water world. It swims immediately to the surface for its first breath of air. The mother assists it if necessary. The calf is about 3 feet (1 meter) long at birth and weighs 25 to 35 pounds (11 to 16 kilograms).

During the first few weeks of life, the calf swims with the tip of one flipper touching the mother's body. The eye directed toward the mother is open, but the one on the other side is kept closed. Perhaps this keeps the infant from being distracted or startled.

Like all mammals, the baby dolphin nurses from its mother. Nursing must often take place while mother and calf are swimming or when the sea is rough. So the calf nurses frequently but very quickly. Its mother's milk glands have special muscles that squirt milk directly into the calf's mouth.

Dolphin calves and adults have few natural enemies. Killer whales and sharks are about the only creatures living in the sea that they need to fear. (Most dolphins live 25 to 35 years in the wild. Killer whales can live as long as 50 years.)

Sleeping in Naps

The sleeping habits of dolphins are unlike those of most other mammals. Instead of sleeping mainly at one time, dolphins take brief naps during both day and night. They may sleep for several minutes every couple of hours, although there does not seem to be a regular pattern. They can sleep while swimming, but their eyes generally open a little bit now and then during the nap.

▶A DOLPHIN'S SENSES

Sight. Though dolphins are aquatic animals, they have surprisingly good vision out of the water. We would expect them to see well under water but poorly in air, just as we can see well in air but poorly (without a face mask) under water.

But a dolphin can catch a fish or ball thrown from a distance of 50 feet (about 15 meters) or more. It will also respond to the movement of a hand at this distance.

It is not easy to tell how well a dolphin sees under water. This is because it can use echolocation below the surface to detect submerged objects. This remarkable ability can substitute for vision. (It is so important to dolphins that it will be discussed at greater length further on.)

Touch. The sense of touch in dolphins is highly developed. Dolphin skin has many nerve endings and is obviously very sensitive. A stranded animal, or one being transported out of water, will show a response to the lightest touch of a finger. Tame dolphins have shown a fondness for being stroked. When large brushes are fastened to flat rocks on the floor of the oceanarium, the dolphins frequently scratch themselves on the brushes with every evidence of enjoyment.

Smell and Taste. So far as is known, dolphins have no sense of smell. It is not surprising that this sense has been lost. A dolphin would have to breathe water in order to smell anything beneath the surface, and the ability to smell airborne odors would hardly be of value.

Most whales are thought not to have much of a sense of taste. However, a dolphin does seem to have taste buds at the base of the tongue. In deciding which fish they will accept, captive animals may be influenced by a sense of taste.

Hearing. Hearing is almost certainly the most important sense of all. Yet dolphins have no outer ear. The tube leading to the inner ear is so small that its opening is like a pinprick on either side of the head. The inner ear, however, is very highly developed.

The first experiments to test the hearing ability of dolphins were conducted at Marineland of Florida in 1952. Working with sound-producing equipment, scientists reported that the dolphins reacted (by swimming faster) to sounds up to 50,000 cycles per second. The upper limit of human hearing in air is only about 20,000 cycles per second.

A much more detailed experiment was performed a few months later with a bottlenose named Annie at Marineland. Annie was trained to come to a feeding station for a fish whenever she heard a sound signal. The researchers found that Annie responded to signals up to 120,000 cycles.

With underwater listening gear, the researchers could also hear her "talking" in the form of whistling and rasping noises. Some of the dolphin calls they later recorded were at the amazingly high frequency of 196,000 cycles per second.

▶ SOUND AND SONAR

Researchers now know that dolphins make a great variety of sounds. But they did not know the exact nature of most of these sounds until they suspended a hydrophone (underwater microphone) in an oceanarium tank where dolphins were kept. In addition to whistles and many forms of rasping and grating noises, the scientists heard the dolphins make barks, yaps, yelps, and mewing sounds. The rasping and grating noises were quite varied. Sometimes they resembled the sound of a door or gate swinging slowly on rusty hinges. This sound could always be heard when the dolphins were investigating some new object in the tank. When this object was the hydrophone, the "rusty hinge" noise was always very loud as a dolphin approached it and seemed to examine it.

The suspicion grew that dolphins could "see" with sound. This is known as **echolocation**. When sounds are sent out from an organ in the dolphin's head, they strike objects and bounce back. The direction of these echoes and the time it takes them to return tells the direction and distance of the objects. Further research has shown that many kinds of dolphins actively use sonar to gather information about their environment.

Bats are also known to have this ability. Even when blindfolded, a bat can avoid obstacles and catch insects on the wing. But if its ears are plugged as well, it is unable to "hear" where it is going. (You can read more about this in the article BATS in Volume B.)

Human use of echolocation has been chiefly in the sea, for water is a much better conductor of sound than air. With sonar (*so*und *na*vigation *r*anging) equipment, it is possible to locate a submarine or a school of fish or to detect an underwater obstacle. Sonar is also used to determine the depth of water under a ship. (You can read about this in more detail in the article RADAR AND SONAR in Volume QR.)

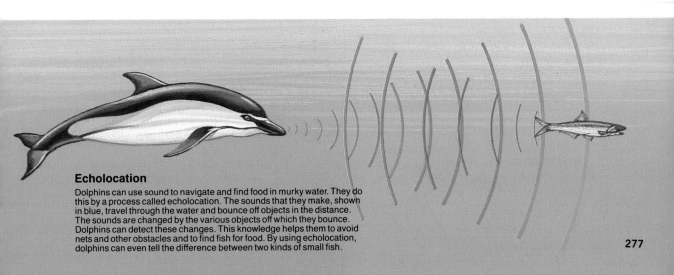

Echolocation

Dolphins can use sound to navigate and find food in murky water. They do this by a process called echolocation. The sounds that they make, shown in blue, travel through the water and bounce off objects in the distance. The sounds are changed by the various objects off which they bounce. Dolphins can detect these changes. This knowledge helps them to avoid nets and other obstacles and to find fish for food. By using echolocation, dolphins can even tell the difference between two kinds of small fish.

Dolphins' capacity to enjoy people makes them unique among wild animals. They seek out swimmers and boaters, apparently just for human companionship.

▶ DOLPHINS AND PEOPLE

Dolphins are "wild animals." In their natural state they are as free-living and untamed as deer or wolves. Yet unlike most wild creatures, they will voluntarily associate with people. Every seafarer knows how dolphins accompany boats and ships. They are not seeking food. Apparently they join up for company and sport. Even more remarkable are the dolphins that become friendly with human bathers. Tales of this have even come down to us from ancient times. A boy on a dolphin seen on Greek coins and vases tells of such a friendship.

Perhaps this friendliness accounts in part for the belief that dolphins will save a drowning person. There is no good evidence that this happens. If, by chance, a swimmer has been nudged or shoved, it seems most likely that this was done in play. However, dolphins are known to aid their own kind. An injured animal may be held at the surface between two of its companions.

Dolphin Play and Intelligence

Sometimes, when a ground swell is rolling in to shore, dolphins are seen riding the waves. When the water becomes shallow and a crest begins to form, they dive out of the wave and swim seaward to catch another. This is one form of play.

In captivity dolphins have invented a number of games. They use whatever objects are available, such as a feather shed by a bird. A dolphin will release the feather near the jet of water entering the tank. The feather drifts into the jet and goes shooting off. The dolphin pursues it, catches it, brings it back, and again releases it into the jet.

A small rubber inner tube can be tossed for a game of catch to someone standing by the tank. Tossed back, it may be caught on a dolphin's snout to "make a ringer." This is a game the dolphins taught people to play with them. Sometimes the dolphin had to toss the ring several times before the human player learned to throw it back, instead of dropping it in the water for the dolphin to fetch. Such creative play is a sign of intelligence.

Dolphins in captivity have also shown the ability to recognize themselves in a mirror. This self-recognition, another sign of intelligence, is a trait previously seen only in humans and the great apes.

Protecting Dolphins

The single threat to the world's dolphin population—and it is a serious one—comes from tuna fishing. Because schools of the yellowfin tuna often swim underneath schools of dolphins, the fishing nets are set around both. When the nets are pulled in, the dolphins are captured along with the tuna, and they drown. Hundreds of thousands of dolphins have been killed in this way. But the Marine Mammal Protection Act, passed by the U.S. Congress in 1972, restricts the number of dolphins that U.S. fishing fleets can kill yearly. New nets have been designed with a type of "gateway" at the top that permits the dolphins to escape while the tuna remain inside. In addition, a tuna boycott led major U.S. tuna companies to agree in 1990 to catch only tuna that swim separately from dolphins, further protecting these animals.

F. G. WOOD, JR.
U.S. Naval Missile Center

See also WHALES.

DOMINICA

Dominica is a small island nation, one of the Windward Islands of the Caribbean Sea. It is named for the Latin *Dies Dominica* (Day of the Lord), because Christopher Columbus first sighted the island on a Sunday in 1493. Beginning in the 1720's, Dominica changed hands four times between the British and the French. After 1783 it fell firmly under British rule until gaining independence in 1978.

People. Some 69,000 people live on Dominica, including 3,000 people of Carib Indian descent. But most Dominicans are descendants of black Africans brought from West Africa in the 1700's to work as slaves on the island's coffee and sugar plantations. Dominica's official language is English, although Creole, a French-based dialect, is also widely spoken. Nearly 80 percent of Dominicans are Roman Catholics; 15 percent are Protestants.

Land. Called the Nature Island of the Caribbean, Dominica offers very lush vegetation and nearly 200 species of birds and other animals. Tropical forests cover much of its mountainous interior. It is also home to several active volcanoes. The climate is mildly tropical. The port of Roseau is Dominica's capital and largest city.

FACTS and figures

COMMONWEALTH OF DOMINICA is the official name of the country.

LOCATION: Caribbean Sea.

AREA: 290 sq mi (751 km²).

POPULATION: 69,000 (estimate).

CAPITAL AND LARGEST CITY: Roseau.

MAJOR LANGUAGE: English (official).

MAJOR RELIGIOUS GROUP: Roman Catholic.

GOVERNMENT: Parliamentary democracy. **Head of state**—president. **Head of government**—prime minister. **Legislature**—House of Assembly.

CHIEF PRODUCTS: Agricultural—bananas, citrus fruits, mangoes, coconuts, cacao. **Manufactured**—processed food, furniture, shoes.

MONETARY UNIT: East Caribbean dollar (1 dollar = 100 cents).

Economy. Most Dominicans work in agriculture, fishing, and forestry; food processing; and trade. To raise revenue, the government is promoting tourism. Those who visit come to hike, dive, watch the whales, or attend the island's famous World Creole Music Festival. The addition of a giant stadium is expected to help Dominica attract world-class sporting events. Although better off in economic terms than many Caribbean countries, Dominica suffers from high unemployment, and nearly a third of its people are poor.

History and Government. Dominica was ruled for nearly 200 years by the British. In the 1800's, under British rule, Dominica's black population had little say in the way the island was governed. This began to change in the 1920's, and in 1967 Dominica was given control of its internal politics. In 1978, Dominica became an independent republic and a parliamentary democracy within the British Commonwealth. After independence, Eugenia Charles, the Caribbean's first female prime minister, led Dominica for 15 years.

In January 2004, Roosevelt Skerrit of the Dominican Labour Party (DLP) was appointed prime minister, replacing Pierre Charles, who died in office. General elections held in May 2005 resulted in a victory for the DLP and a first election as prime minister for Skerrit, who will serve a 5-year term.

Reviewed by LENNOX HONYCHURCH
Author, *The Caribbean People*

DOMINICAN REPUBLIC

The Dominican Republic is the second largest nation in the West Indies, after Cuba. Located in the Caribbean Sea between Cuba and Puerto Rico, it occupies the eastern two-thirds of the island of Hispaniola, which it shares with the nation of Haiti. The Dominican Republic takes its name from its capital, Santo Domingo (Saint Dominic), which was founded by the Spanish in 1496.

▶ PEOPLE

The majority of the Dominican people are mulattoes (persons of mixed black African and white ancestry). Most of the remainder are blacks of pure African ancestry or whites of Spanish descent.

Language and Religion. All Dominicans speak Spanish, and some people who live near the border with Haiti also speak Creole (a mixture of French and African languages with some Spanish and English words). English is also widely spoken.

Almost all of the people are Roman Catholic. *Romerías* (religious pilgrimages) from the countryside to town churches are a yearly event. Although Roman Catholicism is the official religion, the constitution guarantees freedom of worship.

Education. School attendance is required for children from age 7 to 14. Most large communities have elementary and secondary schools. The Autonomous University of Santo Domingo, founded in 1538, claims to be the oldest university in the Americas.

Way of Life. Dominicans are about evenly divided between urban and rural dwellers. The typical Dominican farm or village home is a small, simple house with a thatched roof. *Pastelitos* (pastries filled with fish or meat), *sancocho* (a stew of meat and vegetables), pork roasted on a spit, and *piñonate* (a coconut and milk dessert) are among the common dishes of the Dominican home.

Baseball is the national sport, and a number of Dominicans play in the major leagues

Top: Most Dominicans are of mixed Spanish and African ancestry. *Below:* The Bahoruco mountain range rises above the village of La Ciénaga on the Caribbean Sea.

in the United States. Dominican music and dance mirror their Spanish and African origins. The national dance is called the merengue.

▶ LAND

The terrain of the Dominican Republic is dominated by the Cordillera Central (central mountain range) and several smaller ranges, which run east and west. Luxurious green valleys lie between the mountains.

Along the northern coast, a narrow coastal plain ends suddenly at the base of a low mountain range, which rises sharply to about 4,000 feet (1,200 meters) and then descends to the pine-covered slopes of the Cibao to fertile lowlands.

The Cordillera Central is the country's most impressive landform. Pico Duarte, the highest peak in the West Indies, rises there to 10,414 feet (3,174 meters). Streams have cut deeply into the mountain slopes and formed many valleys and canyons.

The Neiba Valley is a lowland area in the southwest corner of the country. This region is flanked by two mountain ranges that rise steeply from the Caribbean. Lake Enriquillo lies below sea level in a plain at the bottom of the Bahoruco mountains. The lake, surrounded by tropical forests, is a popular hunting and fishing ground. Two rivers, the Yaque del Norte and the Yuna, drain the Cibao lowland. The Yaque del Sur flows to the Caribbean through a small valley west of the city of Santo Domingo.

Climate. The Dominican Republic lies in the belt of the northeast trade winds. A tropical country, it is warm or hot most of the time, with an average annual temperature of 77°F (25°C). Fresh ocean breezes bring cooler temperatures at night, especially near the coast.

About 70 inches (1,780 millimeters) of rain fall in the northern coastal region each year. The southern and southwestern regions receive a yearly average rainfall of 45 inches (1,140 millimeters).

The Dominican Republic's tropical climate and white sand beaches make it a popular destination for tourists.

Natural Resources. The Dominican Republic has many valuable natural resources. The most important among them are iron, nickel, gold, and silver.

▶ ECONOMY

The Dominicans who live in villages work in crafts and trades—pottery, shoe, and brick making; carpentry; and shopkeeping. In Santo Domingo the people hold jobs in trade, commerce, government, and construction. Tourism has become a major year-round industry.

Sugarcane is the leading commercial crop. The largest plantations are found in the coastal lowland around Santo Domingo and near Santiago and Puerto Plata, in the north. Coffee, cotton, and cacao are other major commercial crops. Quality tobacco is grown in many areas, including the Cibao lowland.

Thousands of small farms are owned by individual families. They produce rice, beans, potatoes, corn, bananas, and dairy products and raise livestock. Other foodstuffs must be imported. Cattle are valued for their meat and hides. Fishing is important along the coast.

The sugar plantations provide raw material for the country's largest industry, sugar processing. Bagasse (cane fiber) is used in making paper. Other agricultural products are processed, and small factories turn out a variety of consumer goods. But many manufactured items must be imported.

Industrial free-trade zones are located at San Pedro de Macorís and La Romana, east of Santo Domingo. In these zones, Dominican workers assemble electrical and electronic components, clothing, footwear, and other semifinished goods for re-export.

When the Spaniards arrived in Hispaniola, they found gold and silver in stream gravels. After a long period of neglect, these precious metals are being mined once again and have become a major export. Nickel and iron ore are mined and concentrated into ferronickel for export.

▶ **MAJOR CITIES**

Santo Domingo, the capital and largest city of the Dominican Republic, dates from 1496. It is the oldest permanent European settlement in the New World. It has a population of about 3 million. From 1936 to 1961 it was called Ciudad Trujillo, in honor of the country's dictator at that time.

Santo Domingo is a modern city of dazzling white mansions, hotels, shops, monuments, fountains, and handsome, broad

Santo Domingo, the republic's capital and largest city, was founded in 1496. It is the oldest permanent European settlement in the New World.

avenues. In 1930 a hurricane destroyed much of the city, although the national cathedral—begun in 1514 and the oldest church in the New World—survived. Some records show that the remains of Christopher Columbus, who died in Spain in 1506, were taken to Santo Domingo and buried in this cathedral in the early 1540's.

▶ **GOVERNMENT**

The country's constitution, ratified in 1996, provides for three branches of federal government—executive, legislative, and judicial. The executive branch is headed by a president, who serves as both head of state and government. The president is assisted by a cabinet of ministers chosen by him. The legislature, the Congreso Nacional (National Congress) has two houses—the Chamber of Deputies and the Senate. Direct elections to choose a president, vice president, and members of the legislature are held every four years. The judicial branch is headed by the Supreme Court. Governments for each of the 29 provinces are headed by governors appointed by the president. Municipalities are governed by elected councils.

FACTS and figures

DOMINICAN REPUBLIC (República Dominicana) is the official name of the country.

LOCATION: Eastern two-thirds of the island of Hispaniola in the Caribbean Sea.

AREA: 18,815 sq mi (48,730 km²).

POPULATION: 8,700,000 (estimate).

CAPITAL AND LARGEST CITY: Santo Domingo.

MAJOR LANGUAGE: Spanish.

MAJOR RELIGIOUS GROUP: Roman Catholic.

GOVERNMENT: Republic. **Head of state and government**—president. **Legislature**—Congreso Nacional (National Congress, composed of the Senate and Chamber of Deputies).

CHIEF PRODUCTS: Agricultural—sugarcane, coffee, cotton, cacao, tobacco, rice, beans, potatoes, corn, bananas, livestock, dairy products. **Manufactured**—processed sugar, textiles, cement, tobacco products. **Mineral**—iron, nickel, gold, silver.

MONETARY UNIT: Dominican peso (1 peso = 100 centavos).

▶ HISTORY

More than 1 million Arawak Indians once lived in large and well-organized villages in Hispaniola. The Indians were expert at fishing and cleared the woodland with stone axes to grow cassava (a starchy root), sweet potatoes, and cotton. They also worked soft metals, such as gold and silver. Their metalwork captivated the explorer Christopher Columbus, who claimed the island for Spain in 1492.

For a time, Hispaniola was Spain's leading trade center in the New World. But disease, earthquakes, hurricanes, and battles with the natives weakened the young colony. Most of the Spanish settlers withdrew to the area around Santo Domingo. But the island also attracted other European settlers and adventurers. In 1697, Spain was forced to recognize French control of the western part of the island (now Haiti). As a result two distinct and different cultures grew side by side—one Afro-Spanish, the other Afro-French.

Dominican independence was not easily won. The area was a Spanish colony until 1795. Control then alternated between France, Spain, and Haiti, which gained independence in 1804 after a slave revolt. The Dominican Republic declared its independence in 1844. Constantly threatened by Haiti, its government asked Spain to make the country a Spanish colony again in 1861. But independence was re-established in 1865.

Rafael Hipólito Mejía of the Dominican Revolutionary Party served one term (2000–04) as president of the Dominican Republic.

After independence, lawful government was the exception rather than the rule in Dominican political life. Dictator followed dictator and revolt followed revolt. The country's debts to other nations grew so fast that by 1905 the Dominican government agreed to allow the United States to collect its customs duties to pay these debts and stabilize the economy. After further violence, the United States sent Marines to occupy the whole country. The Dominican Republic was a U.S. protectorate from 1916 to 1924. Order was restored. But many Dominicans resented the occupation, and the Marines were withdrawn in 1924. The United States continued to collect Dominican customs duties until 1941.

In 1930, President Horacio Vásquez's efforts to assure his own re-election caused a revolt, successfully led by Rafael Leonidas Trujillo Molina, a man of humble origins, who had risen to colonel in the U.S.-trained National Guard. Trujillo quickly assumed the powers of a dictator.

The Trujillo dictatorship lasted from 1930 to 1961. Progress was made in providing public services, and in agricultural and industrial production. But Trujillo ruled to enrich himself and those of the army and upper classes who supported him. He was friendly to the United States, but he amended the constitution to keep himself in power. He was assassinated in 1961.

Democratic elections for president held in 1962 resulted in the victory of Juan Bosch. His government, however, was overthrown by the military in 1963. A revolt by Bosch's supporters in 1965 led to civil war. The United States, fearing expanded Communist influence, sent troops to the country. In new elections held in 1966, Bosch was defeated for the presidency by Joaquín Balaguer. Foreign troops were withdrawn that same year. Balaguer was re-elected in 1970 and 1974, but in 1978 he was defeated by Antonio Guzmán. Guzmán was succeeded as president by Salvador Jorge Blanco in 1982.

Recent Events. Balaguer was again elected president in 1986 and 1990. In 1994 he won a close contest marred by charges of fraud. To offset this, a special half-term election was held in 1996, which was won by Leonel Fernández Reyna. In 2000, Fernández was defeated by the opposition candidate Rafael Hipólito Mejía, a populist representing the Dominican Revolutionary Party. But in 2004, Fernández was returned to power.

HERBERT L. RAU, JR.
Chicago State University

DOMINOES

"Dominoes" is the name of many kinds of games that are played with flat, rectangular blocks or tiles that are also called dominoes. Early forms of dominoes first appeared in China, perhaps as early as the 1100's, and used blocks as dice. These games eventually spread to Europe, where the more familiar forms developed by the 1700's.

A domino has a long side that is twice the length of its short side. One face is divided by a line through the middle, so that there are two squares. Each square is marked with dots, or pips, or is left blank. The standard set has 28 pieces. The 6–6 domino, with six pips in each square, is the highest pair. Larger sets are also made with 9–9, 12–12, or 15–15 pairs, but most games are based on a 6–6 set.

At the beginning of any game, the dominoes are mixed face down. Each player then draws enough dominoes to give him or her the number needed to play the particular game. Any dominoes not drawn remain as the stock. There are many different games of dominoes, but draw dominoes is one of the most popular.

Draw Dominoes. Two or more people may play draw dominoes, but the best game is two-handed. Each player draws a predetermined number of dominoes (usually seven). Before selecting their dominoes, the players each draw one from the stock; the one who draws the domino with the most pips plays first.

The first player lays one domino face-up in the center of the table. This domino has two open ends, either of which is matched with a domino of the same number of pips by the next player. The pattern formed by the dominoes played is called the **layout**. A domino may be placed against an open end either to continue a straight line or to make a right-angle turn to keep the layout from running off the table. A domino that has the same number of pips on both ends is called a **doublet** and may be played crosswise to provide two open ends where there was only one before.

The players take turns, going around the table clockwise. If a player does not have a

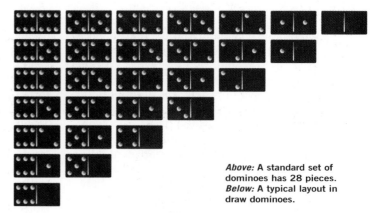

Above: A standard set of dominoes has 28 pieces. *Below:* A typical layout in draw dominoes.

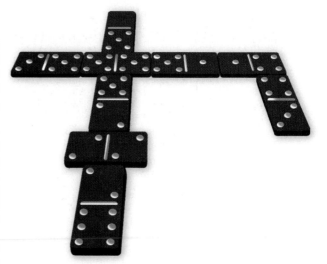

domino to match one of the open ends of the layout, he or she draws from the stock until a matching piece is found. If no matching piece is found among the stock, the player passes his or her turn to the next player.

The player who gets rid of all his or her dominoes first wins the deal. If play ends in a block (no player can play off a domino), the one who has the smallest number of pips on the dominoes remaining in his or her hand is the winner. If two tie for the low score, there is no score for the deal.

The winner scores the total number of pips on all the dominoes remaining in the hands of the loser or losers. When play ends in a block, there is no deduction for the dominoes left in the winner's hand. The first player to score 100 wins the game. Some players prefer to settle each deal as a separate game.

CHARLES H. GOREN
Author, *Goren's Hoyle*

DONATELLO (1386?–1466)

A leading figure of the early Renaissance in Italy was the sculptor Donatello. He was one of the first artists to study the art of ancient Greece and Rome, which had been largely ignored during the Middle Ages. Combining the forms of classical art with his own ideas, Donatello created sculptures that influenced artists for generations.

Donatello was born in Florence about 1386. The son of a wool comber, his real name was Donato di Niccolò di Betto Bardi. His first training was in a goldsmith's shop, but at age 17 he became an apprentice to the famous sculptor Ghiberti. In 1407 he began work at Florence Cathedral, where he carved a series of biblical figures. These statues were much more lifelike than the stiff sculptures of the Middle Ages. Donatello received many commissions from churches and private patrons. He decorated tombs and pulpits and made portrait busts and monuments. He also carved many reliefs—carvings raised from a flat surface. Using his knowledge of the new science of perspective, Donatello gave the illusion of depth to these reliefs.

This marble statue of a prophet was carved for Florence Cathedral by Donatello, a founder of Italian Renaissance sculpture. The statue is nicknamed *Zuccone* ("Pumpkin Head").

Donatello was greatly influenced by the ancient works of art that he saw during two trips to Rome, in about 1409 and 1432–33. This influence can be seen in his elegant and graceful bronze life-size statue of David. Another important bronze is in Padua. Known as *Gattamelata*, it is a statue of a Roman general on horseback.

Donatello died on December 13, 1466.

Reviewed by HOWARD HIBBARD
Columbia University

DONIZETTI, GAETANO (1797–1848)

Gaetano Donizetti was one of the most popular opera composers of the first half of the 1800's. He was born on November 29, 1797, near the Italian city of Bergamo. He studied music with Johannes Simon Mayr, a well-known composer of Italian operas.

Donizetti followed many of the operatic traditions established by the great Italian opera composer Gioacchino Rossini. Like Rossini, Donizetti wrote both serious and comic operas. His serious operas were usually based on historical or literary topics. For example, *Anna Bolena* (1830) is based on the tragic story of Anne Boleyn, wife of England's Henry VIII. *Maria Stuarda* (1835) deals with the similarly tragic life of Mary Queen of Scots. Donizetti's most popular serious opera is *Lucia di Lammermoor* (1835), based on Sir Walter Scott's *The Bride of Lammermoor*. It concludes with the stunning Mad Scene, in which Lucia's insanity is portrayed by her elaborate vocal displays.

Today Donizetti is better known for his comic operas depicting the antics of ordinary people, such as *The Elixir of Love* (1832) and *Don Pasquale* (1843). In *The Elixir of Love*, for example, Nemorino buys a love potion guaranteed to win his beloved Adina. Comic confusion erupts as the "love potion" turns out to be only wine, with no magic properties to soften Adina's heart.

Donizetti died in Bergamo on April 8, 1848. He had written more than seventy operas, as well as symphonies, chamber music, masses, and works for piano. His operas were performed all over Italy and also in London, Paris, and Vienna. In his serious operas, Donizetti introduced new levels of dramatic realism. His comic operas are light and airy, full of charming music and comic twists that continue to delight modern audiences.

WENDY HELLER
New England Conservatory of Music

DONKEYS. See HORSES (Related Animals).

DONNE, JOHN (1572–1631)

One of England's greatest poets, John Donne was born in London in 1572. His parents were Roman Catholics at a time when Catholicism was suppressed in England; his mother was related to the Catholic martyr Thomas More. Educated by Jesuits, Donne entered Oxford University at age 11 but due to his religion was not granted a degree.

In the 1590's Donne studied law in London's Inns of Court. Known as "Jack" Donne, a ladies' man, he wrote a number of love poems. Among the most famous are "A Valediction Forbidding Mourning," "The Extasy," "The Canonization," and "The Sun Rising." He often joined religious and seemingly unrelated images in a style that was later called metaphysical poetry.

In 1598 he became secretary to Sir Thomas Egerton, a well-known government official. He fell passionately in love with Lady Egerton's 16-year-old niece, Ann More, and secretly married her. He was dismissed from his post for this and was thrown into prison by Ann's father. After his release he lived in poverty and ill health for more than a decade. In 1615, to gain advancement under King James I, he became a priest in the Church of England. Eventually, he became dean of St. Paul's Cathedral (1621). Ann died in childbirth in 1617, and he never remarried.

Donne became the most famous preacher of his day. Besides sermons and other religious prose, he wrote sacred poems, including *Holy Sonnets,* "A Hymn to God the Father," and "Good Friday, 1613: Riding Westward." After rising from his deathbed to deliver a final sermon, he died in London on March 31, 1631.

> No man is an island, entire of itself; every man is a piece of the continent, a part of the main; … any man's death diminishes me, because I am involved in mankind; and therefore never send to know for whom the bell tolls; it tolls for thee.
>
> From *Devotions upon Emergent Occasions*

JAY L. HALIO
University of Delaware

DOOLITTLE, JAMES. See WORLD WAR II (Profiles: Allied Powers).

DORÉ, GUSTAVE (1832–1883)

The French artist Gustave Doré was one of the most imaginative and popular book illustrators of the 1800's. Doré was born in Strasbourg on January 6, 1832. From the time he was a small boy, Doré loved to draw, and his exceptional talent quickly became apparent. At age 15 Doré moved to Paris, where he lived for the rest of his life. The lively sense of humor in his sketches attracted the attention of a Parisian publisher, who offered him a job drawing caricatures (comically exaggerated pictures) for a magazine.

Doré is best known for his illustrations of literary classics. His first effort, for an 1854 edition of Rabelais's *Gargantua and Pantagruel,* was an immediate success. In all, he illustrated nearly one hundred books, including Cervantes' *Don Quixote* (1863), Perrault's *Fairy Tales* (1862), and the Bible (1866).

Doré's favorite medium was wood engraving, although he also made many lithographs. He usually drew directly on the woodblock, and an engraver cut the block for printing.

Doré wanted above all to be appreciated as a painter. He exhibited his paintings in Paris

Illustration by Doré for *Little Red Riding-Hood*.

with little success. In London, however, he had a greater following, and he opened his Doré Gallery there in 1869.

Doré's visits to London led to the publication of one of his most fascinating books, *London. A Pilgrimage* (1872), which records life in England's capital, from the poor people living in the slums to the upper classes living in their elegant homes. Doré died in Paris on January 23, 1883.

HELEN MULES
Metropolitan Museum of Art

DOS PASSOS, JOHN (1896–1970)

John Dos Passos was a leading figure in American literature in the 1920's and 1930's. He is best known for *U.S.A.*, a trilogy (series of three novels) covering thirty years of American life.

Dos Passos was born in Chicago, Illinois, on January 14, 1896. He spent much of his early life traveling in Europe with his mother. After graduating from Harvard University in 1916, he studied architecture in Spain, then served as an ambulance driver in World War I (1914–18). His first novels were based on his experiences in the war.

Throughout the 1920's, Dos Passos was involved in modern-art movements and left-wing (radical) politics. He first won wide attention with the novel *Manhattan Transfer* (1925), a portrait of New York City told through dozens of related sketches. He also wrote several plays and published essays in left-wing magazines.

Along with many other writers and intellectuals of his time, Dos Passos was disillusioned with postwar American life. The stock market crash of 1929 and the Great Depression that followed convinced him that fundamental change was necessary in American society.

In the 1930's, Dos Passos published his most important books, the three novels of the *U.S.A.* trilogy. These three volumes, *The 42nd Parallel* (1930), *1919* (1932), and *The Big Money* (1936), describe what Dos Passos saw as the decline of the United States into a nation of commerce and greed. The books were notable for the experimental techniques Dos Passos used. Weaving together fact and fiction, *U.S.A.* offers a panoramic chronicle of American life in the first three decades of the 1900's.

Dos Passos broke with the left in the late 1930's, and he gradually moved toward a more conservative point of view. The many novels, biographies, and books of history he wrote in these later years were celebrations of the American past and of American individualism. He died in Baltimore, Maryland, on September 28, 1970.

PETER CONN
Author, *Literature in America: An Illustrated History*

DOSTOEVSKI, FËDOR (1821–1881)

Fëdor Dostoevski was one of Russia's greatest novelists. His deep insights into human nature greatly influenced later writers. His novels are filled with suspense and action. They portray the suffering of characters who are in some way injured by society and who rebel by breaking its laws.

Dostoevski was born in Moscow on October 30, 1821. After attending engineering college in St. Petersburg, he became an army engineer but resigned at age 22 to pursue a writing career. His first novel, *Poor Folk* (1846), was an immediate success.

In 1849, Dostoevski was arrested for attending meetings that criticized the government. He was condemned to death, but moments before his execution his sentence was changed to four years of hard labor in Siberia, followed by a period of service in the Siberian army.

After his return to St. Petersburg in 1859, unsuccessful business ventures and his addiction to gambling led Dostoevski into debt. He  also suffered from epileptic attacks. His marriage to Anna Snitkin in 1867 brought him some peace. The couple traveled abroad to avoid creditors, and Dostoevski continued to write.

Dostoevski's four greatest novels were published between 1866 and 1880. *Crime and Punishment* (1866) explores the psychology of a murder. *The Idiot* (1868) provides a portrait of a good man living in a flawed world. *The Possessed* (1872) describes political upheaval in Russia. *The Brothers Karamazov* (1880) tells of four brothers and the events surrounding their father's murder. All four novels are considered masterpieces of world literature.

Dostoevski died in St. Petersburg on January 28, 1881.

THAÏS S. LINDSTROM
Author, *A Concise History of Russian Literature*

DOUGLAS, STEPHEN A. (1813–1861)

Stephen Arnold Douglas was a politician and a leading Democrat in the years before the Civil War. Born on April 23, 1813, in Brandon, Vermont, he later settled in Illinois, where he became a lawyer and entered politics. A superb campaigner, Douglas was elected district attorney in 1835, state legislator in 1836 and 1837, state supreme court judge in 1841, and U.S. representative in 1843. In 1847 he became a U.S. senator.

Douglas was often called the Little Giant because of his massive head and short legs. Nevertheless, he was ambitious and confident and a powerful orator. As chairman of the Senate committee on territories, he promoted the idea of popular sovereignty, which would allow the settlers of a territory to decide whether or not to permit slavery. Douglas himself had no strong feelings about slavery. He helped pass the Compromise of 1850, which included popular sovereignty for the New Mexico and Utah territories. Then in 1854, he pushed for popular sovereignty in Kansas and Nebraska. When Kansas became a slaveholding state, many people were angered by the extension of slavery and took action by forming the Republican Party.

In 1858, Abraham Lincoln, an Illinois Republican, challenged Douglas for his Senate seat, and the two participated in a series of now-famous debates. Although Douglas won the election, the debates damaged his popularity in the South, while they gave Lincoln national recognition. In 1860, Democrats in the North nominated Douglas for the presidency, but Southerners opposed him. Lincoln, the Republican nominee, was elected president.

Douglas pleaded for a peaceful compromise between North and South. But when the Civil War broke out in 1861, he strongly urged his followers to support Lincoln and the Union. He died in Chicago, Illinois, on June 3, 1861.

ARI HOOGENBOOM
City University of New York, Brooklyn College

See also KANSAS-NEBRASKA ACT; LINCOLN, ABRAHAM (The Lincoln-Douglas Debates).

DOUGLAS, WILLIAM O. (1898–1980)

William O. Douglas served as an associate justice (1939–75) of the U.S. Supreme Court for 36 years, the longest term in the Court's history. He is remembered for his commitment to civil rights and for defending governmental protection of personal rights and freedoms, as described in the First Amendment.

William Orville Douglas was born on October 16, 1898, in Maine, Minnesota. His family later moved to Yakima, Washington, where William grew up in poverty and became sensitive to the needs of the poor and disadvantaged. After graduating from Whitman College (1920) in Washington and Columbia Law School (1925) in New York City, he taught at Columbia and Yale universities, specializing in business law.

In 1937, Douglas was named chairman of the Securities and Exchange Commission by his good friend President Franklin D. Roosevelt. Then in 1939, Roosevelt appointed him to the Supreme Court.

Douglas became a controversial figure on the Court. He supported people's right to privacy, but he was criticized by conservatives who objected to his tolerant attitudes on issues concerning obscenity and civil disobedience and to his concern for the protection of accused criminals.

Among Douglas' most influential opinions were *Federal Power Commission* v. *Hope Natural Gas Company* (1942), which set a precedent in federal rate regulation, and *Griswold* v. *Connecticut* (1965), which overturned a state law against the use of birth control. His professional publications include *A Living Bill of Rights* (1961), *Points of Rebellion* (1970), and *The Court Years* (1980). A naturalist by avocation, Douglas also published several books on nature and conservation, such as *Of Men and Mountains* (1950). He died on January 19, 1980.

GEORGE CAREY
Georgetown University

DOUGLASS, FREDERICK (1817–1895)

Frederick Douglass was one of the most dynamic leaders of the abolition movement against slavery in the United States. He was born Frederick Augustus Washington Bailey in 1817 in Tuckahoe, Maryland, the son of a white father and a slave mother. He learned to read and write while working as a house servant in Baltimore, Maryland. Later he was put to work in the Baltimore shipyards. Determined to gain his freedom, he declared, "I wish myself a beast, a bird, anything rather than a slave." In 1838 he escaped north to New Bedford, Massachusetts, and changed his name to Douglass.

He made his first public speech in 1841 at a meeting of the Massachusetts Anti-Slavery Society. The audience was deeply moved by his story, although some doubted that such a well-spoken man could have been a slave. Douglass then wrote the autobiographical *Narrative of the Life of Frederick Douglass* (1845), which established him as one of America's leading orators and writers.

In 1845, Douglass traveled to England to lecture, earning enough money to buy his freedom. He later settled in Rochester, New York, and began publishing an antislavery newspaper, *North Star* (1847–51), later called *Frederick Douglass's Paper* (1851–60). His Rochester home became a refuge on the Underground Railroad.

When the Civil War (1861–65) broke out, President Abraham Lincoln authorized Douglass to organize two regiments of black soldiers. Douglass later served as a U.S. marshal for the District of Columbia (1877–81) and as minister to Haiti (1889–91). He died on February 20, 1895. His home at 1411 W. 11th Street, S.E., Washington, D.C., is preserved as a national memorial.

DANIEL S. DAVIS
Author, *Struggle for Freedom: The History of Black Americans*

See also ABOLITION MOVEMENT; AMERICAN LITERATURE (Slave Narratives); UNDERGROUND RAILROAD.

DOVE, RITA FRANCES. See OHIO (Famous People).
DOVER. See DELAWARE (Cities).

DOVES AND PIGEONS

The names "dove" and "pigeon" are interchangeable; they refer to any of more than 300 species of birds belonging to the Columbidae family. They are found on all continents except Antarctica in habitats ranging from urban areas to backyards to lush tropical forests. The species commonly seen on city streets is the rock pigeon (formerly called rock dove).

Characteristics of Doves and Pigeons. Doves and pigeons are short-legged birds with short necks and small heads. The smallest species is the plain-breasted ground dove of Central and South America, which grows to about 6 inches (15 centimeters) in length. The largest is the Victoria crowned pigeon of New Guinea, which can reach up to almost 30 inches (76 centimeters) in length.

The feathers of North American species range in color from reddish to combinations of grays and whites or mottled browns and black. Many European species have green feathers, some with purple, orange, or blue.

Doves and pigeons eat mostly seeds and fruit, although a few eat insects. Members of the Columbidae family are the only North American birds that can drink water by sucking; other birds can drink only by dipping their bills in water and tipping their heads back so the water will run down their throats.

These birds typically make low-pitched, mournful calls. Some species, such as the

Rock pigeon

mourning dove of North America, make a whistling sound with their wings when they take flight. Others create a sharp, slapping noise by beating their wings together during mating displays.

Rock pigeons are famous for their ability to return to their homes from hundreds of miles away. Studies suggest they may use a variety of clues, including the sun, the Earth's magnetic field, and polarized light. Because of this homing ability, domesticated rock pigeons, called homing, or carrier, pigeons, have been used for many years to carry messages. Racing these birds is a popular sport.

Victoria crowned pigeon

The Lives of Doves and Pigeons. During the breeding season, adult males will puff out their throat feathers and strut aggressively in front of females. Doves and pigeons will sometimes breed with the same individual for more than one mating season.

Pairs nest on the ground, on ledges, on bridge supports, or in rock cavities. The female builds the nest, using grass, twigs, and other material provided by the male.

Females lay one or two pale, oval eggs, and the parents take turns incubating them. When the young hatch, both parents feed them with "crop milk," a special substance secreted from the lining of their crops (part of the digestive tract that stores food before it is digested).

Worldwide, many species of doves and pigeons are hunted. Many are threatened with extinction, particularly those native to small islands. The passenger pigeon, another North American species, once had numbers of more than 2 billion, but it was hunted into extinction in the early 1900's.

ALLISON CHILDS WELLS
Natural Resources Council of Maine

DOWN SYNDROME

Down syndrome is a genetic disorder caused by the presence of an extra chromosome. The syndrome is named for John Langdon Down, an English physician who first wrote about the disorder in 1866. It occurs in approximately 1 of 800 births.

Chromosomes are cell structures that are composed of genes—the basic units that carry inherited characteristics. Chromosomes are numbered and arranged in 23 pairs. Most children who are born with Down syndrome have an extra chromosome number 21. Because there are three rather than two chromosomes, the disorder is often referred to as **trisomy 21**. For unknown reasons, older women have a greater chance of having a baby with Down syndrome.

Children with Down syndrome have distinguishing physical features, such as eyes slanting upward at the outer corners, flattening of the bridge of the nose, or small hands. More than one-third of children with Down syndrome have heart disorders, most of which can be corrected with surgery. Most people with Down syndrome have some, but not all, of these physical traits.

Children with Down syndrome usually have mild to moderate mental retardation. Compared with other children, youngsters with Down syndrome tend to be slower in learning to walk and talk. Still, children with Down syndrome have more similarities to other children than they have differences. They attend school, and most grow up to live independent and productive lives.

Although Down syndrome can now be detected before birth, there is still no cure. However, children with the disorder usually benefit from a caring home environment and special educational programs that include sensory stimulation, exercises to improve muscle function, and opportunities to increase their intellectual function.

CAROL MATTSON PORTH
Author, *Pathophysiology: Concepts of Altered Health States*

DOYLE, SIR ARTHUR CONAN
(1859–1930)

Arthur Conan Doyle, creator of the master detective Sherlock Holmes, was born on May 22, 1859, in Edinburgh, Scotland. His grandfather and uncles were distinguished artists. His father, however, earned a small salary as an architect for the Scottish government, and Arthur, his younger brother, and his six sisters were raised in poverty.

In 1877, Arthur entered Edinburgh University as a medical student. One of his professors there, Dr. Joseph Bell, was noted for the remarkable accuracy with which he diagnosed his patients' illnesses. It was Bell who inspired the character of Sherlock Holmes, whose powers of deduction help him solve the most baffling cases.

Young Doyle worked his way through medical school as a physician's assistant and as a ship's doctor on a seal-hunting expedition to the Arctic. After becoming a physician in 1881, he shipped out to sea again, this time on a trading voyage to Africa. But his most reliable source of income, even in these early days, was his short-story writing. He sold his first story, an adventure tale about diamond hunting in South Africa, when he was 20 years old. His sales were steady, although they did not make him rich, and he achieved some fame as a storyteller.

In 1882, Doyle began a medical practice in Southsea, a suburb of Portsmouth, England. This practice was busy but not profitable, and early in 1891 he set himself up in London as an eye specialist.

In the meantime, he had written his first published novel, *A Study in Scarlet* (1887), in which he introduced his immortal characters, the brilliant consulting detective Sherlock Holmes and his companion Dr. Watson. Yet it was not for this work that he first won popular and critical recognition as a novelist, but for *Micah Clarke* (1889), a historical romance set in England in the 1600's. This book was followed by his best-known historical romance, *The White Company* (1890), a story of English soldiers during the Hundred Years' War. These and other historical novels were the books in which Doyle took the greatest pride, but they are little read today.

Not one eye patient ever consulted Doyle in his London office, and he spent all of his time writing. His works suddenly became so successful that in August 1891 he gave up medicine entirely. It was at this time that he began writing a series of short stories about Sherlock Holmes for a new magazine called the *Strand*. With these stories, collected as *The Adventures of Sherlock Holmes*, he developed and popularized the modern detective story.

Within a year, Sherlock Holmes made Doyle wealthy and world famous. But Doyle grew tired of his creation, and in the story *The Final Problem* (1893), Holmes was killed in a struggle with his archenemy, the evil Professor Moriarty.

After Holmes's "death," Doyle wrote stories about the medical profession, an autobiographical novel called *The Stark Munro Letters* (1895), and *The Exploits of Brigadier Gerard* (1896), about a cavalry officer in Napoleon's army, among many other very popular books. When the Boer War broke out in 1899, he helped organize a field hospital and went to South Africa with it as a doctor. On his return to England, he wrote a book defending British conduct in the war, and for this he was knighted in 1902.

But Sherlock Holmes remained so popular with readers that Doyle revived him. *The Hound of the Baskervilles,* the most famous Sherlock Holmes novel, was serialized in the *Strand* in 1901–1902. The last book featuring the detective, *The Casebook of Sherlock Holmes,* appeared in 1927.

In the years before World War I, Doyle wrote more nonfiction and a number of plays, which he produced himself. He also wrote science fiction, the best of which is *The Lost World* (1912). He ran twice for Parliament and lost, solved several real-life mysteries, and, though happily married, worked to make divorce laws more liberal.

After his brother and eldest son died in World War I, Doyle converted to spiritualism, the religious belief that the living can communicate with the dead through persons called mediums. He spent the rest of his life writing books and lecturing the world over on this subject. His autobiography, *Memories and Adventures*, was published in 1924. He died on July 7, 1930, at the age of 71.

JACK W. TRACY
Author, *The Encyclopaedia Sherlockiana*

A scene from a Sherlock Holmes story follows.

THE RED-HEADED LEAGUE

Sherlock Holmes was famous for his powers of observation and deduction. This means that he was able to draw very accurate conclusions about a person by carefully observing his or her dress and appearance. Holmes's unique abilities are demonstrated in this scene from "The Red-Headed League" in which a client visits the great detective in his rooms at 221B Baker Street, London. The story is narrated by Holmes's friend Dr. Watson.

Our visitor bore every mark of being an average commonplace British tradesman, obese, pompous, and slow. He wore rather baggy gray shepherd's check trousers, a not over-clean black frock-coat, unbuttoned in the front, and a drab waistcoat with a heavy brassy Albert chain, and a square pierced bit of metal dangling down as an ornament. A frayed top-hat and a faded brown overcoat with a wrinkled velvet collar lay upon a chair beside him. Altogether, look as I would, there was nothing remarkable about the man save his blazing red head, and the expression of extreme chagrin and discontent upon his features.

Sherlock Holmes's quick eye took in my occupation, and he shook his head with a smile as he noticed my questioning glances. "Beyond the obvious facts that he has at some time done manual labour, that he takes snuff, that he is a Freemason, that he has been in China, and that he has done a considerable amount of writing lately, I can deduce nothing else."

Mr. Jabez Wilson started up in his chair, with his forefinger upon the paper, but his eyes upon my companion.

"How, in the name of good-fortune, did you know all that, Mr. Holmes?" he asked. "How did you know, for example, that I did manual labour? It's as true as gospel, for I began as a ship's carpenter."

"Your hands, my dear sir. Your right hand is quite a size larger than your left. You have worked with it, and the muscles are more developed."

"Well, the snuff, then, and the Freemasonry?"

"I won't insult your intelligence by telling you how I read that, especially as, rather against the strict rules of your order, you use an arc-and-compass breastpin."

"Ah, of course, I forgot that. But the writing?"

"What else can be indicated by that right cuff so very shiny for five inches, and the left one with the smooth patch near the elbow where you rest it upon the desk?"

"Well, but China?"

"The fish that you have tattooed immediately above your right wrist could only have been done in China. I have made a small study of tattoo marks and have even contributed to the literature of the subject. That trick of staining the fishes' scales of a delicate pink is quite peculiar to China. When, in addition, I see a Chinese coin hanging from your watch-chain, the matter becomes even more simple."

Mr. Jabez Wilson laughed heavily. "Well, I never!" said he. "I thought at first that you had done something clever, but I see that there was nothing in it, after all."

DRAFT, OR CONSCRIPTION

A draft (conscription) law requires people to serve in the armed forces. Since ancient times, armies have consisted either entirely of volunteers or a mixed force of volunteers and draftees.

The Draft in the United States. During the American Revolution (1775–83), George Washington led a largely volunteer national army, but the 13 states required some men to serve in local militias. For most of the 1800's, the United States relied totally on volunteers for its small regular army and its part-time National Guard (the successor to state militias). It relied mostly on volunteers for its wartime armies. The country changed course, however, during the Civil War (1861–65), when volunteering began to decline. Both the Confederacy (Southern states) and the Union (Northern states) passed conscription acts.

In both the North and South, people in certain jobs, such as ministers, did not have to serve. Draftees could hire substitutes or pay a large sum of money to avoid service. Because wealthy people could avoid serving and the poor could not, opponents in both the North and South said the draft made the Civil War a "rich man's war but a poor man's fight." In the North, there were anti-draft riots. The unpopular draft provided few soldiers. Most Civil War soldiers were volunteers.

It was not until World War I (1914–18) that the United States raised a wartime army mainly through conscription. The Selective Service Act of 1917 created the Selective Service System to administer the draft. The act forbade substitutes and avoidance fees and provided for men between 18 and 45 to be drafted by lottery (random selection by number). Draft boards then decided who among those called would serve and who would be deferred (not called upon to serve at that time). Deferments were meant for people who were needed by their families or who did crucial work in a war industry. The law classified those who objected to war based on their religion as **conscientious objectors** to violence. They were allowed to serve unarmed in noncombat branches. The World War I army was a mixed force: 72 percent were draftees and 28 percent were volunteers.

Between World Wars I and II, the United States returned to its peacetime tradition of a small volunteer regular army and part-time National Guard. But in 1940, when Nazi Germany invaded Western Europe, Congress adopted the country's first prewar national draft. It was similar to the 1917 draft but applied at first to men aged 21 to 35. After the United States entered the war in 1941, the draft was expanded to include men aged 18 to 37. It permitted conscientious objectors to serve in noncombat military branches or civilian public service camps. Once again the United States had a mixed force of draftees and volunteers. The country drafted 10 million men between 1940 and 1945; 6 million men and 350,000 women enlisted.

Changes in the Draft. When the World War II draft law expired in 1947, the armed forces briefly returned to solely voluntary enlistment. Then in 1948, Congress adopted a selective draft that required 21 months of military training and service for draftees, most of whom were between the ages of 18 and 21. There were many exemptions and deferments, including deferments for college students.

During most of the Cold War with the Soviet Union, the United States relied on a mixed force of draftees and volunteers. In the Korean War (1950–53) and the Vietnam War (1965–73), draftees were assigned two-year tours of duty. In 1969, nearly 90 percent of the U.S. infantry riflemen fighting in Vietnam were draftees. That year, growing protest against the war and inequality in the draft led to reforms in selective service.

The reforms abolished student deferments, established a draft lottery for men aged 19 or 20, and allowed more men to qualify as conscientious objectors. However, draft evasion, flight, and protest continued, and several thousand people were put in prison.

Congress ended the draft in 1973 and draft registration in 1975. Since 1973, the United States has maintained an all-volunteer force. But in 1980, when the Soviet Union invaded Afghanistan, Congress reinstated compulsory draft registration for men aged 18 to 25. The draft has not resumed, however. That would require approval by Congress.

JOHN WHITECLAY CHAMBERS II
Rutgers University
Author, *To Raise an Army: The Draft Comes to Modern America*

See also PEACE MOVEMENTS.

DRAGONFLIES

Visit a pond on a sunny summer day and you are sure to see dragonflies. With their big round heads and long slender bodies, these fast-flying insects look like miniature helicopters zooming back and forth along the water's edge.

There are about 6,500 species of dragonflies, which belong to the order Odonata. They live on every continent except Antarctica.

Fossil evidence shows that the first dragonfly-like insects appeared on Earth about 325 million years ago. The largest of these had wingspans of about 30 inches (75 centimeters). Flying insects virtually identical to the dragonflies of today were buzzing around 200 million years ago, during the Jurassic period.

Characteristics of Dragonflies. Adult dragonflies have long, thin bodies with 10 segments in the abdomen; three pairs of legs; two enormous compound eyes; and a pair of sensory antennae. They also have two pairs of long, narrow wings marked by a network of fine veins. Their wingspans can reach about 5½ inches (14 centimeters), and they can fly up to 35 miles (56 kilometers) an hour. At rest, dragonflies hold their wings out flat on either side of their body. Many species are brightly colored.

Dragonflies are fierce predators and will eat most other kinds of insects. They seize their prey with sharp, serrated jaws. (The name "Odonata" means "toothed ones.")

Damselflies, a related group, also belong to the Odonata order. They look similar to dragonflies but are smaller and more slender, and they fold their wings back over their body when not in flight.

The Lives of Dragonflies. Dragonflies typically begin their lives in the water, where they hatch from eggs. The young wingless dragonflies, called **nymphs**, look like long-legged beetles. They live underwater for months or even years, molting, or shedding, their outer skin at intervals as they grow larger. They use a hooked, extendable part of their mouth called the **labium** to snatch up a wide variety of prey, including zooplankton, snails, water beetles, small fish, tadpoles, and even other dragonfly nymphs.

When they are ready to take on their winged adult form, nymphs emerge from the water. They cling to reeds, stones, or other ob-

Above: Dragonflies have large heads, long bodies, and two pairs of wings that they hold out to their sides when resting. *Left:* Damselflies are smaller and more slender than dragonflies, and they fold their wings together above their body when resting.

jects as they molt one last time. The free-flying adults may have as little as a week or as long as several months to mate before they die. In some species, males will protect a particular patch of open water by sitting on a nearby perch or by buzzing back and forth over it. Males will also engage in spectacular aerial fights over territory or a female. After mating, the female dips the tip of her abdomen into the water over and over, or shakes it just above the surface, to deposit her eggs. The eggs may hatch in a few days or not until the following spring, beginning the dragonflies' life cycle again.

CYNTHIA BERGER
Author, *Wild Guide: Dragonflies*

DRAGONS

Fire-breathing dragons have lived in people's imaginations for thousands of years. Dragons were thought to combine the features of many different animals—the scaly body and long tail of a reptile, the claws of lions, batlike wings, and jaws like a crocodile's. When they were not stealing maidens or terrorizing villages, these solitary creatures were said to live in caves, where they guarded great treasures.

Dragons around the World. Dragons are featured in the myths and legends of many cultures. Ancient depictions of dragonlike creatures have been found on Babylon's Ishtar Gate, in Egyptian hieroglyphic writing, and in Chinese scroll paintings. In Greek mythology, the Chimera was a cave-dwelling, fire-breathing dragon with a goat's body, a lion's head, and a snake's tail. Chinese dragons had long, twisting reptilian bodies and short, clawed feet, but they also had turned-up snouts, whiskers, antlers, and hairy ears. They were kindhearted creatures who symbolized rain clouds and brought good fortune. Dragons in the Middle East were thought to cause eclipses by devouring the moon. In Aztec mythology and art, dragons had bird and serpent features (such as in the feathered serpent god Quetzalcóatl) and represented both good and evil. In ancient India, it was said that men and boys hunted dragons in the foothills of the Himalayas to gather glittering jewels from the creatures' skulls.

Persian epics abound with tales of heroes fighting gold-guarding dragons. A famous European legend concerns Saint George, the patron saint of England, who supposedly killed a dragon to save the daughter of a Libyan king. Numerous other tales told of medieval knights (including King Arthur), saints, and other heroes who destroyed the evil monsters in their lairs.

Origins of Dragon Myths. Some scholars suggest that the idea of dragons developed out of primitive human fears of dangerous animals such as large snakes and birds of prey. Dragons may have also been inspired by early discoveries of the fossils of extinct animals. For example, many fossil dinosaur skulls found in China have horns and jaws that resemble the dragons depicted in ancient Chinese art. In Europe, fossils of huge cave bears, surrounded by heaps of smaller bones, may have led to tales of great dragons lurking in caves and preying on humans. The famous dragon statue at Klagenfurt, Austria

Tales of dragons have been told in cultures around the world. According to one legend, Saint George killed a dragon to save the daughter of a king.

(1590), was based on the skull of an Ice Age woolly rhinoceros discovered in Germany about 1330. When fossil hunters in the American West first found fossils of large, winged dinosaurs (later named pterosaurs), they called them "flying dragons." And scientists have even found that calcite crystals sometimes form in ancient skulls, which may explain the jewels said to be found in the heads of dragons.

ADRIENNE MAYOR
Folklorist

Queen Elizabeth I bestows knighthood on Francis Drake after his voyage around the world. Drake is shown kneeling on the deck of his ship, the *Golden Hind*.

DRAKE, SIR FRANCIS (1540?–1596)

Francis Drake was one of England's greatest sailors. He was born about 1540 near Tavistock, England, and at an early age was apprenticed to a ship's captain. In 1567, Drake commanded his own ship on a trading expedition to the West Indies. The tiny English fleet was attacked by the Spanish. In the fight only Drake's ship and one other escaped. After that battle, Drake felt that he had a score to settle with the Spaniards.

Drake's private feud with Spain fitted in perfectly with the plans of Queen Elizabeth I. The nations of Europe were engaged in a struggle for new lands and for control of the seas. Spain, especially, had rich colonies in America. Spanish galleons brought home treasures that made Spain wealthy and powerful. Elizabeth wanted King Philip II of Spain to respect England's growing sea power. Besides, she felt that the English treasury could well use some Spanish gold.

In 1572, Drake landed in Panama with two ships and 73 men. He took the town of Nombre de Dios from the surprised Spanish soldiers and captured 30 tons of silver destined for King Philip. When Drake returned to England, he was both rich and famous.

In 1577, Drake won the Queen's permission for another expedition—this time to the Pacific Ocean. No English ship had ever ventured into the Pacific. Drake sailed through the Strait of Magellan and into the body of water that now bears his name—the Drake Passage.

He sailed north and attacked the Spanish settlements in Chile and Peru. Then, when his ship the *Golden Hind* could hold no more gold and silver, Drake headed farther north. He sailed about as far as Vancouver Island, looking in vain for a passage to the Atlantic Ocean.

How was Drake to get back to England? He could not return by the same route. The Spaniards would surely be waiting for him. One choice remained—to cross the vast Pacific Ocean and sail around the world. Only Ferdinand Magellan had done this before.

After stopping at the Spice Islands (Moluccas), Drake arrived back in England in 1580. The voyage had taken three years. Queen Elizabeth knighted Drake. He was elected mayor of Plymouth and a member of Parliament.

Soon, however, all Europe was buzzing with news about the armada that Spain was building to invade England. With 30 ships, Drake sailed right into the harbor of Cadiz, Spain, and set fire to many of the ships being built there. Laughingly he boasted that he had singed (burned) the King of Spain's beard. In 1588 the armada of more than 130 ships sailed into the English Channel. Drake was vice admiral of the fleet that destroyed many of the Spanish ships. Only about half of the great armada returned home. King Philip's hope of conquering England was ruined.

Drake set out for the West Indies again in 1595. It was to be his last voyage. On January 28, 1596, he died and was buried at sea.

THOMAS W. PERRY
Boston College

DRAMA

Drama is a type of literature that tells a story through the dialogue and action of its characters and is designed to be performed in front of a live audience. Drama has existed for thousands of years in almost every culture. Because drama allows the audience to enter imaginatively into the lives of the characters, it is an important way for people to know and understand the world around them.

Drama had its beginnings in religion. Early peoples used rhythm, music, and dance to worship gods of the sun and the moon, of the seasons, the harvest, or the hunt. Sometimes masks were used that made people appear more like the animals or spirits they were imitating. Dances, then story and dialogue (conversations) grew out of these imitations. Eventually stories came to be valued for their own sake rather than for their religious content, and drama and other forms of literature were born.

Drama can be divided according to whether it emphasizes the serious or the comic or a mixture of the two elements. Serious plays are often called **tragedies**, especially if they end with the death of the leading character, but sometimes they are merely called dramas. Comic plays, or **comedies**, em-

Drama has many faces.
Above left: Blue Man Group.
Above: Laurence Olivier in Shakespeare's *Hamlet*.
Left: A masked character in a Japanese Noh play.

phasize the ridiculous aspects of human behavior. Mixed types most often end happily. The most common of the mixed types are **melodrama** and **tragicomedy**. A melodrama is a suspenseful story in which a villain threatens an admirable character, but good eventually triumphs over evil. A tragicomedy tells a serious story that ends happily.

Drama has developed differently in various parts of the world and during various periods of history.

▶ CHINESE DRAMA

In China, performances that incorporated dance, music, and ritual go back as far as 1500 B.C. Performances originally occurred in temples, and when secular (nonreligious) theater developed, the playhouse was a platform with a roof that resembled that of a temple.

The most popular form of Chinese theater, called **Beijing Opera**, developed about A.D. 1800. These plays are based on myths, history, legends, or domestic situations. The written text is not as important as the acting. Actors improvise freely, cutting and changing the script as they wish. Lines of dialogue are delivered through a combination of speaking, chanting, and singing. The characters follow standard types, such as the young female, the old lady, the young man, the old man, and the warrior.

Music and colorful costumes are used in Beijing Opera, but the only stage properties, or **props**, are a wooden table and a few chairs. With these few items, as well as some symbolic props, the stage can represent a throne room, a mountain, a chariot, or just about any other kind of scene. The people in charge of the props wear ordinary clothes and change the scenes in full view of the audience.

▶ **JAPANESE DRAMA**

Japanese drama was influenced by the Chinese. But the Japanese people were more aware of social and economic rank than the Chinese. They created a drama for the nobility called **Noh**, or Nō, and a popular drama called **Kabuki**. Noh plays, which developed in the late A.D. 1300's, are ceremonial. A chorus (group of actors) sits on the stage—a platform with a temple roof—and chants the

Masks representing comedy and tragedy are the internationally recognized symbols of drama.

connecting parts of the story. All the principal characters wear masks.

Kabuki is younger than Noh. A woman dancer named Okuni is credited with beginning Kabuki about 1600. The plays are concerned with daily life as well as mythical subjects. At first women were permitted to perform in the plays, but the government later forbade them.

Noh plays keep to old methods, subjects, and costumes. Kabuki is freer and appeals to popular taste.

▶ **INDIAN DRAMA**

Indian, or Hindu, drama was divided into two general kinds. An outdoor festival celebrated the lives of kings who became gods. A partly religious, poetic drama was performed in palaces.

Indian drama existed before A.D. 100, but no one knows its exact age. The finest drama is *Shakuntala*, written by Kalidasa during the A.D. 400's. This and another play called *The Little Clay Cart* (300's–700's) are the best-known examples of Indian drama.

Performances were given on specially built, raised platforms, with draperies as background. The actors were excellent pantomimes and suggested their own scenery through descriptive movement.

▶ **ANCIENT GREEK DRAMA**

Ancient Greek drama has influenced the course of modern playwriting more than the drama of any other culture. It was born in festivals and rituals honoring the god Dionysus. These festivals included **dithyrambs**, in which a chorus and choral leader sang and danced a hymn to Dionysus. These dithyrambs gradually developed into plays, and in 534 B.C. Athens instituted a contest for tragedy. That date is said to mark the beginning of theater in the Western world.

Greek plays were performed in large outdoor theaters that could hold up to 20,000 spectators. The audience sat on a hillside, and at the base of the hill was a large circle called the **orchestra** that served as the performance space. Behind the orchestra was the *skene*, a building that was used for the entrances of

---

WONDER QUESTION

What is the most frequently performed drama in history?

Although an exact number is impossible to determine, the most frequently performed play is probably William Shakespeare's tragedy *Hamlet*. First produced in 1600–01 in London, *Hamlet* has since been performed around the world. It has been translated into dozens of languages and staged in a variety of settings, from the traditional medieval castle to a modern corporate boardroom. The complex title character has attracted and challenged the outstanding actors of every period. The play's timeless themes and the beauty of its language seem to appeal to nearly every generation and culture.

In ancient Greece, actors performed before an audience seated on a hillside. Drama is performed the same way today at a theater in Epidaurus dating from the 300's B.C.

the actors, for changing costumes and masks, and for scenic background. The *deus ex machina* ("god from a machine") was operated from the roof of the *skene*. The machine lowered into the orchestra a god who could step into the play to untangle the plot or deliver a final judgment on the characters.

Although the plays featured many female characters, all the performers were male and all wore masks that covered the entire head. The plays were divided into scenes, between which choral passages were sung and danced by a group of 15 performers.

Greek tragedies were based on myths and legends. Though thousands of Greek tragedies were written, only about 30 survive. Most of these surviving plays were written by the three greatest Greek tragedians—Aeschylus, Sophocles, and Euripides. Aeschylus is best known for *The Oresteia*, a trilogy of plays showing the evolution of the concept of justice. Sophocles, the most revered tragedian, wrote the famous plays *Oedipus Rex* and *Antigone*. Euripides wrote controversial plays, such as *Medea* and *The Bacchae*, that questioned traditional values.

Comedy was also important in ancient Greek drama. The leading writer of comedy was Aristophanes, a master of satire and farce. **Satire** is the use of ridicule to expose the follies and vices of humankind. The humor in a **farce** is based on exaggeration. Two of Aristophanes' best-known comedies, *The Frogs* (405 B.C.) and *Lysistrata* (411 B.C.),

comment on absurd conditions of his day. For more information on the drama of ancient Greece, see GREECE, LITERATURE OF in Volume G.

▶ ROMAN AND MEDIEVAL DRAMA

Plays by only three Roman dramatists have survived. Plautus and Terence wrote comedies, while Seneca wrote tragedies. All their plays were based on Greek models, and they in turn significantly influenced the plays of Shakespeare's time.

By the beginning of the Middle Ages in the A.D. 500's, the Christian Church had become a dominant force and had condemned all forms of drama. There was no organized theater in Rome. Actors and entertainers became wanderers. During the next centuries many traveling minstrels, comedians, jugglers, and clowns performed throughout Europe. During the Christmas season, mummers (villagers and farmers playing buffoons) performed in the manor houses of wealthy people.

In the 900's, the church began introducing dramatic scenes into its services to illustrate its teachings more vividly. For the first time the resurrection of Jesus and other episodes from the Bible were enacted before the people. At first, these plays were performed inside the churches and were acted, in Latin, by the clergy and choirboys. When the plays moved out into courtyards and town squares, they were performed in the **vernacular** (the

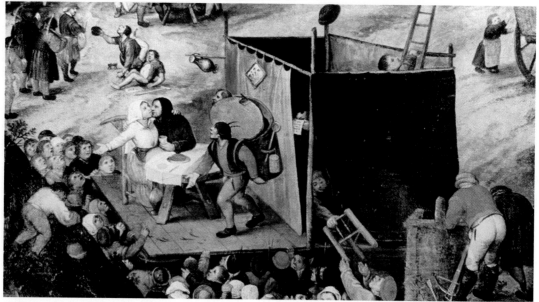

Medieval players performed at village festivals on wagons drawn from one location to another or on raised platforms that served as stage, scenery, and dressing room.

local language) by members of the community. There were three main types of medieval drama. **Miracle plays** portrayed episodes from the lives of saints. **Mystery plays** were based on biblical incidents. And **morality plays** focused on ordinary people and demonstrated the desirability of virtue over vice.

Trade guilds (associations) began to compete with one another in presenting festivals of religious plays. In some towns, the plays were performed on wagons drawn from one location to another. The wagons represented tombs, stables, houses, thrones and palaces, the mouth of hell, and other settings in the plays. In other towns, the plays were performed on large, fixed platforms.

▶ RENAISSANCE DRAMA

The Renaissance began in Italy during the 1300's and gradually spread throughout Europe. The word "renaissance" means

The plays of William Shakespeare tower above those of the many other talented dramatists of the Renaissance.

"rebirth," and the period of the Renaissance was characterized by a renewed interest in art, literature, and learning.

Until the 1550's, drama continued to focus on religious issues. After the Protestant Reformation, rulers throughout Europe banned plays with religious subject matter. However, due to the Renaissance, a secular form of theater was emerging. At schools and colleges, people were studying the old Roman plays and were writing imitations of them.

In Italy *commedia dell'arte* (comedy of professional players) emerged as entertainment for the lower classes. This form used only the outline of a plot, with the actors improvising the dialogue and stage business. *Commedia dell'arte* relied on stock, or type, characters including, among others, Dottore, a ridiculous Doctor of Bologna; Il Capitano, a boastful Spanish captain; Pantalone, a foolish merchant from Venice; and the two servants Brighella and Arlecchino.

The best Renaissance drama occurred in England during the reign of Elizabeth I (1558–1603). The first public theater in England, the Red Lion, was built in 1567. Many of William Shakespeare's plays were performed at the Globe, the most famous Elizabethan theater, which opened in London in 1599. In these theaters, the audience stood in an open-air yard called the pit, in front of or around the sides of the stage; or they were seated in boxes around and above the stage. Little scenery was used, but the costumes were rich and colorful.

Among the early Renaissance playwrights were Thomas Kyd and Christopher Marlowe. Marlowe's powerful blank (unrhymed) verse in *Tamburlaine the Great* (1587), *The Tragical History of the Life and Death of Dr. Faustus* (1588–93), *The Jew of Malta* (about 1589), and *Edward II* (1592) opened the way for Shakespeare.

William Shakespeare was the outstanding genius of his time. He is credited with writing 38 plays, and among his best are *Hamlet* (1600–01), *Othello* (1604–05), *King Lear* (1605–06), *Macbeth* (1605–06), and *The Tempest* (1610–11). His use of words and his mastery of dramatic action have never been surpassed. For more information, see the biography of William Shakespeare in Volume S.

Shakespeare overshadowed the many other talented writers of the era—writers such as Ben Jonson, John Fletcher, Francis Beaumont, John Webster, John Ford, and Thomas Dekker.

▸ **DRAMA IN SPAIN AND FRANCE**

Lope de Vega is often considered the foremost Spanish dramatist. It is estimated that he wrote between 800 and 1,800 plays. His plays, such as *The Foolish Lady* (1613) and *The Sheep Well* (1614), are filled with action and intrigue. Another major writer was Pedro Calderón de la Barca. Among his poetic dramas are *Life Is a Dream* (1636) and *The Mayor of Zalamea* (1642).

Unlike the rest of Europe, Spain did not outlaw religious drama, and both Lope de Vega and Calderón wrote numerous religious plays. Since these plays were performed as part of the church's festival of Corpus Christi and since they celebrate the Christian sacraments, they are known as *autos sacramentales*.

In France, drama did not thrive until the 1630's, when playwrights sought to return to the literary traditions of Greece and Rome. Eventually they adopted an approach to writing plays in which strict rules were followed. Among the demands, some of the most important were that all plays should be written in five acts, that all deaths and violence should occur offstage, and that the unities of time, place, and action should be observed. (That is, a play had to be about a single event and take place in one day and in one location.) This style of writing is usually called **neoclassicism**.

Pierre Corneille, in his *Le Cid* (1637), ushered in the greatest era of French playwriting. *Le Cid* was extremely popular, but it violated many of the new rules and provoked a bitter argument that ended in strong criticism of Corneille. Thereafter, the rules were generally accepted and dominated European standards for the next 150 years. French neoclassical tragedy reached its highest point with Jean Racine. His *Phèdre* (1677), a story about a woman's overpowering love for her stepson, is usually considered the greatest of all French tragedies.

French comedy reached its peak with the plays of Jean Baptiste Poquelin, who took the stage name of Molière. Molière was an actor, playwright, and director of a theatrical company. Molière's plays were great favorites with the French court. *School for Wives* (1662), *Tartuffe* (1664), *The Doctor in Spite of Himself* (1666), *The Miser* (1668), and *The Imaginary Invalid* (1673) are still much admired for their wit, characterizations, and commentary on contemporary life and manners. *Tartuffe*, which satirizes religious

French playwright and actor Molière, shown here as Julius Caesar, wrote witty social commentaries that were favorites with the French court.

hypocrisy, was so controversial that it was banned for several years.

▶ THE RESTORATION AND 1700'S

Oliver Cromwell's Puritan revolution in England had closed the theaters for 18 years because the Puritans considered the theater immoral. On the restoration of the monarchy in 1660, Charles II reopened the theaters, and new plays were written. For the most part they were devoted to the manners of the times, and they were performed for the entertainment of the upper classes. The plays were

Most French dramatists of the 1700's modeled their plays on those of Corneille, Racine, and Molière. The best of the playwrights from the 1700's was Pierre Beaumarchais, author of *The Barber of Seville* (1775) and *The Marriage of Figaro* (1783).

Germany's first important dramatist was Gotthold Ephraim Lessing, who achieved fame with *Miss Sara Sampson* (1755), a domestic tragedy set in England, and *Minna von Barnhelm* (1767), a comedy about lovers divided by economic and political forces.

▶ ROMANTICISM

In the late 1700's, the neoclassical style of writing was gradually replaced by **romanticism**, a movement that looked to the plays of Shakespeare as ideals of dramatic writing. The unities of time and place made way for large-scale historical stories in which feeling and instinct were considered the best bases for human behavior. Romanticism created a heroic and colorful vision of life.

Faust, by Johann Wolfgang von Goethe, is perhaps the greatest of all romantic dramas. In its depiction of its hero's search for fullfillment, it reflects the sweeping themes associated with romanticism.

Romanticism first developed in Germany. Perhaps the greatest of all romantic dramas is *Faust* (part I, 1808; part II, 1831), by Johann Wolfgang von Goethe. It depicts its hero's

sophisticated and witty, full of gossip and courtship. William Wycherley set the style for the period with *The Country Wife* (1675) and *The Plain Dealer* (1676). After him came William Congreve, whose *Love for Love* (1695) and *The Way of the World* (1700) established him as the foremost writer of Restoration comedy.

Much of this comic spirit was recaptured when *She Stoops to Conquer* (1773), by Oliver Goldsmith, was produced. It was followed by Richard Brinsley Sheridan's *The Rivals* (1775) and *The School for Scandal* (1777).

search for fulfillment. Friedrich von Schiller wrote a number of plays about significant historical figures, such as *Don Carlos* (1787), *Mary Stuart* (1800), and *Wilhelm Tell* (1804).

Due to the continuing influence of neoclassicism, romanticism arrived late in France. Victor Hugo's *Hernani* (1830) created a major storm of protest because it deliberately violated the neoclassical rules. Another popular writer of romantic drama in France was Alexandre Dumas *père* ("father"). In Russia, Aleksandr Pushkin wrote that country's most important romantic drama, *Boris Godunov* (1825).

▶ REALISM

The romantic writers set their plays in picturesque and exotic regions. The realists turned to the familiar and the everyday, to the known instead of the imagined world.

In France, realistic drama was introduced in the 1850's by Alexandre Dumas *fils* ("son") and Emile Augier, who treated such contemporary issues as the rights of illegitimate children and the influence of the church in politics. They always defended accepted moral standards and did little to disturb the prejudices of their audiences. It remained for the Norwegian Henrik Ibsen to shock audiences so deeply that he came to be considered the father of modern theater.

Although Ibsen's subjects did not differ greatly from those of Dumas and Augier, he was the most controversial playwright of the period because he always questioned accepted social conventions and moral standards. For example, *A Doll's House* (1879) ends with the heroine leaving her husband and small children—a deeply shocking action in Ibsen's time—so that she can search out truth for herself. Similar unconventional behavior is found in plays such as *Ghosts* (1881), *The Wild Duck* (1884), and *Hedda Gabler* (1890).

In England, George Bernard Shaw made drama a vehicle for discussion and ideas. Shaw differed from Ibsen in writing comedies, rather than serious plays, in which he discredited accepted prejudices. Among the best known of his many plays are *Arms and the Man* (1894), *Man and Superman* (1903), *Major Barbara* (1905), and *Pygmalion* (1912). Shaw's plays sometimes seem too talkative, but it is witty talk, about worthwhile ideas. Oscar Wilde was also a great master of wit. He rivaled Shaw in brilliant dialogue, especially in *Lady Windermere's Fan* (1892) and *The Importance of Being Earnest* (1895).

Next to Shaw, John Galsworthy was the most popular of the realists in England. He used the stage to show up injustice and human follies. Among his best plays are *The Silver Box* (1906) and *Strife* (1909).

In Germany, Gerhart Hauptmann brought new life to drama with his realistic plays *Before Sunrise* (1889) and *The Weavers* (1892), which emphasized the plight of workers. In Austria, Arthur Schnitzler, a doctor by profession, brought the objectivity of his consult-

Henrik Ibsen's *A Doll's House* shocked audiences of its day because of its heroine's unconventional behavior. Ibsen continually questioned accepted moral standards.

ing room to such plays as *Anatol* (1893) and *Reigen* (1903).

In Russia, Nikolai Gogol began the trend toward realism with his comedy *The Inspector General* (1836), a satire on Russian provincial life and government corruption. *A Month in the Country* (1850), by Ivan Turgenev, was the first Russian play to focus realistically on the mental and emotional lives of the characters. The great period of Russian theater is usually said to have begun with the Moscow Art Theater and the plays of Anton Chekhov, especially *The Sea Gull* (1896), *The Three Sisters* (1901), and *The Cherry Orchard* (1904). All depict with great compassion the aimless lives of ineffectual characters.

While realism was gaining acceptance, another more demanding approach to writing, called **naturalism**, was developing in France. Its primary advocate was Émile Zola, who admired the realists but thought they distorted truth through too much concern for theatrical effects. In plays such as *Thérèse*

Raquin (1873), Zola championed a kind of drama that showed the results of heredity and environment in human behavior. He argued that playwrights should be as objective as scientists in their observation of life. Some of Zola's followers said that dramatists should merely place a "slice of life" on the stage. Few naturalist plays won audience acceptance.

In Sweden, August Strindberg called himself a naturalist for a time. His plays *The Father* (1887) and *Miss Julie* (1888) develop one of Strindberg's favorite themes, the struggle between men and women for dominance. Strindberg later wrote a number of nonrealistic plays that were to influence much drama in the 1900's. These plays, which include *A Dream Play* (1902) and *The Ghost Sonata* (1907), borrowed many of their effects from dreams and nightmares.

▶ EUROPEAN DRAMA IN THE 1900'S

Strindberg's later plays were related to two other approaches to playwriting—**symbolism** and **expressionism**. The symbolists believed that those things one can observe directly—the primary concern of the realists and naturalists—are unimportant. Rather, they argued, we live in a world so mysterious that we can never fully understand it, and we can only suggest those perceptions we do have through symbols. The major symbolist playwrights were Maurice Maeterlinck, best

known for *Pelléas and Mélisande* (1892) and *The Blue Bird* (1908)—a play about the search for happiness—and Paul Claudel, who used religious symbols in such plays as *The Tidings Brought to Mary* (1912). Symbolism was primarily used in France.

Expressionism was primarily used in German drama. The expressionists believed that the human spirit had been distorted by industrialized society. They wished to create a "new society," so that a "new man" could develop freely. Expressionist drama often depicted characters as having standardized, mechanical responses. In performance, the visual elements often included distorted shapes, unnatural colors, and mechanical movements to suggest how life had been perverted. The German playwrights Georg Kaiser and Ernst Toller were major expressionist writers. In his expressionist play *R.U.R.* (for "Rossum's Universal Robots," 1921), the Czech dramatist Karel Čapek invented the word and the concept of robots.

In Germany during the 1920's, expressionism gave way to **epic theater**, popularized by Bertolt Brecht. Brecht used a combination of narrative devices, slide projections, songs, and dialogue to provoke audiences into thinking about and evaluating what they saw in the theater. He wanted them to go out and change society. Among Brecht's best-known plays are *The Threepenny Opera* (1928), *Mother Courage and Her Children* (1938–39), and *The Good Woman of Setzuan* (1938–40).

Following World War II, German dramatists often focused on guilt and responsibility. Perhaps the best of these writers was the Swiss-born Friedrich Dürrenmatt, whose plays include *The Visit* (1956) and *The Physicists* (1962). During the 1960's, German playwrights developed "documentary drama" or "theater of fact," based on actual events and with dialogue often taken from transcripts of court trials or hearings. Writers of this type of play include Peter Weiss,

In satirical plays such as *The Threepenny Opera*, Bertolt Brecht sought to make audiences aware of social ills.

Heinar Kipphardt, and Rolf Hochhuth. Since the 1970's, German dramatists have taken a very critical view of society, depicting it as selfish, depraved, and unjust, especially to the working classes. Among these recent writers are Franz Xaver Kroetz and the Austrian Thomas Bernhard.

During the early 1900's, Irish drama underwent a renaissance. Major playwrights included William Butler Yeats (*Cathleen ni Houlihan*, 1902) and Lady Augusta Gregory (*Kincora*, 1905), both of whom wrote plays about Irish myths and peasants. John Millington Synge, in plays such as *Riders to the Sea* (1904) and *The Playboy of the Western World* (1907), used distinctive language to create a poetic realism. Sean O'Casey blended comedy and tragedy in *The Plough and the Stars* (1926) and other works.

In Spain, Federico García Lorca wrote the finest plays since the Spanish Golden Age of Lope de Vega and Calderón. Works such as *Blood Wedding* (1933), *Yerma* (1934), and *The House of Bernarda Alba* (1936) have strong female characters and rich, poetic imagery.

In England, Noël Coward wrote sophisticated comedies reflecting the spirit of the 1920's and 1930's. Among his best works are *Hay Fever* (1925), *Private Lives* (1930), and *Blithe Spirit* (1941). Verse drama (plays written in a poetic meter) also flourished in England from the 1930's to the 1950's. Successful verse dramas include T. S. Eliot's *Murder in the Cathedral* (1935), a dramatization of the martyrdom of Saint Thomas à Becket, and Christopher Fry's comedy *The Lady's Not for Burning* (1949).

By the mid-1950's, English drama seemed to be on the decline, but a revival began with *Look Back in Anger* (1956), a play by John Osborne that attacked British values and class consciousness. Osborne was the first and most important of Britain's "angry young men," who wrote of discontented working-class people. In the following decades, several

The English dramatist Tom Stoppard wrote "comedies of ideas" that featured clever use of language.

British playwrights achieved international acclaim, including Peter Shaffer, author of *Equus* (1973) and *Amadeus* (1979). However, the two most praised were Tom Stoppard and Harold Pinter. Stoppard was known for his "comedies of ideas" and clever use of language, as seen in *Rosencrantz and Guildenstern Are Dead* (1967), *The Real Thing* (1982), and *Arcadia* (1993). Pinter wrote plays with an air of mystery or menace, and in works such as *The Homecoming* (1965) and *Old Times* (1971) he combined unexplained or ambiguous motivations with authentic, seemingly natural dialogue. Other successful British playwrights of this time included Alan Ayckbourn, David Hare, Caryl Churchill, and Martin McDonagh.

One recurring theme of drama in the 1900's was the inability of human beings to find certainty because each person has a unique personal version of the truth. One of the first dramatists to develop this theme was the Italian Luigi Pirandello in such plays as *Right You Are If You Think You Are* (1917) and *Six Characters in Search of an Author* (1921). Following World War II, French playwrights in particular were concerned about the lack of certainty in life. Jean-Paul Sartre, in plays such as *The Flies* (1943) and *No Exit* (1944), sought to demonstrate that there are no dependable external guides for human behavior and that all of us must find and live by our own values. This philosophy is usually called **existentialism**.

This view was further developed by a group of writers called **absurdists**, who believed that human beings are trapped in a world where all ideas and actions are meaningless. The major absurdist dramatists included the Nobel Prize winner Samuel Beckett, with plays such as *Waiting for Godot* (1953) and *Endgame* (1957); Eugene Ionesco, author of *The Chairs* (1952) and *Rhinoceros* (1960); and Jean Genet, author of *The Balcony* (1956).

Later writers were not as bleak as the absurdists. Italy's Dario Fo, winner of the 1997

Classic American dramas of the mid-1900's include Tennessee Williams' *A Streetcar Named Desire* (*left*) and Arthur Miller's *Death of a Salesman* (*above*).

Nobel Prize, wrote acclaimed social and political satires such as *The Accidental Death of an Anarchist* (1970). In the 1990's, French dramatist Yasmine Reza earned international praise for plays such as *Art* (1994).

▶ EARLY AMERICAN DRAMA

During its early years American drama was mainly borrowed from England. Also from England came the Puritan idea of the theater as evil, which held back its development. Thus theater in New England lagged behind theater in Virginia and the Carolinas.

In 1752, the first professional company arrived in Williamsburg, Virginia, but it was not until 1787 that an important play was written by an American. This was *The Contrast*, by Royall Tyler. William Dunlap wrote or translated many plays, notably *André* (1798), about a Revolutionary War spy.

American playwriting never reached great heights in the 1800's, but some notable plays were written, including *Fashion* (1845), by Anna Cora Mowatt, and *Uncle Tom's Cabin* (1852), adapted by George L. Aiken from Harriet Beecher Stowe's novel. Throughout the 1800's melodrama was the most popular kind of theater, and the form reached its peak in the works of Augustin Daly (*Under the Gaslight*, 1867) and the British-born Dion Boucicault (*The Octoroon*, 1859).

▶ AMERICAN DRAMA OF THE 1900'S

In the early 1900's, theater in the United States was controlled by people interested primarily in profit. Writers with new ideas had little opportunity to see their work performed. But slowly the feeling grew that a new and more creative kind of theater was needed. As a result, a number of "art" or "little" theaters were founded. These new theaters provided an outlet for new writers, among them Eugene O'Neill. In 1920, O'Neill's play *Beyond the Horizon* won the first of his four Pulitzer Prizes. One of O'Neill's best plays, *Long Day's Journey into Night* (1941), deals with his family's troubled relationships. Other successful pre-World War II American playwrights included Robert E. Sherwood, Maxwell Anderson, Lillian Hellman, Clifford Odets, William Saroyan, and Thornton Wilder, author of the continually popular play *Our Town* (1938).

After World War II, two new writers gained international fame. Tennessee Williams, in *The Glass Menagerie* (1945), *A Streetcar Named Desire* (1947), and *Cat on a Hot Tin Roof* (1954), showed sensitive characters attempting to cope with the harsh realities of their world. Arthur Miller, in *Death of a Salesman* (1949) and *The Crucible* (1953), portrayed characters destroyed by the prejudices and distorted values of their society.

Other major dramatists of the postwar period included William Inge and Edward Albee, winner of three Pulitzer Prizes and author of *Who's Afraid of Virginia Woolf?* (1962).

The 1950's saw the emergence of "off-Broadway" theaters (small New York City theaters located away from the main theatrical district), and the 1960's saw the development of still more out-of-the-way, or "off-off-Broadway," theaters. In addition, the 1960's brought the establishment of numerous professional theaters (regional companies) in cities throughout the United States.

In addition to recent hits from London, most plays now seen on Broadway were first performed off-Broadway or in regional theaters. Among the prominent playwrights who have emerged from these theaters are Sam Shepard (*Buried Child*, 1978), Lanford Wilson (*Talley's Folly*, 1979), Beth Henley (*Crimes of the Heart*, 1979), David Mamet (*Glengarry Glen Ross*, 1983), Marsha Norman (*'night Mother*, 1983), Wendy Wasserstein (*The Heidi Chronicles*, 1988), and Paula Vogel (*How I Learned to Drive*, 1997). Each of these plays won the Pulitzer Prize.

Since Lorraine Hansberry's *A Raisin in the Sun* (1959)—a poignant story of an African American family—an increasing number of playwrights have addressed the concerns of minority groups. One of the most successful has been August Wilson, who won Pulitzer Prizes for *Fences* (1985) and *The Piano Lesson* (1987). In an attempt to document and examine the African American experience, Wilson wrote a cycle of plays, each set during a different decade of the 1900's. Louis Valdez was the most influential Hispanic American playwright, and his *Zoot Suit* (1978) was the first Hispanic play performed on Broadway. The leading Asian dramatist of the late 1900's was David Henry Hwang, best known for *M. Butterfly* (1988). There have also been a number of plays dealing

The Piano Lesson is one of a cycle of plays by the American playwright August Wilson that examine the African American experience.

with homosexuality, most notably Tony Kushner's Pulitzer Prize-winning *Angels in America* (1992).

Throughout the 1990's and into the 2000's, American drama continued to grow in diverse ways. Individuals and theater companies began composing "performance pieces," in which dialogue is less important than images, movement, or sound. Instead of seeing a traditional story, the audience experiences visual images that may arouse different associations in each spectator's mind. Practitioners of this kind of theater include Robert Wilson, Blue Man Group, and the Canadian company Cirque du Soléil ("Circus of the Sun"). There were also a number of plays performed by a single actor, often based on the performer's own life. Such writers and performers include Anna Deavere Smith and Eric Bogosian.

ROBERT E. GARD
University of Wisconsin, Madison
Revised by JOHN FLEMING
Texas State University

See also MUSICAL THEATER; PLAYS; THEATER.

Instead of traditional dialogue, Cirque du Soléil uses acrobatics, music, and dance to engage the audience.

Ballet at the Paris Opera, completed in 1877 by French artist Edgar Degas, shows the different effects that can be achieved by the use of pastels.

DRAWING

Drawing is an art form used to create an image or design. Drawings are made in many different ways for many different purposes. An artist might create a drawing to be a completed work of art. Or a drawing might be made as a plan for another type of art work, such as a painting or sculpture. Often an artist will quickly make sketches, or first drawings, with a pencil or charcoal to show the main idea or image. Later, these sketches can be used for more detailed and complete drawings. Sketching helps students· and artists practice and develop skill in making lines and shapes.

▶DRAWING MATERIALS

Artists can select from many types of materials to create their drawings. Images can be created with pencil, charcoal, pastel, ink, felt tip marker, or any combination of these materials. With the exception of charcoal, all are produced in a variety of colors. The dry mediums of charcoal, pencil, and pastel are available in a range of hardness, each of which produces a different effect. Pencils, pens, and brushes come in a variety of widths designed to make different kinds of lines.

Paper is the most commonly used surface to draw on, but almost any suitable material can be used. Prehistoric people drew on clay or on the stone walls of caves. Artists in the Middle Ages drew on parchment, made from the skin of sheep. Today, most drawing papers are manufactured from wood pulp and are available in an assortment of colors, weights, and sizes. Drawing papers vary in absorbency and texture. The paper will affect the way the sketch or drawing will look. Smooth papers highlight fine detail and delicate shading. Coarse papers are used when more texture is desired.

Pencil

The pencil is the most common medium used to make drawings. The "lead" in a pencil is actually a synthetic material called graphite. Pencils with very hard leads are called H pencils and are graded by number according to the hardness of the lead. An 8H pencil would be harder than a 2H pencil. Pencils with very soft lead are called B pencils and are also graded by number, indicating the softness of the lead. An 8B pencil would have a softer lead than a 2B pencil. Artists choose pencils with varying degrees of hardness or softness to achieve desired effects. For example, a 3H pencil would make a thin, smooth line, while a 6B pencil would make a very dark, broad line.

DEVELOPMENT OF A STILL LIFE DRAWING

(1)

In order to draw this vase of flowers, the artist must study it carefully, noting its characteristics.

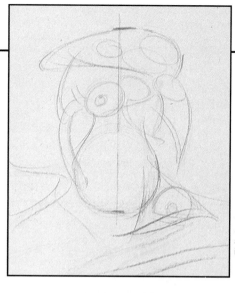

(2)

The artist first draws a rough sketch of the vase of flowers, using a sketching pencil, and fills in basic shapes and outlines. At this stage, detail is not important.

(3)

Next, the artist refines the lines and shapes. Crosshatching and several tones of color are added.

(4)

More colors are applied and rubbed in with fingertips to further define forms. At this stage it is easy to imagine what the completed drawing will look like.

(5)

The forms are made lighter or darker to show where the light is coming from and where the shadows are. The artist adds more detail, textures, and color to complete the drawing.

MATERIALS USED IN DRAWING

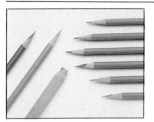

Pencil is the most common medium used for drawing. Pencils can be hard or soft and can create various effects.

Pencil marks made over rubber cement will disappear when cement is removed.

A soft pencil used on smooth paper, then erased, creates a gradated tone.

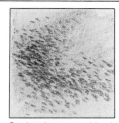

Gradated tones combined with stippling produce a textured effect.

Charcoal is manufactured in hard, medium, or soft sticks, as well as in pencil form.

Charcoal applied to textured paper results in a rough effect.

Crisscrossing lines (crosshatching) adds texture to a drawing.

Using a finger to spread charcoal varies the tone in a drawing.

Pastels are powdered pigments of color mixed with gum or resin to form a stick.

Rubbing pastel with a finger gives a hazy effect to the tone.

Twisting the hand while using a pastel stick results in a line of varied width.

Different edges of the pastel stick can be used when crosshatching.

Pen and ink allows an artist to achieve a variety of effects because of the wide selection of pens and inks that is available.

Different amounts of pressure create lines of different widths.

When ink is washed on with a brush, then scraped with a razor, texture is achieved.

Varying brush strokes and a dry brush combine to create a soft effect.

Felt tip markers are made of strips of felt soaked in water-based colors and put into plastic casings.

Drawing through a piece of tissue paper will result in a blurred effect.

Tone can be achieved by making a wash (thinning the colors with water).

Soft tones can be achieved by using tone on both sides of thin paper.

The use of pencil allows the artist to make clear, continuous lines, called contours, when outlining shapes. These give the drawing a very calm appearance. When lines are broken into small pieces, or small rough marks are drawn (**stippling**), the picture seems to give off energy or suggest movement.

Pencils are particularly suitable for showing a solid, three-dimensional object on the flat surface of the paper. The artist uses shading (or gradated tones) to show how light falls on the object. Those areas that are closest to the source of light are made lighter. Those areas that are turned away from the light are made darker. This is called **modeling.** When the artist rubs the pencil point, or edge, on the paper, the tones are gradually changed by varying the amount of pressure applied. By rubbing the pencil tones with the finger or by partially erasing them, the artist can make additional tones.

Some masters of pencil drawing include Leonardo da Vinci (1452–1519), Jean Auguste Dominique Ingres (1780–1867), and Pablo Picasso (1881–1973).

Charcoal

The artist uses charcoal when vigorous, bold drawings are desired. The charcoal stick or pencil is an ideal medium for the beginning art student. The variety of lines and tones that can be created is endless. Another advantage of drawing with charcoal is that the drawing can be changed easily. A special eraser, called a kneaded eraser, can be used to rub off the charcoal.

Charcoal is manufactured in hard, medium, or soft sticks, as well as in pencil form. It is made from burnt sticks of willow wood that have turned into carbon. Charcoal is most effective on coarse-grained papers such as watercolor paper.

The artist can rub charcoal on large areas of the paper, making flat, medium to dark tones. These tones can be blended by smudging with the fingers. Different tones can also be created by **crosshatching,** the technique of making lines in one direction and crossing them at right angles with other lines.

A fixative should be sprayed on a completed charcoal drawing or sketch to prevent smearing. Famous drawings in charcoal were made by the artists Vincent van Gogh (1853–1890) and Henri Matisse (1869–1954).

Pastels

Pastels are powdered pigments of color mixed with gum or resin to form a stick. An artist uses pastels when an immediate effect is desired. That is, by simply applying the color stick to the paper, the artist achieves the full effect of the color immediately. With oil or other paints, the colors must dry before the artist can see the results.

Pastels are excellent for sketches on which to base future work in other mediums. The artists of the 1800's favored pastel drawings to make descriptive portraits. Pastels are used alone, as well as with other mediums, to achieve unusual and varied effects.

Pastels are manufactured in grades from soft to hard, but all are softer than pencil or chalk. When the pastel stick is rubbed on pastel paper, the pure color is released. Pastel paper is manufactured specially for pastel drawing and comes in a variety of colors.

Light, delicate tones can be achieved by crosshatching. Rubbing the pastel with a fingertip will also create various tones. The artist can twist the pastel stick to draw lines of different widths. Paper **torchons,** which are made of heavy rolled paper and look like pencils with pastels instead of lead, are used to apply the pastel when the artist wants to create clear edges and lines. Torchons place the color down exactly where the artist wants it to go. The quality of a pastel drawing is often unique in tone and richness.

A fixative should be sprayed on a finished pastel drawing to prevent the soft color from smearing.

Masters of pastel drawing include Edgar Degas (1834–1917) and Odilon Redon (1840–1916).

Pen and Ink

Pen and ink is a versatile medium offering the artist a number of ways to create line drawings. Clear precise lines, strong dark lines, and energetic lines can be made. Very detailed forms are characteristic of pen and ink drawings.

The steel pen point (nib) placed in a pen holder has become a popular drawing tool for the artist and student. The pen points come in many sizes, allowing a wide range of marks and textures. To make wider lines, an artist uses a brush and ink. Lines drawn at one angle, crosshatching, small dots of ink, and

A mixed-media drawing begins with a rough sketch in pencil or charcoal. The artist then uses a variety of mediums to fill in the details, sometimes applying one over another.

scribbles of ink are but a few techniques that change the character of the drawing.

Black waterproof India ink is commonly used, but other colors of ink are readily available. Smooth, hard papers are preferred for ink drawings so that the edges of the lines remain sharp. When ink is made into a wash (ink and water) and applied with a brush, softer lines and tones can be created.

Ink drawings have been very popular through the years because they are so rich in line texture and detail. Masters of pen and ink drawing include Leonardo da Vinci (1452–1519), Michelangelo (1475–1564), Honoré Daumier (1808–1879), and Pablo Picasso (1881–1973).

Felt Tip Markers

The felt tip marker has become a popular drawing medium. Felt tip markers are made of strips of felt soaked in waterbased colors and put into plastic casings, so that they look like ballpoint pens. The medium is favored by commercial artists and illustrators because the color is very strong. Felt tip pens are often used when quick sketches are needed. They are also useful to artists drawing outdoor landscapes, groups of people, or buildings. The student who carries a small pad, ready for the unexpected subject, can work quickly with a felt tip pen.

Felt tip pens are best for bold, strong qualities of color and line. Tones are more difficult to create. The felt tip pen is often used with other mediums.

Mixed Media

A combination of several mediums is often used to create drawings. Such mixed-media drawings may utilize a variety of techniques as well. Because of the various effects created by using the different mediums, an artist can create exactly the result desired.

▶ LEARNING TO DRAW

Drawing in any medium is an activity that involves eye-hand responses. It is therefore referred to as a muscular activity requiring physical action. It requires a sharp eye, the ability to remember what is seen, and a sure hand.

Since drawing is the first step toward becoming an artist, most students choose to take special courses in drawing techniques. Artists continually practice the development of their drawing skills.

JERROLD SCHOENBLUM
Manhattan Community College
City University of New York

PERSPECTIVE IN DRAWING

Perspective is the science of creating the appearance of depth on a flat surface. The paper that an artist uses has only two dimensions: height and width. To make a drawing appear to have the third dimension—depth— the artist uses perspective.

Some ancient peoples tried to capture the appearance of depth in their paintings. But nothing scientific was known about perspective until the 15th century. At that time an Italian architect-sculptor named Filippo Brunelleschi (1377–1446) developed a set of rules that he taught to other Renaissance artists. Although Brunelleschi's rules have since been expanded, they are still the basis of the science of perspective.

Perspective is called a science because there is a specific body of rules for its use. The rules separate perspective into two types: **linear** and **aerial.** To create a good illusion of depth in a drawing, the artist must use both types of perspective.

In linear perspective, lines that are parallel seem to get closer to each other as they recede into space. If you have ever driven down a straight highway, you have probably noticed that the road appears to get narrower in the distance. Eventually the sides of the highway seem to meet. Linear perspective is also based on the idea that objects appear to grow smaller in the distance. If you watch a ship sailing away, the ship will appear smaller and smaller in the distance, until you can no longer see it. In nature, these illusions help us judge distances. Linear perspective is an imitation of these illusions.

Aerial perspective deals with atmosphere. Because of light and moisture in the air, colors appear to fade in the distance. Objects that are close to us seem crisp and clear. At a distance, the same objects look soft and pale. In drawing, the artist uses bright colors and sharp, clear lines to portray objects that appear nearer. The artist uses softer lines and pale colors to draw objects that appear to be far away.

▶VISION AND PERSPECTIVE

Perspective is based on how we see objects in space. Our eyes allow us to see only a certain distance ahead and much less to either side. Many times our vision is blocked—by a wall, building, or other object. But if we go to the beach and look straight out at the ocean, we have the chance to see as far and wide as is humanly possible.

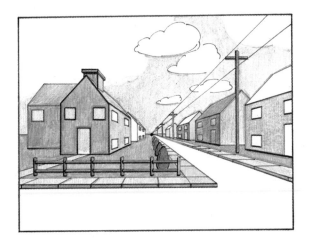

On a very wet day the ocean and the sky seem to blend into bluish gray mist in the distance. To imitate this effect, the artist would use aerial perspective. On a clear day we see a line where the sea and sky seem to meet. This line, called the **horizon,** is the point where our vision ends. If we were watching two parallel rows of battleships sailing over the horizon, we would notice that the rows seem to sail closer to each other in the distance. Imitating this illusion in drawing requires the use of linear perspective.

The horizon is at eye level. The exact point on the horizon where parallel lines seem to meet is called the **vanishing point.** Linear perspective is based on the fact that receding parallel lines, if continued indefinitely, appear to meet at a vanishing point on the horizon.

In most drawings that use perspective, there are one or two vanishing points. In one-point linear perspective, all receding lines are drawn to meet at the vanishing point on the horizon line, usually near the center of human vision. In two-point perspective, the vanishing points are located at the widest spots on the horizon that the eye can perceive. Three-point linear perspective is used for objects that are not upright. Its use requires the artist to combine one- and two-point perspective.

Reviewed by JERROLD SCHOENBLUM
Manhattan Community College
City University of New York

Objects drawn on a flat surface can be given the appearance of depth by the use of perspective. In the top drawing, all of the lines of perspective meet at one vanishing point. That is called one-point perspective. In the bottom drawing, two-point perspective has been used and the lines vanish in two directions.

DRAWING, HISTORY OF

When we speak of drawing as an art form, we are referring mainly to an artist's use of line to make a picture. However, the definition of drawing can be expanded to include the use of color, shading, and other elements in addition to line.

Drawings can be made as finished works of art, but they are also made for other reasons. One of the first main functions of drawing has been as a first step in the preparation of a work of art in another medium, such as painting, sculpture, or architecture. The study of drawing has also served as the basic form of training for work in all of the arts.

The history of drawing is as old as the history of humankind. People drew pictures even before they learned how to write. Like other art forms, drawing has changed and developed through history, with each new style growing out of the style that came before it. This evolution of drawing styles closely parallels the development of painting. As drawing styles changed, so did drawing materials. (For a discussion of drawing materials and techniques, see the preceding article DRAWING.)

▶ EARLY HISTORY

The earliest known drawings, dating from 30,000 to 10,000 B.C., were found on the walls of caves in France and Spain. Other examples of early drawing are designs that were scratched, carved, or painted on the surfaces of primitive tools.

Ancient Egyptians (beginning about 3000 B.C.) decorated the walls of their temples and tombs with scenes of daily life. These drawings had a flat, linear style. Texts written on papyrus—an early form of paper—were illustrated with similar designs in pen and ink.

Nearly all that survives to show the drawing and painting skills of the ancient Greeks are their decorated pottery vases. These great works of art show the Greeks' ability to draw graceful figures and decorative lines.

▶ THE MIDDLE AGES

In the Middle Ages, from about the 5th to the 15th century, art was produced mainly to glorify God and to teach religion. Painting and drawing merged in the illustration of Bibles and prayer books produced by monks. These beautifully decorated manuscripts were hand-

The great Renaissance artist Michelangelo sketched these drawings in red chalk as a first step in preparing one of his paintings for the Sistine Chapel.

lettered on vellum (calfskin), or later, on paper. Those made for royalty contained miniature paintings ornamented with gold. Those made for less wealthy persons were decorated with pen-and-ink drawings. The flat, linear forms often resembled the ornamental patterns made by metalworkers.

Drawings were used in the preparatory stages of a work of art during the Middle Ages, but few survive. Paper was not made in Europe until the 12th century, and at first it was expensive and difficult to obtain. Artists sometimes drew on prepared animal skins such as parchment or vellum, but these were also expensive. For centuries, artists made their preparatory drawings on tablets made of slate, wood, or wax, which were thrown away or reused. Some painters made their preparatory drawings directly on the panel or wall that was to be painted, and these were covered in the final stage of painting.

Drawings had another important function during the Middle Ages. They helped artists keep a record of images they frequently used. Pen-and-ink drawings of the human figure, costumes, plants and animals, and many other forms were collected in model books. Artists then copied the drawings instead of working directly from live models or from nature.

▶ THE RENAISSANCE

Modern drawing in Europe began in 15th-century Italy, during the period known as the Renaissance. A special love of drawing was born at this time. The production of drawings increased steadily, both because paper had become easier to obtain and because of the new importance attached to drawing.

Drawing came to be considered the foundation for work in all the arts. Art students first trained in drawing before going on to painting, sculpture, or architecture. Drawing was used as a tool for the study of nature, which was becoming increasingly important. Artists carefully studied the physical structure of the human body for the first time and began to draw from nude models. The portrayal of the human figure became increasingly realistic.

Above: The 16th-century German artist Albrecht Dürer drew highly detailed watercolor studies from nature. Below: The Baroque artist Rembrandt van Rijn used pen and brown ink for this drawing of the Dutch countryside.

Above: Jean-Antoine Watteau, a French rococo artist, made these sensitive studies of heads using red and black chalks. Right: The 19th-century French artist J.-A.-D. Ingres employed a new medium—the pencil—to create this finished portrait of a young family.

The need for preparatory drawings also grew during the Renaissance. In Italy, many large-scale paintings were produced to decorate the interiors of churches, palaces, and public buildings. Paintings of this size required extensive preparation, and drawings were an important step in creating the finished work. The artist often made a very detailed working drawing before beginning to paint.

Renaissance artists continued to use pen and ink for drawing. But they turned increasingly to softer materials, such as black and red chalks and charcoal, to make larger drawings and to achieve a greater variety of effects. Shading was introduced to suggest solids and textures. Among the most celebrated draftsmen (masters of drawing) of this period are Michelangelo and Leonardo da Vinci.

The Renaissance in Northern Europe

Artists living in Northern Europe (Germany, France, The Netherlands) in the 16th century gradually absorbed some of the ideas and styles that were first developed in Italy. Albrecht Dürer, the great draftsman and printmaker of Germany, was one of the first to travel to Italy, and he inspired others to make the same journey. Yet the Northern artistic tradition remained different from the Italian. While Italians produced many working studies to prepare their paintings, Northerners made many more finished drawings as works of art for sale. Portraits and landscape drawings were especially popular. Northern artists also portrayed their subjects with greater interest in realism. Dürer's precise studies of people, animals, landscapes, and plants, especially those rendered in watercolor and in chalk, are outstanding examples, as are the portrait drawings of Hans Holbein the Younger of Switzerland. Holbein's black chalk drawings of members of the English Court are masterful in their simple realism.

▶THE 17th AND 18th CENTURIES

The precision and control of Renaissance drawings were replaced in the Baroque period by livelier forms and by bolder use of materials. Chalk and pen lines became freer and more flowing, and washes of ink and watercolor were used. The drawings of Peter Paul Rubens of Flanders, who was inspired by the

Italian painters, are good examples of 17th-century art. His larger-than-life figures seem to burst through the surface of the picture.

Holland had its greatest period of artistic flowering in the 17th century. Rembrandt van Rijn, the most famous painter and printmaker of Amsterdam, was one of the world's greatest draftsmen. He was able to convey form, movement, and emotion with just a few simple pen lines. Dutch artists made a specialty of landscape painting. They often went into the countryside with sketchbook in hand and produced finished drawings or studies for paintings to be completed in the studio.

The rococo period of the 18th century was dominated by French taste and culture. Decorative lines and cheerful subjects are characteristic of the work of Jean-Antoine Watteau and François Boucher. Both artists often drew with red, black, and white chalks, sometimes combining all three.

▶THE 19th AND 20th CENTURIES

Many different styles developed side by side during the 1800's. Pencils were first manufactured early in the century, and they became the preferred drawing tools of many. The French artist Jean-Auguste-Dominique Ingres produced highly finished portrait drawings in this medium. Francisco Goya of Spain is known for his expressive drawings rendered with brush and black and gray wash. Late in

the century Edgar Degas led the realist movement in France. He experimented with various drawing techniques (oil on paper, pastel, and crayon, for example) with very original results. Everyday scenes, ballet dancers, and horse races were among his favorite subjects.

The tradition of academic training founded on drawing had dominated European art since the Renaissance. In the last quarter of the 19th century, artists began to question the merits of this training. The change began with the impressionists, who painted directly on the canvas without using preparatory drawings.

The liberation of art from past traditions in the 20th century has meant that the definition of drawing has also been expanded. It can be almost anything an artist wishes it to be. All the art movements in the 20th century in Europe and in America are represented in the drawing medium: from cubism (Pablo Picasso) to abstract expressionism (Jackson Pollock), fauvism (Henri Matisse) to postmodernism (Robert Rauschenberg). Artists continue to express themselves through drawing, just as our ancestors felt the impulse to draw on their cave walls so many years ago.

HELEN B. MULES
Associate Curator of Drawings
The Metropolitan Museum of Art

See also PAINTING; names of individual artists, such as LEONARDO DA VINCI; and art of individual countries, such as ITALY, ART AND ARCHITECTURE OF.

In the 20th century, artists working in a wide variety of styles have expressed themselves through drawing. This 1943 drawing in China ink of two pigeons is by Pablo Picasso, a master of modern art.

DREAMING

A dream is a special kind of mental experience. It seems as real at the time as something that actually happens. While it lasts, dreamers believe they act and react. The body stays quietly asleep, but the thinking part of the brain is very active.

Some people claim they never dream, but research shows that all people dream several times each night. During eight hours of sleep, the average person is dreaming a total of about one to two hours. Some people simply have more trouble remembering their dreams. People who wake up quickly seem to recall their dreams better than those who awaken slowly.

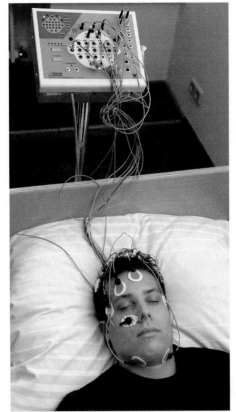

An EEG records the electrical impulses given off by the brain of a volunteer. Sleep researchers study the patterns of these impulses to learn about dreaming.

▶ STUDYING DREAMS

Scientists have learned how many dreams a person has in one night and how long each dream lasts by studying volunteers while they are sleeping. They do this with a machine called an **electroencephalograph (EEG)**.

An EEG records the electrical impulses given off by the brain. These impulses vary with each of the brain's activities, so that different patterns occur when a person is awake, sleeping lightly, sleeping deeply, or dreaming. The impulses can be measured by pasting wires to a person's head beside each eye and under the chin. The other ends of the wires are connected to the EEG, which records the electrical impulses and displays them on a computer screen.

When a person falls asleep, the brain waves become large and slow. When the sleeper begins to dream, the waves speed up, the eyes begin to move rapidly, and the chin muscle becomes relaxed. When the dream is over the eyes are quiet again, the chin muscle has tone, and brain waves become large and slow.

The picture of the sleep patterns recorded by the EEG is called an **electroencephalogram**.

Because dreaming affects more than brain processes, the EEG may be attached to other parts of the body during dream experiments to record the dreamer's heart rhythm, breathing patterns, and leg muscle activity. (An exciting dream will cause the dreamer's eyes to dart rapidly, the heart to beat faster, and blood pressure to increase.)

The EEG tells when a dream occurs but never what the dream is about. That can be told only by the dreamer. When the EEG indicates that a person is dreaming, researchers must wake the person and ask for a report. (If they wait until the dream has ended, the person will not be able to recall as much.)

Research with the EEG has shown scientists that there is a close relationship between having a dream and the rhythms of sleep. Everyone passes through periods that include both deep and light sleep. For most people, each period of these cycles lasts about 1 ½ to 2 hours. At the end of each, there is a period of dreaming. Anyone who sleeps eight hours a night has about four or five dream periods. Each dream may have different scenes lasting anywhere from 5 to 50 minutes.

Researchers can also determine when dreaming is happening from observing eye movements. **Rapid eye movement (REM)** is the most important sign that a person is dreaming. During a dream, the eyes move rapidly back and forth behind closed eyelids. Dreaming sleep is called REM sleep.

Research with blind people also shows the relationship between dreams and eye movements. When people have been blind all their lives, their eyes do not move when they

Awake	Sleeping without Dreaming	Dreaming

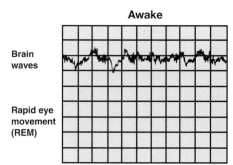 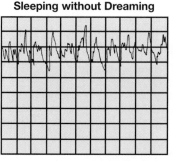 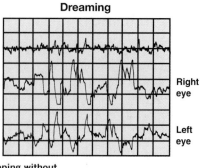

Brain waves

Rapid eye movement (REM)

Right eye

Left eye

The brain wave patterns recorded by an EEG reveal when a person is awake, sleeping without dreaming, and dreaming. When people fall asleep the brain waves become large and slow. They speed up when a person begins to dream. REM, measured by another machine, is the most important sign that a person is dreaming. During a dream, the eyes move back and forth rapidly under the lids.

dream. These people only feel or hear what is happening in their dreams.

Scientists have also discovered that four out of every five dreams are in color. But people describe most dreams as gray or black and white. As dreams fade from memory, they lose their color.

Experiments show that there is no definite connection between what people eat or drink and the kind of dreams they have. Studies tested this idea by having people go to bed hungry or thirsty. These people's dreams had little or nothing to do with thirst or hunger. Other experiments proved that eating spicy foods before going to bed does not cause nightmares.

Nightmares are experienced by almost everyone. These are long, frightening dreams that seem to be very lifelike. The dreamer may dream, for example, of monsters, wild animals, dangerous people, running from danger, or falling from a cliff. Sometimes normal, everyday objects become frightening parts of such dreams.

Nightmares generally occur in the last hours of nighttime sleep. They are usually more frequent when a person is under stress and may also occur during traumatic events such as war. Nightmares are also more common during childhood. At least half of all children experience them. They occur less frequently as the person learns how to handle frightening events.

▶ **THE NEED FOR DREAMS**

One group of researchers decided to see what would happen if they stopped people from dreaming. As soon as the EEG registered a dream pattern, researchers woke the

sleeper. They did this all night for several nights, every time the person started to dream. (Even though they were awakened whenever they were about to dream, the people taking part got a fairly normal amount of deep sleep during the night.)

The experiment revealed that people who were not allowed to dream kept trying more often to start REM sleep. They were nervous, easily upset, and hungrier the next day. As soon as they were allowed to sleep without interruptions, they lost their nervousness and felt normal again. But when they began to sleep normally, they had more dreams than usual. It was as if they were catching up on their dreams.

To check these findings, the researchers did a control experiment. Again they woke people during the night, but only during their non-dreaming sleep periods. These people did not change their daytime behavior. And when they were allowed to sleep without interruptions, the number of their dreams did not increase.

Experiments like these led scientists to ask if dreams serve a purpose. Some researchers believe that dreaming helps people live normal lives because they are able to work out their emotional problems through their dreams. Others think that dreams help strengthen new learning by storing it in memory. Another theory suggests that dreams help remove ridiculous or irrational thoughts from people's minds, so that they think more clearly and act sensibly when they are awake.

Reviewed by ROSALIND D. CARTWRIGHT
Author, *Crisis Dreaming: Using Your Dreams to Solve Your Problems*

See also PSYCHOLOGY; SLEEP.

Left: A dipper dredge collects spoil with a toothed bucket, or dipper, at the end of a dipper stick, which is supported and lifted by a boom. *Above:* A ladder bucket dredge uses a continuous loop of buckets—which looks like a staircase in the middle of the boat—that moves around a frame. As the buckets revolve, they scoop up spoil from the waterway.

DREDGES

The water in harbors, rivers, and lakes often contains a large amount of mud and silt that settles on the bottom. If enough of this material builds up, the water becomes too shallow for ships to use. To keep the waterways open, the mud and silt must be scooped up and removed from time to time. The machines used for this task are called dredges.

Dredges do other kinds of excavating work. They dig up valuable ores from lake and river bottoms. Often they are used to bring up sand and gravel for construction work. Environmental dredging removes contaminated sediment. However, care must be taken to prevent spillage.

Before the steam engine was invented, dredging was a very slow and difficult operation. All sorts of ways were tried to keep mud and silt from clogging the waterways.

The earliest type of dredge, dating back many centuries, was the scoop—a large, strong bag made of leather with small holes pierced in it. The mouth of the bag was held open by an iron hoop that also acted as a scooping blade. The bag was attached to one end of a long pole that was mounted on a pivot at one edge of a barge. To operate the dredge, the crew lowered the bag to the bottom and pulled it along with a rope. When the bag was swung into the air, some of the water in its load ran out through the holes. The mud and silt that had been dug up (called **spoil**) stayed in the bag. The spoil was dumped into barges to be carried away. Since the bags wore out quickly, many dredges used metal buckets, or ladles, instead. They resembled the digging bucket of a modern power shovel. Some of them even had hinged bottoms that opened up to dump the spoil.

Dredges like these worked too slowly to keep up with the mud and silt that rapidly piled up in some rivers and harbors. Many seaports became clogged and unusable.

The Dutch were especially plagued by silting in their harbors, because so much of their country is made up of waterways. As early as the year 1400, they used rakes and harrows to stir up the silt, which was then washed away by the current. Sometimes special ships called *krabbelaars* (scrapers) ran along the rivers or through the harbors, scraping up mud and silt with tools attached to their bottoms.

Sometimes rivers were dammed up by sluice gates. When the water had backed up high enough, the sluice gates were opened. The sudden rush of water loosened and carried away much of the silt.

In the 16th century a machine called a grab dredge was invented. It dug up spoil with a "clamshell" bucket. This machine was still used in Venice as late as the 19th century.

Faster-working dredges were made that had scooping buckets attached to a revolving wheel or a continuous loop. Wheel dredges were not too successful. They could be used only in water shallow enough for them to reach the bottom, and the mud thrown up often clogged the shaft of the wheel. The first use of a loop, or chain, of buckets for dredging was in a machine called the mud-mill, invented in the Netherlands in 1589. It consisted of a boat with two treadmills that drove the chain. Beginning in 1622, horses were used for power to drive the chain.

For breaking up ledges of rock or other hard materials on the river bottom, a large, heavy spike was often used. The spike was suspended from a barge or pontoon and driven again and again into the rock until it was broken up.

Not until the invention of the steam engine did dredges become efficient. The first steam dredge was a ladle dredge built in England late in the 18th century. A few years later, steam power was used to run a bucket dredge in Philadelphia. This was Oliver Evans' famous *Orukter Amphibolos* ("amphibious digger"), which could move about under its own power on land as well as in the water.

Another advance in dredging was made possible by the invention of the centrifugal pump in the middle of the 19th century. The pump was used on a suction dredge (also called a hydraulic dredge). This machine sucks up mud and silt like a vacuum cleaner and squirts it into a container with small holes. The water drains through the holes, leaving the mud and silt, which is then carried away in barges.

▶ MODERN DREDGING

The dredges used today are mostly improved versions of the old types of dredges. Some of these machines are mounted on ship hulls and can sail about under their own power. Others are mounted on floating plat-forms that have to be towed about in the water. Today's dredges may be powered by steam engines, internal-combustion engines, hydraulic systems, pneumatic systems, or electric power.

The **dipper dredge** is a seagoing version of the common steam shovel. A dipper on the end of a dipper stick is attached to a long boom that can be raised and lowered. The steel cutting teeth of the dipper bite into the spoil. When the boom is raised and swung over a barge, the hinged bottom of the dipper opens and dumps its load into the barge.

Modern **grab dredges** operate in much the same way as those that were used in the 16th century, except that the modern dredges are powered by engines. Two types of grabbing buckets are used on these dredges—the "clamshell" and the "orange-peel." The clam bucket has two hinged parts that open to scoop up the mud; the orange-peel bucket has three hinged parts.

The **ladder bucket dredge** (also called the chain, or bucket, dredge) scoops up mud and silt with a continuous loop of buckets. The buckets are mounted on a long steel frame, which is lowered to the bottom. As each bucket reaches the bottom, it is filled with spoil. It travels back to the surface, and at the top of the frame, it upends, spilling its load onto a barge.

Suction, or hydraulic, dredges are used where large amounts of soft material, such as sand or mud, must be removed. The spoil that is sucked up is either dumped into barges or pumped through a pipeline to the shore.

The old method of stirring up spoil and letting it float away on the current is still in use. Rakes, harrows, mechanical stirrers, and water jets are used for this.

If much digging has to be done in any spot, the dredge must be held in position so that it will not float away. In deep water, anchors hold the dredge in place. Otherwise, dredges are held in place by heavy beams, called spuds, that stand on the bottom of the waterway.

There is one type of deep-water dredge that moves about freely. This is the drag, or hopper dredge, used in mining manganese and other ores from the sea bottom.

WALTER BUEHR
Author, *The First Book of Machines*
Reviewed by SAMUEL D. STICKLE
Formerly, Great Lakes Dredge and Dock Co.

DRED SCOTT DECISION

In the Dred Scott case of 1857, the United States Supreme Court made one of its most famous and controversial decisions. The court declared that it was unconstitutional for Congress to outlaw slavery in United States territories. In addition the court said that no slave could claim United States citizenship.

Background of the Case. Dred Scott (1795?–1858) was a slave owned by Elizabeth Blow of Missouri. In 1833 she sold Scott to an army surgeon, John Emerson. Emerson took Scott to the free state of Illinois and later to Wisconsin Territory, where slavery was outlawed by the Missouri Compromise (1820). In 1838, Emerson brought Scott back to Missouri.

After Emerson died in 1843, Scott turned to the sons of his former owner, Elizabeth Blow, for help. Taylor Blow and H. T. Blow were abolitionists—people who thought slaves should be freed. But instead of setting Scott free, the Blows decided to test the burning question—could a slave who had lived in places where slavery was outlawed sue for his freedom and win? Scott first sued for freedom in the Missouri courts in 1846. But the Missouri Supreme Court ruled against him.

Meanwhile the Blows had transferred Scott's ownership to Emerson's brother-in-law, John Sanford. Sanford lived in New York. Since federal courts had the right to decide cases between citizens of different states, Scott could now sue for his freedom in a federal court—that is, he could if he were a citizen. The New York court said he was not. Scott's lawyers appealed to the Supreme Court.

The Decision. On March 6, 1857, the United States Supreme Court delivered its decision. The vote was seven to two.

Chief Justice Roger B. Taney's opinion, which was given as that of the court, dealt with three main questions. The first was whether blacks—slave or free—could be citizens. Taney said that they could not. He argued that the authors of the Constitution had considered blacks ''a subordinate and inferior class of beings.'' Thus the Constitution had not meant blacks to be citizens.

The second question had to do with Congress' right to outlaw slavery in a territory. Scott claimed he was a free man because he had lived in the Wisconsin Territory at a time

The case of Dred Scott, a slave who sued his owner for his freedom in 1846, led to one of the U.S. Supreme Court's most famous and controversial decisions.

when the Missouri Compromise outlawed slavery there. But according to Taney, the Missouri Compromise was unconstitutional. Congress had no more right to outlaw slavery, he said, than it did to take away a person's land or cattle or other property.

Finally, Taney asked whether Scott became free by living in Illinois, where there was a state law against slavery. His answer was that since Scott had returned to Missouri and brought suit there, Missouri law should decide whether Scott was slave or free. According to Missouri law, Scott's residence in Illinois did not make him free. Scott was still a slave and was not a citizen of Missouri; therefore he was not entitled to use federal courts.

Effects of the Decision. The decision of the Supreme Court settled little, and instead aroused a violent uproar throughout the country. Scott's abolitionist owners promptly freed him. But his case had already upset the shaky balance by which compromisers had tried to hold together a nation half slave, half free—and it brought the Civil War closer.

Reviewed by RICHARD B. MORRIS
Columbia University

See also MISSOURI COMPROMISE.

DREISER, THEODORE (1871–1945)

Novelist Theodore Dreiser was a leader in the literary movement known as naturalism. He was also one of the first American writers to portray modern urban life.

The American author Theodore Dreiser was a leader in the literary style known as naturalism. His best-known novel is *An American Tragedy* (1925).

Dreiser was born in Terre Haute, Indiana, on August 27, 1871, the ninth child of poor parents. After a year of school at the University of Indiana, he worked as a reporter in Chicago, St. Louis, and Pittsburgh. His early poverty instilled in him a fascination with wealth and power; he wanted money and the freedom it seemed to buy. At the same time, his readings in the philosophy known as Social Darwinism convinced him that life is a struggle between impersonal forces over which individuals have little control. In the end, he believed, success and failure are merely the result of fate and circumstance. This point of view, which in literature is called naturalism, governed Dreiser's writing throughout much of his career.

Dreiser's first novel, *Sister Carrie* (1900), was a turning point in American literature. Driven by the desire for comfort and luxury, Carrie Meeber, the book's penniless heroine, grasps at every opportunity to improve herself. She is indifferent to the demands of conventional morality. She becomes the mistress of two men and at the novel's conclusion has become a successful actress.

Some early readers found the book shocking, in part because of Dreiser's refusal to condemn Carrie for her actions, and in part because of the novel's frank portrayal of city life. At the turn of the century, the United States was becoming an increasingly urban society. Dreiser, more than any writer before him, saw the nation's cities as a rich source of fiction. His large novel brought together the immigrants and workers, the theaters and sweatshops, the trolley cars and taxis that filled the urban scene. Dreiser gave voice to people and events that had previously been excluded from American fiction.

When Dreiser's publishers realized how controversial *Sister Carrie* would be, they refused to promote it. As a result, the book was a commercial failure; Dreiser did not publish another novel for more than ten years. During that time he supported himself as a journalist and magazine editor. His next novels, including *Jennie Gerhardt* (1911) and *The Financier* (1912), were also attacked for their so-called immorality. It was only when he published *An American Tragedy* that Dreiser gained widespread recognition as a major novelist.

Based on actual events, *An American Tragedy* tells the story of Clyde Griffiths, an ambitious young man who desperately wants to escape from the shabby life in which his family is trapped. When Roberta, a factory worker whom he has made pregnant, demands marriage, Clyde murders her so that he will have a chance to marry a wealthy woman. Although Clyde plans the crime carefully, he is quickly captured, convicted, and executed.

Dreiser's unflinching honesty, and the long neglect he suffered, made him a heroic figure among younger writers. Sinclair Lewis, who in 1930 became the first American to win the Nobel prize for literature, said that the prize should have gone to Dreiser.

In the last twenty years of his life, Dreiser became more active in politics. In the late 1920's and throughout the 1930's he expressed admiration for socialist and communist political systems. He visited the Soviet Union and wrote favorably about it in *Dreiser Looks at Russia* (1928). Later he traveled around the United States and published *Tragic America* (1931), a record of his disillusionment with American values. He died in Hollywood, California, on December 28, 1945.

PETER CONN
Author, *Literature in America:
An Illustrated History*

DREW, CHARLES R. (1904–1950)

Charles Richard Drew, an American surgeon, gave the world the techniques of processing and storing blood for future use. His achievement made it possible to maintain supplies of blood for long periods of time.

Born in Washington, D.C., on June 3, 1904, Drew was raised in poverty and attended segregated schools. He entered Amherst College on an athletic scholarship and later attended medical school at McGill University in Montreal, Canada. There and at Columbia University in New York City he studied the techniques and problems of blood transfusion. Drew discovered that, unlike whole blood, blood plasma (the liquid part of the blood without cells) can be dried and stored for long periods without spoiling. For this work Drew became, in 1940, the first African-American man in the United States to be awarded a doctor of science degree.

When World War II broke out in Europe in 1939, Drew helped establish a system to supply Great Britain with blood plasma for its wounded soldiers. After the United States joined Great Britain in the war, Drew directed an American Red Cross program to supply blood to the U.S. Army and Navy. Some white people objected to white soldiers receiving blood from African-American or other non-white people. Although there was no scientific evidence that showed that blood from different races was different blood, the Army, Navy, and Red Cross bowed to political pressure and agreed to set up segregated blood banks. This practice was against everything Charles Drew had learned or believed about medicine. After only a few months directing the program, he resigned.

In the following years, Drew served as head of surgery at Howard University Medical School, as chief of surgery at Freedmen's Hospital nearby, and as a surgical consultant to the U.S. Army. On April 1, 1950, he was killed at the age of 45 in an automobile accident near Burlington, North Carolina.

JIM HASKINS
Author, *One More River to Cross: The Stories of Twelve Black Americans*

DREYFUS, ALFRED (1859–1935)

The court-martial of French Army captain Alfred Dreyfus caused the most scandalous political crisis in the history of France's Third Republic.

Dreyfus, the son of a Jewish manufacturer, was born on October 9, 1859, in Mulhouse, France. He decided on a career in the army and eventually became an officer.

The Dreyfus Affair—as the episode is now called—erupted on October 15, 1894, the day Dreyfus was arrested and accused of selling military secrets to the Germans. Although the evidence against him was weak, Dreyfus was quickly convicted of treason and sentenced to life imprisonment on Devil's Island.

Dreyfus remained in prison for more than four years, even though evidence later proved that another officer, Major Esterhazy, was the traitor. Esterhazy was brought to trial but remarkably was acquitted. The French generals would not admit that they had made a mistake. The honor of the French Army was at stake. Besides, they did not like the idea of Dreyfus—a Jew—as an officer.

By then the case had become a public issue. It involved the church and the government, as well as the army. Some people believed Dreyfus innocent, but many thought him a "Jewish traitor." A brave few defended him. In 1898 the newspaper *l'Aurore* printed a letter titled *J'accuse* ("I Accuse"), by the novelist Émile Zola. Zola accused officials of hiding the truth. Because of this, Zola was forced to flee from France. Then a French officer, Colonel Henry, admitted having forged documents to incriminate Dreyfus.

In 1899, Dreyfus was granted a new trial. Again he was found guilty, but this time the government stepped in and pardoned him. It was not until 1906, however, that Dreyfus was cleared of all charges. He later served in World War I as a lieutenant colonel. He died in Paris on July 12, 1935. To this day the Dreyfus Affair remains a forceful symbol of social injustice and the contemptible power of institutionalized anti-Semitism.

Reviewed by ALBERT DE VIDAS
Fairfield University

A professional driving instructor reviews the rules of the road with a student driver as part of the student's behind-the-wheel driver education.

DRIVER EDUCATION

North America's highways are among the safest in the world, yet traffic crashes result in thousands of deaths and cost many billions of dollars each year. Driver education is one of the most effective ways of dealing with these problems, because properly trained drivers have fewer crashes.

The best way to learn to drive is with a licensed, professional driving instructor. In the United States and Canada, many school systems and licensed commercial schools offer driver education. The typical course for teenagers includes a minimum of 30 hours of classroom instruction and 6 hours of behind-the-wheel practice with a licensed driver education instructor. Most of those under 18 years of age who apply for drivers' licenses in the United States have completed a state-approved driver education course.

▶ LEARNING TO DRIVE

Driver education is usually offered to teenagers who have reached, or are approaching, the legal driving age in the state or province in which they live. Students may have to purchase an instruction permit to enroll in the course.

In the classroom, students use textbooks as well as a driver's manual, workbook, videos, and computers. They are taught the basics of driving and how to share the road safely with other drivers. They learn to identify and respond to traffic control signals and to recognize road signs, which can indicate special hazards or guide drivers to where they want to go. They also learn driving maneuvers they will practice during their behind-the-wheel training. In class, the driving instructor explains how drivers can be impaired by alcohol and drugs, or by being tired or angry. Impaired drivers often cause serious crashes.

In the behind-the-wheel phase, students learn how to control a vehicle while driving in busy traffic, as well as how to park and turn the vehicle around in tight spaces. They also learn how to handle emergencies and spot and avoid dangers. Most, if not all, driver education cars have a separate brake for the instructor in case the instructor must take control of the car. Some programs also use a multiple-car driving range where students drive cars while the instructor communicates by radio. This allows students to practice driving in a safe environment without an instructor in the car.

Some driver education programs also use driving simulators, which have controls similar to those of an automobile. The simulator may project driving situations on one screen for all to see, or on individual computer screens. Students demonstrate their knowledge and skill by reacting to the situations on the screen. Their reactions are recorded, and the instructor uses the information to help students learn to correct the mistakes they make.

When they have completed their driver education, teenage drivers in most U.S. states and Canadian provinces must continue practice driving with a licensed adult in the car for a minimum period of time. During this time, new drivers can continue practicing the good driving

SAMPLE DRIVING TEST QUESTIONS

1. You are driving on a highway with a 65 mph (105 kph) speed limit. Most of the other drivers are going 70 mph (113 kph) or faster. You may legally drive
   a. 70 mph (113 kph) or faster to keep pace with the other vehicles.
   b. no faster than 65 mph (105 kph).
   c. between 65 mph (105 kph) and 70 mph (113 kph).

2. You see a school bus in front of you in your lane and it is stopped with red lights flashing. You should
   a. slow down and carefully pass it.
   b. stop as long as the red lights are flashing.
   c. pass the bus when you think all the children have left it.

3. You want to make a left turn. You must use your turn signal during the last ____ feet before you turn.
   a. 50 feet (15.24 meters)
   b. 75 feet (22.86 meters)
   c. 100 feet (30.48 meters)

4. You may legally block a traffic intersection
   a. under no circumstances.
   b. after 5 P.M.
   c. if you entered the intersection when the light turned green.

5. If you drive faster than other drivers on a two-way road and keep passing other vehicles, you will
   a. increase your chances of a crash.
   b. reach your destination quicker and safer.
   c. improve traffic flow.

6. The most important sense used when driving is your sense of
   a. taste.
   b. hearing.
   c. sight.

7. You may drive off the paved road to pass another car
   a. under no circumstances.
   b. if the car ahead of you is going too slow.
   c. if the vehicle ahead of you is turning left.

8. When you reach an intersection, crosswalk, or railroad crossing, you should always
   a. stop and listen.
   b. look to the sides of your vehicle to see what is coming; search left, front, and right for pedestrians, traffic, or trains.
   c. slowly pass cars that seem to have stopped for no reason.

9. When you approach a YIELD traffic signal you must
   a. yield to traffic in the cross street.
   b. stop and check vehicles behind you.
   c. take the right of way.

10. Traffic traveling in the same direction is separated by
   a. a yellow line.
   b. broken white lines.
   c. double yellow lines.

11. The most important safety features in a vehicle are
   a. the accelerator and brake.
   b. seatbelts and airbags.
   c. windshield wipers and wiper fluid.

12. With GDL, you
   a. do not have to take a driving test.
   b. you initially practice driving with an adult in the car and gradually learn to drive unsupervised.
   c. must drive every day.

Answers: 1 (b); 2 (b); 3 (c); 4 (a); 5 (a); 6 (c); 7 (a); 8 (b); 9 (a); 10 (b); 11 (b); 12 (b).

habits learned in driver education. They then progress to driving in more complex situations without adult driver supervision and finally to getting a license with full privileges. This process, called graduated driver licensing (GDL), has been shown to reduce crashes involving young drivers in the United States and other countries.

▶ DRIVING FOR LIFE

Driver education is the first step in a lifetime of driving. Practicing good driving habits rather than developing bad ones can result in fewer traffic violations and crashes. Drivers who have a poor driving record pay a lot more for car insurance. A traffic court may also require them to take a driver improvement course.

In addition to basic driving instruction, both younger drivers and adults can benefit from "defensive" driving courses. Defensive drivers view every situation as potentially dangerous and adjust their driving to avoid crashes. They learn that careful driving saves lives.

ELIZABETH WEAVER SHEPARD
President, The American Driver and Traffic Safety Education Association

See also AUTOMOBILES; TRAFFIC CONTROL; TRUCKS AND TRUCKING.

Drought is a shortage of water caused by abnormally dry climate conditions. During the recent long drought in Africa, famine and thirst forced people to migrate.

DROUGHT

A drought is a condition of significantly below-normal water levels in the ground, lakes, reservoirs, and rivers. The most obvious effect of drought is crop failure. In less-developed nations—where local agriculture is barely enough to feed the population—drought-caused crop failure may result in the deaths of many people from starvation and malnutrition. In any area stricken by drought, the possibility of forest fires and grass fires is greatly increased; soils dry out and may be blown away by winds; and animals may die of thirst.

▶THE OCCURRENCE OF DROUGHT

Drought occurs when the major forces involved in the earth's water-balance cycle take more water away from the ground than precipitation adds. (Precipitation is rain, snow, sleet

and hail.) Groundwater is lost mostly through evaporation and transpiration, which is the use of groundwater by plants in their food-making process. When there is not enough rain (or other precipitation) to balance the loss, a drought occurs.

Drought often occurs during periods of extreme heat that totally dry out the land. Or, drought can occur when temperatures are cooler but when there is very little rain.

The most important cause of drought is a change of the regular weather pattern. When the normal storm track moves away from an area, there are fewer storms to bring rain, and drought becomes possible. Forecasting droughts is very difficult, though, because scientists are not sure why these storm tracks move from year to year.

While drought is a condition of below-normal water levels, different parts of the world can have greatly different "normal" conditions. For example, Seattle, Washington, has a normal rainfall of 38.6 inches (980 millimeters) per year, while Cairo, Egypt, has a normal rainfall of 1.1 inches (27.9 millimeters) per year. So, an amount of rain that is well below normal in Seattle can easily be much above normal if it fell in Cairo.

What people consider a drought can change depending on how people use water. An abnormally dry period of one month may not even be noticed by someone who lives in a city. But the same abnormally dry month can have severe effects on a farmer's livelihood if it happens during the crop-growing season.

Dry periods that are part of an area's normal weather pattern are not considered droughts. For example, Seattle does not get a steady stream of rain during the year. The city usually has warm, dry summers and rainy or snowy winters. Even though summers are dry, the dry period is not considered to be a drought because that is part of Seattle's normal weather pattern.

▶THE DURATION OF DROUGHTS

Droughts can be short and last only a few weeks. Or, they can drag on for years.

An example of a long drought occurred in the Sahel region of north central Africa. Rainfall was below normal in this area from 1968 through 1984. Many people have been forced to leave the Sahel in search of food and water. It became so dry there that some parts of the area, which used to be farmland, have now become part of the Sahara desert.

A much shorter drought happened in the summer of 1980 in the United States. This drought started in June in Texas and moved eastward all summer until it reached the East Coast in early September. Much of the southern United States quickly dried out, even though the South had had a very wet spring. The drought was marked by extremely hot temperatures. From late June through early August, temperatures near Dallas, Texas, reached 100°F (38°C) or higher for 42 consecutive days. Throughout the drought-stricken area, crops, livestock, and nearly 1,300 people died because of the heat.

Another type of drought hit New York City during the summer of 1985. There was enough rain to keep the grass green and crops growing on nearby farms. But the city's reservoirs were at dangerously low levels because there had been very little snow or rain during the previous winter. Winter precipitation is very important for keeping reservoirs full. This is because the loss of water to evaporation and transpiration is lowest during the cold season. So, during the winter, relatively more precipitation winds up in reservoirs than during the summer.

▶ **HUMAN ACTIVITY AND DROUGHT**

People can do things that make drought worse. In the Sahel region of Africa, people cut down many trees. Trees absorb some of the sun's heat. Without the trees, some scientists think, temperatures were hotter in north central Africa than they were when the forests were still there. So, human actions—in this case, the cutting of trees—probably worsened the effects of drought.

Some scientists also believe that the residents of New York City made their drought worse by using much more water than residents of other cities normally use. The city's reservoirs were drained very quickly. Finally, city authorities had to order people to stop watering lawns, washing cars, and otherwise using water unnecessarily. These steps were taken so that the half-filled reservoirs would have enough water to last through the summer months.

Careful conservation of the water supply is perhaps the best way that people can prepare for the possibility of drought. However, during periods of good rainfall, people tend to forget that drought can occur quickly and can quite rapidly reduce the water supply.

ROBERT A. WEISMAN
State University of New York at Albany

DRUG ABUSE

A drug is a substance intended to fight a disease. But drugs are also substances that affect the structure or function of the body, as well as mood or behavior. Drugs given to a person by a medical professional are referred to as medicines or prescription drugs. Drug abuse is the nonmedical use of a prescription drug, or the use of an illegal substance, that interferes with normal functioning.

People are allowed by law to use a variety of substances that are, in fact, drugs. Coffee contains a drug called caffeine. Alcohol is a drug. It affects a person's body and the way he or she feels. But like other drugs, it can be dangerous if used too often or in too great amounts. (Problems with alcohol use are covered in a separate article, ALCOHOLISM, in Volume A.) Nicotine, the drug contained in tobacco, increases heart rate and blood pressure and restricts blood flow to the heart muscle. Nicotine is highly addictive, which means that it is hard for people to stop using it once they start.

People have known about drugs and their powerful effects for thousands of years. The use of drugs certainly is not new, but most people support the laws and customs that say it is unwise for people to take drugs unless they are ill. However, the misuse of drugs, including underage drinking and cigarette smoking, is a common problem in many societies. Drug abuse confronts many societies and is associated with many consequences, including injury, poor health, family disruption, and emotional problems.

▶ **CAUSES**

Particularly since the 1960's, drug abuse has become a major problem in the United States and throughout the world. The reasons

A group of students rally to demonstrate their opposition to drug abuse. Antidrug campaigns have been shown to increase awareness of the dangers of drug use.

people, especially youngsters, get involved in using drugs are complicated. Young people want to be independent and make their own decisions. They do not like to be told what to do, and they are likely to disobey their parents or teachers just to be rebellious. The use of drugs goes far beyond just being rebellious, however.

One very common excuse for taking drugs is "All my friends take drugs, and I want to be with them and do what they are doing." For some, wanting to be liked and to fit in can cause adolescents to try a drug offered even when they do not want to. Others take drugs to make them feel less anxious. They take drugs rather than try to deal with the issues that are troubling them. In these cases, drug use becomes a problem and leads to even more stress. Most young people who try drugs soon stop, but some find that they cannot, even if they want to.

▶ THE ABUSED DRUGS

Alcohol and tobacco are the most commonly abused drugs among young people. Some other abused drugs have been in our society for many years, while others are "popular" only for a short time. The most commonly abused illegal drugs are described below.

Marijuana

Marijuana is the most widely used illegal drug among young people. It is produced from the dried leaves and flowers of the cannabis plant. Tetrahydrocannabinol (THC) is the main ingredient in marijuana. When people use marijuana, they have difficulty doing tasks that require concentration or coordination. They are likely to forget what they said or did just a few minutes earlier. Marijuana changes brain messages that affect how a person perceives what is going on around them. Most people who have studied marijuana think that it is not as harmful as other drugs but that it is still dangerous, both to the people who use it and to the people around them. Like many other abused drugs, it is against the law to use marijuana or even to have it in one's possession.

Marijuana has been used for its medicinal value in the past, and recent studies have demonstrated its potential as a medicine. Accordingly, various U.S. states have sought through ballot amendment or initiative or through legislation to authorize the use of marijuana strictly for medicinal purposes. Some such motions have passed. In 2001, Canada became the first nation to allow its citizens to use marijuana for medicinal purposes under certain conditions. Such use of marijuana remains extremely controversial, however, and a topic for continued debate and research. In addition, the actions of the various states in legalizing the use of marijuana as a medicine have been challenged in the nation's courts.

Stimulants

A stimulant is a general name for a drug that speeds up nervous system activity and causes the heart to beat faster. Stimulants make a person more talkative and feel more alert but also anxious. Some stimulants—such as caffeine, which is found in coffee, tea, and some soft drinks in small amounts—are mild. Four types of stimulant drugs are described below.

Amphetamines. Amphetamines are a type of stimulant drug. People may become addicted to amphetamines because the drugs make them feel self-confident and able to stay awake for a long time. Gradually they find that they must take regular and ever-larger doses. Otherwise, they feel exhausted and depressed. They cannot perform their usual activities, such as work or study. In time, some users think of nothing else but getting the amphetamines into their bodies.

Methamphetamine. The number of users of methamphetamine, a dependency-producing drug that is closely related to the amphetamines, has grown in recent years. Methamphetamine affects the brain and body. Hyperthermia (overheating) and convulsions as a result of methamphetamine use can cause death. Long-term effects can include addiction, stroke, anxiety, confusion, paranoia, hallucinations, and mood changes.

Cocaine. Cocaine is a white powder made from the coca plant. Cocaine can cause someone's heart to beat abnormally fast and at an unsteady rate. Use of cocaine also narrows blood vessels, reducing the flow of blood and oxygen to the heart. Cocaine users experience a temporary sense of happiness and increased energy. To maintain these feelings they must use more and more cocaine, which can lead to convulsions, depression, paranoia, or death. Cocaine in rock form is called crack.

Ecstasy. The chemical name for ecstasy, which was being used increasingly by teenagers as the 21st century began, is MDMA. It can produce both stimulant and hallucinogenic effects, which last approximately three to six hours; though confusion, depression, sleep problems, anxiety, and paranoia have been reported to occur even weeks after the drug is taken. Ecstasy can be extremely dangerous in high doses. It can cause a marked increase in body temperature leading to muscle breakdown and kidney and cardiovascular system failure. MDMA use may also lead to heart attacks, strokes, brain damage, and seizures.

Depressants

Drugs known as depressants slow down the body or produce drowsiness or sleep. They include tranquilizers and medicines, called sedatives or barbiturates, that produce sleep. These drugs can cause unconsciousness or even death. Quaaludes, tablets or capsules of methaqualone, are an example of a depressant drug.

Heroin

Heroin is an infrequently used drug that has very serious consequences. It not only causes physical dependence, but also causes the person using it to develop tolerance, so that more and more of the drug is needed. Perhaps the greatest danger of heroin is that an overdose can lead to almost immediate death.

Hallucinogens

Hallucinogens cause very odd, distorted, and unreal sensations, known as hallucinations. People who take hallucinogenic drugs may hear or see things that cannot be heard or seen by anyone else. Most people who take these drugs find the experience extremely frightening. LSD is one of the best known of the hallucinogens.

PCP

Users of PCP, which is sometimes called angel dust, become confused or violent and lose coordination. This condition may last up to eight hours, but regular use of PCP can lead to more serious problems lasting for weeks or months.

Inhalants

Inhaling vapors from glue, cleaning fluid, gasoline, or other chemicals is extremely dangerous. It causes excitement or violent behavior at first, and sometimes hallucinations, convulsions, loss of consciousness, and death.

Prescription Drugs

Despite their beneficial effects, prescription drugs can be abused. Many patients simply fail to follow the directions for taking a particular drug or take the drug in improper amounts. The wrong drug, or the wrong amount of the right one, can make an illness worse, destroy blood cells, damage the body, or cause death.

Left: A customs official searches for illegal drug shipments at the U.S.-Mexico border. *Above:* Teens at risk for drug abuse attend a counseling session.

Painkillers—including the drug OxyContin that has been given to cancer patients—are known to be especially abused. It has also been discovered that antibiotics may be over-prescribed for common childhood conditions, including ear infections. Bacteria can gain resistance to antibiotics over time, and unnecessary prescriptions can shorten the effectiveness of antibiotics in one's body.

Ritalin is the most commonly prescribed drug for treating attention deficit disorder in children. Its advantage is that it helps children concentrate. Its disadvantage is that it can have damaging side effects. Concern has grown that too many children may be taking the drug unnecessarily.

▶ HARMFUL EFFECTS OF DRUGS

Drug use has both immediate effects and long-term consequences—the chance that negative things will happen in the far future. It is often difficult for young people to think about the long-term consequences of drug use. One immediate serious danger of taking some drugs is the possibility of taking so much that the dose is fatal. Some drugs can cause a person to become violent. Other drugs can cause people to lose control of themselves and their behavior. People who take drugs may place themselves in dangerous situations or endanger others, especially if they are driving a car.

A person who takes a drug for a while may not be able to stop it without experiencing dangerous physical effects. Such a person is said to be physically dependent. Many people find that they very much want to go on using a particular drug, even though they are not physically dependent on it. They will not be ill if they do not get the drug. But if they can get it, they find it difficult or impossible not to take it.

At first a person may need only a small amount of a drug to get the desired effect. But with continued use, the body becomes accustomed to the drug, and more is needed to get the same effect. The person is said to have developed a tolerance to the drug.

Those who take drugs by injecting them into their veins or under the skin with a needle run risks of infection. These people are especially at risk for both infectious hepatitis and AIDS (acquired immune deficiency syndrome). These two diseases are caused by a virus that can be carried on a needle.

Sometimes people who start taking drugs find that they have lost interest in everything else. They are comfortable only when they are with other people who are also taking drugs. This feeling keeps them from doing many things they would otherwise enjoy. Such a person may do something that can seriously hurt his or her future, such as getting into trouble with the law or failing in school.

Drug abuse has also had a damaging effect on society. Drug users often turn to crime to support their drug habit. Drug-related crime waves have struck many U.S. cities. The suburbs have been struck by drug problems as well. U.S. prisons are filled with offenders serving time for drug-related crimes. The cost of fighting drug abuse is extremely high.

▶ ANTIDRUG CAMPAIGNS AND TREATMENT

Parents, schools, and young people themselves have established various programs to increase awareness of the problems of using drugs. Information about drugs and their effects is now available from teachers, doctors, and other sources in almost every community of the United States. Group discussions concerning the drug problem can also be very helpful. Anyone thinking of taking drugs should ask "Why do I want to do this?" They then should ask for help from friends or family. The family can assist by planning supportive activities. When enough people learn that drugs are dangerous and do more harm than good, they will see the wisdom of not becoming involved with them.

There is a treatment process for those who abuse drugs. The initial step involves detoxifying (stopping the patient from using the drug). Withdrawal symptoms must then be treated. Next, the patient receives help in staying off the drug. At times, a long-acting, less-dangerous medication may be administered as a substitute. The patient then escapes withdrawal symptoms and can be tapered off the substitute drug slowly.

Federal, state, and local governments have passed laws and established their own programs to combat drug abuse. Federal drug enforcement efforts are directed at keeping shipments of illegal drugs out of the United States. The United Nations and national governments seek to fight the problem on the international level.

DANA L. FARNSWORTH, M.D.
Former Director of University Health Services
Harvard University

Reviewed by AMELIA M. ARRIA
Center for Substance Abuse Research (CESAR)
University of Maryland, College Park

See also ALCOHOLISM; DRUGS; JUVENILE CRIME; NARCOTICS.

DRUGS

Drugs, also known as medicines, are substances used for the cure, relief, treatment, diagnosis, or prevention of disease. They play an important role in everyone's life from birth until death and can help people lead healthier and longer lives. Many of the diseases that were fatal years ago are nonexistent today due to the development of medicines to treat or prevent them.

There are many different types of drugs, and they are often classified according to their effect on the body. Some common examples of medicines in use today include antibiotics to fight infections, analgesics for pain relief, antihypertensives to lower high blood pressure, and antiasthmatics to treat asthma.

This article discusses prescription and nonprescription drugs and their uses. Illegal drugs and the overuse of medications are the subject of the article DRUG ABUSE. The articles ALCOHOLISM and NARCOTICS discuss the effects of and treatments for dependence on these specific drugs.

Most medications have at least three different names—a chemical name, a generic name, and a trade or brand name. The chemical name is a complex name that describes its molecular structure. The generic name is a name assigned to it by an official agency, and the pharmaceutical company that makes the medicine chooses the brand or trade name. For example, the crystalline compound $C_8H_9NO_2$ is a generic product called acetaminophen that is marketed as Tylenol ®.

▶ PRESCRIPTION AND NONPRESCRIPTION DRUGS

By law, drugs are divided into two categories—prescription and nonprescription, or over-the-counter (OTC), drugs. Prescription drugs are considered safe only when used under the supervision of a licensed professional such as a physician, dentist, or podiatrist. These drugs are usually ordered by the doctor on a prescription and obtained by the patient from a pharmacist. Some prescription drugs, such as narcotics, have special controls on them because they have a high potential for abuse. In the United States, the Food and Drug Administration (FDA) is the government agency that decides which drugs require a prescription and which may be sold over the counter.

Nonprescription drugs are those considered safe for use without medical supervision. They are also called OTC or proprietary drugs and are available from pharmacies as well as grocery stores, convenience stores, and even vending machines. Common OTC medicines include pain relievers such as aspirin or ibuprofen, acne preparations, and cough or cold products.

In the past, most advertising to consumers for medicines involved nonprescription drugs. Today, however, much advertising is aimed at increasing consumer awareness of available prescription medications. In addition, numerous dietary supplements and herbal products are now available without a prescription. Many of these preparations contain active ingredients, which can produce effects in the body similar to other medications. Because of this, anyone taking these products should follow the instructions of the physician and pharmacist about the use of the drug.

The dried leaves of the foxglove plant are the source of digitalis, used as a heart medicine since the Middle Ages.

▶ WHERE DRUGS COME FROM

In the past, most drugs were obtained from plants and animals. For example, the heart medicine digitalis was isolated from the foxglove plant, and insulin for diabetes was produced from the organs of pigs and cows. The majority of drugs used in medicine today, however, are produced in the laboratories of large pharmaceutical manufacturers. In these laboratories, medicines are designed and synthetically (artificially) produced for numerous medical disorders. Recently, the fields of biotechnology and genetic engineering have opened the door for new drug development. Biotechnology is the manipulation of living things (organisms) to provide desirable products for human use. Most of the insulin currently used for treating diabetes is produced using biotechnology, which reduces the need for animal-derived products. In the future, the Human Genome Project will further enhance the development of medicinal products. This project identifies all the genes on human chromosomes, which will allow researchers to develop precise new ways to prevent, diagnose, and treat many diseases such as cancer, Alzheimer's, diabetes, and heart disease.

▶ HOW DRUGS WORK

To produce its effect in the body, a drug either mimics, stimulates, or antagonizes (counteracts) a normally occurring biological function. Most drugs affect one or more of the body's organ systems by combining with structures known as receptors. Many drugs work in the central nervous system, which includes the brain and spinal cord. For example, the pain-relieving drug morphine can block pain signals that travel along the nerves. Stimulant drugs such as caffeine can speed up signals in the nervous system. Cardiovascular drugs can act on the heart and blood vessels. For example, cardiovascular drugs called antihypertensives can help dilate (expand) blood vessels, thus lowering blood pressure.

Medications such as diuretics affect the kidneys and help rid the body of excess water. Hormones such as insulin are given when the body does not produce them in sufficient quantity. Other hormones are used to prevent pregnancy when given as birth-control pills. Numerous drugs—antibiotics that kill bacteria or vaccines that prevent serious diseases such as smallpox—work throughout the body. In addition, specialized drugs help diagnose certain diseases and are given to patients as they undergo testing.

The science dealing with the properties of drugs and the way they act on particular organs in the body is called **pharmacology**. The way a drug produces its effect on the body is called its **mechanism of action**. Scientists often know what a drug does but do not totally understand why until many years later. For example, it was known for a long time that opium and morphine could relieve pain, but it was not until more information about brain chemistry was discovered that their mechanisms of action were determined.

Medicines come in a variety of dosage forms, including tablets and capsules to be taken by mouth (oral), liquids, ointments and creams for application to the skin, tablets that are dissolved under the tongue (sublingual), eye drops, ear drops, or medicines that are inhaled such as those used for treating breathing problems. Medications can also be injected directly into the bloodstream or into muscle tissue. Some dosage forms are placed into body cavities or applied to the skin with a patch.

▶ SIDE EFFECTS

Unfortunately, most drugs cannot differentiate between healthy cells and diseased cells. Because of this, they can cause side effects, or adverse drug reactions. Side effects are a major concern. The potential benefit of a medicine must always be weighed against its potential to cause harm. It has been estimated that 2 million people in the United States are hospitalized each year due to side effects from medications and that approximately 100,000 die from these effects. Side effects can be more common in elderly people because of changes that occur in the body as one ages. A drug may cause mild side effects such as drowsiness and dizziness or severe ones such as bleeding or heart damage.

Medicines—both prescription and nonprescription as well as dietary supplements—can interact with each other and even with some foods to produce adverse effects. To prevent unwanted drug interactions, patients should keep their doctor and pharmacist informed about all the medicines they are taking. Many drug products should be avoided by people with certain medical conditions, including diabetes or high blood pressure. In addition, some people are allergic to some medicines and can have serious reactions when they

take them. It is very important to carefully follow instructions for taking medication and read the labeling and product information provided by the pharmacist to avoid potential problems.

▶ THE PHARMACEUTICAL INDUSTRY

Over the past 250 years, drug development in the United States has gone from trial and error to a very technical and scientific-based process. In early times, pharmacists would make various medications by compounding, or mixing together, medicinal ingredients in their laboratories or pharmacies. Over the years, this compounding function moved

A pharmacist helps a customer choose an over-the-counter (OTC) medicine. OTC drugs do not require a prescription.

from the pharmacy to large-scale manufacturing firms. During and after World War I (1914–18), the pharmaceutical industry began to grow in the United States, eventually becoming the largest in the world. Along the way numerous discoveries were made, including insulin in 1921, penicillin in 1928, blood thinners in 1940, the polio vaccine in the 1950's, birth control pills in the 1960's, cancer chemotherapy in the 1970's, and biotechnology medicines in the 1990's.

The discovery and approval process for most new drugs takes about ten years. Before a new drug is tested in humans, it is first studied in animals to be sure it is safe. Human

A technician tests the sterility of conditions in a pharmaceutical lab. Drug products must be manufactured according to strict government standards.

volve thousands of patients and is designed to better determine the drug's safety, effectiveness, and proper dosage in treating a specific disease. Based on the test findings, the Food and Drug Administration (FDA) decides whether or not to approve the new drug for human use.

The maker of a new drug is granted a patent, which gives the manufacturer exclusive rights to market and sell the new drug. Drug patents last for 17 years, but since it usually takes ten years to develop and test a new drug, the drug manufacturer has about seven years to be the only maker of the new drug. After that time, generic forms of the drug can be made. A generic drug product contains essentially the same ingredients as the original brand-name drug but is much less expensive. After a new drug reaches the marketplace, its effects continue to be monitored to make sure it remains safe and effective.

▶ PATIENT INFORMATION

Your doctor and pharmacist are the first sources to consult for information about medicines. Other sources include your local library, the drug manufacturer, and Internet sites sponsored by such government agencies as the National Institutes of Health.

RICHARD P. HOFFMANN
Drug Information Consultant
Author, *Ask the Pharmacist*

See also ANESTHESIA; ANTIBIOTICS; ANTIBODIES AND ANTIGENS; PLANTS.

drug testing consists of three phases. In Phase One, a small number (20–80) of healthy people are studied. The first phase of studies is designed to determine if the drug is toxic (poisonous) to humans, how the drug is handled by the human body, and what the safe dose is. During Phase Two testing, approximately 100–200 patients with a particular disease are treated with the new drug to determine if the drug helps cure or improve the patient's condition. Phase Three may in-

GUIDELINES FOR THE SAFE USE OF MEDICINES*

Before taking a new medicine, a person should ask the doctor or the pharmacist the following questions:

1. What is the name of the medicine and what is it for? Is this the brand name or the generic name?

2. If it is the brand name, is a generic version of this medicine available?

3. How and when do I take it, and for how long?

4. What foods, drinks, other medicines, dietary supplements, or activities should I avoid while taking this medicine?

5. When should I expect the medicine to begin to work, and how will I know if it is working? Are there any tests required with this medicine?

6. Are there any side effects? If so, what are they and what should I do if they occur?

7. Will this medicine work safely with the other prescription and nonprescription medicines I am taking? Will it work safely with any dietary or herbal supplements I am taking?

8. Can I get a refill and, if so, when and how often?

9. How should I store this medicine?

10. Is any written information available about the medicine?

*Source: National Council on Patient Information and Education.

DRUM

The drum is one of the oldest and most widely used of all musical instruments. From very ancient times, people experimented with different rhythms and sought a simple instrument with which to accompany their dances. At first they used hollow logs, which they beat with their hands.

A drum has been found that was played in Egypt almost 4,000 years ago, and there is evidence that primitive drums existed about 3,000 years before the birth of Christ. The ancient Greeks used some form of drum in the worship of Cybele and Bacchus. The Romans borrowed the instrument from the Greeks and brought it to the countries of the West. The earliest picture of an English drum dates back to the 12th century.

Drums have been made in many different shapes and sizes. They have been used for a variety of purposes—making music, dancing, sending messages, and fighting wars. Drums are found in every symphony orchestra, jazz band, and marching band.

The drum is a percussion instrument. This means that it is played by striking the surface of the instrument with the hands or with sticks. A drum is made by stretching some kind of skin over a frame or hollow vessel. When an object beats upon the tightly stretched skin, sounds are produced.

Snare Drum

The snare, or side, drum is one of the most popular of all drums, probably because it can produce such a wide variety of sound effects. It is made of either calfskin or plastic that is stretched over the top and bottom of a round wood or metal frame. Across the bottom, or snare, head are stretched strips of catgut or wire called snares. The drummer strikes the top, or batter, head with two wooden sticks. This causes the snare head to vibrate, and a bright, clear sound is produced.

If drummers wish, they can make snare drums sound like tom-toms. They do this by moving a special lever that loosens the snares and drops them farther away from the snare head. Then, when the sticks strike the surface, the sound produced is low and muffled.

The most familiar of all snare-drum strokes is the roll. It is played by striking the batter head with both sticks in rapid alternation. The skillful snare drummer can start softly and slowly and can increase the sound and speed to produce a great booming roll, that can be heard far away.

When the snare drum is used in a dance band, the drummer will sometimes play it with two brushes instead of the usual wooden sticks. These brushes look like little whisk brooms made of stiff wire. When they are rubbed across the surface of the batter head

No marching band is complete without the deep-toned boom of the base drum (*background*) and the sprightly rat-a-tat-tat of the snare drums (*foreground*).

Rock musicians often use a variety of drums. A set of modern drums, *below*, typically includes a tenor drum (1), a bass drum (2), and snare drums (3), as well as cymbals. The bass drum is sounded through the action of foot pedals.

of the drum, they make a swishing, soft sound that is especially suitable for dance music.

The snare drum is often used in military parades. It is attached to a strap at the drummer's left side—hence the drum's other name, the side drum.

Tenor Drum

The tenor drum is heard most often in parades and at football games. The heads of the tenor drum are about the same size as those of the snare drum, but the frame is much deeper. Since it does not have snares, it gives a lower and darker sound than the brilliant snare drum.

Bass Drum

The largest member of the drum family is the bass drum. Its two heads, made of calfskin or plastic, are stretched over wooden frames 60 to 90 centimeters (2 to 3 feet) in diameter. Among the world's largest bass drums are the wheel-mounted Big Bass Drum —3.2 meters (10½ feet) in diameter—at Disneyland in California and Big Bertha—2.5 meters (8¼ feet) in diameter—played by the Longhorn Band of the University of Texas at Austin.

The heads on the bass drum are much

thicker and looser than those on smaller drums. Usually it is played with a single stick that has a soft, felt-padded head. The sound of the bass drum is very deep and booming, and most of the time it is played with single strokes. To play a roll, drummers use either a special stick with two heads that they hold in the middle and wiggle back and forth or two sticks that they strike quickly one after the other. A roll on the bass drum sounds like a great roar of thunder.

The bass drum used in a dance band is smaller than the one used in a symphony orchestra. Dance bands have only one drummer, who must play several instruments at the same time. The drummer plays the bass drum with the foot, using a pedal to which is attached a short padded stick.

Scotch Drum

Everyone notices the antics of drummers who play the Scotch drums in parades. These drums look like thin bass drums strapped to the players' chests. Drummers play them with two padded sticks that they hold by leather thongs. The thongs allow the drummers to do all sorts of fancy tricks while playing. They twirl one stick while they beat the drum with the other. The Scotch drum is not used in every musical group, but it is an important member of marching bands and drum and bugle corps.

Tambourine

The drum known today as the tambourine is exactly the same as it was when it was first used more than 2,000 years ago. Carvings on ancient vases show tambourines no different from the ones we know. From references in the Bible, we can be certain that this instrument was played during the feasts and ceremonies of the ancient Hebrews.

The tambourine has only a single head, stretched over a shallow, wooden hoop. Set in the hoop are little metal disks called jingles. Unlike other kinds of drums, the tambourine is seldom played with sticks. Instead, players strike it with their hands or their knees, jiggle it in the air, or rub a thumb around the edge to make the jingles vibrate.

The tambourine is widely used by the dancers of Spain and Latin America. The beating and shaking of the gay tambourines that accent the rhythms of these spirited dances are often their only accompaniment.

Kettledrum or Timpani

If you were to strike the snare, tenor, bass, or Scotch drum or the tambourine, you would not be able to tell what note you heard. In other words, you could not tell whether the note was a B flat or an F sharp or any other note because these drums do not have definite pitch. The kettledrum is different from all other drums in one very important way. It is the only drum that is tuned to pitch and can produce a definite note.

TAMBOURINE

BONGO DRUMS

TAMBORA

KETTLEDRUM (TIMPANI)

TIMBALES

BASS DRUM

Most modern symphony orchestras use at least three kettledrums, or timpani. There are three sizes—small, medium, and large—making possible a wide range of pitch. Within the last hundred years, some composers have begun writing for four or even more timpani. In an orchestra there is only one timpanist, who is often kept very busy.

The kettledrum is made of a single calfskin or a plastic head stretched over a hollow, hemisphere-shaped bowl of copper or some other metal. The skin is first stretched over a ring that is attached to the kettle or bowl with

Music is vital to many aspects of African tribal life. These drummers, playing long drums and cylindrical drums, are part of a funeral procession in the Ivory Coast.

T-shaped screws. When these screws are tightened or loosened, the tension of the skin changes and different notes can be sounded. The tighter the skin, the higher the pitch; the looser the skin, the lower the pitch.

The kettledrum, like the other drums, came from Asia. In the 12th and 13th centuries, during the Crusades, the European knights found their Eastern enemies riding to battle with kettledrums hanging on both sides of their saddles. These ancient drums were made of animal skins stretched over gourds, or dried fruit shells, and they were beaten to frighten the enemy. When the knights returned from the Crusades, they brought the drum back to Europe with them. Europeans found it better to stretch the skin over a metal bowl rather than over a gourd, and the kettledrum soon came to look just the way it does today.

The kettledrum is played with two wooden mallets with heads of felt, rubber, or some other soft material.

Latin-American Drums

Until recently, drums came from the countries of Asia and Africa. During the 20th century, there has been a new migration of drums, this time from the countries of South America. These Latin-American drums and other percussion instruments give us the exciting beats and rhythms of dances like the cha-cha and rumba (Cuba), merengue (Dominican Republic), and salsa (Puerto Rico).

Most Latin-American drums have only one head, the other being left open. They are played not only with sticks but with the fingers, knuckles, and palms. **Timbales** look like small metal snare drums except that they have only a batter head with neither a snare head nor snares. Dance-band drummers have a pair among their drums because of the importance of timbales in Latin-American dances. The drummer plays not only on the heads of the timbales but on the metal frames as well, producing a wide variety of sounds.

Bongo drums resemble a pair of small timbales connected by a bar. Many people who are not drummers enjoy trying out Latin-American beats on a set of bongos.

The **tambora** is a modern version of the traditional **conga drum.** It has a narrow barrel-like frame and is played in the same way as other Latin-American drums. It is considered the national instrument of the Dominican Republic.

MELVIN BERGER
Co-author, *Music in Perspective*
See also PERCUSSION INSTRUMENTS.

DRY CLEANING

Dry cleaning is a method of removing dirt and soils from fabrics without washing them in water. Many fabrics such as polyester and rayon shrink, become discolored, or lose their shape when they are washed in water. They should be cleaned or dry cleaned with carefully controlled temperature and agitation.

Dry cleaning is not really "dry," because liquids called **solvents** are used in the process. Solvents can dissolve dirt as well as greases and oils that are not soluble in water.

The Process. When items arrive at a professional dry cleaning plant, they are inspected for damage and stains that may need special chemical treatment. Next they are sorted according to fabric and color. The garments are then placed in the dry cleaning machine, which is similar to a washing machine except it does both washing and drying. Because of the high cost of solvent, as well as environmental concerns, solvent is not dumped down the drain. It is used repeatedly.

As the machine gently tumbles the clothes, synthetic solvent passes through them, removing greases and oils. The solvent is mixed with a detergent that helps loosen the dirt and float it away. Special detergent additives remove water-soluble soil. The solvent goes into a filter to be purified and back into the machine again.

The machine then spins the clothes at a high speed until most of the solvent is removed. Warm air is added as the clothes tumble to evaporate the remaining solvent, leaving the clothes dry. The evaporated solvent is trapped and passed over cold coils to condense it back into a liquid for reuse.

After drying, the garments go to a spotter, who takes out any stains that are left using special chemicals and a steam gun. The garments then go to the pressing department where steam is applied to soften the fabric, remove wrinkles, and restore shape. Finally each garment is inspected, tagged, and placed in a protective bag to await customer pickup.

History. Turpentine was the first solvent to replace water for cleaning fabrics around 1700. The first dry cleaning plant opened in Paris, France, in 1845. During the 1860's the dry cleaning business spread to the United States. By this time, petroleum solvents had been developed.

Clothing that has been dry cleaned is placed on a hanger, wrapped in a protective bag, and hung on a conveyor rack to await customer pickup.

Early dry cleaning had some serious problems. The petroleum solvents were a safety hazard because they could burst into flame. The cleaning fluids removed only grease, oil, and tar spots. Many other stains would come out only if the garment was scrubbed hard in hot water. Many clothes came back from the cleaner damaged.

Over time, dry cleaning techniques improved. Synthetic solvents, particularly perchloroethylene (commonly known as perc) revolutionized the dry cleaning industry. These solvents dissolve greases and other dirt better and evaporate faster than previously used products. After World War II (1939–45), thousands of small quick-service shops sprang up all over the United States and Canada.

Environmental Concerns. Small amounts of perc can contaminate groundwater or drinking water. It must therefore be handled as a hazardous waste. And because perc releases hazardous vapors, dry cleaners must also comply with the National Emission Standard for Hazardous Air Pollutants.

Newer, alternative cleaning systems have been developed, including wet cleaning (using water and detergents), Green Earth (methyl siloxane), and liquid carbon dioxide. These new systems generally have good cleaning performance and are safer and more environmentally friendly.

LEONARD KLIEGMAN
President, Kliegman Brothers, Inc.
Reviewed by CINDY MCCOMAS
University of Minnesota

See also DETERGENTS AND SOAP; LAUNDRY.

DRYDEN, JOHN (1631–1700)

John Dryden was England's leading poet, critic, and dramatist during the Restoration, the period following the return of the monarchy to power. His often satirical work focused on the social, political, and religious issues of his day.

Dryden was born on August 9, 1631, in Aldwinkle, Northamptonshire. He won a scholarship to Westminster School in London and later attended Trinity College in Cambridge, where he received his B.A. in 1654. His father died soon after and left him a small inheritance. In 1663, Dryden married Lady Elizabeth Howard. They had three sons.

Much of Dryden's early career was spent in search of a patron (someone who would support him while he wrote). His poetry first praised Oliver Cromwell, who ruled England after King Charles I was beheaded in 1649, and then—when the monarchy was restored in 1660—King Charles II. With the reopening of the theaters during the Restoration, new opportunities arose for writers. Dryden achieved fame with both comedies and tragedies, most of them in the form of rhyming couplets (two lines of verse containing a complete thought).

In 1668, Dryden was appointed poet laureate. That same year, he published an essay, *Of Dramatic Poesy*, which led the English writer and dictionary maker Samuel Johnson to call him the father of English criticism.

The writings for which Dryden is chiefly remembered were published during the 1670's and 1680's. His most famous play, *All for Love* (1677), retells the tragedy of Antony and Cleopatra. In 1681 he wrote *Absalom and Achitophel*, a playful poem with a serious political aim. In it, Dryden defends the future James II, a Catholic, against those who sought to keep him from the throne. In *MacFlecknoe* (1682), he ridicules a rival poet.

In 1685, Dryden converted to Roman Catholicism, thereby losing the laureateship when King James II was deposed in 1688. During the last decade of his life, Dryden translated the works of classic authors such as Vergil and Plutarch. Dryden died in London on May 1, 1700, and was buried in Westminster Abbey.

DAYTON HASKIN
Boston College

DRY TORTUGAS NATIONAL PARK. See FLORIDA (Places of Interest).

DU BARRY, MADAME (1743–1793)

Madame du Barry was a famously beautiful mistress of the French king Louis XV. She was born Jeanne Bécu on August 19, 1743, in Vaucouleurs, France. Her mother, Anne Bécu, was a cook. Her father was probably Jeane Baptiste Gormand of Vaubernier, a friar from the convent of Picpus. Until the age of 15, Jeanne was educated in the convent of Saint-Aure in Paris.

In 1763, while working in a shop, Jeanne became the mistress of a nobleman, Jean du Barry, who introduced her to aristocratic society. Eventually, King Louis took notice of her. In 1768, Jeanne married Guillaume, Jean's brother, and became the Countess du Barry, a title she needed to be formally accepted at the king's court.

Jeanne soon became Louis XV's mistress. She never acquired the political influence enjoyed by the king's previous companion, the Marquise de Pompadour. But Louis lavished her with gifts, including a mansion at Louveciennes. Jeanne became a patron of the arts, employing the talents of the neoclassical architect Claude Nicolas Ledoux and the rococo painter Jean-Honoré Fragonard, among others.

After Louis XV died in 1774, his grandson and successor, Louis XVI, confined Jeanne to a convent for two years. Afterward, she became the mistress of the duke of Brissac. Brissac was killed in 1792 during the French Revolution. Jeanne, also considered an enemy of the revolution, was sentenced to death the following year. She was executed by guillotine on December 8, 1793.

JEREMY BLACK
University of Exeter

DUBINSKY, DAVID. See LABOR MOVEMENT (Profiles).

DUBLIN

Dublin, the capital of the Republic of Ireland, extends around Dublin Bay from the suburb of Dalkey in the south to Howth in the north. The River Liffey snakes through the center of the city, dividing it in two. Over 1 million people, a quarter of the Republic's population, live in Dublin and its suburbs. Its name comes from the "dark pool" (*Dubh Linn*) that formed where the Liffey met another river that once ran through the city. Rainfall in Dublin is high and occurs evenly throughout the year; the climate is mild.

The City. Many of Dublin's most magnificent public buildings were built in the 1700's. These include Leinster House (now the home of the Irish Parliament), the Bank of Ireland, and the Four Courts, the seat of the High Court of Justice. However, the most notable reminders of the 1700's in Dublin are the elegant tree-lined streets and terraces around Merrion Square. Many grand buildings also surround St. Stephen's Green, a spacious haven of lawns, flowers, and fountains in the heart of the city.

Earlier structures include Dublin Castle and St. Patrick's Cathedral, which contains a memorial to the Dublin-born writer Jonathan Swift, author of *Gulliver's Travels* (1726). Dublin's oldest university, Trinity College, was founded in 1592. Playwrights Oliver Goldsmith and Samuel Beckett are among its many famous students. The college houses the Book of Kells, the most richly decorated of Ireland's medieval manuscripts.

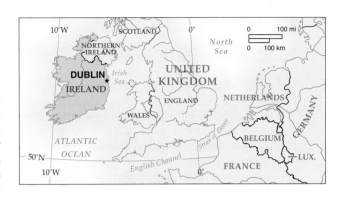

Against a backdrop of stately buildings is Dublin's O'Connell bridge, one of many that people use to cross the River Liffey, which divides the city into two parts.

Dublin has an international airport, and it is possible to travel within the city's suburbs by bus, train, or tram.

Economic Activity. Dublin is Ireland's most important commercial city, as well as its principal port. The Guinness brewery, founded in 1759 and now one of the largest breweries in Europe, exports beers to more than 120 countries. Other industries include textiles, electrical goods, financial services, whisky distilling, glass manufacture, and food processing. Dublin is also a center for culture and tourism, most notably since the 1990's when many old buildings were restored and converted to shops and restaurants, especially in the lively Temple Bar area.

History. Excavations in the Wood Quay part of the city revealed that the Vikings founded Dublin as a trading settlement in approximately 841. After a series of skirmishes, they gradually integrated with the native Irish. The Anglo-Normans invaded in the 1100's, began to construct Dublin Castle in the 1200's, and made the city the center of English rule. In the 1600's, Dublin was the refuge of Huguenots (French Protestants) who were fleeing religious persecution in France. The 1700's were a time of relative wealth, when the Irish gentry remodeled Dublin into one of the most elegant cities in Europe.

In the 1800's, Dublin changed from a mostly Protestant city to a Roman Catholic stronghold, mainly due to immigration from other parts of Ireland. Nationalist sympathies grew, leading to the 1916 Easter Rising against British rule, when armed campaigners for Irish independence occupied the Post Office and other public buildings. In 1922, Dublin was declared the capital of the Irish Free State, which later became known as the Irish Republic.

SUSAN RICHARDSON
Writer and Lecturer

DU BOIS, W. E. B. (1868–1963)

The African American author and sociologist W. E. B. Du Bois (pronounced doo BOYS) was an early civil rights advocate. Du Bois believed that educated blacks should lead the fight against racial discrimination through aggressive political activism.

William Edward Burghardt Du Bois was born in Great Barrington, Massachusetts, on February 23, 1868, to Dutch-African and French parents. He graduated from Fisk University in Nashville, Tennessee, in 1888. He then attended Harvard University, in Cambridge, Massachusetts, obtaining a bachelor's degree (1890), a master's degree (1891), and a doctorate in sociology (1895). From 1897 to 1910 he taught at Atlanta University.

In 1903, Du Bois launched his challenge to Booker T. Washington, then the unquestioned black civil rights leader, by publishing his book of essays, *The Souls of Black Folk*. This book made the prophetic statement that "the problem of the twentieth century is the problem of the color line." Du Bois' call for full equality for black people contrasted with Washington's emphasis on industrial training for blacks and near silence on the questions of social and political equality.

In 1905 Du Bois founded an organization of black intellectuals called the Niagara Movement. When Du Bois cofounded the National Association for the Advancement of Colored People (NAACP) in 1909, the two organizations merged into one.

Du Bois joined the NAACP's staff as director of publications and research. He founded *The Crisis* magazine, which he edited from 1910 to 1934, using it as a national forum for his ideas. He wrote numerous books and articles, and he spoke extensively. He organized the first of a series of Pan-African congresses, beginning in 1919, to unify blacks throughout the world in protest against racism and colonialism.

After World War II (1939–45), Du Bois participated in the conference that led to the founding of the United Nations. In 1961, he moved to Ghana. He died in Accra, Ghana, at the age of 95, on August 27, 1963.

DENTON L. WATSON
Director of Public Relations, NAACP

DUCHAMP, MARCEL (1887–1968)

The French artist Marcel Duchamp devoted his career to changing how people thought about art. For Duchamp, the ideas, or concepts, behind a work of art were more important than traditional values of beauty and craftsmanship. His radical, often humorous work strongly influenced later generations of modern artists.

Marcel Duchamp was born in Blainville, France, on July 28, 1887. He studied painting in Paris from 1904 to 1905 and had his first exhibition in 1909.

His first major work, *Nude Descending a Staircase, No. 2*, sparked a storm of controversy at the 1913 Armory Show in New York City. The painting captured the successive motions of a descending figure as a series of overlapping abstract shapes. It was widely criticized for its mechanical portrayal of such a classic subject.

Duchamp moved to New York City in 1915. He became active in the new and experimental art movement known as dada (nonsense). He edited several dada magazines and developed his concept of "ready-made" art. These were works he "created" by taking ordinary objects, such as a snow shovel or a hat rack, and adding his signature and a title to them. These "ready-mades," such as *Bicycle Wheel* (1913), forced people to think about what qualifies as a work of art—and why.

Duchamp's most challenging work was *The Bride Stripped Bare by Her Bachelors, Even*, or *The Large Glass* (1915–23). In this towering construction, painted on two panes of glass, Duchamp used mechanical and abstract images to comment on romantic love. After this work, which he declared to be "definitively unfinished," Duchamp claimed that he was no longer interested in making art.

Duchamp did eventually return to art, but on a very limited basis. He died in Paris, France, on October 2, 1968.

MICHAEL R. TAYLOR
Muriel and Philip Berman Curator of Modern Art
Philadelphia Museum of Art

DUCKBILL. See PLATYPUS AND SPINY ANTEATERS.

DUCKS, GEESE, AND SWANS

There is not another group of birds that is as well known as the family Anatidae—the waterfowl. No matter where you live, it is likely there are waterfowl—ducks, geese, or swans—nearby.

There are 148 species in the Anatidae family with 57 species living in North America. All of these waterfowl share certain physical features. They all have short legs with webbed feet that help them swim and dive. The majority of them have flattened bills with specialized edges that are used for picking up food from the water and straining it.

All waterfowl, or "wildfowl" as they are called in European countries, have outer feathers that are very oily. The oil is produced by a **preen gland** located just over the tail. The oil is worked into the feathers by the bill in an act called **preening.** If you watch a duck, goose, or swan at rest, you will see that the bird seems to "bite" the top of the tail then comb its feathers with its bill. It is actually waterproofing its feathers with the oil.

Beneath the outer feathers is a lining of **down** (small fluffy feathers) plus a layer of fat, which provide insulation. Because the oiled outer feathers do not allow water to pass through, the inner lining of down rarely gets wet. That is why waterfowl are able to swim and still remain warm and dry during the winter, while we humans stand shivering on the shoreline!

Nearly all the waterfowl are strong fliers. They may fly thousands of miles during the spring and fall migration seasons. You have probably seen migrating geese flying overhead in a V-formation, or wild ducks making rest stops in city and country ponds. In some cases, especially in the Southern Hemisphere, some types of waterfowl do not migrate and spend their entire lives in the same area.

Individual species that travel south in the fall, and back north each spring, will fly as far as 9,600 kilometers (6,000 miles) one way. The blue-winged teal, a small duck, makes this long trip from its nesting grounds in the far north to its wintering place in the Southern Hemisphere.

Waterfowl often travel well-defined flight paths. In North America there are four such wide paths known as "flyways." They are called the Atlantic, Mississippi, Central, and Pacific flyways. These flyways were determined by biologists who studied banded waterfowl.

Another interesting feature common to waterfowl is their habit of **imprinting.** This means that a baby duck, goose, or swan will identify anything near it after hatching—from a chicken to a human being—as its parent. Experiments have shown that any large, moving object, even a balloon or a puppet, will be treated as a parent by a downy youngster. It is difficult to return orphaned birds to the wild once they are imprinted by anything other than their natural parents.

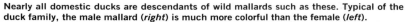

Nearly all domestic ducks are descendants of wild mallards such as these. Typical of the duck family, the male mallard (*right*) is much more colorful than the female (*left*).

Ducks are the best known of the waterfowl and have the most variety in their color patterns and body types. The smallest duck weighs no more than 0.5 kilogram (about 1 pound), while the largest duck can weigh up to 7 kilograms (about 15 pounds).

Molting. Twice each year all ducks get new feathers. This is called **molting.** (Swans and geese molt only once a year.) When ducks molt, after nesting has begun, the males (called **drakes**) gather in small groups and lose their bright colors. At this time they resemble the less colorful females (properly called **hens**). During this period the ducks cannot fly and will spend most of their time on the water or well hidden in marshes. The females lose their feathers more slowly but also undergo a complete molt by late summer.

No sooner do the males grow new flight feathers than they again undergo another molt. This time, however, they can fly. The second set of annual feathers brings back the colorful plumage of the drakes. Male ducks are easy to identify because they possess the brighter colors of the two sexes.

Life Cycle. Ducks choose their mates on their wintering grounds and during the northward migrations in the spring. The males are very colorful at this time. Ducks pair up for that nesting season only, then choose a new mate the following year.

Ducks most often nest in grassy hollows or in marshes. Sometimes the nests are built in tree cavities. A clutch, or group of eggs, usually consists of five to twelve eggs. After an incubation period of three to four weeks, the baby ducks (called **ducklings**) hatch. They can run and swim just a few hours later.

The main enemies of young ducks (and duck eggs) are raccoons, skunks, foxes, crows, gulls, and snapping turtles. Human beings also threaten ducks. Water pollution results in habitat loss and poisoning. Some ducks die from accidentally eating lead shotgun pellets left by duck hunters.

Types of Ducks. Scientists divide the various kinds of ducks into seven tribes, or subgroups. They are: whistling ducks, dabbling ducks, freshwater diving ducks, stiff-tailed ducks, diving sea ducks, perching ducks, and eiders.

The whistling ducks are also called tree ducks. They have very long necks, stand upright, and get their name from their habit of occasionally nesting in trees. They make high-pitched whistling sounds, especially when flying. These ducks live in warm climates.

Dabbling ducks feed from the water's surface, usually by tipping up their bodies and putting their heads underwater. They also feed on dry land. These ducks feed mainly on vegetable matter such as plants, seeds, nuts, grains, and roots. They also have the ability to jump from the water directly into flight. Mallards, pintails, wigeons, shovelers, teal, and black ducks belong to this tribe.

Freshwater diving ducks are most often found on large lakes and rivers. They get their food by diving for animals such as crustaceans, mollusks, and fish. Divers must run across the water's surface, like an airplane going down a runway, before taking flight.

Stiff-tailed ducks are also excellent divers. They are so named because they typically hold their sharply tapered tails straight up. This contrasts with their stubby bodies and large heads. They, too, mainly eat small animals. The little ruddy duck lays the largest eggs of any duck in relation to its body size.

Diving sea ducks include the scoters, goldeneyes, buffleheads, and the fish-eating ducks, or mergansers. Many of these ducks are also found in inland freshwaters at migration times. The mergansers have long, narrow bills with rough edges that enable them to hold slippery fish.

The beautiful wood duck is one of North America's perching ducks. It nests in trees, sometimes far from water. Its Asian counterpart is the colorful mandarin duck.

Eiders are residents of the Arctic coast where their nesting down is collected by natives. It is then sold for use in sleeping bags and clothing. Eiders spend much of their time at sea where they feed on mussels.

Shimmering colors, streaks of vivid white, and an unusual crested head make the male wood duck one of the showiest birds in the waterfowl family.

▶GEESE

Fourteen varieties of geese can be found throughout the world. Nearly all of them live in the Northern Hemisphere and make long migrations in the winter, though they do not fly as far as most ducks.

In body size, geese are generally larger than ducks and smaller than swans. The weight of adult birds ranges from 1 to 9 kilograms (about 2 to 20 pounds). Unlike ducks, it is not easy to distinguish the male (called the **gander**) from the female (properly called the **goose**). Both birds have identical coloring.

Geese are highly gregarious, which means they like to be in the company of their own kind. On the wintering grounds massive flocks of 20,000 or more birds are sometimes seen.

Mating Habits. Males and females mate for life, although if one dies, the other will often find another mate. The youngsters, called **goslings,** stay with their parents throughout their first year of life. Most geese do not mate until they are three years old.

Male geese establish the nesting territory and defend it from intruders and predators. The nests are built of grasses, twigs, and reeds. They are often located along the shoreline, in grasses or reeds, or atop muskrat houses. The nest is lined with down from the female's breast. Four to seven eggs are in the usual clutch, and they hatch in three to four weeks. Unlike the male duck, the gander stays with the female and helps protect and raise the offspring. After hatching it takes from 40 to 85 days for the young to begin flying.

Migration. Canada geese and various other species fly in a V-formation, or wedge. The wedge has a leader, and each successive goose flies slightly to the left or right of the leader to form the V. The movement of air by the wings of each bird makes the task of flying a bit easier for the bird in back of it. Obviously, the leader has to do the most work. On long flights several leaders will take turns at the job.

Eating Habits. Like most waterfowl, geese eat many types of vegetation. Their bills are also equipped for clipping grasses and leaves. They frequently stop in cornfields to pick up leftover grain. They sometimes cause problems on golf courses where they pluck the green grass, roots and all.

Types of Geese. The Canada goose is North America's best-known species of goose. Throughout the continent there are eleven sub-

The loud honking and the V-shaped flying formation of migrating Canada geese have come to mark the changing of the seasons. These attractive birds are easily identified by their black heads and white cheeks.

types of Canada geese that look very much alike but differ in size. The smallest, called the cackling goose, weighs from 1 to 2 kilograms (about 2 to 4 pounds). The largest, the giant Canada goose, can grow to 7 kilograms (almost 16 pounds) or more.

Geese vary greatly in colors. Canada geese and brants, small marine geese, are sometimes referred to as "black geese" because of their many black feathers. "Gray geese," such as the white-fronted goose and the rare emperor goose, have feathers that range from gray to white.

The beautiful snow goose and the small Ross's goose are pure white. Often these geese will not have pure colors until their second or third years of life because it takes a long time for the adult plumage to develop. The blue goose is a color phase of the snow goose. The tiny Ross's goose also has the distinction of being the world's smallest goose—a mere 1.3 kilograms (less than 3 pounds).

Goose Hunting. Geese, like ducks, are heavily hunted in the United States and Canada. Economically they are very important to people in places such as the Chesapeake Bay region in Maryland, Delaware, and Virginia where millions of dollars are spent by visitors who come to see and hunt them.

Goose down, which is collected from dead birds, is also important for insulation in winter clothes. However, synthetic products have made expensive down clothing and sleeping bags less popular.

Most of the world's geese are present in high numbers, assuring their survival. Only the Hawaiian goose, or "nene," is endangered. This species almost became extinct in the 1950's. Only through human concern for them have their numbers increased since that time.

▶ SWANS

The graceful, long-necked swans are the largest of all flying birds. They weigh from 3 kilograms (about 7 pounds) to as much as 21 kilograms (more than 46 pounds).

Like the geese, the male and female swans have identical coloring. Only during the nesting season can the female (called the **pen**) be easily distinguished from the male (called the **cob**). The male acts as the nest protector while the female incubates the eggs.

Swans mate for life and form close family bonds. Both birds protect the young, called **cygnets,** as they move around a marsh or lake on daily food-gathering activities.

Swans feed on vegetable matter and will hunt on dry land for grains. In the water they often tip up like dabbling ducks, sticking their long necks to the bottom of a pond to get to their meals.

Like geese, swans fly in V-patterns on long flights. Like diving ducks and geese, they must run, either on land or atop the water, for a short distance before becoming airborne.

Types of Swans. There are eight species of swans around the world; five live in the Northern Hemisphere. All except one of the swans are mostly white. The exception is the coscoroba swan of the Southern Hemisphere, which is entirely black except for its white wing tips. The coscoroba—named because its call sounds like it is saying "kos-kor-oo-bah"—is also the smallest of the swans. It weighs only about 3 kilograms (7 pounds) at maturity.

The biggest migrating swan is the trumpeter swan of Alaska, Canada, and the western United States. At 18 kilograms (almost 40 pounds) it is probably the largest long-distance flier of all birds. The mute swan, a native of Europe that was introduced to the United States, grows slightly larger and can fly, but it does not migrate. The whistling swan, which lives in eastern North America, closely resembles the trumpeter.

Swan Legends. Of all the waterfowl, the beauty and mystery of the swans have best captured people's attentions through the ages. In Greek mythology the swan was believed to have great powers, enabling it to foretell the future. The constellation Cygnus, also known as the Northern Cross, was believed by the Greeks to be a swan with its wings outstretched and its long neck pointing south. In the ballet *Swan Lake* a prince, who goes hunting for wild swans, watches as they turn into maidens. In England the easily domesticated mute swan is a bird of royalty, and it graces ponds on many private estates.

THOMAS D. FEGELY
Author, *Wonders of Wild Ducks;*
Wonders of Geese and Swans
See also BIRDS; HOMING AND MIGRATION; POULTRY.

Young swans do not resemble their graceful parents until they are about 5 months old. Hans Christian Andersen's story *The Ugly Duckling* is based on this fact.

In one of the most famous duels in history, Aaron Burr, the challenger, fatally wounded Alexander Hamilton on July 11, 1804.

DUELS AND DUELING

A duel is a fight with deadly weapons between two people who have arranged their combat in advance. Duels were usually held to settle a dispute or point of honor, and they followed fixed rules. Sometimes young nobles also fought duels as a sport. So popular did this deadly sport become that in France between 1588 and 1608, around 4,000 people were killed in duels. Between 1798 and 1860, more American naval officers died in duels than in battle.

An early form of dueling, called judicial dueling, or trial by battle, was first carried on in the 6th century by German tribes as a way of administering justice. But it was not until the late Middle Ages (especially the 12th through 15th centuries) that rulers encouraged trial by combat or duel to settle a variety of disputes. Nobles and knights, or their "champions" (substitutes chosen to fight for them), took part in tournaments before the king and court. People of the Middle Ages believed that God would be on the side of the good and just party in these duels.

The medieval tournaments were run according to a strict set of rules. The challenger threw down a gauntlet (glove), which the opponent picked up to signify that the challenge was accepted. In England the person chal-lenged had a right to choose the weapons. The weapons might be lances, swords, knives, battle-axes, or maces. Sometimes all of these weapons would be used in a single tournament.

There were always some people who did not approve of dueling. In 1547, King Henry II of France forbade tournaments after his favorite knight was killed. The Roman Catholic Church was so opposed to dueling that it began to refuse religious burial to duelists who were killed. But nobles continued to meet secretly and fight "duels of honor," in which the offended party sought "satisfaction" for an insult.

The custom of having "seconds"—friends who arranged and supervised the duels—developed in the 16th century. Later a surgeon was also usually present at a duel to attend a wounded participant. Duels often took place in a remote location at dawn to avoid discovery.

In France in the late 16th and early 17th centuries, a minor difference of opinion, a harsh word, or an imagined insult was enough to bring on a duel. Royal proclamations were issued announcing heavy punishments—including banishment from France—to duelists. In 1643, King Louis XIV ordered the death penalty for men caught dueling. Still the duels continued.

Dueling was not as popular in England as in France. Nevertheless, during the reign of Charles II (1660–85), some 200 duels, in which 75 men were killed, took place.

Toward the end of the 18th century, the pistol replaced the sword as the favorite dueling weapon in England. Dueling pistols were made with fine workmanship and ornate decoration, although they were not as accurate or as powerful as modern pistols.

The use of dueling pistols may actually account for the smaller number of people killed in duels after 1750. Most duels with guns were fought with the participants standing from 8 to 12 paces apart. In France the distance was often as much as 25 to 30 paces. It took a very good marksman to hit someone at that distance.

Duels were fought in England's American colonies, too. As early as 1621 a duel was fought at Plymouth Colony. Dueling was es-

DUELS IN LITERATURE

Sir Walter Scott wrote about medieval tournaments in *Ivanhoe* and other historical novels.

William Shakespeare used dueling with swords in his plays, notably in *Hamlet* between Hamlet and Laertes, and in *Romeo and Juliet* between Romeo and Tybalt.

Miguel de Cervantes Saavedra made fun of the knightly custom of dueling when his hero, Don Quixote, dueled against windmills.

Casanova, the Italian adventurer, left in his celebrated memoirs accounts of the duels he fought for love.

Don Juan, the legendary Spaniard who fought many duels for love, was used as the hero of works by George Bernard Shaw and Lord Byron.

Alexandre Dumas used the duel in many of his novels, including *The Count of Monte Cristo* and *The Three Musketeers*.

pecially popular in the United States after the American Revolutionary War. Gentlemen usually favored pistols as dueling weapons. Less refined Americans used rifles, lances, harpoons, bowie knives, army rifles, and in the case of Western gunfighters, .45-caliber revolvers. But almost half the duels fought before the United States Civil War were fought by politicians and journalists.

The most famous American duel was the one in which former secretary of the treasury Alexander Hamilton was killed by former vice president Aaron Burr on July 11, 1804, in Weehawken, New Jersey. Burr had accused Hamilton of making false statements about him. Some people say that Hamilton fired in the air. Burr, however, shot to kill, and Hamilton later died of his wound.

By the middle of the 19th century, most European nations had given up dueling. Dueling clubs continued to exist, but duels were fought as a sport, not to the death. In 1844, British Army regulations stated that an officer would lose rank if caught dueling or if it were proved that he knew about a duel and did not try to stop it. Other European nations had even stricter laws. By 1900, dueling had become illegal in most of the United States, and the ancient contests eventually vanished.

Reviewed by Lt. Col. W. C. Smith
United States Military Academy

See also Fencing; Knights, Knighthood, and Chivalry.

DULCIMER. See Stringed Instruments.

DULLES, JOHN FOSTER. See Washington, D.C. (Famous People).

DULUTH. See Minnesota (Cities).

HISTORIC DUELS

1093 Godfrey Baynard, Count of Beaumont, killed William of Eu with a sword after accusing him of treason against William II of England.

1547 La Châtaigeraie was killed by Comte de Jarnac, favorite of King Henry II of France, after Jarnac accused his adversary of slander.

1772 Richard Brinsley Sheridan was wounded in a sword duel with Thomas Mathews over rivalry for the affection of Elizabeth Linley.

1798 William Pitt dueled with George Tierney over a debate concerning the navy; they exchanged shots without hitting each other.

1804 Aaron Burr accused Alexander Hamilton of making false accusations about him and killed him in a duel with pistols.

1806 Andrew Jackson killed Charles Dickinson in a pistol duel after Dickinson had denounced him in the press.

1820 Commodore James Barron challenged Commodore Stephen Decatur of the United States Navy when Decatur refused to reinstate Barron, who had been court-martialed. Decatur was shot to death.

1829 The Duke of Wellington fought a duel with Lord Winchelsea, who had charged him with dishonesty. Both fired wild.

1837 Russian poet Aleksander Pushkin was fatally shot by Baron George D'Anthes Heeckeren. The duel resulted from Pushkin's suspicion that the baron was in love with his wife.

1838 Congressman Jonathan Cilley was shot by his colleague William Graves after a political argument.

DUMAS, ALEXANDRE PÈRE (1802–1870) AND ALEXANDRE FILS (1824–1895)

Two of the most popular French writers of the 1800's were a father and son both named Alexandre Dumas. The world knows them as Dumas *père* ("father") and Dumas *fils* ("son").

Dumas *père* was born on July 24, 1802, at Villers-Cotterêts, a market town northeast of Paris. He was partly of African descent, his father's mother having been a black slave in Haiti. Dumas was only 4 years old when his father, who had served as a general under Napoleon, died. Dumas had a very sketchy education and later worked as a law clerk. In 1829, he wrote the first romantic drama to be produced in France, *Henri III et sa cour* (*Henry III and his Court*). It was a tremendous success, as were several of his later plays.

Dumas produced more than 200 novels during his lifetime, but today he is chiefly remembered for those he wrote in the 1840's. Most of them were based on historical events, such as *The Three Musketeers* (1844) and *Chicot the Jester* (1846). But one of the most famous, *The Count of Monte Cristo* (1844–45), was set in Dumas's own time.

Dumas loved adventure in real life as well as in fiction. He fought in the Revolution of 1830—an adventure described in his *Mémoires*—and took part in Garibaldi's daring expedition to liberate Sicily in 1860. He also traveled widely in Russia and North Africa.

Dumas *fils* was born in Paris on July 27, 1824. He, too, became a dramatist, but his plays were more serious than his father's. Dumas *père* used to say that in their case, the father was younger than the son.

Dumas *fils* is best known for his novel and play *La Dame aux camélias* (1848). The play, known as *Camille* in English, was the basis for Verdi's opera *La Traviata*.

Alexandre Dumas *père*

Alexandre Dumas *fils*

Dumas *père* died at his son's house, near Dieppe, on December 5, 1870. Dumas *fils* died on November 27, 1895.

F. W. J. HEMMINGS
Author, *Alexander Dumas: The King of Romance*

THE THREE MUSKETEERS

Alexandre Dumas's historical novel *The Three Musketeers* is full of adventure and intrigue. It tells the story of young D'Artagnan, who goes to Paris in 1625 to join the king's musketeers. Soon after he arrives, he challenges the best of the musketeers—Athos, Porthos, and Aramis, "the three inseparables"—to duels. They are about to begin the contest when a company of the Cardinal's guards, led by Jussac, appears and orders them to stop. The musketeers are only three, against five guards, but they refuse. D'Artagnan declares he will fight alongside the musketeers. The following excerpt picks up the story from there.

"Will you make up your minds?" cried Jussac, for the third time.

"It is done, gentlemen," said Athos.

"And what have you determined?" asked Jussac.

"We are going to have the honour to charge you," replied Aramis, lifting his hat with one hand and drawing his sword with the other.

"Ah, you resist!" cried Jussac.

"*Sangdieu!* does that astonish you?"

And the nine combatants fell upon each other with a fury which was not devoid of method.

Athos engaged a certain Cahusac, a favourite of the Cardinal; Porthos engaged Bicarat; while Aramis saw himself faced with two adversaries; as for D'Artagnan, he found himself matched against Jussac himself. The heart of the young Gascon was beating as though it would burst, not with fear—he felt not a shadow of that—but with emulation; he fought like an enraged tiger, turning round his adversary and constantly changing his ground. Jussac, as the saying went, was an epicure of the sword, and had practised much; however, he had all the trouble in the world to defend himself against so agile and leaping an adversary who set ordinary rules at defiance. This struggle ended by making Jussac impatient. Angry at being held in check by an adversary he looked upon as a boy, he became excited, and began to commit faults. D'Artagnan, who, in default of practice, had excellent theory, redoubled his agility. Jussac, wishing to terminate the affair, made a terrible lunge at his adversary, who parried the thrust, and, as Jussac was recovering himself, gliding like a serpent under his blade, ran his rapier through his body. Jussac fell all of a heap. D'Artagnan then threw an uneasy and rapid glance over the field of battle.

Aramis had already killed one of his adversaries; but the other was pressing him keenly. However, Aramis was not in difficulties, and could still defend himself.

Porthos had just received a wound through the arm, and had run Bicarat through the thigh. But neither wound was serious. Athos, wounded again by Cahusac, was growing rapidly paler, but did not yield an inch; only he had changed his sword to his left hand.

D'Artagnan, according to the laws of duelling at that period, was at liberty to help a friend. While looking to see which of his companions he should aid, he caught a glance from Athos. Athos would sooner have died than have called for help, but his eyes seemed to ask for support. D'Artagnan comprehended this, and sprang with a terrible bound on the flank of Cahusac, shouting: "My turn, sir; I mean to kill you!"

Cahusac turned round; it was high time, for Athos, sustained only by his supreme courage, fell upon his knee.

"*Sangdieu!*" cried he to D'Artagnan, "do not kill him, young man; I have an old affair to settle with him when I am cured and well. Disarm him only. That's right!"

This exclamation sprang from Athos on seeing the sword of Cahusac dashed twenty paces from him. D'Artagnan and Cahusac both darted after it, but D'Artagnan being the quicker, arrived first, and placed his foot upon it.

Cahusac then ran to the guard who had been killed, seized on his rapier, and was returning to D'Artagnan; but he met Athos on the way, who had recovered breath, and who, fearing that D'Artagnan would slay his enemy, wished to recommence the combat.

D'Artagnan understood that Athos wished to be left alone. In fact, a few seconds afterwards Cahusac fell, run through the throat. At the same moment Aramis held his sword to the chest of his adversary, who was on the ground, and forced him to ask for mercy.

DUNBAR, PAUL LAURENCE
(1872–1906)

Paul Laurence Dunbar was one of the first African American authors to receive widespread acclaim. His works, written in standard English as well as in dialect, were popular with black and white readers alike.

Paul Laurence Dunbar was born on June 27, 1872, in Dayton, Ohio. He was the son of former slaves. His father escaped to Canada before the Civil War but returned to the United States to fight for the North. He died when Paul was 12.

Paul's mother washed and ironed clothes to support him and his two half-brothers. While she worked she would tell Paul stories, and he began writing his own poetry by the age of 6. Dunbar was popular at school and wrote poems for the school paper. Orville Wright, the aviation pioneer, was one of his classmates. Wright helped Dunbar with algebra and Dunbar helped Wright with poetry. Dunbar was the only African American student in his high school class. He was president of the literary society and editor of the student newspaper.

Because he was black, the only work Dunbar could find after graduation was running an elevator for $4 a week. His poems were printed in newspapers, and the first collection of his poems was published in 1893 under the title *Oak and Ivy*. He paid the publishing costs himself. The same year, Frederick Douglass, famous abolitionist and former minister to Haiti, employed Dunbar in the Haiti Building at the Chicago World's Fair.

Two prominent Toledo citizens paid for the publication of Dunbar's second book of poems, *Majors and Minors* (1895). *Lyrics of Lowly Life*, which included a selection of poems from his first two books and an introduction by the prominent American novelist and critic William Dean Howells, followed a year later and brought Dunbar widespread popularity. The years from 1898 to 1903 were filled with critical and popular success. "When Malindy Sings," inspired by his mother, is the best known of his poems, many of which were set to music.

Dunbar gave many recitals of his poetry in both the United States and England. He also wrote short stories, several novels, and the lyrics for a number of successful musicals. During 1897 and 1898 he served as an assistant in the Library of Congress. In 1898 he married Alice Ruth Moore, a teacher and poet. He died in Dayton on February 9, 1906.

Reviewed by CHARLES NILON
University of Colorado (Boulder)

A STARRY NIGHT

A cloud fell down from the heavens,
And broke on the mountain's brow;
It scattered the dusky fragments
All over the vale below.

The moon and the stars were anxious
To know what its fate might be;
So they rushed to the azure op'ning,
And all peered down to see.

PAUL LAURENCE DUNBAR

DUNCAN, ISADORA
(1877–1927)

American dancer and choreographer Isadora Duncan became famous for her revolt against the formal training and costuming of classical ballet. She created her own expressive style, which laid the foundations for what came to be called modern dance. Her work raised the public's respect for dance, which she regarded as a sacred art.

Dora Angela Duncan was born in San Francisco, California, on May 26, 1877, into an artistic family. As a teenager she taught ballroom dance at her own school. After dancing in musical theater in Chicago and New York, she departed for Europe in 1899. She first gained fame while touring with the famous American dancer Loie Fuller. Then she embarked on a remarkable solo career. By 1904 she had won international acclaim.

Duncan used natural movements, such as skips, hops, and runs, in her dances. Her use of her arms—influenced by the motion of wind and waves—was expressive and free. Rather than portraying a character such as a princess or goddess, she danced as herself. She rejected the confining corset, tights, and pointe shoes worn by ballerinas. Inspired by the clothing worn in ancient Greece, she chose instead to dance barefoot, dressed in a simple tunic. Instead of using traditional

Isadora Duncan, shown leading a troupe of dancers in an outdoor performance, pioneered an expressive style that laid the foundations for modern dance.

dance pieces, she interpreted the music of the great classical composers. She founded dance schools in Germany, France, and Russia that offered free training in her style of dance.

Duncan was killed in an accident on September 14, 1927, in Nice, France. Her long scarf got caught in a wheel of the car in which she was riding, and she died instantly of a broken neck. Thousands of mourners attended her burial in Paris.

PATRICIA BEAMAN
Department of Dance
Tisch School of the Arts, New York University

DUNHAM, KATHERINE. See DANCE (Profiles).

DUNIWAY, ABIGAIL. See OREGON (Famous People).

DUODECIMAL SYSTEM. See NUMERALS AND NUMERATION SYSTEMS.

DU PONT FAMILY. See DELAWARE (Famous People).

DÜRER, ALBRECHT (1471–1528)

The German artist Albrecht Dürer did more than any other to bring the art and ideas of the Renaissance to northern Europe. He became the most honored and respected artist in northern Europe—not just for his skill but for his scholarship as well.

Dürer was born in Nuremberg on May 21, 1471. Until he was 15 he worked with his father, a goldsmith. Then he served as apprentice to the artist Michel Wolgemut (1434–1519) for three years. During this time Dürer became skilled in techniques of woodcut and engraving. In 1490 he left home to travel.

Dürer was married in 1494. He went to Venice later that year and again in 1505. There he saw works of the great masters of the Italian Renaissance, and his own work began to show their influence. He combined the detailed Gothic characteristics of his native German style with the classical harmony of Italian art. Dürer's engraving *Saint Jerome in His Study* shows the scholarly saint studying at his desk in a simple and orderly room. The German love of detail and concern with mystery and death are also present.

Dürer learned not only from the art of Renaissance Italy but also from the theories of scholars. He had friends throughout Europe, including Giovanni Bellini and Martin Luther. He became well educated in mathematics, geometry, Latin, and literature. Emperor Maximilian respected Dürer so much that he made the artist court painter and awarded him a pension for life.

Although he did many excellent drawings and paintings, including portraits and landscape watercolors, Dürer is best known for his detailed work in woodcut and engraving. He was the greatest master of the engraving technique, in which a drawing is cut into a copper plate, inked, and printed on paper.

After Maximilian died, Dürer wanted to make certain that the new Holy Roman emperor, Charles V, would renew his pension. So he went to the Netherlands to attend the coronation of the new ruler. When he arrived at the court, Charles treated him with great respect. Then, Dürer returned to Nuremberg and spent his last years there, developing and writing about his theories of art and beauty. He died on April 6, 1528.

Reviewed by LOLA B. GELLMAN
Queensborough Community College

DURHAM. See NORTH CAROLINA (Cities).
DU SABLE, JEAN BAPTISTE POINT. See CHICAGO (Famous People).

The craftsmanship of German artist Albrecht Dürer is evident in these two examples of his engravings: *Saint Jerome in His Study* (*left*) and *The Prodigal Son* (*right*).

DUST

Dust is not just the lint you find under the bed and in the corners of rooms. Dust is everywhere—in cities, on farms, and in the air.

Dust particles are very small. Many are less than one-tenth the width of a human hair. Dust is made up of tiny particles from many sources, including minerals; compounds from evaporated gasoline and paint solvents; and organic matter such as bacteria, spores, pollen, animal dander, and bits of fibers.

A great deal of dust makes its way into the atmosphere because it is so small and light. Natural sources of atmospheric dust include volcanic eruptions, dust storms, and forest fires. Human activities also release tiny particles into the air. For example, the cultivation of arid (dry) lands removes native plants and stirs up the soil. The small dust particles in the soil can then be lifted into the air by the wind. Smoke from factories and car exhaust contains dust particles that are spewed into the air. And we stir up roadside dust while driving.

Dust provides some benefits. It is dust in the atmosphere that creates the beautiful colors of a sunrise or sunset. Light from the sun is filtered by the dust particles and bent in different ways, creating the colored sky. Dust particles play a role in the formation of rain and snow clouds; they provide the nuclei around which water and ice crystals form. Dust is also in the soil of a garden, helping the plants grow.

But dust also has a negative side. Dust—especially from non-natural sources—can cause breathing problems in some people. High levels of dust in the atmosphere may also alter local or global weather patterns. Dust affects the way the sun's radiant energy passes through the atmosphere to Earth and back, often causing cooler temperatures. And dust blowing from the desert into the ocean has caused fish kills.

Whether it is a component of a beautiful sand dune or the smog that covers large cities, dust is part of our world.

Reviewed by JENNIFER M. MANGAN
National Center for Atmospheric Research

DUST BOWL

The Dust Bowl refers to the southern Great Plains of the United States, where dust storms swept across the land during the 1930's. Extending approximately 400 miles (640 kilometers) from north to south and 300 miles (480 kilometers) from east to west, the Dust Bowl encompassed southeastern Colorado, northeastern New Mexico, western Kansas, and the panhandles of Texas and Oklahoma. The region received its name after a large dust storm, known as a black blizzard, struck the area on April 14, 1935.

The Causes. In 1803, the United States acquired from France most of the Great Plains—the land between the Mississippi River and the Rocky Mountains. And until the late 1860's, the Great Plains represented the American frontier.

In 1862, the U.S. Congress passed the Homestead Act, promising a parcel of free land to any adult male who would live on it and make it productive. Settlers began pouring into the region, and by 1890 about 6 million people had settled on the grasslands of the Great Plains. The settlers replaced the grass with wheat and other crops they could grow and sell for a profit.

The plains were productive when there was plenty of rainfall. But they were also subject to serious drought and bitter winters. Furthermore, the shallow root systems of the new crops, combined with the churning of tractors and plows that loosened the soil, made the land vulnerable to the blowing wind. The erosion was made worse by inadequate soil-conservation practices. By the early 1930's, middle America was plagued not only by dust storms but by a worldwide economic collapse that became known as the Great Depression.

The Storms. In 1931, drought struck the southern Great Plains, and the following year wind erosion became a common problem for the region. During the worst storms, the dust drifted like snow, halted road and railway travel, and made breathing difficult. Work crews sometimes shoveled the railway tracks clear of drifted dust so the trains could pass.

Residents sealed windows with tape or putty and hung wet sheets in front of windows to filter the air. Others spread sheets over their furniture, wedged rags under doors, and covered keyholes to keep the dirt out of their homes. Electric lights dimmed to a faint glow along streets during the day. Poor visibility made travel hazardous during a dust storm, as soil drifted across highways and railroad tracks. Some storms sifted dust on ships far out in the Atlantic Ocean.

Federal Aid. The wind erosion conditions in the southern Great Plains became so serious that farmers looked to the federal government for technical and financial support. In 1935, the Forest Service began the Shelterbelt Project or Prairie States Forestry Project, which involved planting strips of trees called shelterbelts on selected farms. As the trees grew, they protected fields and farm homes from the wind and slowed the blowing soil. By the time the project ended in 1942, the Forest Service had planted nearly 19,000 miles (30,000 kilometers) of shelterbelts.

The Soil Conservation Service (SCS), also established in 1935, encouraged farmers to adopt proper conservation techniques. By the late 1930's the SCS had helped farmers bring their blowing lands under control. Most farmers who followed the technical advice of the SCS adopted proper plowing and planting techniques, such as contour plowing, terracing, and strip cropping, that helped protect the soil from the wind. The soil-conservation practices promoted by the SCS were designed to restore the Dust Bowl to pre-drought conditions.

The Resettlement Administration (RA) and its successor, the Farm Security Administration (FSA), worked to restore blowing fields and rangelands to grass. In 1935, the RA began a land-purchase program to buy the worst wind-eroded lands in order to restore them with the most effective soil-conservation techniques. (Many of these restored lands have since become national grasslands, administered by the National Forest System.) Then the federal government rented those lands to cattlemen, thereby returning a portion of the region to a grazing economy while ensuring the preservation of the soil.

Restoration. Precipitation increased during 1938, and the wheat, grass, and cotton grew and helped hold the soil against the wind. As a result, the dust storms diminished in number and intensity. By the spring of 1939, less than 10 million acres (4 million hectares) were still subject to severe wind erosion, down from 50 million acres (20 million hectares) in 1935. During the early 1940's normal precipitation returned to the southern Great Plains. Crops, grass, and weeds covered much of the land and protected it from blowing with the wind.

The dust storms of the 1930's forced farmers and the federal government to use all the technical expertise and financial resources they could command to bring the wind erosion problem under control. The lives of the men, women, and children who lived on the southern Great Plains during the 1930's would be forever marked by the drought and dust that gave the region the name Dust Bowl.

R. Douglas Hurt
Iowa State University

DUTCH AND FLEMISH ART

The artists of the Low Countries developed no original style of painting until the 15th century. At that time the dukes of Burgundy brought the many small territories of the area under one government. The dukes encouraged national art by buying the works of painters, goldsmiths, and tapestry weavers. Architects and sculptors continued to work in styles similar to those of foreign artists, but the painters developed a completely original tradition that rivaled the art of any other country.

In 1609 the Low Countries were divided. The Dutch lived in the north in Holland (now the Kingdom of the Netherlands). The southern part became Flanders (now Belgium and part of northern France), where the Flemish people lived. Before the division Dutch and Flemish painting had been very similar. After the division their styles remained much the same, but their favorite subjects changed. The Dutch, who were mostly Protestant, no longer painted religious pictures; the Catholic Flemish still did.

The artists of the Low Countries tried to paint things exactly as they looked. When you look at the work of these 15th-century artists, you can almost feel the softness of velvet, the hard crust of a loaf of bread, the fuzz on a peach. They painted the tiniest details of objects around them: wrinkles in a face, the feathers of a bird, the folds of a dress. They painted everyday objects with the same loving attention they gave to the glow of gold and the radiance of precious jewels.

The Dutch sculptor Claus Sluter (late 14th century) influenced styles of sculpture and painting all over northern Europe. He was interested in all the things that make one person or thing look different from another.

▶ THE 15TH CENTURY

Among the many artists who worked for the dukes of Burgundy were the three Limburg brothers. They were born in the Netherlands, and before 1399 they were in Paris studying with a goldsmith. Their work marks the height of the international style. The international style was a blend of Franco-Flemish and Italian styles. At the time painting in Flanders was done in illuminated

April, from an early 15th-century manuscript by the Limburg brothers. Condé Museum, Chantilly, France.

manuscripts—handwritten and illustrated books. The Limburgs' illuminations show not only the elegant festivities of the nobility but also the everyday work of common people.

The Limburgs painted the most realistic landscapes of the time. And more important, they helped introduce a new kind of realistic painting done on wooden panels or canvas instead of in small manuscripts. Although more portraits were done, painters' favorite subjects were still the old familiar Bible stories.

The greatest Flemish painter of the 15th century was Jan van Eyck (1370?–1440?). He was born in a Dutch town but set up his workshop in the city of Bruges in Flanders. He was the official court painter of the Duke of Burgundy. With his older brother, Hubert van Eyck (1366?–1426), about whom we know very little, Jan painted the famous altarpiece in Ghent, *The Adoration of the Lamb*. Finished in 1432, this large, detailed work is

Madonna with the Chancellor Rolin (1430–35) by Van Eyck. Louvre, Paris.

one of the masterpieces of early Flemish painting.

The Van Eycks perfected the technique of oil painting. It was Jan's use of this medium that made possible the many tiny details in his paintings. Some details are so small that a magnifying glass must be used to see them.

Jan's technique was to put layer upon layer of oil paint over a white base. In this way he got bright jewel-like colors. He is probably most famous for his amazing ability to make such subjects as cloth, jewels, marble, and flowers look real. He also knew how to paint landscapes that seem filled with real air and light. He knew that colors in the distance look paler and that things look hazier near the horizon. All this attention to detail does not, however, detract from the main subject of his paintings. The religious story or the personality of the people in his portraits remain most important.

Another artist who helped form the tradition of Flemish realism and influenced Jan van Eyck is known as the Master of Flémalle. It is not certain, but he was probably Robert Campin (1375?–1444), who had a successful workshop in Tournai, Flanders. He was the first to paint religious stories in the setting of an ordinary home. He also showed landscapes and city views through an open window. While Jan van Eyck painted the Virgin Mary as the Queen of Heaven, the Master of Flémalle pictured her as a middle-class mother. Although the settings are simple, the paintings are filled with many symbolic details. **Symbolism**—using one object to stand for another object or an idea—is used in all Flemish paintings of the century. For example, the dog stands for loyalty.

Another important painter of the 15th century was Rogier van der Weyden (1399?–1464). He was probably trained in the workshop of the Master of Flémalle. By the middle of the century, he was the leading painter in the city of Brussels. While the Van Eycks were interested in everything in the world around us, Rogier was interested in the world inside us. He explored human feelings and realistically represented strong, religious emotions. He knew how to show the red and tearful eyes of a person crying. Like all Flemish artists, he was interested in detail and rich color.

In spite of the importance of the Van Eycks, it was the paintings of the Master of Flémalle and of Rogier van der Weyden that inspired most of the artists working in Flanders for the rest of the century. The only real follower of the Van Eycks was Petrus Christus (1420?–72?). Sometimes said to have been Jan's pupil, Christus continued his careful style and sense of space. He was also interested in the work of the Master of Flémalle and Van der Weyden.

Born in the Netherlands, Dierik Bouts (1410?–75) soon moved to Flanders. His realistic scenes and many fine portraits were

Mourning Monk, a statue by Claus Sluter, was completed in 1411 for the tomb of Philip the Bold. Dijon Museum.

done in wonderful rich color. His figures are much less emotional than those of Rogier. Hugo van der Goes (1440?–82) was one of the most talented of the Flemish artists. His most famous painting, *The Portinari Altarpiece,* was done for an Italian banker. It was immediately sent to Florence, Italy, where the rich color, fine oil technique, and realism of Flemish art were admired and copied.

One of the most popular artists of the period was Hans Memling (about 1430?–94). He was born in Germany but was probably a pupil of Rogier van der Weyden. He spent most of his life in Bruges, Flanders, where he painted the sweet, refined Madonnas (mother and child) that are world famous. The last master of the Bruges school was Gerard David (1460?–1523), who came from the Netherlands and followed the style of Rogier van der Weyden.

One of the few painters of the 15th century who was born in the Netherlands and stayed there was Geertgen tot Sint Jans (1465?–95?). His name means "little Gerard of the Brethren of Saint John." The Brethren of Saint John were a group of monks with whom Geertgen lived. His style was simpler and less detailed than that of other Flemish artists of his time.

Another important artist who was born and lived in the Netherlands was Hieronymus Bosch (1450?–1516). His unusual, imaginative style influenced later Flemish as well as Dutch art. Like many artists of the late 15th century, Bosch was concerned with death and sin. He often painted weird combinations of animals, fish, human beings, plants, and objects. His vivid imagination also produced violent pictures of Bible stories.

▶ THE 16TH CENTURY

The 16th century was a period of religious and political struggle in the Low Countries. The area had come under the control of Spain. The Netherlands objected to the rule of the Spanish Catholic kings. The Protestants wanted the right to worship in their own way. They felt that old traditions of local independence were not protected by these foreign kings. In 1568 a war that was to last 39 years began between the Netherlands and Spain. By 1609 the Netherlands had won independence. The Southern provinces—Flanders—stayed under Spanish rule.

During this century there were two main trends in art—Italianism and realism. Interest in the Italian Renaissance was great, and many artists went to Italy. They came back and painted pictures of classical subjects, such as mythology, in styles borrowed from Leonardo da Vinci and Michelangelo. Although these early borrowings from Italy were not always successful, many good portraits and designs for tapestries were produced in this period.

The greatest and most original artist of the 16th century was not influenced by Italy. He was the Flemish artist Pieter Bruegel (1525?–69). While Bruegel does represent the trend of realism, often his imaginative paintings of real people and events reflect the influence of Bosch. Many of Bruegel's pictures illustrate the simple life of Flemish peasants and show them working in the fields or making merry. He illustrated the months of the year, stories, and proverbs. Whatever the subject, Bruegel's paintings are filled with rhythm and movement. This is as true of his dancing people as it is of a view of a countryside stretching far into the distance. Bruegel's interest in painting the countryside or landscape was to be shared by many painters in the 17th century.

▶ THE 17TH CENTURY

In Flanders the Catholic Church, encouraged by the Spanish governors, tried to awaken interest in religion through art. Flemish art dealt mostly with religion. The Church and aristocratic community ordered more paintings than ever before. But the great cost of war was to put an end to the immense wealth of the Flemish cities.

The most important Flemish painter of the century was Peter Paul Rubens (1577–1640). During his lifetime he was famous not only as an artist but also as a diplomat and a man of great learning. Honored by the kings of England, Spain, and France, he was court painter to the Spanish governor of Flanders.

Rubens set up a huge workshop in Antwerp, where he employed many assistants. Sometimes Rubens painted pictures entirely by himself, but much of the time he simply put finishing touches on the paintings of his assistants. His paintings were richly colored, dramatic, and filled with movement.

The international fame of Flemish art was also due to one of Rubens' pupils, Anthony van Dyck (1599–1641). Van Dyck was famous for his portraits of nobility and royalty. Part of his great success was no doubt due to the fact that he did not hesitate to flatter the great ladies and gentlemen who posed for him. Although less forceful than Rubens, Van Dyck was better at capturing the sitter's personality. The exactness with which he painted the appearance of rich materials

Flemish painters liked to show the tiniest details. The Master of Flémalle made everything in his *Nativity* (1425?), in foreground and background, crystal-clear. Dijon Museum.

Rogier van der Weyden painted no landscape background on *The Descent from the Cross* (1435?), but every twist of cloth is sharply drawn. Prado, Madrid.

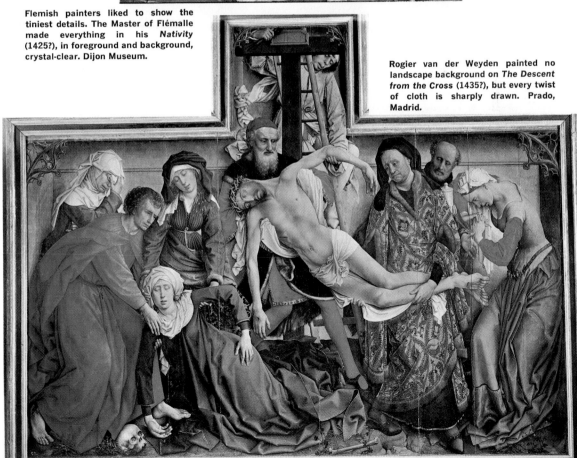

Children's Games (1560) by Pieter Bruegel. Vienna Museum.

Left: *The Last Supper* (1465) by Dierik Bouts. St. Peter's, Louvain. Right: *Saint John the Baptist in the Wilderness* (1490?) by Geertgen tot Sint Jans. Berlin.

Temptation of Saint Anthony (around 1500) by Hieronymus Bosch. National Museum of Fine Arts, Lisbon.

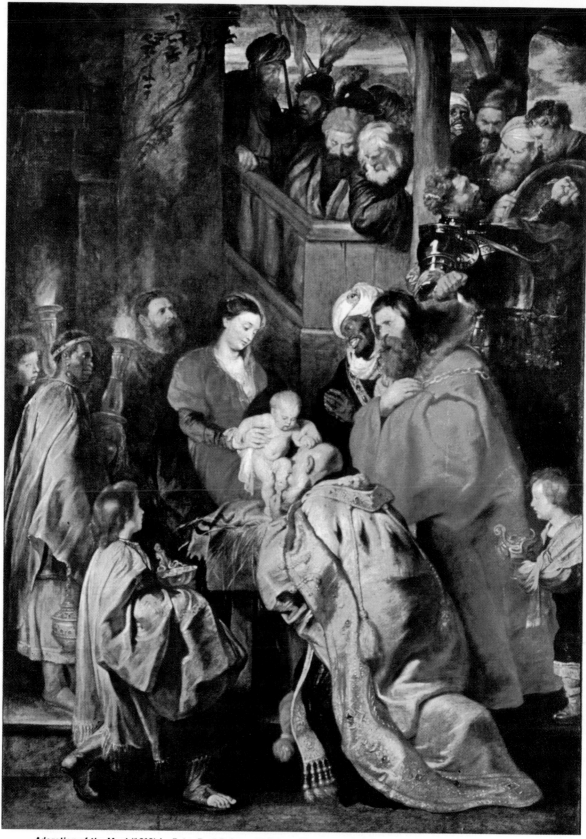

Adoration of the Magi (1619) by Peter Paul Rubens. Boijmans Museum, Rotterdam.

such as satins and velvets was in the tradition set by the Van Eycks. Van Dyck spent 9 years in England, and his portrait style was influential there for a long time.

The new Dutch Republic was growing rich from its large merchant fleet, which sailed all over the world. Trade with places as far away as China and America made port cities like Amsterdam very rich. Because the country was a republic, there was no aristocracy to buy artists' work. The official Protestant religion forbade the decoration of churches with most types of traditional painting and sculpture. Therefore the church could no longer ask artists to paint religious pictures. It was the rich merchants and shopkeepers who now commissioned paintings. They were proud of their new political freedom and they loved pictures of themselves and their way of life. This new rich class kept many artists very busy.

Unlike the Flemish artists, not many Dutch artists traveled to Italy. But in the beginning of the 17th century, there were some who did. These artists were especially interested in the dramatic use of light and action in the paintings of the Italian artist Caravaggio (1573–1610). The most talented member of this group—called the Utrecht school—was Hendrick Terbrugghen (1588–1629). Many of the works of the Utrecht painters were on religious or mythological themes. These painters were important for bringing Italian ideas to Holland. Great masters like Frans Hals and Rembrandt were to use many of these ideas successfully.

Portraiture was one of the most popular forms of art in the 17th century. Frans Hals (1580?–1666) is famous for his lifelike portraits. Painted with quick brush strokes, his laughing, smiling people probably reflect Hals's own good nature. Besides portraits of individuals, Hals did many portraits of groups. The group portrait was a Dutch invention. The members of societies, guilds, and military organizations were proud of their achievements. They had their pictures painted together—just as today a class in school has a group photograph taken.

Some of Hals's paintings show people drinking and making merry in taverns. Paintings of this kind that show everyday life are called **genre** painting. Some artists painted gay scenes of rich burghers (townspeople) similar to those of Frans Hals. Others like Adriaen van Ostade (1610–85) and his pupil Jan Steen (1626–79) painted scenes of peasant life and merrymaking. Their pictures are full of the rush and bustle of life. Quite different are the calm scenes of family life portrayed by Pieter de Hooch (1629–84?) and Gerard Terborch (1617–81).

The finest of the painters of interior scenes was Jan Vermeer (1632–75). He portrayed objects in detail with great calm and dignity. He loved to show the glitter of metal and the shine of cloth as well as the effect of light in a room. His use of light adds a feeling of quiet drama to his paintings. Vermeer also painted a very famous picture of his native town, Delft.

Many artists painted nothing but landscapes. These scenes were popular because art buyers liked pictures of the countryside and coast, which they knew so well. They painted the flat Dutch countryside and rivers, capturing the misty air. Other artists like Jacob van Ruysdael (1628?–82) painted landscape with a new sense of drama—probably inspired by Rembrandt. Meindert Hobbema (1638–1709) was the last of the great painters of purely Dutch landscape.

In a nation that grew rich because of its large fleet of trade ships, paintings of harbors and boats were also very popular. Painters such as Willem van de Velde (1611–93) specialized in this kind of picture. Other artists did nothing but paintings of things—or still lifes. The term "still life" was invented by the Dutch. Objects such as dishes, flowers, and fruits were interestingly arranged and painted in a realistic way.

Most artists of the 17th century specialized in one type of painting. However, Rembrandt van Rijn (1606–69), the greatest Dutch artist of all, was a master of many kinds of painting—portraits, landscape, genre, and religious subjects. He is also famous for his beautiful etchings. Etchings are prints that are made from a metal plate. Grooves are burned with acid into the plate, and ink is forced into the grooves. The ink is printed onto paper by a press. Printmakers before Rembrandt sketched their ideas first with pencil or pen, but Rembrandt worked directly on the etching plate. This change al-

Abraham's Sacrifice (1655),
an etching by Rembrandt.
This print is in the Dussel-
dorf State Museum.

lowed the printmaker to express his ideas in one creative act.

Rembrandt was too great an artist to keep within the limits of a national style. His paintings do not always show the usual Dutch feeling for clarity and order. Rembrandt would select the most dramatic moment of a story, and many of his paintings are filled with excitement. Part of the drama is obtained by his use of light, inspired by Caravaggio. But Caravaggio's light has a definite source, while Rembrandt's light seems to come from no specific place. By means of this heavenly light, Rembrandt draws the viewer's attention to the central figure and the parts of the painting that reflect it.

As he grew older Rembrandt became less interested in scenes of dramatic action. Instead he was interested in the inner drama of people's feelings and emotions.

▶ THE MODERN PERIOD

During the 18th century Dutch artists continued to paint landscapes and marine scenes. However, the quality of these paintings declined. In Flanders painting was even less inspired. But in the 19th century there was a revival of the arts in Flanders, probably caused by independence from Spain. Both Belgium and Holland may be proud of several modern artists of international fame.

An outstanding Belgian artist was James Ensor (1860–1949). Greatly influenced by Bosch and Brueghel, Ensor painted pictures that were both sad and fantastic. His works influenced the expressionists of the 20th century. **Expressionism** is a style that stresses the artist's feelings about himself and the world. Line and color are often exaggerated and distorted.

Saint Sebastian (1625) by Terbrugghen. Allen Memorial Art Museum, Oberlin, Ohio.

Portrait of Charles I Hunting (1635) by Anthony van Dyck. Louvre, Paris.

The Syndics of the Cloth Guild (1662) by Rembrandt. Rijksmuseum, Amsterdam.

Artist in His Studio (1665–70) by Jan Vermeer. Czernin Gallery, Vienna.

Above, *The Avenue, Middelharnis, Holland* (1689) by Meindert Hobbema. National Gallery, London.

Portrait of a Married Couple (1621?) by Frans Hals. Rijksmuseum, Amsterdam.

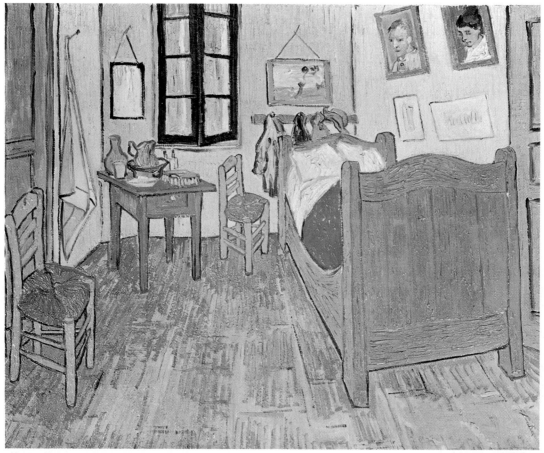

Above, *Vincent's Room at Arles* (1888) by van Gogh. Louvre, Paris. Below, *Composition* (1921) by Piet Mondrian. Museum of Modern Art, New York.

Even more important to the creation of expressionism were the works of the Dutch painter Vincent van Gogh (1853–90). He never stayed in one place nor held a job for long. His restlessness and loneliness are expressed in his paintings. Quickly applying his bright colors, Van Gogh made vivid, swirling designs that have a nervous quality.

Dutch artists also contributed to the international movement of abstract art—art that does not represent actual objects. The most important of the Dutch abstractionists was Piet Mondrian (1872–1944). In 1911 Mondrian stopped painting realistic landscapes. He developed a style in which he divided his canvases into rectangles and squares, painting each shape a simple blue, red, yellow, or white. The calm, balance, and order of this artist's works are certainly part of the Dutch tradition.

ROBERT WELSH
University of Toronto

See also ARCHITECTURE; GERMANY, ART AND ARCHITECTURE OF; PAINTING; SCULPTURE.

DUTCH AND FLEMISH MUSIC

During most of the 15th and 16th centuries, the Dutch and Flemish musicians of the Low Countries led all of Europe in musical genius. The Low Countries of that time included present-day Belgium, the Netherlands, Luxembourg, and part of the eastern border region of France.

▶ ## THE BURGUNDIAN PERIOD

The dukes of Burgundy ruled over this entire region, and one of them, Philip the Good, became one of the most powerful and wealthy men in Europe. Philip was a great lover of all the arts, but especially of music. His musical establishment, called a chapel, was the envy of every other monarch and prince. The finest singers, composers, and instrumentalists were in his service. People came from far and near to hear the glorious music. Thus the first flowering of Low Country music is called the Burgundian period.

The finest musicians of Europe came from the provinces of Flanders, Brabant, and Hainaut. Duke Philip's heir, Duke Charles the Bold, continued to love and cultivate the arts. His court was a place of color, liveliness, and song. The chapel always numbered from 15 to 25 or more musicians, besides a more informal group made up of minstrels, hurdy-gurdy players, and trumpeters.

The Burgundian dukes maintained no fixed residence, but moved freely throughout the Low Countries, setting up court wherever they went. Their musicians always went along with them, even to the battlefield. When their soldiers were victorious, the chapel sang a *Te Deum* ("We Praise Thee, God"). But if things went badly, the choir was ready to chant a Requiem Mass for those who had died.

Famous Burgundian Composers

Two of the greatest musicians of the Burgundian period, Gilles Binchois (1400?–60) and Antoine Busnois (?–1492), served the last two dukes of Burgundy. But the greatest musician of them all, Guillaume Dufay (1400?–74), spent much of his life in Italy, where music was beginning to be greatly appreciated. The music of these Burgundians has a very beautiful sound. Usually the highest part is a sweet, free-flowing melody while two or three lower voices or instruments supply the accompaniment beneath it. Pictures of the time show singers and instrumentalists grouped around a single large book, called a choir book if the music was performed in church or a *chansonnier* if the occasion was a social one.

During the Burgundian period and for many years afterward, musical training was carried on principally in the choir schools of the great cathedrals. Among the finest were those in Antwerp and Bruges, both Flemish cities, and in Tournai and Cambrai in the French border region. Hundreds of talented boys were trained in these schools. There they sang lovely music with the cathedral choirs in return for the best of musical educations. Dufay was a choirboy at Cambrai, Binchois probably at Tournai.

Sacred Music

The mass had become the most important musical form and was chosen by composers for some of their finest works, as was the symphony in the time of Haydn, Mozart, and Beethoven. The mass as a musical form usually has five sections, or movements: *Kyrie, Gloria, Credo, Sanctus,* and *Agnus Dei.* Today in many Catholic churches one can still hear masses sung much as they were in the 16th century. The term "motet" was applied to most of the sacred compositions that were not part of the mass.

Usually this sacred music was written for four or sometimes five voice parts. Often it was based upon some well-known melody, like a section of Gregorian chant, or even a popular song of the day, which sometimes was sung in long notes by the tenor. One of the most popular songs on which masses were based was *L'Homme armé* ("The Armed Man"), and scarcely a composer from Dufay to the mid-16th century failed to use this tune in a mass. If the use of a popular song as part of a religious composition seems odd to us, we must remember that this was still a time when the Church was very close to every aspect of daily life, and so such a custom probably seemed quite natural and no irreverence was intended. Probably it was thought that the song had been sanctified by its use in church music.

▶THE FLEMISH PERIOD

The second half of the 15th century and most of the 16th is generally called the Flemish period. It is sometimes known as the Franco-Flemish period because so many musicians continued to come from the disputed Franco-Flemish border region.

Jean d'Ockeghem

The first great musician of the new generation was Jean d'Ockeghem (1430?–95), who was a choirboy at the Antwerp cathedral, but served the kings of France during most of his life. Ockeghem was a great teacher as well as composer, and many of the leading younger musicians of the time studied with him. He was greatly loved and respected, especially by his students. At his death several laments were written and set to music, the finest one by Josquin des Prez.

Josquin des Prez

The greatest of all the Low Country musicians, Josquin des Prez (1450?–1521), was a man so advanced in his ideas that he has been called the first modern composer. He enjoyed great renown in his lifetime, and the passing centuries have added to his fame. Josquin was a master of all the craftsmanship and musical cunning that had long marked

Lute Player and Woman Playing the Harp, by Israel van Meckenem (1450–1503).

Low Country music; but, more important, he felt that beauty was as necessary to music as fine workmanship. As a consequence, his masses, motets, and chansons are an especial joy to hear. Josquin was very sensitive to the sound and meaning of words, which he tried to express in his music. Many musical traits that we now take for granted appeared strongly for the first time in Josquin's compositions—firm cadences, full chords, clearly defined and organized structures. Few composers have ever matched this great Netherlander.

A Famous Musical Theorist

Since musical scenes were a favorite subject for most of the great painters of the 15th and 16th centuries, much that we know about Renaissance music comes from pictures. There are also some diaries that describe the times, and books that tell how to become skilled in music. Johannes Tinctoris (1436–1511), a Flemish musician and writer on musical theory, left several such books that tell us how greatly respected the musicians were during their lifetimes. In 1477 he wrote: "At the present time . . . there flourish, by some heavenly influence or because of diligent practice, countless composers . . . . Nearly all the works of these men exhale such sweetness that in my opinion they are to be considered suitable not only for men and heroes, but even for the immortal gods."

Obrecht and Isaac

Josquin's great contemporary, the composer Jacob Obrecht (1452–1505), came from Holland, but worked in several Flemish towns and later in Italy, where he died of the plague. Heinrich Isaac (1450?–1517) had an especially brilliant career abroad. In Florence, Italy, he served at the court of Lorenzo the Magnificent, greatest member of the Medici family. After Lorenzo's death Isaac was called to serve Emperor Maximilian of Austria, who preferred Flemish musicians above all others. Both Obrecht and Isaac wrote many wonderful masses and motets, as well as delightful songs to enjoy on social occasions.

The Spread of Low Country Music

After Josquin's death the musical seeds planted in Italy, Austria, Spain, and France

Family Group by Jan Miense Molenaer (1605?–68).

by the Dutch and Flemish musicians began to bear wonderful fruit. Native composers in all these countries arose to carry on the great Netherlands tradition. For at least 70 years more, however, Low Country musicians were successful all over Europe. They included Adrian Willaert (1490?–1562), Nicolas Gombert (1490?–1556), and Jacob Arcadelt (1505?–1567?). But best of all the Netherlanders who came after Josquin was Roland de Lassus (1532–94). A truly international composer, Lassus worked in almost every European country before he was called to Munich in 1556. He was revered in his day in the same manner as was his Italian contemporary, Palestrina.

The End of a Great Musical Era

The last of the line of Low Country Renaissance musicians was Jan Pieters Sweelinck (1562–1621), a Hollander whose organ playing at Amsterdam attracted people from all over Europe. Many pupils, especially from Germany, flocked there to study with him. The long line of great German organists was Sweelinck's bequest to the future of European music.

By the 1600's the great age of Dutch and Flemish music was past, and only occasionally does the name of a later-day Belgian or Hollander recall the glories of the Renaissance. Jean Baptiste Loeillet early in the 1700's, François Joseph Gossec and André Ernest Modeste Grétry two generations later, and César Franck in the late 1800's are all important Low Country musical figures.

LOUISE E. CUYLER
Chairman, Department of Musicology
University of Michigan

See also RENAISSANCE MUSIC.

DUTCH GUIANA. See SURINAME.

DUTCH WEST INDIES. See NETHERLANDS (Overseas Territories).

DVD. See VIDEO RECORDING.

DVOŘÁK, ANTONÍN (1841–1904)

Composer Antonín Dvořák sought to capture in his music the spirit of his native Bohemia, a province that is now part of the Czech Republic.

Antonín Leopold Dvořák was born near Prague on September 8, 1841. Even as a young boy, Antonín loved music and learned to play the violin. Unwilling to follow in his father's footsteps as an innkeeper and butcher, he went to Prague when he was 16 to study the organ and music composition. Antonín supported himself by playing the violin and viola in cafés and the opera house.

Dvořák's first important work, a choral piece called *Hymnus* (1873), attracted wide attention. The support of such established composers as Johannes Brahms, Franz Liszt, and Bedřich Smetana helped Dvořák's reputation spread. After the publication of his first set of *Slavonic Dances* (1878), Dvořák became Bohemia's best-known composer.

Dvořák composed in nearly all forms of music, both vocal (operas, songs, choral works) and instrumental (symphonies, concertos, chamber music, piano pieces). Though his musical style was influenced by such masters as Ludwig van Beethoven and Johannes Brahms, many of his compositions express the spirit of folk music—in particular, the rhythms and melodies of his native Bohemia.

Dvořák made many successful trips to England during his lifetime. In 1884 he conducted his *Stabat Mater* (1877) in London, to great applause. He composed his oratorio *Saint Ludmila* (1886) and a requiem (1890) for the English people. In 1891, Cambridge University awarded him an honorary Doctor of Music degree.

Between 1892 and 1895, Dvořák taught in New York City. During this period he composed the symphony entitled *From the New World*, his most celebrated work. Dvořák also composed his famous cello concerto and the popular piano piece "Humoresque" while he was in the United States.

On his return to Prague, Dvořák taught at the Prague Conservatory, and in 1901 he was made its artistic director. The same year, his most successful opera, *Rusalka (The Water-Nymph)*, was given its first performance at the National Theater in Prague. He died in Prague on May 1, 1904.

Reviewed by SYLVAN SUSKIN
Oberlin College Conservatory of Music

DWARFISM

Dwarfism is extreme short stature caused by a medical condition. Dwarfs range in height from 2 feet 8 inches to 4 feet 10 inches (81 to 147 centimeters). About 250,000 dwarfs live in the United States.

Several hundred conditions leading to dwarfism have been identified. In the United States today, the conditions most commonly associated with dwarfism include genetic (inherited) conditions and metabolic (hormonal) disorders. Extreme neglect and abuse may also prevent growth. To diagnose dwarfism, a specialist reviews X-ray pictures, blood tests, and genetic studies. Once the type of dwarfism has been identified, the spe-

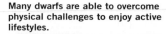

Many dwarfs are able to overcome physical challenges to enjoy active lifestyles.

cialist can give medical advice. He or she may also put the family in contact with people who have similar conditions and who lead satisfying lives.

Disproportionate Dwarfism. Some types of dwarfism involve disproportion. That is, the arms and legs or the trunk (the main part of the body) are short in relation to other parts of the body. Nearly every case is caused by genetic conditions that interfere with the growth of bone, cartilage, and connective tissue. This type of dwarfism occurs in about 1 in 10,000 births.

Some people with disproportionate dwarfism have spinal compression and degenerative joint disease (which causes pain and difficulty walking), reduced lung function, and hearing problems. These complications are often treatable. Some young dwarfs undergo a complex procedure to lengthen the limbs. But most choose to accept their dwarf identity.

Proportionate Dwarfism. A person with proportionate dwarfism is shorter overall than a person of average height. However, the arms, legs, trunk, and head are the same size in relation to each other as would be expected in an average-size person. This kind of dwarfism results from hormonal deficiencies, chromosomal abnormalities, poor nutrition, emotional neglect or abuse, or disease.

Proportionate dwarfism is often treatable. If the cause is the lack of growth hormone, injections of synthetic growth hormone during childhood may increase height.

Some forms of proportionate dwarfism have almost disappeared in Western nations. However, because of poor nutrition, certain types of dwarfism that are "diseases of poverty" still occur in many places.

Terms. Accepted terms include **persons with dwarfism**, **short-statured persons**, and **dwarfs** (not dwarves). **Little person** is also acceptable, and a shorter version, **LP**, is often used by members of Little People of America, a support group for people of short stature and their families. The term **midget**, formerly used to refer to proportionate dwarfs, is now considered unacceptable.

Social Factors. Dwarfs have faced discrimination and prejudice. In early times, dwarfs were often kept at royal courts to provide entertainment. Even later, jobs as entertainers or circus performers were often the only occupations available to dwarfs. However, throughout history, people of very short stature have excelled in diverse fields.

Conditions for dwarfs have improved dramatically. Helpful developments include disability legislation, new educational and economic opportunities, and medical advances. In addition, advocacy groups have appeared in countries around the world.

Although dwarfs look different, intellectually and emotionally they do not differ from others. Dwarfs are members of families in which their parents, siblings, spouses, and children may be short or tall. They pursue all kinds of careers and are active in their communities. Despite the physical, medical, and social challenges they face, dwarfs are able to lead productive and rewarding lives.

BETTY ADELSON
Author, *The Lives of Dwarfs*

DYES AND DYEING

Dyes give color to fabrics and other materials. Since ancient times, they have been an important item of trade between nations. The needs of dyers to find better ways of applying dyes and the search for new dyes added greatly to the world's scientific knowledge. Thanks to dyes, we have colors of every kind in our clothing and in many things we use every day.

The most important use of dyes is for coloring textiles. But large quantities are used to color other materials, including paper products, plastics, leather, drugs, cosmetics, and foods. The dye usually is used to make products more attractive. It can also serve a functional purpose. For example, dyes are used for identification, as in flags and uniforms.

Dyes can even be used for purposes other than coloring. For example, gentian violet, a purple dye, has been used as a medicine in the treatment of some infections. Dyes have

also helped doctors discover many disease organisms by making them visible through a microscope. By making the structures of cells easier to distinguish, dyes have helped biolo-

Many different color dyes, both natural and synthetic, are sold in local markets, such as this one in Kathmandu, Nepal.

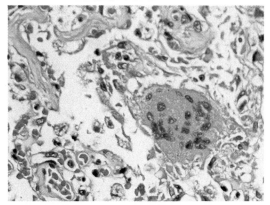

Dyes are used in medicine to make cell structures easier to distinguish through a microscope. This slide shows disease-damaged lung cells.

gists learn many things about plant and animal life.

Color was used in an interesting way in national elections held in Iraq in 2005. After casting their ballots, voters were asked to dip their index fingers in a solution of purple dye. The colored fingers of those who voted were easy to spot, thus preventing them from voting more than once. Coloring their fingers would have been of no use if the color could be washed off easily. Therefore a dye was chosen. When used this way, the dye binds with the outer layer of skin and wears away over time.

A woman displays the purple dye used to identify people who had cast their votes in elections held in Iraq in 2005.

When something is **dyed**, chemical or physical forces hold the color molecule firmly to the material. A dye is called **fast** when the molecules of the dye and the material to be dyed bind together tightly. If these forces are not holding the color fast, the material is **stained**, not dyed.

Many dyes stick firmly to some materials but are easily washed out of others. For example, some dyes can be applied to wool in such a way that they are not easily removed, while the same dyes will only stain cotton. That is, the dye molecules can be removed from the cotton by washing. But other dyes are **colorfast** on cotton. Still others are effective only for dyeing synthetic fibers.

When there is no holding force between a dye and the material to be dyed—or when the holding force is too weak—a substance called a **mordant** may be added. The word "mordant" comes from the Latin *mordere* ("to bite"). The mordant makes the dye "bite" harder into the material being dyed. It helps bind the dye to the material. Sometimes mordants also affect the shade of color that is produced by the dye.

▶ **HISTORY OF DYES**

For centuries people did not know much about what took place when a dye was applied to a fabric. Only when chemists and physicists had gained enough knowledge could the process of dyeing be understood thoroughly. But even without scientific knowledge, people got remarkable results with their dyes.

Dyes of the Ancient World

Ancient people used dyes of vegetable origin to color their bodies, believing that certain colors, notably red, could drive out evil spirits or illness. In many regions of the world, a plant commonly known as henna was used to provide red, orange, and brown dyes. People applied these dyes to their skin and hair, as well as to textiles.

The earliest written record of the use of natural dyes, dated 2600 B.C., was found in China. In 331 B.C., Alexander the Great mentions finding purple robes dating to 541 B.C. Since very early times, people have used plant juices to color their fabrics. Fabrics found in Near and Middle Eastern archaeological sites show that the ancient cultures of the eastern Mediterranean region were well practiced in the use of natural dyes. Ancient civilizations also knew of mordants and frequently used them.

The important dyes used in the Mediterranean civilizations (before A.D. 500) were obtained entirely from the animal or plant world. These dyes included indigo, kermes, madder root, saffron, and Tyrian purple.

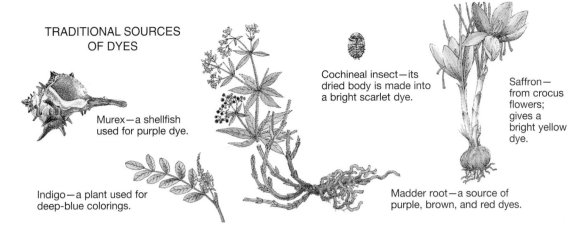

TRADITIONAL SOURCES OF DYES

Murex—a shellfish used for purple dye.

Cochineal insect—its dried body is made into a bright scarlet dye.

Saffron—from crocus flowers; gives a bright yellow dye.

Indigo—a plant used for deep-blue colorings.

Madder root—a source of purple, brown, and red dyes.

Indigo, obtained from a plant grown in India, Java, China, and Japan, gave a deep bright blue color. This beautiful color is still used, although the dye is now made synthetically. A dye very similar to indigo was obtained from a plant known as **woad**.

Kermes, which gave a reddish-purple color, was extracted from the bodies of insects found on the leaves of the kermes oak. This tree is common in southern Europe, North Africa, and the Middle East. Kermes was one of the main sources of red dye in ancient times. When combined with different mordants, kermes gave shades of scarlet, crimson, or purple.

Madder root, which comes from a prickly vine native to the Middle East, was called the dyer's root in ancient times. It was used to dye cotton and wool purple, brown, and red. **Saffron**, extracted from certain crocus flowers, gave a bright yellow dye. **Tyrian purple**, probably discovered about 1600 B.C., was taken from the shellfish *Murex brandaris* found in the Mediterranean Sea. It was called the purple of the ancients. About 12,000 snails were needed to obtain a very small quantity of the dye. This made Tyrian purple too expensive to be used on anything but the robes of kings. The color has now come to be called royal purple as well as Tyrian purple. Other dyes may have been known in the ancient world, but these were the most important. They continued to be used for many centuries.

Dyes from the New World

The discovery of America and of a sea route around the Cape of Good Hope had a great impact on world trade. Many dyes from plants and animals of America became known to the rest of the world. Dyes were also brought from India around Africa to Europe.

In 1518 the Spanish brought a new dye—**cochineal**—to Europe from Mexico. Cochineal, like kermes, is made from the dried bodies of insects. Cochineal bugs are small, scaly insects often found on cactus plants. They give a bright scarlet dye, which is ten times stronger than kermes. After the discovery of cochineal, kermes almost disappeared from use.

Logwood, which comes from a tree in the West Indies and Central America, was discovered by the Spanish early in the 1500's. It is used to dye fabrics dark blue, purple, or black. When used with a mordant of iron or tannin, it gives an especially rich black color. It is still sometimes used to dye silk black.

Yellow dye was obtained from the wood known as fustic. The tree is a member of the mulberry family and is found in the West Indies and the lands around the Caribbean Sea. Its coloring matter is called **morin**, and it is used for dyeing cotton and wool. Fustic is the more important of the two kinds of wood used to obtain yellow dye. The other kind is the wood of the southern European sumac tree. This tree belongs to the same plant family as poison ivy and the cashew nut tree.

Another yellow dye, **annatto**, was obtained from the fleshy pulp around the seeds of the annatto tree, which is also found in the tropics. Annatto is used now as a coloring for foods such as butter and cheese. It also used to be a dye for cotton.

A tree that was already well known in Europe was found in abundance in the New World. This was the brazilwood tree. In the year 1500, a Portuguese expedition led by Pedro Alvares Cabral reached the eastern coast of South America. The explorers found so many brazilwood trees there that they called the area *terra de brasil* ("the land of the brazilwood"). This is the origin of the name "Brazil." The wood of the tree yields **brazilein**, which can be used to dye fabrics pink, purple, or crimson.

Old Dyeing Methods

For many centuries the methods used in dyeing were carefully guarded secrets, passed on by word of mouth. But around the 1500's, associations, or guilds, of dyers began to keep written records of their methods of dyeing. The written records give a clear picture of the art of dyeing at that time. The methods had remained unchanged for at least 1,500 years.

In India, a boy stands among rows of dyed silk threads hanging outdoors to dry. Coloring textiles is the most important use of dyes.

Ancient and medieval dyers produced various shades of color mainly by using the three primary colors—blue, red, and yellow. Blue was obtained from indigo or woad. Red was obtained from kermes, cochineal, or madder root. Yellow was obtained mostly from saffron. Reds and yellows were usually dyed after the fabric had been treated with the mineral **alum**, which was used as a mordant. Alum appears to have been used as a mordant for thousands of years. The Egyptians, Greeks, and Romans used it.

Green, brown, violet, and other shades of color were obtained by combining primary colors and sometimes by adding alum as a mordant. Black, too, could be obtained by combining the primary colors. But most ancient and medieval dyers produced black by using a mixture of iron and tannic acid.

Origin of Synthetic Dyes

Synthetic dyes have also been called coal-tar dyes. This is because they are made from materials extracted from coal tar. Coal tar is a black, sticky substance obtained when bituminous coal is heated to make coke.

Today, at least 1,500 synthetic dyes are used in the textile industry. Many other synthetic dyes have been made in the past century but have been replaced with improved dyes.

The first synthetic dye was discovered in 1856 by a young English chemist, William Henry Perkin. As a child in school, Perkin became very interested in chemistry and decided to make it his career. He entered the Royal College of Chemistry in London at the age of 15. Three years later Perkin discovered the first synthetic dye. During an experiment he accidentally produced a black, sticky substance. When Perkin treated this substance with alcohol, it turned to a violet-colored solution. Perkin found that this solution would dye silk and wool. He called the substance **mauve** and set up a small plant to produce and sell it as a dye. Perkin's discovery was important because dyers no longer had to depend on substances found in nature. It was the beginning of the synthetic dye industry.

The first synthetic dye was discovered in England, but Germany soon became a leader in the field. In 1914 nearly 90 percent of the world's synthetic dyes were made in Germany. This worldwide German monopoly was broken by World War I (1914–18). The German export trade was cut off by the Allied blockade. Germany's old customers learned how to make their own dyes. A vast amount of research produced large dye industries in England, France, Switzerland, and the United States. Germany never fully regained its lead.

Synthetic dyes are usually cheaper than natural dyes. They also offer more consistent results and a wider range of shades of color.

Dyes can be applied to fabrics as well as fibers. They provide the vibrant red, green, blue, and other colors seen in these ruffles.

Indigo was first made artificially in 1897. Since then synthetic indigo has replaced the dye from natural sources, except where local artisans maintain the traditional practices. Turkey red, made from madder root, was artificially produced as early as 1868. Synthetic Tyrian purple was produced in 1906 but did not become commercially important.

▶ APPLYING TEXTILE DYES

Dyes can be applied to textile fibers and fabrics by two processes—dyeing and printing. The two processes are often combined to produce the commercial fabrics used in clothing and furnishings.

Textile Dyeing

Fabrics are dyed by being immersed in a liquid solution called a **dye liquor** or **dye bath**. Some textile fibers, such as cotton and wool, can be dyed as raw fibers, as spun yarn, or as woven cloth.

Before dyeing is begun, the fiber must be cleaned thoroughly to remove grease and other substances that might prevent the dye from penetrating and binding to the material.

Dyeing used to be done by hand-dipping the material in a dye bath. Today most dyeing is done in machines. There are two main types of dyeing machines. In one, the yarn or cloth is moved about in the dye bath by mechanical means. In the second type, the material to be dyed (usually raw fiber or yarn) is held still and the dyeing solution is circulated through it.

Three things are important in dyeing. First, the dye solution must spread throughout the fibers to dye the fabric evenly. This is called **diffusion**. Second, after the dye penetrates the fibers, it must be held to them firmly and not washed away by either the dye bath itself or by later washing or soaking in water. The force that holds the dye to the fibers is called **affinity**. Third, the dye must be fast; that is, it must not be easy to remove after the dyeing is completed.

A **fast color** is one that is not removed by washing or rubbing, or sunlight, perspiration, or bleach. The kind of fastness needed for a particular fabric varies with the different uses of the fabric. Fastness to sunlight, for example, is far more important for window curtains than for underclothing. Fastness to washing is more important for work clothes than for furniture coverings that are not washed often.

Fastness is the result of a secure bond between the dye molecule and the atoms of the fiber. This means that the atoms of the dye must be in a specific position with respect to

A textile worker in the Cook Islands applies a blue dye to create a pattern on a piece of fabric.

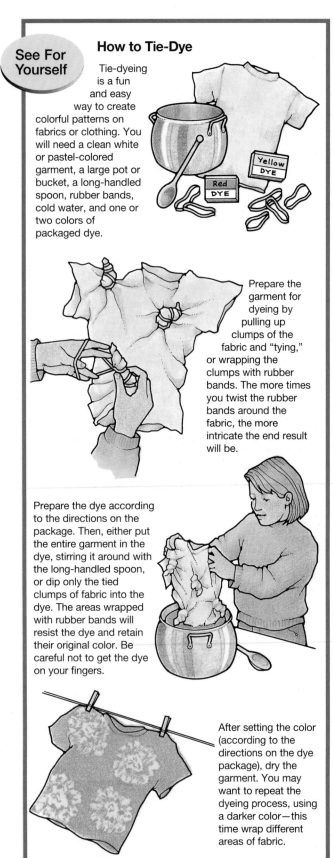

See For Yourself

Tie-dyeing is a fun and easy way to create colorful patterns on fabrics or clothing. You will need a clean white or pastel-colored garment, a large pot or bucket, a long-handled spoon, rubber bands, cold water, and one or two colors of packaged dye.

Prepare the garment for dyeing by pulling up clumps of the fabric and "tying," or wrapping the clumps with rubber bands. The more times you twist the rubber bands around the fabric, the more intricate the end result will be.

Prepare the dye according to the directions on the package. Then, either put the entire garment in the dye, stirring it around with the long-handled spoon, or dip only the tied clumps of fabric into the dye. The areas wrapped with rubber bands will resist the dye and retain their original color. Be careful not to get the dye on your fingers.

After setting the color (according to the directions on the dye package), dry the garment. You may want to repeat the dyeing process, using a darker color—this time wrap different areas of fabric.

the atoms of the material so that the two substances are held together firmly.

There are four classes of fibers, each of which needs different kinds of dyes. The classes are animal, or protein, fibers, such as wool or silk; vegetable (cellulose) fibers, such as cotton or linen; regenerated fibers, such as rayon; and synthetic fibers, such as nylon or polyester.

There are about a dozen important kinds of commercial dyes. Some are used for dyeing many kinds of materials, while some are used mainly with one type of material. **Acid dyes**, for instance, are good for dyeing wool. But they do not work well when applied to the other major natural textile fiber, cotton.

Some dyes are applied without using mordants or other chemical treatments to hold them in the material. **Direct dyes**, used on cotton and rayon, are of this type. Their fastness for washing is rather poor, but the fastness can be improved by chemical treatments after dyeing. **Mordant dyes**, on the other hand, must be combined with a mordant (usually a metal salt) to bind them to the material. The color and the mordant are applied separately. In the material the two substances react chemically to form a compound called a **lake**, which cannot be dissolved out of the material. The exact color of the dyed material depends on the kind of metal used as a mordant. **Vat dyes** need no mordants. They react with the oxygen of the air to form new compounds. These new compounds do not dissolve in water, and they cannot be washed out of the fiber. Vat dyes can be used on either animal or plant fibers, but they are particularly good for dyeing cotton.

Newer dyes, called **disperse dyes**, were developed for coloring synthetic fibers. They are held in the fibers by physical forces. Other recently developed dyes are **fiber reactive dyes**, which attach to fibers by chemical bonds. Fiber reactive dyes are very important for dyeing cotton and wool. The dyes named are only a few of the many available for textile dyeing. There are even colorless dyes, called **fluorescent brightening dyes**. They are used to make white textile fabrics whiter and in laundry detergents to make a whiter wash.

Dyeing problems can become complicated when cloth containing more than one kind of fiber must be dyed. Cloth woven of different fibers may be dyed either a solid color or several colors, depending on the kind of dye mixture used. If a multicolored effect is wanted, a dye mixture can be made in which each separate dye will act only on the fiber for which it has an affinity. Thus, with a cloth made of six different kinds of fiber, a dyer can produce a cloth of six colors by using one dye mixture. On the other hand, if the cloth is to be a solid color, a dye solution can be mixed that will dye all the fibers the same color.

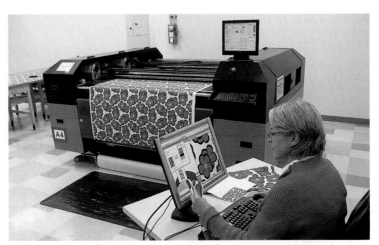

New methods of textile printing include digital printing. With these systems, textile designs can be created on a computer and then printed on fabric.

Textile Printing

Textile printing is a method of applying dye to certain areas of a fabric. A pattern is formed as areas of different colors are printed next to each other. It is much quicker and cheaper to produce colored patterns by printing than by weaving threads of different colors together. Cotton is printed more often than silk, rayon, and acetate.

To keep the coloring from spreading out and spoiling the design, the dye is mixed with a paste that does not spread. Most often it is applied to the fabric through stencils or screens. The dye paste can also be applied with a paintbrush or by using carved blocks.

WONDER QUESTION

What makes dyes fade?

Dyes fade because they lose their power to absorb light. Every color has its own particular wavelength of light. White light is a mixture of lights of all visible wavelengths. A dye has color because it absorbs some wavelengths and reflects the rest. A red shirt looks red because its dye absorbs all wavelengths of light except red, which it reflects. A dye that does not absorb any of the visible wavelengths of light looks white or colorless. The particular wavelengths a dye absorbs depends on the way the atoms in the dye's molecules are arranged. A change in the position of even one atom can cause a dye molecule to stop absorbing light.

When a dyed object, such as a shirt, is exposed to sunlight, the energy of the sunlight bit by bit knocks atoms out of position in the dye molecules. In time, so many molecules lose their color that the whole object becomes faded.

Color can be printed on fabrics in several other ways, too. A mordant can be applied in the desired pattern, and then a mordant dye is used. The mordant dye will stick only in the pattern and can be washed off the other parts of the cloth, leaving them undyed. Or the pattern can be created by using a **resist**, a substance that keeps parts of the cloth from being dyed. Various types of mechanical resists (such as batik wax) can be applied to the cloth. A pattern develops by repeated applications of resist and dye.

The discharge method is the reverse of the resist method. A dyed fabric is printed with a substance that removes the dye. This gives a dyed background with a pattern that is the color of the original fabric.

New methods of textile printing continue to be developed to keep pace with the growth of synthetic textiles. The most recent, transfer printing, involves the migration of colored patterns or metallic foils from a sheet of paper to fabric by heating. Digital printing enables designers to design printed textiles directly on the computer, using digitally controlled effects such as blurring, layering, and reflection.

GUILIANA C. TESORO
Massachusetts Institute of Technology
Reviewed by CHARLOTTE HAMLIN
University of Massachusetts, Dartmouth

See also FIBERS; TEXTILES.

DYLAN, BOB. See ROCK MUSIC (Profiles).

DYNAMITE. See EXPLOSIVES.

DYSLEXIA. See LEARNING DISORDERS.

Index

HOW TO USE THE DICTIONARY INDEX

See the beginning of the blue pages in Volume 1.

D (fourth letter of the English alphabet) **D:**1 *see also* Alphabet

Da capo (musical term) **B:**70; **M:**536

Dacca (Bangladesh) *see* Dhaka

Dachau concentration camp (Germany) **H:**174

Dachshunds (dogs) **D:**252–53
  picture(s) **D:**244

Dacia (Roman province in southeastern Europe) **R:**296, 299

Dacko, David (Central African political leader) **C:**171

Dacron (synthetic fiber) **N:**437; **R:**334

Dactylic hexameter (meter in poetry) **P:**353

Dactyls (metrical feet in poetry) **P:**351

Dadaism (modern literature and art movement) **M:**393
  Duchamp, Marcel **D:**344
  France, literature of **F:**442
  sculpture **S:**104
  surrealism **S:**518

Daddah, Moktar Ould (president of Mauritania) **M:**180

Daddy longlegs (arachnids) **A:**348

Dadié, Bernard B. (Ivorian writer) **I:**421

Daedalus (human-powered airplane)
  picture(s) **A:**570

Daedalus (in Greek mythology) **A:**37; **G:**366

Daffodil (flowering plant)
  picture(s) **G:**43

"Daffodils" (poem by William Wordsworth) **W:**242

Dafne (first opera) **B:**70

Da Gama, Vasco *see* Gama, Vasco da

Daggers (weapons)
  picture(s) **D:**73

Dagomba (a people of Africa) **G:**194

Daguerre, Louis (French photographer) **C:**466; **D:**2; **P:**211

Daguerreotypes (first permanent photographs) **C:**466; **D:**2; **P:**211
  picture(s)
    earliest taken in North America **C:**466

Dahl, Roald (British author) **C:**230 *profile*
  picture(s) **C:**230

Dahlias (flowers) **G:**49

Dahlonega (gold mining settlement in Georgia) **G:**145

Dahlonega Gold Museum (Georgia) **G:**140

Dahnā, Ad (desert region of Saudi Arabia) **S:**58c

Dahomey (African kingdom) **B:**143, 144

Dahomey (modern African country) *see* Benin

Dahshûr (Egypt) **E:**108

Daily Values (DV's) (on food labels) **N:**428

Daimler, Gottlieb (German inventor) **A:**540; **I:**265; **M:**498; **T:**286

Daimyo (Japanese feudal lords) **J:**43

Dairy cattle **C:**153–54; **D:**3–7
  picture(s) **C:**54; **D:**89; **N:**120b; **V:**308, 312; **W:**193, 199

Dairy herd improvement associations **D:**6

Dairying and dairy products **D:**3–11 *see also* Butter; Cheese; Ice cream; Milk; Yogurt
  Canada **C:**64
  cattle **C:**153–54
  cooking **C:**542–43
  fat content **O:**80
  food shopping **F:**349
  food supply **F:**350
  important agricultural products **A:**90, 94–95
  livestock **L:**273
  Netherlands **N:**120b

Vermont **V:**306, 312, 319
What is "Grade A" milk? **D:**9
Wisconsin is leading producer **W:**192, 201
  picture(s)
    dairy farms **C:**510; **F:**50–51; **V:**308; **W:**193
    processing plant **M:**332

Daisy Girl Scouts **G:**215
  picture(s) **G:**215

Daisy Miller (book by Henry James) **J:**20

Dakar (Senegal) **S:**118
  picture(s) **S:**117

Dakota Indians *see* Sioux

Dakota Territory (in United States history) **N:**334; **S:**325–26

Dakota War (1862) **M:**338

Daladier, Édouard (French statesman) **W:**295

Dalai Lama (title of Tibetan Buddhist leaders) **B:**425, 427; **D:**12; **T:**189, 190, 191
  picture(s) **D:**12

Dale, Chester (American banker and art patron) **N:**37

Dale, Sir Thomas (English governor of Jamestown) **J:**23

Daley, Richard J. (mayor of Chicago) **D:**12

Daley, Richard M. (mayor of Chicago) **D:**12

Daley, William M. (American political figure) **D:**12

Daley family (American political family) **D:**12

Dalhousie, 9th Earl of (British governor of Canada) **O:**247

Dalhousie University (Halifax, Nova Scotia) **N:**355

Dali, Salvador (Spanish painter) **D:**13; **M:**395; **S:**385
  picture(s)
    The Persistence of Memory (painting) **D:**13

Dalits (formerly **Untouchables**) (people in India) **H:**139; **I:**119, 133

Dal Lake (Kashmir) **K:**197
  picture(s) **K:**197

Dallam-Hartley XIT Museum (Dalhart, Texas) **T:**132

Dallapiccola, Luigi (Italian composer) **I:**412

Dallas (Texas) **C:**321; **D:**14; **T:**134
  picture(s) **D:**14; **T:**125
    airport **N:**304
    Cotton Bowl **T:**130

Dallas, George Mifflin (American politician) **V:**326 *profile*

Dallas Cup (youth soccer) **S:**222

Dall sheep **S:**147
  picture(s) **A:**145

Dalmatians (dogs)
  picture(s) **D:**247

Dalton (unit of measurement) **A:**486

Dalton, John (English chemist and physicist) **D:**15
  atomic theory in history of chemistry **A:**486; **C:**209
  atomic theory in history of physics **P:**234
  science, milestones in **S:**73
  picture(s) **D:**15

Dalton, Roque (Salvadoran writer) **E:**198

Daltrey, Roger (British rock musician) **R:**263

Daly, Augustin (American playwright) **D:**306

Daly, Marcus (Irish-born American financier) **M:**428, 440–41 *profile*

Dama de Baza (Spanish sculpture)
  picture(s) **S:**380

Damages (in civil law cases) **C:**574, 576

Damascus (Syria) **I:**351; **M:**303; **S:**549, 551
  picture(s) **S:**551

Damascus steel swords **I:**337; **T:**332

Damask (textile) **S:**551

Damasus, Saint (pope) R:292
Damasus II (pope) R:292
Dame (British title) K:277
Dame schools E:81; T:38
Damien, Father (Joseph Damien de Veuster) (Belgian priest and missionary in Hawaii) H:61 *profile*
   picture(s) H:61
Damietta (branch of the Nile River) N:261
"Damn the torpedoes–full speed ahead!" (said by Farragut at Battle of Mobile Bay, 1864) F:62
Damon and Pythias (in Greek legend) G:366
Dampier, William (English explorer) E:411
Dams D:16–21
   artificial lakes L:27
   beaver dams B:110–12
   canals C:89
   Columbia River (Washington) W:21, 27, 28
   Delta Plan (the Netherlands) N:120a
   flood control F:257; R:238
   Grand Coulee Dam W:22
   Johnstown Flood J:124
   Middle East M:302
   notable dams, list of D:21
   Ohio River O:78
   Tennessee T:76
   Three Gorges Dam (China) Y:353
   waterpower P:421; R:239–40; W:69–70
   Why don't we get all our electric power from water? W:70
   picture(s) F:257
      Garrison Dam (North Dakota) N:325
      Grand Coulee Dam (Washington) I:340
      Itaipú Dam (Brazil–Paraguay) P:64, 422
      Kootenay River (British Columbia) C:61
      TVA dam in Tennessee T:78
Damselfish
   picture(s) O:24
Damselflies (insects) D:294
   picture(s) D:294
Dana, Richard Henry (American writer) A:210
Danaë (in Greek mythology) G:365
Danakil (a people of Eritrea) E:316
Danakil desert (Eritrea) E:316
Danbury (Connecticut)
   first hat factory in the United States H:47
Danby (Vermont) V:312
Dance D:22–33
   arts of the United States U:99
   ballet B:25–33
   bee "dances" B:120
   colonial life in America C:412
   folk dance F:299–303
   folklore F:304
   Hawaiian hula H:55
   Irish step dancing I:322
   music *see* Dance music
   Paraguayan bottle dance P:63
   roller disco R:282
   theater of India T:162
   picture(s)
      Australian Aborigines A:7
      Balinese dancer I:206
      Ballet Folklórica (Mexico) L:72
      Guinea G:406b
      Mexican dancing in Arizona A:397
      Native Americans' ceremonial dances M:545; R:145
      Paraguayan children in traditional dress P:62
      Thailand S:328; T:151
Dance Class (painting by Degas)
   picture(s) D:86
Dance music
   drums, use of D:337–38, 338–39, 340
   Latin-American folk music for the dance L:72
   play-party tunes of folk music F:326
   Spain S:392a
   Strauss, Johann, Jr. S:466

Dance of Death (series of woodcut prints by Holbein) H:159d
Dance suite (musical composition) B:72
Dance Theater of Harlem B:33
Dandelions
   growth P:312
   seed, dispersal of P:313
   wine made from F:281
   picture(s) W:105
"Dandelions" (poem by Frances M. Frost) F:123
Dander (of animals) A:190
Dandie Dinmont terriers (dogs) D:248
   picture(s) D:248
Dandruff (dead skin shed by the scalp) H:6–7
Dandy roll (part of a papermaking machine) P:56
Danegeld (tribute of gold or silver) V:342, 343; W:174
Danelaw (section of England under Viking rule) E:237–38; V:342
Danes (Teutonic Norsemen and Vikings) D:112
   Alfred the Great and the Danes A:179
   invasions of England E:237–38
   rulers of England, list of E:236
Daniel (Biblical character) B:157, 159, 163
   Apocryphal additions to Book of Daniel B:163
   story of Daniel in the lion's den B:172–73
Daniel in the Lion's Den (Bible story) B:172–73
Daniel-Johnson Dam (Quebec, Canada)
   picture(s) D:17
Daniels, Charles M. (American athlete) S:536
Danish language D:108
Dannay, Frederic (American author) *see* Queen, Ellery
D'Annunzio, Gabriele (Italian writer and poet) I:408
Dan Patch (racehorse) H:235
Dante 2 (robot)
   picture(s) C:485
Dante Alighieri (Italian poet) D:34; I:387, 405–6
   wanted restoration of the Holy Roman Empire H:179
   picture(s)
      painting of Dante D:34
Dante and His Book (painting by Domenico di Michelino)
   picture(s) I:404
Danton, George Jacques (French revolutionary leader) F:470 *profile, 471, 472*
Danube River (Europe) D:35; E:346; R:241
   Austria A:520
   Budapest B:422a–422b
   Bulgaria B:443
   Germany G:154
   Hungary H:296
   Romania's major waterway R:297
   Slovakia S:200
   map(s) D:35
   picture(s) E:348; R:241
Danville (Virginia) V:352
Danzig (Poland) *see* Gdańsk
Danziger, Paula (American author) C:230 *profile*
Dao (Taoist religious precept) *see* Tao
Daoud Khan, Mohammed (Afghan general and political leader) A:44
Daphne (in Greek mythology) G:366
Daphni, church of (near Athens, Greece) B:492–93
DAR *see* Daughters of the American Revolution, National Society of the
Daravica, Mount (Serbia and Montenegro) S:124
Darby, Abraham (English inventor) I:218
Dardanelles, Strait of the (Turkey) T:345
Dardanelles Campaign (World War I) W:283–84
Dare, Virginia (first English child born in America) T:166
   Fort Raleigh National Historic Site N:318
Daredevils (circus performers) C:308
Dar es Salaam (capital of Tanzania) T:19
   picture(s) T:19
Darfur (region of Sudan) S:480
Darhan (Mongolia) M:418
Dari (language) A:43

Darién (jungle area, Panama–Colombia)   **P:**46
  Balboa's name for Panama   **B:**20
Darío, Rubén (Nicaraguan poet)   **L:**69
Darius I (the Great) (king of Persia)   **D:**36; **I:**308; **P:**154, 155
Darius III (king of Persia)   **A:**178; **D:**36; **P:**155
Darjeeling (India)   **H:**138; **I:**123
Dark Ages *see* Middle Ages
Dark and Bloody Ground (Kentucky)   **O:**271
Dark field microscopes   **M:**284
Dark matter (in galaxies)   **A:**474; **S:**368
Dark nebulas (in astronomy)   **N:**96
Darkroom, digital *see* Digital darkroom
Darmstadtium (element)   **E:**172
Darnley, Henry Stuart, Lord (husband of Mary, Queen of Scots)   **M:**118
Darrow, Charles (American patent holder for Monopoly game)   **G:**14
Darrow, Clarence Seward (American lawyer)   **D:**36; **I:**59; **S:**84
  picture(s)   **D:**36
Darrow, Frank E. (American doll maker)   **D:**268
Darsan (Hindu temple attendance)   **H:**140
D'Artagnan (friend of the three main characters in *The Three Musketeers*)   **D:**351–52
Darters (fish)   **F:**195
Dartmouth (Nova Scotia)   **N:**352
Dartmouth College (Hanover, New Hampshire)   **N:**155; **O:**231
Darts (game)   **D:**37; **G:**18
  picture(s)   **D:**37
Darts (in sewing)   **C:**376
Darvon (drug)   **N:**15
Darwin (capital of Northern Territory, Australia)   **A:**506, 513, 517
Darwin, Charles Robert (English naturalist)   **D:**38–39
  adaptation of animals to environment   **L:**197–98
  atheism   **A:**476b
  Chile, visit to   **C:**254
  English literature   **E:**284
  evolution, theory of   **E:**374, 375, 376, 377; **S:**67
  Galápagos Islands   **E:**66
  human origins, study of   **A:**359
  Huxley, Thomas H., supported   **H:**310
  Indians, journal entry on   **I:**199
  influence on study of biology   **B:**203
  Lyell's theories in geology, influenced by   **G:**110
  nature, study of   **N:**70
  science, milestones in   **S:**72
  picture(s)   **B:**202; **D:**38; **F:**385; **S:**73
Darwin's rheas (flightless birds)   **O:**244
Das, Jibanananda (Indian poet)   **I:**142
Dashara (Hindu festival)   **H:**141; **I:**122
Dashboard (of an automobile)   **A:**546
Dashes (punctuation marks)   **P:**542
Dash for Cash (race horse)   **H:**234
Da Silva, Luiz Inácio Lula (president of Brazil)   **B:**384
Das Kapital (book by Karl Marx)   **C:**103; **M:**117
Data (facts)   **S:**439, 440–42
  graphs   **G:**309–13
  opinion polls   **O:**169
  psychologists, goals of   **P:**500
Database management systems   **D:**40
Databases (organized collections of data)   **C:**483–84, 491; **D:**39–40
Data compression (in telecommunications)   **T:**49
Date (fruit)   **D:**41
  Iraq is the world's largest producer   **I:**313
Date line, International *see* International date line
Dating (of archaeological sites)   **A:**357
Dating (social)   **A:**25
Dating, radiometric *see* Radiometric dating
Daudet, Alphonse (French novelist)   **F:**441
Daugherty, Harry M. (American politician)   **C:**547; **H:**31, 32, 33
Daughtercards (computer components)   **C:**481
Daughter isotopes (of radioactive elements)   **R:**74
  table(s)   **R:**75

Daughters of Charity (secular nursing order)   **N:**420
Daughters of the American Revolution, National Society of the (DAR)   **G:**76, 76d
Daumier, Honoré (French artist)   **D:**42; **F:**429
  hero of lithography   **G:**308
  political cartoonist   **C:**127
  realism in illustrations   **I:**80; **R:**115
  picture(s)
    drawing of lawyer   **D:**42
Dauphin (title of eldest son of a French king)   **J:**110
Davenant, Sir William (English poet and dramatist)   **O:**142
Davenport (Iowa)   **I:**299
Davenport, Thomas (American inventor)   **E:**154
David (king of Israel)   **B:**161; **D:**42; **J:**102
  David and Goliath (Bible story)   **B:**169–70; **G:**202
  Jerusalem   **J:**84
  Psalms (first hymns)   **H:**320
  statues   **M:**257
  tomb in Jerusalem   **J:**82
  Twenty-Third Psalm   **P:**431
  picture(s)   **B:**163; **J:**102
    statues   **I:**398; **S:**99
David (statue by Bernini)   **B:**65, 152; **S:**100
  picture(s)   **B:**65
David (statue by Donatello)
  picture(s)   **S:**99
David (statue by Michelangelo)   **F:**258–59; **I:**397; **M:**257
  picture(s)   **I:**398; **S:**99
David, Gerard (Dutch painter)   **D:**360
David, Jacques Louis (French painter)   **F:**428; **P:**27, 29
  picture(s)
    Coronation of Napoleon, The (painting)   **N:**11
    Madame Julie Récamier (painting)   **P:**26
    Oath of the Horatii (painting)   **F:**428
    portrait of Napoleon I   **N:**10
David and Goliath (Bible story)   **B:**169–70; **G:**202
David Copperfield (book by Charles Dickens)   **D:**151
  excerpt from   **D:**152–53
David Kalakaua (king of Hawaii) *see* Kalakaua
Davie, Donald (English poet)   **E:**290
Davies, Peter Maxwell (English composer)   **E:**293
Dávila, Pedrarias (Spanish colonial governor) *see* Pedrarias Dávila
Da Vinci, Leonardo (Italian painter, architect, and inventor) *see* Leonardo da Vinci
Davis, Benjamin O. (American army officer)   **A:**79c; **U:**117; **W:**35 *profile*
Davis, Benjamin O., Jr. (American Air Force officer)   **W:**35 *profile*
Davis, Bette (American film actress)   **M:**487 *profile*
Davis, Henry C. (American officer)   **N:**23
Davis, Jefferson (president of the Confederate States of America)   **D:**43
  Civil War   **C:**332, 336, 495, 496
  home at Beauvoir, near Biloxi (Mississippi)   **M:**358
  Kentucky birthplace   **K:**212,
  Montgomery (Alabama) home   **A:**138
  picture(s)   **C:**336, 495; **D:**43
Davis, John (English navigator)   **N:**338
Davis, John William (American lawyer and politician)   **C:**547
Davis, Miles (American jazz trumpeter)   **I:**74 *profile;* **J:**62–63, 64
  picture(s)   **I:**74; **J:**64
Davis, Mount (Pennsylvania)   **P:**127, 128
Davis, Rebecca Harding (American writer)   **A:**212
Davis, Thomas (Irish poet)   **I:**326
Davis Cup (in tennis)   **T:**99
Davis Dam (Arizona)   **N:**125
Davis Mountains (Texas)   **T:**126
Davy, Sir Humphry (English chemist)   **D:**44
  aluminum's existence predicted by   **A:**194f
  anesthesia   **A:**254; **M:**208a
  battery, electric   **E:**138
  discoveries of new elements   **C:**209

electric arc light   **I:**284
 Faraday was his protégé   **F:**47
 leather tanning discoveries   **L:**111
 magnesium, work with   **M:**27
Dawes, Charles G. (American statesman and financier)   **D:44;**
    V:329 *profile*
 picture(s)   **V:**328
Dawes, William (American patriot)   **R:**193, 198
Dawes Act (United States, 1887)   **M:**440
Dawes Plan   **D:**44
Dawn (space probe)   **C:**451
Dawson City (Yukon Territory)   **Y:**373, 374, 375
Day (measure of time)   **C:**13; **W:**115 *see also* Day and night;
    Rotation (of astronomical bodies)
 early time measurement   **T:**200
 Earth's period of rotation   **E:**9
 international date line   **I:**266
Dayaks (a people of Borneo)   **B:**336; **I:**206; **M:**54, 55
Day and night (light and darkness)
 Arctic has long periods of darkness and daylight   **A:**379;
    F:136
 daylight saving time   **T:**203
 equator   **E:**308
 hibernation cued by   **H:**128
 length of during the seasons   **S:**109, 110–11
 migration determined by length of day   **H:**200
Day and Night (woodcut by Escher)   **E:**320
 picture(s)   **E:**320
Day camps   **C:**49
Day care (of children by paid adults)   **D:45**
 kindergarten and nursery schools   **K:**250
 picture(s)   **F:**40
Day Lewis, C. (English poet)   **E:**288
Daylighting (passive use of solar energy)   **S:**239
Daylight saving time (DST)   **T:**203
Day of Atonement *see* Yom Kippur
Day of the Dead (holiday) *see* Día de los Muertos, El
Day of the Race (holiday) *see* Día de la Raza, El
Daypacks (for hiking)   **H:**135
Dayparts (divisions of a television broadcast day)   **T:**68
Day schools   **P:**443
Days of the week   **D:46**
 calendar   **C:**13–17
 in French   **F:**434
 in Italian   **I:**405
 names honor Norse gods   **N:**280
 sabbath for different religions   **R:**153
 in Spanish   **S:**391
Daytona (Florida)   **A:**537
Daytona Beach (Florida)   **F:**270
 picture(s)   **F:**270
Dayton Accord (1995)   **B:**338; **S:**127; **Y:**369
D batteries   **B:**103a; **E:**143
DC *see* Direct current
D.C. *see* District of Columbia
DC-3 *see* Douglas DC-3
DC Comics (publisher)   **C:**453
D-Day (in World War II)   **B:**103f; **W:**310–11
 Eisenhower's historic decision   **E:**123
 how named   **D:**1
 What does "D day" mean?   **W:**310
 picture(s)   **B:**103f; **W:**311
DDT (pesticide)   **F:**33; **M:**52
Deaconesses (early church workers concerned with nursing)
    N:420
Deacons (of the church)   **C:**289; **R:**285–86
Dead, Day of the (holiday) *see* Día de los Muertos, El
Dead Christ, The (painting by Holbein)   **H:**159d
Deadlines (for newspaper editions)   **N:**202
Deadly nightshade (plant) *see* Belladonna
Dead reckoning (method of navigation)   **A:**118; **N:**76
 migration of animals   **H:**201
Dead Sea (Israel–Jordan)   **I:**371; **J:**130; **L:**26, 29–30
 picture(s)   **L:**25

Dead Sea Scrolls   **B:**163; **D:47**
 picture(s)   **B:**164
Dead Souls (novel by Gogol)   **N:**360; **R:**381
Deadwood (South Dakota)   **G:**252; **S:**319, 320, 325, 327
 picture(s)   **S:**320
Deaf, education of the   **D:**50–51, 179
 Bell, Alexander G., was teacher   **B:**139
 Keller, Helen   **K:**203
 teaching deaf people to speak   **S:**395–96
Deaf culture   **D:**50
Deafness   **D:48–51** *see also* Ear; Hearing
 Beethoven   **B:**122
 biotechnology, uses of   **B:**214
 computer assistance   **C:**485
 disabilities, people with   **D:**178, 179, 180
 Edison, Thomas Alva   **E:**70
 hearing-ear dogs   **D:**257
 hearing problems   **E:**6
 teletypewriters   **T:**374
Dean, Christopher (British ice dancer)   **O:**107 *profile*
 picture(s)   **O:**107
Dean, H. Trendley (American dentist)   **F:**288
Dean, James (American actor)   **I:**156 *profile*
 picture(s)   **I:**156
Dean, Jay Hanna (Dizzy) (American baseball player and sports
    commentator)   **A:**418 *profile*
Dean, John Wesley, III (American public official)   **W:**60 *profile*
 picture(s)   **W:**60
Dearborn (Michigan)   **D:**142; **M:**262, 265
 picture(s)
  Henry Ford Museum   **M:**262
Death   **D:51** *see also* Funeral customs
 aging   **A:**82–83
 children's literature, treatment in   **C:**238
 dogs linked to in mythology   **D:**245
 family problems   **F:**41–42
 funeral customs   **F:**493–95
 grief   **G:**380
 hibernation conditions are close to death   **H:**128
 mythology about   **M:**573
 suicide   **S:**485
Death camas (plant)   **P:**316
Death of a Salesman (play by Arthur Miller)   **A:**218
 picture(s)   **D:**306
Death of the Virgin (painting)
 picture(s)   **I:**401
Death penalty *see* Capital punishment
Death rate *see* Mortality
Death star (theoretical companion star to the sun)   **D:**177
Death Valley (California)   **C:**18, 19; **D:**126
 picture(s)   **N:**284
  mirage on   **M:**341
Death Valley National Park (California)   **C:**28
 picture(s)   **C:**21
DeBakey, Michael Ellis (American surgeon)   **T:**138–39 *profile*
Debates   **D:52** *see also* Public speaking
 Congressional bill amendments   **U:**167
 debating the motion in parliamentary procedure   **P:**82
 Kennedy-Nixon television debates   **K:**208
Debit (in bookkeeping)   **B:**311
Debit cards   **C:**582
Deborah (Biblical character)   **B:**159
De Brazza's monkeys
 picture(s)   **M:**420
Debrecen (Hungary)   **H:**297
Debris flows (landslides)   **A:**558
de Broglie, Louis-Victor (French physicist)   **E:**163; **P:**238
De Bruijn, Inge (Dutch swimmer)   **O:**119
Debs, Eugene V. (American labor and political leader)   **D:53;**
    L:14 *profile*
 Pullman strike   **R:**88
 picture(s)   **L:**14
Debt
 credit cards   **C:**582

Debt (cont.)
 imprisonment of English debtors **T:**178
 inflation benefits debtors **I:**227
 national budget **E:**62–63
 Public Debt, Bureau of the **T:**294
Debugging (in computer programming) **C:**489
Debundscha (Cameroon) **C:**40
Deburau, Jean-Gaspard (French mime) **C:**386
Debussy, Claude (French composer) **D:53; F:**447
 chamber music **C:**184
 musical impressionism **M:**398
 opera **O:**148
 Pelléas et Mélisande (opera) **O:**160–61
 picture(s) **D:**53
Deby, Idris (president of Chad) **C:**181
Decaffeinated coffee **C:**397
Decaffeinated tea **T:**35
Decalogue *see* Ten Commandments
Decameron (book of short stories by Boccaccio) **I:**406; **S:**161
Decapods (crustaceans) **C:**601; **L:**280
Decathlon (track and field event) **O:**106, 107; **T:**258
 world record **T:**261
 picture(s) **T:**263
Decay (Decomposition) (of plants and animals) **E:**54, 299; **L:**205; **S:**236, 237
Decay, radioactive *see* Radioactive decay
Decay, tooth *see* Cavities
Deccan plateau (India) **I:**121, 124, 128
Deccan Traps (hills, India) **I:**124
Deceleration (loss of speed) **M:**474
 human body, effects on **S:**341
December (12th month of the year) **D:54–55**
 Christmas **C:**297, 300, 301
Decembrists (in Russian history) **R:**370
Deci, Edward (American psychologist) **P:**510
Decibels (units measuring sound) **D:**48; **N:**271; **S:**259
Deciduous trees **T:**307–8
 forest biomes **B:**208, 210; **P:**319
 forests, animal life in **A:**274
 forests, kinds of trees in **F:**374, 376
 leaves of deciduous plants **L:**114
 picture(s)
  autumn **L:**115
  forest biomes **P:**321
Decimal calendar (in French history) **T:**201
Decimal classification (of books) **L:**182–83
Decimal point **F:**400
Decimals **D:**56; **F:400–402; N:**402
 arithmetic **A:**390
 changing measurements of the metric system **W:**111
 percentage **P:**145
Decimal system (counting system based on ten) **D:**56; **N:**407
 abacus **A:**2–3
 dollar **D:**261
Decision-based automation **A:**530, 531
Decision making **T:**205
Decius (Roman emperor) **C:**288
Decks (of playing cards) **C:**107
Declaration of Human Rights *see* Universal Declaration of Human Rights
Declaration of Independence **D:57–68**
 Adams, Samuel, was signer **A:**20
 American literature, place in **A:**205
 civil rights **C:**325
 Continental Congress **C:**536
 defended by John Adams **A:**13
 Enlightenment, Age of **E:**297
 founders of the United States **F:**392
 gives new dignity to American cause **R:**202
 Hancock signed first in extra-large letters **H:**17
 human rights **H:**285
 Independence Day commemorates **I:**112
 Jefferson, Thomas, was author of **J:**67
 Lee, Richard Henry and Francis Lightfoot, were only brothers to sign **L:**127

 Liberty Bell was rung to celebrate **L:**170
 Locke's political ideas **L:**281
 National Archives **N:**24
 Rhode Island's declaration (May 4, 1776) **R:**225
 Seneca Falls Woman's Rights document parallels **W:**212
 signatures prized by autograph collectors **A:**527; **D:**62
 signed in Independence Hall **I:**113
 slave trade condemned in first draft **S:**194
 text of **D:**62, 64
 what the Declaration says **D:60–62**
 picture(s) **D:**63
  draft in Jefferson's writing **J:**66
  presented by the drafting committee **A:**15
Declaration of Rights and Sentiments (women's rights) **S:**424; **W:**212
Declaration of the Rights of Man and of the Citizen (French bill of rights adopted in 1789) **E:**297; **F:**469
Declaratory Act (Great Britain, 1766) **D:**58
Decomposition *see* Decay
Decompression sickness *see* Bends, the
Decongestants (drugs) **A:**191
Deconstructivism (in architecture) **A:**376
Decorating (of homes) *see* Interior design
Decoration Day *see* Memorial Day
Decorations (for special occasions)
 Christmas **C:**297–98
 parties **P:**88, 91
Decorations (of honor) **D:69–71** *see also* Medals
Decorative arts **D:72–79** *see also* Design; Industrial arts
 Byzantine **B:**487–94
 China, art of **C:**276–77
 Easter eggs **E:**44
 enameling **E:**205
 flower arranging **F:**278–79
 folk art **F:**292–98
 furniture **F:**506
 interior design **I:**257–61
 Islamic art **I:**358–59
 Japanese origami **O:**228–30
 mosaic **M:**464
 needlecraft **N:**97–101
 papier-mâché **P:**58b–58c
 pottery **P:**407–13
 rubbings **R:**348b–349
 stained-glass windows **S:**417–18
 tapestry **T:**20–22
 wood carving **W:**228
De Cosmos, Amor (Canadian provincial premier) **B:**406d
De Coster, Charles (Belgian writer) *see* Coster, Charles de
Decoys (wooden models of game birds and fish) **F:**295
Decrescendo (musical term) **M:**536, 538
Dedication, Feast of the *see* Hanukkah
Deductibles (on insurance policies) **I:**251
Deductions (from income tax) **I:**111
Deductive arguments (in logic) **L:**289–90
Deed (Title) (document of land ownership) **R:**112d–113
Deep Blue (computer) **C:**492
 picture(s) **C:**492
Deep-fat frying (of food) **C:**542
Deep Impact (space probe) **C:**452; **S:**359, 360
Deep-sea diving **E:**415; **U:21–27** *see also* Scuba diving; Skin diving; Underwater exploration
 compared to skin diving **S:**186
 Cousteau, Jacques-Yves **C:**577
 Piccard, Auguste **P:**244
Deep-sea fish **B:**205; **F:**182, 183; **O:**26–27
Deep Space 1 (space probe) **S:**353
 picture(s) **S:**351
Deep Space Network (DSN) (of radio telescopes) **R:**73
Deep Throat (name for Watergate informer) **W:**61
Deep-water swamps **W:**146
Deer (hoofed mammals) **D:80–82**
 antler regrowth **H:**220

barking deer **K:**259
domestication of **H:**220
elk and moose are the largest members of the deer family
    E:193
fawn's spots are camouflage **M:**74
hoofed mammals **H:**218–19
Irish elk of Ice Age **I:**12
livestock **L:**273
Mississippi **M:**353
reindeer and caribou **R:**138
reproduction **M:**67
wolves helped keep numbers in check **W:**211
diagram(s)
    barking deer **K:**259
    leg and hoof **F:**80
picture(s) **D:**80, 81, 82
    black-tailed deer **B:**209
    hind foot **H:**218
    mule deer **A:**269
    white-tailed deer **C:**512
Deere, John (American industrialist) **I:**75, 222; **V:**318 *profile*
Deerfield (Massachusetts) **C:**422; **M:**144
Deerfly
    picture(s) **I:**234
Deer mice **H:**128; **M:**67, 69–70; **R:**277
Deerslayer, The (novel by James Fenimore Cooper) **C:**549
Deerstalker (kind of hat) **H:**46
Deer ticks **T:**192
    picture(s) **V:**284
De facto segregation **S:**113, 115
De Falla, Manuel (Spanish composer and pianist) *see* Falla,
    Manuel de
Defects (in crystals) **M:**152–53; **T:**274
Defendant (in law) **C:**574; **L:**90
Defense (of animals and plants) *see* Protective devices
Defense, United States Department of **D:**83–84; **P:**447
    largest civil service employer **C:**331
    United States, Armed Forces of the **U:**100–101
    United States Air Force **U:**107–10
Defense attorneys **L:**91
Defense Nuclear Facilities Safety Board **E:**217
Defense Nuclear Nonproliferation, Office for (United States)
    E:218
Defense program (in North America)
    Canadian participation **C:**70
    New Mexico's economy **N:**186
Defense Programs, Office of (United States) **E:**218
Defensins (proteins) **A:**312
Defensive driving courses **D:**327
Defensive missiles **M:**348
Deferments (from the military draft) **D:**293
Defibrillator (device to control the heartbeat) **A:**199; **H:**84
Deficiency diseases **D:**197
    anemia **D:**188
    malnutrition **N:**429
    medicine, history of **M:**208c
    mineral deficiency **V:**371–73
    vitamin deficiency **V:**370b–370d
Deficit, national **E:**62–63
Definite proportions, law of (in chemistry) **A:**483
Deflation (removal of ground surface sediments by wind)
    D:128
Deflation (of prices) *see* Inflation and deflation
Defoe, Daniel (English journalist and novelist) **D:**84–85;
    E:279
    children's literature **C:**232
    published the first magazine (*The Review*) **M:**19
    Robinson Crusoe, excerpt from **D:**85
    Robinson Crusoe set on one of Chile's islands **C:**254
    Robinson Crusoe was first major English novel **F:**115
    style and themes of his novels **N:**359
De Forest, Lee (American inventor) **R:**58
Deforestation (loss of forests) **C:**524
    destruction of animal habitats **E:**209, 426

logging restrictions **L:**342
    picture(s) **C:**525
Deformation (in topology) **T:**236
Degas, Edgar (French painter) **D:**86; **F:**431
    drawing, history of **D:**318
    impressionism **I:**103, 105
    modern art **M:**388
    picture(s)
        Ballet at the Paris Opera (drawing) **D:**308
        Blue Dancers (drawing) **F:**430
        Dance Class (painting) **D:**86
        The Tub (drawing) **I:**105
De Gaulle, Charles (French general and political leader)
    D:86–87
    Fourth and Fifth Republics **F:**419–20
    Free French forces organized **F:**419; **W:**298
    picture(s)
        liberation of Paris **F:**419; **W:**312
        with President Truman **T:**325
Degenerative diseases **D:**187, 195
Degradable plastics **P:**326–27, 329
Degradation (decreased land quality) **F:**351
Degrees (units of measure)
    latitude and longitude **L:**77, 78
    measurement of angles **G:**121
    measurement of time zones **T:**202–3
    temperature scales **H:**86
Degrees (university and college) **U:**220–21
Dehydration (drying by mechanical means)
    food in space **S:**343
    food preservation **F:**340
    milk **D:**9
    mummies, Egyptian **M:**512
Dehydration (loss of moisture from the body) **S:**5
Deimos (moon of Mars) **M:**109; **P:**279; **S:**52
Deinonychus (dinosaur) **D:**171
Deirdre (heroine of Irish legend) **I:**325
Deir el-Bahri (Egyptian temple) **A:**365; **E:**109, 114
Deism (system of thought) **R:**293
Déjeuner sur l'herbe (painting by Manet) **M:**78
De jure segregation **S:**113
De Kalb, Baron (German general in the American Revolution)
    see Kalb, Johann
Dekalux (unit of measurement) **L:**237
de Klerk, Frederik Willem (president of South Africa) **S:**273
    picture(s) **S:**273
De Kooning, Willem (American painter) **M:**396b; **U:**134
    picture(s)
        A Tree Grows in Naples (painting) **M:**396
De Koven, Reginald (American composer) **M:**553; **O:**167
Delacroix, Eugène (French painter) **D:**87; **F:**429; **P:**29
    illustration, his art as **I:**80
    romanticism in painting **P:**29
    watercolor painting **W:**56
    picture(s)
        Chopin, Frédéric, portrait of **R:**302
        Horses Coming out of the Sea (painting) **D:**87
        Liberty Leading the People (painting) **F:**429
        Orphan Girl at the Cemetery (painting) **P:**27
De la Huerta, Dolores (American labor leader) **H:**148
De la Madrid Hurtado, Miguel (Mexican political leader)
    M:252
De la Mare, Walter (British author and anthologist)
    "Little Red Riding-Hood" **F:**29–32
    quotation from **N:**276
    "Silver" **F:**123
Delany, Martin Robinson (African American leader, physician,
    and army officer) **C:**344 *profile*
    picture(s) **W:**138
Delany, Samuel R., Jr. (American author) **S:**82
De Large, Robert (American politician)
    picture(s) **U:**143
De la Roche, Mazo (Canadian author) **O:**135
de la Rúa, Fernando (Argentine president) **A:**386d
Delaunay, Robert (French painter) **C:**612

DeLaval, Carl Gustaf (Swedish engineer) *see* Laval, Carl Gustav de
Delaware   **D:**88–102
  colonial historic sites   **C:**422
  Declaration of Independence signers   **D:**65
  thirteen American colonies   **T:**176
  map(s)   **D:**97
  picture(s)
    Amish farm   **D:**90
    boats docking at Lewes   **D:**88
    Brandywine Creek   **D:**90
    commemorative quarter   **C:**400
    dairy farm   **D:**89
    Delaware Agricultural Museum   **D:**94
    Dover   **D:**99
    Dover's Olde Dover Days   **D:**93
    Fort Christina Park   **D:**96
    Hagley Museum and Library   **D:**94
    Nemours   **D:**89
    New Castle   **D:**98
    Rehoboth Beach   **D:**89, 92
    University of Delaware   **D:**93
    wildlife refuge   **D:**91
    Wilmington   **D:**98
    Winterthur Museum and Gardens   **D:**96
    Zwaanendael Museum   **D:**96
Delaware (Indians of North America)   **I:**179
  Delaware   **D:**92
  New Jersey   **N:**175, 176
Delaware, University of   **D:**93, 94
  picture(s)   **D:**93
Delaware Agricultural Museum (Dover, Delaware)
  picture(s)   **D:**94
Delaware Memorial Bridge   **D:**98
Delaware River (United States)   **R:**241
  Pennsylvania   **P:**128, 133
  river system in Delaware   **D:**90
  Washington's crossing during campaign for Trenton   **R:**202
Delaware Water Gap (New Jersey–Pennsylvania)   **N:**166, 172; **P:**134
Delay, Tom (United States congressman)   **B:**469
Delegated powers (of the United States government)   **U:**162
Delegates (to presidential conventions)   **E:**129
De Lesseps, Ferdinand, Vicomte (French businessman) *see* Lesseps, Ferdinand de
Delftware (pottery)   **P:**412
Delgado, José Matías (Roman Catholic priest and Salvadoran patriot)   **E:**198
Delhi (India)   **D:**103–5; **I:**129
  picture(s)   **I:**129
    Chandni Chowk   **D:**104
    Pearl Mosque   **I:**139
    Raj Path   **D:**104
    tomb of emperor Humayun   **D:**103
Delibes, Léo (French composer)   **F:**447
Delibes, Miguel (Spanish novelist)   **S:**392
Delicatessen
  automated meat slicers   **A:**530
Delilah (Biblical character)   **B:**159
DeLillo, Don (American writer)   **F:**116
Delinquency, juvenile *see* Juvenile crime
Delirium (mental condition)   **M:**222
Delius, Frederick (English composer)   **E:**293
Della Porta, Giambattista (Italian scientist) *see* Porta, Giambattista della
Della Quercia, Jacopo (Italian sculptor) *see* Quercia, Jacopo della
Della Robbia, Luca (Florentine sculptor)   **S:**100
  medallions on Brunelleschi's colonnade for Foundling Hospital   **R:**164
  picture(s)
    Madonna and Angels (sculpture)   **S:**98
    medallions on Brunelleschi's colonnade for Foundling Hospital   **R:**165

Della Robbia family (Italian sculptors and ceramists)   **R:**164
Dells of the Wisconsin *see* Wisconsin Dells
Delmarva Peninsula (United States)   **D:**90; **V:**346
Delmonico's (restaurant in New York City)   **R:**186
Delos (Greece)   **I:**364
Delphi (Greece)   **G:**363
  picture(s)
    Athena, Temple of   **A:**229
Delphinidae (Delphinids) (mammal family of dolphins and whales)
  picture(s)   **D:**275
Delphiniums *see* Larkspur
Delta kite   **K:**266b
Delta Plan (the Netherlands)   **N:**120a
Deltas (earth deposits at river mouths)   **R:**236
  erosion by water   **E:**318
  Ganges-Brahmaputra Delta of India   **G:**25
  Mississippi River   **M:**350
  Nile River   **N:**261
  picture(s)
    Nile River   **E:**18
Delta wing (of high-speed planes)   **A:**112
DeLucas, Lawrence (American astronaut)
  picture(s)   **S:**344
Delusions (form of mental illness)   **M:**223
Delvaux, Paul (Belgian painter)   **B:**133
Demand, law of (in economics)   **D:**120; **E:**56
Demand deposits (banking)   **B:**56–57
Demantoid (gemstone)   **G:**69
Demarcation, Line of *see* Tordesillas, Treaty of
Dementia (mental condition)   **M:**222–23
  Alzheimer's disease   **A:**196
  Variant Creutzfeldt-Jakob disease   **D:**208–9
Demerol (drug)   **N:**15
Demeter (Ceres) (Greek goddess)   **G:**363
  origin of the word "cereal"   **G:**280
  picture(s)   **G:**360
Demian (book by Hermann Hesse)   **H:**125
Demigods (in Greek mythology)   **G:**363
Demilitarized Zone (DMZ) (in Vietnam)   **V:**336
De Mille, Agnes (American dancer and choreographer)   **B:**32
De Mille, Cecil B. (American film producer and director)   **M:**493 *profile*
Deming, William Edwards (American management expert)   **W:**346 *profile*
Demirel, Süleyman (prime minister of Turkey)   **T:**349
Democracy   **D:**105–7; **G:**273
  ancient Athens   **A:**238; **G:**341–42
  Aristotle's idea of   **G:**273
  Bill of Rights   **B:**181–84
  Depression, Great, impact of   **D:**120
  education in early Athens a preparation for   **E:**77
  education plays an important role in   **E:**74
  elections in democratic societies   **E:**126–27
  Fascism contrasted with   **F:**63
  First Amendment freedoms   **F:**163
  Homestead Act (1862) gave free land   **P:**516
  how legislatures function   **L:**137
  human rights   **H:**285
  Iceland's Althing was first democratic parliament   **I:**37
  initiative, referendum, and recall   **O:**212, 214
  Jacksonian   **J:**6
  journalism, duties of   **J:**136, 137
  Latin America   **L:**57, 59
  Mayflower Compact   **P:**345; **T:**171
  parliamentary procedure   **P:**81–82
  pioneer experience in America   **P:**261
  police, role of   **P:**368
  political parties   **P:**369–73
  poverty reduction   **P:**420
  propaganda   **P:**489
  Puritan legacies   **P:**551
  Roman Catholic Church and   **R:**294
  Solon founded Athenian democracy   **S:**253

town meetings in Massachusetts Bay Colony   T:173
United States government   U:161
Democratic Party (in the United States)   P:370, 371
Bryan, William Jennings   B:416
Depression, Great   D:120
elections   E:128
labor movement   L:18
Nast popularized donkey as symbol   C:127; N:17
Who were the Barnburners?   V:274
picture(s)
political cartoon on party symbol   P:371
poster from 1856 campaign   P:370
Democratic Republic of Congo *see* Congo, Democratic Republic of
Democrat-Republican Party (in the United States)   P:370; U:178
Democritus (Greek philosopher)   C:207; P:234; S:68
Demodulator (of a television receiver)   T:63
Demographics (study of populations)   S:439
Demography (statistical study of population)   G:102; P:385; S:231
Demoiselles d'Avignon, Les (painting by Picasso)
picture(s)   M:390
Demolition derby (competition in which old cars smash into each other)   F:14
Demonstrations and protests
Chinese students   C:272–73
civil rights movement   C:330
Greenpeace   G:374b
Kent State University (1970)   N:262d; O:77
Korea, South   K:303
Wisconsin, University of   W:207
picture(s)
abortion-rights protest   C:327
anti-fur march   A:261
Bulgarian pro-democracy demonstration   B:446
California gun-control demonstration   D:105
Canadian national unity   C:69
Chinese students   C:273
civil rights of African Americans   A:79i, 79n
German Green Party   P:373
gun control   G:426
nuclear weapons   N:379
Vietnam War   J:122; P:105; W:206
Demonstrative pronouns   P:92
Demosthenes (Greek orator)   G:357; O:190
Demotic (everyday form of Greek language)   G:331
Demotic writing (cursive writing developed from hieratic)   H:130, 131
picture(s)   H:131
Dempsey, Jack (American boxer)   B:351, 352 *profile;* C:442 *profile*
picture(s)   B:352; C:442
Dempster Highway (Canada)   Y:372
Denali National Park and Preserve (Alaska)   A:148
picture(s)   N:47
Denarius (Roman coin)   M:413
Denatured alcohol   A:172
Denby, Edwin (American politician)   C:547
Dendi (language)   A:56
Dendrites (branch-shaped ice crystals)   R:95
Dendrites (of neurons)   B:362; N:117, 118
Dendrochronology (Tree-ring dating)   A:357; R:76
clues about past climate   C:363
picture(s)   P:312
Dendur, Temple of (Metropolitan Museum of Art, New York City)   M:239
Dené (Native Americans) *see* Athapascan language family
Deneb (star)   C:531; S:429
Dengue hemorrhagic fever   V:284
Deng Xiaoping (Teng Hsiao-ping) (Chinese political leader)   C:272, 273; D:107
picture(s)   D:107
Denham, Dixon (British explorer of Africa)   S:7
Denier (thickness of a synthetic fiber)   F:111

De Niro, Robert (American film actor)   M:487 *profile*
Denishawn (school for dancers)   D:31, 32
De Nittis, Giuseppe (Italian painter)   I:105
Denmark   D:108–13; S:58f–58g
ballet   B:31–32
Christian (kings)   C:286
Copenhagen   C:551–52
counted cross-stitch   N:98
East India Company   E:47
Faroe Islands   I:365
Frederick (kings)   F:460
Greenland   G:371–74a
Iceland   I:37
mummies found in bogs   M:513
Scandinavian literature   S:58h, 58i
World War II   W:296, 316
map(s)   D:109
picture(s)
child eating ice cream   D:108
Copenhagen   D:108
Egeskov Castle   D:113
Faroe Islands   I:367
fishing industry   D:111
flag   F:230
Øresund Bridge   D:111
windmill   D:110
Denner, Johann (German flute and clarinet maker)   C:348
Denominations, religious *see* Sects
Denominator (of a fraction)   F:397, 398
Denotation (of a word)   S:116
Density (in physics)   M:173, 175
floating and buoyancy   F:250, 252, 253
plastics   P:323
seawater   O:38
Density (of light)
diagram(s)   L:216
Density, population *see* Population density
Dental assistant   D:116
Dental caries (disease of the teeth)   D:114, 115; T:44
care of the teeth   H:76
fluoridation   F:288–89
Dental hygienist   D:114, 116
Dental laboratory technician   D:116
Dental pulp (soft substance of teeth)   T:43
Dent corn   C:558
Dentin (hard substance of teeth)   I:415; T:43
Dentistry   D:114–16
gold used in   G:248
hypnotism, use of   H:327, 328
lasers, uses of   L:46c
orthodontics   O:232–33
silver amalgams used in   S:178
teeth   T:44
ultrasound, uses of   S:265
picture(s)   D:114; H:76
Denver (capital of Colorado)   C:430, 435, 436, 439; D:116–17
United States Mint   M:340
picture(s)   C:431, 440; D:117
wagon train (1886)   C:442
Denver, James (governor of the Kansas Territory)   D:117
Denver, University of (Denver, Colorado)   C:435
Denver International Airport (Denver, Colorado)   C:439; D:117
Denys le Petit (monk)   C:16
Deoxyribonucleic acid *see* DNA
Deoxyribonucleotides (nucleic acid chains)   B:298
Deoxyribose (body sugar)   B:298
De Paola, Tomie (American author and illustrator)   C:230–31 *profile*
picture(s)
illustration from *Merry Christmas, Strega Nona*   C:236
Departments (local political units in France)   F:411
Department stores   D:118; R:188, 189
credit cards   C:582

Department stores (cont.)
picture(s)
Macy's **N:**218
Dependence (on drugs) **D:**332; **N:**15 *see also* Alcoholism
Dependencies (of Australia and New Zealand) **C:**461
Dependencies (of the United Kingdom) **C:**461; **U:**61–62
Dependent variable (in psychological research) **P:**503
Deposition (in geology) **E:**16; **G:**99
Deposits, bank **B:**56–57
DePreist, James (American orchestra conductor) **O:**214
profile
Depressants (drugs) **D:**331
Depression (mental state) **P:**509
emotions **E:**203, 204
grief **G:**380
mood disorders **M:**221, 225
suicide **S:**485
Depression, Great (1929–1939) **D:**119–20, 121, 122; **U:**29, 193–95
American literature during **A:**216
bank failures **B:**58
California **C:**33
Dust Bowl **D:**355–56
homelessness **H:**183
Hoover's administration **H:**224–25
inflation and deflation **I:**226
outlaws **O:**263
prohibition, end of **P:**485
Roosevelt's New Deal program **N:**138h; **R:**323–24
picture(s)
breadline **D:**119
mother and children **W:**273
soup kitchen **R:**324
unemployed **H:**224
Depressions and recessions **D:**121–22; **E:**61–62 *see also*
Depression, Great; Inflation and deflation
inflation and deflation **I:**226
Panic of 1837 **V:**271, 273–74
panics due to stock speculation **S:**455
unemployment insurance **U:**29
Depth charges (antisubmarine weapons) **S:**474
Depth of field (in photography) **P:**201, 213
Depth perception (stereoscopic vision) **E:**429
De Quincey, Thomas (English essayist) **E:**284; **N:**273
Derain, André (French painter) **M:**388, 390
Derby (hat)
picture(s) **H:**45
Derbyshire, J. H. (English athlete) **S:**536
Deregulation (removal or reduction of government controls)
savings and loan industry **B:**54
De Rerum Natura (poem by Lucretius) **L:**75
Dermatitis (Eczema) (skin condition) **D:**123
Dermatology (the study of the skin) **D:**123–24
Dermis (inner layer of skin) **B:**276
Dermoptera (order of mammals)
picture(s)
flying lemur as example **M:**66
Derricks (hoisting machines) **H:**159b; **P:**169, 170
Derringers (small guns)
picture(s) **G:**418
Desalting (Desalination) *see* Water desalting
Descartes, René (French mathematician and philosopher) **D:**124
algebra **A:**184
analytic geometry **M:**165–66
Cartesian dualism **P:**190
Christina (queen of Sweden) **C:**295
idea of separation of mind and body **M:**226
"I think, therefore I am" **F:**438
physics, history of **P:**234
psychology **P:**506
picture(s) **P:**505
Descent from the Cross, The (painting by Giotto)
picture(s) **P:**19

Descent from the Cross, The (painting by Rogier van der Weyden)
picture(s) **D:**361
Descent stage (part of spacecraft) **S:**340g–340h
Descent with modification (evidence of evolution) **E:**374
Deschamps, Marie (Canadian Supreme Court justice)
picture(s) **S:**505
Desegregation *see* Segregation
Deseret (Mormon settlement, Utah) **U:**255; **Y:**363
Desert animals **A:**274; **D:**129
Arizona wildlife **A:**396
biomes **B:**207
California wildlife **C:**21–22
camels **C:**39
kangaroo rats and pocket mice **R:**276
lizards **L:**277
sand cats **C:**144
snakes **S:**209, 210
picture(s) **A:**275
birds **B:**241
Desert Fox *see* Rommel, Erwin
Desert foxes *see* Fennecs
Desertification (loss of fertile land to the desert) **B:**212; **D:**130, 131
Desert Laboratory (Tucson, Arizona) **A:**397–98
Desert plants **D:**128–29; **P:**319
Arizona wildlife **A:**396
biomes **B:**207
cacti **C:**4–5
structural defenses **P:**316
picture(s) **N:**67; **P:**320
Deserts **D:**125–31
Arizona **A:**394
Asia **A:**438e–438f, 438g
biomes **B:**207
climate, types of **C:**362, 363
intermittent rivers **R:**237
irrigation **I:**339–41
nomadic life **N:**272
North America **N:**290, 291
oases **O:**2–3
polar desert in the tundra **T:**331
Sahara **A:**47; **S:**6–7
soils **S:**237
Sudan (northeast central Africa) **S:**478
picture(s)
Arabian Peninsula **A:**346; **S:**58a
Mexico's Central Desert **M:**244
Nevada **N:**124
oases **E:**299
people in desert **C:**364
Rub' al Khali (Saudi Arabia) **A:**438f
Thar Desert (India) **I:**125
Desert Storm, Operation *see* Persian Gulf War
De Sica, Vittorio (Italian film director) **M:**493
Design **D:**132–37 *see also* Decorative arts
airplanes **A:**120–21, 567
automobiles **A:**536, 544, 552–53
book design **B:**328, 329
bottles **B:**346
building construction **B:**436
Byzantine patterns **B:**490
clothing industry **C:**381
collage **C:**402
commercial art **C:**456–58
decorative arts as **D:**79
dyes used in textile printing **D:**381
fans **F:**46
fashion designer **F:**66, 69–70
Finland is a center for modern design **F:**138
flower arranging **F:**278–79
folk art **F:**292–98
furniture **F:**506–17
glass **G:**231

graphic arts: Japanese prints **G:**303
illuminated manuscripts **I:**77–78
industrial **I:**213–15
integrated circuits **T:**278
interior design **I:**257–61
Islamic art **I:**355
jewelry **J:**94–100
mechanical drawing **M:**200
mechanical engineers design engines **E:**226
newspaper page design **N:**201
play production **P:**336
sculpture **S:**90–105
trademarked products' design protected **T:**266
Designated hitter (in baseball) **B:**80
DeSilva, Ashanti (first human being to undergo gene therapy)
   G:88–89
Desire Under the Elms (play by Eugene O'Neill) **O:**122
Desjardins, Peter (American diver) **D:**229
Desks (furniture)
   picture(s) **F:**513
Desktop computers *see* Personal computers
Desktop publishing **C:**484; **I:**83; **O:**57; **P:**209
De Smet, Pierre-Jean (Belgian-born missionary) **M:**441 *profile*
Des Moines (capital of Iowa) **I:**299
Desmoulins, Camille (French revolutionary leader) **F:**468
De Soto, Hernando (Spanish explorer) **D:**138; **E:**407; **I:**202
   Alabama **A:**139
   Arkansas **A:**415
   Florida **F:**271
   Georgia **G:**144
   Louisiana **L:**326
   Mississippi **M:**359
   Mississippi River **M:**364
   map(s)
      exploration routes **D:**138
De Soto National Forest (Mississippi) **M:**358
Despotism (government by ruler with unlimited authority)
   G:273
Des Prez, Josquin (Flemish composer) *see* Josquin des Prez
Dessalines, Jean-Jacques (Haitian revolutionary and emperor)
   H:11
Desserts
   ice cream **I:**21–22
   party refreshments **P:**89, 91
Dessert wines **W:**190a
De Stijl (Dutch art movement) **M:**393, 410
Destroyers (ships) **S:**153–54; **U:**114
Destroying angel amanitas (poisonous mushrooms) **M:**529
Detachment (army troop unit) **U:**104
Detectives
   community police **P:**363
   Federal Bureau of Investigation **F:**76–77
   Pinkerton, Allan **C:**221
   postal inspectors **P:**400
Detective stories *see* Mystery and detective stories
Détente (relaxation of tensions between nations) **C:**401; **U:**43
Detention camps (in World War II) **A:**460, 461; **W:**304
Detention centers (for juvenile offenders) **J:**169, 170
   picture(s) **J:**169
Detergents **D:**139–41
   dry cleaning **D:**341
   environment, pollution of **E:**301
Determinatives (type of ideogram) **C:**613; **H:**130
Determiners (in grammar) **G:**289
Deterrence (country's military buildup to ward off attacks)
   N:378
Deterrence (to discourage people from committing crimes)
   C:586
Deterritorialization (weakening of the tie between culture and
   place) **A:**305
Detonation (explosion) **E:**420
Detonator (explosive charge) **E:**420–21
Detoxification (treatment for drug abuse) **D:**333

Detroit (Michigan) **D:**142; **M:**258, 263, 264, 265
   center of American automobile industry **A:**554
   General Motors complex **A:**376
   population decline **U:**96
   War of 1812 **W:**9
   picture(s) **M:**268
      Renaissance Center **D:**142; **M:**259
Detroit Industry (frescoes by Rivera) **R:**235
   picture(s) **M:**264
Detroit River (Michigan–Ontario) **L:**33
Deucalion (in Greek mythology) **G:**364–65
Deuce (in tennis scoring) **T:**89
Deukmejian, George, Jr. (American public official) **A:**421
Deusdedit I, Saint *see* Adeodatus I, Saint
Deus ex machina (in Greek drama) **D:**299
Deuterium (hydrogen isotope) **A:**486; **H:**316
   heavy water **N:**370
   nuclear energy **N:**367, 373
   nuclear weapons **N:**375
Deuteronomy (book of the Old Testament) **B:**159
Deutsches Museum (Munich, Germany) **M:**523
Deutschlandlied (national anthem of Germany) **N:**18
Deuxième Bureau (French intelligence service) **S:**407
Devadasi (Indian dancers) **D:**26
De Valera, Eamon (president of Ireland) **I:**324
   picture(s) **I:**324; **P:**459
De Valois, Dame Ninette (British choreographer) **B:**30, 31
DeVarona, Donna (American swimmer) **S:**537 *profile*
   picture(s) **S:**537
Developable Column (sculpture by Pevsner)
   picture(s) **M:**393
Developing (in photography) **P:**199, 202, 208–9, 211
   compact disc production uses similar process **S:**267a
Developing countries **D:**143
   agriculture **A:**92–93; **F:**49
   blindness, causes of **B:**256–57
   death rates **P:**387
   Depression, Great **D:**120
   disasters, effects of **D:**183
   education **E:**74
   food supply **F:**350, 351
   foreign aid **F:**370
   forest use **F:**377
   globalization's effects on **G:**238; **O:**220
   housing problems **H:**190
   imperialism **I:**100–102
   industrial development **I:**224–25
   livestock **L:**271
   manufacturing, development of **M:**89
   natural resources, use of **N:**66
   Peace Corps **P:**104
   poverty **P:**418–20
   United Nations interest in **U:**71
   water supply **W:**74, 75, 76
   World Bank loans **B:**55
Development (in motion picture production) **M:**480
Development (in music) **M:**541
Development (of an organism) **B:**196
Developmental psychology **P:**504
Devi, Mahasweta (Indian author) **I:**142
Deviation IQ (mental ability test score) **T:**118
Devil Dogs (nickname for United States Marines) **U:**123
Devilfish *see* Manta rays
De Villepin, Dominique (premier of France) **F:**420
Devils Canyon (Montana)
   picture(s) **M:**430
Devil's Hole pupfish **A:**275
Devil's Island (French Guiana) **F:**466
Devils Tower National Monument (Wyoming) **W:**334, 342
   first national monument **N:**45
   picture(s) **N:**50; **W:**335
      lava formations **V:**382
Devil's Triangle *see* Bermuda Triangle
Devol, George (American inventor) **R:**253

Devolution (surrender of power to local authorities by a central government) **S:**88
Devonian period (in geology) **E:**25, 27; **F:**386, 387
 Age of Fish **F:**184
 mass extinction **E:**425
 prehistoric animals **P:**433
 picture(s)
  drifting continents **G:**112
 table(s) **F:**384
Devonport (Tasmania, Australia) **A:**513
Dew **F:**291; **W:**84
Dewar flask (type of vacuum bottle) **V:**265
Dewberries **G:**301
Dewclaws (toes) **D:**241; **H:**216
Dewey, George (American admiral) **D:144; P:**188; **S:**392c
 picture(s) **D:**144
Dewey, John (American philosopher and educator) **D:144**
 development of kindergarten **K:**249–50
 psychology, schools of **P:**506
Dewey, Melvil (American librarian) **L:**180
Dewey, Nelson (American political figure) **W:**205
Dewey, Thomas E. (American politician) **M:**272 *profile;* **N:**225; **R:**326; **T:**326
Dewey Decimal Classification (of books) **L:**182–83
DEW line *see* Distant Early Warning line
Dew point (saturation temperature) **F:**290; **W:**84
 cloud formation **C:**382
 how to make a dew point apparatus **W:**84
Dexter Avenue King Memorial Baptist Church (Montgomery, Alabama) **A:**138
Dexterity puzzles **P:**554
Dextrose (Glucose) (kind of sugar) **B:**298; **S:**482
Dhahran (Saudi Arabia) **S:**58b
Dhaka (Bangladesh) **B:**50
 picture(s) **B:**50
Dharma (Hindu laws of conduct) **H:**140; **R:**149
Dhivehi (language) **M:**60
Dhu Nuwas (Yemenite prince) **J:**104
Diabetes (disease) **D:145,** 186
 bacteria-made insulin, use of **G:**83
 blindness, cause of **B:**256
 discovery of insulin by Banting **B:**59
 endocrinology **B:**188
 glands, disorders of **G:**228
 hormone disorders **H:**228
 obesity is a major health concern **F:**338; **O:**6
Diacritical marks (to show pronunciation) **P:**486
Día de la Raza, El (Day of the Race) (Hispanic holiday) **H:**167
Día de los Muertos, El (Day of the Dead) (Hispanic holiday) **H:**146; **M:**241
Día de los Reyes, El (Three Kings Day) (Hispanic holiday) **H:**145–46; **L:**56
Diaghilev, Sergei (Russian ballet producer) **B:**29–30
Diagnosis (of disease) **D:**199–205, 237
 cancer **C:**93
 diabetes **D:**145
 examining the heart **H:**85
 imaging, diagnostic **I:**85–86
 medicine **M:**204, 208d
 science, modern **S:**73–74
 surgery **S:**514
 X-rays **X:**350
Diagnostic and Statistical Manual of Mental Disorders, Fourth Edition (DSM-IV) **M:**221
Diagnostic tests **T:**119
Dialects
 Castilian Spanish **S:**386
 Chinese language **C:**258
 French **F:**433–34
 German **G:**174
 Greece, language of **G:**353
 Italian language, development of **I:**404–5
 pronunciation **P:**486
Dialogue (literary form) **D:**149; **G:**357

Dialogues of Plato, The (conversations between Socrates and his students) **P:**330
Dial thermometers **T:**163–64
 picture(s) **T:**163
Dial tone (of telephones) **T:**53
Dialysis
 electrodialysis **W:**75
 hemodialysis **K:**244
Diameter (of a circle) **G:**122
Diamond, Donna (American illustrator)
 picture(s)
  illustration for *Bridge to Terabithia* **C:**238
Diamond dust (fog made of ice crystals) *see* Ice fog
Diamond Head (volcanic crater in Honolulu, Hawaii)
 picture(s) **H:**56, 58, 215
Diamond Jubilee (of Queen Victoria) **V:**332a
Diamond ring effect (of solar eclipses) **E:**51
 picture(s) **E:**51
Diamonds **D:146–48; G:**69, 70–71, 73, 74
 abrasive for grinding and polishing **G:**391
 Africa **A:**49
 amulets **G:**72
 Antwerp (Belgium) is center of diamond trade **B:**134
 Arkansas **A:**410, 414
 carbon, form of **C:**106
 Congo, Democratic Republic of **C:**501
 crystals **C:**603
 jewelry, history of **J:**98
 mining **M:**324
 Mohs' scale of relative hardness of gems **G:**70; **M:**315–16
 powder metallurgy **M:**236
 South Africa **S:**273
 picture(s) **D:**146; **G:**74
  crystals **M:**152, 315
  cutting and polishing **D:**147
  necklace **G:**69
  rough diamonds **D:**147
Diamond State (nickname for Arkansas) **A:**407
Diamond Sutra (Buddhist book)
 picture(s)
  woodcut from **G:**302
Diana (Roman goddess) *see* Artemis
Diana, Princess of Wales **D:148; E:**192, 255
 revived interest in women's hat fashions **H:**47
 picture(s) **E:**254; **H:**47
  mourners paying tribute **E:**255
  with victims of land mines **D:**148
Diaphone (fog signal) **L:**229
Diaphragm (birth control device) **B:**250b
Diaphragm (muscle) **B:**283
 hiccups **B:**300
 mammals' unique characteristics **M:**65
 voice training **V:**377
Diaphragm (of a camera) **P:**201, 210
Diaphragm (of a telephone transmitter) **T:**53
Diaries **D:149–50**
 Adams, John Quincy **A:**16
 American literature **A:**202–3
 English diarists **E:**276
 Frank, Anne **F:**453
Diarra, Seydou (Ivorian prime minister) **I:**421
Diarrhea **D:**165, 206
Diary of a Madman, The (book by Lu Xun) **C:**279
Diary of a Young Girl (book by Anne Frank) **D:**149–50; **F:**453
 picture(s) **D:**149
Dias, Bartholomeu (Portuguese explorer) **A:**66; **E:**404; **P:**394
Diaspora (of the Jews) **J:**84, 103
Diastole (action of the heart) **H:**82
Diastolic pressure (of blood) **D:**195
Diathermy (treatment that creates heat) **M:**288
Diatomite (mineral)
 Nevada is a leading producer **N:**131

Diatoms (kind of algae) A:181
    plankton O:23–24; P:283, 284
    picture(s) A:181; L:195; M:275
Diatonic (musical term) M:532, 536
Diaz, David (American illustrator)
    picture(s)
        illustration for Smoky Night C:11
Díaz, Porfirio (Mexican president) M:250
    Indians, American I:194, 195
    picture(s) M:250
Diaz de Bivar, Rodrigo (Spanish national hero) see Cid, The
Díaz del Castillo, Bernal (Spanish explorer) L:66
Díaz de Solís, Juan (Spanish explorer) see Solís, Juan Díaz de
Díaz Ordaz, Gustavo (Mexican president) M:251
Dibiasi, Klaus (Italian diver) D:229
Dice G:15
Dick, A. B. (American inventor) O:58
Dick, Ayzik Meir (Yiddish publisher) Y:360
Dick Act (United States, 1903) N:42
Dickens, Charles (English writer) D:151–54; E:285–86; F:115
    A Christmas Carol C:299; G:200
    contributions to the detective story M:566
    David Copperfield, excerpt from D:152–53
    Hard Times set in Manchester U:59
    Oliver Twist, excerpt from D:153–54
    themes of his novels N:359
    wrote about hardships of factory workers I:219
    picture(s) D:151
        A Christmas Carol G:199
Dickinson, Charles (American attorney) J:4
Dickinson, Emily (American poet) A:211; D:154–55
    "A Bird Came Down the Walk" D:155
    free verse P:350
    "I'll Tell You How the Sun Rose" D:155
    poetry, opinion on P:349
    picture(s) A:207; D:154; P:350
Dickinson, John (American statesman and writer) D:96, 100
    profile; N:22
Dickinson Mansion (Delaware) D:96
Dickson, William K. L. (American inventor) E:73; M:487
Dick Tracy (comic strip)
    picture(s) C:128
    board game G:22
Dicotyledons (Dicots) (seed plants) F:283; L:113; P:302
    picture(s) P:307
Dictation machines O:58
Dictatorship G:274
    Caesar, Julius C:6
    elections are essential to appearance of lawful rule
        E:128
    Fascism F:63–64
    Hitler, Adolf H:153–54
    Latin America L:57, 58–59
    Lenin's views C:473
    Mussolini, Benito M:556
    Nazism N:79
    propaganda P:489
    rise of dictators before World War II W:294–96
    violations of civil rights C:325
Dictionaries D:156–57
    building a vocabulary V:374
    electronic typewriters with dictionary programs T:373
    Johnson's dictionary J:124
    pronunciation, guide to S:395
    scientific names T:29
    spelling, use in S:398, 400
    Webster, Noah W:99
Dictionary (game) G:17
Dictionary of National Biography R:129
Dictionary of Occupational Titles V:376
Diderot, Denis (French philosopher) E:207, 296–97 profile,
        297; F:439
    picture(s) E:296
Didion, Joan (American writer) A:219
Dido (queen of Carthage) A:36

Dido and Aeneas (opera by Purcell) E:292
Didrikson, Babe (Mildred Didrikson Zaharias) (American athlete)
        G:258 profile, 260–61; T:263
    picture(s) G:258
Didymus see Thomas, Saint
Die casting (type of molding) D:159
    of metals M:234
    zinc alloys Z:385
Diefenbaker, John George (Canadian statesman) D:158
Diefenbaker, Lake (Saskatchewan) S:43
Diem, Ngo Dinh see Ngo Dinh Diem
Dien Bien Phu (fortress, Vietnam) G:93; V:334d, 335–36
Dieppe Raid (1942) W:307
Dies (for shaping and cutting materials) D:158–59
    brick making B:392
    bronze and brass, forging of B:410
    jewelry stamping J:97
    metalworking M:234, 235–36
    plastics P:325
    steel wire I:337
    wire W:191
Dies, Martin (American political figure) U:13
Diesel, Rudolf (German inventor) D:160; I:281
Diesel engines D:160–62; E:230
    automobiles A:548
    locomotives L:286–87
    railroads R:81
    ships S:154, 159
    submarines S:475
    trucks T:319, 322
    picture(s)
        locomotives L:285
Diesel fuel F:487
Diesel locomotives D:162; L:286–87; R:80
    picture(s) L:285; R:80
Diet (legislative assembly)
    Japanese National Diet J:40
Diet (special plan or way of eating) see also Nutrition
    aging affected by A:84–85
    brain, health tips about B:366
    cancer prevention C:95
    circulatory system disorders, prevention of C:306
    diseases, treatment of D:209
    food F:329–38
    health H:74–75
    health foods H:79
    human beings H:282
    obesity, treatment of O:6
    people eat an amazing variety of foods F:332
    phenylketonuria, treatment of D:199; R:191
    reducing diets N:429
    salt in the diet S:23
    vegetarianism V:293–94
    world rice consumption R:227
Dietary Guidelines (advice for Americans) N:428
Dietary laws
    Jewish J:146b
Dietary Reference Intakes (DRI's) (standards for nutrition of
        healthy individuals) N:427–28; V:373
    table(s)
        vitamins and minerals V:372
Dietary supplements D:334, 335
Dietetics (study of how body uses foods) N:424
    dieticians work in hospitals H:250
    mathematics in careers M:161
Dietrich, Marlene (German-American actress and singer)
        M:487 profile
    picture(s) M:487
Difference (in subtraction) A:389
Differential (set of gears) A:550
Differentiation (of cells) D:195–96; E:98
Diffraction (of light) L:216–18
Diffraction gratings (for measuring light wavelengths) S:489
Diffuse nebulas (in astronomy) N:96
Diffuse reflection (of light) L:213

Diffusion (in physics) **G:**59
 osmosis **O:**239–41
 principle used in dyeing process **D:**379
 processes in animal cells **C:**161
Digestive system (of the body) **B:**280–82; **D:163–65**
 allergies **A:**190
 ants **A:**320
 bacteria **B:**12
 Beaumont's studies of **B:**109
 birds **B:**222–23
 burps, stomach growls, and intestinal gas **B:**301
 circulatory system's role in digestion **C:**304, 306
 experiments and other science activities **E:**396
 fiber's importance in diet **N:**427
 fish **F:**191
 glands **G:**226–27
 insects **I:**238
 liver: how it works **L:**268–69
 lymphatic system closely associated with **L:**349–50
 osmosis **O:**241
 peptic ulcer **D:**198–99
 rabbits and hares **R:**24–25
 smooth muscles **B:**279; **M:**519–20
 stomach **S:**460–61
 stomachs of ruminants (cud-chewing animals) **H:**218
 teeth help digestion **T:**42
Digests (type of magazine) **M:**16, 20
"Digging" (poem by Seamus Heaney) **I:**328
Digital audio data transmission **R:**61
Digital audio recording **H:**132–33; **R:**124; **S:**267a
 picture(s)
  digital music players **R:**122, 123, 124
Digital audio tape (DAT) **S:**267b
Digital audio tape players **S:**267a
Digital camcorders **V:**332g
Digital cameras **C:**467; **P:**199, 200–201, 203, 205–6, 209,
  213, 216, 218
 diagram(s)
  how a digital camera captures an image **P:**204
 picture(s) **P:**205
Digital clocks **C:**370–71, 372
Digital communications **C:**468; **I:**286
Digital compact cassette (DCC) **S:**267b
Digital compositing (in motion picture special effects) **M:**484
Digital darkroom (using image-editing software on digital
  photographs) **P:**209, 216–17
Digital instruments (in airplanes) **A:**120
Digital integrated circuits **T:**277
Digitalis (drug) **H:**83, 120; **L:**118; **P:**297
 where drugs come from **D:**334
Digital keyboards (musical instruments) **P:**242
 picture(s) **P:**242
Digital Millennium Copyright Act (United States, 1998) **C:**555
Digital mode (of transistors) **T:**276
Digital photography *see* Digital cameras
Digital radio **R:**55
Digital subtraction angiography (X-ray technique) **I:**86
Digital synthesizers **E:**156; **K:**239
 picture(s) **K:**239
Digital technology **C:**481, 491
 electronic music **E:**157
 electronics **E:**160
 telecommunications **T:**48–50
 textile printing **D:**381
 picture(s)
  textile printing **D:**381
Digital television **C:**469; **T:**66–67
Digital transmission (of cellular telephones) **T:**56
Digital video discs (Digital versatile discs; DVD's) and players
  V:332f–332g
 communication **C:**467
 computers **C:**482
 high-fidelity systems **H:**133
 lasers **L:**46c
 television **T:**66
 video games **V:**332b
 diagram(s)
  how a DVD player works **V:**332f
Digital video recorders (DVR's) *see* Personal video recorders
Digital video recording **V:**332e–332g, 332i
Digital video star projector **P:**271–72
Digital watches **W:**45
 picture(s) **W:**45
Digits (symbols used to represent numbers) **N:**403
Dihedral (angle at which airplane wings are attached) **A:**111
Dik-diks (mammals) **H:**219
Dikes (embankments) **F:**257 *see also* Levees
 Netherlands **N:**120a
Dikes (rock masses in which diamonds are found) **G:**71
Dili (capital of East Timor) **T:**208
Dillinger, John (American bank robber) **I:**156 *profile*
Dillon, Leo and Diane (American illustrators) **C:**231 *profile*
 picture(s) **C:**231
DiMaggio, Joe (American baseball player) **B:**88 *profile*
 picture(s) **B:**88
Dimbovița River (Romania) **B:**421
Dime novels (early paperback books) **C:**579; **P:**58a
Dimensions **T:**204
 multidimensional figures **G:**126–27
 table(s)
  geometric figures **G:**127
Dime stores *see* Variety stores
Dimethyl ether **C:**201
Diminished interval (in music) **M:**536
Diminuendo (musical term) **M:**536
Dimlang, Mount (Nigeria) **N:**255
Dimples (in the cheeks)
 picture(s) **G:**80
Dinaric Alps **A:**194d; **E:**345
Diné (Indians of North America) *see* Navajo
Dinesen, Isak (Danish novelist) **D:**112; **S:**58i
Dinezon, Jacob (Yiddish novelist) **Y:**361
Dingoes (wild dogs of Australia) **A:**506
Dining cars (of railroads) **R:**82
 picture(s) **R:**81
Dinka (language) **A:**56
Dinka (people) **S:**478
Dinners and dining
 table manners **E:**338
Dinnerware (cups, plates, and bowls) **P:**413
Dinoflagellates (algae) **A:**181; **O:**23–24; **P:**283–84
 picture(s) **A:**181
Dinosaur National Monument (Utah–Colorado) **C:**438; **U:**250
 museum built around dinosaur bones **D:**166
 picture(s) **U:**250
Dinosaurs **D:166–77** *see also* Fossils
 asteroid-caused extinction theory **C:**364, 450; **E:**28,
  426; **F:**387; **G:**112
 birds are descended from **B:**247
 Earth's history **E:**28–29
 evolved in Triassic period **F:**387
 fossil tracks **F:**382
 largest collection of skeletons in North America **C:**53
 largest extinct animals **A:**271
 mass extinction **E:**426
 prehistoric animals **P:**433, 434
 What was the deadliest dinosaur that ever walked the
  earth? **D:**171
 picture(s) **P:**433
  asteroid-caused extinction theory **G:**111
  children's museums **M:**526
  embryo skeleton and reconstruction **F:**386
  footprints **F:**382
  Indianapolis Children's Museum **I:**148
  natural history museums **M:**523
  Tyrannosaurus rex jaw **F:**386
  Tyrannosaurus rex skeleton **P:**432
Dinwiddie, Robert (British colonial officer) **W:**38
Diocese (church district) **C:**133; **E:**45; **R:**284

Diocletian (Roman emperor)   C:288; R:286, 317
Diode lasers *see* Semiconductor lasers
Diodes (P-n junctions) (in electronics)   E:159; T:275–76 *see also* Light-emitting diodes
  photoelectricity   P:196, 197
  thermometers   T:164
  diagram(s)   T:275
Diodes (two-part vacuum tubes)   R:58
Dioecious plants (bearing either male or female flowers)   F:283
Diogenes (woodcut by Carpi)   G:304
Diola (a people of Africa)   S:117
Diomedes (in Greek legend)   G:367
Dione (moon of Saturn)
  picture(s)   O:11
Dionysius, Saint (pope)   R:292
Dionysus (Bacchus) (Greek god)   D:298; G:72, 363, 366
  picture(s)   G:361
Diophantus (Greek mathematician)   A:184; M:163
Dior, Christian (French fashion designer)   C:379
Diorama (three-dimensional scene)   D:2
Diori, Hamani (Niger president)   N:252
Dioscorus (antipope)   R:292
Diouf, Abdou (president of Senegal)   S:118
Dioula (language)   I:417
Dioxins (group of toxic chemicals)   H:72, 73; W:65
Dipendra (crown prince of Nepal)   N:110
Diphtheria (disease)   D:191–92
Diphthongs (two vowels sounded together)   P:486
Diplodocus (dinosaur)   D:173
  picture(s)   D:166
Diplomacy (practice of carrying on relations between nations)   I:269
  diplomatic passports   P:96
  foreign service   F:371
  Franklin's career   F:456–58
  United States president   U:170
Diplomystus (extinct fish)
  picture(s)   E:425
Dipper *see* Big Dipper
Dipper dredge   D:322
  picture(s)   D:321
Dirac, Paul (English physicist)   P:238
Direct current (DC) (in electricity)   E:144–45
  electric generators   E:133–34
  electric motors   E:153
Direct democracy (form of government)   D:105
  town meetings   M:515
Direct dyes   D:380
Directed election (system enforced by autocratic governments)   G:274
Direction
  gyroscope   G:436–38
  maps   M:94
  motion   M:476
  navigation   N:72–77
  navigation of animals   H:202
  radar techniques of finding   R:39
Directional drilling (for oil) *see* Whipstocking
Direct lineal descent (in genealogy)   G:76
Directly observed therapy (DOT) (in health care)   T:329
Direct marketing   A:30; M:34–35
Directors (of museums)   M:526
Directors (of plays)   P:337, 338; T:157
  how to give plays   P:336
Directors of photography (for motion pictures)   M:481
Directory (government of France, 1795–99)   F:472–73
Direct primary system (of elections)   E:131
  Oregon system   O:212
Direct taxes   T:25
Dirigibles *see* Airships
Dirt motorcycles   M:498–99
Dirty bombs   F:36

Disabilities, people with   D:178–80
  blindness   B:255–58
  Boy Scout programs for the handicapped   B:360
  buses can be equipped with ramps or lifts   B:460
  camping, organized   C:49
  cerebral palsy   D:190
  computer assistance   C:485
  deaf people   D:48–51
  dogs for assistance   D:256–57
  dwarfism   D:374–75
  education   E:85
  ham radio equipment for   R:62
  Hansen, Rick, and "Man in Motion" tour   B:406d
  Holocaust, many executed in   W:298
  occupational therapy   O:14–15
  Paralympic Games   O:115
  retardation, mental   R:189–91
  speech disorders   S:397–98
  typewriters help with disabilities   T:374
  universal home design   O:100
  welfare, public   W:120
  picture(s)
    dolls with disabilities   D:271
    educational mainstreaming   E:86
    veterans' rehabilitation programs   V:322
Disability, presidential (in the United States)   P:452
Disability insurance *see* Insurance, disability
Disabled American Veterans (DAV)   U:121
Disappointment, The (ballad opera)   M:552
Disappointment River (Mackenzie's name for what is now the Mackenzie River, Canada)   F:521
Disarmament   D:181–82 *see also* Nuclear disarmament
  Cold War   C:401
  Kellogg-Briand Pact (1928)   C:548
  League of Nations   L:95
  nuclear weapons   N:378–79
  peace movements   P:105–6
Disasters (unforeseen events that cause destruction and suffering)   D:183–85 *see also* Hurricanes; Indian Ocean tsunami (2004)
  Amateur Radio Emergency Service   R:62
  Army's peacetime duties include disaster relief   U:102
  famine   F:44–45
  floods   F:254–57
  foreign aid   F:370
  homelessness can be caused by   H:183
  influenza pandemic (1918–19)   I:228
  Johnstown Flood   J:124
  National Guard called to help   N:42
  notable disasters, table of   D:184
  poverty, causes of   P:419
  Red Cross services   R:126–27
  Senegalese ferry disaster (2002)   S:118
  space exploration and travel   S:352
  volunteerism   V:389
  What caused the *Titanic* tragedy?   O:33
  Which of the following qualifies as a disaster?   D:185
Disc brakes (of automobiles)   A:550–51
Disc dog competitions   D:253
Discharge method (of printing textiles)   D:381
Disciples, Twelve *see* Apostles, The
Discipline (of children) *see* Child development
Disc (Disk) jockeys (people who conduct programs of musical recordings)   R:60, 262b
  picture(s)   R:60
Disco dancing   D:27, 29; R:264
Discount stores   R:188
Discoveries (in geography) *see* Exploration and discovery; individual country, state, and province articles
Discovery (ship of Henry Hudson)   H:274
Discovery (ship that carried colonists to America)   J:22; T:168
Discovery (United States space shuttle)   S:340j, 346, 348, 364, 365
  Glenn, John, and studies of older people in space   G:235
  picture(s)   S:364, 365

Discovery clubs (of Camp Fire Boys and Girls)   **C:**43
   picture(s)   **C:**42
Discovery learning (in education)   **L:**100
Discrete sources *see* Radio stars
Discrimination
   African American history   **A:**79b, 79h–79i
   civil rights   **C:**325–27
   civil rights movement   **C:**328–30
   dwarfism   **D:**375
   Hispanic Americans   **H:**148, 149
   homosexual people   **H:**204
   IQ scores affected by   **I:**254
   NAACP's fight against   **N:**26
   Oriental Exclusion Acts   **O:**228
   racism   **R:**34b
   segregation   **S:**113–15
   United States, remains a problem in the   **U:**99
   women's rights movement   **W:**212–15
Discs *see* Compact discs; Videodiscs
Disc tumbler locks   **L:**283
Discus (fish)   **F:**198
Discussion groups (of people using e-mail) *see* Newsgroups
Discussions (by panels of speakers)   **D:**52 *see also*
      Parliamentary procedure
Discus throw (field event)   **T:**257, 258
   world records   **T:**261
   picture(s)   **T:**252
Discus-Thrower (statue by Myron)   **G:**349
   picture(s)   **G:**345
Disease, prevention of   **D:**210–13; **M:**203
   cancer, prevention of   **C:**95
   circulatory system   **C:**306
   disaster relief   **D:**185
   health   **H:**76–77
   holistic medicine   **H:**171
   immune system   **I:**95–98
   obesity   **O:**6
   occupational health and safety   **O:**13
   protecting care-giver of bleeding person   **F:**159
   public health   **H:**77; **P:**515–16
   teeth, caring for   **T:**44
   vaccination and inoculation   **V:**260–61
   vector-borne diseases   **V:**285
Diseases   **D:**186–213 *see also* Medicine; the names of
      diseases
   alcoholism   **A:**173
   allergies   **A:**190–91
   animal diseases *see* Animal diseases
   animals pass to people   **A:**287
   antibiotics   **A:**306–12
   bacteria as cause   **B:**11, 12
   bioterrorism   **T:**115
   blood, disorders of the   **B:**262
   brain disorders   **B:**368–69
   cancer   **C:**92–95
   Can just one virus make you sick?   **V:**368
   carriers   **V:**282–85
   deafness caused by childhood diseases   **D:**48
   dermatological conditions   **D:**123–24
   descriptions of some diseases   **D:**188–209
   diagnosis   **D:**199–205
   drug treatments   **D:**333
   European diseases brought to Inuit   **I:**275
   globalization's increased trade and travel help spread
      G:239
   heart, disorders of the   **H:**82–85
   hereditary diseases   **G:**80–81, 87–88
   Indian population reduced by European diseases   **I:**162,
      176, 189, 205
   liver, disorders of the   **L:**269–70
   lung diseases   **L:**345
   lymphatic system, disorders of   **L:**350
   malaria   **M:**51–52
   mental illness   **M:**221–26

   mosquitoes as carriers of   **M:**471
   "notifiable" diseases   **P:**513
   nutrition and disease   **N:**429–30
   occupational diseases   **O:**13
   parasitic fungi   **F:**498, 499
   plant diseases *see* Plant diseases
   prevention of *see* Disease, prevention of
   public health   **P:**512–16
   "quarantinable" diseases   **P:**514–15
   sanitation measures to prevent   **S:**33
   treatment   **D:**205–9
   vaccination and inoculation   **V:**260–61
   vectors of disease   **V:**282–85
   viruses   **V:**361–70a
   vitamin deficiency diseases   **V:**370b–370d
   water pollution   **W:**64–65, 76
Diseases, animal *see* Animal diseases
Diseases, mental *see* Mental illness
Diseases, plant *see* Plant diseases
Disentanglement puzzles   **P:**554
Dish antennas (for television reception)   **T:**48, 63, 66
   microwave communication   **M:**288
   satellites, artificial   **S:**54
   picture(s)
      microwave communication   **M:**287
Dishwashers (kitchen appliances)   **A:**532
   picture(s)   **A:**533
Disinfectants   **D:**214 *see also* Antiseptics
   iodine   **I:**287
   water treatment   **S:**33; **W:**76
Disjoint sets (in mathematics)   **S:**128
Disk (of a galaxy)   **M:**309
Disk drive (computer system peripheral)   **C:**481, 491
   lubrication   **L:**335
   magnetic devices   **M:**33
Disk florets (of composite flowers)   **F:**283
Disk harrows   **F:**54, 55, 60
Disk jockeys *see* Disc jockeys
Disk plows   **F:**54
Disks (of cartilage)   **S:**184b
Disks, computer   **C:**481
Dislocations (crystal defects)   **M:**152–53
Dislocations (injuries)   **F:**160
Disney, Walt (American film producer)   **D:**215–16
   animated cartoons   **A:**290–91; **M:**493
Disneyland (Anaheim, California)   **C:**28; **D:**216; **L:**305; **P:**79
   picture(s)   **C:**28; **D:**215
Disneyland (near Paris, France)   **P:**79
Disneyland (Tokyo, Japan)   **P:**79; **T:**219
Disney World (officially **Walt Disney World,** near Orlando,
      Florida)   **D:**216; **F:**270; **P:**79
   picture(s)
      EPCOT Center   **F:**261
      map   **M:**94
Dispatchers (people who monitor traffic)
   ambulances   **A:**199
   railroads   **R:**86
   picture(s)
      railroads   **R:**85
Disperse dyes   **D:**380
Dispersion (of light)   **L:**215, 223–24
Displaced persons *see* Refugees
Display (courtship behavior of birds)   **B:**216, 228
Display ads (in newspapers)   **N:**203
Disposable cameras *see* One-time-use cameras
"Disposable culture" (in which good products are thrown away)
      A:35
Dispositions (juvenile court decisions)   **J:**170
Disputation (a formal debate)   **E:**80–81
Disraeli, Benjamin (1st Earl of Beaconsfield, English statesman
      and novelist)   **D:**217; **E:**251; **V:**332a
   Gladstone was a political opponent of   **G:**225
   picture(s)   **D:**217
Dissected Till Plains (area of Kansas and Missouri)   **K:**178;
      M:368

Dissecting microscopes see Stereoscopic microscopes
Dissenters (Nonconformists) (religious group outside Church of
    England)
    Defoe, Daniel D:84
    Puritans in New England C:417; P:551
    schools E:83
Dissertation (research project) U:221
Dissonance (in music) M:398, 536
Distance learning (through the Internet) C:488
Distance Measuring Equipment (DME) (navigation device in
    airplanes) A:118
Distant Early Warning line (DEW) C:70
Distemper (artist's paint) P:30
Distillate fuel oil see Heating oil
Distillation D:218–19
    chemical terms C:204
    fractional distillation of petroleum P:172
    gasoline obtained from petroleum G:62
    kerosene obtained from petroleum K:235
    liquid gases L:253
    metals, refining of M:234
    perfumes P:151
    seawater purification K:309; M:302
    water desalting W:75
    whiskey and other distilled beverages W:161
    wood yields chemicals W:227
    zinc, refining of Z:385
Distinguished Flying Cross (American award)
    picture(s) D:70
Distinguished Service Cross (American award)
    picture(s) D:70
Distinguished Service Medal of the National Aeronautics and
    Space Administration (American award) D:71
    picture(s) D:70
Distortion (of space) R:143
    map projections M:97
Distributed computing (of computers in networks) C:494
Distribution (of motion pictures) M:486
Distribution transformers (of electric currents) T:271
Distributive properties (of numbers) N:399
Distributor (of an automobile) A:548; I:264
District attorneys see Prosecutors
District courts U:170
District of Columbia (United States) W:29–36 see also
        Washington, D.C.
    Maryland donated the land M:120
    slavery abolished C:340
    slave trade abolished by Compromise of 1850 C:479
    voting rights U:159
Ditches (fortifications) F:378
Dithyramb (Greek poetry) D:298
Dityatin, Aleksandr (Soviet gymnast) O:113
Diuretics (drugs) D:334; O:116
Diurnal motion (of the stars as seen from Earth) P:271
Divali (Hindu festival) H:141; I:122; R:155
Divan Japonais (lithograph by Toulouse-Lautrec) G:306
Divergent margins (of the oceans) E:18
Diverging lenses L:145, 149
    diagram(s) L:143
Diversion dams D:16, 20
Diversion programs (to prevent juvenile crime) J:169
Diversity, biological P:434
Diversity, cultural A:300, 304, 305
Divertimento (musical form) M:541
Divide, Continental see Continental Divide
Dividend (in arithmetic) A:390
Dividends (shares in a company's profits) B:471; S:454
Dividers (measuring tools) T:230
Divine Comedy, The (by Dante Alighieri) D:34; I:406
    picture(s)
        picture of Dante with book D:34
Divine Liturgy see Holy Liturgy
Divine right of kings (doctrine sanctioning king's right to rule)
    French Revolution put an end to F:467, 473
Diving D:220–29; O:106–7, 119–20 see also Skin diving

Diving, deep-sea see Deep-sea diving
Diving, scuba see Scuba diving
Diving, skin see Skin diving
Diving bells (devices allowing people to walk on the ocean floor)
    U:26
    picture(s) U:26
Division (army combat unit) U:104
Division (in biological classification) L:209
Division (in mathematics)
    abacus A:2
    algebra A:182, 183
    arithmetic A:390
    decimal fractions F:401–2
    fractions F:399–400
    number systems N:398, 401
Divisionism (in art) P:27
Division of powers (in United States Constitution) U:162
Divisor (in arithmetic) A:390
Divorce D:230–31
    children's literature, treatment in C:238
    family F:41
Dix, Dorothea Lynde (American social reformer) D:231
    picture(s) D:231
Dixie (name for South) A:130
"Dixie" (song by Dan Emmett) N:22–23
Dixiecrat Party (in the United States) see States' Rights Party
Dixieland (New Orleans jazz) J:59
Dixon, Jeremiah (English surveyor) M:135
Djakarta (capital of Indonesia) see Jakarta
Djebel Chambi (highest point in Tunisia) T:334
Djenné (Mali) P:411
Djerma (a people of Africa) N:251
Djibouti D:232–33
    map(s) D:233
    picture(s)
        city of Djibouti D:232
        flag F:230
Djibouti (capital of the Republic of Djibouti) D:232, 233
    picture(s) D:232
Djindjic, Zoran (prime minister of Serbia) S:127
DME see Distance Measuring Equipment
DMZ see Demilitarized Zone
DNA (Deoxyribonucleic acid) (in body cells) B:297, 298
    aging A:84
    biochemistry B:187, 189–90
    biological studies B:199, 203
    biotechnology B:213
    body, human B:274
    in cell nucleus C:160; L:200
    chemical composition of viruses V:362, 365, 367
    forensic science F:76, 372, 373; G:85–86
    genetics E:376; G:77–78, 79, 82–83, 87, 91
    Human Genome Project G:86
    hydrogen bonds W:50
    microbiology M:279
    Neanderthals not ancestors of modern humans P:442
    paleoanthropologists study DNA of human ancestors
        A:301
    plants P:300, 301
    science, milestones in S:74
    species identification K:259
    diagram(s) B:298, 299
    picture(s) G:77, 89
        analysis used in crime fighting C:586; F:76
        separated by electrophoresis B:189
DNA fingerprinting G:85–86, 91
DNA markers (unique segments of DNA) G:87
DNA polymerase (enzyme) B:189
DNA sequencing B:189
DN class (of iceboats) I:20
    picture(s) I:19
Dnieper River (Europe) K:245; R:241, 362; U:9
Dniester River (Europe) M:402
Dnipropetrovs'k (Ukraine) U:10
D.O. (Doctor of osteopathy) (medical degree) D:234

Do a Good Turn Daily (Scout slogan) **B:**358
Doak, Samuel (American educator) **T:**78
Dobell, Sir William (Australian artist) **A:**501
Doberman pinschers (dogs) **D:**247, 256
 picture(s) **D:**247
Dobruja (Romania) **R:**297, 300
Dobsonflies
 picture(s) **I:**244, 245
Doby, Larry (American baseball player) **S:**310 *profile*
 picture(s) **S:**311
Docents (in museums) **M:**526
d'Ockeghem, Jean (Flemish composer and teacher) *see*
 Ockeghem, Jean d'
Docking (spaceflight maneuver) **S:**340d
Dock Street Theater (Charleston, South Carolina) **S:**306
Doctor (form of address for Doctor of Medicine, M.D., or Doctor
 of Philosophy, Ph.D.) **A:**21
Doctorate (academic degree) **U:**221, 223
Doctor blade (in gravure printing) **P:**477
Doctor De Soto (book by William Steig)
 picture(s) **C:**242
Doctors **D:**234–39
 astronauts, care of **S:**340h, 340L
 Australia's flying service **A:**500
 Blackwell, Elizabeth, was first woman doctor in the United
  States **B:**253
 diagnosis and treatment of disease **D:**199–209
 disease prevention **D:**211
 hospitals **H:**249
 Is the Surgeon General really a surgeon? **D:**236
 medicine **M:**203–10
 mental health professions **M:**225
 physician-assisted suicide **S:**485
 regular checkups for good health **H:**77
 research **R:**181
 surgery **S:**512–15
 picture(s)
  Australia's flying service **A:**499
Dr. Seuss (American author and illustrator) *see* Seuss, Dr.
Doctors without Borders (aid agency) **D:**185
Dr. Zhivago (novel by Boris Pasternak) **R:**384
Doctrine (body of defined truth of the Roman Catholic Church)
 R:284, 286–87
Documentary drama (in German literature) **D:**304–5
Documentary photography **P:**214, 215
Documentary videos **V:**332h
Dodders (plants) **P:**288; **W:**104
 picture(s) **P:**287
Dodecahedron (twelve-faced geometric figure) **G:**123
Dodecanese (Aegean islands) **I:**364
Dodge, Grenville Mellen (American railroad engineer) **I:**302
 profile
Dodge, Henry (American territorial governor) **W:**205
Dodge, Mary Mapes (American writer and editor) **C:**231
 profile; **M:**17
Dodge Caravan (automobile)
 picture(s) **A:**545
Dodge City (Kansas) **K:**184
 on the Chisholm Trail for cattle drives **O:**282
 Earp, Wyatt **E:**7
 picture(s) **K:**184
Dodgson, Charles Lutwidge *see* Carroll, Lewis
Dodo birds (extinct birds) **E:**426
Dodoma (Tanzania) **T:**19
Dodsworth (novel by Sinclair Lewis) **L:**162
Doe, Samuel K. (president of Liberia) **L:**168
Doenitz, Karl (German admiral) **W:**302 *profile,* 316
 picture(s) **W:**302
Does (female deer) **D:**80
Doesburg, Theo van (Dutch artist) **M:**393
Dog days (hot summer days) **D:**256
Doge (Venetian official) **R:**157–58
Doges, Palace of the (Venice, Italy) **V:**301
Dog family *see* Canidae
Dog fighting **D:**251

Dogfish (sharks) **S:**143–44
 picture(s) **F:**185
  how fish swim **F:**198
Dogger Bank (in the North Sea) **F:**216
Doggett's Coat and Badge (boat race) **R:**341
Dogies (orphaned calves) **C:**578
Dogon (a people of Africa)
 Mali **M:**61
Dog on a Leash (painting by Balla)
 picture(s) **M:**390
Dog pounds **D:**258
Dog racing **R:**34a
Dogras (a people of Kashmir) **K:**197, 198
Dogrib (Indians of North America) **I:**188
Dogs **D:**240–60 *see also* Foxes; Wolves; the names of dogs
 artificial selection **E:**379
 The Call of the Wild, excerpt from **L:**299–300
 classification of the domestic dog **T:**28
 dogsledding for mail service **P:**397, 398
 domestication of **A:**287
 guide dogs for the blind **B:**256, 257
 hunting dogs **H:**300
 Laika, dog sent into space **S:**350
 Military Working Dogs **U:**114
 Pavlov's experiment in learning **L:**98; **P:**103
 pets **P:**177
 police dogs **P:**365
 rabies prevention **D:**201
 racing dogs **R:**34a
 ultrasonic sound heard by **S:**265
 What are the dog days? **D:**256
 diagram(s)
  foot bones **F:**81
 picture(s)
  members of the dog family **L:**207
Dog shows *see* Breed shows
Dogsledding **D:**253
 Alaska **A:**144, 156
 Iditarod Trail Sled Dog Race **D:**250
 Inuit **I:**273
 mail routes **P:**397, 398
 picture(s) **A:**378; **D:**253; **I:**276; **N:**410
  Finnish musher **E:**352
Dog star *see* Sirius
Dogwood trees
 buds **T:**309
 picture(s) **B:**403; **M:**367; **N:**307; **P:**313; **S:**299; **T:**301;
  V:347
Doha (capital of Qatar) **Q:**3, 4
Dojo (practice gym for karate) **K:**194
Dolce (musical term) **M:**536
Doldrums (area near the equator) **T:**268; **W:**189
Dole, Elizabeth Hanford (United States government official)
 N:320 *profile*
 picture(s) **L:**3
Dole, Robert Joseph (Bob) (American political figure) **C:**368;
 K:188–89 *profile;* **U:**205
 picture(s) **K:**189
Dole, Sanford Ballard (American lawyer and political leader in
 Hawaii) **H:**61 *profile*
Dolgoruki, Yuri (Russian prince) *see* Yuri Dolgoruki
Dollar (monetary unit) **D:**261–63
 Great Seal of the United States **G:**329
 How can you tell if a bill is counterfeit? **D:**262
 Sacagawea Golden Dollar **S:**2
 Susan B. Anthony dollar **A:**299
Doll Collectors of America, Inc. **D:**271
Dollhouses **D:**264–65
Dollies (small retractable wheels of a semitrailer) **T:**319
Dollies (wheeled platforms for moving objects) **M:**485
Dolls **D:**266–72 *see also* Puppets and marionettes
 dollhouses **D:**264–65
 Festival of Dolls (Japan) **H:**170; **J:**31
 picture(s) **T:**249
  Russian nesting dolls **R:**363

Dolls, Festival of *see* Girls' Day
Doll's House, A (play by Henrik Ibsen)   **D:**303; **I:**2
  picture(s)   **D:**303
Dolly (sheep produced by cloning)   **G:**91; **L:**210
  picture(s)   **G:**91; **I:**277
Dolmetsch, Arnold (French musical authority)   **R:**121
Dolohmwar (highest point in Micronesia)   **M:**280
Dolomites (Alps range in Italy)   **A:**194d
Dolphins and porpoises   **D:**273–78
  echo   **E:**49
  locomotion   **A:**278
  sleep   **S:**198
  sonar system   **S:**265
  tuna and dolphins   **F:**217
  picture(s)
    birth of calf   **D:**276
    bottlenose dolphins   **D:**274, 275
    bouto dolphin   **D:**275
    convergent evolution   **E:**378
    performing dolphins   **D:**273, 278
Domagk, Gerhard (German physician)   **M:**209
Domain name servers (of computers)   **C:**487
Dome of the Rock (Muslim shrine in Jerusalem)   **I:**355; **J:**82, 83
  picture(s)   **P:**40d
Domes (in architecture)
  Byzantine architecture   **A:**370; **B:**490, 491
  Capitol, United States   **C:**105
  Islamic architecture   **A:**370; **I:**356
  planetarium's ceiling   **P:**270
  Rome, architecture of   **A:**369
  Saint Peter's   **A:**372
  Taj Mahal   **T:**12
  picture(s)   **A:**368
Domesday (Doomsday) Book (results of a census in England in 1086)   **E:**238; **W:**174
Domestic animals *see also* the names of domestic animals
  agriculture, history of   **A:**97, 98–99; **F:**336
  American Indians' contribution to world cultures   **I:**166
  bred from wild ancestors   **A:**287
  buffalo and bison   **B:**430
  camels   **C:**39
  cats   **C:**137–40
  cattle   **C:**151–54; **D:**3–7
  dogs   **D:**240–60
  elephants   **E:**183–84
  genetic engineering   **G:**82
  hoofed mammals   **H:**217, 219, 220
  horses   **H:**236–44
  livestock   **L:**271–73
  llamas   **L:**278
  oxen   **O:**286
  prehistoric people domesticated animals   **P:**442
  reindeer and caribou   **R:**138
  sheep   **S:**147
  transportation   **T:**281
Domestic Policy Council (of the United States)   **P:**451
Domestic science *see* Home economics
Domestic violence (violence among members of the same household)   **V:**344
Dominant fifth tone (in music)   **M:**536
Dominant traits (in genetics)   **G:**79
Domingo, Placido (Spanish opera singer)   **O:**140 *profile*
  picture(s)   **O:**140
Domínguez, Francisco Atanasio (Spanish explorer)   **C:**442; **U:**254
Dominic, Saint (Spanish Roman Catholic priest)   **C:**291; **R:**289
Dominica (Caribbean island nation)   **C:**114, 115; **D:**279; **L:**50
  map(s)   **D:**279
  picture(s)
    flag   **F:**230

Dominican Republic   **C:**113, 114, 115; **D:**280–83 *see also* Haiti
  immigration to the United States   **H:**144, 149
  Latin America   **L:**49, 50
  map(s)   **D:**281
  picture(s)
    beach   **D:**281
    flag   **F:**230
    people   **D:**280
    Santo Domingo   **D:**282
    sugarcane farming   **A:**90
    tobacco crop   **A:**91
    village and mountains   **D:**280
Dominicans (religious order)   **C:**291; **R:**289
Dominion Day (July 1) *see* Canada Day
Dominion of New England   **C:**521
Dominions (of the Commonwealth of Nations)   **C:**461
Dominoes (game)   **D:**284; **G:**15
  picture(s)
    Cuban American men playing dominoes   **H:**145
Domitian (Roman emperor)   **R:**316
Doña Barbara (novel by Rómulo Gallegos)   **V:**298
Donatello (Italian sculptor)   **D:**285; **I:**395; **R:**164; **S:**100
  picture(s)
    David (statue)   **S:**99
    Gattamelata (statue)   **I:**395
    Zuccone (statue)   **D:**285
Don Carlos (opera by Giuseppe Verdi)   **O:**153
Donelson, Emily (Jackson's official hostess)   **F:**167–68; **J:**6
  picture(s)   **F:**167
Donelson, John (American pioneer)   **N:**16
Donets Basin (Ukraine)   **U:**9
Donets'k (Ukraine)   **U:**8, 10
Don Giovanni (opera by Mozart)   **O:**153
Dongting Hu (lake, central China)   **L:**30
Dong Yuan (Chinese artist)   **C:**274
Doniphan, Alexander (American soldier)   **M:**239b
Donizetti, Gaetano (Italian composer)   **D:**285; **I:**412; **O:**145
  Lucia di Lammermoor (opera)   **O:**155–56
  picture(s)
    Lucia di Lammermoor (opera)   **O:**157
Don Juan (poem by Lord Byron)   **E:**282
Don Juan (tone poem by Richard Strauss)   **S:**466
Donkeys (burros)   **H:**235, 243
  Nast cartoons   **C:**127; **N:**17
  picture(s)   **H:**242
Donne, John (English poet)   **D:**286; **E:**274–75
Donner party (of pioneers on the California Trail)   **O:**281
Donor countries (providing foreign aid)   **F:**370
Donoso, José (Chilean writer)   **C:**254
Donovan (British rock music performer)   **R:**262c
Don Quixote (novel by Cervantes)   **C:**178; **N:**358–59; **R:**160
  first great novel   **F:**115
  golden age of Spanish literature   **S:**388
  picture(s)   **F:**114; **W:**266
Don Quixote (tone poem by Richard Strauss)   **S:**466
Don River (Russia)   **R:**241
"Don't fire until you see the whites of their eyes" (order of William Prescott)   **R:**200
"Don't give up the ship" (slogan, spoken by James Lawrence)   **W:**10
  Perry's battle flag   **O:**75; **P:**153
Donus (pope)   **R:**292
Doolittle, James Harold (American aviator and army officer)   **W:**300 *profile*, 305
Doomsday Book *see* Domesday Book
Door County (Wisconsin)   **W:**200
Dopamine (neurotransmitter)   **A:**23; **B:**363
Doping (introducing impurities into materials)   **M:**153–54; **T:**274, 277, 278
Doping (use of prohibited drugs by athletes)   **O:**114, 116
Doppler, Christian (Austrian scientist)   **S:**262
Doppler effect (law of physics)   **L:**226
  navigation   **N:**76

Doppler effect (cont.)
   sound   **S:**262–63
   spacecraft tracking   **S:**340L
   wind speed   **W:**90
Doppler radar   **R:**39
   tornado detection   **T:**242
   wind measurement   **W:**189
   picture(s)   **R:**40
Doppler shift (in spectrum)   **U:**215
Dorantes, Esteban (Spanish explorer) *see* Estevanico
Doré, Gustave (French artist)   **D:**286
   picture(s)
      illustration for *Little Red Riding-Hood*   **D:**286
      illustration of London   **I:**220
Doria, Andrea (Genoese statesman)   **G:**95
Doric order (in Greek architecture)   **A:**368; **G:**346, 348
   picture(s)   **G:**346
Dormancy (winter inactivity in cold-blooded animals)   **H:**128
Dormant volcanoes   **V:**381
Dormition, Cathedral of the (Moscow, Russia)   **R:**375
   picture(s)   **R:**376
Dormouse (plural: **dormice**) (rodent)   **H:**127
Dörpfeld, Wilhelm (German archaeologist)   **T:**316
Dorr War (1841, in Rhode Island)   **R:**225
Dorsal fins (of fish)   **F:**188
Dorset (Vermont)   **V:**312
Doryphorus (statue) *see* Spearbearer
Doshi, B. K. (Indian architect)   **I:**139
Dos Passos, John (American novelist)   **A:**216; **D:**287
dos Santos, José Eduardo (Angolan president)   **A:**260
Dostoevski, Fëdor (Russian novelist)   **D:**287; **F:**115; **N:**360;
   R:382
   Saint Petersburg museum   **S:**18b
DOT *see* Directly observed therapy
Do the Right Thing (motion picture, 1989)   **M:**497
Dotted notes (in musical notation)   **M:**535
Douala (Cameroon)   **C:**41
Douay Bible (English version of the Vulgate) *see* Rheims-Douai
   Version
Double-acting cylinders (in hydraulic systems)   **H:**313
Double bar (in musical notation)   **M:**536
Double-barreled shotguns   **G:**421
Double bass (stringed instrument)   **O:**193, 196
   picture(s)   **M:**548
Double bassoon (musical instrument) *see* Contrabassoon
Double crochet stitch (in crocheting)   **C:**591
Doubleday, Abner (American army officer)
   "invention" of baseball   **B:**87
Double-deck elevators   **E:**187
Double Dutch (rope jumping game)
   picture(s)   **G:**18
Double Eagle II (balloon)   **B:**36
   picture(s)   **B:**38
Double Eagle V (balloon)   **B:**36
Double-entry system (in bookkeeping)   **B:**311–12
Double-headed nails   **N:**2
Doubleheader (two baseball games played in one day)   **B:**84
Double helix (form of DNA)   **B:**298; **W:**50
Double Indemnity (motion picture, 1944)   **M:**492
Double indemnity (payment of twice the basic amount
   promised)   **L:**88
Double jeopardy (prosecution twice for the same criminal
   offense)   **B:**182; **L:**88
Double Metamorphosis II (painting by Vaacov Agam)   **P:**32
   picture(s)   **P:**31
Double play (in baseball)   **B:**83
Double stars *see* Binary stars
Doublets (kind of jacket)   **C:**376, 377
Doubt, River of (Brazil) *see* Roosevelt River
Douc monkeys
   picture(s)   **M:**421
Dough, baker's (modeling material)   **C:**354
Dough, bread   **B:**386, 388
   fermentation   **F:**89

Doughboys (World War I soldiers)
   picture(s)   **W:**277
Doughty, Charles (English explorer)   **E:**413
Douglas, James (Buster) (American boxer)   **B:**351
Douglas, Sir James (Canadian fur trader and colonial official)
   B:406d
Douglas, Marjory Stoneman (American environmentalist)
   F:274 *profile*
Douglas, Paul (American businessman)
   picture(s)   **L:**3
Douglas, Stephen A. (American statesman)   **D:**288
   events leading to Civil War   **C:**336
   Illinois   **I:**75
   Kansas-Nebraska Act (1854)   **K:**191
   Lincoln's campaign against   **L:**243–44
   picture(s)   **D:**288
      Lincoln-Douglas debates   **L:**243
Douglas, William O. (associate justice of the Supreme Court)
   D:288
Douglas DC-3 (airplane)   **A:**564–65
   picture(s)   **A:**566; **T:**287
Douglas Duncan collection (of Canadian art)   **N:**40
Douglas fir trees
   British Columbia   **B:**403; **C:**61
   Oregon   **O:**206
   uses of the wood and its grain   **W:**227
   Washington   **W:**18
   picture(s)   **O:**203; **T:**303
      uses of the wood and its grain   **W:**223
Douglass, Frederick (American journalist and anti-slavery
   leader)   **A:**79b, 79g; **D:**289; **S:**196, 197 *profile*
   American literature   **A:**208
   Equal Rights Party   **P:**372
   national historic site   **W:**32
   picture(s)   **A:**6a, 208; **D:**289
Douglas World Cruiser (airplane)   **A:**563
Douro River (Portugal)   **P:**392
Douroucoulis (monkeys)   **M:**422
   picture(s)   **M:**421
Dove, Arthur (American artist)
   picture(s)
      Grandmother (collage)   **D:**137
Dove, Rita Frances (American professor and poet)   **A:**219;
   O:77 *profile*
Dover (capital of Delaware)   **D:**88, 96, 99, 101
   picture(s)   **D:**93, 99
Dover (England)   **E:**233
Dover (New Hampshire)   **N:**159, 160
Dover Air Force Base (Delaware)   **D:**98, 99
Dover sole (fish) *see* Sole
Doves and pigeons   **D:**289–90
   birds of residential areas   **B:**246
   carrier pigeons   **C:**465
   incubation in hot climates   **B:**231
   nearly flightless pigeons   **O:**242
   passenger pigeons are now extinct   **B:**248
   pets   **B:**250a; **P:**178–79
   pigeon's milk   **B:**236
   picture(s)   **B:**234; **D:**289, 290
Dovetailing (in furniture construction)   **F:**506
Dowland, John (English composer)   **E:**292
Down (inner feathers of waterfowl)   **D:**345, 346, 347, 348
Downbeat (musical term)   **M:**536
Down East (nickname for Maine)   **M:**36
Downhill racing (in skiing)   **S:**184e–184f
Downing Street, No. 10 (London)   **L:**293
"Down in Yon Forest" (English carol)   **C:**118
Downloading (putting files on a computer)   **P:**216; **R:**124
Down quark (subatomic particle)   **A:**488, 489
Downs (in football)   **F:**354
Downstage (front of a theater's stage)   **P:**337
Down syndrome   **D:**193, 194, **290**; **G:**80; **R:**190
Doxycycline (antibiotic)   **D:**188

Doyle, Sir Arthur Conan (English doctor and detective-story writer) **D**:291–92; **M**:566
  The Red-Headed League, excerpt from **D**:292
D'Oyly Carte, Richard (English impresario) **G**:208, 209
D. P.'s (Displaced persons) *see* Refugees
Dr. *see* Doctor
Drabble, Margaret (English novelist) **E**:290
Drachma (Greek coin) **M**:413
Dracula (book by Bram Stoker) **L**:130
Draft (Conscription) **D**:293
  French-Canadian opposition **C**:85
  Jews in Russia **J**:106
  New York City Draft Riots during Civil War **C**:342
  Nixon administration **N**:262d
Draft horses **H**:237, 240–41; **L**:272
  picture(s) **H**:240
Drafting (drawing) *see* Mechanical drawing
Drafting (writing) *see* Rough draft
Drag (resistance of air to moving objects)
  aerodynamics **A**:39, 40
  airplane flight **A**:109, 114
  rockets **R**:258
  supersonic flight **S**:500–501, 502
  vacuum lacks air resistance **V**:262
Drag (Hopper) dredge **D**:322
Dragila, Stacy (American athlete) **T**:263
Draglines (earth-moving machinery) **E**:31
Draglines (spun by spiders) **S**:403
Drag nets (used in oceanographic studies) **O**:40
Dragon Boat Festival (China) **H**:163
Dragonflies (insects) **D**:294; **I**:248
  eating habits **I**:236
  metamorphosis **M**:238
  picture(s) **D**:294; **M**:238
    ancient and modern **E**:372
    wings **I**:240
Dragons (legendary creatures) **D**:295
Drag racing (hot-rod cars) **A**:538
  picture(s) **A**:538
Drainage basins (of rivers) **R**:236
Drains (in plumbing) **P**:339
Drais, Baron Karl von (German inventor of early bicycle) **B**:177
Drake, Edwin L. (American oil producer) **F**:487; **P**:168
  picture(s) **P**:140
Drake, Sir Francis (English sailor and explorer) **C**:29; **D**:296; **E**:406
Drake, Frank (American radio astronomer) **R**:70
Drakensberg Mountains (South Africa) **A**:48; **S**:270
Drake Passage (strait connecting Atlantic and Pacific Oceans) **A**:478; **S**:274
Drakes (male ducks) **D**:346
Drama **D**:297–307; **L**:259; **T**:156–62 *see also* Acting; the names of well-known dramatists
  Africa, literature of **A**:76d
  American *see* American drama
  China, literature of **C**:279
  copyright **C**:555
  English *see* English drama
  fiction, origins of **F**:114
  France, literature of **F**:437–38, 440, 442
  German literature **G**:177, 178–79, 181
  Golden Age of Radio **R**:59
  Greek tragedy and comedy **A**:238; **G**:356–57
  Indians, American **I**:189
  Irish National Theatre (Abbey Theatre) **I**:326–27
  Japanese No and Kabuki **J**:32, 53
  Japanese puppet play **J**:32–33, 53
  Korea, North **K**:297
  motion pictures **M**:477–97
  musical theater **M**:552–55
  opera **O**:139–65
  pageants **P**:12
  play production **P**:335–38

Pulitzer Prizes **P**:536–37
puppets and marionettes **P**:545–48
realism **R**:114
Scandinavian literature **S**:58h–58i
Spanish literature **S**:387, 388–89
What is the most frequently performed drama in history? **D**:298
picture(s)
  Indians, American **I**:201
Drama series (television programs) **T**:70
Dramatic monologue (in poetry) **E**:284
Dramatic voice **V**:377
Dramatists *see* Playwrights
Draper, Henry (American astronomer) **A**:472
Draughts (English game of checkers) **C**:192
Draughtsmanship *see* Mechanical drawing
Drava River (Croatia) **C**:588
Draves, Victoria (American diver) **A**:459; **D**:229
Dravidian (language group of Asia) **A**:445; **L**:40
  India, literature of **I**:140
  spoken in southern India **I**:117
Dravidians (a people of India) **I**:117, 131
Drawbridges **B**:398–99
  fortification of a castle **F**:378–79
Drawing **D**:308–14
  animation **A**:288–91
  cartoons **C**:127–29
  engraving **E**:294
  etching **E**:326–27
  Gothic architects' plans of buildings **G**:270–71
  history of **D**:315–18
  mechanical drawing **M**:200
  optical illusions **O**:172–74, 175
  perspective **D**:313–14
  police artists **P**:367
  techniques and uses of the graphic arts **G**:302–8
Drawing (of cotton fibers) **C**:569
Drawing (of metals) **M**:235–36
Drawing Hands (lithograph by Escher) **E**:320
Drawing-room comedy *see* Comedy of manners
Drawknife (tool) **T**:234
Draw looms (weaving) **R**:353
Drayton, Michael (English poet) **E**:272
Dreaming **D**:319–20
  extrasensory perception **E**:428
  health, importance to **H**:75
  sleep **S**:198
Dreamtime (Australian Aboriginal legend) **A**:498
Drebbel, Cornelius van (Dutch inventor) **S**:473
Dredges **D**:321–22
  fishing equipment **F**:218
  oceanography **O**:39
  underwater archaeology **U**:19–20
Dred Scott Decision (1857) **A**:6b, 79f; **D**:323; **U**:185
  Buchanan upheld the decision **B**:419–20
  events leading to Civil War **C**:335
  Missouri, history of **M**:366, 380
  Supreme Court **S**:510
Dreidel (game) **H**:29
  picture(s) **H**:29
Dreiser, Theodore (American novelist) **A**:214; **D**:324; **N**:361; **R**:114
Dresden (Germany) **G**:156
Dresden Codex (Maya book) **M**:186
Dresden diamond **G**:73
Dresden dolls **D**:267
  picture(s) **D**:268
Dresden (Meissen) porcelain **A**:316a; **P**:413
Dress *see* Clothing; Fashion
Dressage (type of riding) **H**:229
  picture(s) **H**:232
Dressing (of furs) **F**:503
Dress rehearsals (of plays) **P**:338
Drew, Charles R. (American surgeon) **D**:325

Dreyfus, Alfred (French army officer) **D:**325; **F:**466
  Dreyfus case in French history **F:**417–18
  Jews, history of **J:**107
  Zola helped in Dreyfus' release **Z:**387
Dreyfuss, Henry (American industrial designer) **I:**215
Dreyse, Johann Nickolaus von (German inventor) **G:**420
Dribbling (in basketball) **B:**95d, 95f
Dried flowers **F:**279
Dried fruits
  baked goods, ingredient in **B:**388
  dates **D:**41
  figs **F:**121
  prunes **P:**108
  seedless grapes **G:**297
Dried milk **D:**9
Dries (fly-fishing lures) **F:**214
Drift (changes in viruses) **I:**228
Driftless Area (Illinois) **I:**64
Drift mining (of coal) **C:**389
Drift nets (for fishing) **F:**218–19
Drift Prairie (North Dakota) **N:**322, 324, 326
Drill bits (tools) **T:**229
Drilling and boring
  mining **M:**320
  natural gas **N:**59
  oceanography **O:**39
  oil wells **P:**168, 169–71
  quarrying **Q:**6
  wells **W:**121–22
  picture(s)
    mechanical mole **T:**340
    natural gas drilling platform **N:**59
Drilling mud (lubricant used in drilling for oil) **P:**170
Drill press (machine tool) **T:**231–32
Drills (baboons) *see* Mandrills
Drills (machines that plant grain) **F:**56, 60
Drills (tools) **T:**229, 231–32, 233
  dental drills **D:**115
  electric drill **T:**230
  picture(s)
    eggbeater drill **T:**229
    electric drill **T:**231
Drinking (of alcoholic beverages) **A:**173
Drip irrigation (direct application of water to plant roots)
  C:524; **F:**351; **W:**74
  picture(s) **C:**524
Drip method (of brewing coffee) **C:**397
Dripstone (cave formations) **C:**156
DRI's *see* Dietary Reference Intakes
Driskill Mountain (Louisiana) **L:**315, 316
Drive-in restaurants **R:**186
Driver education **D:**326–27 *see also* Traffic control
Drivers (part of loudspeakers) **S:**267b
Drive shaft (of an automobile) **A:**549–50; **T:**279
Drive train (of an automobile) **A:**546
  picture(s) **A:**548
Drive wheels (of an automobile) **A:**546
Driving Under the Influence (DUI) *see* Drunk driving
Driving While Impaired (DWI) *see* Drunk driving
Drizzle (kind of precipitation) **R:**94, 95–96
Drnovšek, Janez (president of Slovenia) **S:**204
Drogues (small parachutes to slow spacecraft re-entry)
  S:340d, 340j
Dromaeosaurus (dinosaur) **D:**171
Dromedaries *see* Arabian camels
Drones (male bees) **B:**117, 119
Droop Mountain Battlefield (West Virginia) **W:**134
Drop forging (of metals) **M:**234
Dropsondes (instruments released into the eye of a hurricane)
  H:306
Drosophila *see* Fruit flies
Drought (shortage of water) **D:**328–29
  climate, changes in **C:**364
  desert environments **D:**127

disasters **D:**183, 184, 185
Dust Bowl, causes of **D:**355
environment of prairies **P:**426, 428
Ethiopia **E:**331
famine **F:**44
Kenya **K:**231
Nebraska, history of **N:**94, 95
Niger **N:**252
water supply **W:**73
Drowned mouths (of rivers without deltas) **R:**236–37
Drowning, preventive measures against **S:**5
Drug abuse **D:**329–33
  AIDS is transmitted by intravenous drug abusers **A:**100b
  avoiding health hazards **H:**76
  brain, health tips about **B:**366
  Coast Guard detects drug smugglers **U:**124
  deafness in infants caused by mothers' drug use **D:**48
  dogs sniff out illegal drugs **D:**243, 256; **U:**114
  driving under the influence of drugs **D:**326
  family problems **F:**42
  homelessness **H:**183
  juvenile crime **J:**168, 169
  mental illness **M:**223, 225
  Olympic Games controversy **O:**114, 116
Drug addiction **N:**15 *see also* Alcoholism
  mental illness **M:**223
Drug Enforcement Administration (DEA) **J:**166; **N:**15
Drug industry **D:**335–36
  picture(s) **I:**150; **P:**529
Drugs **D:**333–36
  allergies **A:**191
  ancient medicine **M:**207
  anesthesia **A:**254–57
  antibiotics **A:**306–12
  antidotes for poisons **P:**356
  aspirin **M:**208g
  cancer treatment **C:**94
  circulatory system disorders, treatment of **C:**306
  disease prevention **D:**213
  disease treatment **D:**206–7
  Elion, Gertrude, and pharmaceutical research **I:**282
  Federal Food, Drug, and Cosmetic Act (1938) **F:**345
  medicine **M:**204
  medicines can be poisonous when taken in large amounts
    P:356
  medicines from plants **P:**297
  mental illness, treatment of **M:**225
  narcotics **N:**15
  poisons in the home **P:**356
  protein drugs **B:**213
  religion of early Andean civilization **I:**168
  research **R:**181, 182
  safety **S:**4
  science, modern **S:**74
  stomach disorders, treatment of **S:**461
  picture(s)
    pharmaceutical plant **N:**171
Druids (priests of ancient Gaul and Britain) **C:**164
  Halloween customs taken from **H:**13, 163
  Stonehenge long believed to be a temple **S:**462
Drum (musical instrument) **D:**337–40; **P:**147–48
  Africa, music of **A:**77, 78, 79
  communication method **C:**465
  dance accompaniment **D:**24
  musical instruments, types of **M:**551
  orchestra **O:**194
  picture(s)
    African drums **A:**77; **F:**327
    drummers in Burundi **B:**458
    funeral in Ghana **G:**194
    Haitian manman **L:**71
    Indians, American **I:**183
Drum brakes (of an automobile) **A:**550
  diagram(s) **H:**313

Drumlins (hills formed by glacial deposits)   **G:**225; **I:**8, 14; **M:**138; **N:**213
   picture(s)   **I:**10
Drummer Hoff (book by Ed Emberley)
   picture(s)   **C:**236
Drummond, Lake (Virginia)   **V:**348
Drunk driving   **A:**173
Drupes *see* Stone fruits
Drury Lane Theatre (London, England)   **L:**296
Druzes (Druses) (religious sect)
   Israel   **I:**370
   Lebanon   **L:**120, 122
Dry bulk carriers (ships)   **S:**155
Dry-cargo ships   **S:**154–55
Dry cells *see* D batteries
Dry cleaning   **D:**341
Dryden, John (English critic, poet, and dramatist)   **D:**342; **E:**275–76
   odes   **O:**52
   quoted on Chaucer   **E:**270
Dry distillation   **D:**219
Dry ice (frozen carbon dioxide)
   cloud seeding   **W:**95
   refrigeration   **R:**134
Drying (of foods)   **F:**339–40 *see also* Dehydration
Drying (preparation of leather)   **L:**110
Drying oils   **O:**79, 81
Dry measure   **W:**115, 117
Dry method (of preparing coffee beans)   **C:**396
Drypoint (engraving technique)   **G:**305
Drysdale, Russell (Australian painter)
   picture(s)
      Sunday Evening   **A:**501
Dry Tortugas National Park (Florida)   **F:**270
Drywall screws   **N:**3
Dry wines   **W:**190, 190a
DSA *see* Digital subtraction angiography
DSM-IV (book by the American Psychiatric Association)   **M:**221
DSN *see* Deep Space Network
DST *see* Daylight Saving Time
Dual Alliance (France and Russia)   **W:**277
Dual citizenship   **C:**322
Dual control locks   **L:**282
Duars plain (of Bhutan)   **B:**155a
Duarte, José Napoleón (Salvadoran political leader)   **E:**199
Duarte, Pico (highest peak in the West Indies)   **D:**281
Duarte Frutos, Nicanor (president of Paraguay)   **P:**66
Du Barry, Madame (Jeanne Bécu) (mistress of Louis XV of France)   **D:**342; **L:**311
   picture(s)   **D:**342
Dubayy (state, United Arab Emirates)   **U:**45
Dubcek, Alexander (Czechoslovak political leader)   **C:**624; **S:**202
Dubinsky, David (American labor union official)   **L:**14 *profile*
Dublin (capital of Ireland)   **D:**343; **I:**320, 321, 323
   architecture   **I:**322
   Easter Rising   **I:**324
   picture(s)
      O'Connell Bridge   **D:**343; **I:**321
Dublin, University of (Ireland)
   picture(s)
      library   **I:**318
Dubliners (short stories by Joyce)   **I:**327
Dublin Gate Theatre   **T:**161
Dubnium (element)   **E:**172
Dubois, Ambroise (Flemish-French painter)   **F:**426
Dubois, Raphaël (French scientist)   **B:**205
Du Bois, W. E. B. (African American leader)   **A:**79h, 79i, 79j; **D:**344
   American literature   **A:**214a
   National Association for the Advancement of Colored People (NAACP)   **N:**25
   Spingarn Medal   **S:**409
   picture(s)   **A:**79h, 214a; **N:**25

Dubuffet, Jean (French painter)
   picture(s)
      Nimble Free Hand to the Rescue (painting)   **F:**432
Dubuque (Iowa)   **I:**300
   picture(s)   **I:**299
Dubuque, Julien (French-Canadian pioneer)   **I:**302
Duccio di Buoninsegna (Italian painter)   **I:**394
   picture(s)
      Three Marys at the Sepulcher (painting)   **J:**89
Duce, Il (name for Benito Mussolini)   **M:**556
Duchamp, Marcel (French artist)   **D:**344; **M:**393; **S:**104
Duck-billed dinosaur *see* Hadrosaur
Duckbills *see* Platypuses
Duckpins (bowling game)   **B:**350a
Ducks (amphibious vehicles)   **W:**200
Ducks (waterfowl)   **D:**345, 346
   flightless birds   **O:**242
   pets   **B:**250a
   poultry   **P:**417
   picture(s)
      being treated for oil-spill injury   **P:**176
      mallard ducks   **B:**219; **M:**353
      pets   **B:**249
      poultry   **P:**416
      wood duck   **B:**234
Duckweed (plant)   **P:**294, 302
   picture(s)   **F:**283
Ductility (property of metals)   **M:**233
Dude ranches
   picture(s)   **W:**339
Dudevant, Madame (French novelist) *see* Sand, George
Duels and dueling   **D:**349–50
   fencing   **F:**85–87
   Hamilton and Burr   **H:**16
   Jackson, Andrew   **J:**4
   The Three Musketeers, excerpt from   **D:**351–52
   violence and society   **V:**344
Due process (legal proceedings)   **B:**182; **G:**276; **L:**88
Dufay, Guillaume (Flemish composer)   **C:**283; **D:**371; **F:**444–45; **R:**172
Duffy, Brian (American astronaut)
   picture(s)   **S:**340L, 341
Dufourspitze (mountain, Switzerland)   **S:**543
Dufy, Raoul Ernest Joseph (French painter)
   picture(s)
      Fishing (woodcut print)   **W:**229
Dugongs (aquatic mammals)   **M:**77
   picture(s)   **M:**77
Dugout (in baseball)   **B:**83
Dugouts (canoelike boats)   **C:**101; **T:**281
   picture(s)   **B:**138
Duhalde, Eduardo Alberto (president of Argentina)   **A:**386d
DUI (Driving Under the Influence) *see* Drunk driving
Duich, Lake (Scotland)
   picture(s)   **S:**85
Dukas, Paul Abraham (French composer)   **F:**447
Dukhan (Qatar)   **Q:**4
Dulac, Edmund (English illustrator)   **I:**82
Dulcimer (musical instrument)   **S:**469
   picture(s)   **S:**469
Dulle Griete (famous cannon)   **G:**424
Dulles, John Foster (United States Secretary of State)   **W:**35 *profile*
Dulles International Airport (Virginia)   **V:**353
Duluth (Minnesota)   **M:**326, 335
   picture(s)   **M:**333
Duma (Russian national assembly)   **R:**371; **U:**40
Dumas, Alexandre, *fils* (French writer)   **D:**303, 351; **F:**441
   picture(s)   **D:**351
Dumas, Alexandre, *père* (French writer)   **D:**351–52; **F:**441
   historical romance   **F:**114
   romanticism in French drama   **D:**302; **R:**303
   The Three Musketeers, excerpt from   **D:**351–52
   picture(s)   **D:**351
Dumas, Frederic (French author)   **C:**577

Du Maurier, Dame Daphne (English writer)   M:564
Du Maurier Classic (golf championship)   G:260
Dumbarton Oaks Conference (1944)   U:63
Dumbbells (weights used for exercise)   W:107
Dumbfish (colonial American dish)   C:411
Dummy (in printing)   I:84
Dummy (in ventriloquism)   P:545; V:302
Dumping (of wastes)
  hazardous wastes   H:72, 73
  ocean pollution   O:29
  water pollution   W:65
Dumplings (food made from wheat)   G:281
Dump trucks   E:32; T:321
Dunant, Jean Henri (Swiss philanthropist and founder of the
  Red Cross)   G:93; R:126
Dunbar, Paul Laurence (American poet and novelist)   A:214a;
  D:352–53
  "A Starry Night"   D:353
  picture(s)   D:352
Duncan, Isadora (American dancer)   C:32 profile; D:31, 353
  picture(s)   D:32, 353
Duncan I (king of Scotland)   S:88
Duncan Phyfe furniture
  picture(s)
    room at Winterthur   F:512
Dunciad, The (by Alexander Pope)   P:384
Dune (novel by Frank Herbert)   S:82
Dunedin (New Zealand)   N:236, 241
Dunes
  deserts   D:128, 130
  Great Sand Dunes National Monument (Colorado)   C:438
  Nebraska's Sand Hills   N:84
  Sleeping Bear Dunes National Lakeshore (Michigan)
    M:262
  picture(s)
    Death Valley   C:21
    fences against erosion   E:319
    Indiana Dunes State Park   I:145
    Michigan   M:261
    Sahara ergs   S:6
Dung beetles see Scarabs
Dungeness crabs   C:581
Dunham, Katherine (American dancer, choreographer, and
  ethnologist)   D:31, 32, 33 profile; I:74 profile
  picture(s)   D:33; I:74
Duniway, Abigail Scott (American suffragist)   O:214 profile
  picture(s)   O:214
Dunk (in basketball)   B:95g–95h
Dunking for apples (Halloween game)   H:14
Dunkirk (Dunkerque) (French seaport)   W:298
Dunlap, William (American playwright)   D:306
Dunlop, John Boyd (Scottish inventor)   T:210
Dunmore's War (1774)   W:138
Dunninger, Joseph (American magician and mind reader)
  M:23
Dunstable, John (English composer)   E:291
Duodecimal system (Base-12 system) (of numeration)
  N:408–9
Duodenum (upper part of the small intestine)   D:163, 164
  peptic ulcer   D:198
Duomo (cathedral, Florence, Italy)   F:258
  picture(s)   F:258
Duong Van Minh (Vietnamese political leader)   V:338
Dupin, Amandine (French novelist) see Sand, George
Duplessis, Maurice Le Noblet (Canadian statesman)   Q:15
Duplicate plates (in printing)   P:473
Duplicating machines   O:58–59
Du Pont, Eleuthere Irénée (French-born American industrialist)
  D:100 profile, 102
Du Pont, Lammot (American chemist and inventor)   E:420
Du Pont, Pierre S. (American industrialist)   D:100 profile
  picture(s)   D:101
DuPont Company   D:88, 95, 99, 100, 102
Dura mater (covering of the brain)   B:364
Durán, Roberto (Panamanian boxer)   B:353

Durango and Silverton Narrow Gauge Railroad (Colorado)
  C:438
Duras, Marguerite (French writer)   F:443
Duration (of musical notes)   M:535
Durban (South Africa)   I:161; S:272
Dürer, Albrecht (German artist)   D:354; G:167
  drawing, history of   D:317
  graphic arts   G:303, 305
  Renaissance art   R:171
  watercolor painting   W:55
  woodcut printing   W:229
  picture(s)
    Hare (painting)   A:427
    The Knight, Death, and the Devil (engraving)   G:303
    medieval illustrations   I:79
    The Prodigal Son (engraving)   D:354
    Saint Anthony at Nuremberg (engraving)   G:167
    Saint Jerome in His Study (engraving)   D:354
    Self Portrait (painting)   R:170
    watercolor of irises   W:54
    watercolor studies from nature   D:316
Durga (Hindu goddess)   H:141
Durham (North Carolina)   N:315
Durham Cathedral (England)   A:371; G:266–67
Durham report (recommending self-government for Canada)
  C:83
Durkheim, Émile (French sociologist)   S:231
Dürrenmatt, Friedrich (Swiss dramatist)   D:304; G:181
Durrës (Albania)   A:161
Durum wheat   G:281, 284; W:156, 158
  North Dakota is nation's leading producer   N:322
  picture(s)   W:157
Duryea (automobile)   A:542
Duryea, Charles Edgar (American inventor and manufacturer)
  A:542; T:286
Duryea, James F. (American inventor and manufacturer)
  A:542
Du Sable, Jean Baptiste Point (American pioneer)   C:221
  profile
Duse, Eleonora (Italian actress)   T:160 profile
Dusenberg SSJ (automobile)
  picture(s)   A:542
Dushanbe (capital of Tajikistan)   T:10
Dusky scrub fowl   B:229–30
Düsseldorf (Germany)   G:157; W:307
Dust (specks of solid material that float in the air)   D:355
  air pollution   A:122, 123
  allergies   A:190
  atmosphere contains   A:480
  climate, changes in   C:364
  cloud formation and dust   C:382, 383
  comets, formation of   C:449, 452
  desert dust storms   D:128, 130
  diamond dust for grinding and polishing   D:148
  dinosaurs' extinction is possibly the result of a huge dust
    cloud   D:177
  erosion by wind   E:318
  fog and smog   F:290–91
  galactic dust   U:211
  grain dust is highly combustible   G:286
  Mars' dust storms   M:107, 108
  Mercury's surface   M:229
  meteors   C:449
  radioactive fallout   F:35–36
  picture(s)
    dust storm   D:128
Dust Bowl (region of the United States)   D:355–56; K:189;
  O:96
Dust-cloud hypothesis (theory of the formation of the solar
  system) see Solar system—theories of formation
Dust devils (whirling winds)   T:242; W:188
Dust jacket (of a book)   B:329
Dutch (people of the Netherlands)   N:119
  picture(s)
    costumes, traditional   C:373

Dutch and Flemish music   D:371–73
  Belgium   B:133
  Franco-Flemish style of early French composers
      F:444–45
  Renaissance music   R:172–73
Dutch art   D:357–70; P:23, 24 *see also* Flemish art
  baroque period   B:64, 67–68
  dollhouses   D:264
  drawing, history of   D:318
  Escher, M. C.   E:320
  Hals, Frans   H:15
  Mondrian, Piet   M:410
  pottery   P:412
  Rembrandt   R:156
  Vermeer, Jan   V:305
Dutch Borneo *see* Kalimantan
Dutch East India Company   E:47; J:14
  early stock company   S:455
  Hudson, Henry   H:273–74; T:174
  Indonesia   I:211
  South Africa   S:269, 272
Dutch East Indies   J:14
Dutch elm disease   E:209; P:287, 289
Dutch Guiana *see* Suriname
Dutch in America   C:419; T:174–76
  Delaware, history of   D:96, 100
  homes and housing   H:187, 194
  New Jersey, history of   N:176
  New York, history of   N:221–22
  Tulip Festival (Holland, Michigan)   M:262
  picture(s)
    Pella (Iowa) tulip festival   I:294
Dutch language   N:119–20
  Latin America   L:50
  official language of Flanders   B:130
"Dutch Lullaby, A" (poem by Eugene Field)   F:118
Dutch Reformed Church   C:294; N:120
Dutch West India Company   N:221; T:175
Dutch West Indies *see* Netherlands Antilles
Duties (custom)   I:271
Dutra, Eurico (president of Brazil)   B:384
Dutt, Michael Madhusudan (Indian poet)   I:142
Duty, Honor, Country (West Point motto)   U:106
Duty-free shops (in international airports)   A:127
Duun, Olav (Norwegian writer)   S:58i
Duvalier, François (president of Haiti)   H:11
Duvalier, Jean-Claude (president of Haiti)   H:11
DVD-Audio   R:124
DVD's *see* Digital video discs
Dvina River (Europe) *see* Western Dvina River

Dvořák, Antonin (Czech composer)   C:621; D:374
  picture(s)   C:621
Dwarf elliptical galaxies   U:214
Dwarf galaxies   M:309
Dwarfism (extreme short stature caused by a medical condition)
      D:374–75
  picture(s)   D:374
Dwarfs (in Norse mythology)   N:279, 280
Dwarf sperm whales   W:150
Dwarf stars   S:429–30, 432
Dwarf varieties (of plants)
  apple trees   A:333
  cereal grains   G:286
DWI (Driving While Impaired) *see* Drunk driving
Dwight, James (American tennis player)   T:94
Dyaks (a people of Borneo) *see* Dayaks
Dye lasers *see* Liquid lasers
Dyes and dyeing   D:375–81
  color added to specimens viewed through a microscope
      M:282
  digital subtraction angiography   I:86
  Easter eggs   E:44
  furs   F:503
  ink   I:229
  leather preparation   L:111
  purple dye of meat inspection stamp   M:198
  resins used in   R:184
  textiles   T:142–43
  What makes dyes fade?   D:381
Dyhrenfurth, Norman G. (American mountaineer)   E:371
Dying Swan, The (ballet solo choreographed by Michel Fokine
      and danced by Anna Pavlova)   B:29
Dylan, Bob (American composer and singer)   R:262c, 262d
  profile
  picture(s)   F:328; R:262c
Dynamic braking (of diesel locomotives)   L:287
Dynamics (in music)   M:536, 537
Dynamic system (in chaos theory)   W:93
Dynamite (explosive)   E:419–20, 421, 422
  mining, use in   M:319
  Nobel, Alfred   N:263
Dynamos *see* Electric generators
Dynasties (in Chinese history)   A:240; C:257, 268–70
Dyoplosaurus (dinosaurs)   D:176
Dyslexia (difficulty in learning to read)   D:178; L:107, 108
Dysprosium (element)   E:172
Dysthymic disorder (mental illness)   M:221
Dzhugashvili, Iosif *see* Stalin, Joseph
Dzongkha (Tibetan dialect)   B:155
Dzurinda, Mikuláš (prime minister of Slovakia)   S:202

PHOTO CREDITS

The following list credits the sources of photos used in THE NEW BOOK OF KNOWLEDGE.
Credits are listed, by page, photo by photo—left to right, top to bottom. Wherever appropriate, the
name of the photographer has been listed with the source, the two being separated by a dash. When
two or more photos by different photographers appear on one page, their credits are separated by
semicolons.

Lonely Planet Images; © Robbie Jack—Corbis.
31 © Will Burgess—Reuters/Corbis
32 The Granger Collection; Mary Evans Picture Library; © Jerry Cooke—Corbis.
33 The Granger Collection; © Robbie Jack—Corbis.
34 SuperStock
36 The Granger Collection
37 Art Reference Bureau
38 © Bettmann/Corbis
40 © Jean-Yves Bruel—Masterfile
41 © David Weintraub—Photo Researchers
42 © Burstein Collection/Corbis
43 Corbis
45 © Jeffry W. Myers—H. Armstrong Roberts
46 Northwind Picture Archives
47 The Granger Collection
48 © Harry Sieplinga—HMS Images/The Image Bank/Getty Images
49 © Richard Hutchings—Photo Researchers
53 Photo Researchers
57 © J. Scott Applewhite—AP/Wide World Photos
58 The Granger Collection; National Museum of American History/Smithsonian Institution.
60– © Yale University Art Gallery, New Haven
61
62 The Granger Collection
63 The National Archives
65 The Granger Collection; The Granger Collection; The Granger Collection; © Bettmann/Corbis.
66 The Granger Collection (all photos this page).
67 Photo by Hulton Archive/Getty Images; The Granger Collection; © Corbis.
68 The Granger Collection (all photos this page).
69 © Desjardins—Réalités—Agence TOP; Bonnefoy—Connaissance des Arts, Loo Collection—Agence TOP.
70 © F. L. Kenett—George Rainbird Limited
71 © Roland—Ziolo—Musée Guimet, Paris; Smithsonian Institution, Freer Gallery of Art; The Metropolitan Museum of Art, New York.
72 © Dagli Orti—Archaeological Museum, Rabat/Art Archive; © Erich Lessing—Art Resource, NY; © Victoria & Albert Museum, London/Art Resource, NY; © Indianapolis Museum of Art, Robertine Daniels Art Fund in memory of her husband and son, Richard Monroe Fairbanks, Sr. and Michael Fairbanks/The Bridgeman Art Library; © Erich Lessing—Art Resource, NY; Photo by George Kopp; © Iraq Museum, Baghdad/The Bridgeman Art Library.
73 © Scala/Art Resource, NY; © Victoria & Albert Museum, London/Art Resource, NY; © Dagli Orti—Egyptian Museum, Cairo/Art Archive.
74 © Dagli Orti—Antenna Gallery, Dakar, Senegal/Art Archive; © Werner Forman—Art Resource, NY.
75 © David Forbert—SuperStock; © Werner Forman—Art Resource, NY.
76 © Vanni—Art Resource, NY.
77 © Dagli Orti—Art Archive; © Nimatallah—Art Resource, NY.
78 © Dagli Orti/Private Collection/Art Archive; © Reunion des Musees Nationaux/Art Resource, NY.
79 © New York Historical Society/The Bridgeman Art Library; The Granger Collection; Digital Image © The Museum of Modern Art/Licensed by Scala/Art Resource, NY.
80 © Fred Bavendam—Peter Arnold, Inc.; © Jeff Foott—Bruce Coleman Inc.
81 © Aaron Ferster—Photo Researchers; © Stephen J. Krasemann—Photo Researchers.
82 © Leonard Lee Rue III—Photo Researchers
83 U.S. Department of Defense
85 Courtesy of Wilmington Library, Brandywine Museum, Illustration from The N. C. Wyeth Collection
86 Photographie Giraudon
87 The Phillips Collection, Washington, D.C.
88 © Larry Lefever—Grant Heilman Photography
89 © Tom Payne; © Tom Payne; © Kevin Fleming.
90 © Robin Coventry—Delaware Stock; © Tom Payne.
91 © Tom Payne
92 © Robin Coventry—Delaware Stock; © Everett C. Johnson—Leo de Wys.
93 © Robin Coventry—Delaware Stock; © Kevin Fleming.
94 © Tom Payne; © Kevin Fleming.
95 © Robin Coventry—Delaware Stock
96 © Kevin Fleming; © Tom Payne; © Tom Payne; © Robin Coventry—Delaware Stock.

98 © Tom Payne; © Tom Payne; © David Forbert.
99 © Jeff Gnass
100 © Tom Payne
101 Underwood & Underwood—Corbis-Bettmann; © Archive Photos; Courtesy of PNC Bank, Delaware.
103 © Abbie Enock—Travel Ink/Corbis
104 © Francesco Venturi—Kea Publishing Services Ltd/Corbis; © Jeremy Horner—Corbis.
105 © A. Ramey—Woodfin Camp & Associates
106 Swiss National Tourist Office
107 © Philippe Ledru—Corbis-Sygma
108 © SuperStock; © Steve Vidler—SuperStock.
110 © Picture Box/The Viesti Collection, Inc.
111 © R. Grossmann/Helga Lade—Fotoagentur/Peter Arnold, Inc.; © Jorgen Schytte—BAM/Peter Arnold, Inc.
113 © SuperStock
114 © Bill Aron—Photo Researchers
117 © Phil Degginger—Bruce Coleman Inc.
118 © Jeff Greenberg—PhotoEdit
119 AP/Wide World Photos
120 Farm Security Administration/Library of Congress
121 © Keith Srakocic—AP/Wide World Photos
123 © Laurent—American Hospital of Paris/Photo Researchers
125 ©Roy Ooms—Masterfile; © Frans Lemmens—zefa/Corbis; © George H. H. Huey—Corbis; © Galen Rowell—Peter Arnold, Inc.
128 © China Newsphoto/Reuters/Corbis
129 © Michael & Patricia Fogden—Corbis; © Michael Fogden/OSF/Animals Animals/Earth Scenes.
130 © Frans Lemmens—Peter Arnold, Inc.; © David Else—Lonely Planet Images.
131 © SuperStock
132 © Stephen J. Krasemann—Photo Researchers; © Todd Gipstein—Photo Researchers; © Tom Branch—Photo Researchers; Alfred J. Wyatt—Philadelphia Museum of Art: The Louise and Walter Arensberg Collection.
133 © Joseph Martin—Scala/Art Resource; Hirshhorn Museum, Washington, D.C.; The Brooklyn Museum.
134 © Antonio Frasconi—Harcourt, Brace & World; Alfred J. Wyatt—Philadelphia Museum of Art.
135 Courtesy of Richard Lippold; Courtesy of the Art Institute of Chicago. Gift of the artist Stieglitz Collection.
136 Arts Club of Chicago; Charles Uht—Private Collection, New York.
137 Hirshhorn Museum and Sculpture Garden, Smithsonian Institution; Courtesy, The Museum of Modern Art, New York.
139 From The Homemakers, Watts: NY, 1973, Fisher, Leonard Everett; Courtesy of The Procter & Gamble Company.
140 Courtesy of The Soap and Detergent Association
141 © Dan Budnick—Woodfin Camp & Associates
142 © Jack Novak—SuperStock
143 © Dennis Cox
144 USN/AP/Wide World Photos
145 © ThinkStock/SuperStock
146 © Erica and Harold Van Pelt/© American Museum of Natural History
147 © Benelux Press/Photo Researchers; © SuperStock; © Sahm Doherty—TimePix; © Charles D. Winters—Photo Researchers.
148 © Joao Silva—AP/Wide World Photos
149 © Ann Frank Fonds - Basel—Anne Frank House/Getty Images; Mary Evans Picture Library.
150 © August 12, 2005, Burnt Orange Report/www.burntorangereport.com
151 Hulton/Archive by Getty Images
153 The Granger Collection
154 The Granger Collection
156 From SCHOLASTIC CHILDREN'S DICTIONARY. Published by Scholastic Library Publishing/Scholastic Inc. Copyright © 2002, 1996 by Scholastic Inc. Reprinted by permission.
157 The Granger Collection
153 The Granger Collection
160 © SuperStock
162 © SuperStock
168 © Bruce Selyem—Museum of the Rockies; © Les Stone—Corbis-Sygma; © W. Perry Conway—Tom Stack & Associates.
169 © Gerd Ludwig—Woodfin Camp & Associates; © Museum of the Rockies; © Royal

Tyrell Museum/Alberta Culture & Multiculturalism.
170 © The Carnegie Museum of Natural History
171 © François Gohier—Photo Researchers; © Tom McHugh—Photo Researchers.
173 © Bruce Selyem—Museum of the Rockies; © The Carnegie Museum of Natural History.
174 © Denver Museum of Natural History
175 © The Carnegie Museum of Natural History
177 © David Hardy/Science Photo Library—Photo Researchers
178 © Brian Nicholson, Standard-Examiner/AP/Wide World Photos; © Karen Schiely, Akron Beacon Journal/AP/Wide World Photos.
179 © Garo—Photo Researchers
180 © Mike Derer—AP/Wide World Photos
181 © Michal Heron—Monkmeyer; © Martin Rotker—Taurus; © D. C. Lowe—Medichrome.
183 © Kazuhiro Nogi—AFP/Getty Images
184 © David J. Phillip—AP/Wide World Photos
185 © Wally Santana—AP/Wide World Photos
186– © Dennis Kunkel—Oxford Scientific (OSF)/
187 Photolibrary
186 © Grapes-Michaud—Photo Researchers
187 © LADA/Photo Researchers; © Howard Sochurek—The MedicalFile/PeterArnold,Inc.; © Photodisc Blue/Getty Images.
188 © Dr. Gary Gaugler—Photo Researchers
189 © Michael Newman—PhotoEdit; © D. Gifford—Photo Researchers.
190 © 3D Clinic/Getty Images; © 3D Clinic/Getty Images; © Alfred Pasieka—Peter Arnold, Inc.
192 © D. Lovegrove—Photo Researchers; © Dr. Fred Hossler—Visuals Unlimited.
193 © CDC/PHIL/Corbis
194 © Robert Brenner—PhotoEdit; © Dr. Linda Stannard, UCT/Science Photo Library/Photo Researchers.
196 © Oliver Meckes/Nicole Ottawa—Photo Researchers; © Biophoto Associates/Photo Researchers.
197 © Siri Mills—Oxford Scientific (OSF)/Photolibrary
198 © Will & Deni McIntyre—Photo Researchers; © John M. Daugherty—Photo Researchers.
200 © SIU/Peter Arnold, Inc.
201 © Reza Estakhrian—Stone/Getty Images; © Biophoto Associates/Photo Researchers.
202 © Darlyne A. Murawski—Peter Arnold, Inc.; © Vincent Yu—AP/Wide World Photos.
203 © Charles Gupton—Stone/Getty Images; © Eye of Science/Photo Researchers.
204 © Dr. Freiburger—Peter Arnold, Inc.
205 © Klaus Rose—Das Fotoarchiv/Peter Arnold, Inc.; © Scott Camazine—Photo Researchers.
206 © Andrew Syred—Photo Researchers
207 © Simon Fraser—Photo Researchers
208 © Eric Barbeau—Peter Arnold, Inc.; © Dr. Gary Gaugler—Photo Researchers.
209 © Professors Stanley Prusiner/Fred Cohen, University of California San Francisco Medical School/AP/Wide World Photos; © Alfred Pasieka—Photo Researchers.
211 © Jack Dempsey—AP/Wide World Photos
212 © Lawrence Migdale—Photo Researchers
214 © Cameramann International Ltd.—Skokie Valley Hospital
215 © The Walt Disney Co.
216 © The Walt Disney Co.
217 The Hulton Press, London
219 © Runk/Schoenberger—Grant Heilman Photography
220 © Focus on Sports
224 © Tony Duffy—Allsport Photography
225 © Tony Duffy—Allsport Photography
226 © Focus on Sports
227 © Focus on Sports
228 © Tony Duffy—Allsport Photography
229 © Tony Duffy—Allsport Photography
231 Corbis
232 © Jason Laure; © Sayyid Azim—AP/Wide World Photos.
234 Scala/Art Resource
235 © Barao—Custom Medical Stock Photo; © Michal Heron—The Stock Market; © Randy Duchaine—The Stock Market.
237 © Michal Heron
238 © Will & Deni McIntyre—Photo Researchers
239 © Art Stein—Photo Researchers; © Will & Deni McIntyre—Photo Researchers; © Jean-Pierre Laffont—Corbis-Sygma.
240 © Tim Kiusalaas—Masterfile; The Granger Collection; © Paul Barton—Corbis.
240– © Jodi Jacobson—Peter Arnold, Inc.
241
241 © Lawrence Jackson—AP/Wide World Photos; © John Cancalosi—Peter Arnold, Inc.

242 ©Jeanne White—Photo Researchers; © Jerry Shulman—SuperStock; © Prenzel Photo—Animals Animals; © Gerard Lacz—Peter Arnold, Inc.; Richard Orr; Richard Orr; Richard Orr.

243 © Galen Rowell—Corbis; © Richard Orr; © Richard Orr.

244 © Joe McDonald—Visuals Unlimited; © Myrleen Ferguson Cate—PhotoEdit; © Ulrike Schanz—Photo Researchers; © Ralph Reinhold—Animals Animals; © Gerard Lacz—Peter Arnold, Inc.; © Jerry Shulman—SuperStock; © Lynn Stone—Animals Animals; © BIOS/Peter Arnold, Inc.

245 © Ashmolean Museum, University of Oxford, UK/The Bridgeman Art Library.

246 © Ralph Reinhold—Animals Animals; © David Dalton—FLPA-images.co.uk; © Ralph Reinhold—Animals Animals; © Ulrike Schanz—Animals Animals; © Doris Lechner; © Carolyn A. McKeone—Photo Researchers; © Dale C. Spartas—Corbis.

247 © Henry Ausloos—Animals Animals; © Eunice Percy—Animals Animals; © Robert Dowling—Corbis; © Gerard Lacz—Peter Arnold, Inc.; © Jeanne White—Photo Researchers; © BIOS/Peter Arnold, Inc.; © Eunice Percy—Animals Animals; © Gerard Lacz—Peter Arnold, Inc.

248 © Jerry Shulman—SuperStock; © Info Hund Kramer—Okapia/Photo Researchers; © Info Hund Kramer—Okapia/Photo Researchers; © Ulrike Schanz—Animals Animals; © Gerard Lacz—Peter Arnold, Inc.; © Barbara Hoffmann—Animals Animals; © Jerry Shulman—SuperStock; © Frederic Jacana—Photo Researchers.

249 © J. L. Klein & M. L. Hubert—Okapia/Photo Researchers; © Frederic Jacana—Photo Researchers; © Ulrike Schanz—Animals Animals; © Frederic Jacana—Photo Researchers; © Jeanne White—Photo Researchers; © Gerard Lacz—Peter Arnold, Inc.; © BIOS/Peter Arnold, Inc.

250 © Iditarod Trail Committee

251 © Mitsuaki Iwago—Minden Pictures

252 © Henny Ray Abrams—Reuters/Corbis; © Tomas Ovalle, *Fresno Bee*—AP/Wide World Photos.

253 © Alan & Sandy Carey—Photo Researchers; Courtesy, Christine Johnson; © Al Grillo—AP/Wide World Photos.

254 © Axel-Jacana—Photo Researchers; © Eunice Percy—Animals Animals.

255 © The Illustrated London News Picture Library, UK/The Bridgeman Art Library

257 © Reinhardt/Zeitenspiegel—VISUM/The Image Works; © Lawrence Migdale Photography; © David McNew—Getty Images.

258 © Richard Hutchings—Photo Researchers; © Michael Krasowitz—Taxi/Getty Images.

259 © Jim Corwin—Photo Researchers

260 © Syracuse Newspapers/The Image Works

262 Courtesy, Bureau of Engraving and Printing/U.S. Department of the Treasury

263 © Werner H. Muller—Peter Arnold, Inc.

264 © Bethnal Green Museum, London/The Bridgeman Art Library

265 © Bethnal Green Museum, London/The Bridgeman Art Library

266 Courtesy of Coleco

267 Courtesy of Strong Museum, Rochester, NY; Courtesy of Strong Museum, Rochester, NY; © Daniel Simon—Liaison Agency.

268 © Werner H. Muller—Peter Arnold, Inc. (all photos on page).

269 © Bruce Roberts—Photo Researchers; Courtesy of Strong Museum, Rochester, NY; © Werner H. Muller—Peter Arnold, Inc.; © Daniel Simon—Liaison Agency.

270 Courtesy of Mattel Toys © Mattel, Inc.; © 1986 Hasbro, Inc., All Rights Reserved; Courtesy of Strong Museum, Rochester, NY.

271 Courtesy of Mattel Toys © Mattel, Inc.; Courtesy of Mattel Toys © Mattel, Inc.; Photo by Frances Pellegrini for F.A.O. Schwarz, New York.

272 © Philippe Halsman—Courtesy of Mr. and Mrs. Samuel Pryor; © SuperStock; © Arizona Photographic Assoc., Inc.

273 Sea World

274 © SuperStock

275 © John L. Pontier—Animals Animals; © Norbert Wu—Peter Arnold, Inc.

276 Sea World (all photos on page).

278 © DiMaggio/J. Kalish—Peter Arnold, Inc.

280 © Catherine Karnow—Woodfin Camp & Associates; © M. Timothy O'Keefe—Bruce Coleman Inc.

281 © Look GMBH/eStock Photo

282 © Hank Barone—Houserstock

283 © Aizar Raldes—AFP/Getty Images

285 Scala/Art Resource

286 The Granger Collection

287 North Wind Picture Archives

288 The Granger Collection

289 AP/Wide World Photos; © John Kaprielian—Photo Researchers.

290 © Gavriel Jecan—Corbis

294 © Michael Lustbader—Photo Researchers; © age fotostock/SuperStock.

295 Private Collection/The Bridgeman Art Library

297 © J. A. Kraulis—Masterfile; © Mike Blake—Reuters/Landov; Hulton/Archive by Getty Images; Hulton/Archive by Getty Images.

298 © Francisco Cruz—SuperStock

299 © Costa Manos—Magnum Photos

300 The Granger Collection; Art Resource, NY.

301 © Erich Lessing—Art Resource, NY

302 © Erich Lessing—Art Resource, NY

303 Photofest

304 Everett Collection

305 © George Widman—AP/Wide World Photos

306 Hulton/Archive by Getty Images; © Eric Y. Exit—AP/Wide World Photos

307 Everett Collection; © Max Nash—AP/Wide World Photos.

315 The Metropolitan Museum of Art, New York

316 Graphische Sammlung Albertina, Vienna; (all photos on page).

317 Documentation Photographique de la Reunion des musees nationaux; Museum of Fine Arts, Boston. Purchase, Maria Antoinette Evans Fund.

318 *Cahiers d'Art*, Vol. 26, 1951, reproduced by permission of Christian Zervos, © SPADEM 1966 by French Reproduction Rights, Inc.

319 © Rolf Haid/DPA/Landov

321 © Junebug Clark—Photo Researchers; © Peter & Georgina Bowater—The Image Bank.

323 The Granger Collection

324 Culver Pictures

324 Courtesy of the American Automobile Association

326 © Kevin Seifert, *The Herald Sun*/AP/Wide World Photos

328 © Michael S. Yamashita—Woodfin Camp & Associates

330 © Myleen Ferguson Cate—PhotoEdit

332 © Amy Etra—PhotoEdit; © David Kelly Crow—PhotoEdit.

334 © Stephen R. Swinburne—Stock, Boston

335 © Stephen Ogilvy—Bruce Coleman Inc.

336 © Geoff Tompkinson—Science Photo Library/Photo Researchers

337 © Toby Rankin—The Image Bank

338 © Mark Weiss

340 © Mark & Evelyne Bernheim—Woodfin Camp & Associates

341 © Jeff Greenberg—PhotoEdit

342 © Private Collection, Roger-Violet, Paris/The Bridgeman Art Library

343 © SIME s.a.s./eStock

345 © Harold Hoffman—Photo Researchers

346 © Stephen J. Krasemann—Photo Researchers

347 © Grant Heilman Photography; © Rod Allin—Tom Stack & Associates.

348 © Ronny Jacques—Photo Researchers

349 The Granger Collection

351 The Granger Collection; Mary Evans Picture Library.

352 The Granger Collection

353 © Underwood & Underwood/Corbis

354 The Metropolitan Museum of Art, New York; Art Institute of Chicago, Clarence Buckingham Collection.

356 © Arthur Rothstein—Resettlement Administration/TimePix

357 Giraudon—Rapho Guillumette

358 Giraudon—Rapho Guillumette

359 Art Reference Bureau

361 Giraudon—Rapho Guillumette; Art Reference Bureau.

362 European Art Slide Company; Art Reference Bureau; Art Reference Bureau.

363 Art Reference Bureau

364 European Art Slide Company

366 Marburg—Art Reference Bureau

367 Allen Art Museum, Oberlin, Ohio; Louvre, Paris—Art Reference Bureau; Art Reference Bureau.

368 Art Reference Bureau

369 National Gallery, London—Art Reference Bureau; Art Reference Bureau.

370 Giraudon—Rapho Guillumette; Courtesy, The Museum of Modern Art, New York.

372 The Metropolitan Museum of Art, New York

373 Art Reference Bureau

374 © Myrleen Ferguson Cate—PhotoEdit

375 © Nino Ellison—Taxi/Getty Images

376 © Dr. Sherif Zaki—Photo Researchers; © Andrew Parsons—AP/Wide World Photos.

378 © Bonnie Kamin—Photo Edit

379 © age fotostock/SuperStock; © Paul Dymond—Lonely Planet Images.

381 Courtesy, DuPont Company